Proceedings

International Computer Performance and Dependability Symposium

Proceedings

International Computer Performance and Dependability Symposium

April 24–26, 1995   Erlangen, Germany

Sponsored by

The IEEE Computer Society Technical Committee
on Fault-Tolerant Computing

In cooperation with

IFIP WG 7.3
IFIP WG 10.4
University of Erlangen-Nürnberg
University of Illinois at Urbana-Champaign

IEEE Computer Society Press
Los Alamitos, California

Washington   ●   Brussels   ●   Tokyo

IEEE Computer Society Press
10662 Los Vaqueros Circle
P.O. Box 3014
Los Alamitos, CA 90720-1264

IEEE Computer Society Press Order Number PR07059
Library of Congress Number 94-73915
IEEE Catalog Number 95TH8034
ISBN 0-8186-7059-2 (paper)

Additional copies may be ordered from:

IEEE Computer Society Press	IEEE Service Center	IEEE Computer Society	IEEE Computer Society
Customer Service Center	445 Hoes Lane	13, Avenue de l'Aquilon	Ooshima Building
10662 Los Vaqueros Circle	P.O. Box 1331	B-1200 Brussels	2-19-1 Minami-Aoyama
P.O. Box 3014	Piscataway, NJ 08855-1331	BELGIUM	Minato-ku, Tokyo 107
Los Alamitos, CA 90720-1264	Tel: +1-908-981-1393	Tel: +32-2-770-2198	JAPAN
Tel: +1-714-821-8380	Fax: +1-908-981-9667	Fax: +32-2-770-8505	Tel: +81-3-3408-3118
Fax: +1-714-821-4641			Fax: +81-3-3408-3553
Email: cs.books@computer.org			

Editorial production: Penny Storms
Cover photo: Gertrud Glasow, Erlangen / Cover design: Markus Schwehm, Erlangen
Cover layout: Joseph Daigle/Schenk-Daigle Studios
Printed in the United States of America by McNaughton & Gunn, Inc.

 The Institute of Electrical and Electronics Engineers, Inc.

Table of Contents

Keynote Panel: Future Issues: Designing Computers for High-Performance and Dependability
Moderator: Alain Costes, LAAS-CNRS

Session 1: Dependable Software
Session Chair: Karama Kanoun

Session 2: Operating System Mechanisms
Session Chair: Josep Torrellas

Invited Session: Modeling and Evaluation
Session Chair: Dave Rennels

Session 3: Modelling Theory
Session Chair: Isi Mitrani

v

Session 8: Performance and Reliability Analysis
Session Chair: Edgar Nett

Panel 2: Responsiveness in Automotive and Communication Systems
Moderator: Paul J. Kühn, TU Stuttgart

Session 9: Practical Issues
Session Chair: Kumar Goswami

Session 10: Low-Level Hardware Aspects
Session Chair: Mukesh Singhal

Message from the General Chairs

It is our great pleasure that on behalf of the entire organizing committee we welcome you to the first International Computer Performance and Dependability Symposium IPDS'95. Its aim is to bring together researchers in both areas: computer performance and computer dependability. The idea to organize such a symposium came up when Ravi Iyer visited Erlangen, having been nominated a Humboldt fellow. He convinced us that such a meeting would not only be beneficial for our scientific community but would also be of great benefit to our Computer Science Department since it traditionally always had strong research groups in computer performance evaluation and dependability. Thanks to the efforts of the hard-working program committee led by Ravi a technical program of high quality has been put together. We would like to thank Ravi Iyer and his program committee members for their diligence.

The symposium was preceded by the excellent tutorial on "Tools for Analytical and Experimental Evaluation of Dependable Computers" organized by Jean Arlat. Distinguished speakers were Ravi Iyer, Kishor Trivedi, Johan Karlsson, Dimitri Avresky, William Sanders, Karama Kanoun and E. Thurner. Jean opened the tutorial with his talk on "Analytical and Experimental Evaluation Techniques: How Can They Work Together?". We take the opportunity to thank Jean Arlat and the speakers for their work. The symposium is highlighted by an excellent keynote panel which will explore future issues in the area of our common interest. Another highlight will be the special session of invited papers on fundamental issues in stochastic modeling. Two industry-oriented panels will provide plenty of opportunities for discussions. Special thanks are due to Ambuj Goyal, Dan Lenoski, and Paul Kühn for organizing these panels.

We are grateful for the support we received from many people. We are especially grateful to Wolfgang Hohl, the Finance Chair, who did a tremendous job of preparing the symposium, William Sanders our Publication Chair, Sue Windsor, and our Conference Program Coordinator Fran Wagner. She had the important task of keeping the different actions in line. Our thanks go to Markus Schwehm who did both the fine graphics and artwork of the program and the proceedings, to Kurt Freudenthaler and Axel Klein from Siemens. Last but not least our thanks go to Christine Cetin and Nadja Asid for their secretarial and administrative support and to Jens Guethoff who helped with the preparation of the tool demonstrations. So we warmly welcome all participants and hope you will find the symposium a rewarding and stimulating experience.

Mario Dal Cin
University of Erlangen-Nürnberg

Ulrich Herzog
University of Erlangen-Nürnberg

Message from the Program Chair

Welcome to the First IEEE International Computer Performance and Dependability Symposium, the first international symposium to specifically address the issues of performance and dependability together. Thirty-five papers and two panel sessions are presented, offering a broad range of topics from both theoretical and practical viewpoints. Sixty-three papers were submitted. Each was reviewed by a minimum of three reviewers. The final selection process took place at a meeting in Urbana, IL, in January. Reviews were submitted electronically, which facilitated the use of analytical tools to inform the decision process. The selection process went smoothly, largely due to the diligence of the referees, including over 40 external reviewers. The selection progress was rigorous; the result is, I believe, a program of exceptional quality and interest.

In addition to the selected papers, a distinguished keynote panel considers what the future holds for designing with both high performance and dependability in mind. Two additional panels are included. The first visits the subject of design, focusing on cost-performance versus dependability in the design of workstation-based systems. The second addresses the timely topic of responsiveness in automotive and communications systems. A session of invited papers from three distinguished researchers in the area focuses on the ever-critical area of modeling and evaluation, which is also the topic of a pre-symposium tutorial highlighting evaluation tools.

I am very gratified by the interest this new symposium has generated in the dependability and performance communities. I am especially pleased with the amount of industry interest and support reflected throughout the program. This is an exciting beginning for a new forum with a timely and important objective: the integrated study performance and dependability issues.

In closing, I would like to thank the General Chairs Mario Dal Cin and Ulrich Herzog for their constant support, and all the members of the Organizing Committee and Steering Committee, who provided timely help whenever it was needed. I also thank all the members of the Program Committee for working very hard to shape this fine program. Finally, thanks are due to Michael Chan, Steven VanderLeest, Chitra Natarajan, and Timothy Tsai for their invaluable support during the review process.

R. K. Iyer
University of Illinois at Urbana-Champaign

Organizing Committees

General Co-Chairs

Mario Dal Cin and Ulrich Herzog
University of Erlangen-Nürnberg, Germany

Program Chair

Ravishankar K. Iyer
University of Illinois at Urbana-Champaign, USA

Program Vice-Chair

Martin Reiser
IBM, Zürich, Switzerland

Steering Committee:

J. Abraham, University of Texas, USA
A. Avizienis, *University of California, USA*
G. Balbo, *University di Torino, Italy*
P.-J. Courtois, *AV-Nuclear, Belgium*
D. Ferrari, *University of California, USA*
J.-C. Laprie, *LAAS-CNRS, France*
E. McCluskey, *Stanford University, USA*
J. Meyer, *University of Michigan, USA*
B. Randell, *University of Newcastle, UK*
A. Reuter, *University of Stuttgart, Germany*
H. Schwärtzel, *Siemens AG, Germany*
K. Sevcik, *University of Toronto, Canada*
D. Siewiorek, *CMU, USA*
K. Trivedi, *Duke University, USA*

Finance Chair

Wolfgang Hohl, *University of Erlangen-Nürnberg, Germany*

Registration Chair

Axel Klein, *Siemens AG, München, Germany*

Local Arrangements Chair

Kurt Freudenthaler, *Siemens AG, Erlangen, Germany*

Publication Chair

William H. Sanders, *University of Illinois, USA*

Publicity Chairs

Jean Arlat, *LAAS-CNRS, Toulouse, France*
Wolfgang Hohl, *University of Erlangen-Nürnberg, Germany*

Conference Program Coordinator

Frances R. Wagner, *University of Illinois, USA*

Publication Coordinator

Suellen B. Windsor, *University of Illinois, USA*

Program Committee

J. Arlat, *LAAS-CNRS, France*

F. Baccelli, *INRIA, France*

H. Beilner, *Dortmund University, Germany*

A. Bode, *TU München, Germany*

R. Candlin, *Edinburgh University, UK*

G. Chiola, *University di Torino, Italy*

L. Dowdy, *Vanderbilt University, USA*

R. Geist, *Clemson University, USA*

J. Goldberg, *SRI, USA*

K. Goswami, *Tandem, USA*

A. Goyal, *IBM, USA*

G. Haring, *University of Vienna, Austria*

K. Kanoun, *LAAS-CNRS, France*

T. Kikuno, *Osaka University, Japan*

J. Lala, *Draper Labs, USA*

S. Lavenberg, *IBM, USA*

D. Lenoski, *Silicon Graphics, USA*

Y. Levendel, *AT&T, USA*

J. Liu, *University of Illinois, USA*

R. Marie, *IRISA, France*

I. Mitrani, *University of Newcastle, UK*

D. Reed, *University of Illinois, USA*

A. Reibman, *AT&T, USA*

D. Rennels, *University of California Los Angeles, USA*

W. Sanders, *University of Illinois, USA*

R. Schlichting, *University of Arizona, USA*

H. Schwetman, *University of Texas, USA*

L. Sha, *CMU, USA*

K. Shin, *University of Michigan, USA*

S. Shrivastava, *Newcastle University, UK*

M. Singhal, *Ohio State University, USA*

A. Smith, *University of California at Berkeley, USA*

J. Stankovic, *Massachusetts University, USA*

J. Torrellas, *University of Illinois, USA*

S. Tripathi, *University of Maryland, USA*

Referees

M. Abrams
J. Arlat
D. Avresky
J. Aylor
F. Baccelli
R. Bagrodia
H. Beilner
B. Bharat
R. Bianchini
D.M. Blough
A. Bobbio
A. Bode
J. Brehm
P. Bucholz
R. Candlin
C. Childers
G. Chiola
A. Dahbura
M. Dal Cin
S. Daniel
E. De Souza E Silva
L. Dowdy
K. Fuchs
C. Fuhrman
R. Geist
R. German
J. Goldberg
K. Goswami
A. Goyal
S. Han

G. Haring
B. Haverkort
R. Horst
W-M. Hwu
B.W. Johnson
Y. Kakuda
S.M. Kang
K. Kanoun
W-l. Kao
T. Kikuno
S. Kusumoto
J. Lala
S. Lavenberg
I. Lee
D. Lenoski
Y. Levendel
J. Liu
D. Logothetis
T. Ludwig
M. Lyu
R. Marie
J.F. Meyer
I. Mitrani
R. Muntz
C. Natarajan
J.H. Patel
D. Pradhan
A. Puliafito
D. Reed
A. Reibman

D. Rennels
A. Reuter
J. Rexford
G. Ries
W. Sanders
R.D. Schlichting
H. Schwetman
L. Sha
K.G. Shin
D.P. Siewiorek
L. Simoncini
M. Singhal
A.J. Smith
S.K. Shrivastava
J.A. Stankovic
J. Strosnider
A. Tai
D. Tang
M. Telek
A. Thakur
J. Torrellas
S. Toueg
S.K. Tripathi
K. Trivedi
T. Tsai
A. Van Moorsel
Y-M. Wang
L. Yang
C. Xia

Keynote Panel:

Future Issues: Designing Computers for High-Performance and Dependability

---

Moderator:
Alain Costes, LAAS-CNRS

Panelists:
H. Kopetz, TU Vienna
D. Morgan, Motorola
J.-C. Laprie, LAAS-CNRS
H. Schwärtzel, Siemens AG

Session 1:
Dependable Software

Session Chair: Karama Kanoun

Software Assembly Workbench:
How to Construct Software Like Hardware

Y.Levendel

AT&T Bell Laboratories

Abstract

This paper describes an approach for assembling software by combining reusable building blocks, much in the way hardware is being designed. The approach uses a **Software Assembly Workbench** and is predicated on the existence of a **Network Execution Platform**. The Network Execution Platform is a "network computer" that performs network functions necessary to execute typical services. Its operating system provides access to telecommunication and computing functionality. The Software Assembly Workbench is based on two adjacent software layers, the **Service** (upper) layer and the **Component** (intermediate) layer. These two layers require the implementation of a third (lower) layer, the **Capability** layer, which resides on the Network Execution Platform. Before being shipped for **Execution** on the Network Execution Platform, the software constructed using the two layers of the Software Assembly Workbench is first verified through **Simulation**. Both the execution platform and the application software are instrumented for failure detection and management. The uniqueness of this approach resides in our ability to rapidly create software that can be dependably executed in a distributed telecommunication network.

1. INTRODUCTION

As a result of deregulation, competitive pressures have become prevalent in the telecommunication industry. The entry of foreign and domestic competitors into markets that were previously protected has created price and responsiveness pressures on telecommunication equipment manufacturers. At the same time, deregulation has led to requirements for interworking between products coming from diverse manufacturers. This trend being relatively slow due to the local service providers and the large R&D expenses required by modern telecommunication, it has not yet stabilized and one can only try to predict the outcome. However, other industries that have led the way, such as the computer industry, can provide a valid model. Early on, the computer industry that operated in a semi-monopoly took advantage of its position and led the customers toward larger mainframes that guaranteed the perpetuation of this monopoly by excluding smaller

market entrants. In less than a decade, the era of main frames and of market monopolization has ended and given way to distributed computing and market diversity.

Although the cost of the telecommunication infrastructure is slowing down market trends, one can expect by the turn of this century a similar opening of the telecommunication industry and a proliferation of cheaper distributed network solutions. With the opening of the network, computers that are already present as peripheral equipment will play a larger role in service delivery. As a result of network openness and distribution, **balkanization** of the telecommunication market is around the corner world wide. The main question becomes "What technological solution will best position the telecommunication industry to face this new challenge?" From a business view point, this question becomes **"How to speed up the delivery of proprietary products and services in an open environment?"** At the present time, software being the main bottleneck in cost and time-to-market, it is essential to improve its production process. To address this business imperative, it is essential to develop a technology with two complementary attributes:

a) It provides software production **velocity**
b) It provides differentiation by **customization**

1.1. Constructing Software Like Hardware

The hardware industry has succeeded in defining reusable components that have allowed hardware designers to be more effective in their work, both in terms of design speed and design quality. The hardware logic design is reduced to establishing the connectivity of predefined components and to verifying the correctness of the assembly. In exchange for the use of hardware catalog components, the design is greatly simplified and its phases can be automated. The present paper demonstrates a software construction method similar to hardware design methodologies in that it is based on component reuse to speed up the software assembly.

1.2. Software Reuse

In its most general definition, software reuse is practically unattainable although it may be an attractive goal, and in that sense, it has proved to be an elusive goal. In very specific terms, however, software reuse has achieved high benefits (MS-DOS, LOTUS 1-2-3, etc.). In all success cases, several essential issues must be considered:

a) **Software Components Must Have Large Expansion**. In the last few decades, software abstractions have increased in scope so that each language construct is spanning a larger content. In other words, the assembly equivalent of each construct has been growing. The expansion factor is a measure that expresses the content of a language construct. In that sense, a line of C++ has a larger expansion factor than a line of C. Empirical evidence has shown that software productivity is in direct relation to the expansion factor of the language used [JON81].

b) **Reusable Components Must Be Specialized**. In all disciplines, a high degree of specialization has usually accompanied industrialization. This specialization has resulted in the utilization of reusable parts to compose a product. Crafting industrial objects has become equivalent to building an asset of reusable parts and using these parts to assemble these industrial objects. In software as well, basic objects are being reused (finite number of elementary language constructs) to produce larger entities (programs). The main problem with these reusable constructs is that, in general, they are not specialized enough, and therefore they capture no reusable problem solution knowledge. Large expansion factor is not enough to move software production to the industrial age. However, a combination of large expansion and high specialization is likely to provide a movement toward this industrialization.

c) **Reusability Is Often Traded for Functionality**. Of course, while designing reusable components with a large expansion and a high specialization can provide higher productivity, one is likely to face the question: what if a component cannot provide specific behaviors that may be needed in specific situations? In such a case, three solutions are possible:

1) Forgo the specific required behavior as long as the reusable component still has enough residual merit.
2) Modify the component to adjust its behavior as long as other functionality is not affected.
3) Forgo the benefits of this (and other) reusable component(s) and design software as usual.

Obviously, the first solution is the cheapest one as long as the revenue from the unperturbed component is high enough. In this case, one is trading higher

reusability for lower functionality. Unless, this tradeoff is realistic, there can be no long range value to a software assembly methodology based on reusable components. Fortunately, experimental data in computing and telecommunication has shown that a small percentage of functionality is being used the most [LEV91]. This is the old "80%-20%" (80% use of 20% of the assets) which opens up a hope for succeeding to design components that can **cost effectively** cover **most** of the needs. These are **robust** components.

d) **Reuse Requires Agreement**. For one person to reuse a component designed by someone else, it is necessary for an agreement on the component functionality to exist between the component designer and its user. In the most general case, agreements are impossible to achieve. However, a broad agreement is possible when the economic benefits of such an agreement outweigh the loss of freedom, as it is the case for major operating systems, environments and tools. To further software component reuse, one has to be able to design frameworks of moderate size where agreements are possible and can be maintained. Such frameworks of limited scope can help fill the gap between the two extreme situations mentioned above. In our case, we use design environment tools, the **Software Assembly Workbench**, to capture the domain of agreement.

e) **Domain Analysis Is Key to Reuse**. In most industries, the key to the success of reuse is a careful analysis of the domain of application so that the domain can be decomposed into a set of robust components. This set of reusable components representing the domain is consolidated into a "palette" of components that can be inserted into the Software Assembly Workbench for reuse. The entire scope of our work is predicated on our ability to perform domain analysis and extract from the analysis a robust set of components.

2. SYSTEM ARCHITECTURE

2.1. Execution System: a Client-Server Architecture

As shown in Figure 1 below, the execution system has a client-server architecture composed of **network resources** (servers) and **execution platform** (client). Each network resource provides specific functionality (voice systems, computers, data bases, etc.) which is used to execute a service. The resources and the execution platform are connected through a telecommunication network.

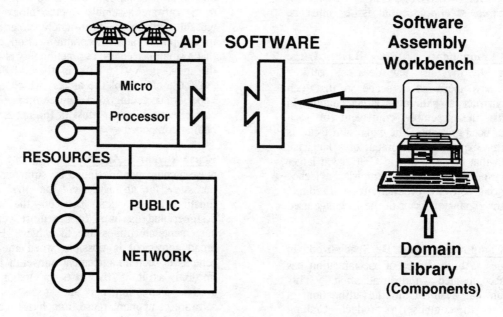

Figure 1. System Architecture

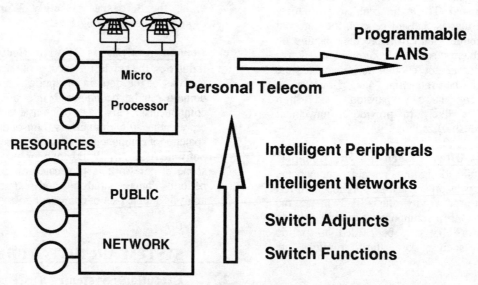

Figure 2. Alternate System Architectures

2.2. Software Assembly Workbench

The Software Assembly Workbench is a software design environment with the following ingredients:

- A Graphical User Interface
- A Visual Representation of a Basic Set ("Palette") of Components
- A Mechanism to Change the Basic Set of Components
- A Visual Software Construction Paradigm to Combine Components
- Incremental Editing Capabilities
- A Simulation Mechanism to Verify the Assembled Software
- A Mechanism to Produce Executable Software

These ingredients are necessary to facilitate the construction of executable software by application programmers.

2.3.   A Range of Application Domains

The techniques described above have been used to control Interactive Voice Systems, PC based call centers, Switching Systems adjuncts, Intelligent Network elements, Multimedia services based on broadband infrastructures (Figure 2). Although these services are diverse both in the application domain and in the telecommunication infrastructure supporting them, they were all addressed by similar software construction techniques.

3.   SOFTWARE ARCHITECTURE

3.1.   Software Layering

On the basis of the existence of the capability layer (API of Figure 1), two additional layers can be derived using domain analysis: the **Component** layer and the **Service** layer. The higher the layer, the easier the programming should be and the larger the revenue potential. In this multilayered software architecture, each layer is insulated from the layer below and is used to construct the layer above it (Table 1).

Table 1. Software Layers

Layer Elements	Used to Construct	Elements Location
Services	-	Software Assembly Workbench
Components	Applications	Software Assembly Workbench
Capabilities	Components	Execution Platform
Primitives	Capabilities	Execution Platform

3.2.   Resource Programmability: A Platform of Capabilities

The resources are programmed with two layers of programming: the **primitives** (lower layer) and the **capabilities** (upper layer). The decision to have two layers was largely accidental and due to the fact that, in our experience, the resources used were already equipped with an "operating system" providing "native" primitives. The capabilities were defined as an additional layer creating more compact operations that would minimize the message load between client and servers. In a long range, these two layers could be merged, as the interfaces between network elements become more standardized.

In the case of Interactive Voice Systems servers, the primitive fall into 4 categories:

- String operations
- Logic programming operations
- Call control operations
- Speech support operations

Sample server capabilities are given in Table 2. Evidently, different capabilities will be necessary for additional application domains. For instance, data functionality will be covered in the following capabilities:
- Business data bases
- Electronic files
- Electronic mail
- Facsimile
- Modem communication
- Input-output
- Directories

Table 2. Voice Server Capabilities

announce	plays an announcement sent from the client
answer	causes the server to go off hook in response to incoming call
code	allows for voice recording of announcements
complete	bridges a transfer to a third party
delete	deletes a voice recording previously coded
disconnect	drops the transferring party after a transfer
flash	assists in the transfer process
halts	terminates a call
init	alerts client of an incoming call
prompt	collects input from a caller
reconnect	return to a caller placed on hold
transfer	connects a call to a third party

In a different application domain, such as multimedia Interactive Video-On-Demand, one can conceive a different set of capabilities. In general, capability definition will be driven by domain definition, will be grouped into resources and will execute on resource servers. The resources being a blend of telecommunication and computing elements, our proposed software and hardware architecture is a good mechanism to achieve the **wedding** of **computing** and **telecommunication** that can unleash new service revenues for the industry [REI94].

4.   A NEW PARADIGM FOR DELIVERING TELECOMMUNICATION SERVICES: THE SOFTWARE ASSEMBLY WORKBENCH

The establishment of a framework to capture domain analysis (the Software Assembly Workbench) opens opportunities to change the way software is constructed. Now, there is room for a new form of programming, Software Assembly, performed by individuals less versed in software design but more qualified in application domains. In telecommunications, this allows an **agent** of the service provider (the operator of a Software Assembly Workbench) to "retail" services to the **end customers**. The service software can now run either on equipment belonging to the service provider or to the end customer. The resources necessary to support a service can belong to the service provider (e.g. telephone directory data base), to the end customer (e.g., customer orders) or to a third party (e.g., computer data bases, processing nodes, etc.).

4.1.   Software Assembly Paradigm

To support rapid and flexible assembly of software applications in a given domain, a familiar composition paradigm is selected. After considering several composition metaphors [PRI93, SEL93], two types of software assembly paradigms were retained: approach No. 1 used control flow diagrams, and approach No. 2 used asynchronous logic diagrams. Both approaches lend themselves well to diagrammatic composition. However, parallel composition constructs are more naturally represented in data flow diagrams [LEE94] and enhanced state diagrams [HAR87].

To construct applications in a given domain, it is assumed that a domain vocabulary and a grammar are defined for the domain. An application domain software is designed by constructing sentences from chosen elements of the vocabulary organized according to the grammar rules.

The domain operators are represented using a palette of icons (Figure 3) that instantiate into components when placed on the design area. A component accepts input events and generates output events upon successful completion or failure of its tasks. A component may be realized using other components or it may internally use a control flow "diagram" to perform its tasks. In this approach there is no sequencing of actions, each component processes events independently from the other components involved in the service. Parallelism is inherent to the event-based interactions between components [AGH86, CHA94, LEE94]. This approach is well suited for the video and multimedia domains where services fequently require the coordinated access of multiple resources from possibly disjoint network elements.

A diagram constructed in this paradigm comprises a set of operators and a set of connections representing associations between output events and input events. An example of such diagram, presented in Figure 3, resembles a logic circuit diagram. However, each connection between operators does not represent an absolute point to point "wire" connection but instead, a potential path for transmitting packets of information (event and data) between two or more operators. Each operator (implemented as a component) may itself be constructed from a set of lower level operators.

4.2.   Software Simulation and Execution

An important characteristic of the Software Assembly Workbench is the ability to seamlessly transition between software simulation and execution. This is a challenging goal that has no analogy in the circuit design, and is possible in software (since software is present at all levels) with certain limitations and compromises.

In the SAW development environment, components can be independently simulated. The simulation of a service instance results from the composite and concurrent execution of small independent simulators that are "wired" according to the service layout diagrams.

Each simulator requires a private execution context (e.g. an execution stack to run its virtual machine). This independent context insures that multiple instances of services can coexist as independent processes competing for network resources. The resource contention is therefore handled at the lowest level in the components hierarchy and does not appear in the service assembly process.

When a service is instantiated a database lookup is used to populate each component with the corresponding customer data. In addition the necessary connections are established between the low level instantiated components and the requested communication ports to establish control of the network capabilities require by the service. Component instantiation occurs iteratively as part of the service initiation process. When all the components data are populated the service is ready to serve its customer.

Events are responsible for coordinating tasks and data exchange (messages) between the constituent components of a service instance. Events are typically generated by the port layer and are distributed (dispatched) to the target components where they destructively modified and passed to the next layer. Component simulators are idle unless directly activated by an event. Component simulators process events concurrently and asynchronously.

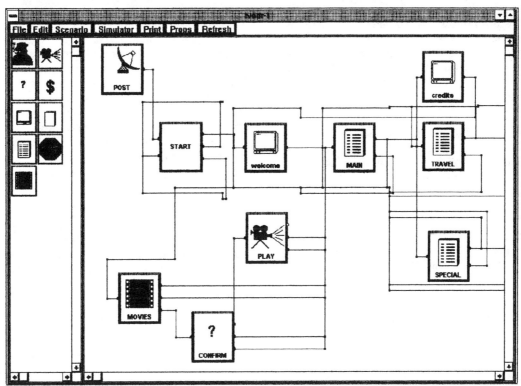

Figure 3. Video service construction from a palette

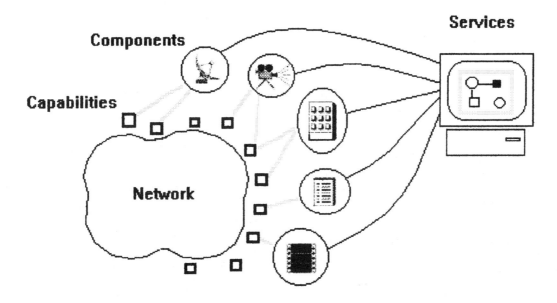

Figure 4. Network Mapping of Software Building Blocks

4.3. Building Block Mapping into the Network

In the network model of Figure 4, we use the following functional mapping: network elements and resources provide a set of capabilities (basic functionality they provide to the network). So different capabilities can reside on separate physical network elements. An intermediate level provides an abstract application domain set of functionality by combining capabilities from one or more network elements into components. This level is a virtual functional domain. Finally services are constructed as the orchestration of component functionality described as a diagram in an assembly paradigm.

4.4. Dynamic Software Architecture

The client-server architecture and the software layering provide the base for capturing the dynamic behavior of the software. The execution of the application software acts like a "conductor" who sequences the resources necessary to perform the functions defined in the components. The component execution will, in turn, trigger the execution of the capabilities that compose it. In that sense, the application software is a representation of the dynamic software architecture of the system.

5. SOFTWARE DEPENDABILITY

5.1. Quality Upfront

Although formal methods have often been advocated for improving the quality of software, we have not found these methods to be cost effective. In the absence of practical more robust methods, constructing software from reusable components contributes to improve the upfront quality of the software by relying on better component quality. Indeed, with time, multiple use of a component tends to improve its quality and that of assemblies using it. On a pragmatic level, reuse will yield more dependable software in the absence of external failures. The method described above was put in service a few months ago, and a significant gain in productivity was observed. In the first three months of use, the technique allowed a gain of productivity of 3:1 without any decline in quality. As in any other case of early introduction, the method and the software production process need to be tuned, which will likely provide additional productivity gains. Our current target is to reach a 10:1 improvement.

5.2. Platform Availability

The system architecture described in Figure 1 separates platform (hardware and software) from the application software generated by the SAW. To ensure platform availability, we decided to depart from the traditional duplex structure and adopt a cluster approach. Duplex and cluster significantly differ in an important element:

a) Duplex availability heavily depends on the sum of failure detection time and switch time (the time it takes to switch from the failing unit to its mate).
b) Cluster availability hinges only on detection time, namely the time it will take to redirect new incoming requests to an active member of the cluster instead of the failing unit.

Besides the commonly used techniques to facilitate the resumption of computation after a cluster unit failure (checkpointing, disk mirroring, machine mirroring, etc.), a reliable watchdog is the critical element of cluster availability since it is the element which limits the detection speed. Using these techniques leads to the possibility to build the platform out of commercial products which is a cheaper alternative. In spite of its importance, the availability of the platform is not the focus of this paper.

5.3. Service Dependability

Each component must include all the basic elements of robustness that are inherited by the assembly every time the component is used. Error handling and ability to monitor usage for revenue generation are two such elements of component robustness. High expected component reusability makes the proper component instrumentation cost effective.

The following basic principles must be adhered to:

a) Errors originating from end user behavior will be handled as a part of the service definition and will be constructed into the service control flow by the service programmer. The reason for this principle is that the recovery actions for this type of error must be determined in conjunction with the customer at service design time.
b) Errors originating from equipment and software failures are handled automatically by inserting software recovery segments and mechanisms. The reason for this decision is that improving service dependability cannot slow down the process of software generation which is highly automated.

5.4. Retry

Services assembled using SAW have, by construction, an inherent level of isolation and protection between service functions. Since each component executes in its own context, errors that first appear in one component can be handled locally without affecting other components nor the execution of other service instances, as long as the proper precautions are taken during code generation. A simple recovery strategy can be devised at the component level: if a typed error occurs, a retry event is issued (e.g. resubmitting the last event corresponding to the error type) to this component and if the error persists, a failure condition is signaled to the parent component in the hierarchy. So automatic retry does not need to be programmed by the service designer but can be handled by the service execution platform.

Since services (and components) are executed independently from one another, it is possible during execution to dynamically replace a faulty service instance (or any faulty component) by a new version of the same service (or component) reinitialized using provisioned data (per customer) and using the last known state-data for this service (or component). This provides a preliminary approach to automatically handle and recover from local faults on a per service or per component basis.

Our approach is predicated on the assumption that appropriate checkpointing and retry can be an acceptable recovery mechanism. The software layering described in Section 2 provides an ideal mechanism for rigorous (and possibly automatic) checkpoint insertion. The software assembled using this layering has a tree structure, the root of the tree being the service and the leaves being capabilities. Each tree node in the hierarchy is a candidate for checkpoint insertion. Checkpoints at capability boundaries can help handle server failures, since a capability controls a server functionality. A component that is composed of several capabilities may control several servers and offers a higher level of checkpointing. Finally, a service that is composed of components provides the highest level of checkpointing. This hierarchy of checkpoints enables a more rigorous escalation strategy execution and an algorithmic way of inserting checkpoints and recovery actions. This possibility of algorithmic design opens the door for the **automation of design and implementation of dependability**, which is a technique in line with the automatic generation of software, since its automation will not slow down software generation.

5.5. Service Software Model

After the service is designed in the SAW and before shipping it to the execution platform, it is <u>expanded</u> in terms of its lowest executable elements, the capabilities. A capability R_iS_j is a request R_i to a resource server S_j. A typical service model (Figure 5) is a directed graph (control flow) composed of decision nodes (D_v, D_w, etc.), computation nodes (C_k, etc.) and capabilities (R_iS_j, R_lS_m, R_pS_q, etc.). The structure is repetitive in that one can model this segment as a succession of: <u>request to a server</u>, followed by a <u>computation node</u> and a <u>decision node</u>. Requests to servers, computation nodes and decision nodes share data structures.

During expansion, component boundaries can be preserved to create the support for a three-level recovery strategy: capability, component and service levels.

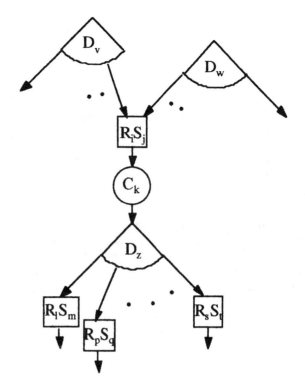

Figure 5. A Typical Service Segment

5.6. Recovery Strategy

With the software model of Figure 5 in mind, a simple strategy can then be put in place:

I. Failure protection is built into the platform execution of the requests to the servers through failure detection and retries. Additional retries can automatically be added into the graph structure based upon redundancy of resources. For instance, multiple voice storage facilities may be available in the network. This mechanism is driven by a service resource table which enumerates alternate resources and their preference in order of cost or quality. Each resource is listed in the table with its alternates and their ordering.

II. A watchdog mechanism is set up to monitor the service execution through <u>heart beat</u>. The heartbeat mechanism is automatically seeded into the service control flow so that it can be monitored.

III. The service state is <u>checkpointed</u> by the watchdog mechanism so that proper action can be taken in case of failure. Again, retry is the privileged route. A two-step strategy is used. First, the service process can be restarted at the closest possible point to the failure: capability, component boundary or even service entry point. Next, the service execution can be moved to a different member of the platform cluster. In both cases, restart must cause the fewest possible perturbations of the service.

IV. Since the platforms can execute multiple services serving a large number of customers, the watchdog mechanism must <u>arbitrate</u> between collisions on resources which would lower service dependability.

The method capitalizes on the recovery libraries introduced by Huang and Kintala [HUA93] by adding the automated instrumentation of the application software.

5.7. Dependability Evaluation
The methods discussed above are highly experimental and it is useful to evaluate their effectiveness without relying on a long field exposure. This desirable acceleration of the dependability testing can be provided by two classic methods: software mechanism for fault insertion in the executable software [CLE86] or model based dependability evaluation [GOS90].

6.   CONCLUSION
A method was presented for the construction of software using reusable components. The saillant advantages of our method are:

a) Software production speed is achieved by visual composition.
b) Contrary to similar other methods, we can generate software which controls multiple resources in a distributed network.
c) Contrary to similar documented methods, the software generated is instrumented for various essential telecommunication tasks: dependability, revenue generation, network measurements, etc.

While the technique is promising in terms of the speed up of software design and has already been put in practice in some AT&T products, two main issues stand on the way of ubiquity:

• our ability to perform efficient domain analysis and derive the best set of components for a given domain.
• more field opportunities to test software techniques instrumented automatically to enhance system dependability.

Both issues are currently being addressed experimentally.

References

[AGH86] Agha, G., *Actors - a model of concurrent computation in distributed systems,* The MIT Press, Cambridge, Massachusetts, 1986.

[CHA94] Chandra, R., A. Gupta, and J.L. Hennessy, "COOL: An Object Based Language for Parallel Programming," *Computer,* pp. 13-26, IEEE, August 1994.

[CLE86] Clement, G.F., and P.K. Giloth, "Evolution of Fault Tolerant Computing in AT&T," *Proceedings of the One-Day Symposium on the Evolution of Fault-Tolerant Computing,* Baden, Austria, 1986.

[GOS80] Goswami K.K., and R.K. Iyer, "Dynamic Load-Sharing Using Predicted Process Resource Requirements," *UILU-ENG-90-2224, UIUC (CSG Technical Report #126),* Coordinated Science Laboratory, University of Illinois, Urbana, Illinois, 23 pages, July 1990.

[HAR87] Harel, D., "Statecharts: A visual formalism for complex systems," *Science of Computer Programming,* Vol. 8, North-Holland, 1987.

[HUA93] Huang, Y., and C. M. R. Kintala, "Software Implemented Fault Tolerance: Technologies and Experience" *Proceedings of the 23rd International Symposium on Fault Tolerant Computing* (FTCS-23), Toulouse, France, June 22-23, 1993.

[JON81] Jones, C., *Programming Productivity,* McGraw-Hill, 1981.

[LEE94] Lee, B., and A.R. Hurson, "Dataflow Architectures and Multithreading," *Computer,* pp. 27-39, IEEE, August 1994.

[LEV91] Levendel, Y. "Reliability Models: Who Needs Them?" *Fourth Reliability Conference,* Invited Address, Denver-Colorado, 1991.

[PRI93] Price, B. A., R. M. Baecker, and I. S. Small, "A Principled Taxonomy of Software Visualization," *Journal of Visual Languages and Computing,* Vol. 4, No. 3, September 1993.

[REI94] Reinardt, A., "The Networks with Smarts," *Byte,* October, 1994.

[SEL93] Selic, B. ,"An Efficient Object-Oriented Variation of the Statecharts Formalism for Distribute Real-Time Systems," *IFIP Conference on Hardware Description Languages and Their Applications,* April 26-28, 1993, Ottawa, Canada.

Dependability Models for Iterative Software Considering Correlation between Successive Inputs

Andrea Bondavalli*, Silvano Chiaradonna*, Felicita Di Giandomenico** and Lorenzo Strigini***

* CNUCE/CNR, Via S. Maria, 36, 56126 Pisa, Italy
** IEI/CNR, Via S. Maria, 46, 56126 Pisa, Italy
***CSR, City University, Northampton Square, London EC1V OHB, UK

Abstract

We consider the dependability of programs of an iterative nature. The dependability of software structures is usually analysed using models that are strongly limited in their realism by the assumptions made to obtain mathematically tractable models and by the lack of experimental data. The assumption of independence between the outcomes of successive executions, which is often false, may lead to significant deviations from the real behaviour of the program under analysis. In this work we present a model in which dependencies among input values of successive iterations are taken into account in studying the dependability of iterative software. We consider also the possibility that repeated, non fatal failures may together cause mission failure. We evaluate the effects of these different hypotheses on 1) the probability of completing a fixed-duration mission, and 2) a performability measure.

1. Introduction

The analysis of the dependability of software structures, including those explicitly designed with the aim of tolerating faults, is the subject of many papers, most recently [2, 6, 8, 11, 12]. However, the realism of the models proposed and therefore their effective utility are limited by the large number of assumptions made to obtain mathematically tractable models and by the lack of experimental data. Among these assumptions, which are quite similar in all the models proposed, one which is clearly not valid in reality is the independence among successive outcomes of repeated executions of a program, that is, the assumption that the failure probability remains constant at each iteration for the entire mission duration.

The data on which most programs operate are represented mathematically as discrete multi-dimensional spaces of finite cardinality with a high numbers of dimensions. For example, a program may read a set of 20 floating-point numbers and have another set of 30 internal variables: it therefore works (in the terminology we use) on an *input space* with 50 dimensions. Experiments and theoretical justifications have shown the existence of contiguous failure regions in the program input space, i.e., connected subsets of the input space such that all the individual points in them cause the program to fail. In addition, it must be observed that in many applications, such as real-time control systems, the input sequences assume the form of trajectories where two successive inputs are very close to each other. For these reasons the inputs which originate failures of the software are very rarely isolated events but more likely grouped in *clusters* [1, 3, 4]. In other types of programs with repeated executions, causes for correlation can be found as well: e.g. periods of peak load in time-shared computers or in communication links could lead, through unusual timing conditions, to a high probability of errors in all the executions that take place during the peak. Last, issues of imperfect recovery (state corruption) and interactions with hardware faults further complicate the problem. For all the classes of applications to which these considerations apply, analyses of software dependability performed assuming independence among successive iterations seem to lead to results excessively diverging from the real behaviour of the analysed system [3, 4].

Another key aspect of software dependability evaluation is the model of the effects of failures on the controlled system. A realistic model should normally consider *sequences* of failures: many physical systems can tolerate "benign failures" (default, presumably safe values of the control outputs from the computer), or even plain incorrect results, if isolated or in short bursts, but a sequence of even "benign" failures such that the system is effectively without feed-back control for a while will often cause actual damage (from stopping a continuous production process to letting an airplane drift out of its safe flight envelope). Predicting the distribution of bursts would be trivial assuming independence, but obviously unrealistic: in reality, failures are going to be grouped into bursts with higher probability than predicted by the independence assumption.

13

In this paper, we try to overcome these limitations by proposing a more realistic evaluation model in which both correlation among successive inputs of the software and sequences of consecutive failures are taken into account. We consider a program (seen as a black box), executed repeatedly for a fixed number of iterations in a mission. We analyse the impact of these new assumptions on two of the various attributes of dependability, namely the probability of surviving missions (reliability at a certain time) and performability. Starting from a typical simplistic model we show the effects obtained by changing 2 hypotheses, first each in isolation and then together. The first is the model of the effects of failures, the other is the independence or correlation among successive inputs of the software.

The structure of the paper is as follows. In Section 2, we survey previous work for modelling correlation, then we describe the class of systems we evaluate, with the assumptions that affect our models. In Section 3 the effects on dependability of the different combinations of hypotheses are described. In Section 4, the problem of identifying proper values of parameters (distributions) for the correlation among successive iterations is discussed and the models are evaluated using some possible distributions. Section 5 contains our conclusions.

2 Background and Assumptions

2.1 Literature

The problem of modelling and evaluating the effects of correlation among the outcomes of successive iterations has been addressed by [7, 13]. [7] models the behaviour of a recovery block structure [10] composed by a primary version, an alternate version and a perfect acceptance test. Assuming that each value in the sequence of inputs is reasonably close to the preceding one, i.e., along each dimension the distance between any two successive points in the sequence of inputs is small compared to the size of the input space (along that dimension), two kinds of failure events of the primary module are distinguished, which we may call:

i) point failure: which happens when the input sequence of the primary enters a failure region,

ii) serial failure: a number of consecutive failures, (with probability 1) after the occurrence of a point failure, i.e., after that the input trajectory enters a failure region.

The number of serial failures subsequent to any point failure is a random variable. Correlation among the successive failures of the alternate are not considered since at the first (point) failure of the alternate the whole scheme fails and the execution stops. From these modelling assumptions a simple Markov chain with discrete time is developed allowing an analytical evaluation of the reliability (MTTF) of

the recovery blocks. [13] analyses the different forms of correlation of the recovery blocks structure, including correlation among the different alternates and among alternates and the acceptance test on the same inputs. To model the correlation among successive inputs these authors make the same assumptions as [7] including the same event set, and use a SRN (Stochastic Reward Net) model to evaluate the effects of input correlation on the MTTF.

2.2 The system

We assume an application of an iterative nature, where a *mission* is composed of a constant number n of iterations of the execution of the program. At each iteration, the program accepts an input and produces an output.

The outcomes of an individual iteration may be: i) *success*, i.e., the delivery of a correct result, ii) a *benign failure* of the program, i.e., an output that is not correct but does not, by itself, cause the entire mission to fail, or iii) a *catastrophic failure*, i.e., an output that causes the immediate failure of the entire mission. Of course in determining if an erroneous outcome is a benign or catastrophic failure the characteristics of the controlled system must be taken into account together with those of the program. We assume here that the execution time of the program is constant, and that as soon as an iteration is over the next iteration is started. This assumption has the same practical effect as those made in [6, 12] where the execution time was described by a combination of exponential variables and a timer was used for aborting those executions that lasted too long; using the mean duration of an iteration as though it was a constant duration yielded a satisfactory approximation.

As already mentioned, we shall show the effects on the dependability when passing from a hypothesis of statistical independence among successive input values to the case in which correlation is assumed. In this context different distributions of the number of consecutive failures will be analysed. The other hypothesis that will be changed regards accounting for sequences of failures in the definition of reliability and performability. In particular, we shall model those cases in which the mission fails not only because of a catastrophic failure but also due to a sequence of more than a given threshold number of consecutive failures. A brief discussion follows to clarify the main issues characterising the context we consider.

Failure Regions: Failure regions are subsets of the program input space I, consisting of contiguous points in the (non continuous) input space.

"A priori" the probability that an input belongs to a failure region is the same for each input; it is clear that some applications should be modelled assuming a different distribution since some parts of the input space may be known to be more prone to failures than others.

In [4] it is shown that the "size" of each failure region F, i.e. the diameters of the subsets $F \subset I$, for specific programs are approximately exponentially distributed. In [3] some two-dimensional views of fault regions (blob defects) are shown for a specific program, and a number of factors affecting the shapes of the faults were identified. The shapes can be often angular, elongated and rectangular. Since there is no evidence for choosing particular sizes and shapes on a general basis our choice will be i) guided by the necessity to simplify the modelling and ii) based on the plausibility and robustness of the models.

Input Sequence: The inputs form a "trajectory": any input value is assumed to be close (but not necessarily contiguous) to the previous one. We have a so called random or deterministic walk trajectory with a small step length. The step length, i.e., the distance between to successive input points, is considered small if the difference of the values of the two points on each dimension of the input space is small compared to the size of the input space in that dimension. If the step length becomes comparable to the size -in each dimension- of the input space (e.g., 50%) then, as shown in [4], we obtain uniform distribution of the inputs and therefore independence.

In such a context many different trajectories may be considered. Examples are 1) the next input is obtained from the previous one by modifying the values on each dimension by a random small quantity, 2) (subcase of 1) a "forward-biased" trajectory: passing from one input to the next the direction may only change slightly, 3) (subcase of 2) a trajectory of points on a straight line, at a random, small distance from each other.

Consecutive Benign Failures : We shall model the effects of sequences of benign failures such that if the sequence is equal or longer than a threshold, n_c, $n_c > 0$, it causes the failure of the entire mission.

The hypotheses we make in modelling sequences of correlated failures are:
1) a single success before the n_c-th consecutive failure will bring the system into a stable state, i.e. the memory of the previous failure sequence is immediately lost;
2) the trajectory of the input sequence is "forward-biased": passing from one input to the next the direction may vary with a small angle;
3) the failure regions are convex.

The main purpose of these assumptions is to simplify the modelling without restricting too much the class of applications that can be modelled. Actually, many control applications (e.g., radar systems or navigation systems) show "forward-biased" trajectories. Assumptions 2) and 3) constrain us to trajectories that, once they have left a failure region, are unlikely to re-enter it soon. They thus allow us to consider as a constant the probability of entering a failure region since 1) the probability of re-entering the failure region just left in a small number of iterations is small, 2) af-

ter an appropriate number of iterations the probability of re-entering that region is equal to the probability of entering any other region. Moreover assumption 3) is also conservative in the sense that, for a given size of a failure region, trajectories become more likely to "stay" longer in the region.

2.3 Dependability indicators

The two attributes of dependability that we will consider are the probability of surviving a mission (reliability after a certain number of executions) and the performability [6, 9, 11, 12]. For some critical applications, the main requirement is a very low probability of failure of a mission. An alternative scenario is that of comparatively non-critical applications, such as somewhat complex transaction-processing or scientific applications. Here the performability figure assumes more importance. For performability measurements, we shall denote M_n the total reward accumulated over a mission, and evaluate the expected total reward $E[M_n]$ (or simply "the performability"). The reward model used as a basis for performability is as follows: successful executions add one unit to the value of M_n; executions producing benign failures add zero; a catastrophic failure reduces the value of M_n to zero.

Instead of considering the probability of "mission survival" separately, one can also include it in the reward model. The reward from a failed mission, in the reward model, could be zero, as in our case, or possibly, a loss exceeding the value of a typical successful mission.

3 Models

After recalling the analysis of the "simplified" case with no correlation and no consideration of effects of sequences of failures, we shall consider the effects of each of our two new assumptions - a positive correlation between failures in successive iterations, and the possibility for repeated "benign" failures to cause a "catastrophic" failure - in isolation and then together.

3.1 Simplifying assumptions

In this case, a mission consists of a sequence of n iterations, and the outcomes of the individual iterations (success, "benign" failure, "catastrophic" failure, with probabilities p_s, p_b, and $p_c = 1 - p_s - p_b$, respectively) are independent events.

Probability of completing a mission. The probability of completing the mission is that of a series of n executions without catastrophic failure, $(1 - p_c)^n$.

Performability. The value of the expected total reward is: $E[M_n] = n * \dfrac{p_s}{1 - p_c} * (1 - p_c)^n$ which is the product of the probability of completing a mission without a catastrophic failure $(1 - p_c)^n$ and the expected number of successes in n iterations $n * \dfrac{p_s}{1 - p_c}$.

3.2 Mission failure from repeated benign failures (with independence between successive iterations)

We now assume that, although the controlled system can survive an individual benign failure of the control computer, any series of n_c or more benign failures in a row will cause the mission to fail. This is a common characteristic of continuous-control systems. In certain cases, the controlled system has enough physical inertia that an individual erroneous output from the control system will not cause the controlled system to move into a prohibited state. For such systems, the probability of an isolated failure with catastrophic consequences is zero. In other cases, although some of the failures of the control system are immediately catastrophic, others (e.g., those where the control system internally detects its own failure and outputs a "safe" value to the controlled system) are not, and only if they are repeated the resulting lack of active control may cause the controlled system to drift into a dangerous state. Of course, in either case the assumption that any sequence of up to n_c -1 failures will be tolerated, and all longer sequences will be catastrophic, is still a simplification of reality, yet more realistic than assuming that a controlled system can tolerate any arbitrary series of "benign" failures.

Probability of completing a mission. Given the independence between successive iterations, we model each iteration of the program as having three possible outcomes: immediate catastrophic failure, with probability p_c, benign failure, with probability p_b, and success with probability $(1 - p_c - p_b)$. The assumption that n_c or more benign failures in a row cause mission failure of course decreases (all model parameters being equal) the probability of surviving a mission. A reasonably tight test of whether the probability of a mission failure due to a series of benign failures, $p_{c\text{-serial}}$, can be neglected, can be obtained as follows. An upper bound on $p_{c\text{-serial}}$ is the probability that a series of iterations without catastrophic failure is followed by a success and then n_c benign failures:

$$\sum_{i=0}^{n-n_c-1} (1 - p_c)^i * p_s * p_b^{n_c} = p_s * p_b^{n_c} * \frac{1 - (1 - p_c)^{n-n_c}}{p_c}$$

The total probability of mission failure is larger than $(1-(1-p_c)^n)$, i.e., of the probability of mission failure if series of benign failures are of no concern. If the upper bound on $p_{c\text{-serial}}$ is negligible in comparison with this lower bound on the probability of mission failure, then it is legitimate to neglect $p_{c\text{-serial}}$ in computing the latter.

Performability. With our hypothesised reward structure, the only effect of the increased probability of mission failure is that a smaller proportion of the missions will be completed. Thus, the value of the performability will be decreased by the same amount as the probability of completing a mission.

3.3 Correlation between successive iterations (without mission failure from repeated benign failures)

We now assume that a failure at an iteration of the program makes it more likely than otherwise that the program will fail at the next iteration as well.

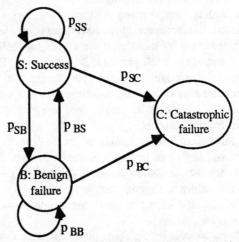

Figure 1. The model for the iterative execution of a system with correlation.

The system can then be modelled, for instance, by the three-state discrete-parameter Markov chain in Figure 1, giving a geometric distribution for the length of stay in failure regions, which would degenerate to the case of independence if $p_{BB}=p_{SB}$ and $p_{BS}=p_{SS}$. If we assume $p_{BB}>p_{SB}$, we would expect the behaviour of the system to be worse than under the independence assumption. This worsening would be due to the fact that the marginal probability of being in the "benign failure" state has increased.

Probability of surviving the mission. There are two possible mechanisms through which an increased probability of spending time in the "benign failure" state can af-

16

fect the completion of missions. We are not considering - yet - the fact that a series of benign failures may cause a mission failure. The other possible mechanism would be one in which the probability of the next iteration producing a catastrophic failure increases if the last iteration produced a failure, albeit benign. This is modelled by setting $p_{BC} > p_{SC}$ in the model. This looks like a realistic assumption in many cases: for instance, one may assume that a benign failure implies that the program has entered a region of its input space where failure in general is especially likely (*per* the assumption of positive correlation), and that a fixed proportion of such failures happens to be immediately catastrophic. However, there are other realistic scenarios, e.g., there may be a controlled system where most erroneous control signals are immediately "catastrophic", but the control system is engineered to detect its own internal errors and then issue a safe output and reset itself to a known state from which the program is likely to proceed correctly. One may then assume that most benign failures are due to this mechanism, and very likely to be followed by successes: $p_{BC} < p_{SC}$ and, indeed, $p_{BB} < p_{BS}$. We will not consider this scenario any further.

It is worth repeating that these are the only two mechanisms through which positive correlation between successive failures may affect the probability of completing a mission. To analyse their separate contributions, we can consider one specific form of positive correlation between successive (benign) failures, i.e., we assume that when input trajectories cross failure regions the "length of stay" (number of execution steps before leaving the region) has a geometric distribution. This is modelled by the Markov chain in Figure 1. Then, assuming that the random variables X_i represent the state of the system at time steps $i = 0, 1, 2, \ldots$, and the initial state of the system is S, i.e. $P(X_0 = S) = 1$, we can write:

$$P(\text{mission success}) = \prod_{i=1}^{n} P(X_i \neq C \mid X_{i-1} \neq C).$$

Each term in the product has the form:

$$P(X_i \neq C \mid X_{i-1} \neq C) =$$
$$= (1 - p_{SC}) * P(X_{i-1} = S \mid X_{i-1} \neq C) +$$
$$+ (1 - p_{BC}) * P(X_{i-1} = B \mid X_{i-1} \neq C) =$$
$$= (1 - p_{SC}) + (p_{SC} - p_{BC}) * \frac{P(X_{i-1} = B)}{P(X_{i-1} \neq C)}.$$

Since the last term in the right-hand product is positive, the sign of the difference $(p_{SC} - p_{BC})$ determines whether the probability of surviving the mission is greater or lower than it would be in case of independence between successive iterations, setting $p_c = p_{SC}$, and $p_b = p_{SB}$.

Performability. The value of the expected total reward will be affected by the increased number of benign failures and, if $p_{BC} > p_{SC}$, also by the increased probability of not completing a mission.

3.4 Correlation between successive iterations, allowing mission failures from repeated benign failures

A model of this more complex case is that in Figure 2.

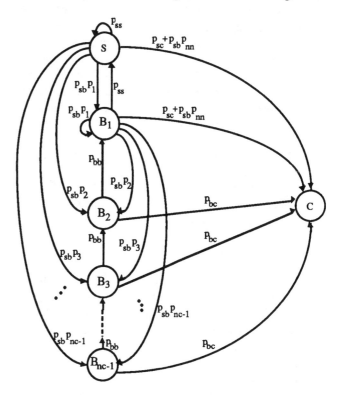

Figure 2. The model for iterative executions with failure clustering.

To model the correlation between successive failures, we assume that after an iteration with success (state S), the program has a probability p_{sb} that the next execution will produce a benign failure (i.e., that the input trajectory has entered a failure region). However, once in a failure region, the probabilities of staying there for one, two or more iterations are given by the parameters p_1, p_2, etc. The parameter p_{nn} designates the probability of staying for n_c iterations or more, i. e. $p_{nn} = 1 - \sum_{i=1}^{n_c-1} p_i$.

So, for instance, with probability $p_{sb}p_2$ the program enters a failure region, represented by state B_2 in our model, from which, unless a catastrophic failure occurs (arc from B_2 to C labelled p_{bc}) it will be compelled to move to B_1, after which it exits the failure region. This explains the role of the states B_1, B_2, etc., all designating a "benign" failure of the last execution. If the sequence of failures were longer than n_c-1, a mission failure would occur. This is described by adding the term $p_{sb}p_{nn}$ to the probability of the transition from S to C.

By choosing the values of the parameters p_i, we assign a distribution function to the variable "number of consecutive failures", conditional on being inside a failure region. Parameters p_{sc} and p_{bc} represent, respectively, the probability of catastrophic failure from state S and from any of the states B_i. Notice that once in B_1 (the last benign failure in the crossing of a failure region), the program may move to another success, or it may enter another failure region: this is modelled by the series of downward arcs issuing from B_1, labelled $p_{sb}p_1$, $p_{sb}p_2$, $p_{sb}p_3$, etc. The probabilities on these arcs are the same as those on the downward arcs issuing from S on the left: the probabilities of the trajectory entering a new failure region is independent of how long ago it left another failure region. This seems appropriate for representing a situation of sparse, small failure regions.

We point out that state C models the failure of a mission due either to crossing a failure region and staying there for at least n_c iterations, or to a "catastrophic" failure. A third cause for mission failure exists, i.e., crossing two or more failure regions without interruption, staying in each for less than n_c failures but so that the total number of consecutive benign failures exceeds n_c-1. This mechanism is not represented by a state in our chain, but rather by a trajectory which, after entering one of the B_i states, and stepping up all the way to B_1, takes one of the downward arcs on from B_1 back to one of the B_i, and does so one or more times until it has spent n_c iterations in the set of the B_i states. In solving the models, we have adopted the simplification of neglecting this kind of events, and developed an analysis, which is detailed in [5], that permits to verify if this simplification is acceptable with respect to the values given to the parameters.

Probability of completing a mission. Under these conditions, the positive correlation between successive iterations will affect the probability of completing a mission in two ways. One is the probability of having n_c consecutive benign failures and the second is the longer stays in failure regions. Inside failure regions we also assume a higher risk of catastrophic failures.

We can use again the expression:

$$P(\text{mission success}) = \prod_{i=1}^{n} P(X_i \neq C \mid X_{i-1} \neq C).$$

Where each term in the product now has the form:

$$P(X_i \neq C \mid X_{i-1} \neq C) =$$

$$= (1 - p_{sc} - p_{nn}*p_{sb}) + (p_{sc} + p_{nn}*p_{sb} - p_{bc})*$$
$$*p(X_{i-1} = B_2 \text{ or...or } X_{i-1} = B_{n_c-1} | X_{i-1} \neq C) =$$
$$= (1 - p_{sc}) +$$
$$+ (p_{sc} - p_{bc})*p(X_{i-1} = B_2 \text{ or.. or } X_{i-1} = B_{n_c-1} | X_{i-1} \neq C) -$$
$$- p_{nn}*p_{sb}*(1 - p(X_{i-1} = B_2 \text{ or.. or } X_{i-1} = B_{n_c-1} | X_{i-1} \neq C)).$$

It can be observed that the first term in this sum represents the case that sequences of (benign) failures do not affect the probability of mission failures. The second term represents the contribution of the higher (or lower, as the case might be) probability of catastrophic failure after a benign failure, compared to that after a successful iteration. The third term represents the probability of mission failure due to sequences of n_c or more consecutive failures.

Performability. In terms of performability, the expected total reward will be affected by:
1) the increased number of benign failures,
2) if $p_{bc} > p_{sc}$, also by the increased probability of not completing a mission due to a catastrophic failure, and
3) the probability of not completing a mission due to sequences of n_c or more consecutive failures.

4. Evaluations results

The model proposed in Section 3.4 is a general one in the sense that it is not tied to any specific distribution of the length of stays in failure regions. As there is no evidence for choosing a particular distribution on a general basis, we show the effect of a few different distribution functions, before discussing the properties that they share.

4.1 Distribution functions for the length of stay in a failure region

The distribution functions we consider are: the *geometric*, a *modified negative binomial* (including the geometric as a particular case), a *modified Poisson* distribution and an *ad hoc* distribution (described later).

4.1.1 Geometric, modified negative binomial and modified Poisson. The geometric distribution, defined as $p_i = q*(1-q)^{i-1}, i = 1, 2, 3, ...,$ for some $q \in (0,1]$, fits very well contexts where most failure regions are of small size. It seems suitable in contexts where: a) high-quality software is used, meaning that the residual failure regions are of small size and so the input trajectory will remain in the failure region for just a few iterations; b) large failure regions can still be present, but the probability that the input trajectory will enter them and stay for many iterations is negligible. The geometric distribution is memoryless. It

models trajectories having at each iteration the same probability q of leaving the failure region, independently of how long they had been in it before.

If the probability of entering a large failure region and staying in it for a considerable number of iterations is not negligible compared to the probability of entering small failure regions, a modified negative binomial distribution function and a modified Poisson distribution function seem to be more appropriate.

The modified negative binomial is defined as $p_i = \binom{i+r-2}{r-1} * q^r * (1-q)^{i-1}, i=1,2,3,...,$ for some $r=1,2,3,....$, and $q \in (0,1]$. The modified Poisson is defined as $p_i = \frac{e^{-\alpha} * \alpha^{i-1}}{(i-1)!}, i=1,2,3,....,$ for some $\alpha > 0$. In the evaluation that we present here, the modified negative binomial is used with parameter r=5.

4.1.2 An ad-hoc distribution.

A further distribution is considered as an example of how ad hoc distribution functions can be derived based on knowledge available in particular cases. Suppose that for a particular application the following knowledge has been obtained:
1) the input space is a discrete two-dimensional (Cartesian) space;
2) failure regions have a square shape with its sides parallel to the axes of the input space;
3) the input trajectory is a straight line crossing the square region failures vertically, horizontally or diagonally.

This ad-hoc distribution can therefore be defined as: $p_i = \frac{i+1}{3i-1} * p_L(i) + \sum_{j=i+1}^{max L} \frac{2}{3j-1} * p_L(j),$ with $i=1,2,3,..,$ where: $p_L(j)$ is the probability that the failure region which the input trajectory has entered is of side length equal to j, $1 \le j \le maxL$, and maxL is the maximum length of the side of a failure region. The expressions $\frac{i+1}{3i-1}$ and $\frac{2}{3j-1}$ are the probabilities that the length of stays in failure regions be i, conditional on being inside a failure region having the side length equal to respectively i and j>i.

Different distributions could be considered for p_L; among these the truncated geometric represents an input space mainly populated by failure regions of small size. In the following numerical evaluation, the truncated geometric distribution and a length of the sides of the failure regions ranging between 2 and 30 will be used.

4.2 Evaluation and discussion

Now we show the results for the probability of mission failure and the performability measure obtained from the model in which correlation between successive iterations, and mission failures from repeated consecutive failures are taken into account.

We use the four distributions described previously to model the correlation among successive inputs and a set of plausible values for the model parameters, as shown in Table 1. The number of iterations in a mission, n, is 10^6 (a realistic number, e.g., for civil avionics where the average duration of one iteration could be 20-50 milliseconds and the mission duration could be around 10 hours).

Parameters and their values	
$p_{sb} = 10^{-5}$	
$p_{sc} = 10^{-9}$	
$p_{ss} = 1 - p_{sb} - p_{sc}$	(notice that
$p_{bc} = 10^{-3}$	$p_{bc} \gg p_{sc}$)
$p_{bb} = 1 - p_{bc}$	
$n_c = 10$	

Table 1. Parameter values used in the numerical evaluation.

The two factors that presumably have the greatest influence on the probability of mission failure (that is, the probability of entering state C in Figure 2) and on the performability are 1) the probability of exceeding a sequence of n_c -1 consecutive failure, p_{nn} and 2) the mean stay in a failure region, once the input trajectory enters it. We shall therefore evaluate the variations in the dependability figures as a function of these two factors, while keeping all others constant.

In Figures 3a and 3b, showing, respectively, the probability of failure and the performability as functions of the probability of exceeding n_c-1, two additional distribution functions p^* and p^{**} have been introduced. Once a value for p_{nn} has been fixed, p^{**}, defined such that $\sum_{i=1}^{n_c-2} p^{**}(i) = 0,$ $p^{**}(n_c - 1) = 1 - p_{nn}$ and $\sum_{i>n_c-1} p^{**}(i) = p_{nn}$, represents one of the two extreme behaviours of an input trajectory: the case in which the input trajectory, once in a failure region, stays in it for at least $(n_c - 1)$ iterations; while p^*, defined such that $p^*(1) = 1 - p_{nn},$ $\sum_{i=2}^{n_c-1} p^*(i) = 0,$ and $\sum_{i>n_c-1} p^*(i) = p_{nn}$, represents the other extreme behaviour in which, once in a failure region, the trajectory may either exit immediately (after one benign failure) or stay in it for at least n_c iterations.

The range of p_{nn} has been limited between 0 and $2 \cdot 10^{-3}$ because higher values would imply a probability of mission failure too high for being acceptable.

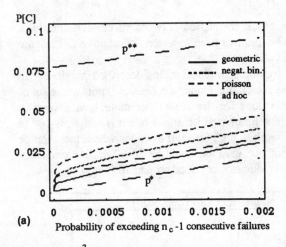

(a)

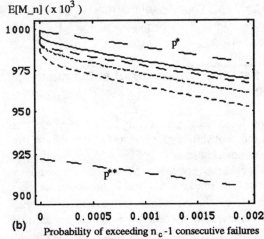

(b)

Figure 3. Probability of mission failure (a) and performability (b) as a function of p_{nn}.

A few observations can be derived related to Figure 3:

1) p^* shows better figures than p^{**} because we set $p_{bc} > p_{sc}$, in the other case the opposite would have been true. Moreover, increasing n_c increases the difference between the probabilities of mission failure implied by the two extreme distributions p^* and p^{**};

2) the distance of the curves for the considered distributions from the curve for p^* depends on the mean stay in failure regions (and on the difference $p_{bc} - p_{sc}$);

3) the value of p_{sb} determines the slope of the curves; higher values imply that the probability of entering a failure region becomes higher and therefore the probability of mission failure increases;

4) as expected, the four distributions we considered are all included in between the two extreme distribution functions and are closer to p^*, since they have been chosen to model a higher probability of short sequences (than of long ones) of consecutive failures;

5) the definition of p^* and p^{**} allows simple tests on the viability of specific applications requiring only an estimate of p_{nn}. The designer of a software application can bound the probability of mission failure and the performability, using p^* and p^{**}. If the worse of the two values obtained is sufficient to satisfy the application requirements, further information regarding the actual distribution becomes unnecessary.

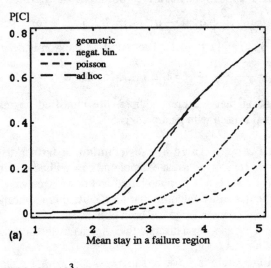

(a)

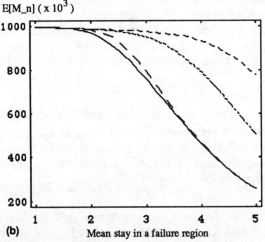

(b)

Figure 4. Probability of mission failure (a) and performability (b) as a function of the mean stay in a failure region (conditional on having entered it).

Figure 4a and 4b show, respectively, the behaviour of the probability of failure and the performability as function of the mean stay in a failure region.

Analysing them we observed that, with the same mean, the distributions with higher variance cause worse behaviour. The figures obtained from the ad hoc distribution are very similar to those obtained from the other distributions. The plots have been made for a range of parameters that extends to unrealistic situations: with the set of parameter values chosen, our plots show that, to obtain probabilities of mission failure up to 10^{-1}, the mean stay in failure regions must be limited to 2-4.

5. Concluding remarks

In this paper, we addressed one of the main causes of the lack of realism of most structural models for predicting the dependability of iterative software. The assumption of independence between the outcomes of successive executions, which is often false, may, in fact, lead to significant deviations of the result obtained from the real behaviour of the program under analysis. We have proposed a model in which both dependencies among input values of successive iterations and the effects of sequences of consecutive failures are taken into account in studying the dependability of iterative software.

The effects of considering failure clusters, and the independence or correlation among successive inputs of the program have been analysed, first the effects of each in isolation and then together. The dependability attributes chosen for the analysis have been the probability of surviving missions (reliability after a certain number of executions) and a performability measure, representative of often conflicting requirements.

The proposed model can accommodate different distributions of the length of stays in failure regions. Therefore a number of distributions have been taken into consideration and their effects on the dependability figures analysed, in particular we used their probability of exceeding a given number of consecutive failures and their mean stay in failure regions. Two distributions representing the two extreme cases have been defined, which produce figures that bound those derived by all the other distributions.

Acknowledgements

This research was supported by the CEC in the framework of the ESPRIT Basic Research Action 6362 "PDCS2" ("Predictably Dependable Computing Systems"). The authors wish also to thank the anonymous reviewers for their useful comments to the initial version of this paper.

References

[1]   P.E. Amman and J.C. Knight, "Data Diversity: An Approach to Software Fault Tolerance," IEEE TC, Vol. C-37, pp. 418-425, 1988.

[2]   J. Arlat, K. Kanoun and J.C. Laprie, "Dependability Modelling and Evaluation of Software Fault-Tolerant Systems," IEEE TC, Vol. C-39, pp. 504-512, 1990.

[3]   P. G. Bishop, "The Variation of Software Survival Time for Different Operational Input Profiles (or why you can wait a long time for a big bug to fail)," in Proc. FTCS-23, Toulouse, France, 1993, pp. 98-107.

[4]   P.G. Bishop and F.D. Pullen, "PODS Revisited - A Study of Software Failure Behaviour," in Proc. FTCS-18, Tokyo, Japan, 1988, pp. 1-8.

[5]   A. Bondavalli, S. Chiaradonna, F. Di Giandomenico and L. Strigini, "Modelling Correlation among Successive Inputs in Software Dependability Analyses," CNUCE/CNR Technical Report No. C94-20, 1994.

[6]   S. Chiaradonna, A. Bondavalli and L. Strigini, "On Performability Modeling and Evaluation of Software Fault Tolerance Structures," in Proc. EDCC1, Berlin, Germany, 1994, pp. 97-114.

[7]   A. Csenski, "Recovery block reliability analysis with failure clustering," in Proc. DCCA-1 (Preprints), Santa Barbara, California, 1989, pp. 33-42.

[8]   J.C. Laprie, J. Arlat, C. Beounes and K. Kanoun, "Definition and Analysis of Hardware-and-Software Fault-Tolerant Architectures," IEEE Computer, Vol. 23, pp. 39-51, 1990.

[9]   J. F. Meyer, "On evaluating the performability of degradable computing systems," IEEE TC, Vol. C-29, pp. 720-731, 1980.

[10]   B. Randell, "System Structure for Software Fault Tolerance," IEEE TSE, Vol. SE-1, pp. 220-232, 1975.

[11]   A. T. Tai, "Performability-Driven Adaptive Fault Tolerance," in Proc. FTCS 24, 1994, pp. 176-185.

[12]   A. T. Tai, A. Avizienis and J. F. Meyer, "Performability Enhancement of Fault-Tolerant Software," IEEE TR, Vol. R-42, pp. 227-237, 1993.

[13]   L.A. Tomek, J.K. Muppala and K.S. Trivedi, "Modeling Correlation in Software Recovery Blocks," IEEE TSE, Vol. SE-19, pp. 1071-1085, 1993.

Session 2:
Operating System Mechanisms

Session Chair: Josep Torrellas

Traffic Dependencies in Client-Server Systems and Their Effect on Performance Prediction

Greg Franks

Department of Systems and Computer Engineering

Carleton University

Ottawa, Ontario, Canada, K1S 5B6

Abstract

Client-server systems are becoming increasingly common in the world today as users move from centralized mainframe facilities to networks of distributed work stations. This form of work demands new performance models as the interactions in client-server systems are more complex than the types supported by classic queueing network solvers such as Mean Value Analysis. However, certain interaction patterns can arise in multi-level client-server systems that require special treatment. This paper describes these interactions (referred to as interlocking here) and how they affect the performance estimates of solution methods using surrogate delays to solve multi-level client-server models. It then describes a method to take interlocking into account when solving the performance models. These corrections often reduce the solution error to close to zero when compared to exact solutions for situations where interlocking is significant.

1 Introduction

Client-server systems are becoming increasingly common in the world today as users move from centralized mainframe facilities to networks of distributed work stations. These systems often use a form of interaction between cooperating agents referred to as the remote procedure call (RPC) [2] or rendezvous. Conventional queueing network models do not represent these systems because of the blocking nature of the remote procedure call. Other techniques, such as Generalized Stochastic Petri Nets [1] and Stochastic Reward Networks [5], do not scale well because of the state-space explosion in the underlying Markov model to handle even moderately sized systems. To overcome this problem, new solution techniques such as Stochastic Rendezvous Networks [13, 14, 8], the Method of Layers [11, 12, 10] and Mobile Servers [4] have been developed. The primary feature of these new solution techniques is that they recognize software contention and the blocking of software processes as well as hardware contention. However, traffic patterns that arise in deeply layered client-server systems are often not handled properly which can result in large errors in the solution of the models. The focus of this paper is one such interaction, referred to as interlocking, where traffic at lower-level servers is constrained by the arrival patterns at intermediate servers.

Interlocking occurs when a client and its server share a common resource; the resource may be either another software server or a hardware device (see Figure 1). Traffic dependencies at the lower-level servers in multiply layered systems in turn affect the prediction of delays. These dependencies arise because the client task can be queued on, blocked on or executing within only one task or device at a time. For the software interlock example, the task `client` can only block waiting for a reply from `server1` or `server2` but not both simultaneously. Similarly, for the device interlock example, the task `client` can either be executing on the processor, or blocked waiting for a reply from `server`. Solutions which ignore interlocking tend to be pessimistic because arrivals from interlocked clients are treated as independent events when in fact they are correlated. Furthermore, these solutions may show that the lower level servers and devices are not fully utilized when in fact they are.

Other authors have recognized that interlocking is a phenomena which must be considered. However, Woodside et al's solver [14] only deals with "send" interlocking (described in greater detail in the next section) while Rolia and Sevcik's solver [10] only accounts for interlocking at the device level. The contribution of this work is in developing a general solution for interlocking effects for all forms of interlocking that arise in these models.

The rest of this paper is as follows: Section 2 describes briefly the layered queueing network models used to solve client-server systems. The interlocking phenomenon itself is described in Section 3. The solution strategy for locating and compensating for interlocking in the performance solvers is described in Section 4 followed by examples in Section 5. Finally, Section 6 summarizes the results.

2 Layered Queueing Network Models

Client-server systems cannot be solved using standard queueing network methods such as product-form Mean Value Analysis (MVA) [9, 7] because of the blocking nature of the remote procedure call. In product-form MVA models, queueing stations are free to accept new requests upon completion of service for a customer. However, in client-server models, queueing

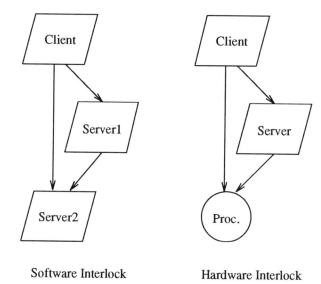

Software Interlock   Hardware Interlock

Figure 1: Simple interlocked case. The parallelograms are software tasks and the circles are devices.

stations block during RPC requests to other stations. Customers to the queueing station issuing the request see the blocking time as an apparent increase in service time. This time is referred to as *"included service time"* here.

The approach taken by both the Stochastic Rendezvous Network and Method of Layers to solve the difficulties introduced by the RPC is to partition the network into a set of submodels and use the method of surrogate delays [6] to propagate delays from one model to the next. The submodels consist of one or more servers and a set of *parents* which consist of all the tasks that call the servers directly (see Figure 2). Each submodel is solved using product-form MVA. Residence times computed for clients at lower levels are then used as included service times for the servers at the next level in the model.

During the solution of a layer, each set of clients is treated as an independent source of customers. However, traffic dependencies from higher levels may in fact cause the flow from one customer to be correlated with the flow from another. For example, when the hardware contention model in Figure 2 is solved, arrivals from the Database and FileSys tasks are treated as independent events. However, an arrival from FileSys to the CPU can only occur as the result of an arrival from Database. Consequently, the lower level submodel introduces more contention delay into the included service times for higher level submodels than is in fact present. Ignoring the correlation always results in pessimistic performance estimates.

3   Interlock Phenomena

This section describes the two forms of interlocking found in client-server systems: *Send* (shown in Figure 3) and *Split* (Figure 4). The overlapped paral-

lelograms labeled t0 in each figure represent a set of pure clients. They cycle continually generating RPC requests along the arcs labeled yab and yac in Figure 3 and yea and yec in Figure 4. The remaining parallelograms in each figure are serving tasks. They may be either pure servers (for example, task t3) or both clients and servers (tasks t1 and t2).

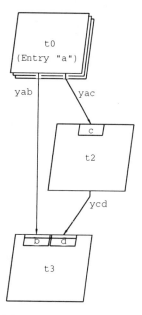

Figure 3: Send interlock. The large parallelograms represent tasks. The small parallelograms enclosed within the task icons are entries.

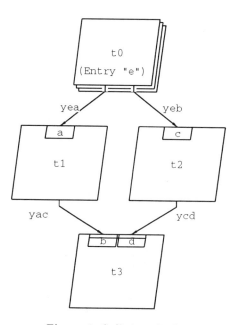

Figure 4: Split interlock.

RPC requests in the layered queueing models described in this paper are always sent to objects called

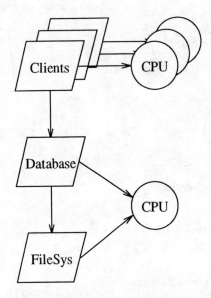

Three-Level Client-Server System

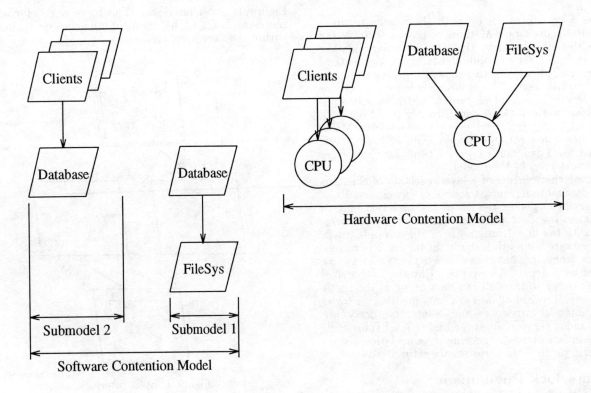

Figure 2: A sample client-server architecture partitioned using the Method of Layers.

"entries" which are shown as the small parallelograms enclosed within each serving task. Entries capture the specific behaviour of a task for each type of request received. Each entry has its own service time parameters and may originate requests to other tasks. Pure client tasks have one implicit entry, which is not shown.

Interlocking arises when a common parent task makes requests to a server through independent nested RPC's or *call paths* which may pass through intermediate servers in the model. The point where the flow splits along independent paths is called the *"split point"*. For example, in Figure 3, the first path consists of the arc labeled yab; the second path consists of the arcs labeled yac and ycd. In Figure 4, the first path is comprised of arcs labeled yea and yac and the second yeb and ycd. In both cases the set of clients labeled t0 are the common parents at the split point in the flow and the task labeled t3 is the common server.

Send interlocking arises when there are one or more direct paths between the common parent and the common server (for example the arc labeled yab in Figure 3). Both the set of client tasks at the split point for the flows, t0, and the intermediate interlocked task, t2, are direct parents of the common server. Split interlocking arises when a common parent task calls independent intermediate tasks which in turn share a common resource. In this case, the split point is not a direct parent of the common resource. In both cases, the common resource may be a device or another task.

Figures 3 and 4 show the very simplest forms of interlocking. More complicated patterns can arise, either by adding more tasks in series along a path, or by adding more paths in parallel. An example of a complex interaction pattern can be found in Section 4.4 below.

3.1 Factors That Affect Performance Estimation

Four factors affect the amount of error introduced into the solution of the model:

1. The number of clients at a common parent split point. Increasing the number of common parents decreases the amount of interlocking.

2. The number of independent paths from the split point to the common resource. Increasing the number of independent paths increases the effect from interlocked flows.

3. The utilization of the interlocked tasks and devices. The error increases with overall utilization.

4. The amount of included service time in the interlocked tasks. Systems with large amounts of included service time close to the split point will show the largest effects from interlocking.

These factors are illustrated in Section 5 with examples.

4 Calculation of Contention with Interlocked Flows

The algorithm to estimate and correct for the interlocked flow rates is split into three parts:

1. The location of interlocking *paths*.

2. The calculation of interlocked flow components.

3. Queue adjustments in the MVA solver.

4.1 Path Finder

Paths in the model consist of nested remote procedure calls from an originating client task to a server. They are located by following the requests made from one task to the next using a depth-first recursive search. By incorporating the call rate information associated with each request while tracing a path, the flow component originated by any parent to any entry can be determined. This information is stored by the solver in an $n_e \times n_e$ *path* matrix where n_e is the total number of entries in the model (see Table 1). Each entry in the matrix stores the number of calls to the destination entry caused by an invocation of source entry. Elements in the matrix are denoted by $path(a, b)$, where a is the source entry and b is the destination. By definition, the diagonal of the matrix is set to 1 indicating that each call to the associated entry causes it to execute once.

Send Interlock			
Src Ent	Destination Entry		
	a	b	c	d
a	1.	1.	1.	0.5
b	0.	1.	0.	0.
c	0.	0.	1.	0.5
d	0.	0.	0.	1.

Table 1: Interlock path matrix for the model shown in Figure 3.

As an example, consider task t0 in Figure 3 and denote it as entry a. During each iteration of this task, entry c on task t2 and entry b on task t3 are each called once. Furthermore, each time entry c is called by entry a, entry d on task t3 is called on average 0.5 times. These numbers make up row one in Table 1.

4.2 Interlocked Flows

The purpose of the interlocked flow finder is to locate all common sources of traffic to a particular *task* in a model since interlocked flows, in general, do not have to go to the same entry. The path matrix table defined in the preceding section is used to meet this objective. Common parents to a task j are located by sequencing through all pairings of incoming arcs that originate from different tasks. The originating entries for each arc, say a and c, are then used as the destination entries in the path table. The table is then searched for source entries belonging to a common task that calls both entries. This algorithm is shown in Figure 5 below.

{ Find parents common to entries a and c. }

common_parent(a, c)

```
    P ← ∅                    {Set of common entries}
    for i ∈ T do             {Search overall tasks T}
        for e ∈ E(i) do      {Search over all entries, E(i)}
            for f ∈ E(i) do
                if path(e, a) × path(f, c) > 0 then
                    P ← P ∪ e
                endif
            endfor
        endfor
    endfor
    return P                 {Return common entries}
end common_parent
```

Figure 5: Common parent finder.

As the path table stores call rates from one entry to another rather than by entry to arc, it is necessary to identify the arcs to the common server by their associated source entries. The flow component from the originating source entry e to the ultimate destination entry of task j is then found using:

$$\lambda_{ec} = \lambda_e \cdot \text{path}(e, a) \cdot y_{ac} \qquad (1)$$

where y_{ac} denotes the number of calls from entry a on task i to entry c on task j, $i \neq j$. Furthermore, the throughput at any particular entry a can be found by the sum:

$$\lambda_a = \sum_{e \in C} \lambda_e \cdot \text{path}(e, a), a \notin C \qquad (2)$$

where C is the set of entries belonging to pure client tasks. In fact, any unique cut-set to the task j can be used in place of C in (2). By knowing the total throughput at an entry a and the throughput at a due to requests from a particular entry e, it is possible to separate flow caused by common parents from flow from other sources.

The common parent finder shown in Figure 5 returns a set of entries (denoted as P) that generate non-zero flow to the entries labeled a and c. This set must be pruned of all entries that do not result in the split in flow. The interlocked flow component, λ^{IL}, is then found by using the expression:

$$\lambda_{ac}^{IL} = y_{ac} \sum_{e \in P} \lambda_e \cdot \text{path}(e, a) \qquad (3)$$

4.3 Interlock Adjustment

The interlock adjustment is accomplished by removing flow which originates from common parents that arrives by different paths to a common server at the point where the queue lengths are being recalculated for Mean Value Analysis. Equation (4) shows

the queue length calculation where L_{mk} is the queue length for chain k at station m, $\mathbf{N}$ is the population vector by chain, W_{mk} is the waiting time for chain k at station m and λ_{mk} is the flow to station m for chain k.

$$L_{mk}(\mathbf{N}) = \lambda_{mk} W_{mk}(\mathbf{N}) \qquad (4)$$

$$\lambda_{mk} = \lambda_{mk}^{IL} + \lambda_{mk}^{NOIL} \qquad (5)$$

Client classes in each submodel of a layered queueing model are represented by separate chains in the underlying MVA model. Flow from a client task corresponding to chain k to the serving station m is found using:

$$\lambda_{mk} = \sum_{a \in E(k)} \sum_{c \in E(m)} \lambda_{ac} \qquad (6)$$

The expression $E(k)$ denotes the set of entries corresponding to task k.

The interlock adjustment separates the flow from common parents from flow from other sources in λ_{mk}. The interlocked flow is then reduced in proportion to the total number of sources (labeled as n_s in (7)) of flow along all chains with interlock. These sources are the tasks at the point where the interlock paths diverge plus the immediate parents of the tasks that lie along the interlocked paths that source non-interlocked flow. In effect, one source out of several that generate the flow rate λ_{mk} is being removed. Equation (4) is then replaced with:

$$L_{mk}(\mathbf{N}) = \left(\frac{n_s - 1}{n_s} \lambda_{mk}^{IL} + \lambda_{mk}^{NOIL} \right) W_{mk}(\mathbf{N}) \qquad (7)$$

4.4 Path Finder Example

Figure 6 shows an example with multiple interlocking paths. The corresponding interlocking path table is shown in Table 2.

Consider task S1. Its entries are h, i and j. Entry h is called by entry c, entry i is called by entry d, and entry j is called by both entries f and g. As entries c and d belong to a common task, the arcs ych and ydi are not separate paths for interlocked flow (task I5 serializes the requests), therefore they are not paired when locating common sources. The set of pairings that must be considered is {(c, f), (c, g), (d, f), (d, g), (f, g)}. For (c, f) the only row that has non-zero entries for the columns c and f is C1. There are no rows that meet the criteria for (c, g). For (d, f), matches are found for rows C1, C2, b and f. This set is pruned to row f only as this entry spans the least number of layers to task S1. Finally, C2 is the only common entry for (d, g) and (f, g). After pruning entries that do not split flow, the path finding algorithm returns the set {C1, f, C2}.

5 Examples

The following examples illustrate the factors identified earlier that affect performance estimation identified earlier and how compensating for interlocked flows improves the solution accuracy. This section concludes with a discussion on how these factors affect performance estimation.

	Complex Interlock										
Src Ent	Destination Entry										
	C1	C2	a	b	c	d	f	g	h	i	j
C1	1.	0.	1.5	0.5	1.5	0.5	0.5	0.	1.5	0.5	0.5
C2	0.	1.	0.	1.	0.	1.	1.	1.	0.	1.	2.
a	0.	0.	1.	0.	1.	0.	0.	0.	1.	0.	0.
b	0.	0.	0.	1.	0.	1.	1.	0.	0.	1.	1.
c	0.	0.	0.	0.	1.	0.	0.	0.	1.	0.	0.
d	0.	0.	0.	0.	0.	1.	0.	0.	0.	1.	0.
f	0.	0.	0.	0.	0.	1.	1.	0.	0.	1.	1.
g	0.	0.	0.	0.	0.	0.	0.	1.	0.	0.	1.
h	0.	0.	0.	0.	0.	0.	0.	0.	1.	0.	0.
i	0.	0.	0.	0.	0.	0.	0.	0.	0.	1.	0.
j	0.	0.	0.	0.	0.	0.	0.	0.	0.	0.	1.

Table 2: Path table for complex example of path finding.

5.1 Example 1: Common Server System (Send Interlock)

Figure 7 shows the same client-server system shown earlier in Figure 2 complete with parameters for the model. Each client runs on its own processor. The central database computer has two tasks running on it called **Database** and **FileSys** (disks are not shown). The service time for both tasks is 1.0 units. The service time at the client tasks is varied from 0.01 units to 100.0 units by powers of 10. The number of clients is varied from 1 to 50. Each client makes one request per cycle on average. This request causes the **DataBase** tasks to make one request to the **FileSys** task. The request parameters are shown next to the appropriate arc on the figure.

The throughputs (among other performance results) were found by an exact Markovian analysis using the GreatSPN [3] Petri Net solver for the cases with one to four clients, by simulation for the cases with ten and fifty clients and by the layered queuing network solver using MVA for all cases with and without the queue length correction for interlocked flows. Without the interlock correction, the relative error ranges up to a maximum of 32.63% as the demand on the database computer increases. However, with the interlocking correction enabled, the maximum error is only 1.61%, with the typical error less than 0.1%. The relative error for all test cases is shown in Table 3.

From Table 3, the largest error occurs with the highest customer demand on the database computer. The reason for this relationship can be seen easily from Figure 8. This graph shows the waiting time versus utilization for the database system when the number of clients was varied from one to four and the client service time was set to 1.0. Without the interlock correction (the points marked with **NOIL**), the included service introduced by the nested RPC limits the utilization of the processor to about 0.67 because the **DataBase** task spends 1 unit of time at the processor and 1 unit of delay for included service. With the interlock correction, the waiting times calculated by the layered queuing network solver and the Markovian an-

alyzer are nearly identical.

5.2 Example 2: Send Interlock

This example is based on the example in the preceding section. However, the service time at the **FileSys** and **DataBase** tasks were varied instead of varying the demand generated by the clients. The number of clients was fixed at 3, and the service time for each client was set to 1 unit. Table 4 shows the service times used and the results for the interlocked and non-interlocked layered queueing network solutions using Mean Value Analysis. As the service time of the **FileSys** task was increased, the relative error in the non-interlocked solution also increased. The utilization at the processor was close to 1.0 for all cases.

5.3 Example 3: Split Interlock

Figure 9 shows the example used earlier in Section 3.1. The parameters for the intermediate tasks, **t1** through **t4** and common server are shown on the figure. The call rates from the common parent **Client** to the intermediate level tasks are shown as $[1/r]$ where r is the number of intermediate tasks (this call rate caused the client throughput to be constant regardless of the number of intermediate tasks for a system with only one client).

Table 5 shows the relative error in throughput for each case (the non-interlocked case is shown in the graph in Figure 10). As the number of clients was increased, the relative error in the layered queueing network solution without the interlocking correction decreased. As the number of independent paths was increased, the error increased.

5.4 Factors that Affect Performance Estimation

Example 3 above demonstrates the effect on solution accuracy caused by the first two factors (common parents and interlocked paths) listed earlier in Section 3.1. The results for the non-interlocked solution are plotted in the graph shown in Figure 10. Increasing the number of clients at the common parent split point decreased the error in the solution without the interlock compensation because, as the num-

n_c	Client Service Time									
	% Error, No interlock					% Error, Interlock				
	0.01	0.10	1.0	10.0	100.0	0.01	0.10	1.0	10.0	100.0
1	32.33	30.78	19.46	1.69	0.02	0.0	0.00	0.00	0.00	0.00
2	32.51	32.39	27.97	3.63	0.04	0.0	0.09	1.47	0.51	0.01
3	32.51	32.51	31.44	6.52	0.06	0.0	0.01	0.48	1.02	0.02
4	32.51	32.51	32.34	10.39	0.08	0.0	0.00	0.04	1.52	0.03
10	32.60†	32.63†	32.55†	30.84†	0.39†	0.16†	0.26†	0.07†	0.67†	0.16†
50	32.60†	32.63†	32.55†	32.59†	24.06†	0.16†	0.26†	0.06†	0.16†	1.61†

Table 3: Relative Error in client throughput versus number of clients, n_c, and varying client service time for the system in Figure 7. The results marked with '†' were compared against simulation runs with a 95% confidence interval of ±1%.

Srv. Time		Exact	No Interlock		Interlock	
s_{DB}	s_{FS}		Util.	% Δ	Util.	% Δ
100.0	0.01	1.	0.7321	26.79	1.	0.00
10.0	0.1	0.9999	0.7348	26.51	0.9994	0.04
1.0	1.0	0.9796	0.6716	31.44	0.9843	0.48
0.1	10.0	0.9922	0.5033	49.28	0.9994	0.73
0.01	100.0	0.9992	0.5	49.96	1.	0.08

Table 4: Utilization and relative error in utilization for the database computer for the service times s_{DB} and s_{FS} of the `DataBase` and `FileSys` tasks respectively. Exact results were generated using Markovian analysis.

n_c	Number of Intermediate Tasks (r)					
	No interlock			Interlock		
	2	3	4	2	3	4
1	5.15	7.15	8.23	0.00	0.00	0.00
2	3.59	6.37	8.11	1.20	0.59	0.12
3	2.61	5.27	7.19	1.65	1.20	0.64
4	2.00	4.26	6.01	1.69	1.62	1.22

Table 5: Relative error in client throughput versus number of clients and number of intermediate tasks for the non-interlocked and interlocked solutions for Figure 9.

ber of clients increased, the likelihood of a request arriving at a common server meeting another request from the same common parent but along a different path decreased. Increasing the number of independent paths increased the solution error caused by interlock flows. When the submodel for the common server is solved without compensating for interlocking, each interlocked call path represents an arrival from an independent source. Increasing the paths increases the number of independent sources.

Example 1 above demonstrates the effect of utilization on a system with send interlocking. As the utilization of the database computer increased, the relative error in the solution also increased. The upper limit of the utilization for the non-interlocked solution, 0.675 in Figure 10, is due to the effect of included service.

Example 2 above shows the effect of included service on the error in the solution. If the bulk of the service time in the interlocked tasks is located at or near the common server (i.e. `DataBase`), then the included service delay will be small and the overall utilization high. However, if the bulk of the service time is in the intermediate task (i.e. `FileSys`), then the included service time at the common parent will be high which will create low utilizations.

6 Conclusions

Ignoring interlocking effects when solving multilevel client-server performance models can have a large impact on the accuracy of the solution of the performance model. There are four factors which affect the relative error: the number tasks involved in the interlock, the number of interlocked paths in the model, the utilization of the interlocked tasks and devices, and the amount of included service in the tasks acting as clients. Increasing the number of tasks associated with the interlocked flow paths, n_s, decreases the relative error as the flow components are adjusted in proportion to $\frac{n_s-1}{n_s}$. Consequently, the error introduced by ignoring interlocking will be quite small as the number of parent tasks increases. Conversely, increasing the number of interlocked paths increases the relative error in the solution because an arrival from an interlocked client task may now encounter its own requests from additional sources. The utilization of the devices and the tasks involved in the interlock also affects solution error. As the utilization goes up, the relative error increases. Finally, systems that have

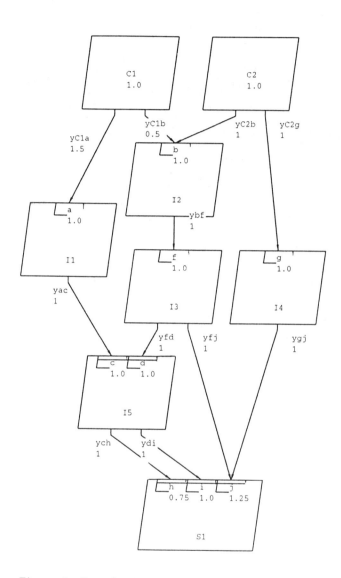

Figure 6: Complex Interlock Case. The number immediately below an arc labels is the arc's call rate. The number associated with an entry label is service time.

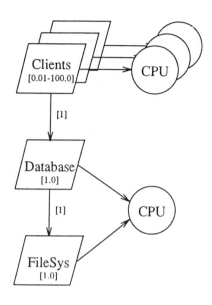

Figure 7: Parameters for example system in Figure 2. Entries are not shown. The numbers inside the brackets denote the service times for entries and the call rates for arcs.

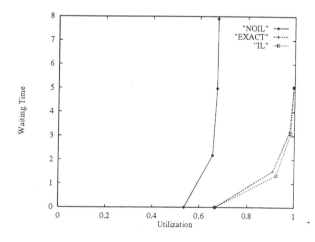

Figure 8: Waiting time versus utilization for three clients. Exact results generated using Markovian analysis are labeled EXACT, and analytic results using layered queueing networks with and without interlock compensation are labeled IL and NOIL respectively.

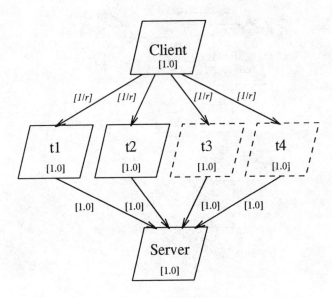

Figure 9: Parameters for split interlock model.

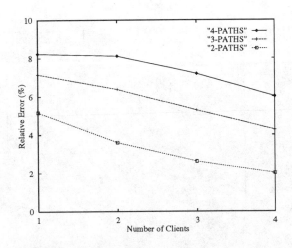

Figure 10: Relative Error versus Number of Clients with two, three and four call paths for the split interlock case shown in Figure 4 and 9.

large amounts of included service time in the tasks where the interlocked flows split will also tend to show larger relative amounts of error. This effect will manifest itself with lower than expected utilizations at the common server.

Interlocking can occur on both tasks and devices. The effect occurs whenever requests from a task split then rejoin at a lower level in the model. Tasks running on a common processor that communicate through remote procedure calls can often be a source of solution error.

The interlock adjustment has been incorporated into a new layered queueing network solver. This paper presents the results of test cases chosen to show dramatically the effects of interlocking. In practice, the interlocking adjustment has been found to improve significantly the accuracy of solutions in over 500 different test cases. Research is continuing on handling the effect for other types of queueing stations, for example, multi-servers.

Acknowledgments

I would like to thank Murray Woodside for his thoughtful comments while preparing this paper. This work has been funded through the Telecommunications Research Institute of Ontario.

References

[1] M. Ajmone Marsan, G. Balbo, G. Chiola, G. Conte, S. Donatelli, and Franceschinis. An introduction to generalized stochastic petri nets. *Microelectronics and Reliability*, 31(4):699–725, 1991.

[2] Andrew D. Birrell and Bruce Jay Nelson. Implementing remote procedure calls. *ACM Transactions on Computer Systems*, 2(1):39–59, February 1984.

[3] G. Chiola. A graphical Petri Net tool for performance analysis. In *Proceedings of the Third International Workshop on Modeling Techniques and Performance Evaluation*, France, May 1987. AFCET.

[4] Michael L. Fontenot. Software congestion, mobile servers, and the hyperbolic model. *IEEE Transactions on Software Engineering*, SE-15(8):947–962, August 1989.

[5] Oliver C. Ibe, Hoon Choi, and Kishor S. Trivedi. Performance evaluation of client-server systems. *IEEE Transactions on Parallel and Distributed Systems*, 4(1):1217–1229, November 1993.

[6] P. A. Jacobson and E. D. Lazowska. Analyzing queueing networks with simultaneous resource possession. *Communications of the ACM*, 25(2):142–151, February 1982.

[7] Edward D. Lazowska, John Zhorjan, Scott G. Graham, and Kenneth C. Sevcik. *Quantitative System Performance; Computer System Analysis Using Queueing Network Models*. Prentice-Hall, Englewood Cliffs, NJ, 1984.

[8] Dorina C. Petriu. Approximate mean value analysis of client–server systems with multi-class requests. In *Proceedings of the 1994 ACM SIGMETRICS Conference on Measurement and Modeling of Computer Systems.*, pages 77–86, Nashville, TN, U.S.A., May 1994. A.C.M. SIGMETRICS.

[9] M. Reiser and S.S. Lavenburg. Mean value analysis of closed multichain queueing networks. *Journal of the Association for Computing Machinery.*, 27(2):313–322, April 1980.

[10] J. A. Rolia and K. C. Sevcik. The method of layers. Submitted for publication in *IEEE Transactions on Software Engineering*, 1994.

[11] Jerome Alexander Rolia. Performance estimates for systems with software servers: The lazy boss method. In Ignacio Casas, editor, *VIII SCCC International Conference On Computer Science*, pages 25–43, Santiago, Chile, July 1988. Chilean Computer Science Society.

[12] Jerome Alexander Rolia. *Predicting the Performance of Software Systems.* PhD thesis, Univerisity of Toronto, Toronto, Ontario, Canada. M5S 1A1, January 1992.

[13] C. Murray Woodside. Throughput calculation for basic stochastic rendezvous networks. *Performance Evaluation*, 9:143–160, 1989.

[14] C. Murray Woodside, John E. Neilson, Dorina C. Petriu, and Shikharesh Majumdar. The stochastic rendezvous network model for performance of synchronous multi-tasking distributed software. *IEEE Transactions on Software Engineering*, 1994. Accepted for publication.

Correctness and Performance of a Multicomputer Operating System

Paul Martin

Rosemary Candlin
Stephen Gilmore

Department of Computer Science
Victoria University of Wellington
New Zealand

Department of Computer Science
University of Edinburgh
Scotland

Abstract

Our discussion here assumes parallel or distributed computer systems that allow dynamic migration of processes between processors. Because the overall performance of these systems is strongly dependent on the overheads of migration, it is vital that migration be implemented as efficiently as possible. However, efficient implementations are often complex implementations and thus we have a conflict between performance and correctness. We cannot make the conflict go away, but we should be able to find ways of describing migration designs such that it is easy for system developers to make changes (for performance reasons) and see straight away what the implications for correctness are.

*We suggest in this paper that the formal specification language **Z** provides just such a way of describing migration designs. To support this suggestion we present an extended example based on the specification of a migration-proof communication protocol. This example is particularly appropriate because the possibility that a communicating process may migrate several times between communications greatly complicates the implementation. Yet we still require that communication should be efficient and correct, i.e. that messages should not be lost or duplicated.*

We make three contributions in this paper. First, we suggest a two-level plan for specification which separates issues of what operations do from when they do it. Second, we outline a rigorous proof style which combines formal statements of assumptions and proof steps with informal reasoning. Third, we show that we can link performance measurements with the specification but that we need to do this via finite state machines.

1 Introduction

A number of studies, for example [5, 7, 10], have shown that the performance of parallel and distributed computer systems can often be substantially improved by dynamic process migration, i.e. the automatic, run-time redistribution of processes to processors. There are a number of distributed operating systems, typically multi-user systems, that support migration, e.g. [1, 2, 4].

Most work has been focussed on the *performance* of systems with migration rather than on their correctness. This is understandable because migrating a process is complex and takes a lot of work:

- Processors must negotiate with each other to decide which processes are to be migrated where.

- Processors offloading work must assemble a network message containing the appropriate pages of code and data, register values, a copy of the user environment, and information about open files.

- Processors accepting work must disassemble network messages and recreate the appropriate processes, their memory segments, user environments, and file tables.

Thus, it is vital that process migration be implemented with the greatest possible efficiency if it is to lead to an improvement (rather than a reduction) in performance.

It seems to us, however, that more attention needs to be given to the *correctness* of systems with migration. When we port our applications to a system with process migration we expect better performance but we also expect the same program output. Unfortunately, it is difficult to uncover incorrect operation in parallel and distributed systems because of the potential for multiple, concurrent operations and the difficulty of reproducing executions. These problems are further compounded by the complexity of process migration which we alluded to above. Our experience has taught us that it requires much thought to find migration designs which are simple enough to be proved correct and yet are still efficient enough to improve system performance.

The aim of the research reported here was to investigate the usefulness of the formal specification language **Z** for describing migration designs. In particular, we examined whether a single description could form the basis for correctness proofs *and also* be related to performance measurements made of the migration implementation. Having such a descriptive method would greatly assist the design of future migration systems.

It would be a very substantial task to construct an operating system with migration that was fully verified in every respect, but we have made a start on formally specifying those parts of the system that are concerned with migration, proving a small number of key properties (Martin [8]) and measuring the performance of those parts (Martin [9]). From this work we have selected examples to present here involving migration-proof inter-processor communication.

Our contribution in this paper is a set of three methods which together make the formal specification language **Z** a convenient and useful way of defining migration systems. First, we describe a way of structuring specifications into two levels: at the lower level the mechanics of operating system functions are described in detail, at the higher level a simplified model of execution is developed that dictates when particular operating system functions are applied. Second, we describe a style of structuring rigorous proofs which allows correctness properties to be shown. The proof style combines a formal statement of assumptions and intermediate proofs steps with informal reasoning. Third, we describe a method for linking 'dynamic' performance measurements made of the implementation with the more 'static' specification via an intermediate step involving finite state machines.

The rest of this paper is organised as follows. We start in Section 2 by describing the six-step plan we used for our investigation. We present an example drawn from the formal specification in Section 3 and then use this example in Section 4 to show how we carried out proofs of correctness. In Section 5 we report our method for relating performance measurements back to the specification. We conclude with a discussion of our results in Section 6.

2 Methodology

We decided that the best way to test the idea that a **Z** specification could be used for correctness proofs and for expressing performance measurements was to apply the idea to a real multicomputer. We describe an approach to designing an operating system for an experimental message-passing multicomputer called the 'Testbed' [6]. This machine has a shared bus over which inter-processor messages and migrating processes pass, and a separate bus for collecting performance data. Hardware-assisted monitoring allows accurate, non-intrusive measurement of low-level operating system functions as well as of higher-level properties of concurrent programs.

The investigation into the relationship between correctness and performance of migration on the Testbed involved the following stages.

1. Designs for the more difficult parts of the operating system, particularly inter-process communication and process migration, were proposed and formulated in **Z**.

2. These formally specified designs were then rigorously proved to have certain desired properties. For instance, it was shown that the protocols for blocking communication always involve synchronisation between communicating processes.

3. The designs were implemented in the Testbed operating system, using an informal argument to show that the code was a good refinement of the specification.

4. The overall operation of the Testbed operating system was described by a set of finite state machines, whose changes of state could be described in terms of the **Z** schemas.

5. Routines in the operating system corresponding to the **Z** schemas under study were instrumented by adding special instructions for generating performance data. A range of synthetic programs was then executed on the Testbed.

6. The performance data collected from the Testbed were analysed, interpreted in terms of the schemas in question, and thus related back to key design decisions made in the first stage.

A number of iterations occurred between the first and second stages as the proofs showed up deficiencies in the original design. We also recommend that the process as a whole should be iterated and the data gathered in the last stage be used to suggest optimisations in the design at the first stage.

3 The Z specification

A typical **Z** specification starts by declaring sets of elements called *types*. These types are assumed to be *basic* and to need no further definition. The specification then proceeds by using the basic types—or compounds defined as functions, relations, or sequences involving the basic types—to define *state schemas*. State schemas are intended to represent aspects of the state of the system being modelled. The main body of the specification then uses set theory and predicate calculus to define *state-modifying schemas*, which represent operations in the system being modelled. A full introduction to the **Z** language can be found in [3].

Our **Z** specification is presented in terms of two conceptual levels. At the lower level, components of operating system functions are represented in detail. An example of a lower level **Z** schema is *Send1* (presented below) which models the mechanics of a step in the inter-processor communication protocol. At the higher level, schemas deal with the question of *when* (rather than *how*) an operation is applied. For instance, the *Send2* schema indicates that a *Send1* schema is applied only when a process's next instruction is to send a message.

We present an example drawn from the specification of the Testbed operating system to illustrate how we have arranged our schemas. Starting at the lower level, we consider the fundamental objects in the system and declare them as **Z** basic types.

[PE, THREAD, CHANNEL]

With reference to Figure 1, the Testbed has multiple processing elements—represented by the type *PE*—each of which executes a copy of the operating system kernel. Programs are written using a language with constructs for parallel programming—the unit of concurrency is represented *THREAD*. Threads communicate data with each other using CSP-style logical channels—represented by the type *CHANNEL*—and each channel has a fixed sender thread and a fixed receiver thread. Notice that the same type *CHANNEL* is used for connections between threads executing on the same processor (channels 1 and 2) and for connections between threads executing on different processors (channel 3), although the latter is more complicated to implement because it requires messages to be passed over the shared bus.

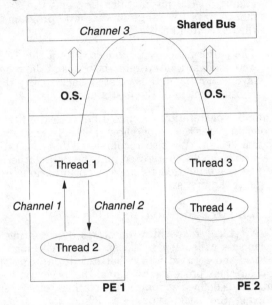

Figure 1: Testbed PEs, threads and channels.

Next we define the specification *state*. This forms the basis for the main part of the specification which consists of *state-modifying operations*. For simplicity we present here only enough state to model the first step in the communication protocol for a sender thread.

```
┌─ State1 ──────────────────────────────────
│ ready_queue : PE ↔ THREAD
│ waiting_sender, waiting_receiver : PE ⇸
│     (CHANNEL ⇸ THREAD)
│ location : PE ⇸ (CHANNEL ⇸ PE)
```

The schema introduces four identifiers—*ready_queue*, *waiting_sender*, *waiting_receiver* and *location*—and, after the colon, their associated types. The type of *ready_queue* is a relation (↔) between processing elements and threads. The types of *waiting_sender* and *waiting_receiver* are partial functions (⇸) from processing elements to partial functions from channels to threads. The type of *location* is a partial function from processing elements to a partial function from channels to processing elements.

Here is how we relate the Testbed to *State1*. When a thread modelled by a specification value t is executing (or is in the queue waiting to execute) on the processing node modelled by a specification value p, we include the

pair (t, p) in the relation *ready_queue*. When a thread is blocked waiting to send a message over a communication channel represented in the model by c, a maplet $p \mapsto \{c \mapsto t\}$ is included in the *waiting_sender* function. The function *waiting_receiver* fulfils a similar role for receiver threads. When the Testbed has a channel connecting a thread executing on processing element p_1 to another thread executing on p_2, then the specification represents this by a maplet $p_1 \mapsto \{c \mapsto p_2\}$ in the function *location*.

Channel communication is implemented on the Testbed using three different kinds of message: 'ready to send' messages, 'ready to receive' messages, and 'data' messages. The first two kinds are used for flow control, the third kind contains the information to be transferred between threads. In the specification we call the generic message type *MSG* and enumerate its values thus:

$$MSG ::= rts \mid rtr \mid data$$

The schema *Send1* specifies the first part of a state-modifying operation which describes the changes that take place when a thread requests to send data over a channel. The schema is parametrised by having input arguments (identifiers with question marks) and output arguments (identifiers with exclamation marks). The declaration $\Delta State1$ is a form of inclusion and introduces instances of the variables defined in *State1* in both normal (unprimed) and primed forms. The unprimed variables represent components of the state *before* the operation. The primed variables represent the state *after* the operation. Thus, *Send1* defines the primed variables of *State1* (and the output argument) in terms of the unprimed variables of *State1* and the input arguments.

```
┌─ Send1 ──────────────────────────────────
│ ΔState1
│ st? : THREAD
│ c? : CHANNEL
│ sp? : PE
│ msgs! : P MSG
├──────────────────────────────────────────
│ c? ∉ dom(waiting_receiver sp?) ⇒
│     ready_queue' = ready_queue \ {sp? ↦ st?} ∧
│     waiting_sender' = waiting_sender ∪
│         {sp? ↦ {c? ↦ st?}} ∧
│     msgs! = if c? ∈ dom(location sp?) then {rts}
│         else ∅
```

We interpret *Send1* informally as follows. The input argument $st?$ specifies a sending thread executing on source processor $sp?$—the channel over which the send is to occur is specified by $c?$. The output argument $msgs!$ is defined in the body of the schema to be the possibly empty *set* (P) of messages that are to be transmitted to another processor by the network interface.

Below the horizontal line dividing the schema declarations from the schema predicates we have an implication (⇒) with one antecedent and three conjoined (∧) consequents. The antecedent is true if there is no receiver thread currently blocked on the channel $c?$ at the sender's processor $sp?$ (dom returns the domain of a function). The first consequent models the removal of the sender thread $st?$ from the ready queue using set difference. The second consequent models the blocking of $st?$. The third consequent models a conditional test—if the location of the other end of channel $c?$ is on a different processor then a 'ready to send' message is added to the output variable $msgs!$ ready to be transmitted to the appropriate processor. Otherwise $msgs!$ is the empty set. The values of $waiting\_receiver$ and $location$ are unchanged by the $Send1$ schema.

Moving up to the higher level of the specification, we introduce the new type $REQUEST$ to model the different communication requests that a user thread may make of the operating system. In each case, the request is accompanied by an argument indicating the appropriate channel.

$REQUEST ::= send \langle\!\langle CHANNEL \rangle\!\rangle$
$\qquad\qquad\quad | \;\; receive \langle\!\langle CHANNEL \rangle\!\rangle$

Next, we show how we have chosen to represent the circumstances in which the $Send1$ schema is applied. This is a two step process: we provide an extended state schema ($State2$) which encapsulates the notion of thread programs as sequences of requests; then we provide a new operation schema ($Send2$) which applies $Send1$ only if certain preconditions are met, i.e. that the sender thread $st?$ is in the ready queue and that $st?$'s next instruction is to send ($head$ is a standard **Z** operator that returns the first element of a sequence).

```
┌─ State2 ─────────────────────────────
│ State1
│ program : THREAD ⇸ seq REQUEST
└──────────────────────────────────────
```

```
┌─ Send2 ──────────────────────────────
│ ΔState2
│ st? : THREAD
│ sp? : PE
│ c? : CHANNEL
│ msgs! : P MSG
├──────────────────────────────────────
│ (sp?, st?) ∈ ready_queue
│ send(c?) = head(program st?)
│ Send1
└──────────────────────────────────────
```

4 Correctness and the specification

Having outlined our formal specification for interprocess communication, we now describe how we constructed proofs to show that migration preserves certain desirable properties of the communication protocol. Our proofs were performed in two phases:

1. In the first phase we assumed that migration was not allowed. We enumerated all legal sequences of communication operations and performed a proof by induction on the number of communications to show that the communication protocol has the desired properties.

2. In the second phase we assumed that migration was allowed. Using the same enumeration of legal sequences of communication operations we performed a proof by induction on the number of migrations to show that migration preserves the desired properties of the communication protocol.

Proofs phase 1

In our specification example we gave only one instance of a communication operation, the operation defined by the $Send$ schemas. In the full specification there are five other operations: a request to receive operation and four operations for exchanging status and flow control messages between processing elements.

The proof is not tractable if we consider *all* sequences of operations simply because there are too many sequences. We limit the number of sequences by considering only those sequences of operations on one (arbitrarily chosen) channel—this is reasonable because channels are independent of each other. We further limit the number of sequences by ruling out subsequences which do not make sense. For example, our model of communication has unidirectional channels so we disallow sequences involving a thread that performs a send request and then a receive request on the same channel. We can express this restriction formally, thus:

$\forall State2; t : THREAD; c : CHANNEL \bullet$
$\quad send(c) \in \mathrm{ran}(program\ t) \Rightarrow$
$\qquad receive(c) \notin \mathrm{ran}(program\ t)$

This says that if a thread t's program includes a request to send on channel c then the program will not also contain a request to receive on c. (ran returns the *range* of a function.)

Having defined legal sequences of communication operations we now enumerate the (legal) subsequences which correspond to a single communication on a given channel. Two example subsequences are:

- (i) A send request followed by (ii) a receive request on the same processor.

- (i) A send request on processing element p_1, (ii) the transmission of a 'ready to send' control message to p_2, (iii) a receive request at p_2, (iv) the transmission of a 'ready to receive' control message to p_1, (v) the transmission of message data to p_2.

Other legal subsequences occur if the receiver makes its request before the sender, or after the sender but before the 'ready to send' message arrives.

Since our inductive proof is based on the number of communications over a channel, let us continue by considering one of the possible subsequences for the first channel communication. Suppose that the subsequence involves a send request followed by a receive request on the same processor. We define the state before the first communication as follows:

$$
\begin{array}{|l}
\hline S0 \\
\hline State2 \\
c? : CHANNEL \\
\hline \forall\, p : PE \bullet c? \notin \mathrm{dom}(waiting\_sender\ p) \land \\
\quad c? \notin \mathrm{dom}(waiting\_receiver\ p) \land \\
\quad c? \notin \mathrm{dom}(location\ p) \\
\hline
\end{array}
$$

Informally, this schema says that there are no senders blocked on channel $c?$, no receivers blocked on channel $c?$, and nothing is known about the locations of the ends of channel $c?$. In the full specification we define an initial state for all channels and we prove that $S0$ can be deduced from that initial state.

We now selectively define the consequences of applying the $Send1$ schema to $S0$ in a new schema $S1$.

$$
\begin{array}{|l}
\hline S1 \\
\hline \Delta State2 \\
c? : CHANNEL \\
st? : THREAD \\
sp? : PE \\
msgs! : \mathbf{P}\,MSG \\
\hline st? \notin \mathrm{ran}\ ready\_queue' \\
(\exists_1\, p : PE \bullet c? \in \mathrm{dom}(waiting\_sender'\ p)) \land \\
\quad (c?, st?) \in waiting\_sender'\ sp? \\
(\forall\, p : PE \bullet c? \notin \mathrm{dom}(waiting\_receiver'\ p)) \\
\hline
\end{array}
$$

Informally, this schema says that the sending thread $st?$ has been removed from the ready queue and blocked on $waiting\_sender$ at exactly one $(\exists_1)$ processing element p. Furthermore, there is no processing element with a receiver blocked on $waiting\_receiver$.

The second part of the subsequence, the receive request, is applied in a like manner to derive another state schema, $S2$ (not shown). We are now able to observe from inspection of $S1$ and $S2$ that the communication subsequence has certain desirable properties. For instance: $S1$ tells us that the sender was blocked, $S2$ tells us that the sender was unblocked, therefore we deduce that communication involved synchronisation—a desirable property for our model of communication.

The full proof proceeds by enumerating all other legal subsequences (for first and subsequent communications) and by showing in each case that the desired properties hold.

Proofs phase 2

In the second phase of the proofs migration is allowed. A similar enumeration of communication subsequences is performed and it is shown for each subsequence that at whatever point a communicating thread migrates, the state of the channel before the migration is (in all essential aspects) the same as the state of the channel after the migration. Thus, we show that migration preserves the desired properties of the communication protocol. All in all, the proofs require some thirty pages of detailed (although somewhat repetitive) working.

5 Performance and the specification

In Section 3 we presented examples from the specification of the Testbed's migration system. In the preceding section we reported how correctness properties can be proved from the specification. We now explain how performance measurements made of the Testbed can be interpreted in terms of the specification.

Performance data is gathered from the Testbed by adding small numbers of extra machine code instructions to the operating system. These instructions write fixed-size data values or *events* to the Testbed's monitoring bus where the events are timestamped from a global clock, buffered, and then centralised at a designated processor for storage and analysis. Events are only 32 bits in size—and half of that space is reserved for the timestamp—so we chose to allocate a small fixed field in each event to identify the location of the event-generating instruction in the operating system. We used the rest of the event to pass arguments, e.g. the channel number during a communication.

How did we decide at which points in the operating system to add event-generating instructions? Essentially, we added instructions to the beginning and end of each section of operating system code that implemented a *module* of the design. For example, suppose the design specified that one processor p_1 sends a request to p_2, waits for a reply, and then processes the reply. We would have events generated by p_1 in four places:

1. At the start of the procedure for generating the request.

2. At the end of the procedure for generating the request.

3. At the start of the procedure for processing the reply.

4. At the end of the procedure for processing the reply.

Thus, when the events were analysed we would be able to compute:

- The delay generating the request $(2 - 1)$.

- The delay produced by two network messages and p_2's processing $(3 - 2)$.

- The delay involved in processing the reply $(4 - 3)$.

- The total time for the request and reply $(4 - 1)$.

These figures might make us decide, for instance, that the first and third delays were so small in comparison with the second delay that we should cache replies at p_1 wherever possible.

This method of placing event-generating instructions around modules works well because each module corresponds to a **Z** schema. That each module has a corresponding schema is not surprising, since the implementation is based (at least informally) on the specification. Thus, we can relate the difference between timestamps on pairs of events to individual schemas.

Relating times to complete communications is more difficult, however. Communication involves the execution of several modules—if threads on different processors are to communicate, for example, then the *Send*1 module, the receive request module and three inter-processor message modules are needed— something which **Z** has difficulty representing explicitly. We *can* deduce legal sequences of schema applications (as we did in the proofs section) but this does not provide a convenient way to express performance measurements. We would like a more 'dynamic' representation of legal sequences of schema applications.

We found that finite state machines (FSMs) offered just such a representation. We informally derived a collection of FSMs from the specification in which:

- Vertices represent operating system states.

- Directed edges represent the commencement or termination of a module and are labelled with the corresponding events.

- Each pair of edges correspond to a module in the specification, and the pair is annotated with the module name.

Figure 2 shows the FSM for communication between threads on different processing nodes. Vertex labels are distinct integers. Edge labels are mnemonics defined for the performance measurements. Module annotations are explained in Table 1. The upper half of the FSM (vertices 1 to 4) represents the modules executed by the sender's processor. Notice that the sender always follows the same execution path, moving through states 1, 2, 3 and 4 before completing the communication and returning to state 1. Only annotations for network modules connect the upper half of the FSM to vertices 5 to 13, the latter showing the two possible execution paths for a receiver processor. The path through vertex 6 shows the execution pattern when the receiver thread requests to communicate before the 'ready to send' message arrives—the path through vertex 11 shows the alternative case.

We developed further FSMs for communication between threads on the same processor and other operating system functions associated with migration. Using the event traces collected during the execution of test programs on the Testbed we then computed the time required to execute each module, attached these times to the FSMs and, simply by summing the times along paths through the FSMs, were able to compute total times for communication and other composite (multi-module) services.

We found the FSMs to be a convenient and natural way to express performance results. For example, most event traces are large and complicated, typically containing interleaved streams of events from multiple pairs of communicating threads. The FSMs, however, made it easy to construct parsers to extract times for particular modules. We also found with the FSMs that it was straightforward to identify the composite modules which imposed the greatest overheads and then to focus in on particular modules (and hence specification schemas) which accounted for large proportions of those overheads.

6 Discussion

The work reported here took about three years to complete and shows that **Z** formal specifications can assist the practical work of designing, implementing, and testing migration systems. The specification that we made for migration on the Testbed multicomputer allowed us to prove a small number of correctness properties and, in the process, find and correct some defects in the original design. The specification also allowed us to interpret the performance measurements that we made of the implementation and to gain insight into which parts of the migration system imposed the greatest overheads.

In order to complete our project, however, we needed to invent some new techniques. First, so that we could perform the proofs we found that our specification needed to be carefully structured so as to separate the details of operating system functionality from the conditions which govern acceptable sequences of operations. Second, we found it appropriate to state the result of each proof step formally, but to reason from step to step informally. This rigorous method allows a suitable degree of precision to be retained without losing the reader in a mass of detailed working. Third, we needed to rely on FSMs to link performance measurements to the specification.

We found **Z** to be a satisfactory, though not perfect, choice for the specification language. In future work on migration systems we would look for more support in the language for structuring the specification—for limiting the scope of variables and defining a clear hierarchy amongst specification objects. We would also seek a language with explicit support for execution sequences—perhaps then we could relate performance to the specification without the need for the intermediate step involving the FSMs.

We found the use of formal methods in general to be beneficial for a number of reasons.

- It is difficult to find migration designs that are efficient and correct. Proofs take time, but not as much as debugging concurrent systems.

- The proof process led us to deeper insights into the migration design and, perhaps surprisingly, resulted in several redundant operations being removed.

- Design prototyping can be conveniently done using the specification—provided an appropriate level of abstraction is used.

If the work reported here has shown the feasibility of our approach then it has also raised a number of issues which deserve further investigation. We are now inspired to see how alternative, more powerful models of communication could be incorporated into the specification, what effect these models have on the complexity of the correctness proofs, and whether the performance of the implementation was better or worse. There are other areas of the Testbed operating system which would benefit from the application of formal methods— in particular the protocols for supporting shared virtual memory. We would like to investigate practical methods for refining the specification into the implementation. It would also be interesting to test our conviction that the specification (and much of the code) is portable.

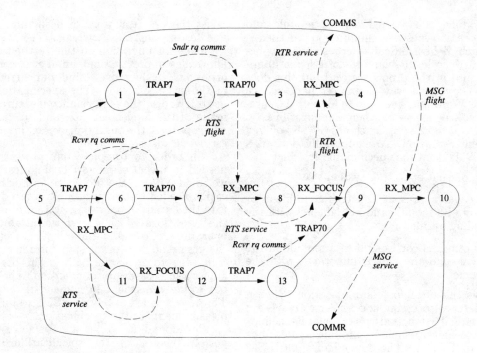

Figure 2: The FSM for remote communication.

Module	Description
Sndr rq comms	Sender thread requests to communicate (*Send1*)
Rcvr rq comms	Receiver thread requests to communicate
RTS flight	'Ready to send' message is transmitted over network
RTS service	Incoming 'ready to send' message is processed
RTR flight	'Ready to receive' message is transmitted over network
RTR service	Incoming 'ready to receive' message is processed
MSG flight	Data message is transmitted over network
MSG service	Incoming data message is processed

Table 1: Modules in the communication protocol.

References

[1] David L. Black. Scheduling Support for Concurrency and Parallelism in the Mach Operating System. *IEEE Computer Magazine*, 23(5):35–43, May 1990.

[2] Andrew Murray Bond. *Adaptive Task Allocation in a Distributed Workstation Environment*. PhD thesis, Department of Computer Science, Victoria University of Wellington, 1993.

[3] Antoni Diller. *Z: An Introduction to Formal Methods*. John Wiley & Sons, second edition, 1994.

[4] Fred Douglis and John Ousterhout. Transparent Process Migration: Design Alternatives and the Sprite Implementation. *Concurrency—Practice and Experience*, 21(8):757–785, August 1991.

[5] Derek L. Eager, Edward D. Lazowska, and John Zahorjan. Adaptive Load Sharing in Homogeneous Distributed Systems. *IEEE Transactions on Software Engineering*, SE-12(5):662–675, May 1986.

[6] Kayhan Imre. *A Performance Monitoring and Analysis Environment for Distributed Memory MIMD Programs*. PhD thesis, University of Edinburgh, 1993.

[7] Miron Livny and Myron Melman. Load Balancing in Homogeneous Broadcast Distributed Systems. In *Proceedings of the ACM Computer Network Performance Symposium*, pages 47–55, April 1982.

[8] Paul Martin. The Formal Specification in **Z** of Task Migration on the Testbed Multicomputer. Technical Report ECS-CSG-2-94, University of Edinburgh, June 1994.

[9] Paul Martin. The Performance Profiling of a Load Balancing Multicomputer. Technical Report ECS-CSG-3-94, University of Edinburgh, June 1994.

[10] Songnian Zhou. A Trace-Driven Simulation Study of Dynamic Load Balancing. *IEEE Transactions on Software Engineering*, 14(9):1327–1341, September 1988.

An Implementation and Performance Measurement of the Progressive Retry Technique

Gaurav Suri *   Yennun Huang *   Yi-Min Wang*   W. Kent Fuchs[†]   Chandra Kintala*

*AT&T Bell Laboratories
600 Mountain Avenue
Murray Hill, NJ 07974

[†]Coordinated Science Laboratory
University of Illinois
Urbana, IL 61801

Abstract

This paper describes a recovery technique called progressive retry for bypassing software faults in message-passing applications. The technique is implemented as reusable modules to provide application-level software fault tolerance. The paper describes the implementation of the technique and presents results from the application of progressive retry to two telecommunications systems. The results presented show that the technique is helpful in reducing the total recovery time for message-passing applications.

1 Introduction

For computer systems designed to provide continuous services to customers, availability is an important performance measure. In such systems, software failures have been observed to be the current major cause of service unavailability [1, 2]. Residual software faults due to untested boundary conditions, unanticipated exceptions and unexpected execution environments have been observed to escape the testing and debugging process and, when triggered during program execution, cause service interruption [3]. It is therefore desirable to have effective on-line retry mechanisms for automatically bypassing software faults and recovering from software failures in order to achieve high availability [4, 5, 6, 7].

Several studies [2, 8, 9] have shown that many software failures in production systems behave in a transient fashion, and so the simplest way to recover from such failures is to restart the system, an approach that we call *environment diversity*. The term *Heisenbug* [1] has been used to refer to the software faults causing transient failures, while the term *Bohrbug* refers to software faults which have deterministic behavior.

Watchd daemon and libft library have been used in several AT&T products to tolerate Heisenbugs [10].

The research of the fourth author was supported in part by the Department of the Navy and managed by the Office of the Chief of Naval Research under Contract N00014-91-J-1283, and in part by the National Aeronautics and Space Administration (NASA) under Grant NASA NAG 1-613, in cooperation with the Illinois Computer Laboratory for Aerospace Systems and Software (ICLASS).

Watchd is a daemon process which monitors system failures like machine crash, process death and process hang. If a machine crashes, all critical applications running on the crashed machine are migrated to another machine. If a process dies (due to bugs in the program), watchd first restarts the process locally. If the restarted process fails again, the process is then migrated to another machine. Libft provides functions for message logging, critical-data checkpointing, fault-tolerant inter-process communication and name services. With libft, an application process can checkpoint its critical data on the local machine as well as on backup machines. Therefore, when a process is restarted, it can restore its checkpointed state and replay its message log to reconstruct its pre-failure state. Watchd keeps track of the dependence between processes. In the event of a failure, the failed process as well as all other processes that depend on it are rolled back in order to guarantee state consistency. Watchd and libft together provides a simple, portable and reusable component for an application to tolerate Heisenbugs.

Our experience has shown that many errors can be successfully tolerated by using the simple rollback-and-retry mechanism provided by watchd and libft. The simple mechanism, although effective, presents some problems. First, the recovery time can be long so that the service disruption due to the recovery can be unbearable. Any process failure results in a global restart. In an application consisting of many processes, a global restart can take a long time before the application returns to normal execution. Therefore, it is desirable to limit the scope of rollback by keeping track of the dynamic inter-process communication patterns and rolling back only the processes which directly communicate with the failed processes in the current checkpoint interval. Second, the simple retry with a deterministic replay of message logs usually reconstructs the application state to the same state as existed before failure. If the state is erroneous and the application behavior is deterministic, the retry and replay will not help. However, if message dependency is recorded, a failed application can replay the messages in a different but consistent order so that the application reaches a new but correct state after retry. In other words, by replaying the message log in a different but consistent order, more software failures may be bypassed.

The above two observations motivate the extension of the rollback-and-retry mechanism provided by watchd and libft. This paper describes a *progressive retry* technique for software failure recovery in message-passing applications[1]. The target applications are continuously-running software systems for which fast recovery is essential and a reasonable amount of run-time overhead may not result in noticeable service quality degradation. Many telecommunications systems fall into this category. There are several reasons that fast recovery is desirable in applications requiring high availability. In the cases where service quality is judged at the user interface level, small "computer down time" involving only a small number of processes may be translated into zero "service down time." Most importantly, when the prolonged unavailability of one part of the system may trigger the boundary conditions in other parts of the system, localized and fast recovery can reduce the possibility of cascading failures which may lead to a catastrophe.

The progressive retry technique is based on checkpointing, rollback, message replaying and message reordering. The goal is to limit the *scope of rollback*: the number of involved processes as well as total rollback distance. The approach consists of several retry steps and gradually increases the scope of rollback when a previous retry fails. The technique is implemented in watchd daemon and libft library.

2 Progressive Retry

The simple example in Fig. 1 is used to illustrate the basic concept of progressive retry. The reader is referred to [12] for a detailed discussion. For the purpose of presentation, we assume every message is logged before it is processed, and is therefore available at the time of recovery. Suppose p_2 detects an error at the point marked "X" in Figure 1 and initiates the progressive retry. In the Step-1 *receiver replaying retry*, p_2 rolls back and replays messages M_a and M_b in exactly the same order as they were processed before the rollback. If the detected error was caused by some transient environmental problems (such as mutual exclusion conflicts, resource unavailability, unexpected signals, etc.) then Step-1 retry may succeed and p_2 can proceed. Under the deterministic assumption, the exact same copy of M_o will be generated during the recovery. Therefore, p_2 does not need to resend M_o and the receiver of M_o, process p_4, does not have to be involved in the retry.

If Step-1 retry fails, then p_2 rolls back again and executes Step-2 *receiver reordering retry* by reordering M_a and M_b in its message log. If the original error was triggered by a boundary condition, then message reordering may be useful for bypassing that condition and thereby recovering from the error. Note that since

[1]We will focus on error recovery in this paper; the issue of error detection is considered elsewhere [10].

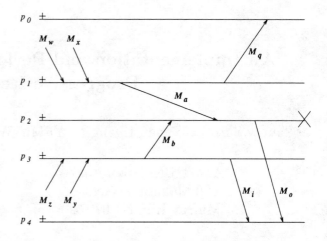

Figure 1: Example for illustrating the basic concept of progressive retry.

message reordering forces a different execution path for p_2, we cannot expect that the same message M_o will still be generated. Such a message is called an *orphan* message [11] and should be discarded. As a result, p_4 should also be rolled back in order to undo the effect of M_o. The message M_i, however, is not an orphan message because its sender is not rolled back. Such a "sent but not yet received message" is called an *in-transit message* [12]. It needs to be processed again by the restarted receiver but its associated processing order information can be discarded.

There are several potentially useful algorithms for reordering the message logs. Random reordering can be used when no knowledge about the possible cause of the software failure is available. If the failure is possibly due to the interleaving of messages from different processes, reordering by grouping the messages from the same process together may be useful. If the software fault might have been triggered by exhausting all available resources, reordering the messages so that every resource is freed at the earliest possible moment can often bypass the boundary condition.

If Step-2 retry fails, then Step-3 *sender replaying retry* will involve in the recovery process all the processes that have sent messages to p_2. In Fig. 1, p_1 (p_3) rolls back and replays M_w and M_x (M_z and M_y) in their original order[2]. Step-3 retry basically gives the messages a second chance to interleave "naturally" with each other, and can be useful for error recovery if the original error was due to some rare message racing conditions. Under the deterministic assumption, the exact same copy of M_q will be generated and so p_0 does not need to be involved in the rollback. In contrast, p_4 needs to roll back because of the orphan message M_o, and M_i remains an in-transit message.

If Step-3 retry still fails, it is suspected that an undetected error might have occurred at p_1 or p_3 and was propagated to p_2 through the erroneous messages

[2]Messages M_w, M_x, M_y and M_z are from processes other than the five processes shown in the Figure.

M_a or M_b to cause the detected error. Step-4 *sender reordering retry* is designed to bypass the software bug that caused the undetected error. In this step, process p_1 rolls back and reorders M_w and M_x, and p_3 rolls back and reorders M_z and M_y. As a result, messages M_a, M_b, M_i, M_o and M_q all become orphan messages and all the five processes in Fig. 1 need to participate in the recovery.

When all previous small-scope retries fail, the objective of localized recovery can no longer be achieved and a large-scope rollback needs to be initiated. All the processes in the system, including the senders of M_w, M_x, M_y and M_z, are rolled back to the latest globally consistent set of checkpoints obtained through coordinated checkpointing [13] or lazy coordination [14]. If a system has been functioning correctly for most of the time and failures are rare events, rolling back the entire system can often recover from the failures. The potential disadvantages of a large-scope rollback include unnecessarily involving healthy critical processes in the rollback and a longer recovery time. In a later section, we show that, for certain systems, the cost of the first four steps of progressive retry is small compared to the cost of a large-scope rollback. For such systems, the five-step progressive retry described in this section is an attractive technique for providing low-cost and efficient software failure recovery.

3 Implementation

The *progressive retry* mechanism is implemented in the *libft* library and the *watchd* daemon [10]. The heart of the system is a centralized *message server* which dynamically keeps track of all the information required for progressive retry. The message server runs as a child of the watchd daemon and uses the checkpointing capabilities of the libft library in order to make its own operation fault-tolerant. The other important components of the progressive retry mechanism are *watchd*, the *throwback agents* and the *recovery management functions* (see Figure 2).

Watchd monitors user processes for failures. As soon as it detects a failure, it restarts the process. It also communicates with the message server to get information about the other processes that need to be restarted. It then kills and restarts those processes. The first action taken by each of the restarted processes is to communicate with the message server and find out the recovery actions that need to be taken. Each process then sets up its recovery status accordingly and proceeds with recovery. The following subsections explain each of these functions in detail.

3.1 Message Server

As described earlier, the message server is the most important component of the progressive retry mechanism. It has the following functions :

- Keep track of the communication graph during failure-free operation,

- Maintain status information for each process in the system, and

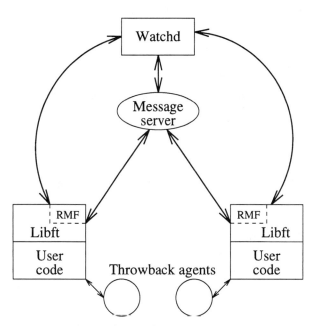

RMF - Recovery Management Functions

Figure 2: Progressive retry system architecture

- Compute the recovery line during failure recovery.

3.1.1 Dynamic Communication Graph

The message server needs to keep track of the message dependencies during normal program execution in order to be able to compute the recovery line during the recovery process. The graph is computed on the basis of the pattern sent to the message server by the receivers of messages in the system. Each process maintains a local communication graph in which it keeps track of all the processes that have sent messages to it so far. Whenever it gets a message from a process that is not present in its local graph, it adds the process to the local graph and also sends the information to the message server so that the global communication graph can be updated.

3.1.2 Process Status Information

When the application is recovering from the failure of a process under progressive retry, the status of other processes is also affected to some degree depending on the communication pattern and the stage of retry the system is in. The processes need to be assigned different status values so that they know whether they have to deterministically replay the pre-failure receiver log , reorder and replay the log, receive in-transit messages from the communication channel or perform as normal processes. The reasons for making these distinctions are explained in Section 3.4.

3.1.3 Recovery Line Computation

Recovery line computation is the first step to be carried out when a failed process restarts and progressive retry needs to be initiated. It involves carrying out the following functions:

- Calculate the retry step number for the system

- Analyze the communication graph, and

- Determine the status of each affected process based on the first two steps

The recovery line computation may result in a change of status for some of the processes in the application. Since all processes run as children of watchd, this information is conveyed to watchd so that it can take appropriate action and restart processes that need a status change.

3.2 Watchd

The basic functions of watchd [10] are to periodically monitor processes to see if they are alive, and to restart failed processes. Under progressive retry watchd is given the following additional responsibilities:

- Invoke the message server to initiate progressive retry when a failed process is brought up again.

- Kill and restart all the processes that require a status change during retry.

3.3 Throwback Agents

The *throwback agents* are invoked on a one-per-process basis and their function is to simulate the presence of *in-transit* messages. If a process is assigned a status which implies that there are pending in-transit messages, these messages need to be resent to it during recovery. The process fires a throwback agent which analyzes the log of the process and sends back to the process all messages that have become in-transit according to the new recovery line. Once all in-transit messages have been re-sent, the throwback agent terminates indicating the completion of recovery at that node.

3.4 Recovery Management Functions

The recovery management functions are a part of *libft* and are responsible for recovery initialization, setup and management for each process in a local manner. The functions in libft that do recovery management are checkpoint(), recover(), recovered(), setlogfile(), ftrecsetup(), ftread() and ftwrite().

ftrecsetup() is the function that sets up the recovery for each process. It communicates with the message server to get the recovery line information. It then uses that information to set its local status value and fire a throwback agent, if required.

The function recovered() returns a value which indicates which stage of recovery the system is in. The stages can be: doing deterministic replay, receiving in-transit messages, or recovery completed. The return

value is used by the process to determine whether it should be receiving messages from the communication channel or retrieving them from the log files. These values, in conjunction with the status values are also used by ftread() and ftwrite(). The function ftread() examines the status value of the process, and based on that value reads the next message either from the log or from the communication channel. Even when reading from the channel, a distinction is made for receiving in-transit messages and new messages. In order to maintain consistency, all in-transit messages from a sender must be received before any new messages can be received from that sender and *fifo* order maintained for the in-transit messages. The received messages are logged before they can be processed. The status value determines whether they are logged in a temporary log file or in the regular log file.

The function ftwrite() sends messages after logging them. The status values indicate whether message comparison needs to be done (in order to verify the deterministic execution assumption) or not, and whether the message actually needs to be sent out on the communication channel at all.

A message in a receiver log file contains five fields: message sequence number, sender id, reference id, message size and message data. Sender id is the number assigned by watchd to each application at start-up time. Sequence number is used during message reordering to ensure that *fifo* order for messages from the same sender is maintained. Reference id is given by ftwrite() and is also used during message reordering. The message structure in the sender log is the same except that it contains the receiver id instead of sender id, and it does not contain the reference id.

4 Experimental Results

Performance measurements for failure-free overhead and recovery time were carried out by applying progressive retry to two telecommunications systems. The two systems used were the REPL [15] file system, and a subsystem of a switched service network system (which we refer to only as System N due to its proprietary nature).

Since most of the source code was unavailable and our objective was to measure the performance, not the effectiveness, we implemented two simulators which use the same software architectures, follow the same communication patterns and generate the same workload conditions as the actual systems. The simulators were also useful for doing controlled fault injection at specific points in the programs.

4.1 General Experimental Setup

The experiments for both the systems studied the performance under two categories :

- measurement of failure-free overhead;

- measurement of recovery time for different steps of progressive retry.

The run time of each simulation was in the order of one hour or more and each measurement was averaged over four runs.

4.2 Performance measurement on System N

The part of System N that we modeled has the communication pattern shown in Figure 3. Nodes A and B report to Node D every 10 seconds. C sends a status report to D every 2 seconds. D periodically reports to F which also receives reports from E every 30 seconds and which in turn reports to G [3].

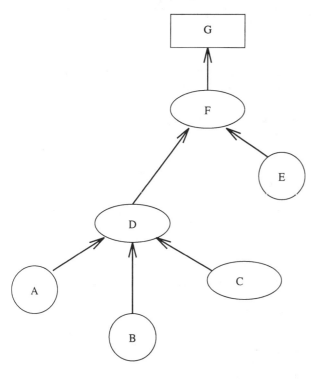

Figure 3: Communication pattern for the part of System N under study

System N uses a coordinated checkpointing scheme where process D is the coordinator. The failure free overhead was measured for two different checkpoint intervals: a checkpoint every 200 messages received by D and every 400 messages. Synchronous logging was used for both sender and receiver logging. The critical data sizes for each of the processes were of the order of a few kilobytes.

The recovery time measurements were done for the checkpoint interval with 400 messages in order to get a worst case measure of timing. Three different failure instants were assumed: failure at 25% of checkpoint interval, at 50% of checkpoint interval and at 75% of checkpoint interval. The failures were injected at the node shown as G in the Figure.

The observations are given in Tables 1 and 2. Table 1 shows the failure-free overhead for System N while Table 2 shows actual recovery time in seconds for step 1 alone, steps 1 & 2, steps 1, 2 & 3, steps 1,

2, 3 & 4, and step 5. Table 2 also shows the recovery times for the first four cases as a percentage of the time taken for step 5 (large-scope rollback recovery) and the number of processes involved at each step.

Table 1: Failure-free overhead for System N

Execution Type	No logging/ checkpointing	Chk&Logging	
		400	200
Time(s)	3040	3137	3140
% overhead	-	3.1%	3.2%

From Table 1, the run time overhead of message logging and checkpointing for system N is about 3%. In case of a failure, the time taken for doing retry is very low compared to the time that large-scale rollback takes, as shown in Table 2. Also note that the number of processes involved in doing steps 1 to 4 is at most 2, compared to 7, which is the number of processes involved in step 5. In most systems, the smaller the number of processes involved in recovery, the less impact the failure has. The results shown here coupled with this observation make the progressive retry technique extremely attractive for use with System N.

System N has been deployed in the field for more than 2 years now. Data obtained from the field has shown that more than 90% of the exceptions (failures) that occurred in the last 2 years have been successfully recovered by steps 1 to 3.

4.3 Performance measurement on REPL

REPL [15] is a collection of file system library functions and server processes that runs on a primary and a backup machine. Applications run on the primary machine and write critical files onto the primary file system. The REPL library intercepts the file system calls, produces update messages and sends the update messages to the REPL server processes, which then transfer the update messages to the REPL processes on the backup node. The backup REPL processes replay the update messages and reproduce the file updates on the backup node. REPL has been used in several telecommunications systems to replicate critical files and databases. The communication graph for REPL is shown in Figure 4.

A normal workload for REPL is a burst mode workload. It receives a burst of messages from an application, then becomes idle for some time and this cycle repeats over and over again. Since the burst frequency depends on the application that is using REPL, it is not possible to define one workload for the system. Thus the experiment has to be conducted for different burst frequencies.

A standard burst size of 10 messages per burst was used for the experiment. The workload was varied between 6 bursts per minute and 1.25 bursts per minute for measuring the recovery time. The failure free overhead was measured for the workload with a frequency of 6 standard bursts per minute, which is the worst

---

[3]The timings used in the simulations were obtained from the specification documents of the system.

Table 2: Recovery times for System N. t:time in seconds, %:recovery time as a percentage of step 5 time, n:number of processes involved

Failure at	Step 1			Steps 1,2			Steps 1-3			Steps 1-4			Step 5	
	t	%	n	t	%	n	t	%	n	t	%	n	t	n
25%-chk	2s	1.4%	1	7s	4.8%	1	16s	11.0%	2	26s	17.9%	2	145s	7
50%-chk	3s	1.1%	1	8s	2.8%	1	18s	6.3%	2	28s	9.8%	2	285s	7
75%-chk	4s	0.9%	1	9s	2.1%	1	20s	4.6%	2	30s	6.9%	2	437s	7

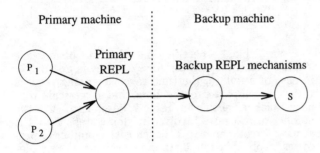

Figure 4: Communication pattern for REPL

case workload due to the high communication frequency.

The failure-free overhead measurements are given in Table 3. Checkpoint intervals of 500 messages, 400 messages and 250 messages per checkpoint were studied. The checkpoint size varied from 10 Kb to about 100Kb. The failure-free overhead for the worst case workload has a maximum value of 10.9%, which is acceptable in most REPL applications.

Table 3: Failure-free overhead for REPL

Execution Type	No logging/ checkpointing	Chk&Logging		
		500	400	250
Time(s)	3092	3387	3398	3432
% overhead	-	9.5%	9.8%	10.9%

Recovery time data was collected for message densities of 6, 3, 2, 1.5 and 1.25 standard bursts per minute (see Figures 5 and 6). For each message density the data was collected for failure rates corresponding to failures at 20% of checkpoint interval, 40% of checkpoint interval, 60% of checkpoint interval and 80% of checkpoint interval. Fault injection was done at the node marked S in the Figure. Figures 5 and 6 present the plots corresponding to failures at 20% and 80% of the checkpoint interval.

From the Figures, we observe that:

- steps 1 and 2 have a low recovery time compared to that of step 5 for all the message densities;

therefore, steps 1 and 2 are very attractive for various message densities;

- step 3 or step 4 of progressive retry could save a lot of recovery time only if the message density is low;

- the later a failure occurs in a checkpoint interval, the lower is the percentage of the recovery time compared with that of the step 5 retry. In other words, if a failure occurs later in a checkpoint interval of a system, progressive retry has a greater impact in reducing the recovery time provided the system successfully recovers at an early step.

5 Concluding Remarks

We have described a 5-step progressive retry technique using message logging as well as checkpointing to limit the scope of rollback and thereby provide a means for achieving localized and fast recovery. The technique is designed for continuously-running software systems which can absorb a certain degree of performance overhead and significantly benefit from reduced service unavailability. Our approach, which is based on the piecewise deterministic execution model, employs message replay to reconstruct state during recovery, message comparison to verify whether the above assumption is true, and message reordering to introduce environment diversity. Progressive retry has been implemented as part of a Software Fault Tolerance Platform developed at AT&T Bell Laboratories to provide automatic, economical, effective and efficient software failure recovery. Experiments conducted using this implementation of progressive retry have shown that the technique can significantly reduce failure recovery time while incurring only small performance overhead. Experience has also shown that incorporating progressive retry is easy as it requires adding only a few lines of code to a program.

Acknowledgements

The authors wish to express their sincere thanks to Chia-Mei Chen for her contribution to the implementation.

References

[1] J. Gray and A. Reuter, *Transaction Processing: Concepts and Techniques.* San Mateo, CA: Morgan Kaufmann Publishers, 1993.

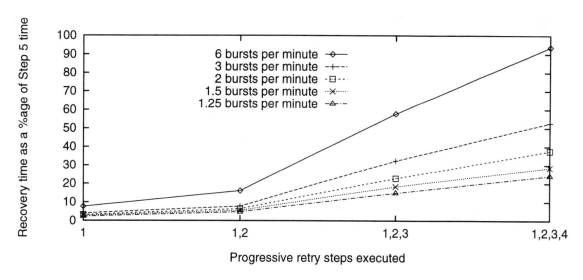

Figure 5: REPL : Time taken for retry (as a percentage of large-scope rollback recovery time) vs. the retry steps executed: failure at 80% checkpoint interval

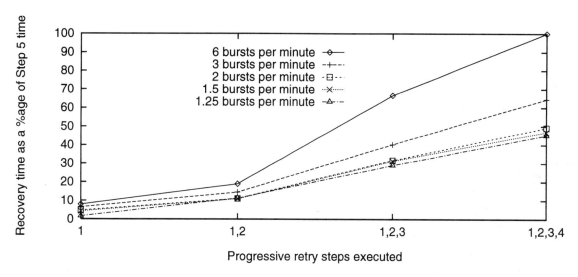

Figure 6: REPL : Time taken for retry (as a percentage of large-scope rollback recovery time) vs. the retry steps executed: failure at 20% checkpoint interval.

[2] J. Gray, "A census of tandem system availability between 1985 and 1990," *IEEE Trans. Reliab.*, Vol. 39, No. 4, pp. 409–418, Oct. 1990.

[3] M. Sullivan and R. Chillarege, "Software defects and their impact on system availability - A study of field failures in operating systems," in *Proc. IEEE Fault-Tolerant Computing Symp.*, pp. 2–9, 1991.

[4] D. Jewett, "Integrity S2: A fault-tolerant UNIX platform," in *Proc. IEEE Fault-Tolerant Computing Symp.*, pp. 512–519, 1991.

[5] J. Gray and D. P. Siewiorek, "High-availability computer systems," *IEEE Comput. Mag.*, pp. 39–48, Sept. 1991.

[6] J. Gray, "Dependable systems." *Keynote Speech, 11th Symp. on Reliable Distr. Syst.*, Oct. 1992.

[7] F. Cristian, "Exception handling and software fault tolerance," *IEEE Trans. Comput.*, Vol. C-31, No. 6, pp. 531–540, June 1982.

[8] E. Adams, "Optimizing preventive service of software products," *IBM J. R&D*, No. 1, pp. 2–14, Jan. 1984.

[9] I. Lee and R. K. Iyer, "Faults, symptoms, and software fault tolerance in the tandem guardian90 operating system," in *Proc. IEEE Fault-Tolerant Computing Symp.*, 1993.

[10] Y. Huang and C. Kintala, "Software implemented fault tolerance: Technologies and experience," in *Proc. IEEE Fault-Tolerant Computing Symp.*, pp. 2–9, June 1993.

[11] R. E. Strom and S. Yemini, "Optimistic recovery in distributed systems," *ACM Trans. Comput. Syst.*, Vol. 3, No. 3, pp. 204–226, Aug. 1985.

[12] Y. M. Wang, Y. Huang, and W. K. Fuchs, "Progressive retry for software error recovery in distributed systems," in *Proc. IEEE Fault-Tolerant Computing Symp.*, pp. 138–144, June 1993.

[13] K. M. Chandy and L. Lamport, "Distributed snapshots: Determining global states of distributed systems," *ACM Trans. Comput. Syst.*, Vol. 3, No. 1, pp. 63–75, Feb. 1985.

[14] Y. M. Wang and W. K. Fuchs, "Lazy checkpoint coordination for bounding rollback propagation," in *Proc. IEEE Symp. Reliable Distributed Syst.*, pp. 78–85, Oct. 1993.

[15] D. Korn, Y. Huang, G. Fowler, and H. Rao, "A user-level replicated file system," in *Proc. Summer '93 USENIX*, pp. 279–290, June 1993.

Invited Session:
Modeling and Evaluation

Session Chair: Dave Rennels

Performability Evaluation: Where It is and What Lies Ahead

J. Meyer

Please see Addendum for this paper.

Stochastic Petri Nets: Accomplishments and Open Problems

G.Balbo

Dipartimento di Informatica

Università di Torino

Corso Svizzera, 185 - I-10149 Torino - Italy

Abstract

Generalized stochastic Petri nets are briefly intro-duced and the work performed since the time of their proposal, to improve their modelling capabilities is surveied according to three directions of research. The open problems that still need to be solved to make this formalism useful for the analysis of real systems are discussed and some directions of future research are suggested.

1 Introduction

Petri nets [90, 1, 89, 92] are a powerful tool for the description and the analysis of systems that exhibit concurrency, synchronization and conflicts. Timed Petri nets [6, 83] in which the basic model is augmented with time specifications are commonly used to evaluate the performance and the reliability of complex systems.

The pioneering works in the area of timed Petri nets were performed by Merlin [76] and Faber, and by Noe and Nutt [88]. In both cases, Petri nets were viewed as a formalism for the description of the global behaviour of complex structures. The nets were used to *tell* all the possible stories that the system could experience also on the basis of their temporal specifications.

Several proposals for incorporating timing informa-tions into PN models have appeared in the literature. In principle, time can be either associated with places or with transitions. In the former case, tokens that are deposited in places become *available* for firing only after a delay that corresponds to the association of time with the place; in this type of models a transition may fire only when all of its input tokens are available and the state change due to its firing happens in zero time. In the latter case, the delay represents the time that takes the activity associated with the transition to complete. Two firing policies have been specified for timed transitions: the first assumes that the to-kens are withdrawn from the input places when the transition starts firing and are deposited in the out-put places at the end of the delay associated with the transition; the second assumes that the tokens are left in the input places for the whole duration of the firing and that the state change takes place in zero time at

*This work was supported in part by the European ESPRIT BRA Project 7269 QMIPS of CEC DG XIII and by Italian Min-istry of University and of Scientific and Technological Research (40% Project).

the end of the delay. It is possible to show that these two ways of specifying time are (almost) equivalent; a discussion of the implication of associating time with places can be found in [91].

Interpreting Petri nets as state/event models, time is naturally associated with activities that induce state changes, hence with the delays incurred before firing transitions. The choices of associating time with tran-sitions and of assuming transition firings to be atomic operations are the most frequent in the literature on timed Petri nets. When random variables are used to specify the firing delays of transitions, timed Petri nets are called Stochastic Petri Nets (SPN).

SPNs were initially proposed assuming exponen-tially distributed firing times and a race execution policy, i.e. selecting to fire the transition whose fir-ing delay is statistically minimum among those of the enabled ones [97, 85, 80]. Under these assumptions it has been proved that the dynamic behaviour of SPNs can be represented by continuous-time homogeneous Markov chains with state spaces isomorphic to the reachability graphs of the nets.

With the aim of extending the modelling power of stochastic Petri nets, Generalized Stochastic Petri Nets (GSPN) were proposed in [4], where two classes of transitions are defined: exponentially dis-tributed *timed* transitions, which are used to model the random delays associated with the execution of activ-ities, and *immediate* transitions, which are devoted to the representation of logical actions that do not consume time. Immediate transitions allow the in-troduction of branching probabilities, independently of timing specifications. When timed and immediate transitions are enabled in the same marking, imme-diate transitions are always assumed to fire first. In GSPNs also the reachability set is partitioned. *Tangi-ble* markings are those in which only timed transitions are enabled; *vanishing* markings are instead those in which at least one immediate transition is enabled. The sojourn times of GSPNs in their tangible states have negative exponential distributions with parame-ters depending on those of the timed transitions they enable; the times spent by the nets in their vanishing markings are instead deterministically null.

Other generalizations of the basic SPN formal-ism that are related with GSPNs are the Extended Stochastic Petri Nets [57] and the Stochastic Activity Networks [77].

GSPNs are among the SPN formalisms that are

0-8186-7059-2/95 $04.00 © 1995 IEEE

most commonly used for the analysis of important problems and a considerable effort has been devoted to their improvement since the time of their original proposal. In this paper we survey these contributions and we provide some indications on the research directions that are most promising for further enlarging the use of this formalism in the area of performance and reliability evaluation of complex systems.

The paper is organized as follows. Section 2 discusses the state of the art of the research on stochastic Petri nets that is relevant for the GSPN formalism. Section 3 highlights the problems that still need to be solved in order to make GSPNs a viable formalism for the analysis of real systems. Section 4 concludes the paper with some general remarks on net modelling. All the discussion contained in the following sections assumes that the reader is familiar with the basic terminology and operational rules of Petri nets for which a comprehensive reference can be found in [84].

2 State of the Art

The discussion of the research related with the GSPN formalism since the time of its proposal is organized in three different parts. First we consider the work done on the representation power of the formalism with an emphasis on the characterization of the stochastic processes underlying these nets. The development of tools for the analysis of GSPN models is discussed in this part of the paper for its contribution to the diffusion of the formalism and for stimulating the research on optimization techniques for the solution of large state space problems. The combinatorial growth of the state space of these models was recognized since the GSPN proposal, as the major obstacle to the use of this formalism in the analysis of real systems. In the second part of our discussion we consider the research that has been conducted in the attempt of overcoming this problem either avoiding the construction of the entire state space or exploiting intrinsic properties of the GSPNs to directly generate reduced state spaces. The third part of this section addresses the work that has been done trying to relate the graph and algebraic properties of the net models with those of their underlying stochastic processes. All the results mentioned in this last part have the common goal of simplifying the construction and the analysis of the probabilistic models on the basis of information coming from the structural analysis of the nets.

In the sequel of the paper we will use the GSPN acronym when discussing results that have been explicitly derived within the framework of GSPN models. Instead, we will use the most generic SPN acronym to address results that have been developed in a more general framework, but that are relevant for the GSPN formalism.

2.1 Markov Chain Description

Since their introduction [59, 80, 79, 97], SPNs (and later on GSPNs [4]) have often been used with the objective of describing the behaviours of complex systems. They turned out to be a convenient graphical notation for the construction of the stochastic processes representing such behaviours.

Having this goal in mind, several authors have proposed extensions of the basic models that improved the expressive power of the formalism. Inhibitor arcs [4, 57], probabilistic arcs [57], marking dependent arc cardinalities [43], and marking dependent firing rates and selection policies [4, 57], are among the features that have been introduced with this purpose.

A considerable effort has been devoted to precisely identify the characteristics of the stochastic processes described with SPNs [41, 47] and to identify the techniques that are better suited for their analysis [34, 17].

2.1.1 Non Markovian Stochastic Petri Nets

The assumption of the negative exponential distribution of firing times was soon felt to be too restrictive for a convenient representation of complex systems and several attempts were made to introduce general firing time distributions in the formalism.

The proposal of GSPN [4] was already motivated by the practical need of including in the model very different firing delays, without hampering the possibility of a convenient solution of the model. In fact, the need of including in the same model bus arbitration features and memory access times for the evaluation of multiprocessor architectures [5] led to the proposal of defining what have been since then called immediate transitions. Immediate transitions made the stochastic process underlying the GSPN semi-Markov, and an embedded Markov chain was identified for the efficient solution of the model.

Exploiting the possibility of encoding into the model (by means of suitable subnets) firing delays characterized by phase-type distributions [86], a simple extension was obtained by proposing special subnet structures that can be easily embedded into GSPN models to account for these type of distributions [30].

In an attempt to extend the class of stochastic processes representable by SPNs, a semi-Markov formulation was proposed by [85, 15] that was however not suited for the modelling of parallel activities due to the lack of memory after every transition firing.

The first useful results concerning SPNs with generally distributed transition delays are presented in [57]. The definition of extended stochastic Petri nets (ESPN) assumes that transitions are partitioned into three classes: exclusive, competitive, and concurrent. Provided that the firing delays of all concurrent transitions are exponentially distributed, and that competitive transitions resample a new firing delay whenever they are enabled, ESPN can be mapped onto semi-Markov processes. In [57] a procedure for analyzing acyclic nets is suggested in which generally distributed firing delays may be associated with concurrent transitions as well. The technique can however be used only for the transient analysis of models (which are not ergodic due to the acyclicity of the net). Moreover, as the authors recognize, the analysis becomes too complex for even medium size nets.

Using a similar approach, an embedded Markov chain technique was later proposed for the analysis of deterministic and stochastic Petri nets (DSPN) [7]. In this case the embedded Markov chain is used for the computation of the steady-state solution of nets in which at most one concurrent transition of constant delay is enabled in any marking.

Relaxing these restrictions on the characteristics of concurrent and competitive transitions, more complex models may be specified. Hence, some work was done in order to precisely define the operational rules of these new models and to understand their impact on the underlying stochastic process [2, 41]. Soon it was recognized that when allowing full generality in the specification of the model the possibility for the computation of analytical or numerical solutions was lost and only simulation could be done to analyze these models [67, 66]

Interesting solution techniques based on the existence of an embedded Markov chain were originally proposed for the DSPNs in [7]. These methods were first improved and optimized in [73]; subsequently, time and space efficient algorithms for the steady state solution of this class of models, based on a subordinated Markov chain were presented in [45]. The transient analysis of DSPN models is presented in [39].

Recently, the class of DSPN models has been extended allowing the transitions to have generally distributed firing times, provided that the constraint of having at most one of these transitions enabled in each marking is still satisfied [65]. This class of models is also called Markov Regenerative SPNs [74, 40] and special formulas for the computation of their steady state solution were recently derived. A systematic study of these classes of models can be found in [44].

2.1.2 Tools

The modelling power of SPN based formalisms attracted the interest of several researchers that employed them for the study of many aspects of real systems. To make these analyses possible, several research groups developed software tools that have been the key for the success of these formalisms [31, 52, 56, 46, 94, 38].

The choice of developing a tool based on a graphical interface for the construction and the analysis of GSPN models [31], led to the implementation of many visualization features that made even more evident the importance of describing the behaviour of complex systems using a net structure. The possibility of "playing" the so-called "token-game" on the net , of animating the movement of tokens on the net while doing discrete event simulation, and of visualizing structural results coming from the theory of classical Petri nets, contributed to the development of a consensus about the importance of using a single model for the qualitative and quantitative analysis of systems.

2.1.3 Improvements

The work on the development of tools for the analysis of very large SPN models provided the basis for understanding even further the implications of the choices made when proposing the formalism. As an example we can mention that when dealing with the problem

of reducing the amount of work related to the generation of vanishing states in GSPN models, a study was conducted on the possibility of firing several immediate transitions simultaneously [13]. This led to a better understanding of the concept of conflict in GSPNs and was the basis for a subsequent revision of the definition of the GSPN formalism that was important for improving the possibility of conducting a qualitative analysis of these models [32].

Always dealing with the problem of managing vanishing markings, accurate studies were performed on the advantages and disadvantages deriving from their removal in terms of complexity of the solution procedure [42, 17]. Additional efforts were also devoted to understand the necessity of immediate transitions and thus to study the possibility of removing them from the model before starting the construction of the reachability graph [34]. Recent results have improved the techniques of multiple firing of immediate transitions and of structural reductions by devising specific optimization algorithms and data structures [87].

Finally extremely large models coming from the analysis of massively-parallel systems with very regular structure of their interconnection networks, led to the implementation of parallel solution methods that on a SIMD architecture allowed the solution of models with millions of states [29].

2.2 State Space Complexity

GSPN models can provide compact representations of extremely complex systems. This is reflected in the sizes of their state spaces that grow combinatorially with the number of places in the nets and of tokens in the initial markings.

This problem has been recognized since the early use of this formalism to study realistic problems. Several approaches have thus been attempted to deal with the state space explosion, ranging from the techniques to efficiently solve the large probabilistic models described with the formalism, to the methods that exploit the structure of the model to devise convenient solution procedures that avoid the construction of the entire state space.

2.2.1 Efficient solution algorithms

Often the models correspond to "open" system representations whose state space grows unbounded. In these cases an efficient solution technique can be implemented if a repetitive structure can be identified within their state spaces [60, 61]. A special class of models of this type is that of the *open synchronized queueing networks* whose solution can be obtained using the matrix geometric method [86].

When the same models have finite populations, i.e. when their state spaces are finite, the solution can be expressed with a matrix product form [62] that generalizes the classical product form solution of closed queueing networks.

2.2.2 Decompositions and Aggregations

A technique for dealing with large GSPN models of complex systems is that of identifying within the model the subnets that correspond to specific functionalities of the real system. This functional decomposition may yield a partition of the model into submodels that enjoy particular properties. One case is that of GSPNs that can be envisioned as collections of subsystems in which synchronization occurs only at the level of their interaction, while the dynamic of the behaviour within each subsystem is only affected by congestion phenomena. In these cases it may be possible, first to characterize the behaviour of each subsystem in isolation solving their corresponding queueing network models, and then to compose these results with "higher level" GSPNs in which each subnet is represented by an equivalent, marking dependent, timed transition. Cases exist in which the procedure can be reversed solving first in isolation a set of GSPN submodels and then a "higher level" queueing network. In [10, 11] several examples of cases of this type are analyzed showing that, while a methodology guiding this approach has not been proposed yet, the ingenuity of the analyst may allow to study systems that are apparently just too complex to be solved.

Some help in this direction is provided by the adoption of the *Queueing Petri Net* formalism that is a generalization of the GSPN one in which situations of "pure" congestion are represented directly into the model with queueing servers [14].

A decomposition technique similar to that commonly used for the solution of queueing networks is that based on time scale considerations in which submodels are identified within a GSPN on the basis of a partition induced by the presence of "slow" transitions. Introducing a threshold criteria that is used to classify the transitions of the GSPN as slow and fast, starting from the original model, a set of intermediate subnets is constructed by temporarily removing all the slow transitions. The resulting subnets are then individually analyzed to compute the probability distributions of their state spaces, subject to different possible initial markings and under the assumption that short term equilibrium is reached in between rare events, when the entire model approaches steady state equilibrium. The partitioning of the GSPN model yields a partition of the corresponding state space. Each element of this partition can be considered as an aggregated state that can be shown to be isomorphic to the reachability set of an aggregated GSPN that may be constructed using a certain ingenuity [9, 8].

A computational improvement of this method is presented in [18] where the subnets are obtained by initially removing from the GSPN the transitions whose firing produces either an increment or a decrement of the number of tokens in the net. These criteria induce a different partition of the original net and an iterative algorithm is presented to compute the corresponding aggregated Markov chain. No attempt is made in this method to construct an aggregated GSPN model that has the aggregated Markov chain isomorphic to its reachability set.

Starting from the same consideration that large Markov chains can be analyzed via state aggregation, a different approach has been proposed in [63, 64] where the concept of *quasi lumpable* Markov chain has been introduced. Bounds on the steady state distribution of the states of these Markov chains are obtained using well known bounded aggregation techniques [51] for the approximate solution of Markov chains with not completely specified state spaces.

2.2.3 Symmetries

When dealing with complex systems, it often happens that their models can be constructed via the replication of many identical submodels. To deal with this problem, coloured Petri nets have been proposed to allow the construction of more compact models [72].

A special class of coloured Petri nets is that of the *Stochastic Well Formed Petri Nets* (SWN) in which restrictions are introduced on the functions that regulate transition firings and colour manipulations [58, 36, 35]. The important feature of SWNs is that the special form of the colour functions allow the direct construction of an aggregated state space. With this formalism the symmetries intrinsic in the model are directly exploited to identify markings that are representative for large groups of other markings having similar characteristics. This often yields dramatic reductions of the state space of the model thus allowing the analysis of quite complex nets. The aggregation method is fully automatized and the direct generation of the aggregated Markov chain is obtained with considerable saving at the level of memory requirements. A significative advantage is also obtained when the reduced state space is still too large for the model to be solved with numerical techniques and we must resort to simulation to obtain the performance indices of the model. A method of symbolic simulation has been developed in which only the aggregated markings are visited during the experiment [38]. When constructing SWN models, redundant colours may be specified for modelling convenience. A particular technique has been developed that removes these redundant colour specifications, thus making the task of the modeller much easier [37]. Concepts similar to those that yielded the definition of SWNs have been used within the framework of Stochastic Activity Networks with the development of methods for directly constructing reduced models targeted to the computation of particular performance indices [95].

2.2.4 Hierarchies

Coloured stochastic Petri nets and SWNs often yield state spaces that are still extremely large even after the exploitation of their intrinsic symmetries to reduce the number of states. To handle these models a hierarchical procedure has been proposed in [21, 22] where the concept of flow equivalent transition is discussed as a characterization of the behaviour of a low level submodel into a higher level one.

A more refined method for the characterization of the submodels is presented in [70] for the case of simple GSPN models. The improvement is obtained by replacing each subnet in the higher level model with a transition with a phase type distribution. To obtain this characterization, the second moment of the time needed by the tokens to "traverse" each subnet is computed feeding the subnet with a traffic process with suitable parameters. These parameters are estimated using an auxiliary net via a recursive application of the flow equivalent aggregation method.

2.2.5 Product Form

Always in the attempt of overcoming the problem of the state space explosion of the Markov chains associated with these models, a class of SPNs has been identified in which the steady state probability distribution of their markings can be expressed with a product form. The characterization of this class of SPNs was first expressed in terms of the special repetitive structures exhibited by their reachability graph [71, 93] and subsequently in terms of structural criteria that can be easily checked by inspecting the incidence matrix of the net [69, 68].

A comparison of the types of models identified with these two criteria showed that they are identical except for pathological cases that can be missed by both methods if they are applied without adequate generalizations [55]. This comparison showed for the first time the possibility of recognizing whether SPNs have product form solution using results from their structural analysis. A complete characterization of this class of models can be found in [19].

As in the case of queueing networks, these results became practically relevant when computational algorithms were developed to make the computation of this solution efficient both in terms of space and time. Also in the case of product form SPNs several algorithms have been devised following convolution and mean value analysis approaches [49, 48, 96].

Particularly important results for the possibilities of applying this techniques to non-product form SPNs are represented by the proof of a series of "arrival" theorems that relate the distributions of tokens seen at the arrival in a given place with the steady state distributions of tokens in the same place computed with the arriving token removed from the net [12]. These arrival theorems are generalizations of their queueing network counterparts since they have been derived for more complex models.

2.2.6 Bounds

When the SPNs that we want to solve cannot be analyzed with the methods that we have discussed before, approximate results can be computed as lower and upper bounds for specific performance indices defined at the net level.

Results in this direction were derived since the beginning of the research on SPNs in an attempt of developing also for these models a "bottleneck analysis" that is classical in queueing networks [81, 82, 20]. The use of linear programming techniques has recently allowed the derivation of a considerable num-

ber of results of this type. Bounding techniques that were originally derived for restricted classes of models [24, 25, 28, 27] are now being extended to larger classes of nets that are becoming extremely interesting also from an application point of view [33, 26].

2.3 Modelling

The problem of mastering the complexity of models of real systems has also been investigated with a somehow different approach driven by the idea that efficient solutions of difficult problems must be sought since the early stage of model construction.

This approach tries to exploit the properties and the structure of the net to guide the solution method. This principle implies that, in order to understand how complex systems work, their behaviours must be considered as the result of the composition of those of individual parts. It follows that in the development of the model, the analyst must maintain a local view of the different components avoiding the direct representation of global system features that, resulting from the interaction of individual parts, could exhibit unexpected behaviours in pathological cases that are difficult to predict. This idea has been the main reason for the revision of the GSPN definition in which restrictions on the specification of marking dependent parameters have been introduced [3, 32].

These general ideas have been recently included in a methodology for the hierarchical construction of large stochastic Petri net models [75] that has been proposed with the explicit goal of using the same hierarchical description also to drive the hierarchical solution of the model. With this methodology a large model is envisioned as the result of the (weak) interaction of many submodels. Each submodel is analyzed in isolation and these individual solutions are exploited to obtain the solution of the whole model.

The idea of a hierarchical composition of submodels to obtain the representation of a complex system is also the basis for a compositional modelling approach that has been proposed in [53, 54]. The Markov chain that underlies the entire model is only formally specified in this approach in terms of the Markov chains (transition probability matrices) of the individual submodels and of certain correcting factors that account for the interactions among the submodels. The complete transition probability matrix is never really constructed thus allowing the solution of extremely large models in a very efficient manner. This solution technique has also the non-trivial advantage of being quite suitable for parallelization. Obviously the solution of the entire models is made easier when the submodels interact in very special ways [23], thus making the correcting factors extremely simple.

3 Future Directions

The amount of work that we have discussed in the previous section shows that the community of researchers working on SPNs is large and alive. After an initial difficulty in accepting this new formalism due to its intrinsic complexity, SPNs are today widely used for the performance and dependability evaluation of many practical systems.

What was originally perceived as a disadvantage is now often appreciated because of the capability of the formalism of describing with precision complex phenomena that are typical of distributed and parallel systems. Moreover, the possibility of using the same model for a qualitative analysis (functional validation) followed by its efficiency and reliability evaluation is understood as an important result in the assessment of real systems. It is a common belief that this possibility should be exploited even further and that more powerful and more user-friendly software tools must be developed to make this integrated study common practice for system designers.

This success highligths also a whole set of new problems since larger and larger models are being built and need to be analyzed. Dealing with large models is obviously difficult since even in the case of bounded nets, the size of their reachability sets can become huge, making the numerical evaluation impossible and the discrete event simulation extremely expensive.

In the survey of the previous section, we have seen that this problem was immediately recognized by the researchers in the field, but so far little progress has been obtained in this direction, event if there is general consensus that the only possibility of successfully dealing with problems of this complexity is that of using a "divide and conquer" approach in which the solution of the entire problem is constructed on the basis of the solutions of the individual submodels. The theory underlying hierarchical solution methods is relatively well understood and applications of hierarchical techniques to specific problems can be found in the literature, but we are still lacking a methodology that can be applied to general problems in a safe and (hopefully) automatic manner. Efforts are needed in this direction with a special emphasis on exploiting the hierarchical construction of the model to drive a hierarchical solution method also when we resort to simulation for computing desired performance indices.

Aggregation/Disaggregation techniques working on the transition probability matrix of the Markov chains underlying most of these models are soundly based on the "Near Decomposability" theory of Courtois [50] that naturally applies to SPN models. Different is instead the situation of solution methods based on the flow equivalent concept coming from product form queueing networks, since a complete theory for product form SPNs has not been developed yet.

This is an important research topic since these techniques have been proved to be computationally efficient in the case of non-product form queueing networks, and since we expect that similar results will be found also in the area of non-product form SPNs. Developing the theory of product form SPNs is thus extremely important since the exact aggregation results that will be found in the case of product form SPNs will be applied to non-product form SPNs with the hope of good accuracy, provided that we have simple criteria to identify product form SPNs and to decide when non-product form SPNs are sufficiently "well behaving" to justify the application of the methods.

A complete characterization of product form SPNs will also contribute to removing the doubts that many analysts still have when dealing with complex SPN models that my hide with their apparent complexity intrinsicly simple behaviours.

Finally a complete understanding of the essence of the theory of product form SPNs may turn out to be extremely important with the development of model construction techniques based on compositionality principles. The construction of complex models as the composition of many small "building blocks" is a tendency that is becoming increasingly common and that is supported by specification tools as well as by theoretical results coming from "box calculus" [16] and from the world of "process algebras" [78]. The nets obtained in this way are likely to exhibit independence properties that can be used to prove the existence of certain types of product form solutions that should be explained by the theory of product form SPNs.

4 Conclusions

SPNs are used to describe complex systems and to construct their probabilistic representation for performance and reliability analyses. The problem of computing the transient and steady state solutions of these models has received considerable attention with a particular emphasis on the possibility of including transitions with arbitrary firing time distributions.

The advantage of net based models, however goes far beyond the modelling power of the formalism, since they provide information useful for automatically classify these models and for deriving preliminary results that can be extremely important to optimize the solution techniques and to develop approximation methods. Invariants results, flow balance equations, and special structures of the reachability graphs of these models are some of the results that we can obtain by the analysis of the graph and algebraic analysis of the net.

Additional efforts are needed in this direction to increase the impact that net based information have on the solution techniques and to improve the cross-fertilization between the qualitative and quantitative analyses fields when the same basic model is used for both types of studies.

References

[1] T. Agerwala. Putting Petri nets to work. *IEEE Computer*, pages 85–94, December 1979.

[2] M. Ajmone Marsan, G. Balbo, A. Bobbio, G. Chiola, G. Conte, and A. Cumani. The effect of execution policies on the semantics and analysis of stochastic Petri nets. *IEEE Transactions on Software Engineering*, 15(7):832–846, July 1989.

[3] M. Ajmone Marsan, G. Balbo, G. Chiola, and G. Conte. Generalized stochastic Petri nets revisited: Random switches and priorities. In *Proc. Intern. Workshop on Petri Nets and Performance Models*, pages 44–53, Madison, WI, USA, August 1987. IEEE-CS Press.

[4] M. Ajmone Marsan, G. Balbo, and G. Conte. A class of generalized stochastic Petri nets for the performance analysis of multiprocessor systems.

ACM Transactions on Computer Systems, 2(1), May 1984.

[5] M. Ajmone Marsan, G. Balbo, and G. Conte. *Performance Models of Multiprocessor Systems.* MIT Press, Cambridge, USA, 1986.

[6] M. Ajmone Marsan, G. Balbo, and K.S. Trivedi, editors. *Proc. Intern. Workshop on Timed Petri Nets*, Torino, Italy, July 1985. IEEE-CS Press.

[7] M. Ajmone Marsan and G. Chiola. On Petri nets with deterministic and exponential transition firing times. In *Proc. 7th European Workshop on Application and Theory of Petri Nets*, pages 151–165, Oxford, England, June 1986.

[8] H. H. Ammar and S.M.R. Islam. Time scale decomposition of a class of generalized stochastic Petri net models. *IEEE Transactions on Software Engineering*, 15(6):809–820, June 1989.

[9] H. H. Ammar and R. W. Liu. Analysis of the generalized stochastic Petri nets by state aggregation. In *Proc. Intern. Workshop on Timed Petri Nets*, pages 88–95, Torino,Italy, Jul 1985.

[10] G. Balbo, S. C. Bruell, and S. Ghanta. Combining queueing network and generalized stochastic Petri net models for the analysis of some software blocking phenomena. *IEEE Transactions on Software Engineering*, 12(4):561–576, April 1986.

[11] G. Balbo, S. C. Bruell, and S. Ghanta. Combining queueing network and generalized stochastic Petri nets for the solution of complex models of system behavior. *IEEE Transactions on Computers*, 37(10):1251–1268, October 1988.

[12] G. Balbo, S. C. Bruell, and M. Sereno. Arrival theorems for product-form stochastic Petri nets. In *Proc. 1994 SIGMETRICS Conference*, Nashville, Tennessee, USA, May 1994. ACM.

[13] G. Balbo, G. Chiola, G. Franceschinis, and G. Molinar Roet. On the efficient construction of the tangible reachability graph of generalized stochastic Petri nets. In *Proc. Intern. Workshop on Petri Nets and Performance Models*, Madison, WI, USA, August 1987. IEEE-CS Press.

[14] F. Bause. Queueing Petri nets: A formalism for the combined qualitative and quantitative analysis of systems. In *Proc. 5th Intern. Workshop on Petri Nets and Performance Models*, pages 14–23, Toulouse, France, October 1993. IEEE-CS Press.

[15] A. Bertoni and M. Torelli. Probabilistic Petri nets and semi-Markov processes. In *Proc. 2nd European workshop on Petri nets*, Bad Honnef, West Germany, September 1981.

[16] E. Best, R. Devillers, and J. Hall. The Petri box calculus: a new causal algebra with multilabel communication. In G. Rozenberg, editor, *Advances in Petri Nets*, volume 609 of *LNCS*, pages 21–69. Springer Verlag, 1992.

[17] A. Blakemore. The cost of eliminating vanishing markings from generalized stochastic Petri nets. In *Proc. 3rd Intern. Workshop on Petri Nets and Performance Models*, Kyoto, Japan, December 1989. IEEE-CS Press.

[18] A. Blakemore and S.K. Tripathi. Automated time scale decomposition and analysis of stochastic Petri nets. In *Proc. 5th Intern. Workshop on Petri Nets and Performance Models*, pages 248–257, Toulouse, France, October 1993. IEEE-CS Press.

[19] R.J. Boucherie. A characterization of independence for competing Markov chains with applications to stochastic Petri nets. In *Proc. 5th Intern. Workshop on Petri Nets and Performance Models*, pages 117–126, Toulouse, France, October 1993. IEEE-CS Press.

[20] S.C. Bruell and S. Ghanta. Throughput bounds for generalized stochastic Petri net models. In *Proc. Intern. Workshop on Timed Petri Nets*, Torino, Italy, July 1985. IEEE-CS Press.

[21] P. Buchholz. Aggregation and reduction techniques for hierarchical GCSPNs. In *Proc. 5th Intern. Workshop on Petri Nets and Performance Models*, pages 216–225, Toulouse, France, October 1993. IEEE-CS Press.

[22] P. Buchholz. Hierarchies in colored GSPNs. In *Proc. 14th Intern. Conference on Application and Theory of Petri Nets*, LNCS, Chicago, Illinois, June 1993. Springer Verlag.

[23] P. Buchholz. Hierarchical high level Petri nets for complex system analysis. In *Proc. 15th Intern. Conference on Applications and Theory of Petri Nets*, number 185 in LNCS, Zaragoza, Spain, 1994. Springer-Verlag.

[24] J. Campos, G. Chiola, J.M. Colom, and M. Silva. Tight polynomial bounds for steady-state performance of marked graphs. In *Proc. 3rd Intern. Workshop on Petri Nets and Performance Models*, Kyoto, Japan, December 1989. IEEE-CS Press.

[25] J. Campos, G. Chiola, and M. Silva. Properties and steady-state performance bounds for Petri nets with unique repetitive firing count vector. In *Proc. 3rd Intern. Workshop on Petri Nets and Performance Models*, Kyoto, Japan, December 1989. IEEE-CS Press.

[26] J. Campos, J.M. Colom, H. Jungnitz, and M. Silva. A general iterative technique for approximate throughput computation of stochastic marked graphs. In *Proc. 5th Intern. Workshop on Petri Nets and Performance Models*, pages 138–147, Toulouse, France, October 1993. IEEE-CS Press.

[27] J. Campos, B. Sanchez, and M. Silva. Throughput lower bounds for Markovian Petri nets: Transformation techniques. In *Proc. 4th Intern. Workshop on Petri Nets and Performance Models*, pages 322–331, Melbourne, Australia, December 1991. IEEE-CS Press.

[28] J. Campos and M. Silva. Throughput upper bounds for Markovian Petri nets: Embedded subnets and queueing networks. In *Proc. 4th Intern. Workshop on Petri Nets and Performance Models*, pages 312–321, Melbourne, Australia, December 1991. IEEE-CS Press.

[29] S. Caselli, G. Conte, M. Fontanesi, and F. Bonardi. Experiences on SIMD massively parallel GSPN analysis. In *Proc. 7th Intern. Conference on Modelling Techniques and Tools for Computer Performance Evaluation*, Vienna, Austria, May 1994. Springer Verlag.

[30] P. Chen, S.C. Bruell, and G. Balbo. Alternative methods for incorporating non-exponential distributions into stochastic Petri nets. In *Proc. 3rd Intern. Workshop on Petri Nets and Performance Models*, pages 187–197, Kyoto, Japan, December 1989. IEEE-CS Press.

[31] G. Chiola. A software package for the analysis of generalized stochastic Petri net models. In *Proc. Intern. Workshop on Timed Petri Nets*, Torino, Italy, July 1985. IEEE-CS Press.

[32] G. Chiola, M. Ajmone Marsan, G. Balbo, and G. Conte. Generalized stochastic Petri nets: A definition at the net level and its implications. *IEEE Transactions on Software Engineering*, 19(2):89–107, February 1993.

[33] G. Chiola, C. Anglano, J. Campos, J.M. Colom, and M. Silva. Operational analysis of timed Petri nets and applications to the computation of performance bounds. In *Proc. 5th Intern. Workshop on Petri Nets and Performance Models*, Toulouse, France, October 1993. IEEE-CS Press.

[34] G. Chiola, S. Donatelli, and G. Franceschinis. GSPN versus SPN: what is the actual role of immediate transitions? In *Proc. 4th Intern. Workshop on Petri Nets and Performance Models*, pages 20–31, Melbourne, Australia, December 1991. IEEE-CS Press.

[35] G. Chiola, C. Dutheillet, G. Franceschinis, and S. Haddad. Stochastic Well-Formed coloured nets for symmetric modelling applications. *IEEE Transactions on Computers*, 42(11), November 1993.

[36] G. Chiola and G. Franceschinis. Colored GSPN models and automatic symmetry detection. In *Proc. 3rd Intern. Workshop on Petri Nets and Performance Models*, Kyoto, Japan, December 1989. IEEE-CS Press.

[37] G. Chiola and G. Franceschinis. A structural colour simplification in Well-Formed coloured nets. In *Proc. 4th Intern. Workshop on Petri Nets and Performance Models*, pages 144–153, Melbourne, Australia, December 1991. IEEE-CS Press.

[38] G. Chiola, G. Franceschinis, R. Gaeta, and M. Ribaudo. GreatSPN1.7: GRaphical Editor and Analyzer for Timed and Stochastic Petri Nets. accepted for pubblication on Performance Evaluation.

[39] H. Choi, G. Kulkarni, and K.S. Trivedi. Transient analysis of deterministic and stochastic petri nets. In *Proc. 14th Intern. Conference on Application and Theory of Petri Nets*, Chicago, Illinois, June 1993. Springer Verlag.

[40] H. Choi, V.S. Kulkarni, and K.S. Trivedi. Markov regenerative stochastic petri nets. In *Proc. of Performance 93*, Rome, Italy, September 1993.

[41] G. Ciardo. Toward a definition of modeling power for stochastic Petri net models. In *Proc. Intern. Workshop on Petri Nets and Performance Models*, Madison, WI, USA, August 1987. IEEE-CS Press.

[42] G. Ciardo. *Analysis of large Petri net models.* PhD thesis, Department of Computer Science, Duke University, Durham, NC, USA, 1989. Ph. D. Thesis.

[43] G. Ciardo. Petri nets with marking dependent arc cardinality: Properties and analysis. In *Proc. 15th Intern. Conference on Applications and Theory of Petri Nets*, number 185 in LNCS, Zaragoza, Spain, 1994. Springer-Verlag.

[44] G. Ciardo, R. German, and C. Lindemann. A characterization of the stochastic process underlying a stochastic Petri net. In *Proc. 5th Intern. Workshop on Petri Nets and Performance Models*, pages 170–179, Toulouse, France, October 1993. IEEE-CS Press.

[45] G. Ciardo and C. Lindemann. Analysis of deterministic and stochastic Petri nets. In *Proc. 5th Intern. Workshop on Petri Nets and Performance Models*, pages 160–169, Toulouse, France, October 1993. IEEE-CS Press.

[46] G. Ciardo, J. Muppala, and K.S. Trivedi. SPNP: Stochastic Petri net package. In *Proc. 3rd Intern. Workshop on Petri Nets and Performance Models*, Kyoto, Japan, December 1989. IEEE-CS Press.

[47] G. Ciardo, J. Muppala, and K.S. Trivedi. On the solution of GSPN reward models. *Performance Evaluation*, 12(4):237–253, July 1991.

[48] J.L. Coleman. Algorithms for product-form stochastic Petri nets - a new approach. In *Proc. 5th Intern. Workshop on Petri Nets and Performance Models*, Toulouse, France, October 1993. IEEE-CS Press.

[49] J.L. Coleman. *Stochastic Petri Nets with Product Form Equilibrium Distributions*. PhD thesis, University of Adelaide, Adelaide, Australia, December 1993. Ph.D. Thesis.

[50] P.J. Courtois. *Decomposability: Queueing and Computer Systems Applications*. Academic Press, New York, 1977.

[51] P.J. Courtois and P. Semal. Bounds on conditional steady-state distributions in large Markovian and queueing models. In O.J. Boxma, J.W. Cohen, and H.C. Tijms, editors, *Teletraffic Analysis and Computer Performance Evaluation*, pages 499–520. Elsevier Science Publ. (North Holland), 1986.

[52] A. Cumani. Esp - a package for the evaluation of stochastic Petri nets with phase-type distributed transition times. In *Proc. Intern. Workshop on Timed Petri Nets*, Torino, Italy, July 1985. IEEE-CS Press.

[53] S. Donatelli. Superposed Stochastic Automata: a class of stochastic Petri nets amenable to parallel solution. In *Proc. 4th Intern. Workshop on Petri Nets and Performance Models*, pages 54–63, Melbourne, Australia, December 1991. IEEE-CS Press.

[54] S. Donatelli. Superposed generalized stochastic Petri nets: definition and efficient solution. In *Proc. of the 15th Intern. Conference on Applications and Theory of Petri Nets*, number 185 in Lecture Notes in Computer Science. Springer-Verlag, 1994.

[55] S. Donatelli and M. Sereno. *On the Product Form Solution for Stochastic Petri Nets*, pages 154–172. LNCS, N. 616. Springer Verlag, Sheffield, England, June 1992.

[56] J.B. Dugan, A. Bobbio, and G. Ciardo K.S. Trivedi. The design of a unified package for the solution of stochastic Petri net models. In *Proc. Intern. Workshop on Timed Petri Nets*, Torino, Italy, July 1985. IEEE-CS Press.

[57] J.B. Dugan, K.S. Trivedi, R.M. Geist, and V.F. Nicola. Extended stochastic Petri nets: Applications and analysis. In *Proc. PERFORMANCE '84*, Paris, France, December 1984.

[58] C. Dutheillet and S. Haddad. Aggregation and disaggregation of states in colored stochastic Petri nets: Application to a multiprocessor architecture. In *Proc. 3rd Intern. Workshop on Petri Nets and Performance Models*, Kyoto, Japan, December 1989. IEEE-CS Press.

[59] G. Florin and S. Natkin. Les reseaux de Petri stochastiques. *Technique et Science Informatiques*, 4(1), February 1985.

[60] G. Florin and S. Natkin. On open synchronized queueing networks. In *Proc. Intern. Workshop on Timed Petri Nets*, Torino, Italy, July 1985. IEEE-CS Press.

[61] G. Florin and S. Natkin. A necessary and sufficient saturation condition for open synchronized queueing networks. In *Proc. Intern. Workshop on Petri Nets and Performance Models*, pages 4–13, Madison, WI, USA, August 1987. IEEE-CS Press.

[62] G. Florin and S. Natkin. Matrix product form solution for closed synchronized queueing networks. In *Proc. 3rd Intern. Workshop on Petri Nets and Performance Models*, pages 29–39, Kyoto, Japan, December 1989. IEEE-CS Press.

[63] G. Franceschinis and R.R. Muntz. Bounds for quasi-lumpable Markov chains. In *Proc. Performance 93*, Rome, Italy, September 1993.

[64] G. Franceschinis and R.R. Muntz. Computing bounds for the performance indices of quasi-lumpable stochastic Well-Formed nets. In *Proc. 5th Intern. Workshop on Petri Nets and Performance Models*, Toulouse, France, October 1993. IEEE-CS Press.

[65] R. German and C. Lindemann. Analysis of stochastic Petri nets by the method of supplementary variables. In *Proc. of Performance 93*, Rome, Italy, September 1993.

[66] P. J. Haas and G. S. Shedler. Regenerative stochastic Petri nets. *Performance Evaluation*, 6(3):189–204, September 1986.

[67] P.J. Haas and G.S. Shedler. Regenerative simulation of stochastic Petri nets. In *Proc. Intern. Workshop on Timed Petri Nets*, Torino, Italy, July 1985. IEEE-CS Press.

[68] W. Henderson and D. Lucic. Exact results in the aggregation and disaggregation of stochastic Petri nets. In *Proc. 4th Intern. Workshop on Petri Nets and Performance Models*, pages 166–175, Melbourne, Australia, December 1991. IEEE-CS Press.

[69] W. Henderson and P.G. Taylor. Aggregation methods in exact performance analysis of stochastic Petri nets. In *Proc. 3rd Intern. Workshop on Petri Nets and Performance Models*, pages 12–18, Kyoto, Japan, December 1989. IEEE-CS Press.

[70] G. Klas. *Hierarchical Solution of Generalized Stochastic Petri Nets by Means of Traffic Processes*, pages 279–288. LNCS, N. 616. Springer Verlag, Sheffield, England, June 1992.

[71] A.A. Lazar and T.G. Robertazzi. Markovian Petri net protocols with product form solution. *Performance Evaluation*, 12:67–77, 1991.

[72] C. Lin and D.C. Marinescu. On stochastic high level Petri nets. In *Proc. Intern. Workshop on Petri Nets and Performance Models*, Madison, WI, USA, August 1987. IEEE-CS Press.

[73] C. Lindemann. An improved numerical algorithm for calculating steady-state solutions of Deterministic and Stochastic Petri net models. In *Proc. 4th Intern. Workshop on Petri Nets and Performance Models*, pages 176,185, Melbourne, Australia, December 1991. IEEE-CS Press.

[74] V. Mainkar, H. Choi, and K. Trivedi. Sensitivity analysis of Markov regenerative stochastic Petri nets. In *Proc. 5th Intern. Workshop on Petri Nets and Performance Models*, Toulouse, France, October 1993. IEEE-CS Press.

[75] M. Malhotra and K.S. Trivedi. A methodology for formal expression of hierarchy in model solution. In *Proc. 5th Intern. Workshop on Petri Nets and Performance Models*, pages 258–267, Toulouse, France, October 1993. IEEE-CS Press.

[76] P. M. Merlin and D. J. Farber. Recoverability of communication protocols: Implications of a theoretical study. *IEEE Transactions on Communications*, 24(9):1036–1043, September 1976.

[77] J. F. Meyer, A. Movaghar, and W. H. Sanders. Stochastic activity networks: Structure, behavior, and application. In *Proc. Intern. Workshop on Timed Petri Nets*, pages 106–115, Torino,Italy, July 1985.

[78] R. Milner. *Communication and concurrency*. Prentice Hall, 1989.

[79] M. K. Molloy. Performance analysis using stochastic Petri nets. *IEEE Transaction on Computers*, 31(9):913–917, September 1982.

[80] M.K. Molloy. *On the Integration of Delay and Throughput Measures in Distributed Processing Models*. PhD thesis, UCLA, Los Angeles, CA, 1981. Ph.D. Thesis.

[81] M.K. Molloy. Fast bounds for stochastic Petri nets. In *Proc. Intern. Workshop on Timed Petri Nets*, Torino, Italy, July 1985. IEEE-CS Press.

[82] M.K. Molloy. Structurally bounded stochastic Petri nets. In *Proc. Intern. Workshop on Petri Nets and Performance Models*, pages 156–163, Madison, WI, USA, August 1987. IEEE-CS Press.

[83] M.K. Molloy, T. Murata, and M.K. Vernon, editors. *Proc. Intern. Workshop on Petri Nets and Performance Models*, Madison, Wisconsin, August 1987. IEEE-CS Press.

[84] T. Murata. Petri nets: properties, analysis, and applications. *Proceedings of the IEEE*, 77(4):541–580, April 1989.

[85] S. Natkin. *Les Reseaux de Petri Stochastiques et leur Application a l'Evaluation des Systemes Informatiques*. PhD thesis, CNAM, Paris, France, 1980. These de Docteur Ingegneur.

[86] M.F. Neuts. *Matrix Geometric Solutions in Stochastic Models*. Johns Hopkins University Press, Baltimore, MD, 1981.

[87] D.S. Nielsen and L. Kleinrock. Data structures and algorithms for extended state space and structural level reduction of the gspn model. In *Proc. 15th Intern. Conference on Applications and Theory of Petri Nets*, number 185 in LNCS, Zaragoza, Spain, 1994. Springer-Verlag.

[88] J. D. Noe and G. J. Nutt. Macro e-nets representation of parallel systems. *IEEE Transactions on Computers*, 31(9):718–727, August 1973.

[89] J.L. Peterson. *Petri Net Theory and the Modeling of Systems*. Prentice-Hall, Englewood Cliffs, NJ, 1981.

[90] C.A. Petri. Communication with automata. Technical Report RADC-TR-65-377, Rome Air Dev. Center, New York, NY, 1966.

[91] C. Ramchandani. *Analysis of Asynchronous Concurrent Systems by Timed Petri Nets*. PhD thesis, MIT, Cambridge, MA, 1974. Ph.D. Thesis.

[92] W. Reisig. *Petri Nets: an Introduction*. Springer Verlag, 1985.

[93] T.G. Robertazzi. *Computer Networks and Systems: Queueing Theory and Performance Evaluation*. Springer Verlag, 1991.

[94] W. H. Sanders and J. F. Meyer. METASAN: a performability evaluation tool based on stochastic activity networks. In *Proc. ACM/IEEE–CS Fall Joint Computer Conference*, November 1986.

[95] W.H. Sanders and J.F. Meyer. Reduced base model construction methods for stochastic activity networks. In *Proc. 3rd Intern. Workshop on Petri Nets and Performance Models*, Kyoto, Japan, December 1989. IEEE-CS Press.

[96] M. Sereno and G. Balbo. Computational algorithms for product form solution stochastic Petri nets. In *Proc. 5th Intern. Workshop on Petri Nets and Performance Models*, Toulouse, France, October 1993. IEEE-CS Press.

[97] F. J. W. Symons. Introduction to numerical Petri nets, a general graphical model of concurrent processing systems. *Australian Telecommunications Research*, 14(1):28–33, January 1980.

Structural Performance Analysis of Stochastic Petri Nets*

Manuel Silva   and   Javier Campos
Departamento de Ingeniería Eléctrica e Informática
Centro Politécnico Superior de la Universidad de Zaragoza
María de Luna, 3, 50015 Zaragoza, Spain

Abstract

Structure performance analysis theory and techniques is an essay to avoid the computational complexity problem associated to Markovian and discrete event simulation techniques. Even if a finished conceptual and technical framework is not yet available, important benefits have been obtained not only from performance but also from correctness analysis point of view. In this survey we overview some of the achievements developed by the authors and collaborators towards a structure theory for performance evaluation of net based models. Concepts and techniques for the computation of performance bounds and approximate and exact evaluation are described in a semiformal/illustrative way through a selected collection of examples.

1 Introduction

Petri nets consist of a few simple objects, relations, and rules to model discrete event dynamic systems with potentially very complex behaviours. Therefore qualitative/logical analysis of net models has been traditionally a problem to which much attention has been devoted. Roughly speaking these analysis techniques fall into the following categories [20, 23]: (1) *enumeration*, in which the state space is (partially) explored; (2) *transformation*, where the basic idea is to transform the original system into another under some "equivalence" notion and easier to analyse; (3) *structural*, where the key point is to obtain the maximum of information about the behaviour reasoning on the net structure (i.e., the static) and the initial marking (essentially considered as a parameter); and (4) *simulation*, where one or several behaviours are explored.

Petri nets have been provided with several timed stochastic interpretations leading to performance models, that can be viewed as *queueing networks with choices and synchronizations* [5]. Performance analysis techniques of timed stochastic interpretation can be also classified into analogous groups. Enumeration techniques are strongly related to techniques in which certain *Markov chains* are solved. Simulation is now essentially a chapter of *discrete event dynamic systems simulation*. Transformation techniques are not too much developed and the existing methods are deeply based on structural concepts and objects. This invited survey overviews and illustrates some of the achievements towards a structure theory for performance computation of net based models. It is heavily based on the work carried out by our group.

As general remarks, we want to point out two important facts: (a) today we have *not* a full-fledged/finished theory for structural computation of performance figures, but several important concepts and techniques are already available; nevertheless several new algorithms improving the more classical approaches are computationally much less complex (even with polynomial time complexity in several cases!); and (b) the interleaving of correctness and performance analysis concepts and techniques has already produced several benefits, that we can summarize as follows [22]:

(1) *Introduction of new concepts for the analysis of autonomous (non-timed, in our context) net systems*, as the liveness bound of a transition (a quantitative generalization of the classical liveness concept, strongly related to the notion of number of servers in a station in steady-state).

(2) *Bridges between logical and performance properties*, as that existing between the existence of home spaces (often required for correctness) and ergodicity of the stochastic model. In section 4, the analysis technique taken as example introduces an elaborated bridge for a class of nets be-

*This work has been partially supported by the projects CICYT TIC-94-0242 of the Spanish Plan Nacional de Investigación, and Esprit BRA Project 7269 (QMIPS) and Human Capital programme CT94-0452 (MATCH) of the European Community.

61

tween synchronic distances (a correctness notion) and potential ergodicity (a performance notion).

(3) *Performance analysis suggests new results for the correctness analysis of autonomous net models.* This is the case, for example, of the so called rank theorems, that allow to characterize, in polynomial time, structural liveness and boundedness of certain net classes (e.g., equal conflict [27, 26]; deterministic systems of sequential processes [21]).

(4) *Untimed net systems analysis techniques allow the development of new performance analysis techniques* in which full state exploration and/or simulation are not needed.

In other words, the interleaving of correctness and performance analysis theories produces a synergic situation, in which each one contributes to the development of the other.

The rest of the paper, through a selected collection of examples, shows concepts and techniques for the structural analysis of performance net models. We assume the reader is familiar with the general concepts and notation on (stochastic) Petri net systems [20, 5, 23, 25].

2 Performance bounds

In this section, we consider the computation of performance bounds for the steady-state behaviour of stochastic Petri net systems under *weak ergodicity* assumption for the firing and the marking processes [4] and with infinite-server semantics. We denote by $\overline{M}$ and $\vec{\sigma}^*$ the *limit average marking* and the *limit throughput* vector, respectively. For each transition t_i, the inverse of its throughput, $\Gamma^{(i)} = 1/\sigma^*(t_i)$, is called *mean interfiring time* of t_i.

If no assumption is made on the probability distribution of transition service times, *insensitive* bounds for the limit throughput can be derived based on some structural characteristics of the model. Such results are presented in section 2.2. Some improvements are briefly presented in section 2.3. The structural concepts needed to derive the performance results are introduced in section 2.1.

As an example of application of the results included in this section, we consider the Petri net model of a multiple-bus multiprocessor with external common memory depicted in Fig. 1 (three processors, three external common memories, and two buses). We assume that the common memory request rates of all processors are equal, and that the three common memories

Figure 1: A multiple-bus multiprocessor with external common memory and its Petri net representation.

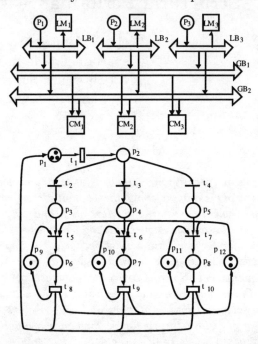

have different access times and they are requested with different probabilities.

2.1 Structural basis

If C denotes the incidence matrix of the net, vectors $Y \geq 0$ such that $Y^T \cdot C = 0$ ($X \geq 0$ such that $C \cdot X = 0$) are called *P-semiflows* or conservative components (*T-semiflows* or consistent components). The *support* of a P-semiflow (T-semiflow) is defined as $||Y|| = \{p \in P \mid Y(p) \neq 0\}$ ($||X|| = \{t \in T \mid X(t) \neq 0\}$). A (P- or T-) semiflow is called *minimal* if it has minimal support (i.e., non strictly included in another).

The *visit ratio* of transition t_j with respect to t_i, $v_j^{(i)}$, is the average number of times t_j is visited (fired) for each visit to (firing of) the reference transition t_i. The vector of visit ratios of a bounded system must be a T-semiflow (the input weighted flow to each place must be equal to the output weighted flow). The visit ratios of transitions in *equal conflict*, i.e., such that their preconditions are the same ($PRE[t_j] = PRE[t_k]$) must be fixed by the corresponding routing rates. For instance, for the net in Fig. 1, the following equations hold: $r_3 v_2^{(i)} - r_2 v_3^{(i)} = 0$; $r_4 v_2^{(i)} - r_2 v_4^{(i)} = 0$, where r_2, r_3, and r_4 are the routing rates of t_2, t_3, and t_4. In summary, the next result can be stated:

Theorem 2.1 [10] *The vector of visit ratios with re-*

spect to transition t_i of a live and bounded net system must be a solution of:

$$C \cdot \vec{v}^{(i)} = 0; \quad R \cdot \vec{v}^{(i)} = 0; \quad v_i^{(i)} = 1$$

where C is the incidence matrix and R is a matrix that relates the visit ratios of transitions in equal conflict ($PRE[t_j] = PRE[t_k]$) according to the corresponding routing rates.

Equations in the above theorem have been shown to characterize a unique vector $\vec{v}^{(i)}$ for important net subclasses [5, 10] (a condition over the rank of C and the number of equal conflicts underlies these cases).

The *average service demand* from transition t_j with respect to t_i is defined as $D_j^{(i)} = s_j v_j^{(i)}$.

The performance of a net with infinite-server semantics of transitions depends on the maximum degree of enabling of the transitions, the *enabling bound*. Interpreting the net transitions as queueing stations, the *liveness bound*, $L(t)$, is a lower bound of the number of servers in steady state. The liveness bound is just a numerical refinement of the classical liveness concept in Petri nets ($L(t) > 0$ iff t is live) required for performance computations.

Definition 2.1 *Let* $\langle \mathcal{N}, M_0 \rangle$ *be a net system.*

The enabling bound of a transition t *of* $\mathcal{N}$ *is* $E(t) \overset{\text{def}}{=}$ $\max\{k \mid \exists M \in R(\mathcal{N}, M_0) : M \geq k PRE[t]\}$.

The liveness bound of a transition t *is* $L(t) \overset{\text{def}}{=}$ $\max\{k \mid \forall M' \in R(\mathcal{N}, M_0), \exists M \in R(\mathcal{N}, M') : M \geq k PRE[t]\}$.

The structural enabling bound of a transition t *is:* $SE(t) \overset{\text{def}}{=} \max\{k \mid M_0 + C \cdot \vec{\sigma} \geq k PRE[t]; \vec{\sigma} \geq 0\}$.

Note that the definition of structural enabling bound reduces to the formulation of a linear programming problem. The following result relates the above three concepts:

Theorem 2.2 [4] *Let* $\langle \mathcal{N}, M_0 \rangle$ *be a net system, then for every transition* t *of* $\mathcal{N}$, $SE(t) \geq E(t) \geq L(t)$.

The interest of the above property lies in the fact that for those net systems whose exact liveness bounds of transitions cannot be efficiently computed, upper bounds (i.e., optimistic values) can be always obtained by solving some linear programming problems, i.e., by computing the structural enabling bounds.

2.2 Computation of insensitive bounds

If, in addition of weak ergodicity, we assume that the *residence time* of a token at each place (time spent

by the token within the place) is bounded[1], the following result can be derived from Little's law and the basic properties of P-semiflows:

Theorem 2.3 [10] *For any live and bounded system, a lower bound for the mean interfiring time* $\Gamma^{(i)}$ *of transition* t_i *can be computed by the following linear programming problem:*

$$
\begin{aligned}
\Gamma^{(i)} \geq \quad &\text{maximum} \quad Y^T \cdot PRE \cdot \vec{D}^{(i)} \\
&\text{subject to} \quad Y^T \cdot C = 0 \\
&\qquad\qquad\quad Y^T \cdot M_0 = 1 \qquad \text{(LPP1)} \\
&\qquad\qquad\quad Y \geq 0
\end{aligned}
$$

Let us consider, for instance, the Petri net model in Fig. 1. The application of (LPP1) gives:

$$
\Gamma^{(1)} \geq \max \left\{ \begin{array}{l} \frac{s_1 v_1^{(1)} + s_8 v_8^{(1)} + s_9 v_9^{(1)} + s_{10} v_{10}^{(1)}}{3}, \\[2mm] \frac{s_8 v_8^{(1)} + s_9 v_9^{(1)} + s_{10} v_{10}^{(1)}}{2}, \\[2mm] \frac{s_8 v_8^{(1)}}{1}, \frac{s_9 v_9^{(1)}}{1}, \frac{s_{10} v_{10}^{(1)}}{1} \end{array} \right\} \quad (1)
$$

The quantities under the max operator above represent, for this particular case, the mean interfiring time, normalized for transition t_1, computed at each of the isolated subnets generated by the minimal P-semiflows of the net, assuming that all the nodes are delay stations (infinite-server semantics). Therefore, the lower bound for the mean interfiring time of t_1 in the original net system given by (1) is computed looking at the "slowest subsystem" generated by the P-semiflows, considered in isolation (with delay nodes).

For instance, if the common memory request mean time of each processor is $s_1 = 1$ modelled by transition t_1 with infinite-server semantics, the three memories have access times with mean $s_8 = 1$, $s_9 = 2$, and $s_{10} = 5$, and they are requested with routing rates $r_2 = 6$, $r_3 = 3$, and $r_4 = 1$, respectively, the bound given by (1) is $\Gamma^{(1)} \geq 0.9$, i.e., the throughput of t_1 is less than or equal to 1.1111. If exponentially distributed service times are assumed for timed transitions, the exact throughput of transitions t_1 can be computed by solving the embedded CTMC, and is equal to 0.8471 (i.e., the bound is 31% above).

With respect to the lower bound on throughput, the following result can be stated:

Theorem 2.4 [10] *For any live and bounded system, an upper bound for the mean interfiring time* $\Gamma^{(i)}$ *of*

---

[1]This condition is assured for live and bounded net systems if a *locally fair* consumption of tokens at each place is assumed (for instance, FIFO discipline or random order for the selection of the token).

transition t_i is given by: $\Gamma^{(i)} \leq \sum_{j=1}^{m} D_j^{(i)}$. *If the system is free choice, then the bound can be improved:* $\Gamma^{(i)} \leq \sum_{j=1}^{m} \frac{D_j^{(i)}}{SE(t_j)}$.

In the general case, the bound corresponds to a complete sequentialization of all the transition services. In the free-choice case, internal self-concurrency at transitions is considered by dividing each average service demand by the corresponding structural enabling bound.

In the case of the net in Fig. 1, which is not free choice, the lower bound on throughput of t_1 given by the inverse of $\sum_{j=1}^{m} D_j^{(1)}$ is 0.3704. This bound is 56% below the exact value for exponential service times (this pessimistic bound is close to the exact value for special probability distributions with very large coefficient of variation; see [3]).

2.3 Some improvements of the bounds

In previous section, only P-semiflows and enabling bounds from the net structure and mean service times from stochastic timing have been used for the computation of bounds. The improvement of such bounds can be addressed in two ways: (1) by introducing a greater amount of structural information or/and (2) by taking into account the probability distribution function of service times.

In [7], some improvements derived just from the first approach (the structural one) were derived. For instance, other structural linear marking relations than those derived from P-semiflows (mainly those derived from *traps*) were used as additional constraints for the linear programming bound computation. The addition of *implicit places* was shown to be another interesting tool for the improvement of structure-based performance bounds.

With respect to the second approach, i.e., that based on the use of the distribution function of service times, the reader is referred to [8] for an example. There, an improvement of throughput lower bounds for NBUE service distributions (thus, in particular, for exponential) is presented by using a kit of *transformation rules* to produce local pessimistic temporal behaviour. In general, the rules lead to an approximation for throughput, and in particular cases to some improvements of the lower bound.

We have selected to present here an improvement that can be considered a mixture of structural and stochastic interpretation approaches. The throughput upper bound presented in the previous section (theorem 2.3) is based on the computation of the mean in-

terfiring time of transitions of subnets generated by P-semiflows considered in isolation. Since infinite-server semantics is considered for the isolated subnet, the real (unknown) residence time at places is lower bounded by the service time of transitions, but waiting time due to synchronizations is not considered at all.

In the paragraphs below, we briefly present (the interested reader is referred to [11] for a detailed exposition) how the bound for the residence time at places can be improved taking into account not only the service time but also a part of the queueing (in places) time due to synchronizations: the time in queue when $L(t)$ servers is the maximum available at each transition t. In other words, we consider also the isolated subnets but with finite-server semantics for transitions (with $L(t)$ servers).

Since we are looking for very efficient computation, we restrict ourselves to analyse some subnets (that we call *RP-components*) isomorphous to product-form queueing networks. RP-components are subnets generated by P-semiflows with the structure of a strongly connected *state machine* (state machines are ordinary Petri nets whose transitions have only one input and only one output place) with the additional constraint that for any pair of transitions in conflict in the subnet, these transitions must be in equal conflict in the whole net.

The idea is that, if $\Gamma^{(i)}$ is the exact mean interfiring time of t_i in the whole net system, $\Gamma_{Y_L}^{(i)}$ is the exact mean interfiring time of t_i in the isolated RP-component generated by a minimal P-semiflow Y, with $L(t)$–server semantics for each involved transition t, and $\Gamma_{Y_\infty}^{(i)}$ is the value of the objective function of (LPP1) corresponding to Y, then, $\Gamma^{(i)} \geq \Gamma_{Y_L}^{(i)} \geq \Gamma_{Y_\infty}^{(i)}$ (provided some additional technical points that are presented in detail in [11]). In other words, the knowledge of the liveness bound of transitions for a given net can allow to improve the throughput upper bound computed in theorem 2.3 by investing an additional computational effort. For the example in Fig. 1, the optimal value of (LPP1) was obtained for the minimal P-semiflow Y_1 that covers the subset of places $\{p_1, p_2, p_3, p_4, p_5, p_6, p_7, p_8\}$. If we consider the RP-component generated by Y_1 with single-server semantics for transitions t_8, t_9, and t_{10} (note that $L(t_8) = L(t_9) = L(t_{10}) = 1$), we obtain (by using, for instance, the *mean value analysis* algorithm) that the throughput of t_1 is less than or equal to 0.8648 (remember that the previous bound was 1.1111). Now, the bound is only 2% above the exact value (0.8471).

All the techniques presented in this section for the computation of bounds are based on the knowledge of

Figure 2: An MG, its decomposition in aggregated systems, and the basic skeleton.

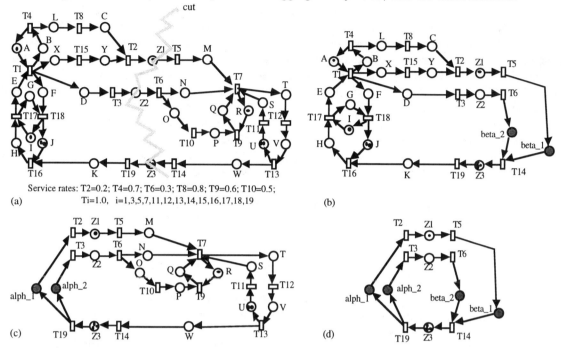

Service rates: T2=0.2; T4=0.7; T6=0.3; T8=0.8; T9=0.6; T10=0.5;
Ti=1.0, i=1,3,5,7,11,12,13,14,15,16,17,18,19

(a)

(b)

(c)

(d)

the vector of visit ratios, but the structural computation of that vector is only possible for some net subclasses [10]. A general, but less intuitive, statement for the computation of bounds (without the explicit use of visit ratios) can be found in [12].

3 Approximate analysis

In this section, we present a general iterative technique for approximate throughput computation. In order to simplify the presentation we restrict to the consideration of stochastic strongly connected *marked graphs* (MG's). MG's are ordinary Petri nets whose places have only one input and only one output transition. Similar results can be found in the literature for other net subclasses [19, 16]. Hierarchical aggregation approximation techniques have been developed in [17, 2]. The approach presented here has two basic foundations. First, a deep understanding of the qualitative behaviour of MG's leads to a general (structural) decomposition technique. Second, after the decomposition phase, an iterative response time approximation method is applied for the computation of the throughput.

3.1 Structural decomposition

The basic idea is the following: a strongly connected and live MG (see Fig. 2.a) is split into two *aggregable* subsystems $\mathcal{N}_{A_1}$ and $\mathcal{N}_{A_2}$ (those in Figs. 2.b and 2.c without the shaded places) by a *cut* Q defined through some places ($Q = \{Z1, Z2, Z3\}$, in Fig. 2.a). Input and output transitions to places of the cut are called *interface transitions* ($T2$, $T5$, $T3$, $T6$, $T19$, and $T14$ in Fig. 2.a). The goal is to add *something* (the shaded places in Figs. 2.b and 2.c) to each aggregable subsystem summarizing the behaviour of the other aggregable subsystem, leading to what we call the *aggregated subsystems*, $\mathcal{AS}_1$ and $\mathcal{AS}_2$ (Figs. 2.b and 2.c). More precisely, the objective is to obtain aggregated subsystems whose reachability sets are projections of the whole system reachability set on the corresponding preserved places.

The method to derive the aggregated subsystem from the aggregable one consists of two steps: (1) add a place to the aggregable subsystem from each interface transition t to each interface transition t' such that there exists a path from t to t' in the original net (see the shaded places in Fig. 2); and (2) compute the minimum initial marking of the places added in the previous step such that the reachability set of the aggregated subsystem is the projection of the whole system reachability set on the corresponding preserved places.

For the computation of the initial marking of the shaded places, let us consider the aggregable subsystem $\mathcal{N}_{A_i}$. We derive from this system a directed graph $G_{A_i} = (V, E)$ as follows. Each vertex corresponds to a transition of the net. There exists a directed arc between two vertices if and only if there exists a place in the net connecting the two transitions that represent the two vertices. The sense of the arc is the sense of the tokens' flow between the transitions through the place. Each arc has a non-negative cost equal to the initial marking of the place that represents. Moreover, we add an arc $t \to t$ for each vertex t with a cost equal to ∞.

If we apply the algorithm of R.W. Floyd to solve the *all-pairs shortest paths* problem [1] to the directed graph G_{A_i}, we obtain for each ordered pair of interface transitions (t, t') the smallest length of any path from t to t', denoted length(t, t') (if this value is equal to ∞, there is no path from t to t'). Observe, that length$(t, t') = \min\{\sum_{p_j \in \pi} M_0[p_j] \mid \pi$ is a path from t to $t'\}$. The computational complexity of this algorithm is $O(m^3)$, where m is the number of transitions of the considered net. We add a place p from t to t' if length$(t, t') \neq \infty$, with initial marking $m_0[p] = \text{length}(t, t')$.

Additionally, a *basic skeleton* system $\mathcal{BS}$ can be defined including only the cut, the interface transitions, and the shaded places (Fig. 2.d).

For the previously explained decomposition, the following result can be proven:

Theorem 3.1 [6] *Let $\langle \mathcal{N}, M_0 \rangle$ be a strongly connected and live MG, $Q \subseteq P$ a cut of $\mathcal{N}$, and $\mathcal{AS}_i$ be the aggregated subsystems. Then, the reachability set of $\mathcal{AS}_i$ is the projection of that of $\langle \mathcal{N}, M_0 \rangle$ on the preserved places.*

Very informally, the above theorem states that the structural decomposition technique leads to "exact qualitative aggregation": firing sequences and reachable markings on aggregated subsystems are the projections of the original one (the same can be stated as a corollary for the basic skeleton).

3.2 Iterative approximation algorithm

The technique for an approximate computation of the throughput that we comment here is, basically, a *response time approximation* method (other techniques as subrogate delays or Marie's method could also be used). The interface transitions of $\mathcal{N}_j$ in $\mathcal{AS}_i$ approximate the response time of all the subsystem

$\mathcal{N}_j$ ($i = 1, 2; j \neq i$). A direct (non-iterative) method to compute the constant service rates of such interface transitions in order to represent the aggregation of the subnet gives, in general, low accuracy. Therefore, we are forced to define a *fixed-point search iterative process*, with the possible drawback of the presence of convergence and efficiency problems. Even if we have not a convergence formal proof, experimentally the method converged for all considered cases, and typically in a maximum of three to five iterations (i.e., very efficiently).

In the iterative algorithm, the CTMC's underlying both aggregated subsystems are solved alternatively until throughput convergence is achieved. Each time that an aggregated subsystem is solved, only its throughput and the ratios among the service rates of some interface transitions are estimated (see the details in [6]). After that, a scale factor for these service rates is computed, by using the basic skeleton system (in such a way that the throughput of the basic skeleton and the throughput of the aggregated subsystem, computed before, are the same). A linear search of the scale factor must be implemented, but in a net system with very few states (the basic skeleton). In each iteration of this linear search, the basic skeleton may be solved by deriving the underlying CTMC.

Let us consider again the MG depicted in Fig. 2.a. The exact value of the throughput is equal to 0.138341 (if single-server semantics is assumed). The approximated value, obtained after five iteration steps, is 0.138343 (the error is 0.064333%). The following additional fact must be remarked: the underlying CTMC's of $\mathcal{AS}_1$ (Figs. 2.b), $\mathcal{AS}_2$ (Figs. 2.c), and the basic skeleton (Fig. 2.d) have 8288, 3440, and 231 states, respectively, while the original MG has 89358 states.

4 Exact analysis

Product-form solutions for the exact steady-state distribution of very restricted classes of stochastic Petri nets have been developed in similar terms to the classical results existing for queueing networks. In some cases, the conditions for the existence of a product-form solution can be checked at the structural level. However, in order to build that solution, a state space level computation must be done in many cases (see in [14] a comparison of several approaches).

An alternative approach, based on the rewriting of the infinitesimal generator of the embedded Markov chain from a Kronecker expression in terms of the infinitesimal generators of smaller components of the system, has been presented in [13]. Even if the solution is based on the recognition of net components that interact through transition synchronization, the method cannot be considered as a fully structural technique.

In this section, we present an efficient exact solution for a particular Petri net subclass mainly based on structural concepts. The presentation is deliberately more technical than before just to present a more detailed flash of concepts and their interleaving leading to new techniques. We consider stochastic Petri net systems with exponential service times constructed from cooperating sequential components (state machines) communicating with buffers (places). Some interesting qualitative results that can be derived from structure of these nets are presented in section 4.1. In particular, necessary and sufficient conditions for "potential ergodicity" (existence of a stochastic interpretation that can lead to ergodic systems) are studied. In section 4.2, necessary and sufficient ergodicity conditions and the steady-state performance measures are computed.

First, we recall the formal definition of the subclass we are going to deal with.

Definition 4.1 *A Petri net system* $\langle \mathcal{N}, M_0 \rangle = \langle \cup_{i=1}^q P_i \cup B, \cup_{i=1}^q T_i, Pre, Post, M_0 \rangle$ *is a deterministic system of sequential processes (deterministic system, DS for short) iff*

i) $P_i \cap P_j = \emptyset, T_i \cap T_j = \emptyset, P_i \cap B = \emptyset, i, j = 1, \ldots, q; i \neq j;$

ii) $\langle \mathcal{SM}_i, M_{0i} \rangle = \langle P_i, T_i, Pre_i, Post_i, M_{0i} \rangle, i = 1, \ldots, q,$ *are strongly connected and 1–bounded state machines, where* $Pre_i, Post_i$ *and* M_{0i} *are the restrictions of* $Pre, Post$ *and* M_0 *to* P_i *and* T_i; *and*

iii) *the set* B *of buffers is such that* $\forall b \in B$:

    a) $^\bullet b \neq \emptyset, b^\bullet \neq \emptyset$;

    b) $\exists i, j \in \{1, \ldots, q\}, i \neq j$ *such that* $^\bullet b \subset T_i$ *and* $b^\bullet \subset T_j$; *and*

    c) $\forall p \in \cup_{i=1}^q P_i : t, t' \in p^\bullet \Rightarrow Pre(b, t) = Pre(b, t').$

A totally open deterministic system of sequential processes (totally open system, TOS for short) is a DS without circuits containing buffers.

The first two items of the previous definition state that a DS is composed by a set of state machines ($\mathcal{SM}_i, i = 1, \ldots, q$) and a set of buffers ($B$). By item *iii.a*, buffers are neither source nor sink places. An input and output-private condition for buffers is expressed by *iii.b*. Due to requirement *iii.c*, the marking of buffers does not disturb the decisions taken by a state machine (this fact justifies the word "deterministic" in the name of the class).

4.1 Structural concepts

Some interesting qualitative results can be derived from the structure of these nets. In theorem 4.1, consistency (necessary condition for ergodicity) is shown to collapse with existence of home state for this subclass of nets. The rest of this section is devoted to the study of necessary and sufficient conditions for the "potential ergodicity": existence of a stochastic interpretation that can lead to ergodic systems.

The following theorem relates, for TOS's, a behavioural property (existence of home state) with a structural one (consistency).

Theorem 4.1 [9] *Let* $\langle \mathcal{N}, M_0 \rangle$ *be a TOS. Then* $\mathcal{N}$ *is consistent iff* M_0 *is a home state.*

Consistency is known to be a necessary condition for the marking ergodicity of a live stochastic Petri net system. Since there exist non consistent TOS's, it is convenient to check consistency (a polynomial time computation) of the TOS before computing ergodicity conditions. Taking into account the above remark, the following result with practical interest can be stated:

Theorem 4.2 [9] *There exist TOS's that are marking non ergodic for all timing interpretation. In particular, non-consistent systems are always marking non-ergodic.*

Unfortunately, it cannot be stated that for all consistent TOS, there exists an stochastic interpretation such that the resulting system is ergodic.

Let us now recall the concept of *global synchronic distance relation*. If two subsets of transitions are in global synchronic distance relation then it is not possible to fire an infinite number of times some transition of the first subset without firing any transition of the second subset, and vice versa. Even more, if two subsets of transitions are in global synchronic distance relation they behave like if they were included in a *regulation circuit* [18, 24]. This equivalence relation is used below for finding necessary and sufficient conditions for the existence of a stochastic interpretation that makes ergodic a TOS.

Definition 4.2 *Let* $\langle \mathcal{N}, M_0 \rangle$ *be a Petri net and* T_1, T_2 *subsets of transitions.* T_1, T_2 *are in global synchronic*

Figure 3: A TOS that admits stochastic timings making ergodic the system.

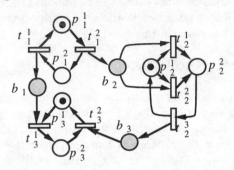

distance relation, $(T_1, T_2) \in SDR$, iff $\exists W_1, W_2 \in \mathbb{N}^m$ vectors which express the weights associated with the transitions of the subsets T_1 and T_2 (i.e., $\|W_1\| = T_1$ and $\|W_2\| = T_2$) and $\exists k \in \mathbb{N}$ such that

$$\sup_{\substack{\sigma \in L(\mathcal{N}, M) \\ M \in R(\mathcal{N}, M_0)}} |(W_1 - W_2)^T \cdot \vec{\sigma}| \leq k$$

For characterizing the possible existence of a timing interpretation making a given TOS ergodic, let us give local rules that will be composed step by step for a large system. The first one gives necessary and sufficient conditions for the existence of a stochastic timing interpretation that makes ergodic a system composed by two state machines.

Theorem 4.3 [9] *Let* $\langle \mathcal{N}, M_0 \rangle = \langle P_1 \cup P_2 \cup B, T_1 \cup T_2, Pre, Post, M_0 \rangle$ *be a TOS composed by two state machines and a set of buffers* B *such that* $\forall b \in B$: $^\bullet b \subseteq T_1, b^\bullet \subseteq T_2$. *Then, there exists a stochastic interpretation making marking ergodic the system if and only if: (i)* $\mathcal{N}$ *is consistent and (ii)* $\forall b_i, b_j \in B$: $(^\bullet b_i, ^\bullet b_j) \in SDR$ *and* $(b_i{}^\bullet, b_j{}^\bullet) \in SDR$.

In case of TOS's composed by two state machines, if (i) and (ii) of the above theorem hold then the marking of all the buffers can be always computed from the marking of one buffer and the marking of the state machines. With the object of computing ergodicity conditions for a larger system including $\mathcal{N}$ as a subsystem, if (i) and (ii) hold, from the performance point of view, we can suppose without loss of generality that the two state machines are communicating with at most one buffer.

Let us now give the "transitivity rule" for three state machines communicating with buffers like in Fig. 3. This rule completes the stating of necessary and sufficient conditions for the existence of a stochastic timing that makes ergodic a given TOS.

Theorem 4.4 [9] *Let* $\langle \mathcal{N}, M_0 \rangle = \langle \cup_{i=1}^3 P_i \cup \cup_{i=1}^3 \{b_i\}, \cup_{i=1}^3 T_i, Pre, Post, M_0 \rangle$ *be a TOS composed by three state machines and three buffers such that* $^\bullet b_1 \subseteq T_1, b_1{}^\bullet \subseteq T_3, ^\bullet b_2 \subseteq T_1, b_2{}^\bullet \subseteq T_2, ^\bullet b_3 \subseteq T_2,$ *and* $b_3{}^\bullet \subseteq T_3$. *Then, there exists a stochastic interpretation making ergodic the system if and only if: (i)* $\mathcal{N}$ *is consistent and (ii)* $^\bullet b_1, ^\bullet b_2) \in SDR, (b_2{}^\bullet, ^\bullet b_3) \in SDR,$ $(b_1{}^\bullet, b_3{}^\bullet) \in SDR$.

If (i) and (ii) of the above theorem hold, then the marking of b_3 can be always computed from the marking of b_1, b_2 and the marking of the state machines. With the object of computing conditions for a larger system including $\mathcal{N}$ as a subsystem, if (i) and (ii) hold, the state machine $\mathcal{SM}_2$ and the buffers b_2, b_3 can be substituted by a unique buffer.

Theorems 4.3 and 4.4 provide rules for an iterative reduction of buffers of a TOS. These rules preserve the possibility of existence of a timing that makes the system ergodic if the necessary and sufficient conditions (stated in the mentioned theorems) hold.

Therefore the existence of a stochastic timing that makes a TOS ergodic is characterized in terms of pure structural conditions: consistency and some synchronic distance relations.

4.2 Ergodicity characterization and steady-state solution

Let us now consider a different problem: given a TOS, once that the previous conditions have been checked, we want to know if ergodicity conditions hold for a given timing. We study these conditions and the steady-state throughput of the system under ergodicity assumption.

In [15], an ergodicity theorem is proved for a particular class of open synchronized queueing networks. Let us recall now the concept of *saturated net* and the adaptation of the above-mentioned theorem for TOS's.

Definition 4.3 *Let* $\langle \mathcal{N}, M_0 \rangle$ *be an and* b *one of its buffers. The net obtained from* $\langle \mathcal{N}, M_0 \rangle$ *by deleting the buffer* b *and its adjacent arcs is called the saturated system according to* b.

Note that the saturated system according to b behaves like $\langle \mathcal{N}, M_0 \rangle$ in the case in which the buffer b is always marked.

Theorem 4.5 [15] *Let* $\langle \mathcal{N}, M_0 \rangle$ *be a TOS, and* $\vec{\sigma}^*_{(b)}$ *be the limit vector of transition throughputs of the saturated net according to* b.

1. Let $B' \subseteq B$ be the subset of buffers the marking of which can vary independently. If $POST[b]\cdot\vec{\sigma}^*_{(b)} < PRE[b]\cdot\vec{\sigma}^*_{(b)}$, $\forall b \in B'$, then the associated Markov process is positive recurrent.

2. If there exists a buffer b such that $POST[b]\cdot\vec{\sigma}^*_{(b)} > PRE[b]\cdot\vec{\sigma}^*_{(b)}$, then the associated Markov process is transient.

Part 1 of theorem 4.5 means that for each buffer the input flow must be less than the service rate of the output state machine.

Let us illustrate the numerical computation of the ergodicity criterion with the net in Fig. 3. The left and right hand side expressions of theorem 4.5.1 for buffer b_2 can be computed considering the state machines $\mathcal{SM}_1$ and $\mathcal{SM}_2$ in isolation:

$$POST[b_2]\cdot\vec{\sigma}^*_{(b_2)}=\frac{\lambda^1_1\lambda^2_1}{\lambda^1_1+\lambda^2_1}; \quad PRE[b_2]\cdot\vec{\sigma}^*_{(b_2)}=\frac{(\lambda^1_2+\lambda^2_2)\lambda^3_2}{\lambda^1_2+\lambda^2_2+\lambda^3_2}$$

where λ^i_j is the rate of the exponentially distributed random variable associated with transition t^i_j. We assume that the conflict at place p^1_2 is solved in favour of transition t^1_2 with probability $\lambda^1_2/(\lambda^1_2+\lambda^2_2)$ and in favour of t^2_2 with probability $\lambda^2_2/(\lambda^1_2+\lambda^2_2)$.

The same computation for the buffer b_1 leads to the expressions:

$$POST[b_1]T\cdot\vec{\sigma}^*_{(b_1)}=\frac{\lambda^1_1\lambda^2_1}{\lambda^1_1+\lambda^2_1}; \quad PRE[b_1]T\cdot\vec{\sigma}^*_{(b_1)}=\frac{\lambda^1_3\lambda^2_3}{\lambda^1_3+\lambda^2_3}$$

The marking of buffer b_3 linearly depends on the marking of the other buffers, so it must not be considered. Then, the system is ergodic if and only if:

$$\frac{\lambda^1_1\lambda^2_1}{\lambda^1_1+\lambda^2_1}<\min\left\{\frac{(\lambda^1_2+\lambda^2_2)\lambda^3_2}{\lambda^1_2+\lambda^2_2+\lambda^3_2},\frac{\lambda^1_3\lambda^2_3}{\lambda^1_3+\lambda^2_3}\right\}$$

Let us suppose now that the system ergodicity conditions given in theorem 4.5 are satisfied. The following theorem gives a method for computing efficiently the steady-state behaviour of the connected machines of a TOS. The idea is as follows. A partial order relation can be introduced on the set of strongly connected components of the system (set of sequential processes) as follows: a sequential process $\mathcal{SM}_i$ is "greater" than other $\mathcal{SM}_j$ iff there exists a directed path from nodes of $\mathcal{SM}_i$ to nodes of $\mathcal{SM}_j$. Maximal elements of this partial order are sequential processes that have not any input buffer.

Theorem 4.6 [9] *Let $\langle\mathcal{N},M_0\rangle$ be a TOS. If its marking process is ergodic then:*

i) *If $\mathcal{SM}_i$ has not any input buffer then the limit average marking of each place and the limit throughput of transitions can be computed solving the following marking invariant and flow equations:*

$$\sum_{p\in P_i}\overline{M}(p)=1;$$
$$\sigma^*(t)=\lambda_t\overline{M}(p), \text{ if } Pre(p,t)=1,\forall t\in T_i$$
$$\sum_{t\in{}^\bullet p}\sigma^*(t)=\sum_{t\in p^\bullet}\sigma^*(t),\forall p\in P_i$$

where $\sigma^*(t)$ is the limit throughput of transition t, λ_t is the rate of the exponentially distributed random variable associated with t, and $\overline{M}(p)$ is the limit average marking of place p.

ii) *If $\mathcal{SM}_j$ has input buffers that are output buffers of the state machines $\mathcal{SM}_{i_1},\dots,\mathcal{SM}_{i_r}$ then the limit average marking of each place and the limit throughput of transitions can be computed solving the equations:*

$$\sum_{p\in P_j}\overline{M}(p)=1;$$
$$\sigma^*(t)=\lambda_t\overline{M}(p), \text{ if } Pre(p,t)=1,\forall t\in T_j:{}^\bullet t\cap B=\emptyset;$$
$$\sum_{t\in p^\bullet}\sigma^*(t)=\sum_{t'\in{}^\bullet p}\sigma^*(t'),\forall b\in B:b^\bullet\subset T_j\wedge{}^\bullet b\subset T_{i_1}\cup\dots\cup T_{i_r};$$
$$\sum_{t\in{}^\bullet p}\sigma^*(t)=\sum_{t\in p^\bullet}\sigma^*(t),\forall p\in P_j$$

We remark that the application of the method described in the above theorem has polynomial time complexity.

As an example, let us consider once more the net in Fig. 3. In this case, there exists one state machine without input buffers: $\mathcal{SM}_1$. Marking invariant and flow equations for this machine have the form:

$$\overline{M}(p^1_1)+\overline{M}(p^2_1)=1;$$
$$\sigma^*(t^1_1)=\lambda^1_1\overline{M}(p^2_1); \ \sigma^*(t^2_1)=\lambda^2_1\overline{M}(p^1_1); \ \sigma^*(t^1_1)=\sigma^*(t^2_1)$$

This system can be solved, obtaining:

$$\overline{M}(p^1_1)=\frac{\lambda^1_1}{\lambda^1_1+\lambda^2_1}; \ \overline{M}(p^2_1)=\frac{\lambda^2_1}{\lambda^1_1+\lambda^2_1};$$
$$\sigma^*(t^1_1)=\sigma^*(t^2_1)=\frac{\lambda^1_1\lambda^2_1}{\lambda^1_1+\lambda^2_1}$$

Now, for computing the steady-state measures of the other state machines under the assumption of ergodicity, it is necessary to take into account that

$$\sigma^*(t^2_1)=\sigma^*(t^1_2)+\sigma^*(t^2_2) \quad \text{and} \quad \sigma^*(t^1_3)=\sigma^*(t^1_1)$$

that is, the input flow of tokens to each buffer in steady-state must be equal to the output flow, and:

$$\overline{M}(p^1_2)=1-\overline{M}(p^2_2); \quad \overline{M}(p^2_2)=\frac{\lambda^1_1\lambda^2_1}{(\lambda^1_1+\lambda^2_1)\lambda^3_2};$$
$$\sigma^*(t^1_2)=\frac{\lambda^1_1\lambda^2_1\lambda^1_2}{(\lambda^1_1+\lambda^2_1)(\lambda^1_2+\lambda^2_2)}; \ \sigma^*(t^2_2)=\frac{\lambda^1_1\lambda^2_1\lambda^2_2}{(\lambda^1_1+\lambda^2_1)(\lambda^1_2+\lambda^2_2)};$$
$$\sigma^*(t^3_2)=\sigma^*(t^1_3)=\sigma^*(t^2_3)=\frac{\lambda^1_1\lambda^2_1}{\lambda^1_1+\lambda^2_1}$$

Thus, the throughput of transitions and the average marking of places can be computed in polynomial time on the net size.

References

[1] A. V. Aho, J. E. Hopcroft, and J. D. Ullman. *Data Structures and Algorithms*. Addison-Wesley, 1983.

[2] P. Buchholz. Aggregation and reduction techniques for hierarchical GCSPNs. In *Proceedings of the 5th International Workshop on Petri Nets and Performance Models*, pages 216–225, Toulouse, France, October 1993. IEEE-Computer Society Press.

[3] J. Campos, G. Chiola, J. M. Colom, and M. Silva. Properties and performance bounds for timed marked graphs. *IEEE Transactions on Circuits and Systems—I: Fundamental Theory and Applications*, 39(5):386–401, May 1992.

[4] J. Campos, G. Chiola, and M. Silva. Ergodicity and throughput bounds of Petri nets with unique consistent firing count vector. *IEEE Transactions on Software Engineering*, 17(2):117–125, February 1991.

[5] J. Campos, G. Chiola, and M. Silva. Properties and performance bounds for closed free choice synchronized monoclass queueing networks. *IEEE Transactions on Automatic Control*, 36(12):1368–1382, December 1991.

[6] J. Campos, J. M. Colom, H. Jungnitz, and M. Silva. Approximate throughput computation of stochastic marked graphs. *IEEE Transactions on Software Engineering*, 20(7):526–535, July 1994.

[7] J. Campos, J. M. Colom, and M. Silva. Improving throughput upper bounds for net based models of manufacturing systems. In J. C. Gentina and S. G. Tzafestas, editors, *Robotics and Flexible Manufacturing Systems*, pages 281–294. Elsevier Science Publishers B.V. (North-Holland), Amsterdam, The Netherlands, 1992.

[8] J. Campos, B. Sánchez, and M. Silva. Throughput lower bounds for Markovian Petri nets: Transformation techniques. In *Proceedings of the 4rd International Workshop on Petri Nets and Performance Models*, pages 322–331, Melbourne, Australia, December 1991. IEEE-Computer Society Press.

[9] J. Campos and M. Silva. Steady-state performance evaluation of totally open systems of Markovian sequential processes. In M. Cosnard and C. Girault, editors, *Decentralized Systems*, pages 427–438. Elsevier Science Publishers B.V. (North-Holland), Amsterdam, The Netherlands, 1990.

[10] J. Campos and M. Silva. Structural techniques and performance bounds of stochastic Petri net models. In G. Rozenberg, editor, *Advances in Petri Nets 1992*, volume 609 of *Lecture Notes in Computer Science*, pages 352–391. Springer-Verlag, Berlin, 1992.

[11] J. Campos and M. Silva. Embedded product-form queueing networks and the improvement of performance bounds for Petri net systems. *Performance Evaluation*, 18(1):3–19, July 1993.

[12] G. Chiola, C. Anglano, J. Campos, J. M. Colom, and M. Silva. Operational analysis of timed Petri nets and application to the computation of performance bounds. In *Proceedings of the 5th International Workshop on Petri Nets and Performance Models*, pages 128–137, Toulouse, France, October 1993. IEEE-Computer Society Press.

[13] S. Donatelli. Superposed generalized stochastic Petri nets: Definition and efficient solution. In R. Valette, editor, *Application and Theory of Petri Nets 1994*, volume 815 of *LNCS*. Springer-Verlag, Berlin, 1994.

[14] S. Donatelli and M. Sereno. On the product form solution for stochastic Petri nets. In K. Jensen, editor, *Application and Theory of Petri Nets 1992*, volume 616 of *LNCS*, pages 154–172. Springer-Verlag, Berlin, 1992.

[15] G. Florin and S. Natkin. Necessary and sufficient ergodicity condition for open synchronized queueing networks. *IEEE Transactions on Software Engineering*, 15(4):367–380, April 1989.

[16] H. Jungnitz, A. Desrochers, and M. Silva. Approximation techniques for stochastic macroplace/macrotransition nets. In *Proceedings of the QMIPS Workshop on Stochastic Petri Nets*, pages 118–146, Sophia Antipolis, France, November 1992. INRIA. To appear in *Flexible Manufacturing Systems*.

[17] H. Jungnitz, B. Sánchez, and M. Silva. Approximate throughput computation of stochastic marked graphs. *Journal of Parallel and Distributed Computing*, 15:282–295, 1992.

[18] W. E. Kluge and K. Lautenbach. The orderly resolution of memory access conflicts among competing channel processes. *IEEE Transactions on Computers*, 31:194–207, March 1982.

[19] Y. Li and C. M. Woodside. Performance Petri net analysis of communications protocol software by delay-equivalent aggregation. In *Proceedings of the 4th International Workshop on Petri Nets and Performance Models*, pages 64–73, Melbourne, Australia, December 1991. IEEE-Computer Society Press.

[20] T. Murata. Petri nets: Properties, analysis, and applications. *Proceedings of the IEEE*, 77(4):541–580, April 1989.

[21] L. Recalde, E. Teruel, and M. Silva. On well-formedness analysis: The case of DSSP. Research Report GISI-RR-95-1, DIEI. Univ. Zaragoza, January 1995. Submitted for publication.

[22] M. Silva. Interleaving functional and performance structural analysis of net models. In M. Ajmone Marsan, editor, *Application and Theory of Petri Nets 1993*, volume 691 of *LNCS*, pages 17–23. Springer-Verlag, Berlin, 1993.

[23] M. Silva. Introducing Petri nets. In *Practice of Petri Nets in Manufacturing*, chapter 1. Chapman & Hall, 1993.

[24] M. Silva and J. M. Colom. On the computation of structural synchronic invariants in P/T nets. In G. Rozenberg, editor, *Advances in Petri Nets 1988*, volume 340 of *LNCS*, pages 386–417. Springer-Verlag, Berlin, 1988.

[25] M. Silva and E. Teruel. Analysis of autonomous Petri nets with bulk services and arrivals. In G. Cohen and J.P. Quadrat, editors, *Analysis and Optimization of Systems: Discrete Event Systems*, volume 199 of *Lecture Notes in Control and Information Sciences*, pages 131–143. Springer-Verlag, London, 1994.

[26] E. Teruel and M. Silva. Structure theory of Equal Conflict systems. Research Report GISI-RR-93-22, DIEI. Univ. Zaragoza, 1993. Revised in March 1994. To appear in *Theoretical Computer Science*.

[27] E. Teruel and M. Silva. Well-formedness of Equal Conflict systems. In R. Valette, editor, *Application and Theory of Petri Nets 1994*, volume 815 of *LNCS*, pages 491–510. Springer-Verlag, Berlin, 1994.

Session 3:
Modelling Theory

Session Chair: Isi Mitrani

Matrix-Geometric Solution of Infinite Stochastic Petri Nets

Boudewijn R. Haverkort
University of Twente, Department of Computer Science
P.O. Box 217, 7500 AE Enschede, the Netherlands
E-mail: b.r.h.m.haverkort@cs.utwente.nl

Abstract

In this paper we characterize a class of stochastic Petri nets that can be solved using matrix geometric techniques. Advantages of such an approach are that very efficient mathematical technique become available for practical usage, as well as that the problem of large state spaces can be circumvented.

We first characterize the class of stochastic Petri nets of interest by formally defining a number of constraints that have to be fulfilled. We then discuss the matrix geometric solution technique that can be employed and present some boundary conditions on tool support. We illustrate the practical usage of the class of stochastic Petri nets with two examples: a queueing system with delayed service and a model of connection management in ATM networks.

1 Introduction

Stochastic Petri nets (SPNs) have been used extensively for the performance evaluation of computer and communication systems as well as of flexible manufacturing systems. Many variants have been proposed: stochastic Petri nets (SPNs) [26], generalized stochastic Petri nets [1], stochastic activity networks (SANs) [31], stochastic reward nets (SRNs) [8, 9], deterministic and stochastic Petri nets (DSPNs) [2, 25] and Markov-regenerative SPNs [7]. An overview of the mathematical differences between these many different variants has recently been presented in [11]. These many different variants have been proposed for various reasons: (i) to increase the modelling flexibility by introducing convenient new constructs such as variable arc multiplicities, gates and enabling functions; (ii) to increase the modelling power by allowing more general timing characterizations as compared to the standard SPNs; or (iii) to introduce more structured models so as to make the solution process of the underlying stochastic process an easier task.

A general problem in employing SPNs is the rapid growth of the state space (the largeness problem). Solutions that have been proposed are often based on (approximate) truncation techniques [20] or lumping [4, 5, 6, 31], thereby still performing the solution at the state space level, or they are based on product-form results which allow for an efficient convolution or mean-value analysis style of solution [12, 14]. In all these cases, the "trick" lies in trying to circumvent the generation of the overall state space before solution, or to decrease the size of the state space. In that respect, also simulation avoids the generation of the overall state space.

Besides the above, we should also consider the following. In queueing theory, the steady-state analysis of infinitely large systems is often simpler than analyzing the corresponding finite systems. These considerations have lead to the following approach to tackle the problem of very large but finite state spaces. Instead of generating and solving a very large but finite SPN model, we solve infinitely large CTMCs derived from an SPN model. In doing so, we explicitly avoid generating the overall state space; instead we exploit the repetitive structure of the infinite CTMC. Once we have solved the infinitely large model, we can use the results also for finite versions of the model, albeit not always exactly. Indeed, also in many application areas, such as the analysis of ATM multiplexers, infinitely large models, i.e., infinite buffer models, are used to compute bounds or approximations on finite models [33].

For the infinitely sized models to be easy solvable, we require them to exhibit a regular structure. This limits their applicability, however, it is surprising to see how many models do fulfill these requirements. A class of infinitely large Markovian models which exhibits both an efficient solution, and occurs very often in practice, are the so-called quasi birth-death (QBD) models, as described in [27, 28]. A state-wise specification of such models, however, is cumbersome for many practical applications. We therefore define a class of infinite-state SPNs which has an underlying Markov chain of the QBD type. We discuss the mapping of such SPNs to a compact description of the QBD process and discuss an efficient matrix geometric solution technique.

Important other work in this direction has been re-

72

ported by Florin and Natkin. In [16] they present so-called "one-place unbounded SPNs" and prove the existance of an underlying QBD structure. In [15] they elaborate on ergodicity conditions of such SPNs. The SPNs addressed are restricted in the sense that transitions have constant firing rates, arc multiplicities are always 1 (monovaluated nets), and unbounded places may not be the origin of inhibitor arcs. Then, in [17], they discuss the ergodicity of "multiple-place unbounded SPNs". Also such SPNs may have un underlying QBD, however, when the so-called "marking-space dimension" is larger than 1, the block matrices $\mathbf{A}_0$ through $\mathbf{A}_2$ are infinitely large themselves (see Section 3). Finally, in [18], they discuss matrix product-from solution for closed, i.e., bounded, stochastic Petri nets. Concluding, our proposed class of SPNs is larger than the class proposed by Florin and Natkin (see the rest of this paper), however, this comes at the cost of more difficulty in deriving the underlying QBD structure.

Recent work by Berson and Muntz is also of interest to our work [3]. They present an approach to detect block-M|G|1 and block-G|M|1 structures directly from models specified using a state-machine specification language. For 2-dimensional models they are able to decide on the (in)finiteness and on the block structure of the models, directly from the specification. For larger-dimensional models they can only do so by further restricting the specification language.

Two performance evaluation tools have been reported in the literature that employ matrix geometric techniques. With the tool MAGIC [32], CTMCs with a QBD structure can be defined at the state level and solved efficiently. With the tool Xmgm, higher-level, user-oriented, constructs are provided that allow for a more user-friendly model specification of QBD models [21]. In this paper we propose to go a step further, namely to use SPNs for the specification of a class of models that allows for a matrix geometric solution.

Regarding the applicability of our approach, we see good opportunities in the field of broadband communication systems, such as ATM systems, where relatively simple multiplexers or switches are used in combination with intricate arrival processes. Also in the field of queues with breakdowns, our approach seem to be well applicable. In section 5 we will see examples in these directions.

This paper is further organized as follows. The special class of SPNs is defined in Section 2. The underlying QBD process is described in Section 3, together with an efficient solution technique. A proposal for a tool supporting this class of SPNs is outlined in Section 4. Two applications are presented in Section 5. Section 6 concludes the paper.

2 Infinite stochastic Petri nets

We discuss notation and terminology in Section 2.1. The restricting requirements are given in Section 2.2. They are discussed in Section 2.3.

2.1 Preliminaries

We consider a class of SPNs similar to the class of SRNs as defined by Ciardo *et al.* [8, 9].

Without loss of generality we assume that the SPN under study, denoted *SPN*, has a set $P = \{p_0, p_1, \cdots, p_n\}$ of places of which only p_0 may contain an infinitely large number of tokens. A distribution of tokens over the places is called a marking and denoted $\underline{\mu} = (m_0, \underline{m}) = (m_0, m_1, \cdots, m_n)$. The set of all possible markings is denote $\mathcal{S} = I\!\!N \times \mathcal{M}$, i.e., $m_0 \in I\!\!N$ and $\underline{m} \in \mathcal{M}$. Clearly, $|I\!\!N| = \infty$ and $|\mathcal{M}| < \infty$. The set of transitions is denoted T.

We now define *level* $\mathcal{S}(k)$ to be the set of markings such that place p_0 contains k tokens, i.e., $\mathcal{S}(k) = \{\underline{\mu} = (m_0, \underline{m}) \in \mathcal{S} | m_0 = k\}$. The levels $\mathcal{S}(k)$, $k \in I\!\!N$ constitute a partition of the overall state space: $\mathcal{S} = \bigcup_{k=0}^{\infty} \mathcal{S}(k)$ and $\mathcal{S}(k) \cap \mathcal{S}(l) = \emptyset, k \neq l$. For ease in notation, we also introduce $\mathcal{S}'(k) = \{\underline{m} | (k, \underline{m}) \in \mathcal{S}(k)\}$.

We furthermore define the following two *leads to* relations. We denote $\underline{\mu} \xrightarrow{t} \underline{\mu}'$ if transition t is enabled in $\underline{\mu}$ and, upon firing, leads to marking $\underline{\mu}'$. The firing rate of t is not important. We denote $\underline{\mu} \xrightarrow{t,\lambda} \underline{\mu}'$ if transition $t \in T$ is enabled in $\underline{\mu}$ and, upon firing, with rate λ, leads to marking $\underline{\mu}'$.

2.2 Requirements: formal definition

We now define a number of requirements on the SPN structure and transition firing behaviour. It should be noted that these requirements are sufficient, rather than necessary, for the SPNs to have an underlying QBD-structure.

Requirement 1. Given *SPN*, there exists a $\kappa \in I\!\!N$ such that for all $k, l \geq \kappa$: $\mathcal{S}'(k) = \mathcal{S}'(l)$. We denote $L = |\mathcal{S}'(\kappa)|$.

Requirement 2. Given *SPN* and κ as defined above, the following requirements should hold for the so-called *repeating portion* of the state space:

1. intra-level equivalence:
   $\forall k, l \geq \kappa, t \in T, \lambda \in I\!\!R^+$: if $(k, \underline{m}) \xrightarrow{t,\lambda} (k, \underline{m}')$ then $(l, \underline{m}) \xrightarrow{t,\lambda} (l, \underline{m}')$;

2. inter-level one-step increases only:
   $\forall k \geq \kappa, \exists t \in T: (k, \underline{m}) \xrightarrow{t} (k+1, \underline{m}')$;

$\forall k \geq \kappa,\ \exists t \in T,\ \lambda \in I\!R^+$: if $(k,\underline{m}) \xrightarrow{t,\lambda} (k+1,\underline{m}')$ then $(k+1,\underline{m}) \xrightarrow{t,\lambda} (k+2,\underline{m}')$;

$\forall k \geq \kappa,\ \forall i \in I\!N, i \geq 2,\ \not\exists t \in T$: $(k,\underline{m}) \xrightarrow{t} (k+i,\underline{m}')$;

3. inter-level one-step decreases only:

$\forall k > \kappa,\ \exists t \in T$: $(k+1,\underline{m}) \xrightarrow{t} (k,\underline{m}')$;

$\forall k > \kappa,\ \exists t \in T,\ \lambda \in I\!R^+$: if $(k+2,\underline{m}) \xrightarrow{t,\lambda} (k+1,\underline{m}')$ then $(k+1,\underline{m}) \xrightarrow{t,\lambda} (k,\underline{m}')$;

$\forall k > \kappa,\ \forall i \in I\!N, i \geq 2,\ \not\exists t \in T$: $(k+i,\underline{m}) \xrightarrow{t} (k,\underline{m}')$;

Requirement 3. Given *SPN* and κ as defined above, for the so-called *boundary portion* of the state space the following requirements should hold:

1. no boundary jumping:

$\forall k < \kappa - 1, \forall l > \kappa,\ \not\exists t_1 \in T$: $(k,\underline{m}) \xrightarrow{t_1} (l,\underline{m}')$;

$\forall k < \kappa - 1, \forall l > \kappa,\ \not\exists t_2 \in T$: $(l,\underline{m}) \xrightarrow{t_2} (k,\underline{m}')$;

2. only boundary crossing:

$\exists t_1, t_2 \in T$: $(\kappa-1,\underline{m}_1) \xrightarrow{t_1} (\kappa,\underline{m}'_1)$, $(\kappa,\underline{m}_2) \xrightarrow{t_2} (\kappa-1,\underline{m}'_2)$;

2.3 Requirements: discussion

Although the requirements to be posed on the SPN models are exact in themselves, it is good to discuss them in a more informal way.

Requirement 1 states that, starting from a certain level κ onwards, all levels are the same as far as the non-infinite places are concerned; they only differ in the number of tokens in place p_0. It is for this reason that the levels $k \geq \kappa$ are often called the repeating portion (levels) of the state space. The levels $k < \kappa$ are denoted the boundary portion (levels) of the state space. In Figure 1 we depict the overall state space and its partitioning in levels. We have tried to visualize the fact that starting from level κ onwards, the levels are similar to each other. Levels 0 through $\kappa - 1$ can be totally different from each other. In between states from levels 0 through $\kappa - 1$ all kinds of transitions may occur. That is why we can also see these boundary levels as one aggregated boundary level (Requirement 1).

Transitions can occur within a level, and between levels. Since the repeating levels are always the same, apart from the level number itself, all internal transitions in one level, must have similar equivalents in other repeating levels. There are no transitions possible between non-neighbouring levels. There have to exist up-

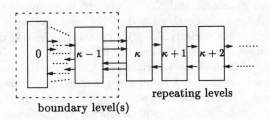

Figure 1: State space partitioning in levels

and down-going transitions between neighbouring levels. Also, for the repeating levels, their interaction with neighbouring levels is always the same (Requirement 2).

The transitions between the boundary levels and the repeating levels only take place in levels $\kappa - 1$ and κ, however, they may have any form (Requirement 3).

Regarding the levels as "super states" one easily sees the similarity with the well-known state spaces of birth-death queueing models. It is this similarity that has named a stochastic process on such a "levelized" state space a quasi birth-death model.

The stated requirements are sufficient, however, not always necessary. One might imagine SPNs which have a slightly different structure that still allow for a matrix geometric solution.

3 Matrix geometric solution

We start with a state space partitioning in Section 3.1. Then, in Section 3.2, we derive a matrix geometric solution for the steady-state probabilities, and in Section 3.3 we discuss the algorithmic aspects. The derivation of reward-based measures is discussed in Section 3.4. Finally, we discuss how results for infinite models can be used to derive (approximate) results for finite models in Section 3.5.

3.1 State space partitioning

Referring to Figure 1, it is easy to see that the generator matrix $\mathbf{Q}$ of the QBD has the following form:

$$\begin{pmatrix} \mathbf{B}_{0,0} & \cdots & \mathbf{B}_{0,\kappa-1} & 0 & 0 & \cdots \\ \mathbf{B}_{1,0} & \cdots & \mathbf{B}_{1,\kappa-1} & 0 & 0 & \cdots \\ \vdots & \vdots & \vdots & \vdots & \vdots & \vdots \\ \mathbf{B}_{\kappa-1,0} & \cdots & \mathbf{B}_{\kappa-1,\kappa-1} & \mathbf{B}_{\kappa-1,\kappa} & 0 & \cdots \\ 0 & \cdots & \mathbf{B}_{\kappa,\kappa-1} & \mathbf{B}_{\kappa,\kappa} & \mathbf{B}_{\kappa,\kappa+1} & 0 \\ 0 & \cdots & 0 & \mathbf{B}_{\kappa+1,\kappa} & \mathbf{B}_{\kappa+1,\kappa+1} & \mathbf{B}_{\kappa+1,\kappa+2} \\ & & 0 & \cdots & 0 & 0 & \mathbf{B}_{\kappa+2,\kappa+1} \\ \vdots & \vdots & \vdots & \vdots & \vdots & \ddots \end{pmatrix}$$

Now, by the requirements posed on the intra- and inter-level transitions, we have

$$\begin{cases} \mathbf{A}_0 = \mathbf{B}_{k,k+1}, & k = \kappa, \kappa+1\cdots, \\ \mathbf{A}_1 = \mathbf{B}_{k,k}, & k = \kappa+1, \kappa+2\cdots, \\ \mathbf{A}_2 = \mathbf{B}_{k,k-1}, & k = \kappa+1, \kappa+2\cdots. \end{cases}$$

Using this notation, we may write $\mathbf{Q}$ as follows:

$$\mathbf{Q} = \begin{pmatrix} \mathbf{B}_{0,0} & \cdots & \mathbf{B}_{0,\kappa-1} & 0 & \cdots & \cdots \\ \vdots & \cdots & \vdots & 0 & \cdots & \cdots \\ \mathbf{B}_{\kappa-1,0} & \cdots & \mathbf{B}_{\kappa-1,\kappa-1} & \mathbf{B}_{\kappa-1,\kappa} & 0 & \cdots \\ 0 & 0 & \mathbf{B}_{\kappa,\kappa-1} & \mathbf{B}_{\kappa,\kappa} & \mathbf{A}_0 & \cdots \\ 0 & 0 & 0 & \mathbf{A}_2 & \mathbf{A}_1 & \cdots \\ 0 & 0 & 0 & 0 & \mathbf{A}_2 & \cdots \\ \vdots & \vdots & \vdots & \vdots & \vdots & \ddots \end{pmatrix}.$$

3.2 Steady-state probabilities

When the CTMC would have been finite, we would have calculated the steady-state probability row vector $\underline{\pi}$ by numerically solving the global balance equations (GBEs):

$$\underline{\pi}\mathbf{Q} = \underline{0}, \text{ and } \underline{\pi}\underline{1}^{\mathrm{T}} = 1, \qquad (1)$$

where the right part is a normalisation, i.e., $\underline{1}^{\mathrm{T}} = (1, \cdots, 1)^{\mathrm{T}}$. In the infinite case, we start from the same equations. First, we partition $\underline{\pi}$ according the states belonging to the various levels, i.e., $\underline{\pi} = (\underline{z}_0, \underline{z}_1, \cdots, \underline{z}_{\kappa-1}, \underline{z}_\kappa, \underline{z}_{\kappa+1}, \cdots)$. Substituting this in (1), we obtain

$$\begin{array}{lll} (a): i = 0, \cdots, \kappa-2: & \sum_{j=0}^{\kappa-1} \underline{z}_j \mathbf{B}_{j,i} = \underline{0}, \\ (b): i = \kappa-1: & \sum_{j=0}^{\kappa} \underline{z}_j \mathbf{B}_{j,i} = \underline{0}, \\ (c): i = \kappa: & \sum_{j=\kappa-1}^{\kappa+1} \underline{z}_j \mathbf{B}_{j,i} = \underline{0}, & (2) \\ (d): i = \kappa+1, \cdots: & \sum_{j=0}^{2} \underline{z}_{i+j-1} \mathbf{A}_j = \underline{0}, \\ (e): \text{normalisation}: & \sum_{i=0}^{\infty} \underline{z}_i \cdot \underline{1}^{\mathrm{T}} = 1. \end{array}$$

We now try to exploit the regular structure in the state space in the solution process. In particular, looking at (2.d), it seems that for the state probabilities $\underline{z}_i$, $i = \kappa, \kappa+1, \cdots$, only the neighbouring levels are of importance. We know this situation from the birth-death process for the M|M|1 queue. For that case, it is well-known that $\pi_{i+1} = \rho\pi_i$, with π_i the probability of having i customers in the system and $\rho = \lambda/\mu$ the traffic intensity. In a similar way, we can *assume* that

$$\underline{z}_{\kappa+1} = \underline{z}_\kappa \mathbf{R}, \quad \underline{z}_{\kappa+2} = \underline{z}_{\kappa+1}\mathbf{R} = \underline{z}_\kappa \mathbf{R}^2, \cdots, \qquad (3)$$

or, equivalently,

$$\underline{z}_{\kappa+i} = \underline{z}_\kappa \mathbf{R}^i, i \in \mathbb{N}, \qquad (4)$$

where $\mathbf{R}$ is an $L \times L$ matrix relating the steady-state probability vector at level $\kappa+i$ to the steady-state probability vector at level $\kappa+i-1$ $(i = 1, 2, \cdots)$. To validate

the above assumption, we have to substitute it in Equation 2(d). For $i \in \mathbb{N}$, we find

$$\begin{aligned} \underline{z}_{\kappa+i}\mathbf{A}_0 + \underline{z}_{\kappa+i+1}\mathbf{A}_1 + \underline{z}_{\kappa+i+2}\mathbf{A}_2 &= \mathbf{0} \Leftrightarrow \\ \underline{z}_\kappa \mathbf{R}^i\mathbf{A}_0 + \underline{z}_\kappa \mathbf{R}^{i+1}\mathbf{A}_1 + \underline{z}_\kappa \mathbf{R}^{i+2}\mathbf{A}_2) &= \mathbf{0} \Leftrightarrow \\ \underline{z}_\kappa \mathbf{R}^i(\mathbf{A}_0 + \mathbf{R}\mathbf{A}_1 + \mathbf{R}^2\mathbf{A}_2) &= \mathbf{0}. \quad (5) \end{aligned}$$

For these three multiplicative terms to yield zero, at least one of them must equal zero. If $\underline{z}_\kappa$ would be zero, all higher level probabilities would be zero as well. This can not be the case. A similar reasoning is valid for $\mathbf{R}$ so that we have to conclude that assumption (3) is valid, if $\mathbf{R}$ satisfies the matrix polynomial

$$\mathbf{A}_0 + \mathbf{R}\mathbf{A}_1 + \mathbf{R}^2\mathbf{A}_2 = \mathbf{0}. \qquad (6)$$

In case $i = \kappa$, (2.c) can be rewritten to incorporate assumption (3), because $\underline{z}_{\kappa+1}$ can be rewritten in terms of $\underline{z}_\kappa$ and $\mathbf{B}_{\kappa+1,\kappa} = \mathbf{A}_2$:

$$\sum_{j=\kappa-1}^{\kappa+1} \underline{z}_j \mathbf{B}_{j,\kappa} = \underline{z}_{\kappa-1}\mathbf{B}_{\kappa-1,\kappa} + \underline{z}_\kappa(\mathbf{B}_{\kappa,\kappa} + \mathbf{R}\mathbf{A}_2) = \underline{0}. \quad (7)$$

With this substitution, (2.a–c) comprises a system of $\kappa+1$ linear vector equations with as many unknown vectors. However, as these vectors are still dependent, the normalisation (2.e) has to be integrated in it, to yield a unique solution. This normalisation can be rewritten as follows:

$$\begin{aligned} \sum_{i=0}^{\infty} \underline{z}_i \underline{1}^{\mathrm{T}} &= \sum_{i=0}^{\kappa-1} \underline{z}_i \underline{1}^{\mathrm{T}} + \sum_{i=\kappa}^{\infty} (\underline{z}_\kappa \mathbf{R}^i)\underline{1}^{\mathrm{T}} \\ &= \sum_{i=0}^{\kappa-1} \underline{z}_i \underline{1}^{\mathrm{T}} + \underline{z}_\kappa \mathbf{R}^\kappa(\mathbf{I} - \mathbf{R})^{-1}\underline{1}^{\mathrm{T}} = 1. \quad (8) \end{aligned}$$

3.3 Algorithm

To summarize, the following steps should be undertaken in the solution process:

S0. From the *SPN*, derive κ, $\mathbf{A}_i$ $(i = 0, 1, 2)$ and $\mathbf{B}_{ij}$ $(i, j = 0, \cdots, \kappa)$.

S1. Compute $\mathbf{R}$ from the matrix polynomial (6);

S2. Solve the linear system (2.a–c), using (7) and (8);

S3. Compute $\underline{z}_{\kappa+i}$ as $\underline{z}_\kappa \mathbf{R}^i$.

Step **S0** typically requires software tool support, which is dealt with separately in Section 4.

Step **S1** is normally done via an iterative approach. Starting with $\mathbf{R}(0) = -\mathbf{A}_0\mathbf{A}_1^{-1}$, we obtain successive approximations of $\mathbf{R}$ as follows:

$$\mathbf{R}(k+1) = -(\mathbf{A}_0 + \mathbf{R}^2(k)\mathbf{A}_2)\mathbf{A}_1^{-1}. \qquad (9)$$

The iteration is stopped whenever $\|\mathbf{R}(k) - \mathbf{R}(k+1)\| < \epsilon$. It can be shown that the sequence $\{\mathbf{R}(k), k = 0, 1, \cdots\}$ is entry-wise nondecreasing, and that it converges monotonically to the matrix $\mathbf{R}$ [27]. Substantial speed-up can be gained when using the new algorithm of Latouche and Ramaswami, as illustrated in [33].

If series of performance analyses need to be performed (parametric analysis), speed-up can be gained if these analyses are ordered in increasing order of system utilisation. The $\mathbf{R}$-matrix of a previous analysis can then be used as initial value for the next analysis. Although we have not (yet) automated this, experience has shown that the required number of steps in the iteration decreases, albeit not dramatically.

Step **S2** is normally done via Gaussian elimination or Gauss-Seidel iteration (or SOR), depending on the size of the system. Our experience is that the boundary part of the model is usually of such a size that Gaussian elimination is well feasible [24, 33].

Step **S3** is only performed when required (see also Section 3.4).

3.4 Reward-based measures

Once the steady-state probabilities are known, reward-based measures can be computed easily. Let $r : \mathbb{N} \times \mathcal{M} \to \mathbb{R}$ denote a real-valued reward function defined on the state space of the model. The steady-state expected reward rate is then computed as

$$E[r] = \sum_{i=0}^{\infty} \sum_{\underline{m} \in \mathcal{S}'(i)} z_{i,\underline{m}} r(i, \underline{m}).$$

If the rewards are only dependent on the level number and not on the inter-level state, i.e., if $r(i, \underline{m}) = r(i, \underline{m}')$, for all $\underline{m}, \underline{m}' \in \mathcal{S}'(i)$ given fixed $i \in \mathbb{N}$, then we write $r(i) = r(i, \underline{m})$ and consequently

$$E[r] = \sum_{i=0}^{\infty} r(i)(\underline{z}_i \underline{1}^{\mathrm{T}}).$$

If $r(i) = i$, further reductions in complexity can be reached, using results for the geometric series, thus avoiding explicit calculation of the state probabilities and the infinite summation.

3.5 Finite models

CTMCs with infinite state space are often used to obtain bounds or approximations for models with a large but finite state space. Two steps need to be undertaken to accomplish this:

Infinite model solution. The infinite-size model is solved, for instance with matrix geometric techniques, yielding $\underline{\pi} = (\underline{z}_0, \underline{z}_1, \cdots)$;

Renormalisation. A new probability vector $\underline{u} = (\underline{u}_0, \underline{u}_1, \cdots, \underline{u}_F)$ is defined, with $\underline{u}_i = \Phi_F \underline{z}_i$ ($i = 0, \cdots, F$), and $\Phi_F = (\sum_{i=0}^{F} \underline{z}_i \underline{1}^{\mathrm{T}})^{-1}$. In doing so, $\underline{u}$ is a probability vector on the levels 0 through F.

Under many circumstances, $\underline{u}$ provides a good approximation for the exact steady-state proabilities of a finite model on levels 0 through F (see [34]). When certain quasi-reversibility properties hold, the renormalization is even exact [20, 23].

Finally, it should be noted that also for a class of *finite* QBD models, matrix geometric solutions apply directly [28, Chapter 4], [19]. These, of course, could also be applied when appropriate.

4 Tool support

A prerequisite to make any performance evaluation technique really usable is to have software tool support for it available. Such tools should (i) allow users to specify their models at a high-level of abstraction; (ii) automatically derive the, often more detailed, underlying mathematical model; (iii) solve the mathematical model in the most appropriate way; and (iv) present the solution results in terms of the original high-level model.

For the class of SPN model at hand, this implies that users should be able to specify, at SPN level, a model and that the tool finds out whether the requirements are met or not. If so, the matrix geometric solution technique can be employed. If the requirements are not met, various ways can be chosen. The tool can just indicate so, and stop the analysis, possibly also indicating where "it went wrong". A different approach might be to analyze the model using either a simulation approach, or a numerical approach with a truncated version of the model on a very large but still finite state space.

One practical problem that comes along here is that the requirements 1–3 may be easy to write down, they are not easily verified in general. As an example of this, consider a marking-dependent transition between two neighbouring levels in the repeating portion of the state space. If the transition has different rates between different neighbouring levels, Requirement 2.1 is not fulfilled. However, it very much depends on the way the marking dependent transition rate is specified, whether this can be checked in finite time or not.

When inhibitor arcs and enabling functions are allowed, in its most general setting, the verification problem might even be undecidable (see also [3]). Therefore, the given requirements should be interpreted as being sufficient to allow for the efficient solution. However, we are free to pose extra requirements, which ease the task of verifying whether a certain SPN passes the test or not, albeit possibly at the cost of less modelling flexibility. As an example of this, not allowing for marking dependent transition rates, will ease the task of verification.

Another problem is the determination of κ. Although this is often easy for a human being, doing this for instance "by inspection" of the upper left part of the matrix $\mathbf{Q}$, for a computer program this is less easy to do. In particular, the state space generation order plays an important role here; it should be done level-by-level. One way to solve this, might be to have the tool user indicate the value of κ. An indicated value that is too large does not spoil the solution process, however, it becomes slightly inefficient. An indicated value of κ that is too small will not yield correct results.

The aim of this paper is to present a class of infintely large SPNs which allow for an efficient solution. In a later paper we will report about the tooling effort we undertake. For the time being, we have used our tool for matrix geometric methods, i.e., Xmgm [21], for the solution of the underlying infinite CTMCs, i.e., for steps **S1** through **S3**. Step **S0** has been performed manually.

5   Applications

In this section we discuss two applications. The first application, a single server queueing system with delayed service, is presented in Section 5.1. Then, in Section 5.2, we discuss an application from the area of B-ISDN.

5.1   Queueing with delayed service

Considers a single server queueing system (see Figure 2) at which customers arrive as a Poisson process with rate λ via transition **arr** and are served with rate μ via transition **serve**.

Before service, arriving customers are stored in a **buffer**. Service is not immediately granted to an arriving customer, even not is the server is idle at that time (a token in place **sleep**). Only after there are at least T (for threshold) customers queued, the server awakes and starts its duties. This is enforced by an enabling predicate associated with the immediate transition **wake-up**: #buffer $\geq T$. The server subsequently remains awake until the buffer becomes empty, after which it resumes sleeping.

For a threshold $T = 3$, the corresponding CTMC is given in Figure 3. From the models, it can easily be seen that they fulfill Requirements 1–3 with $\kappa = T = 3$.

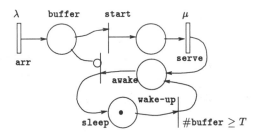

Figure 2: SPN of a single server queueing system with delayed service

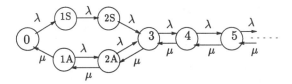

Figure 3: CTMC of the single server queueing system with delayed service; $T = 3$

The generator matrix then has the following form:

$$
\mathbf{Q} = \left(
\begin{array}{ccccc|cc|c}
-\Sigma & \lambda & 0 & 0 & 0 & & & \cdots \\
\hline
0 & -\Sigma & 0 & \lambda & 0 & & & \cdots \\
\mu & 0 & -\Sigma & 0 & \lambda & & & \cdots \\
\hline
0 & 0 & 0 & -\Sigma & 0 & \lambda & & \cdots \\
0 & 0 & \mu & 0 & -\Sigma & \lambda & & \cdots \\
\hline
0 & 0 & 0 & 0 & \mu & -\Sigma & \lambda & \cdots \\
0 & 0 & 0 & 0 & 0 & \mu & -\Sigma & \cdots \\
\hline
0 & 0 & 0 & 0 & 0 & 0 & \mu & \cdots \\
\vdots & \vdots & \vdots & \vdots & \vdots & \vdots & \vdots & \ddots
\end{array}
\right),
$$

where Σ is chosen such that the row sums equal 0. From this matrix we observe that the $L \times L$ **A**-matrices have the following form ($L = 1$): $\mathbf{A}_0 = (\lambda)$, $\mathbf{A}_1 = (-(\lambda + \mu))$ and $\mathbf{A}_2 = (\mu)$. From these matrices we derive $\mu \mathbf{R}^2 - (\lambda + \mu)\mathbf{R} + \lambda = 0$ which has as only valid solution $\mathbf{R} = (\lambda/\mu)$. From this, it once again becomes clear that $\mathbf{R}$ takes over the role of ρ in simpler queueing analysis, such as in the M|M|1 queue.

Denoting $\underline{z}_i = z_i$ ($i = 0$ or $i = 3, 4, \cdots$) and $\underline{z}_i = (z_{i,S}, z_{i,A})$ ($i = 2, 3$), the boundary equations become (from these seven equations, any one of the first six can be omitted):

$$
\left\{
\begin{array}{l}
-\lambda z_0 + \mu z_{1A} = 0, \\
\lambda z_0 - \lambda z_{1S} = 0, \\
-(\lambda + \mu)z_{1A} + \mu z_{2A} = 0, \\
\lambda z_{1S} - \lambda z_{2S} = 0, \\
\lambda z_{1A} - (\lambda + \mu)z_{2A} + \mu z_3 = 0, \\
\lambda z_{2S} + \lambda z_{2A} - (\lambda + \mu)z_3 + \mu z_4 = 0, \\
z_0 + z_{1S} + z_{1A} + z_{2S} + z_{2A} + z_3(1 - \rho)^{-1} = 1.
\end{array}
\right.
$$

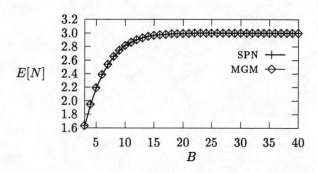

Figure 4: The average number of customers in the system, $E[N]$, as a function of the number of buffer places

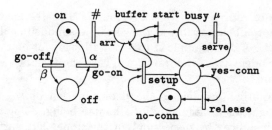

Figure 5: SPN model of OCDR mechanism

Concluding, to solve this SPN model using matrix geometric techniques, for a threshold T, we require a linear system of size $2T$ to be solved, as well as one quadratic equation which, since $L = 1$, can be solved in fixed time.

In contrast, when using a numerical approach based on the global balance equations of a finite SPN model, i.e., a model with a limit of B buffer places, we require a system of linear equations of size $T + B$ to be solved. Especially when B becomes large, the infinite-buffer model with matrix geometric solution is more efficient. Also when the renormalization procedure as outlined in Section 3.5 is used (see below), the matrix gemetric approach becomes more efficient, as for increasing buffer size B, only a renormalization has to be performed, whereas the solution based on the global balance equations has to be totally redone.

As a numerical example, consider the case where $\lambda = 2$, $\mu = 3$, $T = 3$ and, consequently, $\rho = 2/3$. The matrix geometric solution with infinite buffer, i.e., $B = \infty$, results in the following boundary steady-state probabilities:

$$\begin{cases} z_0 = 0.11111, & z_{1A} = 0.07407, & z_{1S} = 0.11111, \\ z_{2A} = 0.12346, & z_{2S} = 0.11111, & z_3 = 0.15638. \end{cases}$$

Using these probabilities, and $z_i = z_3\rho^{i-3}$, $i = 4, 5, \cdots$, we obtain for the average number of customers in the system $E[N] = 3.00$.

In case we have a finite-buffer model, we can also compute $E[N]$ directly from the global balance equations. In Figure 4 we show the average number of customers in such a system as a function of the number of buffer places, as calculated from an SPN model, using the GBEs explicitly (labelled 'SPN'). We also show the renormalized results derived from the infinite-buffer model, according to the procedure proposed in Section 3.5 (labelled 'MGM'). Clearly, the results match

perfectly. This is due to the quasi-reversibility property that holds in this case [20, 23]. A similar conclusion can be drawn for the computation of the buffer-overflow probabilities.

5.2 Connectionless traffic in B-ISDN

An ATM/B-ISDN-based communication infrastructure offers a connection-oriented service. Via two of the ATM adaptation layers 3/4 and 5, also connectionless services can be provided [30]. Packets arriving at the AAL service boundary to make use of such a service, suffer a possible delay from the connection establishment at the ATM service boundary, i.e., a connection set-up delay, unless there already exists a connection when the packet arrives. Once the connection has been established, all buffered packets can be transmitted and the connection can be released. This can be done immediately, or with some delay. The former has as disadvantage that a connection is being maintained when it is not needed, however, it has as advantage that some packets might profit from the fact that there is still a connection when they arrive. Whenever packets arrive in bursts, there is a trade-off between the release delay, the costs and of maintaining an unused connection and the perceived performance (average delay). The above way of implementing connectionless services, has been proposed by Heijenk et al. [22] under the name 'on-demand connection with delayed release' (OCDR).

An SPN model for such a system is given in Figure 5. Packets arrive via transition **arr** and are placed in the **buffer**. The rate of transition **arr** is modulated by an independent on/off-model. A token in place **on** or **off** respectively models the fact that the source is in a burst or not. When in a burst, packets are generated according to a Poisson process with rate λ packets/second. When not in a burst, no packets are generated. The transitions **go-on** and **go-off**, with rates α and β respectively, model the time durations the source remains in the off and on state. The service rate is μ Mbps and the average packet length is denoted l.

If the server is busy, there will be a token in place **busy** and arriving packets have to wait on their turn.

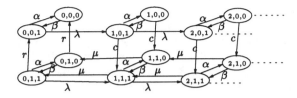

Figure 6: CTMC of the OCDR mechanism

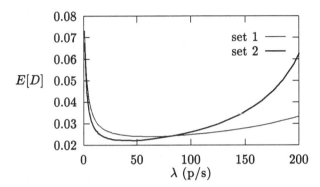

Figure 7: The expected delay $E[D]$ (in seconds) as a function of the arrival rate λ in a burst

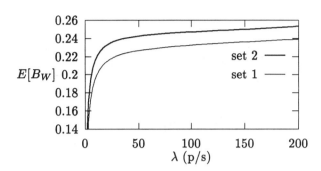

Figure 8: The expected bandwidth $E[B_W]$ (in Mbps) as a function of the arrival rate λ in a burst

If the server is idle, but there is no connection available, signified by a token in place no-conn, a connection will be established, causing a negative exponential delay with average length $1/c$ (transition set-up). Once there is a connection, normal packet transmissions can take place. Once the buffer is empty, the connection is released with a negative exponential delay with average length $1/r$ (transition release).

The corresponding CTMC is given in Figure 6. In this model, the states space $\mathcal{S} = \{(i,j,k)|i \in \mathbb{N}, j, k = 0, 1\}$. Parameter i denotes the number of packets in the system, j denotes whether there is a connection $(j = 1)$ or not $(j = 0)$ and k denotes whether the arrival process is in a burst $(k = 1)$ or not $(k = 0)$. As can be seen from the CTMC, but as can also be verified using Requirements 1–3, this model has a structure that allows for a matrix geometric solution. Every level $\mathcal{S}(l)$ consists of the $L = 4$ states with l packets present, i.e., $\mathcal{S}(l) = \{(l, 0, 0), (l, 0, 1), (l, 1, 0), (l, 1, 1)\}$.

Clearly, $\kappa = 1$ and the boundary equations are given by the global balance equations for the first two levels, i.e., level 0 and 1, plus the normalisation equation, in total yielding a system of 8 linear equations. The $L \times L$ matrix $\mathbf{R}$ with $L = 4$ now has to be solved numerically. If a finite buffer model were used, e.g., with B buffer

places, an underlying finite CTMC can be generated with $4(B + 1)$ states. As measures of interest we could address: (i) the average node delay $E[D]$ (in seconds); (ii) the average reserved bandwidth $E[B_W]$ (in Mbps); and (ii) the expected number of connection establishments per second $E[C]$ (in per-second). All these quantities can be expressed in closed-form using $\mathbf{R}$ and the boundary vector $\underline{z}_0$ (for details, see [22]).

Under the assumption that communication capacity can be claimed in various amounts, the service rate μ can be chosen freely. Given a certain workload, a higher requested transmission speed μ will yield smaller connection times, however, at higher costs per time unit. The parameter μ, therefore, together with the connection release rate r are interesting quantities to control the system performance and cost.

Let us now turn to some numerical results. We assume that $\alpha = 1.0$, $\beta = 0.04$, $c = 10.0$, and $l = 10$ kbit. We address the following two combinations of transmission and release rates: $(\mu, r)_1 = (336.0, 1.0)$ and $(\mu, r)_2 = (236.0, 0.5)$. In the first case, the transmission speed is relatively high, but connections are rapidly released after usage. In the second case, a lower transmission speed is used, but a connection is maintained longer. Therefore, arriving packets have a smaller probability to perceive an extra connection setup delay.

In Figure 7 we depict the expected delay $E[D]$ (in seconds) as a function of the arrival rate λ in a burst. Although for $\lambda \approx 85$ the average delay values coincide $(E[D] \approx 24.5)$, for changing λ's this is certainly not the case. For the first parameter set, the average delay is less sensitive to changes in λ, especially towards higher values. For smaller values of λ, the average delay is smaller for parameter set 2. Suprisingly, the less sensitive solution, requires a smaller average bandwidth as well, as illustrated in Figure 8. The number of connection establishments, however, is higher, as illustrated

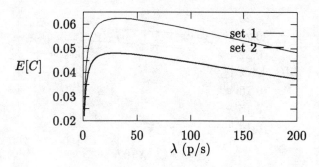

Figure 9: The expected conection setup rate $E[C]$ (in s^{-1}) as a function of the arrival rate λ in a burst

by Figure 9. Since the latter can be associated with costs in a B-ISDN context, the price to be paid for the less sensitive delay behaviour and for the smaller bandwidth consumption is paid here. Also observe, that for higher traffic, the number of connection establishments decreases, i.e., a connection that is once established, is used for a long time since the probability of having a connection and no packets present decreases with larger λ.

Finally, we report on the efficiency of the matrix geometric solution technique. The number of required steps in iteration (9) to calculate $\mathbf{R}$ with accuracy $\epsilon = 10^{-6}$ increases almost linearly with the traffic intensity λ, from a few iterations when λ is very small, to 250 when λ approaches 200. The required computation time to determine $\mathbf{R}$ then ranges from 0.05 through 1.00 seconds. These values are obtained without use of sparse matrices and without the earlier mentioned speed-up that could be obtained when doing multiple analyses.

6   Summary and conclusions

In this paper we have defined a class of infinite SPNs for which an efficient solution technique based on matrix geometric methods is feasible. The requirements to be posed on any SPN to exhibit such a solution are explicitly stated as sufficent conditions. The solution of the steady-state probabilities as well as of reward-based measures, thereby exploiting the QBD structure, is also discussed.

With two examples we have illustrated our approach. From these examples, and from the more general applicability of the theory, we think the newly defined class of SPNs is of importance for many application areas. In order to become practically useful, tool support is

necessary. Some requirements on and suggestions for tools have also been made.

As future research areas we envisage the design and implementation of a tool supporting the presented model class and solution technique. Especially the issue of decidability and the refinement of the requirements will be an important research theme. Also, the refinements should preferably become verifyable at the SPN-level, rather than at the level of the underlying CTMC. Finally, attention should be paid to ergodicity conditions and their *a priori* validation.

Acknowledgements

The author would like to thank the reviewers for their constructive comments on the paper. G.J. Heijenk and W. van Dieten are thanked for the cooperation on the OCDR-example.

References

[1] M. Ajmone Marsan, G. Conte, G. Balbo, "A Class of Generalized Stochastic Petri Nets for the Performance Evaluation of Multiprocessor Systems", *ACM TOCS* **2**(2), pp.93–122, 1984.

[2] M. Ajmone Marsan, G. Chiola, "On Petri Nets with Deterministic and Exponentailly Distributed Firing Times", *LNCS* **266**, Editor: G. Rozenberg, pp.132–145, 1987.

[3] S.S. Berson, R. Munts, "Detecting Block GI|M|1 and Block M|G|1 Matrices from Model Specifications", Technical Report, UCLA, 1994.

[4] P. Buchholz, "Hierarchical Markovian Models: Symmetries and Reduction", in: *Computer Performance Evaluation '92: Modelling Techniques and Tools*, Editors: R. Pooley, J. Hillston, pp.305–319, 1992.

[5] P. Buchholz, "Aggregation and Reduction techniques for Hierarchical GCSPNs", *Proc. of the 5th Int'l Workshop on Petri Nets and Performance Models*, pp.216–225, 1993.

[6] G. Chiola, C. Dutheillet, G. Franceschines, S. Haddad, "Stochastic Well-Formed Colored nets and Symmetric Modelling Applications", *IEEE TSE* **42**(11), pp.1343–1360, 1993.

[7] H. Choi, V.G. Kulkarni, K.S. Trivedi, "Markov-Regenerative Stochastic Petri Nets", in: *Performance '93*, Editors: G. Iazeolla, S.S. Lavenberg, North-Holland, 1993.

[8] G. Ciardo, J. Muppala, K.S. Trivedi, "SPNP: Stochastic Perti Net Package", *Proc. of the 3rd Int'l Workshop on Petri Nets and Performance Models*, pp.142–151, 1989.

[9] G. Ciardo, J. K. Muppala, and K. S. Trivedi, "On the Solution of GSPN Reward Models," *Performance Evaluation* **12**(4), pp.237-254, 1991.

[10] G. Ciardo, K.S. Trivedi, "A Decomposition Approach for Stochastic Reward Net Models", *Performance Evaluation* **18**(1), pp.37–59, 1993.

[11] G. Ciardo, R. German, C. Lindemann, "A Characterization of the Stochastic Process Underlying a Stochastic Petri Net", *IEEE TSE* **20**(7), pp.506–515, 1994.

[12] A.J. Coyle, W. Henderson, C.E.M. Pearce, P.G. Taylor, "Mean-Value Analysis for Batch-Movement Queueing Networks with Product-Form Equilibrium Distributions", *Proc. of the Australia-Japan Workshop on Stochastic Models in Engineering, Technology & Management*, Gold Coast, Australia, July 14–16, 1993, pp.96–106.

[13] W.J. van Dieten, *Performance Evaluation of a Connectionless Protocol over ATM using Matrix Geometric Methods*, University of Twente, Department of Computer Science, 1994.

[14] S. Donatelli, M. Sereno, "On The Product-Form Solution for Stochastic Petri Nets", *Application and Theory of Petri Nets 1992*, Editor: K. Jensen, pp.154–172, Springer Verlag, 1992.

[15] G. Florin, S. Natkin, "On Open Synchronized Queueing Networks", *Proc. of the International Workshop on Timed Petri Nets*, pp.226–223, 1985.

[16] G. Florin, S. Natkin, "One Place Unbounded Stochastic Petri Nets: Ergodicity Criteria and Steady-State Solution", *Journal of Systems and Software* **1**(2), pp.103–115, 1986.

[17] G. Florin, S. Natkin, "A Necessary and Sufficient Saturation Condition for Open Synchronized Queueing Networks", *Proc. of the 2nd Int'l Workshop on Petri Nets and Performance Models*, pp.4–13, 1987.

[18] G. Florin, S. Natkin, "Generalizations of Queueing Network Product-Form Solutions to Stochastic Petri Nets", *IEEE TSE* **17**(2), pp.99–107, 1991.

[19] L. Gün, A.M. Makowski, "Matrix Geometric Solutions for Finite Capacity Queues with Phase-Type Distributions", in: *Performance '87*, Editors: P.J. Courtois, G. Latouche, North-Holland, pp. 269–282, 1988.

[20] B.R. Haverkort, "Approximate Performability and Dependability Modelling using Generalized Stochastic Petri Nets", *Performance Evaluation* **18**(1), pp.61–78, 1993.

[21] B.R. Haverkort, A.P.A. van Moorsel, D.-J. Speelman, "Xmgm: A Performance Analysis Tool Based on Matrix Geometric Methods", in: *Proc. of the 2nd Int'l Workshop on Modelling, Analysis and Simulation of Computer and Telecommunication Systems*, pp.152–157, 1994.

[22] G.J. Heijenk, *Connectionless Communivcations using the Asynchronous Transfer Mode*, Ph.D. thesis, University of Twente, 1995.

[23] F.P. Kelly, *Reversibility and Stochastic Networks*, John Wiley & Sons, 1979.

[24] U. Krieger, B. Müller-Clostermann, M. Sczittnick, "Modelling and Analysis of Communication Systems Based on Computational Methods for Markov Chains", *IEEE JSAC* **8**(9), pp.1630-1648, 1990.

[25] C. Lindemann, "An Improved Numerical Algorithm for Calculating Steady-State Solutions of Deterministic and Stochastic Petri Nets", *Performance Evaluation* **18**(1), pp.79–95, 1993.

[26] M.K. Molloy, "Performance Analysis using Stochastic Petri Nets", *IEEE TC* **31**(9), pp.913–917, 1982.

[27] R. Nelson, "Matrix Geometric Solutions in Markov Models: A Mathematical Tutorial", *IBM Research Report* RC 16777, 1991.

[28] M.F. Neuts, *Matrix Geometric Solutions in Stochastic Models: An Algorithmic Approach*, Johns Hopkins University Press, Baltimore, 1981.

[29] M.F. Neuts, *Structured Stochastic Matrices of M|G|1 Type and Their Applications*, Marcel Dekker Inc., New York, 1989.

[30] R.O. Onvural, *Asynchronous Transfer Mode Networks: Performance Issues*, Artech House, 1994.

[31] W.H. Sanders, J.F. Meyer, "Reduced Base Model Construction for Stochastic Activity Networks", *IEEE JSAC* **9**(1), pp.25–36, 1991.

[32] M.F. Squillante, "MAGIC: A Computer Performance Modelling Tool Based on Matrix-Geometric Techniques", in: *Computer Performance Evaluation: Modelling Techniques and Tools*, Editors: G. Balbo, G. Serazzi, North-Holland, pp.411–425, 1992.

[33] W.J. Stewart, "On the Use of Numerical Methods for ATM Models", in: *Modelling and Performance Evaluation of ATM Technology*, IFIP Transactions C-15, Editors: H. Perros, G. Pujolle, Y. Takahashi, North-Holland, pp.375-396, 1993.

[34] H.C. Tijms, "Heuristics for Finite-Buffer Queues", Research Report 1991-29, Free University, Department of Econometrics, Amsterdam, 1991.

Lumpability and Nearly-Lumpability
in Hierarchical Queueing Networks

P. Buchholz

Informatik IV, Universität Dortmund

D-44221 Dortmund, Germany

Abstract

Hierarchical extended queueing networks (HQNs) have been proposed recently as a model class which allows a very efficient analysis based on an exploitation of the hierarchical model structure in the analysis of the underlying Markov chain (MC). Furthermore the hierarchical structure of the model enables the definition of symmetries due to identical subnets on model level and the automatic generation of a reduced MC resulting from exact or ordinary lumpability. In this paper the notion of symmetries is extended to nearly symmetries at model and submodel level resulting in nearly lumpability of the underlying MC. Bounds on performance quantities for nearly lumpable Markov chains are computed using bounded aggregation in the stationary case.

1 Introduction

Performance and dependability of complex computer and communication systems are often analyzed by means of extended queueing network models. Realistic models often include features which prohibit an analysis based on efficient product-form algorithms, so that the queueing network model has to be mapped on the underlying Markov chain (MC) which can be analyzed using well established numerical techniques. However, this conceptually simple approach usually suffers from the huge state space of the resulting MC which often cannot be handled even with todays high performance computers. Therefore, methods to handle complexity are of great importance. The common way to reduce complexity of MC analysis is to exploit some structure at the level of the generator matrix or, often preferable, at the queueing network level.

Hierarchical extended queueing networks (HQNs) have been proposed recently as an adequate paradigm for the hierarchical specification and related quantitative analysis of complex systems [3]. Furthermore symmetries resulting from identical subnets combined in a symmetric way can be defined at model level and can be used for the automatic generation of an aggregated MC yielding exact results for the non-aggregated MC as shown in [2]. Reduction of submodels of HQNs, based on lumpability and nearly lumpability is considered in [1].

In this paper we combine and extend the former results. Conditions for near-lumpability resulting from nearly symmetric combinations of (nearly) identical subnets are given, the underlying MC is generated and

it is shown, which results on model level can be determined from the reduced MC. Since reduction based on nearly lumpability is only an approximation, it is in particular important to estimate the size of the introduced aggregation error. By using the bounded aggregation approach [9] bounds for the aggregation error of stationary results are computed.

There are some other approaches related to the work presented here. The idea of exact aggregation of MCs based on ordinary lumpability is well known [12,13]. The relation between symmetries in a model specification and lumpability of the underlying MC has first been considered in the Petri net area, resulting in two different approaches. The first (see [6]) is based on Stochastic Well Formed Nets (SWNs), a particular class of colored stochastic Petri Nets which allows the specification of identities and the computation of a reduced (lumped) MC from the specification. The second (see [14]) is based on the hierarchical composition of Stochastic Activity Nets (SANs) allowing the generation of a reduced MC if identical subnets are composed. Both approaches allow only exact aggregation. Approximative analysis of SPNs based on fixpoint computation is considered in [7], however, in this approach bounds cannot be computed.

Our approach relies on extended QN models, the philosophy of hierarchical model specification by combining identical parts in a symmetric way is similar to SANs, although the hierarchy differs significantly and the method of MC generation is completely different. There are also relations to SWNs, since recently papers [10,11] have been published which describe the generation of so called quasi-lumpable MCs from SWNs. The notation of quasi-lumpability is the same as nearly ordinary lumpability defined in [1,4]. However, to the best of our knowledge, no approach which considers lumping of MCs distinguishes between exact and ordinary lumpability. Exact lumpability for MCs is due to Schweitzer [16], who defines also approximate exact lumpability which differs from our definition of nearly exact lumpability. The distinction between ordinary and exact lumpability is important, since both concepts are independent and also different from complete symmetries, although all concepts allow the computation of exact results from the reduced MC. The new contributions of this paper are: An efficient method of computing reduced MCs from HQNs based in particular on nearly exact/ordinary lumpability and the consideration of the reward structure in the aggregation.

The structure of the paper is as follows. In section 2 HQNs and the construction of the underlying MC are introduced. Section 3 summarizes some results and definitions in the context of exact/ordinary lumpability, introduces how to generate a lumpable MC from a HQN specification and shows which results are computable using this MC. In Section 4 the same is done for nearly exact/ordinary lumpability, additionally bounds for the results are determined. An example is presented in Section 5. The paper ends with the conclusions and some directions for future research.

2 Hierarchical Queueing Networks

2.1 Specification of HQNs

The class of HQNs has been introduced in [3]. HQNs are specified in two levels. We distinguish the High Level Model (HLM) describing the connection of J Low Level Models ($LLMs$). The HLM is numbered 0, $LLMs$ receive numbers from 1 to J. In the HLM each LLM is viewed as a "black box", the only information about the internal state is the number of customers which are actually in the LLM. The HLM describes a closed model, including customers from K classes and C chains. The meaning of classes and chains is the same as in standard QNs. Thus the state of the HLM can be described by a $J * K$ dimensional vector $\mathbf{n}$. Component $\mathbf{n}_j(k)$ includes the number of class k customers in LLM j. We assume that customers in a LLM reside there for some time and will eventually leave the LLM. No customers are destroyed or generated in a LLM and at a given time at most one customers leaves.

Dynamic in the HLM is described by customers leaving one LLM and entering another or the same one. This movement is described by (conditional) routing probabilities in the HLM. Let $r(i,k,j,l,\mathbf{n})$ be the probability of a class k customer leaving LLM i and entering LLM j immediately as a class l customer, if the HLM is in state $\mathbf{n}$.

Let N_k be the maximum number of class k customers in the HLM and $N_{j,k}$ be the maximum number of class k customers in LLM j. Thus the state of LLM j as visible in the HLM includes all vectors $\mathbf{n}_j \in \mathbf{N}^K$ with $\mathbf{n}_j(k) \leq N_{j,k}$.

The specification of a single LLM is given by an internal description and the specification of a condensed version of the environment. The environment is realized by a finite capacity source and a sink per class which is allowed to enter the LLM (i.e., $N_{j,k} > 0$ for class k and LLM j). To allow a more flexible use of $LLMs$ we assume that LLM j is specified in isolation. Thus LLM j is specified for a set of customer types K_j with maximum population $N_{j,k}$ for each $k \in K_j$. The source for type $k \in K_j$ generates entities with an exponentially distributed interarrival time with some fictive rate $\lambda > 0$ as long as the type k population does not exceed the capacity $N_{j,k}$, in this case the source is switched off until a type k customers leaves j. Leaving customers are absorbed by a sink. Inside j, customer types are interpreted as chains allowing customers to

have an additional local class identity which is lost upon departure from the LLM. The internal specification of a LLM is given by an extended QN, the only restrictions are that the LLM in combination with the finite capacity source has to be mapped on a finite MC and that the interface behavior is as defined above.

To embed a LLM in an environment the classes of the embedding HLM have to be related to the customer types offered by the LLM. This is done by defining a unique mapping from each $k \in K$ with $N_{j,k} > 0$ on $k' \in K_j$. To allow such a mapping $N_{j,k} \leq N_{j,k'}$ has to hold, or, in other words, a LLM specified in isolation can be used in any environment where the used capacity for the different entities types does not exceed the isolated capacity.

2.2 Computation of the Markov Chain

The MC underlying a HQN can be computed exploiting the hierarchical structure. We start with the generation of the HLM state space Z_0, states are described by vectors $\mathbf{n} \in \mathbf{N}^{J*K}$. Z_0 is generated starting from an initial state $\mathbf{n}_0 \in Z_0$ by computing all successors assuming that a class k customer can leave j whenever $\mathbf{n}_j(k) > 0$ and is routed to another LLM according to the routing probabilities. We assume that Z_0 forms an irreducible, finite state space and that each transition observable in the HLM changes the state (i.e., $r(i,k,i,k,\mathbf{n}) = 0$). The latter assumption is only for notational convenience and can be dropped without any problems (see e.g., [3]). The states in Z_0 determine the maximum populations in the $LLMs$ since $N_{j,k} = \max_{\mathbf{n} \in Z_0}(\mathbf{n}_j(k))$. We define the relations $<$ and $>$ for $\mathbf{n}, \mathbf{n}' \in Z_0$ according to the lexicographical ordering. Let $\mathbf{n} - \mathbf{e}_{i,k} + \mathbf{e}_{j,l}$ be the state which results from $\mathbf{n}$ by a class k customer leaving i and entering j as a class l customer.

Each LLM in combination with the finite capacity source is described as an isolated model. Therefore, the state space and generator matrix for a LLM can be computed in complete isolation. In the sequel we identify $LLMs$ by their number in the HLM and offered customer types by the HLM class which is mapped on these types. It should be noticed that the LLM specification is, apart from the maximum population, independent from the HLM or other $LLMs$. If a LLM specification is used more than once in one or several $HLMs$, then the specification, state space and matrix generation needs to be performed only once.

Let Z_j be the state space which has been generated for j. Z_j can be decomposed into subspaces $Z_j(\mathbf{n})$ according to the population in j. Transitions on $Z_j(\mathbf{n})$ are classified in three different categories. The first category includes transitions internally in j. The corresponding transition rates are collected in matrices $\mathbf{Q}_j^{\mathbf{n}}$ including in the main diagonal the negative sum of transitions rates originated in the subnet. Each $\mathbf{Q}_j^{\mathbf{n}}$ is a $\|Z_j(\mathbf{n})\| \times \|Z_j(\mathbf{n})\|$ matrix ($\|\ldots\|$ describes the cardinality of a set). Transition rates for class k customers departing from j with population $\mathbf{n}$ are collected in matrices $\mathbf{S}_j^{\mathbf{n}}[k]$. Each $\mathbf{S}_j^{\mathbf{n}}[k]$ is a $\|Z_j(\mathbf{n})\| \times \|Z_j(\mathbf{n}-\mathbf{e}_k)\|$ matrix. Transitions specifying arrivals of class k customers to j yielding a new population $\mathbf{n}$, are quantified by conditional probabilities in the matrices $\mathbf{U}_j^{\mathbf{n}}[k]$. All those matrices can be easily computed from a *LLM* specification using an appropriate tool.

The state space Z of the complete HQN is given by substituting each *HLM* state $\mathbf{n}$ by the detailed state spaces of the *LLMs* belonging to $\mathbf{n}$. Thus,

$$Z = \cup_{\mathbf{n} \in Z_0} Z(\mathbf{n}) = \cup_{\mathbf{n} \in Z_0} \times_{j=1}^{J} Z_j(\mathbf{n}_j).$$

According to the *HLM* state the generator matrix $\mathbf{Q}$ of the complete model is decomposed into submatrices $\mathbf{Q}^{\mathbf{n},\mathbf{m}}$ including all transitions between states from $Z(\mathbf{n})$ and $Z(\mathbf{m})$. Each submatrix is computed in two steps, considering first the transitions in the involved *LLMs* and, in the second step, the routing probabilities in the *HLM*. Let $\mathbf{Q}_L^{\mathbf{n}}(i,k,j,l)$ be a matrix including the transition rates of a class k entity leaving i and entering j as a class l entity, when the *HLM* is in state $\mathbf{n}$, without taking care of the routing probabilities (i.e., assuming routing probability 1.0) and $\mathbf{Q}_L^{\mathbf{n}}(0)$ including the transition rates inside the *LLMs*. Matrices $\mathbf{Q}_L^{\mathbf{n}}(i,k,j,l)$ can be computed from the, much smaller, matrices describing *LLMs* using tensor and ordinary products of matrices (see [3] for additional details).

$$\mathbf{Q}_L^{\mathbf{n}}(i,k,j,l) =$$
$$\begin{cases} (\mathbf{I}_{l_i(\mathbf{n})} \otimes \mathbf{S}_i^{\mathbf{n}_i}[k] \otimes \mathbf{I}_{u_i(\mathbf{n})})(\mathbf{I}_{l_j(\mathbf{n})} \otimes \mathbf{U}_j^{\mathbf{m}_j}[l] \otimes \mathbf{I}_{u_j(\mathbf{n})}) \\ \qquad \text{if } i < j \\ (\mathbf{I}_{l_j(\mathbf{n})} \otimes \mathbf{U}_j^{\mathbf{m}_j}[l] \otimes \mathbf{I}_{u_j(\mathbf{n})})(\mathbf{I}_{l_i(\mathbf{n})} \otimes \mathbf{S}_i^{\mathbf{n}_i}[k] \otimes \mathbf{I}_{u_i(\mathbf{n})}) \\ \qquad \text{if } i > j \\ \mathbf{I}_{l_i(\mathbf{n})} \otimes \mathbf{S}_i^{\mathbf{n}_i}[k]\mathbf{U}_i^{\mathbf{m}_i}[l] \otimes \mathbf{I}_{u_i(\mathbf{n})} \\ \qquad \text{if } i = j \end{cases}$$

$$\mathbf{Q}_L^{\mathbf{n}}(0) = \sum_{j=1}^{J} \mathbf{I}_{l_j(\mathbf{n})} \otimes \mathbf{Q}_j^{\mathbf{n}_j} \otimes \mathbf{I}_{u_j(\mathbf{n})}$$

where $l_i(\mathbf{n}) = \prod_{j=1}^{i-1} \|Z_j(\mathbf{n}_j)\|$, $u_i(\mathbf{n}) = \prod_{j=i+1}^{J} \|Z_i(\mathbf{n}_j)\|$ and $\mathbf{m} = \mathbf{n} - \mathbf{e}_{i,k} + \mathbf{e}_{j,l}$.

(1)

To perform the second step we define $r(\mathbf{n}, \mathbf{m} = r(i,k,j,l,\mathbf{n})$ if $\mathbf{m} = \mathbf{n} - \mathbf{e}_{i,k} + \mathbf{e}_{j,l}$ and 0 elsewhere. Thus a single submatrix is given by

$$\mathbf{Q}^{\mathbf{n},\mathbf{m}} = \begin{cases} r(\mathbf{n},\mathbf{m})\mathbf{Q}_L^{\mathbf{n}}(i,k,j,l), \\ \qquad \text{if } \mathbf{m} = \mathbf{n} - \mathbf{e}_{i,k} + \mathbf{e}_{j,l} \ (\mathbf{n} \neq \mathbf{m}), \\ \mathbf{Q}_L^{\mathbf{n}}(0), \\ \qquad \text{if } \mathbf{n} = \mathbf{m}, \\ \mathbf{0}, \\ \qquad \text{elsewhere.} \end{cases}$$

(2)

We assume $\mathbf{Q}$ to be irreducible. The above formulas allow a very efficient computation of the generator matrix and can be exploited for various analysis steps (see [1,2,3]). In particular it can be used to compute exactly or approximately reduced MCs as shown in the sequel of this paper.

3 Exact and Ordinary Lumpability
3.1 Exact and Ordinary Lumpability of MCs

We start with the definition of lumpability on the level of the MC. There are several characterizations, we use the following based on the generator or transition matrix of a MC. Let $\Omega = \{\Omega(1), \ldots, \Omega(N)\}$ be a partition on a state space Z of a finite MC. For a partition Ω on a n dimensional state space Z of a MC we can define a $n \times N$ collector matrix $\mathbf{V}$ element-wise as: $\mathbf{V}(x, X) = 1$ if $x \in \Omega(X)$ and 0 else. $\mathbf{V}$ includes exactly one 1 per row and describes the mapping of states from Z into the partition groups.

Definition 1 *Let $\mathbf{Q}$ be the irreducible generator matrix of a finite MC on state space Z and $\Omega = \{\Omega(1) \ldots \Omega(N)\}$ a partition of the state space with collector matrix $\mathbf{V}$.*

- *Ω is ordinarily lumpable, iff for all $\Omega(X) \in \Omega$ and $x, y \in \Omega(X)$: $(\mathbf{e}_x - \mathbf{e}_y)\mathbf{Q}\mathbf{V} = \mathbf{0}$;*
- *Ω is exactly lumpable, iff for all $\Omega(X) \in \Omega$ and $x, y \in \Omega(X)$: $(\mathbf{e}_x - \mathbf{e}_y)\mathbf{Q}^T\mathbf{V} = \mathbf{0}$;*
- *Ω is strictly lumpable, iff it is ordinarily and exactly lumpable.*

$\mathbf{e}_i$ *is a n-dimensional row vector with 1.0 in position i and 0 elsewhere.*

We use the name lumpable partition for a partition which is exactly or ordinarily lumpable. Lumpability is interesting because it allows the computation of several results for the original MC using a reduced one which is constructed by substituting each partition group of states by a single aggregated state. Before we consider preservation of results, computation of the aggregated generator matrix has to be introduced. For aggregation define a distributor matrix $\mathbf{W}$ belonging to a collector matrix $\mathbf{V}$ as

$$\mathbf{W} = \overline{\mathbf{V}^T}, \qquad (3)$$

where $\bar{\mathbf{A}}$ denotes the matrix $\mathbf{A} \geq \mathbf{0}$ and $\mathbf{A}\mathbf{e}^T > \mathbf{0}$ with each row normalized to 1.0. Let

$$\tilde{\mathbf{Q}} = \mathbf{W}\mathbf{Q}\mathbf{V} \qquad (4)$$

be the generator of the aggregated MC. Let $\mathbf{p}$ and $\tilde{\mathbf{p}}$ be stationary solution vectors of the original and aggregated MC, respectively (i.e., $\mathbf{p}\mathbf{Q} = \mathbf{0}$, $\tilde{\mathbf{p}}\tilde{\mathbf{Q}} = \mathbf{0}$ and $\mathbf{p}\mathbf{e}^T = \tilde{\mathbf{p}}\mathbf{e}^T = 1.0$). The mapping of the original solution into the aggregated state space is given by $\mathbf{p}\mathbf{V}$. The following theorem describes the relation between the solution of the aggregated and the original MC if the aggregation is based on exact/ordinary lumpability.

Theorem 1 *Let Z be the state space of a finite MC with generator matrix $\mathbf{Q}$, let $\Omega = \{\Omega(1), \ldots, \Omega(N)\}$ be a partition on Z, let $\tilde{\mathbf{Q}}$ be the generator matrix of the aggregated MC based on Ω, then the following relations between the results for the aggregated and the original MC hold.*

- *If Ω is an ordinarily lumpable partition, then $\mathbf{p}\mathbf{V} = \tilde{\mathbf{p}}$.*
- *If Ω is an exactly lumpable partition, then $\mathbf{p}(x) = \tilde{\mathbf{p}}(X)/\|\Omega(X)\|$ for all $x \in \Omega(X)$.*

Proof: The proof for stationary results can be found in [12] for ordinary lumpability and in [16,17] for exact lumpability. □

The theorem shows that from a reduced MC resulting from an exactly lumpable partition, the original solution vector can be recreated. If the partition is ordinarily lumpable, only an aggregated version of the solution vector can be computed, which implies that computable results have to depend on the aggregated solution. In the next subsection the results will be interpreted in the context of performance/reliability quantities expressed by HQNs. To be really useful, methods are needed which allow an efficient computation of the reduced MC ideally without first computing the huge original MC.

A special class of MCs which include a strictly lumpable partition, apart from the identity, are MCs which are invariant under a permutation matrix. A permutation matrix $\mathbf{P}$ is a $n \times n$ matrix which includes one element equal to 1 in each row and column. For permutation matrices the relations $\mathbf{P}\mathbf{P}^T = \mathbf{P}^T\mathbf{P} = \mathbf{I}$ hold. Permutation matrices can be used to permute the states of a MC.

Definition 2 *A finite MC with generator matrix $\mathbf{Q}$ is invariant under a permutation represented by a matrix $\mathbf{P}$, if $\mathbf{Q} = \mathbf{P}^T\mathbf{Q}\mathbf{P}$*

Define for a MC with generator matrix $\mathbf{Q}$ $\mathcal{P}$ as the set of permutation matrices under which the MC is invariant.

Theorem 2 *Let Ω be a partition on the state space of a finite MC with generator matrix $\mathbf{Q}$, such that two states x, y are in the same partition group, if a permutation matrix $\mathbf{P} \in \mathcal{P}$ with $\mathbf{P}(x,y) = 1$ exists. Ω is a strictly lumpable partition.*

Proof: The proof can be found in [5]. □

MCs which are invariant under permutation matrices result, in particular, from models including identical parts in a symmetric way. The approaches in [6] and [14] exploit these kind of symmetries, i.e. the MCs are invariant under permutations permuting states in a partition group and aggregation is based on exact and ordinary lumpability.

3.2 Exact and Ordinary Lumpability in HQNs

The usability of lumpability for model reduction relies on two points. First, a partition has to exist which is (nearly) exact/ordinary lumpable and the number of partition groups (states of the aggregated MC) is significantly smaller than the number of states of the original MC. Second, this partition has to be found with a low effort, ideally the aggregated MC is directly computed from the model specification without first generating the original MC. Concerning the first

point it is known that symmetries in a model specification result in invariance under permutations of the underlying MC. Symmetries are common in models from various application areas like parallel computers, computer networks, communication protocols, fault tolerant systems etc. Examples and applications which often show a dramatic reduction of the size of the underlying MC are given in [2,6,14].

The efficient computation of lumpable partitions and the efficient generation of the reduced MC are often more crucial for non-trivial examples. There are two different approaches, the first is to define symmetries (and therefore implicitly also lumpable partitions) in the model specification, the second is to compute a lumpable partition using an algorithmic approach possibly combined with *a priori* knowledge about the model structure. Both approaches have their specific drawbacks. The definition of symmetries in a flat model requires often an experienced user and a complex formalism to specify identities and symmetries. Furthermore model modifications, which are necessary in any kind of practical modeling, become complicated since a local modification might destroy the symmetry and requires a respecification. Computation of lumpable partitions on the MC or state space is theoretically possible, an iterative algorithm is given in [1] which yields the partition with the least number of partition groups as proved in [5]. However, the algorithm requires, first, the computation of the original generator matrix and, second, the construction of lumpable partitions which is often as complex as the analysis of the original MC. Thus, this is not a feasible way of aggregation.

In a hierarchical model the situation is more promising for both approaches. Identities among parts of the model can be implicitly defined by using submodels more than once. Multiple incarnations of one submodel specification in a model is a natural way of hierarchical model design which does not require the user to be aware of defining lumpable partitions. Furthermore, modifications are much easier, since either the submodel type is modified preserving the identity among all incarnations, or the type of a submodel is changed obviously destroying the identity. However, apart from identity we also have to force symmetry among identical submodels to yield lumpable partitions. This is done by an algorithmic approach getting as input identities among submodels and the connection between submodels and producing as output identical and symmetric submodels. Such an approach is possible since the complexity of the interconnection of submodels (i.e., the size of the *HLM* state space) is normally much smaller than the state space of the complete model. The approach, of course, relies on the hierarchical generation of the state space and transition matrices. Candidates for algorithmic generation of lumpable partitions are also state spaces of submodels. Since a submodel state space is much smaller than the state space of the complete model, growing with the product over the sizes of the state spaces of the involved submodels, it is possible to put some effort in submodel reduction and use afterward the reduced submodel in the overall model composition.

3.3 Computation of lumpable partitions

We define lumpable partitions based on identical and symmetric submodels. Identities among $LLMs$ are implicitly given during model specification by using one LLM specification several times in a HLM. Let $\Pi = \{\pi\}$ be a set of permutations on LLM numbers and HLM class indices such that for each $\pi \in \Pi$

- for all $\mathbf{n} \in Z_0$ $\pi(\mathbf{n})^1 \in Z_0$,

- if $\pi(i,k) = (j,l)$ $(1 \leq j, i \leq J, 1 \leq k, l \leq K)$, then i and j result from the same LLM specification and k and l are mapped on the same or identical customer types, and

- $r(i,k,j,l,\mathbf{n}) = r(\pi(i,k,j,l),\pi(\mathbf{n}))$.

The first two conditions assure that only identical parts are permuted and the third condition implies that identical parts are symmetric in the HLM. Π can be computed automatically using the following two steps.

1. Generate a set of permutations Π observing the first and second condition above.

2. Delete those partitions from Π which do not fulfill the third condition.

The set Π is implicitly defined by the modeler using a LLM several times, i.e. the effort for checking the conditions on the routing probabilities is at most proportional to Z_0 the size of the HLM state space which is much smaller than the overall state space Z. Since routing does normally not depend on the complete state of the HLM, which also decreases the effort of checking the condition.

Permutations π can be applied to the detailed state of the HQN. For each π, π_i describes the effect of π on LLM i, thus if $\pi(i,k) = (j,l)$, then $\pi_i(k) = l$ and $\pi_i(z_i)$ is state which results from z_i by changing the type identity of all customers in i as defined by π_i. Let $z = (z_1, \ldots, z_J) \in Z$, $z_j \in Z_j$ is the corresponding state of LLM j. $\pi(z)$ is the state which results from z by permuting the components as specified by π. The i-th component becomes $\pi_i(z_j)$ for $i = \pi(j)$. Since π permutes only identical classes we have for each LLM j, $z \in Z_j$ and permutation π with $i = \pi(j)$:

$$Q_j^{\mathbf{n}}(x,y) = Q_i^{\pi_i(\mathbf{n})}(\pi_i(x), \pi_i(y)),$$
$$S_j^{\mathbf{n}}[k](x,y) = S_i^{\pi_i(\mathbf{n})}[\pi_i(k)](\pi_i(x), \pi_i(y)) \text{ and}$$
$$U_j^{\mathbf{n}}[k](x,y) = U_j^{\pi_i(\mathbf{n})}[\pi_i(k)](\pi_i(x), \pi_i(y)).$$

Thus a partition Ω on Z can be defined by putting $x, y \in Z$ in the same partition group if a permutation $\pi \in \Pi$ exists such that $x = \pi(y)$.

Theorem 3 Ω *is a strictly lumpable partition partition on* $\mathbf{Q}$.

$^1\pi(\mathbf{n})$ results form $\mathbf{n}$ by permuting all LLM and class indices as defined by π. We use in the sequel the notation $\pi(.)$ to indicate the effect of π on the quantity in brackets.

Proof: Following theorem 2 we have to show that $\mathbf{Q}$ is invariant under permutation form Π. The proof is straightforward since all $\pi \in \Pi$ imply complete symmetry on the state space. $\square$

The theorem defines a strictly lumpable partition on Z but it does not include a method to compute the reduced generator matrix preserving as much as possible of the tensor structure. Such a method will be outlined now. Π introduces a partition Ω_0 on Z_0 by putting $\mathbf{n}, \mathbf{m} \in Z_0$ in the same partition group, if a permutation $\pi \in \Pi$ with $\mathbf{n} = \pi(\mathbf{m})$ exists. For each partition group $\Omega_0(X)$ we can define a canonical representation by choosing the lexicographically smallest element of $\Omega_0(X)$. Let $\tilde{\mathbf{n}} = \min(\mathbf{n} \in \Omega_0(X))$ be the canonical representation. It is easy to check that a reduced state space for the HLM results from one state per partition group $\Omega_0(X)$. Let $\tilde{\mathbf{Q}}$ be decomposable into blocks $\tilde{\mathbf{Q}}^{\tilde{\mathbf{n}}, \tilde{\mathbf{m}}}$. On the reduced routing HLM state space routing probabilities can be defined as

$$\tilde{r}(\tilde{\mathbf{n}}, \tilde{\mathbf{m}}) = \sum_{\mathbf{m} \in \Omega_0(X)} r(\tilde{\mathbf{n}}, \mathbf{m}), \text{ where } \tilde{\mathbf{m}} \in \Omega_0(X) \quad (5)$$

We assume that $r(\tilde{\mathbf{n}}, \tilde{\mathbf{n}}) = 0$, for all $\tilde{\mathbf{n}} \in \tilde{Z}_0$. Apart from this aggregation of HLM states we might have an aggregation of states inside the subsets $Z(\mathbf{n})$, if a permutation $\pi \in \Pi$ exists such that $\pi(\mathbf{n}) = \mathbf{n}$ exists. Thus we define partitions $\Omega^{\mathbf{n}}$ such that $z, z' \in Z(\mathbf{n})$ are in the same partition group, if a permutation $\pi \in \Pi$ with $z' = \pi(z)$ exists. For each $\Omega^{\mathbf{n}}$ a collector matrix $\mathbf{V}^{\mathbf{n}}$ and the corresponding distributor matrix $\mathbf{W}^{\mathbf{n}}$ can be defined. The submatrices of $\tilde{\mathbf{Q}}$ can then be expressed as

$$\tilde{\mathbf{Q}}^{\tilde{\mathbf{n}}, \tilde{\mathbf{m}}} = \begin{cases} \tilde{r}(\tilde{\mathbf{n}}, \tilde{\mathbf{m}}) \mathbf{W}^{\tilde{\mathbf{n}}} \mathbf{Q}_L^{\tilde{\mathbf{n}}}(i,k,j,l) \mathbf{V}^{\tilde{\mathbf{m}}}, \\ \qquad \text{if } \tilde{\mathbf{m}} = \tilde{\mathbf{n}} - \mathbf{e}_{i,k} + \mathbf{e}_{j,l} \ (\mathbf{n} \neq \mathbf{m}), \\ \mathbf{W}^{\tilde{\mathbf{n}}} \mathbf{Q}_L^{\tilde{\mathbf{n}}}(0) \mathbf{V}^{\tilde{\mathbf{n}}}, \\ \qquad \text{if } \tilde{\mathbf{n}} = \tilde{\mathbf{m}}, \\ \mathbf{0}, \\ \qquad \text{elsewhere.} \end{cases}$$

$$(6)$$

It is easy to show that $\tilde{\mathbf{Q}}$ results from $\mathbf{Q}$ by aggregation based on strict lumpability. Therefore all stationary results for the original HQN can be computed from the aggregated CTMC. $\tilde{\mathbf{Q}}$ is composed from LLM matrices.

The idea of finding lumpable partitions on a small subset of the state space which are also valid for the complete state space can also be used for the reduction of LLM state spaces. The approach is slightly more complicated than the reduction of the HLM state space and has been introduced in [1] in more detail.

Reduction of a LLM state space should not destroy the information which is used in the HLM about the internal LLM state, therefore the number of customers actually in the LLM has to visible in the state. Thus reduction of LLM j is performed on the subsets $Z_j(\mathbf{n})$.

Let $\tilde{Z}_j(\mathbf{n})$ be this reduced subset of states. A minimal representation of the state space for a *LLM* has to include at least one state per subset. Let Ω_j be a partition of Z_j which consists of a number a subpartitions $\Omega_j^{\mathbf{n}}$, one for each possible population vector $\mathbf{n}$. $\Omega_j^{\mathbf{n}}$ is a partition on $Z_j(\mathbf{n})$. Let $\mathbf{V}_j^{\mathbf{n}}$ be the collector matrix belonging to $\Omega_j^{\mathbf{n}}$. Lumpability now has to be defined according to all the matrices describing a *LLM*. We have to assure

$$\forall \mathbf{n} \text{ with } 0 \leq \mathbf{n}(k) \leq N_{j,k}, \forall 1 \leq k \leq K,$$
$$\forall I \in \{1, \ldots, \|\Omega_j^{\mathbf{n}}\|\}, \text{ and } \forall x, y \in \bar{\Omega}_j^{\mathbf{n}}(X)$$

that for an ordinarily lumpable partition Ω_j

$$|(\mathbf{e}_x - \mathbf{e}_y)\mathbf{Q}_j^{\mathbf{n}}\mathbf{V}_j^{\mathbf{n}}| = 0,$$
$$|(\mathbf{e}_x - \mathbf{e}_y)\mathbf{S}_j^{\mathbf{n}}[k]\mathbf{V}_j^{\mathbf{n}-\mathbf{e}_k}| = 0,$$
$$|(\mathbf{e}_x - \mathbf{e}_y)\mathbf{U}_j^{\mathbf{n}+\mathbf{e}_k}[k]\mathbf{V}_j^{\mathbf{n}+\mathbf{e}_k}| = 0,$$

hold, and for an exactly lumpable partition

$$|(\mathbf{e}_x - \mathbf{e}_y)(\mathbf{Q}_j^{\mathbf{n}})^T\mathbf{V}_j^{\mathbf{n}}| = 0,$$
$$|(\mathbf{e}_x - \mathbf{e}_y)(\mathbf{S}_j^{\mathbf{n}+\mathbf{e}_k}[k])^T\mathbf{V}_j^{\mathbf{n}+\mathbf{e}_k}| = 0,$$
$$|(\mathbf{e}_x - \mathbf{e}_y)(\mathbf{U}_j^{\mathbf{n}}[k])^T\mathbf{V}_j^{\mathbf{n}-\mathbf{e}_k}| = 0,$$

have to hold for all existing population vectors. The partition can be computed by an iterative algorithm, starting with a partition including only one partition group per population and refining this partition until the conditions for lumpability are met (see [1] for details). Since the algorithm is based only on the state space, it is used completely automatically for arbitrary *LLMs*, of course, additional informations about symmetries in the *LLM* can be exploited. Using the collector matrices and corresponding distributor matrices, the matrices for a reduced *LLM* are computed as

$$\tilde{\mathbf{Q}}_j^{\mathbf{n}} = \mathbf{W}_j^{\mathbf{n}}\mathbf{Q}_j^{\mathbf{n}}\mathbf{V}_j^{\mathbf{n}},$$
$$\tilde{\mathbf{U}}_j^{\mathbf{n}}[k] = \mathbf{W}_j^{\mathbf{n}-\mathbf{e}_k}\mathbf{U}_j^{\mathbf{n}}[k]\mathbf{V}_j^{\mathbf{n}},$$
$$\tilde{\mathbf{S}}_j^{\mathbf{n}}[k] = \mathbf{W}_j^{\mathbf{n}}\mathbf{S}_j^{\mathbf{n}}[k]\mathbf{V}_j^{\mathbf{n}-\mathbf{e}_k}.$$

Using the reduced instead of the original *LLM* matrices for the construction of the overall model yields a reduced MC with generator $\tilde{\mathbf{Q}}$. The following theorem has been proved in [1].

Theorem 4 *Let $\tilde{\mathbf{Q}}$ be the generator matrix of a reduced MC computed from reduced LLM matrices which result from an exactly/ordinarily lumpable partition as defined above, then the reduction from $\mathbf{Q}$ to $\tilde{\mathbf{Q}}$ is based on an exactly/ordinarily lumpable partition.*

If a *LLM* specification is used several times, then reduction has to be performed only once. Since the reduction of *LLMs* is completely independent from the environment, reduction can be performed in parallel for several *LLMs* and the *HLM*.

3.4 Computing results from the reduced MC

Normally. the interest of an analysis does not lie directly in the computation of the stationary or transient distribution. Instead the required results are much coarser. A very general concept for the specification of results are reward variables (see [15] for an introduction). The idea is to associate rewards with states or transitions. In MCs it is often sufficient to associate with each state x a reward $\mathbf{y}(x)$. The expectation of steady state reward is given by $\mathbf{p}\mathbf{y}^T$ and the instantaneous reward at time t is computed as $\mathbf{p}(t)\mathbf{y}$, where $\mathbf{y}$ is the vector of rewards. Rewards can be used to express several more application oriented measures like throughput, populations, or interarrival times. Applying theorem 1 yields the following results according to reward computation from the reduced MC.

- If the reduced MC results from ordinary lumpability, then the reward for all states in a partition group has to be identical to gain exact results [13].

- If the reduced MC results from exact lumpability, then stationary results can be computed for an arbitrary reward structure.

4 Nearly Lumpability
4.1 Nearly Exact/Ordinary Lumpability for MCs

The concept of exact/ordinary lumpability is based on identities of aggregated transition rates in the generator matrix. It is natural to define a less strict concept by allowing small differences between aggregated transition rates which yields the following definition for nearly ordinary/exact lumpability.

Definition 3 *Let $\mathbf{Q}$ be the irreducible generator matrix of a finite MC on state space Z and $\Omega = \{\Omega(1) \ldots \Omega(N)\}$ a partition of the state space with collector matrix $\mathbf{V}$.*

- *Ω is $(\epsilon\text{-})$nearly ordinarily lumpable, iff for all $\Omega(X) \in \Omega$ and $x, y \in \Omega(X)$:*
  $|(\mathbf{e}_x - \mathbf{e}_y)\mathbf{Q}\mathbf{V}| \leq \epsilon q_{max}$
- *Ω is $(\epsilon\text{-})$nearly exactly lumpable, iff for all $\Omega(X) \in \Omega$ and $x, y \in \Omega(X)$:*
  $|(\mathbf{e}_x - \mathbf{e}_y)\mathbf{Q}^T\mathbf{V}| \leq \epsilon q_{max}$
- *Ω is $(\epsilon\text{-})$nearly strictly lumpable, iff it is $(\epsilon\text{-})$nearly ordinarily and $(\epsilon\text{-})$nearly exactly lumpable.*

Where $0 < \epsilon << 1.0$ and $q_{max} = \max_{x \in Z}(|\mathbf{Q}(x,x)|)$.

For the aggregated MC resulting from a $(\epsilon\text{-})$nearly exactly/ordinarily lumpable partition Theorem 1 does, of course, not hold, but if ϵ is sufficiently small we can expect a rather good approximation with an error in $O(\epsilon)$. Often it is important to get more information about the aggregation error, e.g. by computing bounds on the error or the results.

Bounds on stationary results can be computed as a particular application of the bounded aggregation method [9]. The approach has been applied to nearly ordinarily lumpable MCs in [4,10]. The approach is based on lower/upper bound for the transition rates of the reduced MC: The corresponding matrices can be defined element-wise as

$$\tilde{\mathbf{Q}}^-(X,Y) = \min_{x\in\Omega(X)}(\sum_{y\in\Omega(Y)}\mathbf{Q}(x,y))$$
$$\tilde{\mathbf{Q}}^+(X,Y) = \max_{x\in\Omega(X)}(\sum_{y\in\Omega(Y)}\mathbf{Q}(x,y))$$

The matrices can be transformed into discrete time transition matrices $\tilde{\mathbf{P}}^- = \tilde{\mathbf{Q}}^-/q_{max} + \mathbf{I}$ and $\tilde{\mathbf{P}}^+ = \tilde{\mathbf{Q}}^+/q_{max} + \mathbf{I}$, where $q_{max} = \max_{X\in\tilde{Z}}|\tilde{\mathbf{Q}}^-(X,X)|$. Bounds on the stationary solution vector $\tilde{\mathbf{p}}$ can be determined as shown in the following theorem (see [9]).

Theorem 5 *Let $\mathbf{P}$ be a N-dimensional, irreducible stochastic matrix and $\mathbf{P}^-$ be a lower bound for $\mathbf{P}$ (i.e. $\mathbf{P}^- \leq \mathbf{P}$), then the steady state probability vector $\mathbf{p}$ of $\mathbf{P}$ can be expressed as $\mathbf{p} = \mathbf{bZ}$, where $\mathbf{Z} = \overline{(\mathbf{I} - \mathbf{P}^-)^{-1}}$, $\mathbf{b} \geq 0$, $\mathbf{be}^T = 1.0$, $\mathbf{b}(x) = 0$ for $x \notin \mathcal{J}$, and $\mathcal{J} = \{x \in \{1,\ldots,N\}, s.t. \exists y : \mathbf{P}(y,x) > \mathbf{P}^-(y,x)\}$. Bounds for $\mathbf{p}$ can be determined as*

$$\max(\min_{z\in\mathcal{J}}\mathbf{Z}(z,x), 1 - \sum_{y\neq x}\max_{z\in\mathcal{J}}\mathbf{Z}(z,y)) \leq \mathbf{p}(x)$$
$$\leq \min(\max_{z\in\mathcal{J}}\mathbf{Z}(z,x), 1 - \sum_{y\neq x}\min_{z\in\mathcal{J}}\mathbf{Z}(z,y))$$

The vectors including upper and lower bounds are denoted by $\mathbf{p}^+$ and $\mathbf{p}^-$, respectively.

A similar theorem with some additional constraints can be defined for the upper bound matrix. An alternative approach for bound computation and some slight extensions is proposed in [10]. We will not introduce this approach here, however, it can obviously be used, since it relies only on the availability of the matrices $\tilde{\mathbf{P}}^-$ and $\tilde{\mathbf{P}}^+$. Bound computation can be expensive for larger matrices $\mathbf{P}^-$.

It should be noticed that the difference $\tilde{\mathbf{P}}^+(X,Y) - \tilde{\mathbf{P}}^-(X,Y) \leq \epsilon$ for nearly ordinarily lumpable partitions. If the partition is only nearly exactly lumpable, then the relation does not hold and the bounds might become bad. For a partition which is nearly exact but not nearly ordinarily lumpable no satisfactory bounds for the stationary solution vector can be computed regardless of the size of ϵ.

4.2 Nearly Lumpability in HQNs

Nearly lumpability in HQNs can be caused by nearly symmetric and identical *LLMs*, reduction of a single *LLM* based on nearly lumpability and by symmetric nearly identical *LLMs*. Of course, also the combination of these concepts is possible.

4.2.1 Nearly symmetric LLMs

Let us start with the first, identical and nearly symmetric *LLMs*. We define a partition Ω resulting from a set of permutations Π which implies the following condition for the routing probabilities for all $\pi \in \Pi$ and some $\epsilon \ll 1$.

$$|r(i,k,j,l,\mathbf{n}) - r(\pi(i,k,j,l),\pi(\mathbf{n}))| \leq \epsilon \quad (7)$$

We can define bounds on the routing probabilities $r^-(\mathbf{n},\mathbf{m})$ and $r^-(\mathbf{n},\mathbf{m})$, using these bounds for the computation of the generator matrix yields bounding matrices $\tilde{\mathbf{Q}}^-$ and $\tilde{\mathbf{Q}}^+$, these bounding matrices can be used to determine bounds for the steady state distribution as shown above.

4.2.2 Nearly lumpable partitions for LLMs

To define nearly exact/ordinary lumpability for an isolated *LLM* we have to extend the definition of exact/ordinary lumpability yielding

$$|(\mathbf{e}_x - \mathbf{e}_y)\mathbf{Q}_j^{\mathbf{n}}\mathbf{V}_j^{\mathbf{n}}| \leq \epsilon q_{max},$$
$$|(\mathbf{e}_x - \mathbf{e}_y)\mathbf{S}_j^{\mathbf{n}}[k]\mathbf{V}_j^{\mathbf{n}-\mathbf{e}_k}| \leq \epsilon q_{max},$$
$$|(\mathbf{e}_x - \mathbf{e}_y)\mathbf{U}_j^{\mathbf{n}+\mathbf{e}_k}[k]\mathbf{V}_j^{\mathbf{n}+\mathbf{e}_k}| \leq \epsilon,$$

for ordinary lumpability and

$$|(\mathbf{e}_x - \mathbf{e}_y)(\mathbf{Q}_j^{\mathbf{n}})^T\mathbf{V}_j^{\mathbf{n}}| \leq \epsilon q_{max},$$
$$|(\mathbf{e}_x - \mathbf{e}_y)(\mathbf{S}_j^{\mathbf{n}+\mathbf{e}_k}[k])^T\mathbf{V}_j^{\mathbf{n}+\mathbf{e}_k}| \leq \epsilon q_{max},$$
$$|(\mathbf{e}_x - \mathbf{e}_y)(\mathbf{U}_j^{\mathbf{n}}[k])^T\mathbf{V}_j^{\mathbf{n}-\mathbf{e}_k}| \leq \epsilon,$$

for exact lumpability (see [1] for further details). The value q_{max} equals $\max_{x\in Z}|\mathbf{Q}(x,x)|$. With the collector and distributor matrices an aggregated *LLM* can be computed. If the aggregated instead of the original *LLM* is used in the *HLM*, then a reduced generator $\tilde{\mathbf{Q}}$ is computed which results from $\mathbf{Q}$ by nearly exact/ordinary lumpability. In the same way lower and upper bounds for the matrix elements of the *LLM* matrices can be computed yielding lower and upper bounds for the matrix $\tilde{\mathbf{Q}}$ when embedded in the *HLM*.

4.2.3 Nearly symmetric and nearly identical LLMs

Symmetry of nearly identical *LLMs* is more complex. The question is how to define nearly identical *LLMs*. We use the following definition. Two *LLMs* i and j are nearly identical, if they can be reduced by a nearly exactly/ordinarily lumpable partition such that

- the state spaces $\tilde{Z}_i(\mathbf{n})$ and $\tilde{Z}_j(\mathbf{n})$ have the same dimension and

- the elements in the $\tilde{\mathbf{S}}-$, $\tilde{\mathbf{Q}}-$ matrices differ at most by ϵq_{max} and the elements in the $\tilde{\mathbf{U}}-$ matrices differ at most by ϵ after appropriate reordering of states.

Under the above conditions the reduced MC and also upper/lower bounds for the elements of the corresponding generator matrix can be computed. Results and bounds on the results for nearly lumpable MCs resulting from HQNs can be computed as shown in section 4.1. If rewards for states in one partition group are different, then for a lower bound the lowest reward, for an upper bound the largest reward and for an approximation an average reward is assigned to the state in the reduced MC representing the partition group. Let $\tilde{\mathbf{y}}^-$ and $\tilde{\mathbf{y}}^+$ the reward vectors including the minimum and maximum reward for each aggregated state and let $\tilde{\mathbf{p}}^-$ and $\tilde{\mathbf{p}}^+$ be the bounds for the aggregated steady state probabilities. $\mathbf{p}$ and $\mathbf{y}$ are the corresponding vectors for the non-reduced

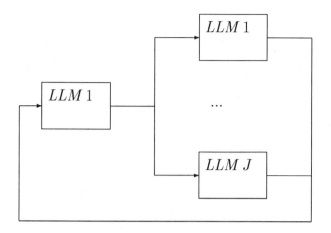

Figure 1: *HLM* structure.

MC. Bounds for the expected reward in steady state can be computed using the matrix $\mathbf{Z}$ and the set of indices $\mathcal{J}$ from theorem 5.

$$\min_{i \in \mathcal{J}}(\mathbf{e}_i \mathbf{Z}(\tilde{\mathbf{y}}^-)^T) \leq \mathbf{p} \mathbf{y}^T \leq \max_{i \in \mathcal{J}}(\mathbf{e}_i \mathbf{Z}(\tilde{\mathbf{y}}^+)^T) \qquad (8)$$

5   An Example

We consider a simple example. The *HLM* is shown in Fig. 1 and structured like a central server including a *LLM* 1 of type 1 and $J - 1$ identical *LLMs* of type 2. The model includes a single customer class with population N, a customer visits first *LLM* 1 chooses afterwards with equal probabilities one of the *LLMs* 2 to j and returns to *LLM* 1. All service times are exponentially distributed.

LLM 1 consists of J_1 identical PS stations. A customer requires a service time with mean λ^{-1} at a station. A newly arriving customer chooses the station with the least number of customers actually served, if this station is not unique, the station with the smallest index is chosen. Observe that due to the latter assumption the stations in the *LLM* are not symmetric, stations with a smaller index will have a higher utilization. Assume that the throughput and mean population for *LLM* 1 should be computed, via Little's theorem the mean sojourn time can be computed from these measures. Thus two reward vectors are needed, first distinguishing states according to the actual population and, second, assigning a reward equal to the number of non-idle stations multiplied with λ to each state.

The *LLMs* 2 to J all include a single station with 2 servers. An arriving customer needs with probability p both servers simultaneously and completes his request after he has been served by both servers. With probability $1 - p$ only 1 server is required. Requests are served in FCFS order. The mean service time in the first case is μ_w, in the second case μ_r. We assume that only the mean population should be computed for the *LLMs* 2 to J, such that rewards are assigned to states according to the mean population in the *LLM*. The

throughput equals $(J - 1)^{-1}$ times the throughput of *LLM* 1.

Let us start with the *HLM*. Since the *LLMs* 2 to J are identical and symmetric the underlying MRP is invariant under permutations changing these *LLM* indices. Exploiting this symmetry the *HLM* state space is reduced significantly. Since the reduction is based on complete symmetries it is based on strict lumpability yielding exact results for arbitrary reward structures.

The next step is the consider exact reduction of the *LLMs*. It has been mentioned that the stations of *LLM* 1 are identical but not symmetric, thus the *LLM* is not invariant under permutations changing the station indices. However, we can still find a partition that is ordinarily lumpable and allows the computation of the required quantities. The structure of *LLM* 1 is introduced first. States can be described by a J_1 dimensional vector $\mathbf{n}$ including in position $\mathbf{n}(i)$ the actual number of customers in station i. From a given state two possible transitions can occur.

- The arrival of a customer when $\sum_{i=1}^{J_1} \mathbf{n}(i) < N$ yielding a new state $\mathbf{m}$ resulting from $\mathbf{n}$ by adding 1 to $\mathbf{n}(i)$ such that $i = \min(j|\mathbf{n}(j) = \min_k(\mathbf{n}(k)))$.

- The departure of a customer yielding a successor state $\mathbf{n} - \mathbf{e}_i$ for some $i \in \{1, \ldots, J_1\}$ where $\mathbf{n}(i) > 0$. The transition rate for each possible departure is μ.

Now, consider the partition which collects states $\mathbf{n}$ and $\mathbf{m}$ in the same partition group, if a permutation of the indices exists such that the vectors are identical after permutation. We show that this partition is ordinarily lumpable. Let $\mathbf{n}$ and $\mathbf{m}$ be two states from a partition group and let π be a permutation transforming $\mathbf{n}$ into $\mathbf{m}$. The population of the *LLM* is the same for both states, therefore an arrival is either possible for all or for none of the states from a partition group. If an arrival occurs, then the successor state is uniquely given as $\mathbf{n}'$ or $\mathbf{m}'$, respectively. It is easy to show that $\mathbf{m}'$ equals $\pi(\mathbf{n}')$ such that both are in the same partition group. Thus the conditions for ordinary lumpability according to arrivals are observed. The situation for departures is similar. First the total departure rate for states from a partition group is the same since the number of idle servers is the same. Each departure from station i corresponds to a departure from station j such that $i = \pi(j)$ and therefore also $\pi(\mathbf{n} - \mathbf{e}_i) = \mathbf{m} - \mathbf{e}_j$ which implies together with identical rates the conditions for ordinary lumpability according to the $\mathbf{S}$- and $\mathbf{Q}$-matrices. Finally, the conditions on the rewards still have to be checked. However, these conditions are satisfied since the mean population and the number of idle servers for states from a partition group are identical. It is worth to mention that the partition is not exactly lumpable, therefore, results specific to a subset of the servers in *LLM* 1 cannot be computed from the reduced model.

The second *LLM* type cannot be specified directly as a standard QN, however, several extensions to QNs exist in the literature that allow the specification of the required behavior. The first observation is that the two servers of the station are identical and symmetric, so that the concrete server identity is not needed, however, an appropriate transformation of the QN specification to the state space might be available which does not distinguish between the servers. The *LLM* can be interpreted as a model of mirrored disk system [18] with two disks. Each disk includes identical information, a request using one server is a *read request* which can be satisfied by one of the disks, a request needing both servers is a *write request* which requires that identical information is written to both disks. Write request which write the same information on both disks are denoted as siblins. We will use the notation read and write request to describe the states of the *LLM*. The subspaces $Z_j(n)$ $(2 \leq j \leq J)$ are all identical for $n \geq 2$ and are different for $n = 1$. $Z_j(1)$ contains the following states.

1. One read request is served by one of the servers;

2. Two write requests are served by the servers, both are siblings;

3. One write request is served by one server, its sibling has completed its task;

For $Z_j(n)$ with $n \geq 2$ we have the following states.

1. Two read requests are served by the servers;

2. One read request and one write request is served, the write request is the first of a pair;

3. One read request and one write request is served, the write request is the second of a pair;

4. Two write request are served, both are siblins;

5. Two write requests are served belonging to different pairs, one request is the first and the other one is the second of a pair;

6. Two write requests are served belonging to different pairs, both are the second of a pair;

We number in the following states as described above. If both servers are not identical or are distinguished, then the state spaces would contain 5 and 9 states, respectively. For this *LLM* type, a lumpable partition which is independent from the parameter settings cannot be found. Assume now that $\mu_w = \mu_r = \mu$ and consider the partition

$$1') \quad (1,3) \quad 2') \quad (2) \quad \text{for } Z_j(1)$$

and

$$1') \ (1,3,6) \quad 2') \ (2,5) \quad 3') \quad (4) \text{ for } Z_j(n) \ n \geq 2 \ .$$

States in brackets belong to one partition group. The partition is ordinarily, but not exactly lumpable. Since states of a subset $Z_j(n)$ all have identical rewards an aggregated representation according to this partition can be computed.

The reduction has to be computed for the *LLM* type and can be used to represent the *LLMs* 2 to J. If $\mu_w = \mu_r = \mu$ and additionally $p = 1 - p = 0.5$, then

N	orig.	red. ($\mu_r \neq \mu_w$)	red. ($\mu_r = \mu_w$)
		$J = 3$	
5	508	184	68
10	4468	1345	402
		$J = 5$	
5	6937	414	123
10	383272	13367	2046

Table 1: State space original and reduced processes

ϵ	p	Throughput		
		lower bound	exact	upper bound
		Throughput		
0.005	0.1	2.345	2.408	2.439
	0.5	1.925	1.953	1.981
0.01	0.1	2.290	2.415	2.476
	0.5	1.900	1.956	2.012
0.05	0.1	1.917	2.466	2.726
	0.5	1.563	1.975	2.335
0.1	0.1	1.568	2.527	2.961
	0.5	1.288	1.998	2.617
		Mean Population		
0.005	0.1	1.575	1.621	1.668
	0.5	1.181	1.202	1.224
0.01	0.1	1.538	1.628	1.720
	0.5	1.162	1.204	1.247
0.05	0.1	1.283	1.681	2.088
	0.5	0.954	1.221	1.679
0.1	0.1	1.046	1.744	2.453
	0.5	0.781	1.241	2.049

Table 2: Bound and exact values for $\mu_r \neq \mu_w$.

an exactly lumpable partition can be found by putting the states 1 and 2 from each subset $Z_j(n)$ $(n \geq 2)$ in partition group, these partition is not ordinarily lumpable.

The small example shows that lumpability and related exact aggregation approaches go beyond complete symmetries in a model. Additionally the reduced representation of a model can be computed efficiently using the methods presented here. To show the effects of reduction Table 1 includes the size of the state space for the original and the two aggregated versions for different values of J and N, J_1 is set to 2 in all cases. For larger populations and number of *LLMs* we get a significant reduction. The generator matrix describing the reduced process can be represented by the matrices for *LLM* types 1 and 2 using tensor operations. Exploiting this representation in iterative numerical analysis approaches as proposed in [3] allows the efficient analysis of fairly large models.

To show the capabilities of nearly lumpability we assume that $\mu_r \approx \mu_w$ such that the above reduction of the state space of *LLM* type 2 is only nearly ordinarily lumpable. We fix the following parameter values $\lambda = 2.0$, $\mu_w = 1.0$ and $\mu_r = 1 + \epsilon$. The model is analyzed for $J = 3$, $N = 5$, $p = 0.1$, 0.5 and $\epsilon = 0.005$, 0.01, 0.05, 0.1. The corresponding bounds and exact results for the throughput and the mean population of LLM 1 are shown in Table 2. The bounds are rather tight in particular for smaller differences in the service requirements.

In a similar way, a nearly ordinarily lumpable partition can be computed when the transition probability from LLM 1 into the $LLMs$ 2 to J is only approximately identical. Apart from the bounds we can also compute approximate solution from the aggregated model, by setting $\tilde{\mathbf{Q}}(X,Y) = 0.5(\tilde{\mathbf{Q}}^+(X,Y) + \tilde{\mathbf{Q}}^-(X,Y))$. The corresponding set of equations can be analyzed by standard means, however, the size of the resulting approximation error is unknown.

6   Conclusion and perspectives

We have presented here a new approach for exact and approximative aggregation in hierarchical queueing networks. It is shown that aggregation can be performed on small parts of a hierarchical model and conditions are preserved when combining this part with an arbitrary environment. The approach extends earlier work in several directions. Conditions for "exact" aggregation are extended by distinguishing exact and ordinary lumpability, approximative aggregation based on nearly exact/ordinary lumpability is introduced and an algorithmic approach for aggregation construction is presented. Although we have presented the technique here in the context of hierarchical queueing networks, it is possible to extend and use it in the context of other modeling paradigms. Aggregation approaches are very important for complex system analysis. In particular we think that a hierarchical approach fits very well in system design since many systems are hierarchically structured. Conditions for lumpability are often met by real systems in particular from the multiprocessor area. In particular it should be pointed out that nearly complete decomposable systems [8] are also nearly lumpable according to our definition.

Acknowledgements

I thank the anonymous referees for their detailed comments.

References

[1] P. Buchholz; The Aggregation of Markovian Submodels in Isolation; *Universität Dortmund, Fachbereich Informatik, Forschungsbericht Nr. 369 (1990) (submitted for publication)*.

[2] P. Buchholz; Hierarchical Markovian Models - Symmetries and Aggregation-; in: J. Hillston, R. Pooley (eds.), *Comp. Perf. Eval. 92, Edinburgh University Press (1993) 305-320*.

[3] P. Buchholz; A Class of Hierarchical Queueing Networks and Their Analysis, *Queueing Systems 15 (1994) 59-80*.

[4] P. Buchholz; Exact and Ordinary Lumpability in Finite Markov Chains; *Journ. of Appl. Prob. 15 (1994) 207-224*.

[5] P. Buchholz; Equivalence Relations for Stochastic Automata Networks; in: W. J. Stewart (ed.), *Computation with Markov Chains, Kluwer (1995) 197-216*.

[6] G. Chiola, C. Dutheillet, G. Franceschinis, S. Haddad; Stochastic Well-Formed Coloured Nets and Multiprocessor modeling Applications; in: K. Jensen, G. Rozenberg (ed.), *High Level Petri Nets. Theo. and Appl., Springer (1991) 504-530*.

[7] G. Ciardo, K. Trivedi; A decomposition approach for stochastic Petri net models; in: *Proc. Int. Workshop of Petri Nets anf Perf. Models, IEEE Press (1991) 74-83*.

[8] P.J. Courtois; Decomposability: Queueing and Computer System Applications; *Academic Press (1977)*.

[9] P.J. Courtois, P. Semal; Bounds for the Positive Eigenvectors of Nonnegative Matrices and Their Approximation by Decomposition; *JACM 31 (1984) 804-825*.

[10] J. Franceschinis, R. Muntz; Bounds for Quasi-Lumpable Markov Chains; *Performance Evaluation 20 (1994) 223-244*.

[11] J. Franceschinis, R. Muntz; Computing bounds for the performance indices of quasi-lumpable Stochastic Well-Formed Nets; *IEEE Trans. on Softw. Eng. 20 (1994) 516-525*.

[12] J.G. Kemeny, J.L. Snell; Finite Markov Chains; *Springer (1976)*.

[13] V. F. Nicola; Lumping in Markov reward processes; *IBM Res. Rep. RC 14719 (1989)*.

[14] W.H. Sanders, J.F. Meyer; Reduced Base Model Construction Methods for Stochastic Activity Networks; *IEEE Journ. on Select. Areas in Comm. 9 (1991) 25-36*.

[15] W.H. Sanders, J.F. Meyer; A unified approach for specifying measures of performance, dependability, and performability; in: A. Avizienis, J. Laprie (eds.), *Dependable Computing for Critical Applications, Springer (1991)*.

[16] P. Schweitzer; Aggregation Methods for Large Markov Chains; *Math. Comp. Perf. and Relia.; (eds.) G. Iazeolla, P. J. Courtois, A. Hordijk; North Holland (1984) 275-285*.

[17] U. Sumita, M. Rieders; Lumpability and Time Reversibility in the Aggregation-Disaggregation Method for large Markov Chains; *Stochastic Models 5 (1989) 63-81*.

[18] D. Towsley, S Chen, S. P. Yu; Performance Analysis of a Fault Tolerant Mirrored Disk System; in: P. J. B. King, I. Mitrani, R. J. Pooley (eds.), *Performance 90, North Holland (1990) 239-253*.

Computation of Absorption Probability Distributions of continuous-time Markov Chains using Regenerative Randomization

Angel Calderón and Juan A. Carrasco

Departament d'Enginyería Electrònica

Universitat Politécnica de Catalunya

Diagonal 647, plta. 9, 08028 Barcelona, Spain

Abstract

Randomization is a popular method for the transient solution of continuous-time Markov models. Its primary advantages over other methods (i.e., ODE solvers) are robustness and ease of implementation. It is however well-known that the performance of the method deteriorates with the "stiffness" of the model: the number of required steps to solve the model up to time t tends to Λt for $\Lambda t \to \infty$, where Λ is the maximum output rate. For measures like the unreliability Λt can be very large for the t of interest, making the randomization method very unefficient. In this paper we consider such measures and propose a new solution method called regenerative randomization *which exploits the regenerative structure of the model and can be far more efficient. Regarding the number of steps required in regenerative randomization we prove that: 1) it is smaller than the number of steps required in standard randomization when the initial distribution is concentrated in a single state, 2) for $\Lambda t \to \infty$, it is upper bounded by a function $O(\log(\Lambda t/\epsilon))$, where ϵ is the desired approximation error bound. Using a reliability example we analyze the performance and stability of the method.*

Keywords: Randomization, continuous-time Markov chains, regenerative models, reliability, transient solution.

1 Introduction

Continuous-time Markov chains (CTMC's) are often used for performance, dependability and performability modeling. The transient analysis of these models is usually significantly more costly than the steady-state analysis, and very costly in absolute terms when the CTMC model is large. This makes the development of efficient transient analysis techniques for CTMC's a research topic of great interest. Commonly used methods are ODE solvers and randomization. Good recent reviews can be found in [Rei88] and [Mal94]. The randomization method (also called uniformization) is numerically very stable and easy to implement. It was first proposed by Jensen [Jen53] and has been applied to analyze performance models [Gra77], [Gro84], dependability models [Koh82], [Rei88], and performability models [Qur93]. The randomization method is based on the following result. Let $X = \{X(t); t \geq 0\}$ be a CTMC with state space Ω; let λ_{ij}, $i, j \in \Omega$ be the transition rates of X and let $\lambda_i = \sum_{j \in \Omega} \lambda_{ij}$, $i \in \Omega$ be the output rates of X. Consider any $\Lambda \geq \max_{i \in \Omega} \lambda_i$ (usually Λ is taken to be $\max_{i \in \Omega} \lambda_i$), and define the discrete-time Markov chain (DTMC) $Y = \{Y_k; k = 0, 1, 2, \ldots\}$ with same state space and initial distribution as X and jump probabilities $q_{ij} = \lambda_{ij}/\Lambda$, $i \neq j$, $q_{ii} = 1 - \lambda_i/\Lambda$. Let $N = \{N(t); t \geq 0\}$ be a Poisson process with arrival rate Λ. Then, $X(t) = Y_{N(t)}$. A recent, short proof of the result with very general conditions on X can be found in [Dij90]. These conditions are satisfied if, as we assume, X is finite.

The randomization equation gives immediately an esqueme for the computation of the transient probabilities of X, but it can also be exploited to compute more complex measures such as the distribution of the interval availability [Sou86], [Rub93] and the distribution of performability [Sou89]. In this paper we assume that X is a transient CTMC with state space $\Omega^t \cup \{a\}$, where a is an absorbing state and all states in Ω^t are transient, and consider the absorption probability by time t, $AP(t) = P[X(t) = a]$. The unreliability is an example of such a measure. Using the randomization equation:

$$AP(t) = \sum_{k=0}^{\infty} P[X(t) = a]\frac{(\Lambda t)^k}{k!}e^{-\Lambda t}.$$

In a practical implementation of the randomization method, the infinite series is approximated by truncating the series up to a given number of randomization steps, K, and the approximation error is bounded:

$$AP^a(t) = \sum_{k=0}^{K} P[X(t) = a]\frac{(\Lambda t)^k}{k!}e^{-\Lambda t},$$

92

$$AP(t) - AP^a(t) \leq \sum_{k=K+1}^{\infty} \frac{(\Lambda t)^k}{k!} e^{-\Lambda t} = AP^\epsilon(t),$$

where $AP^a(t)$ is the approximation and $AP^\epsilon(t)$ upper bounds the approximation error. Taking a large enough M, $AP^\epsilon(t)$ can be computed using a finite number of terms with arbitrary accuracy as:

$$AP^\epsilon(t) \approx \sum_{k=K+1}^{M-1} \frac{(\Lambda t)^k}{k!} e^{-\Lambda t} + \frac{1}{1-\frac{\Lambda t}{M}} \frac{(\Lambda t)^M}{M!} e^{-\Lambda t}.$$

Using the well known result that $N(t)$ has an asymptotic normal distribution with mean and variance Λt, it is easy to show that, for large Λt, the number of steps required in the randomization method is $\approx \Lambda t$, almost independent of the required approximation error. Often we are interested in solving the model for values of t for which Λt is large, and in such cases randomization is unefficient. Consider for instance a reliability model of a repairable fault-tolerant system. For such a model Λ is of the order of the maximum repair rate while the t of interest can be large. With a model including hot restarts, Λ can be as large as $1\,\text{min}^{-1}$, while the t of interest could be 1 year, yielding $\Lambda t = 525,600$. Using the randomization method we are bound to solve Y for more than half a million steps! If X is large this may be *extremely* expensive.

Several approaches have been proposed to alleviate the problem. Miller has used selective randomization to solve reliability models with detailed representation of error handling activities [Mil83]. Reibman and Trivedi [Rei88] have proposed a more general approach based on the multistep concept which works very well when the transition probability matrix is dense. Denoting by Q the transition probability matrix of Y and by $\pi(k)$ the probability distribution row vector of Y at step k, we have $\pi(k + S) = \pi(k)Q^S$, where S is the length of the multistep. Then, computing Q^S explicitly, the number of vector-matrix multiplications can be reduced significantly exploiting the fact that for large Λt the number of $\pi(k)$'s with significant contributions to the randomization formula is of the order of $\sqrt{\Lambda t}$. However, if Q is sparse Q^S can be much denser than Q, and the number of floating point operations can still be large. Adaptive uniformization [Moo93] is a recent method in which the randomization rate is adapted depending on the states in which the randomized DTMC can be in at a given step. For some models, adaptive randomization can be faster than the standard method. In addition, it can be used to solve models with infinite state spaces and not uniformly bounded transition rates. Another recent proposal to speed up the randomization method is steady-state detection [Mal94]. This technique will be efficient if the steady-state is reached fast, but for for many models (for instance, reliability models of repairable fault-tolerant systems) the steady state is reached very slowly and the technique will not help. More recently, we have proposed [Car94] a method

called *regenerative randomization* for the computation of measures like the steady-state availability and the expected interval availability which can be expressed as the transient reward rate or mean interval reward rate of rewarded regenerative CTMC models. Unlike standard randomization, our method is measure specific. In this paper we extend the regenerative randomization method to the computation of $AP(t)$ and investigate its theoretical properties. We show that when the initial distribution of X is concentrated in a single state (a very common case) regenerative randomization requires at most the same number of steps than standard randomization. Furthermore, for large Λt, the number of steps required to achieve an approximation error $\leq \epsilon$ is $O(\log(\Lambda t/\epsilon))$. In Section 2 we derive the regenerative randomization method for $AP(t)$. Section 3 includes the proofs of the theoretical properties of the method. Section 4 analyzes the method compared to standard randomization using a reliability model. Section 5 concludes the paper.

2 Regenerative randomization

Regenerative randomization requires the selection of a transient state $u \in \Omega^t$. Let $\alpha_i = P[X(0) = i] = P[Y_0 = i]$, $i \in \Omega$, and assume $P[X(0) = a] = 0$. Let $\Omega_u^t = \Omega^t - \{u\}$. Let $Z = \{Z_k; k = 0, 1, 2, \ldots\}$ be the transient DTMC following Y from u till reentry in u. The state space of Z is $\Omega^t \cup \{a, b\}$, where both a and b are absorbing states. $Z_0 = u$ and Z enters b when Y enters u. The transition probabilities of Z are:

$$
\begin{aligned}
P[Z_{k+1} = j | Z_k = i] &= P[Y_{k+1} = j | Y_k = i], \\
P[Z_{k+1} = b | Z_k = i] &= P[Y_{k+1} = u | Y_k = i], \\
P[Z_{k+1} = a | Z_k = a] &= P[Y_{k+1} = b | Y_k = b] = 1,
\end{aligned}
$$

with $i \in \Omega^t$, $j \in \Omega_u^t \cup a$.

Let $Z' = \{Z_k'; k = 0, 1, 2, \ldots\}$ be the transient DTMC with state space $\Omega_u^t \cup \{a, b\}$, where both a and b are absorbing states, following Y except that Z' remains in b if Y has been in u. The initial distribution of Z' is $P[Z_0' = i] = \alpha_i$, $i \in \Omega_u^t$, $P[Z_0' = b] = \alpha_u$, and its transition probabilities are:

$$
\begin{aligned}
P[Z_{k+1}' = j | Z_k' = i] &= P[Y_{k+1} = j | Y_k = i], \\
P[Z_{k+1}' = b | Z_k' = i] &= P[Y_{k+1} = u | Y_k = i], \\
P[Z_{k+1}' = a | Z_k' = a] &= P[Y_{k+1} = b | Y_k = b] = 1,
\end{aligned}
$$

with $i \in \Omega_u^t$, $j \in \Omega_u^t \cup \{a\}$.

In the following let $\pi_i(k) = P[Z_k = i]$, $\pi_i'(k) = P[Z_k' = i]$.

The regenerative randomization formula is obtained considering a discrete-time stochastic process $W = \{W_k; k = 0, 1, 2, \ldots\}$, with state space $\{0, 1, 2, \ldots\} \cup \{0', 1', 2', \ldots\} \cup \{a\}$, defined from Y as follows:

$$
W_k = \begin{cases}
l & \text{if } Y_{k-l} = u \wedge Y_m \in \Omega_u^t, k - l < m \leq k \\
k' & \text{if } Y_m \in \Omega_u^t, 0 \leq m \leq k \\
a & \text{if } Y_k = a
\end{cases}
$$

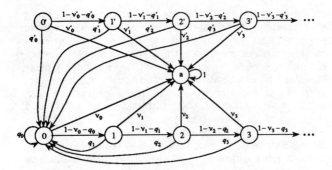

Figure 1: State transition diagram of the DTMC W.

Informally, $W_k = l$ if Y has visited u by time k, has not been absorbed, and has made its last visit to u l steps before the current step, k; $W_k = k'$ if Y has not visited u by time k and has not been absorbed; and $W_k = a$ if Y has been absorbed.

Proposition 1 *Let $a(k) = \sum_{i \in \Omega^t} \pi_i(k)$, $a'(k) = \sum_{i \in \Omega_u^t} \pi_i'(k)$, $v_k = (\pi_a(k+1) - \pi_a(k))/a(k)$, $q_k = (\pi_b(k+1) - \pi_b(k))/a(k)$, $v_k' = (\pi_a'(k+1) - \pi_a'(k))/a'(k)$, $q_k' = (\pi_b'(k+1) - \pi_b'(k))/a'(k)$. Then, W is an homogeneous discrete-time Markov chain with initial probability distribution $P[W_0 = 0] = \alpha_u$, $P[W_0 = 0'] = 1 - \alpha_u$, $P[W_0 = i] = 0$, $i \notin \{0, 0'\}$ and the state transition diagram shown in Figure 1.*

Proof The initial distribution of W follows inmediately from the definition. It is also clear that: 1) $W_k \in \{0, 1, \ldots, k, k', a\}$, 2) from a state l, W can only jump to states a, 0, or $l+1$, and 3) from a state k', W can only jump to states a, 0, or $(k+1)'$. We will compute all transition probabilities at a given step k and show that they only depend on the "from" state.

Case a ($W_k = l, 0 \leq l \leq k$):

$$P[W_{k+1} = a|W_k = l] = \frac{P[W_k = l \wedge W_{k+1} = a]}{P[W_k = l]}$$

$$= \frac{P[Y_{k-l} = u \wedge Y_m \in \Omega_u^t, k - l < m \leq k \wedge Y_{k+1} = a]}{P[Y_{k-l} = u \wedge Y_m \in \Omega_u^t, k - l < m \leq k]}$$

$$= \frac{P[Y_m \in \Omega_u^t, k - l < m \leq k \wedge Y_{k+1} = a|Y_{k-l} = u]}{P[Y_m \in \Omega_u^t, k - l < m \leq k|Y_{k-l} = u]}$$

$$= \frac{P[Z_l \in \Omega^t \wedge Z_{l+1} = a]}{P[Z_l \in \Omega^t]} = \frac{P[Z_{l+1} = a] - P[Z_l = a]}{P[Z_l \in \Omega^t]}$$

$$= \frac{\pi_a(l+1) - \pi_a(l)}{a(l)} = v_l,$$

$$P[W_{k+1} = 0|W_k = l] = \frac{P[W_k = l \wedge W_{k+1} = 0]}{P[W_k = l]}$$

$$= \frac{P[Y_{k-l} = u \wedge Y_m \in \Omega_u^t, k - l < m \leq k \wedge Y_{k+1} = u]}{P[Y_{k-l} = u \wedge Y_m \in \Omega_u^t, k - l < m \leq k]}$$

$$= \frac{P[Y_m \in \Omega_u^t, k - l < m \leq k \wedge Y_{k+1} = u|Y_{k-l} = u]}{P[Y_m \in \Omega_u^t, k - l < m \leq k|Y_{k-l} = u]}$$

$$= \frac{P[Z_l \in \Omega^t \wedge Z_{l+1} = b]}{P[Z_l \in \Omega^t]} = \frac{P[Z_{l+1} = b] - P[Z_l = b]}{P[Z_l \in \Omega^t]}$$

$$= \frac{\pi_b(l+1) - \pi_b(l)}{a(l)} = q_l,$$

$$P[W_{k+1} = l + 1|W_k = l]$$
$$= 1 - P[W_{k+1} = a|W_k = l] - P[W_{k+1} = 0|W_k = l]$$
$$= 1 - v_l - q_l.$$

Case b ($W_k = k'$):

$$P[W_{k+1} = a|W_k = k'] = \frac{P[W_k = k' \wedge W_{k+1} = a]}{P[W_k = k']}$$

$$= \frac{P[Y_m \in \Omega_u^t, 0 \leq m \leq k \wedge Y_{k+1} = a]}{P[Y_m \in \Omega_u^t, 0 \leq m \leq k]}$$

$$= \frac{P[Z_k' \in \Omega_u^t \wedge Z_{k+1}' = a]}{P[Z_k' \in \Omega_u^t]}$$

$$= \frac{P[Z_{k+1}' = a] - P[Z_k' = a]}{P[Z_k' \in \Omega_u^t]}$$

$$= \frac{\pi_a'(k+1) - \pi_a'(k)}{a'(k)} = v_k',$$

$$P[W_{k+1} = 0|W_k = k'] = \frac{P[W_k = k' \wedge W_{k+1} = 0]}{P[W_k = k']}$$

$$= \frac{P[Y_m \in \Omega_u^t, 0 \leq m \leq k \wedge Y_{k+1} = u]}{P[Y_m \in \Omega_u^t, 0 \leq m \leq k]}$$

$$= \frac{P[Z_k' \in \Omega_u^t \wedge Z_{k+1}' = b]}{P[Z_k' \in \Omega_u^t]}$$

$$= \frac{P[Z_{k+1}' = b] - P[Z_k' = b]}{P[Z_k' \in \Omega_u^t]}$$

$$= \frac{\pi_b'(k+1) - \pi_b'(k)}{a'(k)} = q_k',$$

$$P[W_{k+1} = (k+1)'|W_k = k']$$
$$= 1 - P[W_{k+1} = a|W_k = k'] - P[W_{k+1} = 0|W_k = k']$$
$$= 1 - v_k' - q_k'. \;\bigcirc$$

The regenerative randomization formula can now be obtained refining the state description of Y according to W and derandomizing W into a CTMC V. The result is expressed by the following theorem.

Theorem 1 *Let $V = \{V(t); t \geq 0\}$ be the CTMC with state space $\{0, 1, \ldots\} \cup \{0', 1', \ldots\} \cup \{a\}$, initial*

94

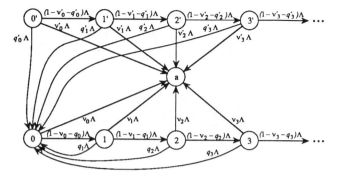

Figure 2: State transition diagram of the CTMC V.

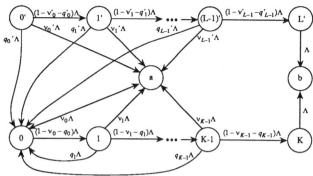

Figure 3: State transition diagram of the CTMC $V_{K,L}$

distribution $P[V(0) = 0] = \alpha_u$, $P[V(0) = 0'] = 1 - \alpha_u$, $P[V(0) = i] = 0$, $i \notin \{0, 0'\}$, *and the state transition diagram shown in Figure 2. Then,* $AP(t) = P[X(t) = a] = P[V(t) = a]$.

Proof Note that $W_k = a$ if and only if $Y_k = a$. Also, $V(t) = W_{N(t)}$. Then:

$$P[X(t) = a] = \sum_{k=0}^{\infty} P[Y_k = a]P[N(t) = k]$$

$$= \sum_{k=0}^{\infty} P[W_k = a]P[N(t) = k] = P[V(t) = a] \bigcirc .$$

The infinite summations of the exact regenerative randomization formula will be truncated assuming that Z has been solved up to step K and Z' has been solved up to step L. The parameters K, L control the computational effort and the approximation error. This is done considering the CTMC $V_{K,L} = \{V_{K,L}(t); t \geq 0\}$ with state space $\{0, 1, \ldots, K\} \cup \{0', 1', \ldots, L'\} \cup \{a, b\}$ defined as follows. $V_{K,L}(t) = V(t)$ if $V(\tau) \in \{0', 1', \ldots, (L-1)'\} \cup \{0, 1, \ldots, K-1\} \cup \{a\}$ for $\tau \in [0, t]$, or $V(t) = L'$ and L' has been entered only once in $[0, t]$ or $V(t) = K$ and K has been entered only once in $[0, t]$; and $V_{K,L}(t) = b$ otherwise.

The state transition diagram of $V_{K,L}$ is given in Figure 3. The absorbing state b represents the behavior of V non captured by the states $\{0, 1, \ldots, K\} \cup \{0', 1' \ldots, L'\} \cup \{a\}$ of $V_{K,L}$. Clearly, from the definition of $V_{K,L}$:

$$P[V_{K,L}(t) = i] \leq P[V(t) = i],$$

$$i \in \{0, 1, \ldots, K\} \cup \{0', 1' \ldots, L'\} \cup \{a\}.$$

Then, a lower bound to $AP(t) = P[X(t) = a] = P[V(t) = a]$ is given by:

$$AP^a(t) = P[V_{K,L}(t) = a], \qquad (1)$$

and the approximation error can be bounded as follows:

$$\begin{aligned} AP(t) - AP^a(t) &= P[V(t) = a] - P[V_{K,L}(t) = a] \\ &\leq P[V_{K,L}(t) = b] = AP^\epsilon(t) \quad (2) \end{aligned}$$

The $V_{K,L}$ model for the transient probabilities of the states a, b can be solved in the Laplace domain (see [Cal94] for details). Then, using (1),(2) and antitransforming analytically whenever possible:

$$\begin{aligned} AP^a(t) &= \sum_{k=0}^{L-1} v'_k a'(k) \sum_{l=k+1}^{\infty} \frac{(\Lambda t)^l}{l!} e^{-\Lambda t} \\ &+ \mathcal{L}^{-1} \left\{ \frac{\tilde{p}_0(s)}{s} \sum_{k=0}^{K-1} v_k a(k) \frac{\Lambda^{k+1}}{(s+\Lambda)^k} \right\} \quad (3) \end{aligned}$$

$$\begin{aligned} AP^\epsilon(t) &= a'(L) \sum_{k=L+1}^{\infty} \frac{(\Lambda t)^k}{k!} e^{-\Lambda t} \\ &+ a(K)\Lambda \mathcal{L}^{-1} \left\{ \frac{\tilde{p}_0(s)}{s} \left(\frac{\Lambda}{s+\Lambda} \right)^K \right\} \quad (4) \end{aligned}$$

$$\tilde{p}_0(s) = \frac{N(s)}{D(s)}, \qquad (5)$$

with

$$\begin{aligned} N(s) &= 1 - \sum_{k=0}^{L-1} a'(k)(s + v'_k \Lambda) \frac{\Lambda^k}{(s+\Lambda)^{k+1}} \\ &\quad - a'(L) \left(\frac{\Lambda}{s+\Lambda} \right)^L \end{aligned}$$

$$\begin{aligned} D(s) &= \sum_{k=0}^{K-1} a(k)(s + v_k \Lambda) \left(\frac{\Lambda}{s+\Lambda} \right)^k \\ &\quad + a(K)\Lambda \left(\frac{\Lambda}{s+\Lambda} \right)^{K-1} \end{aligned}$$

The infinite series in (3), (4) can be approximated with arbitrary accuracy taking a large enough $M > L + 1$ as:

$$\sum_{l=k+1}^{\infty} \frac{(\Lambda t)^l}{l!} e^{-\Lambda t} \approx \sum_{l=k+1}^{M-1} \frac{(\Lambda t)^l}{l!} e^{-\Lambda t} + \delta(M),$$

$$\sum_{k=L+1}^{\infty} \frac{(\Lambda t)^k}{k!} e^{-\Lambda t} \approx \sum_{k=L+1}^{M-1} \frac{(\Lambda t)^k}{k!} e^{-\Lambda t} + \delta(M),$$

$$\delta(M) = \frac{1}{1 - \dfrac{\Lambda t}{M}} \frac{(\Lambda t)^M}{M!} e^{-\Lambda t}.$$

where the $\delta(M)$ terms upper bound the chopped summations.

Regenerative randomization involves in general two truncation parameters. This opens the issue of optimizing the distribution of the total number of steps. We adopt the optimization method which has worked succesfully for other measures [Car94]. In this method, $AP^\epsilon(t)$ is split into two terms; the first, $AP_1^\epsilon(t)$, accounts for the probability of b in $V_{K,L}$ resulting from entries from state L'; the second, $AP_1^\epsilon(t)$, accounts for the entries in b from K. These terms are:

$$AP_1^\epsilon(t) = a'(L) \sum_{k=L+1}^{\infty} \frac{(\Lambda t)^k}{k!} e^{-\Lambda t},$$

$$AP_2^\epsilon(t) = a(K) \Lambda \mathcal{L}^{-1} \left\{ \frac{\tilde{p}_0(s)}{s} \left(\frac{\Lambda}{s + \Lambda} \right)^K \right\}.$$

$AP_1^\epsilon(t)$ can be reduced increasing L; similarly, $AP_2^\epsilon(t)$ can be reduced increasing K. Then, starting with the distribution ($K = 1, L = 1$) we increment K if $AP_2^\epsilon(t) \geq AP_1^\epsilon(t)$, and increment L otherwise. The step is repeated at each (K, L) pair obtained until $AP^\epsilon(t)$ satisfies the accuracy requirements. Using this strategy the contributions to the approximation error bound tend to equalize. Then, at worst, the total number of steps would be close to the minimum (with optimum distribution) number of steps required to achieve half the approximation error bound. Since the dependence of the number of steps on the imposed $AP^\epsilon(t)$ is typically smooth, this guarantees in practice a behavior very close to the optimum.

3 Theoretical properties

We start considering the case $P[X(0) = u] = 1$. In this case $v'_k = q'_k = a'(k) = 0$ and the equations (3-5) are simplified, requiring only the transient solution of the DTMC Z at the steps $k = 0, 1, \ldots, K$. We have the following result:

Theorem 2 When $P[X(0) = u] = 1$ regenerative randomization requires at most the same number of steps than standard randomization.

Proof Let $AP_S^a(t)$ and $AP_R^a(t)$ denote the approximations to $AP(t)$ given by, respectively, standard and regenerative randomization. Let $AP_S^\epsilon(t)$ and $AP_R^\epsilon(t)$ denote the respective error aproximation bounds. By a path analysis, we will show that for the same truncation parameter K (the truncation parameter L is not involved in the randomization formulae for the case considered) $AP_R^a(t) \geq AP_S^a(t)$ and $AP_R^\epsilon(t) \leq AP_S^\epsilon(t)$.

Consider the set of all paths P of the DTMC Y. A path $p \in P$ is a sequence of $L(p)+1$ states, where $L(p)$ denotes the length of the path. Let $p(i)$, $0 \leq i \leq L(p)$ be the ith state of the path p, and let $P[p]$ be the probability of the path p, i.e.:

$$P[p] = P[Y_0 = p(0) \wedge Y_1 = p(1) \wedge \ldots \wedge Y_{L(p)} = p(L(p))].$$

Let P_a^k be the subset of P including all paths of length k which end in state a. Clearly, $P[Y_k = a] = \sum_{p \in P_a^k} P[p]$. Then, we can write $AP_S^a(t)$ as:

$$AP_S^a(t) = \sum_{k=0}^{K} \sum_{p \in P_a^k} P[p] P[N(t) = k]. \tag{6}$$

For $AP_S^\epsilon(t)$ we have:

$$AP_S^\epsilon(t) = \sum_{k=K+1}^{\infty} P[N(t) = k]. \tag{7}$$

Let V_K be the CTMC $V_{K,L}$ particularized to the case considered ($P[X(0) = u] = 1$), and let W_K be the randomized version of V_K, i.e., $V_K(t) = (W_K)_{N(t)}$. W_K can be defined as follows: $(W_K)_k = W_k$ if $W_m \in \{0, 1, \ldots, K-1\} \cup \{a\}$ for $0 \leq m \leq k$ or $W_k = K$ and K has been entered only once; $(W_K)_k = b$ otherwise.

We can write $AP_R^a(t)$ and $AP_R^\epsilon(t)$ as:

$$AP_R^a(t) = \sum_{k=0}^{\infty} P[(W_K)_k = a] P[N(t) = k],$$

$$AP_R^\epsilon(t) = \sum_{k=0}^{\infty} P[(W_K)_k = b] P[N(t) = k].$$

Let $P_a^{k,K}$ be the subset of P including the paths of length k which end in state a and do not give a realization of W_K entering state b. Clearly, $P[(W_K)_k = a] = \sum_{p \in P_a^{k,K}} P[p]$. Since W_K can enter b only after at least $K+1$ steps, $P_a^{k,K} = P_a^k$ for $0 \leq k \leq K$. Then, using (6):

$$AP_R^a(t) = \sum_{k=0}^{\infty} P[(W_K)_k = a] P[N(t) = k]$$

$$= \sum_{k=0}^{\infty} \sum_{p \in P_a^{k,K}} P[p]P[N(t) = k]$$

$$= \sum_{k=0}^{K} \sum_{p \in P_a^k} P[p]P[N(t) = k]$$

$$+ \sum_{k=K+1}^{\infty} \sum_{p \in P_a^{k,K}} P[p]P[N(t) = k]$$

$$= AP_S^a(t) + \sum_{k=K+1}^{\infty} \sum_{p \in P_a^{k,K}} P[p]P[N(t) = k]$$

$$\geq AP_S^a(t).$$

Let $P_b^{k,K}$ be the subset of P including the paths of length k which give a realization of W_K entering state b. Clearly, $P[(W_K)_k = b] = \sum_{p \in P_b^{k,K}} P[p]$, and, since W_K can enter b only after at least $K+1$ steps, $P_b^{k,K} = \phi$ for $0 \leq k \leq K$. Then, using (7):

$$AP_R^{\epsilon}(t) = \sum_{k=0}^{\infty} P[(W_K)_k = b]P[N(t) = k]$$

$$= \sum_{k=0}^{\infty} \sum_{p \in P_b^{k,K}} P[p]P[N(t) = k]$$

$$= \sum_{k=K+1}^{\infty} \sum_{p \in P_b^{k,K}} P[p]P[N(t) = k]$$

$$\leq \sum_{k=K+1}^{\infty} P[N(t) = k] = AP_S^{\epsilon}(t) \bigcirc .$$

An immediate consequence of this result is the following corollary:

Corollary 1 *When X has an initial probability distribution concentrated in a single state, regenerative randomization with an appropriate selection of the regenerative state is better than standard randomization.*

Proof Let $r \in \Omega$ be the initial state of X. Take $u = r$ and apply Theorem 2 $\bigcirc$.

We now study the limiting behavior of regenerative randomization. We will show that the number of steps required to achieve an approximation error bound ϵ is, for $\Lambda t \to \infty$, $O(\log(\Lambda t/\epsilon))$. The proof is done finding a suitable upper bound for $AP^{\epsilon}(t)$ and using spectral properties. The bound is obtained in the following sequence of two propositions. The proofs of these propositions run in parallel with those of similar propositions which appear in [Car94] and are ommited here.

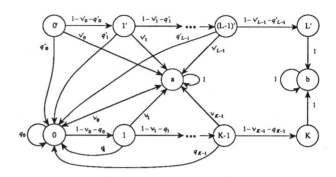

Figure 4: State transition diagram of $W_{K,L}$.

Proposition 2 *Let $W_{K,L} = \{(W_{K,L})_k; k = 0, 1, \ldots\}$ be the DTMC obtained from $V_{K,L}$ under randomization rate Λ, i.e., $V_{K,L}(t) = (W_{K,L})_{N(t)}$ (its state transition diagram is given in Figure 4). Then, $P[(W_{K,L})_k = b] \leq I(k > L)a'(L) + I(k > K)(k - K)a(K).$*

Proposition 3 *The error approximation error bound of regenerative randomization satisfies* $\mathrm{AP}^{\epsilon}(t) < a'(L) + a(K)\Lambda t.$

Theorem 3 *The number of steps required by regenerative randomization to achieve an approximation error bound $\mathrm{AP}^{\epsilon}(t) \leq \epsilon$ is, for $\Lambda t \to \infty$, upper bounded by a function which is $O(\log(\Lambda t/\epsilon))$.*

Proof The proof uses as a basic tool results for the spectrum of non-negative matrices (see, for instance, [Cin75]). Let Q_R be the restriction of the transition probability matrix of Z to its reachable transient states. In general, Q_R may be reducible. Let $Q_1, Q_2, \ldots, Q_M$ be the irreducible submatrices of the normal form of Q_R. Using Frobenius theorem, each Q_i has a real, positive and simple eigenvalue ρ_i such that any other eigenvalue ζ of Q_i satisfies $|\zeta| \leq \rho_i$. The equality can only be given in the case in which Q_i is periodic and, in that case, the eigenvalues ζ with $|\zeta| = \rho_i$ form with ρ_i a equally spaced rotated set of complex numbers. Also, each Q_i has rows which sum less than 1, and $\rho_i < 1$. Let $\rho = \max_{1 \leq i \leq M} \rho_i$. Using this characterization of the eigenvalues of the submatrices Q_i of Q_R, it is easy to prove that $a(k) = \sum_{i \in \Omega} P[Z_k = i]$ is, for $k \to \infty$, upper bounded by a function of the form $A\rho^k$, with $A > 0$. Similarly for Z', let ρ_i', $1 \leq i \leq M'$ be the "dominant" eigenvalues of the irreducible matrices of the normal form of Q_R', the restriction of the transition probability matrix of Z' to its reachable transient states. Let $\rho' = \max_{1 \leq i \leq M'} \rho_i'$, then, for $k \to \infty$, $a'(k)$ is upper bounded by $A'\rho'^k$, with $A' > 0$. Then, using Proposition 3, for $\Lambda t \to \infty$:

$$AP^{\epsilon}(t) < A'\rho'^L + A\rho^K \Lambda t.$$

Let $S = K + L$. Since $K = L$ may not be the optimal distribution, the approximation error for $K = L = S/2$ upper bounds the approximation error achieved with optimal distribution of the steps for a given S. Let $\rho_m = \max\{\rho, \rho'\}$. Then:

$$AP^\epsilon(t) < A'\rho'^{S/2} + A\rho^{S/2}\Lambda t < (A' + A\Lambda t)\rho_m^{S/2}.$$

The number of steps required to achieve an approximation error $\leq \epsilon$ is upper bounded by the S^* satisfying:

$$(A' + A\Lambda t)\rho_m^{S^*/2} = \epsilon.$$

Solving in S^*, considering $\rho_m < 1$:

$$S^* = \frac{2}{\log(1/\rho_m)} \log\left(\frac{A' + A\Lambda t}{\epsilon}\right) = O(\log \frac{\Lambda t}{\epsilon}) \bigcirc.$$

4 Numerical analysis

In this section we illustrate the properties of regenerative randomization and compare its performance with that of standard randomization using a relatively small but representative reliability model. We use the number of randomization steps in Y for SR and the number of steps in Z and Z' ($K+L$) for RR as comparison metric. RR requires the use of a Laplace inversion algorithm. We have used Crump's method [Cru76] with the parameter T of the inversion formula set to $2t$, other parameters set so that the relative antitransform error is smaller than 10^{-8}, and a maximum number of Laplace abscissae to achieve convergence equal to 50. In general, between 20 and 30 transform abscissae have been enough to achieve convergence. RR is implemented by advancing K, L according to the heuristic described at the end of section 2, till the goal relative error is satisfied. Crump's method adds a time complexity $O(m^2)$ per step, where m is the number of abscissae. The significance of this overhead depends on the size of the CTMC X. For the relatively small models of the examples (a few hundred states) the overhead is around 30%. For large models, the overhead would be insignificant.

The example is a fault-tolerant database including two front-ends, two databases and two processing subsystems, each one made up of a switch, a memory and two processors. The fault-tolerant database system is operational if at least one front-end and one database are unfailed and one processing subsystem is operational; a processing subsystem is operational if its switch, its memory and at least one processor are unfailed. Unfailed components of a non-operational processing subsystem and all unfailed components if the system is not operational become dormant. Dormant components do not fail. All components fail with constant rates. Front-ends and databases have failure rate 10^{-4}; switches and memories have failure rate 5×10^{-5}, and processors have failure rate 2×10^{-4}. When a processor fails it contaminates (fails) the operational databases with probability 0.01. For the repair rates we consider two sets of values. In the data

set 1 all components are repaired with rate 1. In the data set 2, databases have repair rate 0.5, front-ends, switches and memories have repair rate 1, and processors have repair rate 5. There is only one repairman which follows a preemptive resume priority strategy with random selection of the component to repair among the failed components with the same repair priority. Front-ends and databases have the highest repair priority, followed next by switches and memories, followed by processors. The measure of interest is the unreliability.

We will consider two initial states for the fault-tolerant database system: s_1 (the state in which all components are unfailed) and s_2 (the state in which only one front-end is failed). Both are operational states and $ur(0) = 0$. For data set 1, $\Lambda \approx 1$; for data set 2, $\Lambda \approx 5$. Table 1 gives the number of required steps under standard randomization (SR) and regenerative randomization (RR) with a *relative* approximation error goal $\epsilon_r = 10^{-5}$ for the data set 1 (repair rates equal) and initial state s_1, taking $u = s_1$ for RR. Table 2 gives the same results for the data set 2 (repair rates unequal). In both cases u is the initial state and RR is guaranteed to require at most the same number of steps as SR. This is confirmed by the numerical results, which show that RR can require significantly less steps than SR also for small and medium Λt. We can also see the benign behavior of RR when t increases. For data set 1, RR is remarkably efficient; for data set 2, RR is less efficient but still significantly more than SR, specially for large Λt. The difference in performance of RR in both cases can be explained by the dispersion of repair rates in the data set 2. In the first case the output rate of *all* the states with failed components is approximately equal to Λ, the probabilities q_{ii} of the DTMC Z are small and Z moves very "fast" to the absorbing state b; then, the quantities $a(k)$ decrease very rapidly with k, and very few steps are enough to achieve a small approximation error (see Proposition 3, which gives an asymptotic upper bound to $AP^\epsilon(t)$ for large Λt). For data set 2 the probabilities q_{ii} of Z are not negligible and more steps are required before $a(k)$ decreases significantly, causing RR to be slower.

The number of steps required under SR is independent on the approximation error for $\Lambda t \to \infty$. The asymptotic bound for the number of required steps under RR when $\Lambda t \to \infty$ given by Theorem 3 suggests a more sensitive behavior of RR in relation to ϵ. Figure 5 shows that behavior for the fault-tolerant database model, initial state s_1, $u = s_1$ and data set 2. We should note that here we fix the relative approximation error bound, whereas the asymptotic behavior of Theorem 3 is established in terms of the absolute approximation error bound. This explains why the number of required steps S^* seems to go asymptotically to a constant value instead of increasing logarithmically with t: for the relatively small values of Λt we consider in the figure, $AP(t)$ is approximately proportional to Λt, transforming the law $A + B \log((\Lambda t)/\epsilon)$ of Theorem 3 into a function independent of Λt, when

Table 1: Number of steps in SR and RR for the unreliability $ur(t)$ of the fault-tolerant database model for data set 1, initial state s_1, $u = s_1$, $\epsilon_r = 10^{-5}$ and several values of t.

t	$ur(t)$	steps	
		SR	RR
0.01	8.000×10^{-8}	5	3
0.1	8.003×10^{-7}	7	4
1	8.021×10^{-6}	12	5
10	8.052×10^{-5}	32	6
100	8.054×10^{-4}	162	6
10^3	8.025×10^{-3}	1,171	6
10^4	7.742×10^{-2}	10,497	6

Table 2: Number of steps in SR and RR with $u = s_1$ for the unreliability $ur(t)$ of the fault-tolerant database model for data set 2, initial state s_1, $u = s_1$, $\epsilon_r = 10^{-5}$ and several values of t.

t	$ur(t)$	steps	
		SR	RR
0.01	8.000×10^{-8}	6	5
0.1	8.003×10^{-7}	10	8
1	8.023×10^{-6}	25	18
10	8.067×10^{-5}	98	69
100	8.074×10^{-4}	631	138
10^3	8.046×10^{-3}	5,376	141
10^4	7.761×10^{-2}	51,090	141

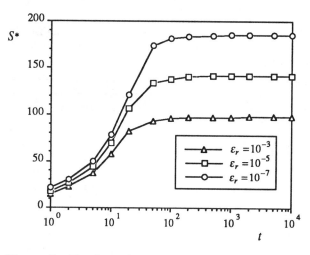

Figure 5: Number of steps in RR with $u = s_1$ for the unreliability $ur(t)$ of the fault-tolerant database model for data set 2, initial state s_1, as a function of the relative error approximation goal ϵ_r and t.

the relative error $\epsilon_r \approx B\Lambda t/\epsilon$ is considered instead of ϵ. The impact of the required relative approximation error bound is quite evident. Thus, it seems that, in RR, solution accuracy can be sensibly traded-off with computational effort, even for large Λt. This is in contrast with SR.

We next consider the fault-tolerant database model with data set 2 and initial state s_2. s_2 is a state which is rarely visited. In such a situation taking the initial state as u may degrade significantly the typical performance of RR, making it very close to SR even though RR is still theoretically better. For the fault-tolerant database model which is highly skewed to state s_1, the choice $u = s_1$ is the reasonable one. This is clearly illustrated by the results obtained with both choices which are given in Table 3. We also give the number of steps required under SR. RR with $u = s_2$ requires almost the same number of steps as SR for all t. In addition, for $t = 10^3, 10^4$ and the choice $(u = s_2)$, Crump's method did not converge, apparently due to cancellation errors caused by the very small rate at which $a(k)$ decreases. This lead us to suspect about the numerical stability of the method. However, by comparing the results given by the Laplace inversion algorithm with the solution of the $V_{K,L}$ model with SR we checked that our implementation of Crump's method was robust whenever it converged (the relative error for both the approximation and the error bound was below 10^{-8} in all cases we have tested). RR with $u = s_1$ requires slightly more steps than SR for small Λt and significantly less for large Λt, exhibiting the "benign" behavior.

5 Conclusions

A new, recently proposed randomization method called *regenerative randomization* has been extended

Table 3: Number of steps in SR, RR with $u = s_1$ and RR with $u = s_2$ for the unreliability $ur(t)$ of the fault-tolerant database model for data set 2, initial state s_2, $\epsilon_r = 10^{-5}$, and several values of t.

		steps		
t	$ur(t)$	SR	RR (s_1)	RR (s_2)
0.01	1.075×10^{-6}	6	9	6
0.1	1.032×10^{-5}	10	15	10
1	7.123×10^{-5}	24	36	24
10	1.807×10^{-4}	97	138	96
100	9.074×10^{-4}	631	258	629
10^3	8.145×10^{-3}	5,376	258	*
10^4	7.770×10^{-2}	51,090	258	*

to the computation of measures of transient CTMC's of the type "absorption probability distribution". An example of such a measure is the unreliability. We have proved that in the common case in which the initial distribution of the model is concentrated in a single state, regenerative randomization (RR) is always better (requires at most the same number of steps) than standard randomization (SR). Using numerical examples it has been shown that RR can be orders of magnitude faster than SR, specially in dependability models which often have "rare" states and, at the same time, frequently visited states which are good candidates for the state u required by RR. The method described here can be also applied to models incorporating performance as well as failure/repair events, e.g., queued servers which can fail. We feel that the solution method we have proposed makes more accesible characteristics of such stiff models which depend on short as well as long term behavior, thus opening a way to explore interesting tradeoffs. We also want to point out that, at the price of an increase in the number of states, non-exponential distributions of very general classes can be accomadated in CTMC's using phase-type distributions [Bob92]. Thus, the application of the method proposed here is not restricted to models with exponential distributions.

References

[Bob92] A. Bobbio and A. Cumani, "ML estimation of the parameters of a PH distribution in triangular canonical form," in *Computer Performance Evaluation: Modelling Techniques and Tools*, Elsevier Science, 1992, pp. 33–46.

[Car94] J. A. Carrasco and A. Calderón, "Regenerative Randomization: Theory and applications," *technical report*, UPC, 1994.

[Cal94] A. Calderón and J. A. Carrasco, "Computation of Absorption Probability Distributions of continuous-time Markov Chains using Regenerative Randomization," *technical report*, UPC, 1994.

[Cin75] E. Çinlar, *Introduction to Stochastic Processes*, Prentice-Hall, 1975, pp. 371–378.

[Cru76] K. S. Crump, "Numerical Inversion of Laplace Transforms Using a Fourier Series Approximation," *Journal of the ACM*, vol. 23, pp. 89–96, 1976.

[Dij90] N. M. Dijk, "On a Simple Proof of Uniformization for Continuous and Discrete-State Continuous-Time Markov Chains," *Adv. Appl. Prob.*, vol. 22, pp. 749–750, 1990.

[Gra77] W. K. Grassmann, "Transient solutions in Markovian queuing systems," *Comput. Operations Res.*, vol. 4, pp. 47–53, 1977.

[Gro84] D. Gross and D. R. Miller, "The randomization technique as a modelling tool and solution procedure for transient Markov processes," *Operations Res.*, vol. 32, pp. 343–361, 1984.

[Jen53] A. Jensen, "Markoff chains as an aid in the study of Markoff processes," *Skand. Akuarietidskrift*, vol. 36, pp. 87–91, 1953.

[Koh82] J. Kohlas, *Stochastic Methods of Operations Research*, Cambridge University Press, Cambridge, 1982.

[Mal94] M. Malhotra, J. K. Muppala and K. S. Trivedi, "Stiffness-Tolerant Methods for Transient Analysis of Stiff Markov Chains," *Microelectron. Reliab.*, vol. 34, no. 11, pp. 1825–1841, 1994.

[Mil83] D. R. Miller, "Reliability Calculation using Randomization for Markovian Fault-Tolerant Computing Systems," in *Proc. 13th IEEE Int. Symp. on Fault-Tolerant Computing, FTCS-13*, 1983, pp 284–289.

[Moo93] A. P. Moorsel and W. H. Sanders, "Adaptive Uniformization", Technical report, University of Arizona, 1993.

[Qur93] M. A. Qureshi and W. H. Sanders, "Reward Model Solution Methods with Impulse and Rate Rewards: An Algorithm and Numerical Results," Technical Report, University of Arizona, 1993.

[Rei88] A. Reibman and K. S. Trivedi, "Numerical Transient Analysis of Markov Models," *Comput. Operations Res.*, vol. 15, pp. 19–36, 1988.

[Rub93] G. Rubino and B. Sericola, "Interval Availability Distribution Computation," in *Proc. 23th Int. Symp. on Fault-Tolerant Computing FTCS-23*, Toulouse, pp. 48–55, June 1993.

[Sou86] E. de Souza e Silva and H. R. Gail, "Calculat-
         ing Cumulative Operational Time Distributions
         of Repairable Computer Systems," *IEEE Trans.
         on Computers*, vol. 35, pp. 322–332, 1986.

[Sou89] E. de Souza e Silva and H. R. Gail, "Calculating
         Availability and Performability Measures of Re-
         pairable Computer Systems using Randomiza-
         tion," *Journal of the ACM*, vol. 34, pp. 179–199,
         1989.

Stochastic Process Algebras as a Tool for Performance and Dependability Modelling*

Holger Hermanns and Ulrich Herzog and Vassilis Mertsiotakis
University of Erlangen-Nürnberg, IMMD VII, Martensstr. 3
91058 Erlangen, Germany

Abstract

The stochastic process-algebra modelling paradigm has been introduced recently as an extension of classical process algebras with timing information aiming mainly at the integration of functional design with quantitative analysis of computer systems. Time is represented by exponentially distributed random variables that are assigned to each activity in the model. Thus, the semantic model of a stochastic process-algebra model can easily be transformed into a continuous time Markov chain which is suitable for computing performance measures as well as dependability measures. The main problem that one encounters frequently in Markov based modelling is the problem of having to solve a huge and stiff Markov chain. In dependability modelling, largeness is caused by lots of detailed and sometimes surplus information stored in the high level model. Stiff Markov chains result when one uses performance related activities together with reliability events in the same model. Various methods to tackle these problems are known, among them the concept of lumpability and decomposition techniques. Recent results in the area of stochastic process-algebras have shown that their theoretical foundations can be related to these concepts. This makes it possible to provide access to these powerful techniques to modellers without requiring a very deeply technical knowledge.

1 Introduction

Performance and dependability evaluation play an important role in the lifecycle of modern computer and communication systems. Most important, these properties are strongly influenced by the functional behaviour of the system and vice versa. This has lead to the development of modelling and specification techniques that are concerned with both, the correct working of a system as well as the question whether it works fast and reliable enough. Stochastic or timed extensions of Petri nets, automaton networks, and graph models are the first and most prominent representatives of this development [1, 39, 40].

All three techniques do have their advantages; in many cases they have proven to be quite valuable yielding realistic results. However, there are still several major problems:

1. Modelling large systems and complex applications the models grow disorderly and often we are faced with the problem of state space explosion.

2. Considering a specific workload usually there are various possibilities to map it onto the given configuration. There is an urgent need to support this important modelling step [3, 23].

3. The full and smooth integration of performance and reliability models into the (mechanized) overall design process is not yet solved sufficiently.

Process algebras are a young and interesting class of abstract programming languages promising for the structured and correct design of complex systems.[1] Their basic intention is to allow the systematic and formal construction of complex systems out of smaller ones. Process algebras support the mechanization of the evaluation procedure: Describing the system behaviour by an (abstract) language, the underlying model is derived automatically, containing all information necessary for the evaluation of characteristic properties.

Process algebras describe the functional behaviour of systems.[2] During several years of research, we showed how to combine both process algebras and stochastic processes. We demonstrated how to develop stochastic process-algebras with generally distributed time intervals [17, 18]. However, in order to present a complete theory and to evaluate the models efficiently, we had to restrict ourselves – for the time being – to Markovian process-algebras. Markovian process-algebras describe the timing behaviour by exponentially distributed time intervals (allowing phase-type modelling). Nevertheless our restricted Markovian approach – and several recent proposals stimulated by our research [6, 15, 26] – seem to be very interesting contributions to overcome the deficiencies disclosed above.

In the past, our work concentrated mainly on developing the necessary theoretical foundation. Now, our interests are moving more towards motivating and using stochastic process-algebras for performance and dependability modelling. Efficient solution techniques have to be developed for our modelling paradigm. Of course, the exploitation of already existing algorithms for well-established modelling techniques, like queuing networks, GSPNs/SRNs/SANs

---

*This research is supported in part by the German National Research Council *DFG* under *SFB 182* and by the Commission of the European Community as *ESPRIT-BRA Project QMIPS*, project no. 7269.

[1]Two of these formal description languages, CSP [27] and CCS [32] are the basis of the quite remarkable programming languages OCCAM and LOTOS.

[2]There are several proposals to add constant time durations to process algebras, for an overview cf. [35]. The objective is then to describe real time systems with deadlines, but not the support of performance modelling.

[8, 31], stochastic graph models [40], or stochastic automaton networks [39] plays an important role. Besides, the large number of existing solution techniques for Markov chains are taken into consideration. Consequently, one possible approach is to apply a *high-level transformation* into another formalism, as it was carried out for ESTELLE in [45] or for three different stochastic process-algebras in [38]. This opens the way to exchange ideas and techniques between two formalisms [12]. The other possibility is to apply a *low-level transformation* into a Markov chain. Primarily, we pursue the latter direction, since this allows us to make use of our established theoretical results (cf. Section 2).

The remaining part of the paper is organized as follows. In Section 2 we introduce the fundamental concepts of the stochastic process-algebra TIPP (timed processes and performability evaluation) developed by our group at the University of Erlangen. Section 3 is devoted to the analysis of the Markov chain underlying a TIPP process. In Section 4 the applicability of stochastic process-algebras to performance and dependability modelling is demonstrated by a case study. Section 5 concludes the paper.

2 The stochastic process-algebra TIPP

In this section we will present the main features of our stochastic process-algebra TIPP. The reader is expected to be familiar with the basic concepts of performance evaluation, reliability theory, and process algebras. A tutorial summarizing the fundamental ideas of stochastic process-algebras has been published at the Performance'93 Conference [17]. Recent research results may be found in [16, 22, 37].

The claim of stochastic process-algebras is to support the systematic description and construction of complex systems. Important features are therefore:

- the composition of components,

- the abstraction of details,

- the interchange of subsystems, and

- the verification of functional and temporal properties.

In order to achieve these objectives we have to provide all elements of a complete process theory (cf. Fig. 1). The syntax of the language allows the modular and compact description of components and their interrelations. The semantic model (usually a labelled transition system) describes precisely and unambiguously the meaning of each language expression. The definition of equivalent behaviour allows one to compare the behaviour of different components and systems with each other. Most important, the axiomatization allows one to provide algebraic laws permitting the comparison of systems (and components) already on the syntactic level. Last not least the semantic model, containing all information, can be analyzed to obtain functional properties (e.g. deadlock, liveness), temporal properties (performance and dependability measures) as well as mixed properties (e.g. probability of deadlock, PDF of tagged event sequences).

It is important to note that the modeller usually sees only the syntactic description and the resulting characteristics, the laws and all other elements and transformations can be mechanized and hidden.

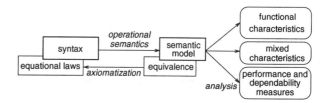

Figure 1: Overview of the stochastic process-algebra approach

2.1 Syntax

The process algebra TIPP – timed processes and performability evaluation – is an extension of the classical abstract languages CSP [27] and CCS [32] including random time variables. The basic elements to describe processes are actions and operators. Actions describe relevant activities of the system; they are considered to be atomic. By means of the operators, process descriptions can be composed from smaller ones in order to yield descriptions of more complex systems. Formally, the ways descriptions can be built are defined by a grammar.

We assume a fixed set of action names $Act := Com \cup \{\tau\}$, where we use τ as a distinguished symbol for internal, invisible actions and Com as the set of regular, visible activities (the communication actions). An action named a can either be exponentially distributed or passive. Exponentially distributed actions – denoted by the action names and the rate (a, λ) – happen instantaneously after a duration that is exponentially distributed with rate λ. Before we define TIPP formally, we give some examples in order to illustrate its expressiveness:

- The sequential arrival of three different jobs is specified by a process *Jobstream* describing explicitly each arrival point before halting:

$$Jobstream := (job_1, \lambda_1).(job_2, \lambda_2).(job_3, \lambda_3).Stop$$

- Consequently, a Poisson-arrival process is defined by an infinite sequence of incoming requests, which can be formulated recursively:

$$Poisson := (in, \lambda).Poisson$$

- Alternative behaviour can be described by the choice operator. As an example an unreliable arrival process may be described by

$$Arriv := (in, \lambda).Arriv + (fail, \varepsilon).Stop$$

Passive actions (denoted by $(a, 1)$) allow the description of receptive behaviour, i.e. the behaviour of components waiting for actions of some partner. For example the behaviour of a faulty and repairable processor may be described as follows:

$$
\begin{aligned}
Proc &:= (in, 1).BusyProc + (fail, \varepsilon).Repair \\
BusyProc &:= (work, \lambda).Proc + (fail, \varepsilon).Repair \\
Repair &:= (diagnose, \delta_1).(repair, \delta_2).Proc
\end{aligned}
$$

Finally the synchronous execution of activities by two communicating components is expressed by the parallel operator, specifying the synchronous actions explicitly. For example, the arrival of a simple job at the above faulty processor may be described as follows:

$$System := (in, \lambda).Stop\|_{\{in\}} Proc$$

More sophisticated examples are shown in Section 2.5 and Section 4.

Definition 2.1 *The set $\mathcal{L}$ of valid system descriptions of TIPP is given by the following grammar, where $a \in Act$, $\lambda \in \mathbb{R}^+$; $S \subseteq Com$, $X \in Var$, Var is a set of process variables.*

$$P ::= Stop \mid (a, \lambda).P \mid P + P \mid P\|_S P \mid$$
$$P\backslash a \mid rec\, X : P \mid X$$

To summarize the intuitive meaning of these basic elements: *Stop* denotes the halting process, the *prefix*ed process $(a, \lambda).P$ behaves as P after the action a has happened. The *choice* operator '+' allows one to model alternative behaviour. By means of the *parallel* operator '$\|_S$' two processes are modelled to proceed independently, but they have to synchronize on actions within S. If no synchronization is forced, we may omit the according index $\emptyset$. The *hiding* operator '\' provides an abstraction mechanism for actions that are internal at a certain level of specification. Infinite behaviour is formally expressed by means of the *recursion* operator '*rec*'. This can be regarded as a compact notation for the recursive equation $X := P$, where X reappears in P. In the remainder of this paper we will frequently use the latter notation, instead of using the *rec*-operator.

2.2 Semantics

The behaviour of a process of this language is formally defined in a structural operational style. The deduction rules in Figure 2 define a labelled transition system (LTS) as a domain for the semantic model, consisting of nodes representing processes and arcs between them. These arcs are labelled with pairs of actions and rates[3]. Each of these arcs ($P \xrightarrow{a,\lambda} Q$) symbolizes that P can evolve to Q by carrying out the action a with rate λ. More detailed motivations and explanations can be found in [17, 22].

2.3 Equivalences

Due to the strict formal semantics of TIPP it is possible to reason about the behaviour of a system in an algebraic setting. For example it is possible to characterize systems with the same functionality, but probably different temporal characteristics. This is formally captured by an equivalence relation called *functional bisimulation* defined in [21]. The idea is that the two systems can simulate each other in any of the states they are going through.

From the performance point of view it is more interesting to classify systems by means of their functional and temporal behaviour, as well. This classification is formally carried out by *Markovian bisimulation* ($\sim_M$) [22], an equivalence relation that abstracts away from different syntactic

[3]An additional third label is used for some subtle management purposes, cf. [22].

$$P \xrightarrow{a,\lambda,w} P' \implies (a,\lambda).P \xrightarrow{a,\lambda,\epsilon} P$$

$$P \xrightarrow{a,\lambda,w} P' \implies P + Q \xrightarrow{a,\lambda,+_l \cdot w} P'$$

$$Q \xrightarrow{a,\lambda,w} Q' \implies P + Q \xrightarrow{a,\lambda,+_r \cdot w} Q'$$

$$P \xrightarrow{a,\lambda,w} P' \wedge (a \notin S) \implies P\|_S Q \xrightarrow{a,\lambda,\|_l \cdot w} P'\|_S Q$$

$$Q \xrightarrow{a,\lambda,w} Q' \wedge (a \notin S) \implies P\|_S Q \xrightarrow{a,\lambda,\|_r \cdot w} P\|_S Q'$$

$$P \xrightarrow{a,\lambda,v} P' \wedge$$
$$Q \xrightarrow{a,\mu,w} Q' \wedge (a \in S) \implies P\|_S Q \xrightarrow{a,\lambda\mu,(v,w)} P'\|_S Q'$$

$$P \xrightarrow{a,\lambda,w} P' \implies P\backslash a \xrightarrow{\tau,\lambda,w} P'\backslash a$$

$$P \xrightarrow{b,\lambda,w} P' \wedge (a \neq b) \implies P\backslash a \xrightarrow{b,\lambda,w} P'\backslash a$$

$$P\{(recX : P)/X\} \xrightarrow{a,\lambda,w} P' \implies recX : P \xrightarrow{a,\lambda,w} P'$$

Figure 2: Semantic rules of TIPP

possibilities to specify the same behaviour. For example, a simple system that works for an exponentially distributed time can be described by $Proc := (work, \lambda).Stop$. If two of them run independently in parallel like in Figure 3, the time until the first process finishes is determined by the minimum of the two random durations. In fact, one of the characteristics of the exponential distributions is that this minimum is also exponentially distributed with rate equal to the sum of the rates. Thus a specialist could describe the behaviour of the two independent processes by $(work, 2\lambda).(work, \lambda).Stop$, exploiting also the memoryless property of the exponential distribution (cf. Figure 3). The fact that these two descriptions are interchangeable is formally captured: they are Markovian bisimulation equivalent.

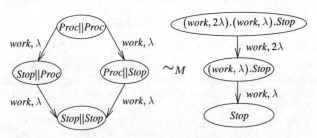

Figure 3: Two different specification of equivalent behaviour

Functional and Markovian bisimulation are congruences, i.e. they allow the exchange of equivalent components that may be specified fairly different *without* changing the overall behaviour of the complex system. This embodies one of the main advantages of the SPA approach, *constructivity*: A complex system can be constructed step by step out of smaller components. These components may be subject of some optimization or manipulation effort – as long as the optimal candidate exhibits equivalent behaviour, the behaviour of the whole system is *not* affected.

Strictly speaking, these equivalences are defined on

TIPP's *semantic* model. They interrelate transition systems rather than syntactic descriptions. Every equivalence class consists of equivalent, but not necessarily identical transition systems. Some of them are smaller, others are larger. This is due to additional information that is irrelevant under the behavioral view of the equivalence.

2.4 Axiomatization

As the states of our transition systems are labelled with the corresponding process descriptions, the bisimulations mentioned above also induce equalities on the *syntactic* level. For Markovian bisimulation this equality can be completely characterized by a set of equational laws (cf. Fig. 4). These laws form the basis of a term rewriting algorithm sketched in Section 2.5 by means of an example.

The laws $\langle\|_0\rangle$, $\langle\|_K\rangle$ and $\langle\|_A\rangle$ are derived from the expansion law $\langle E\rangle$, in order to make the algorithm more efficient. All these laws, together with four additional laws dealing with recursion, form a sound and complete axiomatization of $\sim_M$, as long as no recursion over hiding and parallel composition occurs. The proof is carried out in [22].

$$P + Stop = P \qquad \langle +_0\rangle$$
$$P + Q = Q + P \qquad \langle +_K\rangle$$
$$(P + Q) + R = P + (Q + R) \qquad \langle +_A\rangle$$
$$(a, \lambda).P + (a, \mu).P = (a, \lambda + \mu).P \qquad \langle \lambda\mu\rangle$$

$$Stop\backslash a = Stop \qquad \langle \backslash_0\rangle$$
$$(P + Q)\backslash a = P\backslash a + Q\backslash a \qquad \langle \backslash_+\rangle$$
$$\big((b, \lambda).P\big)\backslash a = (b, \lambda).(P\backslash a) \qquad a \neq b \quad \langle \backslash_{no}\rangle$$
$$\big((a, \lambda).P\big)\backslash a = (\tau, \lambda).(P\backslash a) \qquad \langle \backslash_{yes}\rangle$$

$$P \|_{\{\}} Stop = P \qquad \langle \|_0\rangle$$
$$P \|_S Q = Q \|_S P \qquad \langle \|_K\rangle$$
$$(P \|_S Q) \|_S R = P \|_S (Q \|_S R) \qquad \langle \|_A\rangle$$
$$P \|_S Q = \sum_{a_i \notin S} (a_i, \lambda_i).\big(P_i \|_S Q\big) +$$
$$\sum_{b_j \notin S} (b_j, \mu_j).\big(P \|_S Q_j\big) +$$
$$\sum_{a_i \in S} \sum_{b_j = a_i} (a_i, \lambda_i\mu_j).\big(P_i \|_S Q_j\big) \quad \langle E\rangle$$

$$\text{where } P \equiv \sum_i (a_i, \lambda_i).P_i \text{ and } Q \equiv \sum_j (b_j, \mu_j).Q_j$$

Figure 4: Axiomatization of Markovian bisimulation

2.5 Example for model simplification

Simplifying a system description by term rewriting usually starts with expanding it by $\langle E\rangle$. Afterwards commutativity and associativity of $+$ and $\|_S$ as well as the laws for hiding are used in order to normalize the subterms. Finally the $\langle\lambda\mu\rangle$ law allows the amalgamation of repeated subterms. This procedure is repeated as long as possible. An application of this method can be found in Section 4.3. In order to illustrate the idea, we present a simple example and its transformation.

A simple unreliable process can be modelled as a system going through two alternating phases:

$$P_{up} := (fail, \lambda).P_{down} \qquad P_{down} := (repair, \mu).P_{up}$$

If two or more processes of this type are working in parallel, there is a wide range of possible situations (cf. Fig. 5). As some of them are equivalent, we can use the equational laws in order to fight state space explosion. For example:

$$P_{up}\|P_{up} = (fail, \lambda).P_{down}\|(fail, \lambda).P_{down}$$
$$\overset{\langle E\rangle}{=} (fail, \lambda).(P_{down}\|P_{up}) +$$
$$(fail, \lambda).(P_{up}\|P_{down})$$
$$\overset{\langle\|_K\rangle}{=} (fail, \lambda).(P_{down}\|P_{up}) +$$
$$(fail, \lambda).(P_{down}\|P_{up})$$
$$\overset{\langle\lambda\mu\rangle}{=} (fail, 2\lambda).(P_{down}\|P_{up})$$

$$P_{down}\|P_{down} =$$
$$\vdots$$
$$= (repair, 2\mu).(P_{down}\|P_{up})$$

This leads to a reduction of the transition system without neglecting any relevant information (with respect to Markovian bisimulation). As every transition system embodies a certain continuous time Markov chain, the according state space is also reduced. Hillston [25, 26] has shown that this reduction is in fact a kind of lumping. If two or more identical processes run in parallel, like in our small example, this is a typical candidate. The simplification for this special case is also known as *symmetry exploitation* [42]. Using the equational laws in a term rewriting system is applicable to an arbitrary system description without evident symmetries. An efficient implementation is currently under development.

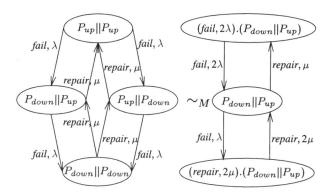

Figure 5: Original and reduced system with two independent processors

3 Performance and dependability evaluation with TIPP

3.1 Reliability and performability measures

Applying the operational semantics rules to a given process description the underlying labelled transition system can be generated. This transition system contains all characteristic information and may be evaluated with respect to the functional behaviour, performance as well as reliability measures. We concentrate on the analysis of reliability and performability aspects and related measures. Hiding the action labels and reducing parallel arcs and loops the transition system leads to a Markov chain which can be described and analyzed via some standard notion and standard measures. Our compact description follows mainly the lines of [20]:

Let $\{X(t); t \geq 0\}$ be a homogeneous continuous time Markov chain and let $S = \{a_i; i = 1, \ldots, n\}$ be the finite state space associated with the model. It is also standard to assume $k + 1$ rewards $\rho_1 > \ldots > \rho_{k+1}$ which may be associated with states or transitions. Besides the well known steady state measures, like throughput, availability or probability of blocking, there are two important classes of transient measures that can be derived out of the state probability distribution and the reward structure:

- Point performability measures

  Let r_i be the reward associated with state a_i. The instantaneous reward at time t is then

  $$Y(t) = \begin{cases} r_i & \text{if } X(t) = a_i \\ 0 & \text{otherwise} \end{cases} \qquad (1)$$

  The point performability $M(t)$ is defined as its expected value

  $$M(t) = E[Y(t)] = \sum_{i=1}^{n} r_i P[X(t) = a_i] \qquad (2)$$

  Various classical measures can be derived from this point performability measure. For example, the point throughput of an action a can be obtained by:

  $$r_i = \sum_j \lambda_j \quad \text{where} \quad (a, \lambda_j) \quad \text{is enabled in state } i$$
  $$(3)$$

- Cumulative reward measures

  When integrating point performability measures over the time, cumulative measures can be obtained. The basis for this is the cumulative reward process $Z(t)$, which is defined by

  $$Z(t) = \int_0^t Y(s) ds \qquad (4)$$

More measures have been defined and may be found in the literature [14, 20, 43]. Analyzing the models and determining characteristic quality measures several technical problems may occur such as state-space explosion and stiffness. Again, the referenced literature deals with these problems and shows solutions. We will briefly summarize the most important techniques and show how to apply them to stochastic process-algebras in the rest of this section.

3.2 Solving the underlying Markov chain

Dependent on the measures to be computed, the basis for further analysis is either the steady state analysis of the underlying Markov chain, or transient analysis. In the former, the following linear equation system has to be solved in order to obtain the steady state probability distribution π:

$$\pi Q = 0 \quad \text{subject to} \quad \sum_{i=1}^{n} \pi_i = 1 \qquad (5)$$

The matrix Q is the infinitesimal generator matrix of the Markov chain underlying a LTS and can straightforwardly be obtained as mentioned above.

There are plenty of different solution methods for the above equations. An overview on direct and iterative solution methods is given in [29]. Usually, the exploitation of information contained in the model reduces the solution effort. The existence of symmetries, regularities, or hierarchies in the model structure enable the use of very efficient algorithms, like the Matrix–Geometric solution method [34], the Spectral–Expansion method [7], Decomposition and Aggregation methods [41] or Tensor–Algebra based methods [36] to name a few.

If steady state analysis is not possible or if time dependent quantities are desired, transient analysis has to be carried out by solving the *Chapmann–Kolmogoroff* differential equation system:

$$\frac{d\pi(t)}{dt} = \pi(t)Q \quad \text{where} \quad \pi(0) = e_1 \qquad (6)$$

Although the above differential equation system has a closed solution

$$\pi(t) = \pi(0)e^{Qt} = \sum_{k=0}^{\infty} \pi(0) \frac{(Qt)^k}{k!} \qquad (7)$$

this way is often avoided because of its numerical instability [19]. Instead, the *randomization technique* is used very frequently. It is based on the transformation of Q into a stochastic matrix of the embedded discrete time Markov chain. Among others, this approach was adopted also by Lindemann [30], who presented a refined randomization technique based on a numerically stable algorithm for the computation of Poisson–probabilities [13].

Unfortunately, in addition to largeness another well known problem arises, especially in performability models, namely the problem of having to solve a stiff differential equation system. Typically, stiffness is caused by transition rates that differ in many orders of magnitude. The above mentioned refined randomization scheme is able to tackle this problem to some extent. Nevertheless, the solution effort remains still relatively high. The use of implicit integration methods is another possibility, but this method is not able to reduce the solution effort either. Therefore, Bobbio/Trivedi [5] have proposed applying decomposition/aggregation techniques based on the approximate decomposition method of Courtois [10] to transient analysis of stiff Markov chains.

Finding appropriate decompositions of the state space usually requires a deep knowledge about the structure of the underlying state space. Therefore, various authors have proposed methods to exploit structural information contained in a high-level model in order to automate this process [2, 4, 11]. Decomposition/aggregation can be carried out either on the state space level or on the high-level model (cf. [9] for an overview). We are concerned with state space level decomposition. The characterization of a class of TIPP–Models that can be analyzed using existing decomposition/aggregation techniques is presented next.

3.3 Decomposable processes

Many algorithms for the computation of the steady–state solution of continuous time or discrete time Markov chains are based on the decomposition of the state space into several distinct partitions. By solving the resulting smaller Markov chains, an approximate solution of the whole model can be obtained using the aggregation technique of Courtois. There are various iterative aggregation methods known which are able to estimate the correct solution very accurately by combining the aggregation technique with iterative solution methods, like SOR, Jacobi, Block–SOR, etc. [44, 29]. Recently, a new approach based on multigrid methods was presented [28].

As the quality of the aggregated solution and the required computation effort for these methods depends strongly on the model structure, we present a characterization of TIPP–processes that can be analyzed efficiently using such methods [24]:

Definition 3.1 *Consider* $P \in \mathcal{L}$, *a process with finite state space.* P *is called* LM–decomposable, *if*

$$P \equiv L \parallel_S M \wedge (\forall a \in S)(L \xrightarrow{a,\cdot} L' \Rightarrow L \equiv L') \quad (8)$$

which denotes that the process L *can only change its state while it is not interacting with the process* M. *Further, we require that the process* L *has also a finite state space and that no free variables occur within* L.

Note that the processes L and M might as well be parallel compositions of other processes. At the first look the above conditions seem to be very restrictive. However, there is a large variety of applications for which this definition applies. As soon as the mapping of a workload to a machine model has to be modelled, where the workload has different arrival rates – in queueing theory commonly referred to as Markov Modulated Poisson Processes [33] – this may easily be modelled by a LM–decomposable process. Actually, the definition of *LM–decomposable* processes was motivated by this class of *workload-to-machine-mapping* models. A more general class of decomposable processes, where explicit modelling of workload is not required, will be presented below.

According to the definition of LM–decomposable processes, two partitioning schemes are possible. On the one side, one natural partitioning scheme is to collect all states where the process L remains unchanged into one partition. By analogy, collecting states where M remains unchanged into one partition leads to the second possible partitioning scheme. For a formal introduction of the possible partitioning schemes the reader is referred to [24].

Another class of processes, where appropriate partitioning schemes can be found in a natural way is the following [24]:

Definition 3.2 *A process* $P \in \mathcal{L}$ *with finite state space is* FR–decomposable, *if* $\exists F, R \subseteq Act$ *where actions in* F, R *have typically low transition rates compared to the other transition rates in the model. The actions sets* F *and* R *should be interpretable as sets of actions that cause failures or carry out repairs, respectively.*

One natural partitioning scheme that can be implied for FR–decomposable processes is the partitioning scheme that results when we require that actions in $F \cup R$ are not allowed within a partition. Moreover, this partitioning scheme would ease the exploitation of the *Near Complete Decomposability* (NCD) property that is often inherent in the Markov chain underlying performability models. In the next section an example is presented that falls in the class of LM–decomposable processes as well as in the class of FR–decomposable processes.

4 A case study

The following case study was presented in [24]. Here, we want to put more emphasis in the modelling aspects rather than in the evaluation results. Additionally, we will show how to reduce the state space by applying the equational laws introduced in Section 2.

The model to be considered represents a multiprocessor mainframe that serves two purposes: on the one side it has to maintain a database and therefore has to process transactions submitted by a number of users, on the other side it is used for program development and has to provide computing capacity to programmers for compiling and testing their programs. As hardware failures occur relatively seldom in comparison to software failures, we will focus on the latter kind of failures and neglect hardware failures [24].

One of the main advantages of process algebras is that they allow the creation of highly modular model descriptions. In our case, we can consider our system as the parallel composition of two components or processes (see Figure 6).

$$System := Load \parallel_A Machine$$

where

$$A := \{user\_job, prog\_job, fail\}$$

The process *Load* represents the system load caused by the database users, the programmers, and the various failures. The mainframe itself is modelled by the *Machine* process.

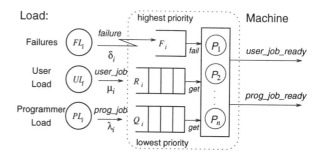

Figure 6: Model structure

4.1 Load modelling

As we want to examine the long term system behaviour dependent on the failure rates and the recovery strategy, we cannot model the various loads as Poisson processes since in a typical application the load varies over time. Therefore, the three arrival streams are modelled by means of a Markov Modulated Poisson Process (MMPP).

$$Load := ProgLoad_1 \|_{\{c\}} UserLoad_1 \|_{\{c\}} FailLoad_1$$

$$
\begin{aligned}
UserLoad_1 &:= (user\_job, \mu_1).UserLoad_1 + \\
&\quad (c, \phi).UserLoad_2 \\
UserLoad_2 &:= (user\_job, \mu_2).UserLoad_2 + \\
&\quad (c, \phi).UserLoad_3 \\
UserLoad_3 &:= (c, \phi).UserLoad_1 \\
&\quad \vdots
\end{aligned}
$$

The processes $UserLoad_i$ and $ProgLoad_i$ generate repeatedly jobs with the rates μ_i and λ_i respectively. By analogy, the process $FailLoad_i$ generates with rate δ_i failures, which can be regarded as special jobs that require all processors and possess preemptive priority over the other job classes. For the sake of simplicity we assume a non-resume policy. Phase changes of the load processes occur with rate ϕ. In phase 3 all load processes are idle.

If we take a closer look at the load process, we may observe that it fulfills exactly the condition (8) because the process $Load$ can change its state only by executing action c, which however is not synchronized with the machine model. Therefore, this model falls in the class of LM–decomposable processes that were introduced in Section 3.3. Moreover, this model represents also a FR–decomposable process with $F = \{fail\}$ and $R = \{repair\}$. As the transition rates of those actions are relatively low, this process can be analyzed efficiently with the approximate decomposition method of Courtois.

4.2 The machine model

The second main component of our model represents the mainframe itself. First, we have to introduce a queue for incoming requests that have to wait until a processor is ready to serve. The processing unit is modelled by the parallel composition of 4 identical processes, each of them modelling one processor.

$$
\begin{aligned}
Machine &:= Queues \|_B (P \|_C P \|_C P \|_C P) \\
Queues &:= F_0 \|_D (R_0 \|_{\{get\_prog\_job\}} Q_0)
\end{aligned}
$$

where

$$
\begin{aligned}
B &= \{get\_user\_job, get\_prog\_job, fail, repair\} \\
C &= \{fail, repair\} \\
D &= \{user\_job, prog\_job, \\
&\qquad get\_user\_job, get\_prog\_job\}
\end{aligned}
$$

4.2.1 The queues

The queuing component is responsible for the buffering of incoming jobs. Additionally, we integrated a scheduling mechanism in this component. Jobs are processed according to a FIFO strategy with priorities. Programmer jobs have the lowest priority, while failures have the highest priority. To each class of jobs a separate queue process is assigned. The queue Q_0 stores the low priority jobs while the queues R_0 and F_0 are for the user jobs and the failures respectively.

$$
\begin{aligned}
Q_0 &:= (prog\_job, 1).Q_1 \\
Q_i &:= (prog\_job, 1).Q_{i+1} \\
&\quad + (get\_prog\_job, \alpha).Q_{i-1} \\
Q_l &:= (get\_prog\_job, \alpha).Q_{l-1} \\
R_0 &:= (user\_job, 1).R_1 \\
&\quad + (get\_prog\_job, 1).R_0 \\
R_i &:= (user\_job, 1).R_{i+1} \\
&\quad + (get\_user\_job, \alpha).R_{i-1} \\
R_l &:= (get\_user\_job, \alpha).R_{l-1} \\
F_0 &:= (fail, 1).F_1 \\
&\quad + (get\_user\_job, 1).F_0 \\
&\quad + (get\_prog\_job, 1).F_0 \\
&\quad + (user\_job, 1).F_0 \\
&\quad + (prog\_job, 1).F_0 \\
F_1 &:= (repair, \beta).F_0
\end{aligned}
$$

The priority mechanism is realized by appropriate synchronization of the three queue processes. The process Q_i for instance is only able to deliver a job to a processor if the other two queues are in state R_0 and F_0. Otherwise, the action get_prog_job is not enabled. Another important fact is that the process F_i prohibits the insertion of new jobs if it is in state F_1, i.e. if a failure occurred.

4.2.2 The processing unit

The system under investigation contains 4 processors. Each processor waits until it can carry out a get action or until a failure occurs. As failures have preemptive priorities over the other two task classes, all processors stop processing if the $fail$ action happens and have to wait until the system will recover.

$$
\begin{aligned}
P &:= (get\_user\_job, 1).P_0 \\
&\quad + (get\_prog\_job, 1).P_1 \\
&\quad + (fail, 1).P_f \\
P_0 &:= (user\_job\_ready, \nu).P \\
&\quad + (fail, 1).P_f \\
P_1 &:= (user\_job\_ready, \xi).P \\
&\quad + (fail, 1).P_f \\
P_f &:= (repair, 1).P
\end{aligned}
$$

4.3 Model simplification

To evaluate the above model, we derive first the semantic model based on the semantic rules of TIPP (see Figure 2). If we do this, we may observe that the reachability set contains much too detailed information. This is due to the representation of the processing component by the parallel composition of 4 identical processes. This is related to the problem of choosing a compact representation of a queuing system's state space. In elementary queuing theory the state space of a queuing system is almost always smaller if the server is represented by one state variable for the whole server instead of one variable for each processor in the server. By analogy, the number of states for our model would be clearly smaller if the processing system is represented by a single process. However, this makes model creation more difficult and error prone. With process algebras like TIPP this can be done systematically using the equational laws and the congruence property of Markovian bisimulation. Moreover, an automation of this task appears to be feasible and is currently under investigation.

In the above case, a simplified version of the server could be obtained as follows:

$$P \parallel_c P \parallel_c P \parallel_c P \stackrel{\langle E \rangle}{=}$$

$$
\begin{aligned}
&(get\_user\_job, 1).(P_0 \parallel_c P \parallel_c P \parallel_c P) &+\\
&(get\_prog\_job, 1).(P_1 \parallel_c P \parallel_c P \parallel_c P) &+\\
&(get\_user\_job, 1).(P \parallel_c P_0 \parallel_c P \parallel_c P) &+\\
&(get\_prog\_job, 1).(P \parallel_c P_1 \parallel_c P \parallel_c P) &+\\
&(get\_user\_job, 1).(P \parallel_c P \parallel_c P_0 \parallel_c P) &+\\
&(get\_prog\_job, 1).(P \parallel_c P \parallel_c P_1 \parallel_c P) &+\\
&(get\_user\_job, 1).(P \parallel_c P \parallel_c P \parallel_c P_0) &+\\
&(get\_prog\_job, 1).(P \parallel_c P \parallel_c P \parallel_c P_1) &+\\
&(fail, 1).(P_f \parallel_c P_f \parallel_c P_f \parallel_c P_f)
\end{aligned}
$$

After the application of the $\langle E \rangle$-law (see Figure 4), the above mentioned disadvantage of modelling the server with 4 processes becomes clear, since the various subprocesses in the above term differ only by the position of the working processor. This information is redundant with respect to Markovian bisimulation. To reduce this process, we have to apply the equational laws $\langle \parallel_A \rangle$, $\langle \parallel_K \rangle$, and $\langle \lambda\mu \rangle$. The result is

$$
\begin{aligned}
&(get\_user\_job, 4).(P_0 \parallel_c P \parallel_c P \parallel_c P) &+\\
&(get\_prog\_job, 4).(P_1 \parallel_c P \parallel_c P \parallel_c P) &+\\
&(fail, 1).(P_f \parallel_c P_f \parallel_c P_f \parallel_c P_f)
\end{aligned}
$$

The same procedure has to be repeated recursively for the processes $P_0 \parallel_c P \parallel_c P \parallel_c P$, $P_1 \parallel_c P \parallel_c P \parallel_c P$, and $P_f \parallel_c P_f \parallel_c P_f \parallel_c P_f$. Finally, we substitute the parallel components by arbitrary process variables and replace the original server component by the simplified version. The decrease of the state space size is immense. Instead of $O(e^p)$ states the simplified model complexity is of order $O(p^2)$, where p is the number of processors.

4.4 Numerical results

Two important aspects that are of some interest considering performability models are: how much does the occurrence of failures influence the performance of the system and how well can different error recovery strategies help in increasing the system availability. To investigate those aspects for the current example, we applied steady state analysis as well as transient analysis to obtain some characteristic performance measures and dependability measures.

Figure 7 shows how the system's availability in the steady state depends on the repair rate β for various failure rates δ_2, whereas Figure 8 presents the transient (point)

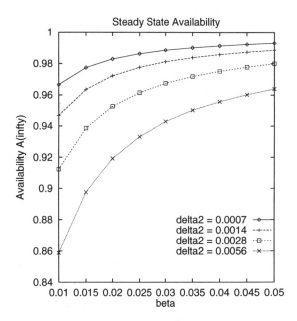

Figure 7:

availability of the system dependent on different repair rates. For more numerical results the interested reader is referred to [24].

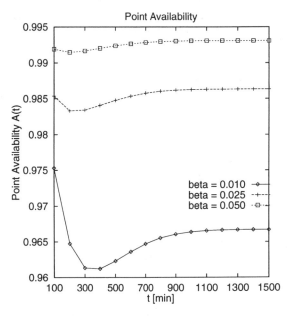

Figure 8:

To obtain the steady state measures we solved the global balance equations of the underlying Markov chain using the Gauß-Seidel method, while for transient analysis we adopted a refined randomization scheme [30].

5 Conclusion and prospects

We presented a formalism for performance and dependability analysis of computer systems based on an extension of a classical process algebra. Exponentially distributed random variables representing duration are attached to each activity in the model. Thus, the resulting semantic model can be transformed into a continuous time Markov chain and this opens the way to make use of many existing solution algorithms.

The major advantages of stochastic process-algebras are their compositionality and their underlying theory. The former gives the user the possibility to build complex systems easily by combining smaller ones using parallel composition for instance. The latter allows one to express similarity or equivalence between models. An equivalence relation (*Markovian bisimulation*) for TIPP was introduced that judges two processes as equivalent with respect to both the functional behaviour as well as the temporal behaviour.

The presented axiomatization allows one to proof the equivalence between models without constructing their state space. This has shown to be especially useful for model simplification. In special cases like the superposition of multiple identical processes in parallel it is relatively easy to implement efficient simplification algorithms based on the axiomatization. For more general structures this deserves a more thorough investigation.

Another future direction in our research will be the examination of more intelligent solution techniques. Here, we could only provide some first concepts how this problem might be approached. We believe that one important link between the theory and the applicability of efficient solution techniques will be the model simplification facility, since many solution algorithms known from the area of Markov chains require a certain structure in the state space, e.g. a two-dimensional state space representation, that might be obtained through model simplification.

References

[1] M. Ajmone Marsan, G. Balbo, and G. Conte. A Class of Generalized Stochastic Petri Nets for the Performance Evaluation of Multiprocessor Systems. *ACM Transactions on Comp. Systems*, 2(2):93–122, 1984.

[2] H. H. Ammar and S. M. Rezaul Islam. Time Scale Decomposition of a Class of GSPN Models, *IEEE Transactions on Software Engineering*, 15(6):809–820, 1989.

[3] H. Beilner. Messung, Modellierung und Bewertung von Rechensystemen. Tutorium, 1985.

[4] A. Blakemore and S. Tripathi. Automated Time Scale Decomposition of SPNs. In *Proc. of the 5th Int. Workshop on Petri Nets and Performance Models*, Toulouse, 1993.

[5] A. Bobbio and K.S. Trivedi. Computing Cumulative Measures of Stiff Markov Chains Using Aggregation. *IEEE Transactions on Computers*, 39(5):1291–1298, 1990.

[6] P. Buchholz. On a Markovian Process Algebra. Tech. Rep. 500/1994, Informatik IV, Universität Dortmund, 1994.

[7] R. Chakka and I. Mitrani. A Numerical Solution Method for Multiprocessor Systems with General Breakdowns and Repairs. In *Proc. of the 6th Int. Conf. on Modelling Techniques and Tools*, Edinburgh, 1992.

[8] G. Ciardo, J. Muppala, and K.S. Trivedi. On the Solution of GSPN Reward Models. *Performance Evaluation*, 12(4):237–254, 1991.

[9] G. Ciardo and K.S. Trivedi. A Decomposition Approach for Stochastic Reward Net Models. *Performance Evaluation*, 18(4):37–59, 1993.

[10] P.J. Courtois. *Decomposability: Queueing and Computer System Applications*. Academic Press, New York, 1977.

[11] J. Couvillion, R. Freire, R. Johnson, W. D. Obal, A. Qureshi, M. Rai, W. H. Sanders, J. E. Tvedt. Performability Modeling with UltraSAN, *IEEE Software*, 8(5):69–80, 1991.

[12] S. Donatelli, J. Hillston, and M. Ribaudo. A Comparison of Performance Evaluation Process Algebra and GSPNs. Tech. Report ECS-CGS-6-94, Dept. of Computer Science, Univ. of Edinburgh, November 1994.

[13] B.L. Fox and P.W. Glynn. Computing Poisson Probabilities. *Comm. of the ACM*, 31(4):440–445, 1988.

[14] H.R. Gail and E. de Souza e Silva. Performability Analysis of Computer Systems: From Model Specification to Solution. *Performance Evaluation*, 14:157–196, 1992.

[15] R. Gorrieri and M. Rocetti. Towards Performance Evaluation in Process Algebras. In *Proc. of the 3rd Int. Conference on Algebraic Methodology and Software Technology*, 1993.

[16] N. Götz. *Stochastic Process Algebras – Integration of Functional Design and Performance Evaluation of Distributed Systems (in German)*. PhD thesis, Univ. of Erlangen, 1994.

[17] N. Götz, U. Herzog, and M. Rettelbach. Multiprocessor and Distributed System Design: The Integration of Functional Specification and Performance Analysis Using Stochastic Process Algebras. In *Tutorial Proc. of the PERFORMANCE '93*, Springer, 1993.

[18] N. Götz, U. Herzog, and M. Rettelbach. TIPP — Introduction and Application to Protocol Performance Analysis. In *Formale Beschreibungstechniken für verteilte Systeme*, Munich, 1993. FOKUS series, Saur publishers.

[19] W. Grassmann. Transient Solutions of Markovian Queues. *Europ. J. Oper. Res*, 1:396–402, 1977.

[20] B. Haverkort, J. Muppala, S. Woolet, and K. Trivedi. Composite Performance and Dependability Analysis. *Performance Evaluation*, 14:197–215, 1992.

[21] H. Hermanns and M. Rettelbach. Markovian Processes go Algebra. Technical Report 10/94, IMMD VII, Universität Erlangen, 1994.

[22] H. Hermanns and M. Rettelbach. Syntax, Semantics, Equivalences, and Axioms for MTIPP. In *Proc. of the 2nd Workshop on Process Algebras and Performance Modelling*, pp. 71–88, Regensberg/Erlangen, July 1994.

[23] U. Herzog. Performance Evaluation and Formal Description. In *Advanced Computer Technology, Reliable Systems and Applications, Proc.*, pp. 750–755. IEEE Press, 1991.

[24] U. Herzog and V. Mertsiotakis. Applying Stochastic Process Algebras to Failure Modelling. In *Proc. of the 2nd Workshop on Process Algebras and Performance Modelling*, pp. 107–126, Regensberg/Erlangen, July 1994.

[25] J. Hillston. Compositional Markovian Modelling Using a Process Algebra. In *Proc. of 2nd. Int. Workshop on the Numerical Solution of Markov Chains*, Raleigh, 1995.

[26] J. Hillston. *A Compositional Approach to Performance Modelling*. PhD thesis, University of Edinburgh, 1994.

[27] C.A.R. Hoare. *Communicating Sequential Processes*. Prentice-Hall, 1985.

[28] G. Horton and S. Leutenegger. A Multi-Level Solution Algorithm for Steady-State Markov Chains. *ACM Performance Evaluation Review*, 22(1):191–200, 1994.

[29] U.R. Krieger, B. Müller-Clostermann, and M. Sczittnick. Modeling and Analysis of Communication Systems Based on Computational Methods for Markov Chains. *IEEE Journal on Selected Areas in Comm.*, 8(9):1630–1648, 1990.

[30] C. Lindemann. Employing the Randomization Technique for Solving Stochastic Petri Net Models. In *Proc. 6. GI/ITG Conf. on Modelling, Measurement and Evaluation of Computing Systems (MMB '91)*, pp. 306–319. Springer, 1991.

[31] J. F. Meyer and W. H. Sanders. Specification and Construction of Performability Models. In *Proc. of the 2nd Int. Workshop on Performability Modeling of Computer and Communication Systems*, Mont. Saint-Michel, France, 1993.

[32] R. Milner. *Communication and Concurrency*. Prentice-Hall, 1989.

[33] P. Naor and U. Yechialy. Queuing Problems with Heterogeneous Arrivals and Service. *Operations Research*, 19:722–734, 1971.

[34] M.F. Neuts. *Matrix–Geometric Solutions in Stochastic Models*. The John Hopkins University Press, 1981.

[35] X. Nicollin and J. Sifakis. An Overview and Synthesis on Timed Process Algebras. In Springer LNCS 600, *Real-Time: Theory in Practice*, 1991.

[36] B.D. Plateau and S.K. Tripathi. Performance Analysis of Synchronisation for Two Communicating Processes. *Performance Evaluation*, 8:35–320, 1988.

[37] M. Rettelbach and M. Siegle. Deriving Lumped Markov Chains from SPA Descriptions. In *Proc. of the 2nd Workshop on Process Algebras and Performance Modelling*, Regensberg/Erlangen, July 1994.

[38] M. Ribaudo. Understanding Stochastic Process Algebras via their GSPN Semantics. In *Proc. of the 2nd Workshop on Process Algebras and Perf. Modelling*, pp. 31–50, Regensberg/Erlangen, 1994.

[39] H. Rudin. From Formal Protocol Specification Towards Automated Performance Prediction. In *Protocol Specification, Testing and Verification*, volume III, pp. 257–269. North Holland (IFIP), 1983.

[40] R. Sahner. *A Hybrid, Combinatorial Method of Solving Performance and Reliability Models*. PhD thesis, Dept. of Comp. Science, Duke Univ., 1986.

[41] P.J. Schweitzer. Aggregation Methods for Large Markov Chains. In *Mathematical Computer Performance and Reliability*, pp. 275–285. North Holland, 1984.

[42] M. Siegle. Reduced Markov Models of Parallel Programs with Replicated Processes. In *Proc. of the 2nd EUROMICRO Workshop on "Parallel and Distributed Processing"*, pp. 126–133, Malaga, Spain, 1994.

[43] R.M. Smith, K.S. Trivedi, and A.V. Ramesh. Perfomability Analysis: Measures, an Algorithm, and a Case Study. *IEEE Transactions on Computers*, 37(4):406–417, April 1988.

[44] W.J. Steward. Recursive Procedures for the Numerical Solution of Markov Chains. In *Queueing Networks with Blocking*, pp. 229–247. Elsevier Science, 1989.

[45] K.S. Trivedi and C.Y. Wang. Integration of Specification for Modelling and Specification for System Design. In *Proc. of the 14th Int. Conf. on Appl. and Theory of Petri Nets*, pp. 473-492. Springer, 1993.

Panel 1:

Cost, Performance, and Reliability Trade-Offs in the Design of General Purpose Computer Systems

Moderator: Dan Lenoski, Silicon Graphics

Session 4:

Non-Markovian Stochastic Petri Nets

Session Chair: Raymond Marie

New Results for the Analysis of Deterministic and Stochastic Petri Nets

Reinhard German
Technische Universität Berlin
Prozeßdatenverarbeitung und Robotik
Franklinstr. 28/29, 10587 Berlin, Germany
e-mail: rge@cs.tu-berlin.de

Abstract

This paper presents new methods for the transient and stationary analysis of stochastic Petri nets with exponentially distributed and deterministic firing delays. The method of supplementary variables is used for the derivation of general state equations which describe the temporal behavior of the underlying stochastic process. Numerical algorithms are presented for the solution of the state equations and illustrated by numerical examples. The results of this paper allow an enhanced performance and reliability analysis based on stochastic Petri net models.

1 Introduction

Deterministic and stochastic Petri nets (DSPNs) [1] represent a graphical method for the modeling of discrete event systems like computer architectures, communication systems, and manufacturing systems. The stochastic extensions to the pure Petri net formalism allow to model and evaluate the performance and dependability of these systems. In DSPNs transitions may fire either without consuming time (*immediate transitions*), after a deterministic time (*deterministic transitions*), or after an exponentially distributed time (*exponential transitions*). Since DSPNs allow to mix deterministic and randomly distributed timing, they are well suited for the modeling of systems in which events occur either after constant or unknown durations (e.g., real-time systems with deterministic events and with failures). This paper presents new results for the transient and stationary analysis of DSPNs using the method of supplementary variables. It is shown how general state equations can be derived and numerically be solved.

As a common structural restriction for the analysis of DSPNs, at most one deterministic transition may be enabled in each marking. Under this restriction the authors of [1] presented a method for the stationary analysis based on the construction of an embedded *Markov chain* (EMC) at memoryless time instants of the underlying stochastic process. In [9] it was shown that the method of *supplementary variables* [6] can also be used for the stationary analysis. Both solution approaches can be generalized in order to deal with more general firing time distributions [9, 4, 5].

Recently, also the transient analysis of DSPNs was investigated. In [3, 4] state equations were derived by considering an underlying *Markov regenerative process*. Although the equations express the solution implicitly, their numerical solution raises computational problems. In [11, 12, 13] several special cases are considered, for which a numerical solution is possible, either in time or in Laplace domain. Additionally, [2] generalizes the solution formulas for more general firing policies of the deterministic transitions.

In [7] it was shown that the method of supplementary variables [6] can be used for the derivation of an alternate set of state equations which describe the transient behavior of the stochastic process which is underlying a DSPN. An iterative numerical method was presented for the analysis of these equations. The state equations and the method were subject to the following three restrictions: 1) at most one deterministic transition may be enabled in each marking, 2) all deterministic transitions have the same firing delay, and 3) deterministic transitions may not be preempted (i.e., may not become disabled by the firing of another transition).

In this paper we first generalize the state equations for DSPNs if restrictions 2 and 3 are relaxed. Then we present several analysis algorithms: i) an iterative algorithm for the transient analysis, ii) a more efficient transient analysis method in a special case, iii) a stationary analysis method, and iv) an approximation method for both the transient and stationary case. Algorithm i) is based on a discretization of the continuous time variables and method ii) can be applied

114

if in the DSPN a sequence of deterministic transitions fires periodically. Furthermore, method iii) can deal with cases which where not considered in [1] whereas method iv) is not subject to any restriction. Methods i) and ii) have been implemented and were added to the software-tool *TimeNET* [8]. TimeNET is a software tool which provides several analysis and simulation components for non-Markovian stochastic Petri nets. Numerical results will be given which were obtained with TimeNET in order to illustrate the transient analysis techniques.

The remainder is organized as follows. In Sec. 2 the considered class of stochastic Petri nets is defined. Sec. 3 and 4 describe the transient and stationary analysis, respectively. In Sec. 5 the approximation technique is presented and in Sec. 6 numerical examples are given.

2 The Considered Class of Stochastic Petri nets

We consider the class of DSPNs as defined in [1]. A DSPN consists of *places*, *transitions*, and *arcs*. Places may contain undistinguishable *tokens*. As already mentioned, the transitions can be divided into *immediate*, *deterministic*, and *exponential transitions*. The arcs are divided into *input*, *output*, and *inhibitor arcs*. The vector representing the number of tokens in each place is refered to as *marking*. Transitions may be *enabled* in a marking. Enabled transitions may *fire* leading to a marking change. The customary enabling and firing rules are adopted. Additionally, it is assumed that all transitions have the firing policy *race with enabling memory* (i.e., the age memory of a transition is set to zero, when it fires or is preempted).

The derivation and solution of the state equations is subject to a few restrictions. Table 1 gives the specific conditions required by each method. The conditions are defined as follows:

1. In each marking no more than one deterministic transition may be enabled.

2. Deterministic transitions may not initially be enabled.

3. A fixed sequence of deterministic transitions fires periodically (cf. Sec. (3.5)).

Condition 2 is not needed for the derivation of state equations, but necessary for the iterative transient analysis. Another important condition is whether a deterministic transition can be *preempted* or not. A transition is said to be preempted if it becomes disabled by the firing of another transition. If deterministic transitions can never be preempted, certain simplifications are possible.

transient analysis, iterative (Sec. 3.4)	cond. 1 + 2
transient analysis, periodic det. firings (Sec. 3.5)	cond. 1 + 3
stationary analysis (Sec. 4)	cond. 1
approximation (Sec. 5)	none

Table 1: Conditions required by each analysis method

3 Transient Analysis of DSPNs
3.1 Notation

The tangible markings of a DSPN constitute the states of an underlying stochastic process. We assume that the number of tangible markings is finite and, thus, the *state space* $\mathcal{S}$ can be enumerated:

$$\mathcal{S} = \{0, \ldots, K\}. \tag{1}$$

T^D denotes the set of all deterministic transitions of the DSPN. The letters c and d are used to denote deterministic transitions: $c, d \in T^D$. Since in each marking at most one deterministic transition may be enabled, the state space $\mathcal{S}$ can be partitioned into the disjoint sets $\mathcal{S}^E$ and $\mathcal{S}^d$, $d \in T^D$. In $\mathcal{S}^E$ only exponential transitions are enabled and in $\mathcal{S}^d$ the deterministic transition d is enabled. The aim of the analysis is to compute the probabilities of each state of the stochastic process. The transient probabilities are denoted as $p_n(t)$, for $n \in \mathcal{S}$, $t \in \mathbb{R}^+$.

State equations can be derived by supplementing the state description by age variables which represent how long a deterministic transition has been enabled. Let X denote the age variable. Then, let $p_n(t, x)$ denote the *age density function* in state n defined as

$$p_n(t, x) = \frac{Pr\left\{\text{state } n \text{ at time } t, x < X \leq x + dx\right\}}{dx},$$
$$\tag{2}$$

for $n \in \mathcal{S}^d$, $d \in T^D$. Note that $p_n(t, x)$ is a probability with respect to t and a (defective) probability density with respect to x. Throughout this paper the variable $t \in \mathbb{R}^+$ will be used for the transient time and the variable x with $0 \leq x \leq \tau^d$ will be used as the age density variable.

In order to give the state equations in matrix notation and to divide between the different types of state transitions, the following vectors and matrices are defined:

- vectors: $\mathbf{p}^E(t)$, $\mathbf{p}^d(t)$, and $\mathbf{p}^d(t, x)$, for $d \in T^D$,

- matrices: $\mathbf{Q}^{E,E}$, $\mathbf{Q}^{E,d}$, $\mathbf{Q}^d$, $\mathbf{Q}^{d,E}$, $\mathbf{Q}^{d,c}$, $\mathbf{\Delta}^{d,E}$, and $\mathbf{\Delta}^{d,c}$, for $c, d \in T^D$.

All vectors are row vectors of dimension $K + 1$ and all matrices are square matrices of dimension $K + 1$. The entries of $\mathbf{p}^E(t)$ corresponding to states of $\mathcal{S}^E$ are given by the transient state probabilities in these states, all other entries are set to zero. The entries of $\mathbf{p}^d(t)$ and $\mathbf{p}^d(t, x)$, for $d \in T^D$, are analogously defined:

$$p_n^E(t) = \begin{cases} p_n(t) & \text{if } n \in \mathcal{S}^E \\ 0 & \text{otherwise} \end{cases}, \quad (3)$$

$$p_n^d(t) = \begin{cases} p_n(t) & \text{if } n \in \mathcal{S}^d \\ 0 & \text{otherwise} \end{cases}, \quad (4)$$

$$p_n^d(t, x) = \begin{cases} p_n(t, x) & \text{if } n \in \mathcal{S}^d \\ 0 & \text{otherwise} \end{cases}. \quad (5)$$

The $\mathbf{Q}$-matrices describe the the exponential state transitions between the corresponding subsets. Let $\lambda_{i,j}$, $i \neq j$ denote the rate from state i to j and $\lambda_{i,i}$ the negative sum of all outgoing rates of state i. The i, j-th entry of matrix $\mathbf{Q}^{a,b}$ is then defined as follows:

$$q_{i,j}^{a,b} = \begin{cases} \lambda_{i,j} & \text{if } i \in \mathcal{S}^a, j \in \mathcal{S}^b \\ 0 & \text{otherwise} \end{cases}. \quad (6)$$

Here, a, b denote variables for either E or a deterministic transition. The matrices $\mathbf{Q}^{d,d}$ and $\mathbf{Q}^d$, $d \in T^D$, are special cases: $\mathbf{Q}^{d,d}$ represents exponential transitions which preempt d and enable it immediately again, whereas $\mathbf{Q}^d$ represents exponential transitions which let d enabled. Similarly, the $\mathbf{\Delta}$-matrices describe the *branching probabilities* of the deterministic state transitions between the corresponding subsets. The branching probabilities describe to which states a deterministic firing leads (including possibly following firings of immediate transitions). Let δ_{ij} denote the probability of branching from state i to j. The i, j-th entry of matrix $\mathbf{\Delta}^{a,b}$ is then defined as follows:

$$\delta_{i,j}^{a,b} = \begin{cases} \delta_{i,j} & \text{if } i \in \mathcal{S}^a, j \in \mathcal{S}^b \\ 0 & \text{otherwise} \end{cases}. \quad (7)$$

The deterministic firing time of a transition $d \in T^D$ is denoted by τ^d. The *cumulative probability distribution function* of the firing time of $d \in T^D$ in isolation is formally given by the unit step function in τ^d and denoted by $F^d(x)$. Allowing generalized functions, the *probability density function* is a unit impulse in τ^d and denoted as $\delta(\tau^d)$. Additionally, the *instantaneous rate* is defined as $\lambda^d(x) = \delta(\tau^d)/F^d(x)$. $\lambda^d(x)$ is undefined for $x \geq \tau^d$, the limit from the left side $x \to \tau^d$ of $\lambda^d(x)$ is given by the unit impulse in τ^d.

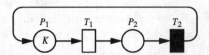

Figure 1: DSPN representing a M/D/1/K queueing system

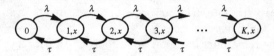

Figure 2: Stochastic process underlying the DSPN

An Example: M/D/1/K Queueing Sytem

In order to illustrate the notation, an example is given. Figure 1 shows a DSPN representing an M/D/1/K queueing system. The exponential transition T_1 models the arrival of customers, the place P_2 the finite capacity of K customers and the deterministic transition T_2 the deterministic service of customers. Figure 2 shows the state graph of the underlying stochastic process. The number of each state corresponds to the number of tokens in P_2. States in which the deterministic transition is active are supplemented by the age variable x. Exponential state transitions are drawn as thin lines labeled with the rate λ and deterministic state transitions are drawn as thick lines labeled with the deterministic firing time τ. In the following the sets, vectors, and matrices are derived for the DSPN.

T^D contains one single transition: $T^D = \{T_2\}$. Each state is uniquely specified by the number of tokens in P_2. The sets of states are given by:

$$\mathcal{S} = \{0, \ldots, K\}, \ \mathcal{S}^E = \{0\}, \text{ and } \mathcal{S}^{T_2} = \{1, \ldots, K\}. \quad (8)$$

Accordingly, the vectors have the form:

$$\mathbf{p}^E(t) = (p_0(t), 0, \ldots, 0), \quad (9)$$

$$\mathbf{p}^{T_2}(t) = (0, p_1(t), \ldots, p_K(t)), \quad (10)$$

$$\mathbf{p}^{T_2}(t, x) = (0, p_1(t, x), \ldots, p_K(t, x)). \quad (11)$$

The $\mathbf{Q}$-matrices describing the exponential state transitions are given by:

$$\mathbf{Q}^{E,E} = \begin{bmatrix} -\lambda & 0 & \cdots & 0 \\ 0 & \cdots & \cdots & 0 \\ \vdots & & & \vdots \\ 0 & \cdots & \cdots & 0 \end{bmatrix}, \quad (12)$$

$$\mathbf{Q}^{E,T_2} = \begin{bmatrix} 0 & \lambda & \cdots & 0 \\ 0 & \cdots & \cdots & 0 \\ \vdots & & & \vdots \\ 0 & \cdots & \cdots & 0 \end{bmatrix}, \quad (13)$$

$$\mathbf{Q}^{T_2} = \begin{bmatrix} 0 & \cdots & \cdots & \cdots & 0 \\ 0 & -\lambda & \lambda & \cdots & 0 \\ \vdots & \ddots & \ddots & \ddots & \vdots \\ \vdots & & & \ddots & -\lambda & \lambda \\ 0 & \cdots & \cdots & 0 & 0 \end{bmatrix}. \quad (14)$$

$\mathbf{Q}^{T_2,E}$ and $\mathbf{Q}^{T_2,T_2}$ contain only zero entries since T_2 can not be preempted. The $\mathbf{\Delta}$-matrices describing the branching probabilities are given by:

$$\mathbf{\Delta}^{T_2,E} = \begin{bmatrix} 0 & \cdots & \cdots & \cdots & 0 \\ 1 & 0 & \cdots & \cdots & 0 \\ 0 & \cdots & \cdots & \cdots & 0 \\ \vdots & & & & \vdots \\ 0 & \cdots & \cdots & \cdots & 0 \end{bmatrix}, \quad (15)$$

$$\mathbf{\Delta}^{T_2,T_2} = \begin{bmatrix} 0 & \cdots & \cdots & \cdots & 0 \\ 0 & \cdots & \cdots & \cdots & 0 \\ 0 & 1 & 0 & \cdots & 0 \\ \vdots & \ddots & \ddots & \ddots & \vdots \\ 0 & \cdots & 0 & 1 & 0 \end{bmatrix}. \quad (16)$$

3.2 The Basic State Equations

Following Cox [6] approach and using the notation introduced in the last section, the *basic state equations* of a DSPN can be derived. These equations describe the temporal behavior of the underlying stochastic process. They express the change of the state probabilities and of the age densities after an infinitesimal small time step dt has elapsed. The change is given in terms of the constant rates of the exponential transitions and of the instantaneous rates of the deterministic transitions. Note that the basic state equations are more general than in the original reference [6], since here deterministic transitions can be preempted. The set of equations contains five different types of vector-matrix equations where each type corresponds to a certain type of state change.

In case a deterministic transition $d \in T^D$ is already enabled, the change of the age densities for $0 \le x < \tau^d$ can be described by:

$$\mathbf{p}^d(t+dt, x+dt) = \mathbf{p}^d(t,x) \cdot \left(\mathbf{I} + \mathbf{Q}^d dt - \lambda^d(x)dt \right) + o(dt). \quad (17)$$

$\mathbf{I}$ denotes the identity matrix and $o(\cdot)$ is a function that goes to zero faster than its argument. The age

densities after time dt depend on the state transitions caused by the exponential transitions enabled in states $n \in \mathcal{S}^d$ (represented by $\mathbf{Q}^d$) and by the firing of d itself (represented by $\lambda^d(x)$). The change of the transient probabilities of states $n \in \mathcal{S}^E$ is described by:

$$\begin{aligned} \mathbf{p}^E(t+dt) = \ & \mathbf{p}^E(t) \cdot \left(\mathbf{I} + \mathbf{Q}^{E,E} dt \right) + \quad (18) \\ & \sum_{d \in T^D} \int_0^{\tau^d} \mathbf{p}^d(t,x) \lambda^d(x) dx \cdot \mathbf{\Delta}^{d,E} dt + \\ & \sum_{d \in T^D} \int_0^{\infty} \mathbf{p}^d(t,x) \cdot \mathbf{Q}^{d,E} dx dt + o(dt). \end{aligned}$$

The state probabilties after time dt depend on the state transitions. The three terms on the right side represent the three possible types of state transitions: firings of exponential transitions enabled in states of $\mathcal{S}^E$, firings of deterministic transitions leading to a state in $\mathcal{S}^E$, and firings of exponential transitions which preempt a deterministic transition leading to a state in $\mathcal{S}^E$, respectively.

We assume that the initial state probability distribution is known and that no deterministic transition was previously enabled. Let the initial distribution be described by the vectors $\mathbf{p}_0^E$, $\mathbf{p}_0^d$, $d \in T^D$. The *initial conditions* are then given by:

$$\mathbf{p}^E(0) = \mathbf{p}_0^E, \ \ \mathbf{p}^d(0) = \mathbf{p}_0^d, \ \ \mathbf{p}^d(0,x) = \mathbf{p}_0^d \cdot \delta(x). \ (19)$$

Note that $\mathbf{p}^d(0,x)$ is a vector of probability density functions in time $t = 0$, given by the Dirac impulse at $x = 0$ and with mass $\mathbf{p}_0^d$. In the instant of time when a deterministic transition d becomes enabled, the age variable is set to zero. The corresponding age density value is given by:

$$\begin{aligned} \mathbf{p}^d(t,0) = \ & \mathbf{p}^E(t) \cdot \mathbf{Q}^{E,d} + \\ & \sum_{c \in T^D} \int_0^{\tau^c} \mathbf{p}^c(t,x) \lambda^c(x) dx \cdot \mathbf{\Delta}^{c,d} + \\ & \sum_{c \in T^D} \int_0^{\infty} \mathbf{p}^c(t,x) \cdot \mathbf{Q}^{c,d} dx. \quad (20) \end{aligned}$$

The three terms on the right side represent the three possible types of state transitions which lead to an enabling of d: firings of exponential transitions enabled in states of $\mathcal{S}^E$ leading to a state in $\mathcal{S}^d$, firings of deterministic transitions leading to a state in $\mathcal{S}^d$, and firings of exponential transitions which preempt a deterministic transition leading to a state in $\mathcal{S}^d$. Finally, the state probabilities of $n \in \mathcal{S}^d$ can be obtained by integrating over the age densities:

$$\mathbf{p}^d(t) = \int_0^{\infty} \mathbf{p}^d(t,x) dx. \quad (21)$$

3.3 The Transient State Equations

Simplifying the basic state equations of the last section leads to the *transient state equations*. This set of equations consist of a system of *partial differential equations* (PDEs), a system of *ordinary differential equations* (ODEs), *initial* and *boundary conditions*, and a system of *integral equations*.

Equation (17) leads to a system of PDEs for $0 < x < \tau^d$:

$$\frac{\partial}{\partial t}\mathbf{p}^d(t,x) + \frac{\partial}{\partial x}\mathbf{p}^d(t,x) = \mathbf{p}^d(t,x) \cdot \mathbf{Q}^d. \qquad (22)$$

Equation (22) is obtained from Eq. (17) by substracting $\mathbf{p}^d(t,x)$ from both sides and by dividing both sides by dt ($\lambda^d(x)$ equals zero for $x < \tau^d$). Equation (18) leads to a system of ODEs:

$$\begin{aligned}\frac{d}{dt}\mathbf{p}^E(t) &= \mathbf{p}^E(t) \cdot \mathbf{Q}^{E,E} + \sum_{d \in T^D} \mathbf{p}^d(t,\tau^d) \cdot \mathbf{\Delta}^{d,E} + \\ &\quad \sum_{d \in T^D} \mathbf{p}^d(t) \cdot \mathbf{Q}^{d,E}.\end{aligned} \qquad (23)$$

Equation (23) is obtained from Eq. (18) by subtracting $\mathbf{p}^E(t)$ from both sides and by dividing both sides by dt. The integrals occuring in Eq. (18) are simplified by using the sifting property of the Dirac impulse and by inserting Eq. (21).

Equation (19) constitutes initial conditions for the differential equations and remains unchanged. The integrals in Eq. (20) can be simplified by using the sifting property of the Dirac impulse and by inserting Eq. (21). The resulting equation represents boundary conditions for the differential equations:

$$\begin{aligned}\mathbf{p}^d(t,0) &= \mathbf{p}^E(t) \cdot \mathbf{Q}^{E,d} + \sum_{c \in T^D} \mathbf{p}^c(t,\tau^c) \cdot \mathbf{\Delta}^{c,d} + \\ &\quad \sum_{c \in T^D} \mathbf{p}^c(t) \cdot \mathbf{Q}^{c,d}.\end{aligned} \qquad (24)$$

Since the age density variable can not become greater than τ^d, the integrals in Eq. (21) are bounded:

$$\mathbf{p}^d(t) = \int_0^{\tau^d} \mathbf{p}^d(t,x)dx. \qquad (25)$$

Equations (22–25) and Eq. (19) uniquely describe the temporal behavior of a DSPN and constitute transient state equations.

Reduction of the PDEs to ODEs

The system of PDEs (22) can be reduced to a system of ODEs, because both time variables t and x increase with the same speed (cf. Eq. (17)). Straight lines with slope one constitute *characteristic lines*, along which the behavior depends just on one variable. The characteristic lines can be defined as:

$$(t,x) = (t_0 + h, x_0 + h), \quad t_0, x_0, h \in \mathbb{R}^+. \qquad (26)$$

t_0 and x_0 are fixed values and h is a parameter. Define $\hat{\mathbf{p}}^d(h)$ as:

$$\hat{\mathbf{p}}^d(h) = \mathbf{p}^d(t_0 + h, x_0 + h) = \mathbf{p}^d(t,x), \qquad (27)$$

representing the age densities along the characteristic lines. The generalized chain rule yields:

$$\begin{aligned}\frac{d}{dh}\hat{\mathbf{p}}^d(h) &= \frac{\partial \mathbf{p}^d(t,x)}{\partial t} \cdot \frac{\partial t}{\partial h} + \frac{\partial \mathbf{p}^d(t,x)}{\partial x} \cdot \frac{\partial x}{\partial h} \\ &= \frac{\partial}{\partial t}\mathbf{p}^d(t,x) + \frac{\partial}{\partial x}\mathbf{p}^d(t,x).\end{aligned} \qquad (28)$$

Substitution of $\mathbf{p}^d(t,x)$ by $\hat{\mathbf{p}}^d(h)$ in Eq. (22) leads to a system of ODEs:

$$\frac{d}{dh}\hat{\mathbf{p}}^d(h) = \hat{\mathbf{p}}^d(h) \cdot \mathbf{Q}^d, \qquad (29)$$

with solution $\hat{\mathbf{p}}^d(h) = \hat{\mathbf{p}}^d(0) \cdot e^{\mathbf{Q}^d \cdot h}$. Backsubstitution leads to:

$$\mathbf{p}^d(t,x) = \mathbf{p}^d(t_0,x_0) \cdot e^{\mathbf{Q}^d \cdot h}. \qquad (30)$$

Equation (30) can be interpreted as follows: if the age densities are known for a given point (t_0, x_0), the age densities at $(t_0 + h, x_0 + h)$ can be obtained by a multiplication with the matrix exponential in h.

3.4 Iterative Solution of the Transient State Equations

For the numerical analysis of the transient state equations discretization is used. A fixed stepsize h is chosen such that it is a divisor of the greatest common divisor of all deterministic delays (assuming that the ratios of the deterministic delays are all rational). Thus, a one-dimensional grid is defined on the definition set of the state probabilities and a two-dimensional grid on the definition set of the age densities. Starting with the values at $t = 0$ it is possible to compute the approximate values at $t = i \cdot h$. The algorithm can be organized such that only the grid values corresponding to one instant of time have to be stored. Numerical experiments show that good results can be obtained if the stepsize is in the order of 1–10% of the smallest deterministic firing time.

The iterative algorithm consists of an initialization step for $i = 0$ and iteration steps from $i - 1$ to i. The following notation is used for the description of the algorithm: i is the step variable over the transient time axis ($t = i \cdot h$) and j is the step variable over the age density variable ($x = j \cdot h$). i goes from zero to a maximum value i_{max} ($t_{max} = i_{max} \cdot h$) and j goes from zero to a maximum value j_{max}^d which is transition-dependent ($\tau^d = j_{max}^d \cdot h$). Additionally, the grid values of the probabilities and age densities are denoted as follows: $\mathbf{p}^d(ih, jh)$ denotes the grid value of the age densities with step variables i and j, $\mathbf{p}^d(ih)$ and $\mathbf{p}^E(ih)$ denote the grid values of the probabilities with step variable i, respectively.

Difficulties arise if a deterministic transition is initially enabled: The age densities $\mathbf{p}^d(0, x)$ are then given by a Dirac impulse (cf. Eq. (19)). Therefore we exclude this case (condition 2 in Sec. 2). Preemption of deterministic transitions is allowed. This complicates the algorithm slightly: since the lower boundary values of the age densities $\mathbf{p}^d(ih, 0)$ can not directly be computed, an iteration over steps 3–5 in each iteration step is necessary to reach a given precision.

Iterative Algorithm

Initialization Step ($i = 0$)

For $i = 0$, all grid values are set according to the initial conditions (19) and condition 2 in Sec. 2: $\mathbf{p}^E(0) = \mathbf{p}_0^E$, $\mathbf{p}^d(0) = \mathbf{0}$, $\mathbf{p}^d(0, jh) = \mathbf{0}$, for $0 \le j \le j_{max}^d$.

Iteration Step ($i - 1 \to i$)

Given that the grid values for $i-1$ are known, the grid values for i can be computed by the following steps:

1. Compute the age densities employing solution formula (30) for the PDEs: $\mathbf{p}^d(ih, jh) = \mathbf{p}^d((i-1)h, (j-1)h) \cdot e^{\mathbf{Q}^d \cdot h}$, for $0 < j \le j_{max}^d$. Randomization [10] is used as a numerical algorithm. Furthermore, set $\mathbf{p}^d(ih, 0) = 0$.

2. Compute the state probabilities $\mathbf{p}^d(ih)$ by numerical integration over the grid values $\mathbf{p}^d(ih, 0) \dots \mathbf{p}^d(ih, j_{max}^d)$. The trapezoidal rule [15] is employed.

3. Compute the state probabilities $\mathbf{p}^E(ih)$ by solving the ODE (23) in ih. Explicit Runge-Kutta of fourth order [15] is used. The grid values $\mathbf{p}^d((i-1)h, j_{max}^d h)$, $\mathbf{p}^d(ih, j_{max}^d h)$, $\mathbf{p}^d((i-1)h)$, $\mathbf{p}^d(ih)$, $\forall d \in T^D$, and $\mathbf{p}^E((i-1)h)$ are required for the computation.

4. Compute $\mathbf{p}^d(ih, 0)$ using the boundary conditions (24). The grid values $\mathbf{p}^d(ih, j_{max}^d h)$, $\mathbf{p}^d(ih)$, $\forall d \in T^D$, and $\mathbf{p}^E(ih)$ are required.

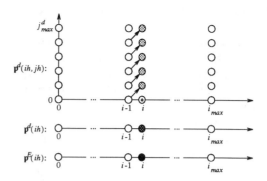

Figure 3: Iterative scheme for the transient solution

5. Correct $\mathbf{p}^d(ih)$ according to the result of step 4.

6. If deterministic transitions can be preempted: check whether the values of $\mathbf{p}^d(ih, 0)$ for all deterministic transitions have reached a precision ϵ (by component-wise comparison of the previous and current values). Continue with step 3 otherwise.

Illustration of the Iterative Algorithm

Figure 3 illustrates the algorithm. It shows the definition sets of the age densities $\mathbf{p}^d(ih, jh)$ and of the probabilities $\mathbf{p}^d(ih)$ and $\mathbf{p}^E(ih)$. Circles visualize grid values. Note that each grid value corresponds to a vector of single values. The initialization step ($i = 0$) gives the leftmost grid values. The iteration step ($i - 1 \to i$) is visualized in the center of the figure: Step 1 yields the grid values $\mathbf{p}^d(ih, jh)$, $0 < j \le j_{max}^d$ (light-grey circles). $\mathbf{p}^d(ih, 0)$ is set to zero (circle with a star inside). Step 2 gives $\mathbf{p}^d(ih)$ (dark-grey circle) and step 3 gives $\mathbf{p}^E(ih)$ (black circle). Step 4 gives a new grid value $\mathbf{p}^d(ih, 0)$ (circle with a star inside), and step 5 a corrected grid value $\mathbf{p}^d(ih)$ (dark-grey circle). An iteration over steps 3–5 is performed until a precision ϵ is obtained. The iteration step ($i - 1 \to i$) is repeated until $i = i_{max}$ is achieved.

3.5 Special Case: Periodic Deterministic Firings

Now a special case is considered in which an easier solution is possible. The applicability conditions are the restrictions 1 and 3 stated in Sec. 2. In a DSPN satisfying restriction 3 a sequence $T_1, \dots, T_n$ of deterministic transitions exists which fire periodically. The sequence is fixed and must not change. Additionally, we require that in each marking a deterministic transition is enabled ($\mathcal{S}^E = \emptyset$) and that the deterministic transitions can not be preempted. For such a DSPN the time instants at which the deterministic transitions fire are fixed and previously known. Condition 3 can automatically be checked considering the matrices defined in Sec. 3.1: $\mathbf{\Delta}^{c,d}$, $c, d \in T^D$ contain the information whether a periodicity exists and $\mathbf{Q}^{c,d}$, $c, d \in T^D$ must not contain non-zero entries. Note that transition invariants can be used as necessary conditions for periodic firings.

In [7] a solution formula was derived for the case that all deterministic transitions have the same firing delay. Similar cases were investigated in [11, 12]. Here we generalize the formula for dealing with periodic sequences of deterministic transitions with possibly different delays. In order to give a comprehensive solution formula, additional notation is introduced: l denotes how often the sequence has fired up to time t, i denotes how many deterministic transitions already have fired during the last period, s denotes the elapsed time since the last firing of a deterministic transition, and $\mathbf{p}(t)$ denotes the vector of all $p_n(t)$, $n \in \mathcal{S}$. The transient probabilities $\mathbf{p}(t)$, $t \geq 0$, are then given by the following successive multiplications:

$$\mathbf{p}(t) = \qquad\qquad\qquad\qquad (31)$$
$$\mathbf{p}(0) \cdot \left(e^{\mathbf{Q}^{T_1} \cdot \tau^{T_1}} \cdot \mathbf{\Delta}^{T_1, T_2} \dots e^{\mathbf{Q}^{T_n} \cdot \tau^{T_n}} \cdot \mathbf{\Delta}^{T_n, T_1} \right)^l \cdot$$
$$e^{\mathbf{Q}^{T_1} \cdot \tau^{T_1}} \cdot \mathbf{\Delta}^{T_1, T_2} \dots e^{\mathbf{Q}^{T_i} \cdot \tau^{T_i}} \cdot \mathbf{\Delta}^{T_i, T_{i+1}} \cdot e^{\mathbf{Q}^{T_{i+1}} \cdot s}.$$

Starting with the initial value $\mathbf{p}(0)$, each matrix exponential describes the evolution caused by exponential and immediate transitions during a deterministic transition is enabled. Each $\mathbf{\Delta}^{c,d}$-matrix represents the branching probabilities caused by the firing of deterministic transitions, possibly followed by immediate transition firings. Using sparse matrix representation and randomization [10], Eq. (31) leads to an efficient transient analysis of DSPNs.

4 Stationary Analysis of DSPNs

A DSPN does not need to possess *steady-state probabilities*: the limits $\lim_{t \to \infty} p_n(t)$ may not be existing. However, it is possible to define *time-averaged limits* p_n, $p_n(x)$, representing the long-term proportion the DSPN spends in its states. The transient state equations can be simplified by eliminating the time variable t. Since these equations describe probabilities which do not change with time t, their solution constitutes *stationary probabilities*. If steady-state probabilities are existing, they are equal to the stationary probabilities or time-averaged limits p_n.

4.1 The Stationary State Equations

The time-averaged limits are defined as:

$$p_n = \lim_{y \to \infty} \frac{1}{y} \int_0^y p_n(t) dt, \qquad (32)$$

$$p_n(x) = \lim_{y \to \infty} \frac{1}{y} \int_0^y p_n(t, x) dt. \qquad (33)$$

The vectors $\mathbf{p}^E$, $\mathbf{p}^d$, and $\mathbf{p}^d(x)$ are the corresponding limits of the vectors defined in Eqns. (3–5), the matrices are defined as in Sec. 3.1.

The transient state equations (22–25) are simplified by taking the time-averaged limit on both sides of the equations. The resulting stationary state equations consist of a system of *ODEs, linear balance* and *boundary conditions*, and *integral equations*. As an additional constraint, we need a *normalization condition*.

The system of PDEs (22) is reduced to the following system of ODEs:

$$\frac{d}{dx} \mathbf{p}^d(x) = \mathbf{p}^d(x) \cdot \mathbf{Q}^d. \qquad (34)$$

The system of ODEs (23) reduces to the following system of linear balance equations:

$$0 = \mathbf{p}^E \cdot \mathbf{Q}^{E,E} + \sum_{d \in T^D} \mathbf{p}^d(\tau^d) \cdot \mathbf{\Delta}^{d,E} + \sum_{d \in T^D} \mathbf{p}^d \cdot \mathbf{Q}^{d,E}. \qquad (35)$$

The boundary conditions (24) simplify to the following linear equations:

$$\mathbf{p}^d(0) = \mathbf{p}^E \cdot \mathbf{Q}^{E,d} + \sum_{c \in T^D} \mathbf{p}^c(\tau^c) \cdot \mathbf{\Delta}^{c,d} + \sum_{c \in T^D} \mathbf{p}^c \cdot \mathbf{Q}^{c,d}. \qquad (36)$$

These boundary conditions contain only unknown constants in contrast to unknown functions. The integral equations (25) reduce to:

$$\mathbf{p}^d = \int_0^{\tau^d} \mathbf{p}^d(x) dx. \qquad (37)$$

Finally, the normalization condition is given by:

$$\sum_{n \in \mathcal{S}} p_n = 1 \qquad (38)$$

Note that this system of equations correctly describes the case of exponential state transitions which preempt a deterministic transition d and lead to a state in which d becomes again enabled (corr. to the rates of matrix $\mathbf{Q}^{d,d}$). This case was not considered in [1].

4.2 Solution of the Stationary State Equations

The stationary probabilities of a DSPN can be obtained by solving Eqns. (34 – 38). The solution can be performed in two steps [9]. First, the ODEs and integral equations have to be solved. The solution is then inserted into the remaining equations, leading to a linear system of equations.

The solution of the ODEs (34) and of the integral equations (37) is given by:

$$\mathbf{p}^d(\tau^d) = \mathbf{p}^d(0) \cdot e^{\mathbf{Q}^d \cdot \tau^d}, \quad \mathbf{p}^d = \mathbf{p}^d(0) \cdot \int_0^{\tau^d} e^{\mathbf{Q}^d \cdot x} dx. \tag{39}$$

The matrix exponential and integral of the matrix exponential can be numerically computed using randomization [10]. Inserting the result of (39) into the Eqns. (35), (36), and (38) leads to a linear system of equations with $K+2$ equations and $K+1$ unknowns. The unknowns are the probabilities p_n, $n \in \mathcal{S}^E$, and the values of $p_n(0)$, $n \in \mathcal{S}^d$, $d \in T^D$. (35) and (36) contain one redundant equation. Therefore one of these single equations can be omitted. The linear system can then be solved with standard techniques. Finally, the values of $p_n(0)$, $n \in \mathcal{S}^d$, $d \in T^D$ have to be inserted into the right side of the second equation in (39) in order to obtain the probabilities $p_n, n \in \mathcal{S}^d, d \in T^D$.

5 Approximate Analysis of DSPNs

In case the restrictions for the numerical analysis are relaxed, approximation techniques can be used. Most commonly, a continuous-time Markov chain (CTMC) is constructed as an approximation of the stochastic process underlying a DSPN. Deterministic delays are replaced by a sequence of exponential phases (Erlang distribution), leading to a CTMC with an expanded state space. In contrast to that, we propose to introduce an artificial timestep and to construct a discrete-time Markov chain (DTMC) as an approximation of the stochastic process underlying a DSPN. In [7] an example was shown where this approach leads to a better precision than the Erlang distribution. In the following a short description of the proposed approach is given.

The timestep (denoted by h) is a divisor of the greatest common divisor of all deterministic delays of the net. All deterministic delays can therefore exactly be represented as multiples of h (assuming again that the ratios of the deterministic delays are all rational). As approximation, we enforce that the exponential transitions may fire at multiples of h only. Thus, a DTMC with an expanded state space is defined. All exponential state transitions of the net can be repre-

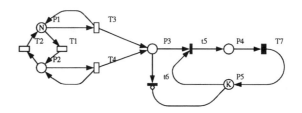

Figure 4: DSPN model of a ΣMMPP/D/1/K queueing system

sented in a generator matrix $\mathbf{Q}$ of a CTMC. Based on that, the stochastic matrix $\mathbf{P}$ containing the one-step transition probabilities of the DTMC can be computed. The probabilities of state transitions caused by the firing of exponential transitions are given by the transient probabilities of the CTMC in the timestep, expressed by the entries of $e^{\mathbf{Q} \cdot h}$. Note that this approach is more general than the approximation of the exponential distributions just by geometric distributions. The transient analysis can be performed by iterating on $\mathbf{P}$ and the stationary analysis by solving the corresponding linear system of equations. Subsequently, the probabilities of the expanded states have to be appropriately summed up.

6 Numerical Examples

The transient analysis algorithms presented in Sec. 3.4 and 3.5 were addded as new solution components to TimeNET [8] and used for numerical experiments. TimeNET runs on Sun and DEC Alpha workstations. The following experiments have been performed on a DEC Alpha workstation (3000 AXP model 800).

6.1 ΣMMPP/D/1/K Queueing System

A DSPN model of a queueing system with deterministic service and finite buffer is considered. The arrival process is a superposition of several identical 2-state Markov modulated Poisson processes (MMPPs). Figure 4 shows the DSPN. The left subnet represents the arrival process: tokens in $P1$ and $P2$ represent MMPPs in low and high levels, respectively. The exponential transitions $T1$–$T4$ have the firing policy *infinite server*, meaning that the actual rate in each marking is obtained by multiplying the rate assigned to the transition with the number of tokens in the corresponding input place. $T1$ and $T2$ represent changes of the levels of the MMPPs, the rates are given by ρ_1 and ρ_2, respectively. $T3$ and $T4$ represent arrivals of customers to the system, the rates are given by λ_1 and λ_2. The right subnet represents the queueing system: tokens in $P3$ model arrived customers, tokens in $P4$

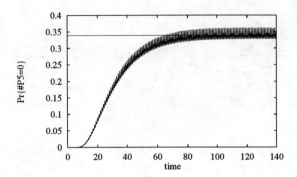

Figure 5: Probability that the buffer is empty

customers waiting for or receiving service, and tokens in $P5$ free buffer places. $T7$ models the service and has a deterministic delay τ. If a customer arrives and no free buffer place is available, the customer is blocked and leaves the system immediately (modeled by the inhibitor arc and immediate transition $t6$). Initially, all K buffer places are free and all N MMPPs are in the low level.

In the following experiments the parameters are chosen according to: $K = 20$, $N = 6$, $\rho_1 = 0.01$, $\rho_2 = 0.1$, $\lambda_1 = 0.2$, $\lambda_2 = 1$, $\tau = 1$. The DSPN has 147 tangible markings. The iterative solution algorithm of Sec. 3.4 can be employed. Figure 5 shows the probability that the buffer is empty (corr. to the probability that no token is in $P5$). The horizontal line shows the stationary result. A stepsize $h = 0.01$ is used. 98 minutes are required for the transient analysis.

6.2 Self-Stabilizing Clock Synchronization

Figure 6 shows a DSPN model taken from [14]. The DSPN models a distributed system consisting of m clocking modules which carry out a fault-tolerant clock-synchronization. All modules are periodically tested and faulty clocks can be adjusted. The system is considered to be *self-stabilizing* if at least f modules are operable. In the DSPN the number of operable modules is represented by tokens in place $P1$. The exponential transitions $T9$ and $T8$ model the failure and repair with rates λ and μ (with infinite-server policy). The deterministic transitions $T10$ and $T11$ represent the time T between two consecutive detections and the detection time δ, respectively. The immediate transitions $t1$, $t2$, $t3$, and $t4$ have weights α, $1 - \alpha$, β, and $1 - \beta$, representing the probabilities of correct detection of the state of the clocking modules.

Since the two deterministic transitions $T10$ and $T11$ fire periodically, the solution formula of Sec. 3.5 can

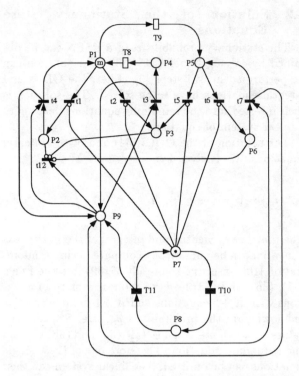

Figure 6: DSPN model of a fault-tolerant clocking system with m modules

be used. In the following sets of experiments the parameters are chosen according to: $m = 40$, $\lambda = 10^{-6}$, $\mu = 10^{-3}$, $\alpha = 0.14$, $\beta = 0.017$, $T = 20$, $\delta = 4$. The DSPN has 13202 tangible markings. Figure 7 shows the probability that at least $f = 10$ clocking modules are operating over a period of 1000 time units. The horizontal line shows the stationary result. 16 minutes were required for the stationary analysis and 21 minutes for the transient analysis.

7 Conclusions

We presented a framework for the transient and stationary analysis of DSPNs. Based on the method of supplementary variables general state equations were derived and several analysis techniques were presented. An approximation technique for more general cases was also given. These results extend the class of stochastic Petri nets which are analytically tractable. Numerical examples were used in order to illustrate the different solution techniques. It should be noted that the presented methods are not restricted to stochastic Petri nets. Stochastic Petri nets were just used as a formalism for the description of stochastic processes.

Several directions are open for further research:

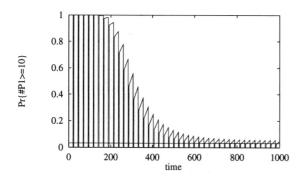

Figure 7: Probability of at least 10 operable modules

More sophisticated numerical subalgorithms can be used (e.g., an adaptive stepsize in contrast to a fixed one, alternate numerical integration techniques). Furthermore, the state equations and solution techniques can be generalized for dealing with general distributions instead of deterministic firing times. However, the restriction that deterministic transitions may not be concurrently enabled is still a major limitation. Therefore, the approximation method should be investigated further. Besides the development of a mathematical description of the method, its precision and costs should be carefully examined.

Acknowledgements

The author would like to thank Jörg Mitzlaff for the implementation of the algorithms.

References

[1] M. Ajmone Marsan, G. Chiola. On Petri Nets with Deterministic and Exponentially Distributed Firing Times. *Advances in Petri Nets 1986, Lecture Notes in Computer Science 266*, pp. 132–145, Springer 1987.

[2] A. Bobbio, M. Telek. Markov Regenerative SPN with Non-Overlapping Activity Cycles. *Int. Performance and Dependability Symp.*, Erlangen, Germany, 1995 (in these proceedings).

[3] H. Choi, V.G. Kulkarni, K. S. Trivedi. Transient Analysis of Deterministic and Stochastic Petri Nets. *Proc. 14th Int. Conf. on Application and Theory of Petri Nets*, Chicago, IL , USA, pp. 166–185, 1993.

[4] H. Choi, V.G. Kulkarni, and K. S. Trivedi. Markov Regenerative Stochastic Petri Nets. *Performance Evaluation*, 20 (1994) 337–357.

[5] G. Ciardo, R. German, C. Lindemann. A Characterization of the Stochastic Process Underlying a Stochastic Petri Net. *IEEE Trans. Softw. Eng.*, 20 (1994) 506–515.

[6] D.R. Cox. The Analysis of Non-Markov Stochastic Processes by the Inclusion of Supplementary Variables. *Proc. Camb. Phil. Soc. (Math. and Phys. Sciences)*, 51 (1955) 433–441.

[7] R. German. Transient Analysis of Deterministic and Stochastic Petri Nets by the Method of Supplementary Variables. *Proc. of the MASCOTS'95*, Durham, NC, USA, pp. 394–398, 1995 (extended version in *Proc. Int. Workshop on the Quality of Communication-Based Systems*, Berlin, Germany, 1994, Kluwer, pp. 105–121, 1995).

[8] R. German, C. Kelling, A. Zimmermann, G. Hommel. TimeNET: A Toolkit for Evaluating Non-Markovian Stochastic Petri Nets. *Performance Evaluation* (forthcoming).

[9] R. German, C. Lindemann. Analysis of Stochastic Petri Nets by the Method of Supplementary Variables. *Performance Evaluation*, 20 (1994) 317–335.

[10] W. K. Grassmann. Finding Transient Solutions in Markovian queueing systems. *Comput. & Ops. Res.*, 4 (1977) 47–53.

[11] D. Logothetis. Transient Analysis of Communication Networks. Ph.D.-Thesis, Duke University, Durham, NC, USA, 1994.

[12] D. Logothetis, K. S. Trivedi. Transient Analysis of the Leaky Bucket Rate Control Scheme Under Poisson and ON-OFF Sources. *Proc. of INFOCOM '94*, Toronto, Canada, 1994.

[13] D. Logothetis, K.S. Trivedi. Time-Dependent Behavior of Redundant Systems with Deterministic Repair. *2nd Int. Workshop Numerical Solution of Markov Chains*, Raleigh, NC, USA, 1995.

[14] M. Lu, D. Zhang, T. Murata. Analysis of Self-Stabilizing Clock Synchronization by Means of Stochastic Petri Nets. *IEEE Trans. on Comp.*, 39 (1990) 597–604.

[15] J. Stoer, R. Burlirsch. *Introduction to Numerical Analysis*. Springer-Verlag, 1980.

Markov Regenerative SPN with Non-Overlapping Activity Cycles

Andrea Bobbio

Dipartimento di Elettronica
Università di Brescia
25123 Brescia, Italy
email: bobbio@icil64.cilea.it

Miklós Telek

Department of Telecommunications
Technical University of Budapest
Budapest, Hungary
email: telek@plan.hit.bme.hu

Abstract

The paper discusses a class of Markov Regenerative Stochastic Petri Nets (MRSPN) characterized by the fact that the stochastic process subordinated to two consecutive regeneration time points is a semi-Markov reward process. This class of SPN's can accommodate transitions with generally distributed firing time and associated memory policy of both enabling and age type, thus generalizing and encompassing all the previous definitions of MRSPN. An unified analytical procedure is developed for the derivation of closed form expressions for the transient and steady state probabilities.
Key words: *Stochastic Petri Nets, semi-Markov Reward Models, Markov regenerative processes.*

1 Introduction

In the usual definition of Stochastic Petri Nets *(SPN)* all the timed transitions have associated an exponential random variable, so that their modeling power is confined to Markovian systems. The analysis of stochastic systems with non-exponential timing is of increasing interest in the literature and requires the development of suitable modeling tools. Recently, some effort has been devoted to generalize the concept of *SPN*, by allowing the firing times to be generally distributed.

An extensive discussion of the semantics of *SPN*'s with generally distributed firing times is in [1], where it is shown that each non-exponential transition should be assigned a *memory policy* chosen among three proposed alternatives: *resampling, enabling* and *age memory*. We refer to this model as *Generally Distributed Transition_SPN (GDT_SPN)*. In general, the stochastic process underlying a *GDT_SPN* is too complex to be analytically tractable, while a simulative solution has been investigated in [16].

With the aim of providing a *modeler's representation* able to automatically generate an *analytical representation* [17], various restrictions of the general *GDT_SPN* model have been discussed in the literature [5]. A classification of *SPN* models, based on the nature of the associated marking process, has been proposed by Ciardo et al. [9].

A particular case of non-Markovian *SPN*, is the class of *Deterministic and SPN (DSPN)* defined in

[3]. A *DSPN* is a non-Markovian *SPN*, where all the transitions are exponential, but in each marking, at most one transition is allowed to have associated a deterministic firing time with enabling memory policy. Only the steady state analysis was elaborated in [3]. An improved steady state algorithm was presented in [20], and some structural extensions were investigated in [10]. Choi et al. [7] have recognized that the marking process underlying a *DSPN* is a Markov Regenerative Process [11] for which a closed form transient solution is available. This observation has opened a very fertile line of research aimed at the definition of solvable classes of models whose underlying marking process is a *Markov Regenerative Process (MRP)*, and therefore referred to as *Markov Regenerative Stochastic Petri Nets (MRSPN)*.

Following this line, Choi et al. [8] have investigated a class of models in which one transition with a generally distributed firing time and enabling memory policy is allowed to be enabled in each marking. German and Lindemann [15] have proposed a numerical solution of the same model based on the method of supplementary variables [12].

In the mentioned references, the generally distributed (or deterministic) transitions must be assigned a firing policy of enabling memory type [1]. The enabling memory policy means [1] that whenever the transition becomes enabled anew, its firing distribution is resampled and the time eventually spent without firing in prior enabling periods is lost. In the language of queueing systems the above mechanism is referred to as *preemptive repeat different (prd)* policy [14, 19].

The possibility of incorporating non-exponential transitions with associated age memory policy has been first explored in [6]. The age memory is able to capture preemptive mechanisms of resume *(prs)* type, where an interrupted activity is recovered by keeping memory of the work already performed, and upon restart, only the residual service needs to be completed. This modeling extension is crucial in con-

---

[1] The enabling memory assumption is relaxed in [10] for vanishing markings only. Since vanishing markings are transversed in zero time, this assumption does not modify the behavior of the marking process versus time

124

nection with fault tolerant and dependable computing systems, where an interrupted task must be resumed from the point it was interrupted.

The paper investigates the nature of GDT_SPN with combined memory policies such that the underlying marking process is a MRP. The timed transitions of the GDT_SPN are partitioned into two subsets: the EXP transitions have an exponentially distributed firing time, while for the GEN transitions the firing time is any random variable (including the deterministic). The *activity cycle* of a GEN transition is the interval of time in which the transition has a non-null memory. We study the case of $MRSPN$ with non overlapping activity cycles, such that the marking process subordinated to two consecutive regeneration time points is a semi-Markov reward process. The proposed model generalizes and encompasses all the previous formulations of $MRSPN$.

In Section 2, the conditions under which the marking process underlying a GDT_SPN is a Markov Regenerative process are set in very general terms. In Section 3, the influence of the memory policy on the activity cycle of a transition is discussed. In Section 4, the subordinated process in a $MRSPN$ with non-overlapping activity cycles is characterized, and a unified analytical solution for the transient and steady state transition probability matrix is proposed in Section 5.

2 Markov Regenerative Stochastic Petri Nets

A marked Petri Net is a tuple $PN = (P, T, I, O, H, M)$, where: $P = \{p_1, p_2, \ldots, p_{np}\}$ is the set of places, $T = \{t_1, t_2, \ldots, t_{nt}\}$ is the set of transitions and I, O and H are the input, the output and the inhibitor functions, respectively. $M = \{m_1, m_2, \ldots, m_{np}\}$ is the marking. The generic entry m_i is the number of tokens in place p_i, in marking M.

Input and output arcs have an arrowhead on their destination, inhibitor arcs have a small circle. A transition is enabled in a marking if each of its ordinary input places contains at least as many tokens as the multiplicity of the input function I and each of its inhibitor input places contains fewer tokens than the multiplicity of the inhibitor function H. An enabled transition fires by removing as many tokens as the multiplicity of the input function I from each ordinary input place, and adding as many tokens as the multiplicity of the output function O to each output place. The number of tokens in an inhibitor input place is not affected.

A marking M' is said to be *immediately reachable* from M, when is generated from M by firing an enabled transition. The reachability set $\mathcal{R}(M_0)$ is the set of all the markings that can be generated from an initial marking M_0 by repeated application of the above rules. If the set T comprises both timed and immediate transitions, $\mathcal{R}(M_0)$ is partitioned into tangible (no immediate transitions are enabled) and vanishing markings. Since the effect of vanishing markings can be incorporated into the tangible ones, according to [2], we do not account in this paper for the presence

of immediate transitions. Let $\mathcal{N}$ be the cardinality of the tangible subset of $\mathcal{R}(M_0)$.

Definition 1 - *A stochastic GDT_SPN is a marked SPN in which [1]:*

- *To any timed transition $t_k \in T$ is associated a random variable γ_k, with cumulative distribution function $G_k(x)$, modeling the time needed by the activity represented by t_k to complete, when considered in isolation.*

- *Each timed transition t_k is attached a memory variable a_k and a memory policy; the memory policy specifies the functional dependence of the memory variable on the past enabling time of the transition.*

- *A initial probability is given on $\mathcal{R}(M_0)$.*

The memory variable a_k, associated to transition t_k, is a functional that depends on the time during which t_k has been enabled. The memory variables together with their memory policy univocally specify how the underlying stochastic process is conditioned upon its past history. The semantics of different memory policies has been discussed in [1] where three alternatives have been proposed and examined.

- *Resampling policy* - The memory variable a_k is reset to zero at any change of marking.

- *Enabling memory policy* - The memory variable a_k accounts for the elapsed time since the last epoch in which t_k has been enabled. When transition t_k is disabled (even without firing) the corresponding enabling memory variable is reset.

- *Age memory policy* - The memory variable a_k accounts for the elapsed time since the last epoch in which t_k has been enabled without firing. The memory variable is reset only when t_k fires (and not when it is simply disabled).

At the entrance in a new tangible marking, the residual firing time is computed for each enabled timed transition given its memory variable, so that the next marking is determined by the minimal residual firing time among the enabled transitions (*race policy* [1]). Because of the memoryless property, the value of the memory variable is irrelevant in determining the residual firing time for exponential transitions, so that the three mentioned policies are completely equivalent in this case. Hence, for an exponential transition t_k, we assume, conventionally, that the corresponding memory variable is always identically zero. We can therefore partition the set of the transitions into EXP transitions with associated an exponential r.v. and identically zero memory variable, and GEN transition with associated any r.v. (including the deterministic case) and memory variable increasing in the enabling markings.

Definition 2 - *The stochastic process underlying a GDT_SPN is called the marking process $\mathcal{M}(x)$ ($x \geq$*

125

0). $\mathcal{M}(x)$ is the marking of the GDT_SPN at time x.

A single realization of the marking process $\mathcal{M}(x)$ can be written as:

$$\mathcal{R} = \{(\tau_0, M_0); (\tau_1, M_1); \ldots; (\tau_i, M_i); \ldots\}$$

where M_{i+1} is a marking immediately reachable from M_i, and $\tau_{i+1} - \tau_i$ is the sojourn time in marking M_i. With the above notation, $\mathcal{M}(x) = M_i$ for $\tau_i \leq x < \tau_{i+1}$.

Assertion 1 - *If at time τ_i^+ of entrance in a tangible marking M_i all the memory variables a_k ($k = 1, 2, \ldots, n_t$) are equal to zero, τ_i is a regeneration time point for the marking process $\mathcal{M}(x)$.*

In fact, if all the memory variables are equal to 0, the future of the marking process is not conditioned upon the past and depends only on the present state; hence, the Markov property holds.

Let us denote by τ_n^* the sequence of the regeneration time points embedded into a realization $\mathcal{R}$. The tangible marking $M_{(n)}$ entered at a regeneration time point τ_n^* is called a regeneration marking. The sequence $(\tau_n^*, M_{(n)})$ is a Markov renewal sequence and the marking process $\mathcal{M}(x)$ is a Markov regenerative process [11, 8, 9]. From Assertion 1 follows that:

i) if all the transitions are EXP all the memory variables are identically zero so that any instant of time is a regeneration time point, and the corresponding process is a *CTMC*;

ii) if at any firing all the memory variables of the GEN transitions are reset, the corresponding process reduces to a semi-Markov process.

iii) only GEN transitions are relevant to determine the occurrence of regeneration time points.

Definition 3 - *A GDT_SPN, for which an embedded Markov renewal sequence $(\tau_n^*, M_{(n)})$ exists, is called a Markov Regenerative Stochastic Petri Net (MRSPN)* [8].

Since $(\tau_n^*, M_{(n)})$ is a Markov renewal sequence, the following equalities hold:

$$Pr\{M_{(n+1)} = j, (\tau_{n+1}^* - \tau_n^*) \leq x \mid$$
$$M_{(n)} = i, \tau_n^*, M_{(n-1)}, \tau_{n-1}^*, \ldots, M_{(0)}, \tau_0^*\} =$$

$$Pr\{M_{(n+1)} = j, (\tau_{n+1}^* - \tau_n^*) \leq x \mid M_{(n)} = i, \tau_n^*\} =$$

$$Pr\{M_{(1)} = j, \tau_1^* \leq x \mid M_{(0)} = i\}$$
$$(1)$$

The first equality expresses the Markov property (i.e. in any regeneration time point the condition on the past is condensed in the present state). The second equality expresses the time homogeneity (i.e. the probability measures are independent of a translation along the time axis). According to [8, 11], we define

the following matrix valued functions $\mathbf{V}(x) = [V_{ij}(x)]$, $\mathbf{K}(x) = [K_{ij}(x)]$ and $\mathbf{E}(x) = [E_{ij}(x)]$ (all of dimension $\mathcal{N} \times \mathcal{N}$), such that:

$$V_{ij}(x) = Pr\{\mathcal{M}(x) = j \mid \mathcal{M}(\tau_0^*) = i\}$$

$$K_{ij}(x) = Pr\{M_{(1)} = j, \tau_1^* \leq x \mid \mathcal{M}(\tau_0^*) = i\} \quad (2)$$

$$E_{ij}(x) = Pr\{\mathcal{M}(x) = j, \tau_1^* > x \mid \mathcal{M}(\tau_0^*) = i\}$$

$\mathbf{V}(x)$ is the transition probability matrix and provides the probability that the stochastic process $\mathcal{M}(x)$ is in marking j at time x given it was in i at $x = 0$. The matrix $\mathbf{K}(x)$ is the *global kernel* of the *MRP* and provides the cdf of the event that the next regeneration time point is τ_1^* and the next regeneration marking is $M_{(1)} = j$ given marking i at $\tau_0^* = 0$. Finally, the matrix $\mathbf{E}(x)$ is the *local kernel* since describes the behavior of the marking process $\mathcal{M}(x)$ inside two consecutive regeneration time points. The generic element $E_{ij}(x)$ provides the probability that the process stays in state j at time x starting from i at $\tau_0^* = 0$ before the next regeneration time point. From the above definitions:

$$\sum_j [K_{ij}(x) + E_{ij}(x)] = 1$$

The transient behavior of the *MRSPN* can be evaluated by solving the following generalized Markov renewal equation (in matrix form) [11, 8]:

$$\mathbf{V}(x) = \mathbf{E}(x) + \mathbf{K} * \mathbf{V}(x) \quad (3)$$

where $\mathbf{K} * \mathbf{V}(x)$ is a convolution matrix, whose (i, j)-th entry is:

$$[\mathbf{K} * \mathbf{V}(x)]_{ij} = \sum_k \int_0^x dK_{ik}(y) V_{kj}(x - y) \quad (4)$$

By denoting the Laplace Stieltjes transform *(LST)* of a function $F(x)$ by $F^\sim(s) = \int_0^\infty e^{-sx} dF(x)$, Equation (3) becomes in the *LST* domain:

$$\mathbf{V}^\sim(s) = \mathbf{E}^\sim(s) + \mathbf{K}^\sim(s) \mathbf{V}^\sim(s) \quad (5)$$

whose solution is:

$$\mathbf{V}^\sim(s) = [\mathbf{I} - \mathbf{K}^\sim(s)]^{-1} \mathbf{E}^\sim(s) \quad (6)$$

If the steady state solution exists, it can be evaluated as $\lim_{s \to 0} \mathbf{V}^\sim(s)$.

As specified by (2), $\mathbf{K}(x)$ and $\mathbf{E}(x)$ depend on the evolution of the marking process between two consecutive regeneration time points. By virtue of the time homogeneity property (1), we can always define the two successive regeneration time points to be $x = \tau_0^* = 0$ and $x = \tau_1^*$.

Definition 4 - *The stochastic process subordinated to state i (denoted by $\mathcal{M}^i(x)$) is the restriction of the marking process $\mathcal{M}(x)$ for $x \leq \tau_1^*$ given $\mathcal{M}(\tau_0^*) = i$:*

$$\mathcal{M}^i(x) = [\mathcal{M}(x) : x \leq \tau_1^*, \mathcal{M}(\tau_0^*) = i]$$

According to Definition 4, $\mathcal{M}^i(x)$ describes the evolution of the PN starting at the regeneration time point $x = 0$ in the regeneration marking i, up to the next regeneration time point τ_1^*. Therefore, $\mathcal{M}^i(x)$ includes all the markings that can be reached from state i before the next regeneration time point. The entries of the i-th row of the matrices $\mathbf{K}(x)$ and $\mathbf{E}(x)$ are determined by $\mathcal{M}^i(x)$.

3 Non-Overlapping Activity Cycles

The analytical tractability of the marking process depends on the structure of the subordinated processes which, in turns, is related to the topology of the PN and to the memory policies of the GEN transitions.

Definition 5 - *A GEN transition is dormant in those markings in which the corresponding memory variable is equal to zero and is active in those markings in which the memory variable is greater than zero. The activity cycle of a GEN transition is the period of time in which a transition is active between two dormant periods.*

Let us consider a single generic GEN transition t_g. The activity cycle of t_g is influenced by its memory policy, and can be characterized in the following way.
Resampling Memory - If t_g is a resampling memory transition, its activity cycle starts as soon as t_g becomes enabled, and ends at the first subsequent firing of any transition (including t_g itself). Therefore, during the activity cycle of a resampling memory transition no change of marking is possible.
Enabling Memory - If t_g is an enabling memory transition its activity cycle starts as soon as t_g becomes enabled when dormant, and ends either when t_g fires, or when it becomes disabled by the firing of a competitive transition. During the activity cycle the marking can change inside the enabling subset of t_g (where the enabling subset is defined as the subset of connected markings in which t_g is enabled). The memory variable associated to t_g grows continuously during the activity cycle starting from 0. We associate a reward variable equal to 1 to all the states in the enabling subset, so that the value of the memory variable is represented by the total accumulated reward.
Age Memory - If t_g is an age memory transition, its activity cycle starts as soon as t_g becomes enabled when dormant, and ends only at the firing of t_g itself. During the activity cycle of an age memory transition there is no restriction on the markings reachable by the marking process. The age memory policy is the only policy in which a transition can be active even in markings in which it is not enabled. During the activity cycle, the memory variable is non-decreasing in the sense that it increases continuously in those markings in which t_g is enabled and maintains its constant positive value in those markings in which t_g is not enabled. In order to track the enabling/disabling condition of t_g during its activity cycle, we introduce a reward (indicator) variable which is equal to 1 in those markings

Table I - Characterization of the activity cycle of a GEN transition t_g

Memory policy	*Resamp.*	*Enabling*	*Age*
start of activity cycle	t_g enabled	t_g enabled when dormant	t_g enabled when dormant
end of activity cycle	firing of any transition	firing or disabling of t_g	firing of t_g
reachable markings	starting marking only	markings in enabling subset	any reachable marking
memory variable	increasing	increasing	increasing or constant

in which t_g is enabled and equal to 0 in those markings in which t_g is not enabled. The memory variable corresponds to the total accumulated reward.

The above features are summarized in Table 1. By virtue of Assertion 1, a regeneration time point for the marking process occurs when a firing causes all the active GEN transitions to become dormant.

Definition 6 - *A transition is dominant if its activity cycle strictly contains the activity cycles of all the active transitions.*

Definition 7 - *A MRSPN with non-overlapping activity cycles is a MRSPN in which all the regeneration periods are dominated by a single transition: any two successive regeneration time points correspond to the start and to the end of the active cycle of the dominant transition.*

Definition 7, includes the possibility that the active cycles of GEN transitions are completely contained into the active cycle of the dominant one, hence allowing the simultaneous enabling of different GEN transitions inside the same subordinated process. In order to make the whole process analytically solvable, we further restrict the subordinated process inside any non-overlapping activity cycle to be semi-Markov.

Assertion 2 - *The subordinated process underlying any non-overlapping activity cycle is semi-Markov if at any firing inside the activity cycle of the dominant transition all the memory variables of the GEN transi-*

tion are reset. This fact happens if the transitions can be partitioned into three classes (exclusive, competitive and concurrent) and only exclusive or competitive transitions are allowed to be GEN [13].

For a regeneration period without internal state transitions (Markovian or semi-Markovian regeneration period) any of the enabled transitions can be chosen to be the dominant one.

4 The Subordinated Process

At $x = \tau_0^* = 0$ a dominant GEN transition t_g (with memory variable a_g and firing time γ_g) starts its activity cycle in state i ($a_g = 0$). The successive regeneration time point τ_1^* is the end of the activity cycle of t_g according to the rules summarized in Table I.

Let $Z^i(x)$ ($x \geq 0$) be the process defined over the states reachable from i during the activity cycle of t_g, and $\underline{r}^i$ the corresponding binary reward vector. We assume in the following that $Z^i(x)$ is a semi-Markov process according to Assertion 2. The subordinated process $\mathcal{M}^i(x)$ (Definition 4) coincides with $Z^i(x)$ when the initial state is state i with probability 1 ($Pr\{Z^i(0) = i\} = 1$). The memory variable a_g increases at a rate r_j^i (which is either equal to 0 or to 1) when $\mathcal{M}^i(x) = j$.

We consider separately the following cases depending whether the dominant transition t_g is of enabling or age memory type.

4.1 Enabling type dominant transition

The dominant GEN transition t_g is of enabling type. The state space of the subordinated process is partitioned into two subsets: R^i contains the states in which t_g is continuously enabled, and R^{ci} contains the states in which t_g becomes disabled by the firing of a competitive transition. The reward vector is equal to 1 for $j \in R^i$ and 0 elsewhere. The next regeneration time point occurs because one of the following two mutually exclusive events:

- t_g fires: this event can be formulated as a completion time problem [4] when the accumulated reward (memory variable) a_g reaches an absorbing barrier equal to the firing requirement γ_g.

- t_g is disabled: this event can be formulated as a first passage time in the subset R^{ci}, and therefore R^{ci} is made absorbing in the subordinated process.

We further particularize the following two cases:

CASE A - no other GEN transitions are activated during the activity cycle of t_g. The subordinated process $Z^i(x)$ is a CTMC.

Case A is the one considered in the *DSPN* model defined in [3, 7, 20], and in the successive extensions to general distributions elaborated in [8, 15]. All the examples reported in the mentioned papers belong to this case.

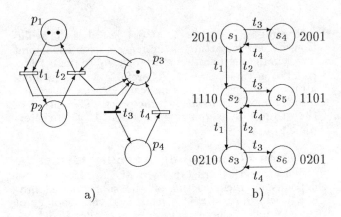

Figure 1 - a) PN of the periodically self tested M/M/1/k; b) corresponding reachability graph.

CASE B - during the activity cycles of t_g, Assertion 2 is satisfied and the subordinated process is a semi-Markov process.

The Markovian (semi-Markovian) regeneration period belongs to Case A (Case B), where R^i contains only the initial state. The steady state analysis of a *MRSPN* with semi-Markovian subordinated process has been considered in [9].

Example 1 - *A periodically self-tested system.*

A system is executing tasks according to a M/M/1/k queue (Figure 1a). Place p_1 represents user thinking and p_2 is the queue including the task under service. t_1 is the exponential submitting time with marking dependent rate $m_1 \lambda$, and t_2 is the exponential service time with rate μ. p_3 represents the system waiting for the test and p_4 the system under test. t_3 is the deterministic testing interval, and t_4 the exponentially distributed test duration with rate δ. When t_3 fires the execution of the M/M/1/k queue is frozen until the test is completed (t_4 fires). The state space of the *PN* of Figure 1a with $k = 2$ customers is in Figure 1b. All the states can be regeneration states, but not all the transitions provide regeneration time points. States s_4, s_5 and s_6 are always regeneration states from which a single EXP transition is enabled (Case A). States s_1 or s_2 or s_3 are regeneration states only when entered by firing t_4, i.e. when the activity cycle of the dominant GEN transition t_3 starts. During the activity cycle of t_3, the subordinated process can move among s_1, s_2 and s_3 which therefore form the subordinated *CTMC* (Case A).

If transitions t_1 and t_2 are GEN with enabling memory policy, the features of states s_4, s_5 and s_6 do not change, while the subordinated process during the activity cycle of t_3 becomes semi-Markovian thus representing a Case B example.

4.2 Age type dominant transition

The situation in which the dominant GEN transition t_g is of age type has been addressed for the first time in [6]. The state space of the subordinated pro-

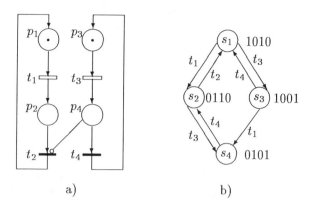

Figure 2 - Preemptive M/G/1/2/2 queue with two classes of customers.

cess R^i contains all the states reachable during the activity cycle of t_g, and the disabling subset R^c is empty (the only criterion for the termination of the activity cycle is the firing of t_g). The reward vector is equal to 1 for the states $j \in R^i$ in which t_g is enabled and 0 for the states $j \in R^i$ in which t_g is not enabled. The firing of t_g can be formulated as a completion time problem [4] when the accumulated reward (memory variable) a_g reaches the firing requirement γ_g. We further particularize the following two cases:

CASE C - During the activity cycle of t_g no other GEN transitions are activated and the subordinated process is a reward CTMC.

CASE D - during the activity cycles of t_g, Assertion 2 is satisfied and the subordinated process is a Reward semi-Markov process.

Example 2 - *Preemptive M/G/1/2/2 with different customers*

In this example, Cases C and D are mixed in a single *PN* [5]. The *PN* of Figure 2a models a M/G/1/2/2 queue in which the jobs submitted by customer 2 have higher priority and preempt the jobs submitted by customer 1. The server has a *prs* service discipline. Place p_1 (p_3) represents customer 1 (2) thinking, while place p_2 (p_4) represent job 1 (2) under service. Transitions t_1 and t_3 are EXP and represent the submission of a job of type 1 or 2, respectively. t_2 and t_4 are GEN transitions, and represent the completion of service of a job of type 1 or 2, respectively. A *prs* service discipline is modeled by assigning to t_2 and t_4 an age memory policy. The inhibitor arc from p_4 to t_2 models the described preemption mechanism: as soon as a type 2 job joins the queue the type 1 job eventually under service is interrupted. The reachability graph of the *PN* of Figure 2a is in Figure 2b. Under a *prs* service, after completion of the type 2 job, the interrupted type 1 job is resumed continuing the new service period from the point reached just before the last interruption. From Figure 2b, it is easily recognized that s_1, s_2 and s_3

can all be regeneration states, while s_4 can never be a regeneration state (in s_4 a type 2 job is always in execution so that its corresponding memory variable a_2 is never 0). Only exponential transitions are enabled in s_1 and the next regeneration states can be either s_2 or s_3 depending whether t_1 or t_3 fires first. From state s_3 the next regeneration marking can be either state s_1 or s_2 depending whether during the execution of the type 2 job a type 1 job does require service (but remains blocked until completion of the type 2 job) or does not. The subordinated process is a $CTMC$, and belongs to Case C. From s_2 the next regeneration state can be only s_1, but multiple cycles (s_2 - s_4) can occur depending whether type 2 jobs arrive to interrupt the execution of the type 1 job. The subordinated process is a SMP (t_4 is GEN), and belongs to case D.

5 Unified Transient Analysis

The global and local kernels $\mathbf{K}(x)$ and $\mathbf{E}(x)$ can be evaluated row by row. In this section, we provide an unified analytical procedure for determining in closed form the entries of a generic row i, given that i is a regeneration marking whose subordinated process is a semi-Markov reward process as described in the previous section.

Let $\mathbf{Q}^i(x) = [Q^i_{k\ell}(x)]$ be the kernel of the subordinated semi-Markov process $(Z^i(x))$. $Z^i(x)$ starts in marking M_i ($Z^i(0) = i$), so that the initial probability vector is $\underline{V}^i_0 = [0, 0, \ldots, 1_i, \ldots, 0]$ (a vector with all the entries equal to 0 but entry i equals to 1). For notational convenience we do not renumber the states in $Z^i(x)$ so that all the subsequent matrix functions have the dimensions ($\mathcal{N} \times \mathcal{N}$) (cardinality of $\mathcal{R}(M_0)$), but with the significant entries located in position (k, ℓ) only, with $k, \ell \in R^i \cup R^{ci}$. We denote by H the time duration until the first embedded time point in $Z^i(x)$ from time $x = 0$.

Let us fix the value of the firing requirement $\gamma_g = w$, and let us define the following matrix functions $\mathbf{P}^i(x, w)$, $\mathbf{F}^i(x, w)$, $\mathbf{D}^i(x, w)$ and $\mathbf{\Delta}^i$:

$$P^i_{k\ell}(x, w) = Pr\{Z^i(x) = \ell \in R^i, \tau_1^* > x \mid \\ Z^i(0) = k \in R^i, \gamma_g = w\}$$

$$F^i_{k\ell}(x, w) = Pr\{Z^i(\tau_1^{*-}) = \ell \in R^i, \tau_1^* \leq x, t_g \text{ fires} \mid \\ Z^i(0) = k \in R^i, \gamma_g = w\}$$

$$D^i_{k\ell}(x, w) = Pr\{Z^i(\tau_1^*) = \ell \in R^{ci}, \tau_1^* \leq x \mid \\ Z^i(0) = k \in R^i, \gamma_g = w\}$$

$$\Delta^i_{k\ell} = Pr\{\text{next tangible marking is } \ell \mid \\ \text{current marking is } k, t_g \text{ fires }\}$$

(7)

By the above definitions, the entries $P^i_{k\ell}(x, w)$ and $F^i_{k\ell}(x, w)$ are significant only for $k, \ell \in R^i$ and are 0 otherwise; the entries $D^i_{k\ell}(x, w)$ are significant for $k \in R^i$ and $\ell \in R^{ci}$, and are 0 otherwise.

- $P^i_{k\ell}(x, w)$ is the probability of being in state $\ell \in R^i$ at time x before absorption either at the barrier w or in the absorbing subset R^{ci}, starting in state $k \in R^i$ at $x = 0$.

- $F^i_{k\ell}(x, w)$ is the probability that t_g fires from state $\ell \in R^i$ (hitting the absorbing barrier w in ℓ) before x, starting in state $k \in R^i$ at $x = 0$.

- $D^i_{k\ell}(x, w)$ is the probability of first passage from a state $k \in R^i$ to a state $\ell \in R^{ci}$ before hitting the barrier w, starting in state $k \in R^i$ at $x = 0$.

- Δ^i is the branching probability matrix and represents the successor tangible marking ℓ that is reached by firing t_g in state $k \in R^i$ (the firing of t_g in the subordinated process $\mathcal{M}^i(x)$, can only occur in a state k in which $r^i_k = 1$).

From (7), it follows for any x:

$$\sum_{\ell \in R^i \cup R^{ci}} [\, P^i_{k\ell}(x, w) + F^i_{k\ell}(x, w) + D^i_{k\ell}(x, w) \,] = 1$$

Given that $G_g(w)$ is the cumulative distribution function of the r.v. γ_g associated to the transition t_g, the elements of the i-th row of matrices $\mathbf{K}(x)$ and $\mathbf{E}(x)$ can be expressed as follows, as a function of the matrices $\mathbf{P}^i(x, w)$, $\mathbf{F}^i(x, w)$ and $\mathbf{D}^i(x, w)$:

$$K_{ij}(x) = \int_{w=0}^{\infty} [\, \sum_{k \in R^i} F^i_{ik}(x, w) \Delta^i_{kj} + D^i_{ij}(x, w) \,] \, dG_g(w) \tag{8}$$

$$E_{ij}(x) = \int_{w=0}^{\infty} P^i_{ij}(x, w) \, dG_g(w)$$

In order to avoid unnecessarily cumbersome notation in the following derivation, we neglect the explicit dependence on the particular subordinated process $Z^i(x)$, by eliminating the superscript i. It is however tacitly intended, that all the quantities $\underline{r}$, $\mathbf{Q}(x)$, $\mathbf{P}(x, w)$, $\mathbf{F}(x, w)$, $\mathbf{D}(x, w)$, Δ, R and R^c refer to the specific process subordinated to the regeneration period starting from state i.

5.1 Derivation of $\mathbf{P}(x, w)$, $\mathbf{F}(x, w)$ and $\mathbf{D}(x, w)$

The derivation of these matrix functions is described in more detail in [21, 6] and follows the same pattern of the completion time analysis presented in [19, 4].

Theorem 1 - *For the firing probability $F_{k\ell}(x, w)$ the following double transform equation holds:*

$$F^{\sim*}_{k\ell}(s, v) = \delta_{k\ell} \frac{r_k [1 - Q^{\sim}_k(s + v\,r_k)]}{s + v\,r_k} + \sum_{u \in R} Q^{\sim}_{ku}(s + v\,r_k) F^{\sim*}_{u\ell}(s, v) \tag{9}$$

Proof - Conditioning on $H = h$ and $\gamma_g = w$, let us define:

$$F_{k\ell}(x, w \,|\, H = h) =$$

$$\begin{cases} \delta_{k\ell} \, U\left(x - \dfrac{w}{r_k}\right) & \text{if}: h\,r_k \geq w \\[2ex] \displaystyle\sum_{u \in R} \frac{dQ_{ku}(h)}{dQ_k(h)} \cdot F_{u\ell}(x - h, w - h\,r_k) & \\[1ex] & \text{if}: h\,r_k < w \end{cases} \tag{10}$$

In (10), two mutually exclusive events are identified. If $r_k \neq 0$ and $h\,r_k \geq w$, a sojourn time equals to w is accumulated before leaving state k, so that the firing time (next regeneration time point) is $\tau_1^* = w/r_k$. If $h\,r_k < w$ then a transition occurs to state u with probability $dQ_{ku}(h)/dQ_k(h)$ and the residual service $(w - h\,r_k)$ should be accomplished starting from state u at time $(x - h)$. Taking the LST transform with respect to x (denoting the transform variable by s), the LT transform with respect to w (denoting the transform variable by v) of (10) and unconditioning with respect to H, (10) becomes (9). $\square$

Theorem 2 - *The state probability $P_{k\ell}(x, w)$ satisfies the following double transform equation:*

$$P^{\sim*}_{k\ell}(s, v) = \delta_{k\ell} \frac{s [1 - Q^{\sim}_k(s + v\,r_k)]}{v(s + v\,r_k)} + \sum_{u \in R} Q^{\sim}_{ku}(s + v\,r_k) P^{\sim*}_{u\ell}(s, v) \tag{11}$$

Proof - Conditioning on $H = h$, and $\gamma_g = w$ let us define:

$$P_{k\ell}(x, w \,|\, H = h) =$$

$$\begin{cases} \delta_{k\ell} \left[U(x) - U\left(x - \dfrac{w}{r_k}\right) \right] & \\[1ex] & \text{if}: h\,r_k \geq w \\[2ex] \delta_{k\ell} \, [U(x) - U(x - h)] + & \\[1ex] \displaystyle\sum_{u \in R} \frac{dQ_{ku}(h)}{dQ_k(h)} P_{u\ell}(x - h, w - h\,r_k) & \\[1ex] & \text{if}: h\,r_k < w \end{cases} \tag{12}$$

The derivation of the matrix function $\mathbf{P}(x, w)$ based on (12) follows the same pattern as for the function $\mathbf{F}(x, w)$ [21]. $\square$

Theorem 3 - *The probability $D_{k\ell}(x, w)$ of first passage into R^c satisfies the following double transform equation:*

$$D_{k\ell}^{\sim *}(s,v) = \frac{1}{v} Q_{kl}^{\sim}(s + v\,r_k) + \sum_{u \in R} Q_{ku}^{\sim}(s + v\,r_k)\, D_{u\ell}^{\sim *}(s,v) \qquad (13)$$

Proof - Conditioning on $H = h$, and $\gamma_g = w$ let us define:

$$D_{k\ell}(x, w \mid H = h) =$$

$$
\begin{cases}
0 & \text{if}: h\,r_k \geq w \\[2ex]
\dfrac{dQ_{k\ell}(h)}{dQ_k(h)} U(x - h) + \\[1ex]
\quad \sum_{u \in R} \dfrac{dQ_{ku}(h)}{dQ_k(h)} D_{u\ell}(x - h, w - h\,r_k) \\[2ex]
& \text{if}: h\,r_k < w
\end{cases}
$$

$$(14)$$

The derivation of the matrix function $\mathbf{D}(x, w)$ based on (14) follows the same pattern as for the function $\mathbf{F}(x, w)$ [21]. $\square$

5.2 The subordinated process is a Reward CTMC

Let us consider the particular case in which the subordinated process $Z(x)$ is a reward $CTMC$ with infinitesimal generator $\mathbf{A} = \{a_{k\ell}\}$. Let us suppose that the states numbered $1, 2, \ldots, m$ belong to R $(1, 2, \ldots, m \in R)$ and the states numbered $m + 1, m + 2, \ldots, n$ belong to R^c $(m + 1, m + 2, \ldots, n \in R^c)$. By this ordering of states $\mathbf{A}$ can be partitioned into the following submatrices $\mathbf{A} = \begin{array}{|c|c|} \hline \mathbf{B} & \mathbf{C} \\ \hline \mathbf{U_1} & \mathbf{U_2} \\ \hline \end{array}$ where $\mathbf{B}$ contains the intensity of the transitions inside R, and $\mathbf{C}$ contains the intensity of the transitions from R to R^c. $\mathbf{U_1}$ and $\mathbf{U_2}$ refer to the portion of the state space not involved in the current subordinated marking process, and are, thus, not influential for the problem at hand. For this reason, their entries can be assumed equal to zero.

Corollary 4 - *The entries of the matrix functions $P_{k\ell}(x, w)$, $F_{k\ell}(x, w)$ and $D_{k\ell}(x, w)$, in double transform domain, take the following expression:*

$$(s + vr_k) F_{k\ell}^{\sim *}(s, v) = \delta_{k\ell}\, r_k + \sum_{u \in R} a_{ku} F_{u\ell}^{\sim *}(s, v)$$

$$(s + vr_k) P_{k\ell}^{\sim *}(s, v) = \delta_{k\ell}\, \frac{s}{v} + \sum_{u \in R} a_{ku} P_{u\ell}^{\sim *}(s, v)$$

$$(s + vr_k) D_{k\ell}^{\sim *}(s, v) = \frac{a_{k\ell}}{v} + \sum_{u \in R} a_{ku} D_{u\ell}^{\sim *}(s, v)$$

$$(15)$$

Proof - The kernel (transition probability matrix) of the given $CTMC$ can be written as:

$$
Q_{k\ell}(x) = \begin{cases}
\dfrac{a_{k\ell}}{-a_{kk}} \left(1 - e^{a_{kk}\, x}\right) & \text{if}: k \neq \ell \\[2ex]
0 & \text{if}: k = \ell
\end{cases}
\qquad (16)
$$

and in LST domain:

$$
Q_{k\ell}^{\sim}(s) = \begin{cases}
\dfrac{a_{k\ell}}{s - a_{kk}} & \text{if}: k \neq \ell \\[2ex]
0 & \text{if}: k = \ell
\end{cases}
\qquad (17)
$$

with $a_{kk} = -\sum_{\ell \in R^i \cup R^{ci}, \ell \neq k} a_{k\ell}$

By substituting (17) into (11), (9) and (13), the corollary is proved. $\square$

Equations (15) can be rewritten in matrix form:

$$\mathbf{F}^{\sim *}(s, v) = (s\mathbf{I} + v\mathbf{R} - \mathbf{B})^{-1} \mathbf{R}$$

$$\mathbf{P}^{\sim *}(s, v) = \frac{s}{v} (s\mathbf{I} + v\mathbf{R} - \mathbf{B})^{-1}$$

$$\mathbf{D}^{\sim *}(s, v) = \frac{1}{v} (s\mathbf{I} + v\mathbf{R} - \mathbf{B})^{-1} \mathbf{C}$$

where $\mathbf{I}$ is the identity matrix and $\mathbf{R}$ is the diagonal matrix of the reward rates (r_k); the dimensions of $\mathbf{I}$, $\mathbf{R}$, $\mathbf{B}$, $\mathbf{F}$ and $\mathbf{P}$ are $(m \times m)$, and the dimensions of $\mathbf{C}$ and $\mathbf{D}$ are $(m \times (n - m))$.

6 Numerical Results

A numerical derivation of the transient state probabilities of the M/D/1/2/2 system described in Example 2 of Section 4.2 is provided. We consider in details the particular case in which the GEN transitions t_2 and t_4 are assumed to be deterministic with duration α, while t_1 and t_3 are EXP with parameter λ [6]. The reachability graph in Figure 2b comprises 4 states. Let us build up the $\mathbf{K}^{\sim}(s)$ and $\mathbf{E}^{\sim}(s)$ matrices row by row, taking into consideration that state s_4 can never be a regeneration marking since a type 2 job with nonzero age memory is always active.

i) - *The starting regeneration state is s_1* - No deterministic transitions are enabled: the state is Markovian and the next regeneration state can be either state s_2 or s_3. The nonzero elements of the 1-st row of matrices $\mathbf{K}^{\sim}(s)$ and $\mathbf{E}^{\sim}(s)$ take the form:

$$K_{12}^{\sim}(s) = \frac{\lambda}{s + 2\lambda} \qquad ; \qquad K_{13}^{\sim}(s) = \frac{\lambda}{s + 2\lambda}$$

$$E_{11}^{\sim}(s) = \frac{s}{s + 2\lambda} \qquad ;$$

ii) - *The starting regeneration state is s_2* - Transition t_2 is deterministic so that the next regeneration time point is the epoch of firing of t_2. The subordinated process $\mathcal{M}^2(x)$ comprises states s_2 and s_4 and is a semi-Markov process (Case D) since t_4 is deterministic. The kernel of the semi-Markov process is:

131

$$Q^\sim(s) = \begin{vmatrix} 0 & 0 & 0 & 0 \\ 0 & 0 & 0 & \dfrac{\lambda}{s+\lambda} \\ 0 & 0 & 0 & 0 \\ 0 & e^{-\alpha s} & 0 & 0 \end{vmatrix}$$

The reward vector is $\underline{r}^{(2)} = [0, 1, 0, 0]$, and the only nonzero entry of the branching probability matrix is $\Delta_{21}^{(2)} = 1$. Applying Equations (9) and (11) we obtain the following results for the nonzero entries:

$$F_{22}^{\sim*}(s,w) = \frac{1}{s+w+\lambda-\lambda e^{-s\alpha}}$$

$$P_{22}^{\sim*}(s,w) = \frac{s/w}{s+w+\lambda-\lambda e^{-s\alpha}}$$

$$P_{24}^{\sim*}(s,w) = \frac{\lambda(1-e^{-s\alpha})/w}{s+w+\lambda-\lambda e^{-s\alpha}}$$

Applying (8), and after inverting the LT transform with respect to w, the LST matrix functions $\mathbf{K}^\sim(s)$ and $\mathbf{E}^\sim(s)$ become:

$$K_{21}^\sim(s) = e^{-\alpha(s+\lambda-\lambda e^{-\alpha s})}$$

$$E_{22}^\sim(s) = \frac{s[1-e^{-\alpha(s+\lambda-\lambda e^{-\alpha s})}]}{s+\lambda-\lambda e^{-\alpha s}}$$

$$E_{24}^\sim(s) = \frac{\lambda(1-e^{-\alpha s})[1-e^{-\alpha(s+\lambda-\lambda e^{-\alpha s})}]}{s+\lambda-\lambda e^{-\alpha s}}$$

iii) - The starting regeneration state is s_3 - The subordinated process $\mathcal{M}^3(x)$ is a $CTMC$ (Case C), hence the results of Section 5.2 apply. The infinitesimal generator of the $CTMC$ is:

$$\mathbf{A} = \begin{vmatrix} 0 & 0 & 0 & 0 \\ 0 & 0 & 0 & 0 \\ 0 & 0 & -\lambda & \lambda \\ 0 & 0 & 0 & 0 \end{vmatrix}$$

and the reward vector is $\underline{r}^{(3)} = [0, 0, 1, 1]$. The branching probabilities arising from the firing of t_4 are $\Delta_{31}^{(3)} = 1$ and $\Delta_{42}^{(3)} = 1$. Applying the first and second equation in (15), the nonzero entries take the form:

$$F_{33}^{\sim*}(s,w) = \frac{1}{s+\lambda+w}$$

$$F_{34}^{\sim*}(s,w) = \frac{\lambda}{(s+w)(s+\lambda+w)}$$

$$P_{33}^{\sim*}(s,w) = \frac{s}{w(s+\lambda+w)}$$

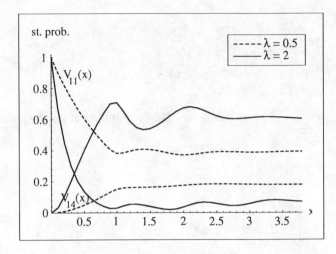

Figure 3 - Transient behavior of the state probabilities for the preemptive M/D/1/2/2 system with different customers.

$$P_{34}^{\sim*}(s,w) = \frac{\lambda s}{w(s+w)(s+\lambda+w)}$$

Inverting the above equations with respect to w, taking into account the branching probabilities, yields:

$$K_{31}^\sim(s) = e^{-\alpha(s+\lambda)}$$

$$K_{32}^\sim(s) = e^{-\alpha s}(1-e^{-\alpha\lambda})$$

$$E_{33}^\sim(s) = \frac{s}{s+\lambda}(1-e^{-\alpha(s+\lambda)})$$

$$E_{34}^\sim(s) = \frac{\lambda}{s+\lambda} - (1-\frac{s}{s+\lambda}e^{-\alpha\lambda})e^{-\alpha s}$$

The time domain probabilities are calculated by first deriving matrix $\mathbf{V}^\sim(s)$ from (6) using a standard package for symbolic analysis (e.g. MATHEMATICA), and then numerically inverting the resulting LST expressions resorting to the Jagerman's method [18]. The plot of the state probabilities versus time for states s_1 and s_4 is reported in Figure 3, for a deterministic service duration $\alpha = 1$ and for two different values of the submitting rate $\lambda = 0.5$ and $\lambda = 2$.

7   Conclusion

The GDT_SPN model, whose semantics has been discussed in [1], provides a natural environment for the definition of a class of analytically tractable $MRSPN$'s. The paper has considered the case of GDT_SPN with non-overlapping activity cycles, such that the marking process subordinated to the activity cycle of the dominant transition is a reward semi-Markov process. The inclusion of a reward variable in the description of the subordinated process has proven to be very effective technique for extending the descriptive power of the model to age memory policies, and for providing a unified procedure for the analytical solution.

Acknowledgements

This work has been partially supported by PHARE-ACCORD under grant No. H-9112-0353 and by OTKA under grant No. W-015859.

References

[1] M. Ajmone Marsan, G. Balbo, A. Bobbio, G. Chiola, G. Conte, and A. Cumani. The effect of execution policies on the semantics and analysis of stochastic Petri nets. *IEEE Transactions on Software Engineering*, SE-15:832–846, 1989.

[2] M. Ajmone Marsan, G. Balbo, and G. Conte. A class of generalized stochastic Petri nets for the performance evaluation of multiprocessor systems. *ACM Transactions on Computer Systems*, 2:93–122, 1984.

[3] M. Ajmone Marsan and G. Chiola. On Petri nets with deterministic and exponentially distributed firing times. In *Lecture Notes in Computer Science*, volume 266, pages 132–145. Springer Verlag, 1987.

[4] A. Bobbio and M. Telek. Task completion time. In *Proceedings 2nd International Workshop on Performability Modelling of Computer and Communication Systems (PMCCS2)*, 1993.

[5] A. Bobbio and M. Telek. Computational restrictions for SPN with generally distributed transition times. In D. Hammer K. Echtle and D. Powell, editors, *First European Dependable Computing Conference (EDCC-1)*, pages 131–148, 1994.

[6] A. Bobbio and M. Telek. Transient analysis of a preemptive resume M/D/1/2/2 through Petri nets. Technical report, Department of Telecommunications - Technical University of Budapest, April 1994.

[7] H. Choi, V.G. Kulkarni, and K. Trivedi. Transient analysis of deterministic and stochastic Petri nets. In *Proceedings of the 14-th International Conference on Application and Theory of Petri Nets*, Chicago, June 1993.

[8] H. Choi, V.G. Kulkarni, and K. Trivedi. Markov regenerative stochastic Petri nets. *Performance Evaluation*, 20:337–357, 1994.

[9] G. Ciardo, R. German, and C. Lindemann. A characterization of the stochastic process underlying a stochastic Petri net. In *Proceedings International Workshop on Petri Nets and Performance Models - PNPM93*, pages 170–179. IEEE Computer Society, 1993.

[10] G. Ciardo and C. Lindemann. Analysis of deterministic and stochastic Petri nets. In *Proceedings International Workshop on Petri Nets and Performance Models - PNPM93*, pages 160–169. IEEE Computer Society, 1993.

[11] E. Cinlar. *Introduction to Stochastic Processes*. Prentice-Hall, Englewood Cliffs, 1975.

[12] D.R. Cox. The analysis of non-markovian stochastic processes by the inclusion of supplementary variables. *Proceedings of the Cambridge Phylosophical Society*, 51:433–440, 1955.

[13] J. Bechta Dugan, K. Trivedi, R. Geist, and V.F. Nicola. Extended stochastic Petri nets: applications and analysis. In *Proceedings PERFORMANCE '84*, Paris, 1984.

[14] D.P. Gaver. A waiting line with interrupted service, including priorities. *Journal of the Royal Statistical Society*, B24:73–90, 1962.

[15] R. German and C. Lindemann. Analysis of stochastic Petri nets by the method of supplementary variables. *Performance Evaluation*, 20: 317–335, 1994.

[16] P.J. Haas and G.S. Shedler. Regenerative stochastic Petri nets. *Performance Evaluation*, 6: 189–204, 1986.

[17] B.R. Haverkort and K. Trivedi. Specification techniques for Markov Reward Models. *Discrete Event Dynamic Systems: Theory and Applications*, 3:219–247, 1993.

[18] D.L. Jagerman. An inversion technique for the Laplace transform. *The Bell System Technical Journal*, 61:1995–2002, October 1982.

[19] V.G. Kulkarni, V.F. Nicola, and K. Trivedi. On modeling the performance and reliability of multimode computer systems. *The Journal of Systems and Software*, 6:175–183, 1986.

[20] C. Lindemann. An improved numerical algorithm for calculating steady-state solutions of deterministic and stochastic Petri net models. *Performance Evaluation*, 18:75–95, 1993.

[21] Miklós Telek. *Some advanced reliability modelling techniques*. Phd Thesis, Hungarian Academy of Science, 1994.

Markov Regenerative Models

Dimitris Logothetis

Kishor S. Trivedi

Antonio Puliafito

GTE Laboratories
40 Sylvan Rd.
MS 40-A
Waltham MA 02174

Center for Adv. Comp. and Comm.
Dept. of Elec. Eng.
Duke University - Box 90291
Durham NC 27708-0291

Ist. di Inform. e Telecom.
Univ. of Catania
Viale A. Doria 6, 95125
ITALY

Abstract

The Markov Regenerative Stochastic Process (MRGP) has been shown to capture the behavior of real systems with both deterministic and exponentially distributed event times. In this paper we survey the MRGP literature and focus on the different solution techniques that can be adopted for their transient analysis. We also discuss the automated generation of MRGPs from Deterministic and Stochastic Petri Nets (DSPNs). Some examples are developed and solved to illustrate the modeling power of MRGPs and DSPNs.

1 Introduction

Modeling is a fundamental aspect in the design process of a complex system as it allows the designer to compare different architectural choices as well as predict the behavior of the system under varying input traffic, service, fault and recovery parameters. Depending on the final target of the analysis and on the complexity of the system, different modeling techniques can be adopted. Model types such as reliability block diagrams and fault trees allow a concise description of the system under study and can be evaluated efficiently, but they cannot easily represent dependencies occurring in real systems.

When a more detailed description of the system is required, Markov models can be adopted as a very powerful modeling framework. Such models are frequently used for performance and reliability analysis as they are capable of capturing various kinds of dependencies that occur in real systems. Markov models are also very useful in evaluating the systems performance in presence of concurrency, synchronization and failures. The analytical tractability of Markov models is based on the exponential assumption of the distribution of the holding time in a given state. This implies that the future evolution of the system depends only on the current state and, based on this assumption, simple and tractable equations can be derived for both transient and steady state analysis.

Nevertheless, the exponential assumption has been regarded as one of the main restrictions in the application of Markov models. In practice there is a very wide range of circumstances in which it is necessary to model phenomenon whose times to occurrence is not exponentially distributed. The hypothesis of exponential distribution thus allows the definition of models which can give a more qualitative rather than quantitative analysis of real systems.

In computer/communication systems, the existence of deterministic or other non-exponentially distributed event times, such as timer expiration, propagation delay, transmission of fixed length packets etc. gives rise to stochastic models that are non-Markovian in nature. A non-Markovian model can be Markovized using phased-type approximation. However, phased-type expansion increases the already large state-space of a real system model. The problem becomes really severe when mixing deterministic times with exponential ones.

An alternative approach is to study the underlying process of such non-Markovian systems. In many cases this process can be shown to be a Markov regenerative one (also known as semi-regenerative process) and therefore Markov renewal theory can be applied for its long-run as well as time-dependent behavior. Recently, several researchers have begun work on transient analysis of Markov regenerative processes (MRGP) [8, 9, 15, 16] as well as on the automated generation of such processes starting from non-Markovian stochastic Petri nets [5, 9, 14, 27] and several applications have been solved in performance/reliability analysis of computer/communication systems [4, 20, 21].

The aim of this paper is to exploit the features of MRGP for performance and reliability analysis of systems. The theoretical framework is described, along with an in-depth analysis of the solution techniques. Computational methods for systems with deterministically and exponentially distributed event times are specially discussed and some interesting applications are presented.

The paper is organized as follows. Section 2 introduces Markov regenerative processes and discusses their mathematical background. Reward models for the previously mentioned stochastic processes are described in Section 3. Section 4 introduces non-Markovian stochastic Petri nets as a tool to automatically generate the underlying stochastic process of a non-Markovian model. In Section 5 we discuss solution methods for the transient analysis of MRGP and in Section 6 we present Petri net examples with special structure that can be solved effectively using the

134

time domain approach. A few concluding remarks and some possible extensions are given in Section 7.

2 Theory of Markov Regenerative Processes

In this section, we review the mathematical background of Markov regenerative process that we use subsequently. We consider discrete state-space processes with state-space $\Omega \subseteq \mathcal{N} = \{0, 1, 2, \cdots, \}$

Definition 1 *A sequence of bivariate random variables $\{(Y_n, T_n)\}$ is called a* Markov Renewal Sequence (MRS) *if:*

1. $T_0 = 0, T_{n+1} \geq T_n; Y_n \in \Omega$

2. $\forall n \geq 0,$
$$P\{Y_{n+1} = j, T_{n+1} - T_n \leq x \mid Y_n = i,$$
$$T_n, Y_{n-1}, T_{n-1}, \cdots, Y_0, T_0\}$$
$$= P\{Y_{n+1} = j, T_{n+1} - T_n \leq x \mid Y_n = i\}$$
$$= P\{Y_1 - j, T_1 \leq x \mid Y_0 = i\} = K_{ij}(x)$$

The matrix $\mathbf{K}(x)$ formed by the elements $K_{ij}(x)$ is called the kernel of the MRS. Define the conditional distribution of T_1, given that $Y_0 = i$ as:

$$H_i(x) = P\{T_1 \leq x | Y_0 = i\} = \sum_{j \in \Omega} K_{ij}(x) \qquad (1)$$

Markov renewal sequences play an important role in the formulation of semi-Markov, Markov renewal and Markov regenerative processes.

Definition 2 *Let $\{(Y_n, T_n), n \geq 0\}$ be a MRS with kernel $\mathbf{K}(x)$. Define $N(t)$ as:*

$$N(t) = \sup\{n \geq 0 : T_n \leq t\} \qquad (2)$$

The continuous-time discrete-state process, $X(t)$, defined by:
$$X(t) = Y_{N(t)}, t \geq 0 \qquad (3)$$

is called a semi-Markov Process (SMP).

Let $V_{ij}(t)$

$$V_{ij}(t) = P\{X(t) = j | X(0) = i\}, t \geq 0 \qquad (4)$$

It can be shown [18] that the conditional probabilities $V_{ij}(t)$ satisfy the following equations:

$$V_{ij}(t) = (1 - H_i(t))\delta_{ij} + \sum_{k \in \Omega} \int_0^t dK_{ik}(u)V_{kj}(t-u) \qquad (5)$$

where δ_{ij} is the Kronecker delta function:

$$\delta_{ij} = \begin{cases} 1 & i = j \\ 0 & \text{otherwise} \end{cases} \qquad (6)$$

The integral

$$K_{ik} * V_{kj}(t) = \int_0^t dK_{ik}(u)V_{kj}(t-u) \qquad (7)$$

is the Stieltjes convolution integral. Equation (5) can be written in matrix form:

$$\mathbf{V}(t) = \mathbf{E}(t) + \int_0^t d\mathbf{K}(s)\mathbf{V}(t-s) = \mathbf{E}(t) + \mathbf{K}(t)^*\mathbf{V}(t) \qquad (8)$$

Matrix $\mathbf{E}(t)$ for the SMP is a diagonal matrix with elements $E_{ii}(t)$ given by:

$$E_{ii}(t) = P\{X(t) = i, T_1 > t | Y_0 = i\} = 1 - H_i(t) \qquad (9)$$

Equation (5) is known as the Markov renewal equation.

Definition 3 *A stochastic process $\{Z(t), t \geq 0\}$ is called a* Markov Regenerative Process (MRGP), *if there exists a Markov renewal sequence $\{(Y_n, T_n), n \geq 0\}$ of random variables such that all the conditional finite dimensional distributions of $\{Z(T_n + t), t \geq 0\}$ given $\{Z(u), 0 \leq u \leq T_n, Y_n = i\}$ are the same as those of $\{Z(t), t \geq 0\}$ given $Y_0 = i$.*

The above definition implies that:

$$P\{Z(T_n + t) = j | Z(u), 0 \leq u \leq T_n, Y_n = i\}$$
$$= P\{Z(t) = j | Y_0 = i\} \qquad (10)$$

From the above definition it is obvious that every SMP is an MRGP. The difference between semi-Markov process and Markov regenerative process can be seen by comparing the sequence T_n with the sequence obtained from the state transition instants L_n of the processes. For the SMP we have $L_{n_{SMP}} = T_n, \forall n$, whereas T_n is just a subsequence of $L_{n_{MRGP}}$. In other words, in a semi-Markov process, every state transition is a regeneration point; however, this is not necessarily true for the Markov regenerative process. The requirement of regeneration at every state transition makes the semi-Markov process of limited interest for transient analysis of systems that involve deterministic parameters as in a communication system.

Figure 1 shows sample paths of an MRGP and its embedded SMP and DTMC. These sample paths correspond to an M/D/1/L+1 queue. Note that in an MRGP sample path (Figure 1 (a)), state is allowed to change between two regeneration points. In the embedded SMP, however (Figure 1 (b)), since every state change is a Markovian regeneration instant, the process keeps the same value until the next regeneration instant. Note, however, that the time spent in the current state (x axis) is retained. If we further ignore the time spent in the current state, we obtain the embedded DTMC (Figure 1 (c)) corresponding to the state sequence of $\{Y_n, n \geq 1\}$ at regeneration epochs.

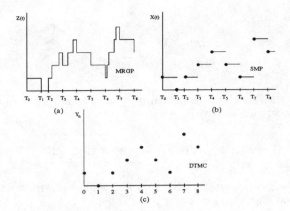

Figure 1: Sample paths of an MRGP and its embedded processes

If we now define $V_{ij}(t)$ as in the case for the semi-Markov process, one can show [18] that for an MRGP:

$$
\begin{aligned}
V_{ij}(t) &= P\{Z(t) = j, T_1 > t | Y_0 = i\} \\
&\quad + \sum_{k \in \Omega} \int_0^t dK_{ik}(u) V_{kj}(t-u) \\
&= E_{ij}(t) + \sum_{k \in \Omega} \int_0^t dK_{ik}(u) V_{kj}(t-u) \quad (11)
\end{aligned}
$$

Note that the semi-Markov and the Markov regenerative process satisfy the same generalized Markov renewal equation (Compare Equations (11) with (5)). The main difference is that matrix $\mathbf{E}(t)$ is diagonal for the SMP (since every state transition instant is a regeneration point) and not diagonal, in general, for the MRGP. Note that $\{Y_n, n \geq 0\}$ is a DTMC with (one-step) transition probability matrix $\mathbf{K}(\infty)$. Matrix $\mathbf{E}(t)$ is called the local kernel, while matrix $\mathbf{K}(t)$ is known as the global kernel of the MRGP.

Assuming an initial probability vector $\mathbf{p}(0)$ we can obtain the system-state probabilities at time t as:

$$
\mathbf{p}(t) = \mathbf{p}(0)\mathbf{V}(t) \quad (12)
$$

3 Markov Regenerative Reward Models (MRRM)

In the previous sections we described various stochastic processes and ways to compute the system-state probabilities at time t. In this section we proceed to define reward models for the previously mentioned stochastic processes. This is done by assigning a reward rate w_i in each state $i \in \Omega$. The process of interest is now $X(t) = w_{Z(t)}$. We can then obtain measures such as distribution of accumulated reward until time t, expected reward rate at time t and steady state expected reward rate. The above definition does not restrict the structure of the underlying process. In [28] the underlying process is taken to be a continuous time Markov chain (CTMC), while in [6] the underlying process is taken to be a semi-Markov process.

We will allow for even more general class of processes, the Markov-regenerative process (MRGP). A variety of measures can be defined based on reward models [26]. In the following we focus on expected reward rate measures (time-dependent and steady-state). In particular, if $p_i(t), i \in \Omega$ are the elements of vector $\mathbf{p}(t)$, (Equation (12)), the expected instantaneous reward rate at time t is given by:

$$
E[X(t)] = \sum_i w_i p_i(t). \quad (13)
$$

Let $Y(t)$ denote the accumulated reward in the interval [0,t). Then $Y(t)$ is given by:

$$
Y(t) = \int_0^t X(\tau)d\tau = \int_0^t w_{Z(\tau)}d\tau
$$

and the expected accumulated reward up to time t can be expressed as:

$$
E[Y(t)] = \sum_i w_i \int_0^t p_i(x)dx. \quad (14)
$$

Finally, if $W(t) = \frac{Y(t)}{t}$ indicates the time averaged accumulated reward, the time averaged reward rate up to time t is given by:

$$
E[W(t)] = \frac{1}{t} \sum_i w_i \int_0^t p_i(x)dx \quad (15)
$$

Steady-state versions of the above can be obtained by taking the limit, as t tends to infinity, of the above expressions. We now turn our attention to the form of the Markov renewal equation for these expected reward measures.

3.1 Transient measures

Let $\mathbf{x}^T(t) = \mathbf{V}(t) \times \mathbf{w}^T$ the vector with elements $E[X(t)|Z(0) = i]$ the expected instantaneous reward rate at time t conditional on the initial state. Multiplying both sides of the generalized Markov renewal equation (Equation (11)) with the column reward rate vector $\mathbf{w}^T$ we obtain

$$
\mathbf{x}^T(t) = \mathbf{f}^T(t) + \int_0^t d\mathbf{K}(x)\mathbf{x}^T(t-x) \quad (16)
$$

where $\mathbf{f}^T(t) = \mathbf{E}(t) \times \mathbf{w}^T$. Taking Laplace Stieltjes Transforms (LSTs) on both sides we obtain a linear system in the s-domain:

$$
[\mathbf{I} - \mathbf{K}^{\sim}(s)]\mathbf{x}^{\sim}(s)^T = \mathbf{f}^{\sim}(s) \quad (17)
$$

where $\mathbf{K}^{\sim}(s) = \int_0^\infty e^{-st} d\mathbf{K}(t)$, $\mathbf{f}^{\sim}(s) = \int_0^\infty e^{-st} d\mathbf{f}(t)$ and $\mathbf{x}^{\sim}(s) = \int_0^\infty e^{-st} d\mathbf{x}(t)$.

In a similar way, the expected accumulated reward up to time t conditional on the initial state can be obtained after integrating Equation (16) from 0 to t.

In the s-domain, the column vector $\mathbf{y}^{\sim}(s)^T$ whose elements are the LST of the expected accumulated reward up to time t, conditional on the initial state can be computed as the solution of the linear system:

$$[\mathbf{I} - \mathbf{K}^{\sim}(s)]\,\mathbf{y}^{\sim}(s)^T = \frac{\mathbf{f}^{\sim}(s)}{s} \tag{18}$$

Finally, the column vector $\mathbf{i}(t)^T$ whose elements are the expected time averaged reward rate up to time t, conditional on the initial state is obtained as simply as $\mathbf{i}(t) = \frac{\mathbf{y}(t)}{t}$. Note that a numerical inversion using Jagerman's method [7, 17] or the Abate and Whitt method [1] will be necessary in order to obtain time domain values of $E[X(t)]$, $E[Y(t)]$ and $\frac{E[Y(t)]}{t}$.

3.2 Steady-state measures

If the embedded DTMC at regeneration points ($\{Y_n, n \geq 0\}$) is aperiodic, irreducible and recurrent non-null then its steady-state probability vector ν is the solution of the linear system $\nu = \nu \mathbf{K}(\infty)$, $\sum_{i \in \Omega} \nu_i = 1$. Let a_{ij} denote the integral $\int_0^\infty E_{ij}(x)dx$. Then it can be shown [18] that the steady-state probabilities π_j of the MRGP are given by:

$$\pi_j = \frac{\sum_{k \in \Omega} \nu_k a_{kj}}{\sum_{k \in \Omega} \nu_k \sum_{l \in \Omega} a_{kl}} \tag{19}$$

The steady-state expected reward rate would then be given as:

$$E[X(\infty)] = \pi \times \mathbf{w}^T \tag{20}$$

4 Model specification

Markov models are frequently used for performance and reliability analysis as they are capable of capturing various kinds of dependencies that occur in such models. Markov models are also very useful in evaluating the systems performance in presence of concurrency, synchronization and failures. Nevertheless, as models of real systems often contain thousand or even millions of states, Markov models experience the major drawback of the largeness of their state spaces.

To overcome this problem, Stochastic Petri nets (SPNs) can be used to generate a large underlying Markov model automatically starting from a concise description [27]. This feature, along with their remarkable flexibility and potential as a modeling tool to analyze the performance and reliability of complex systems comprising concurrency and synchronization, make Petri nets to be viewed as an appropriate model for the qualitative and quantitative study of real systems.

In the last decade, significant research has been conducted and Petri nets have been applied to a large range of real situations. Many extensions to the basic PN introduced by C. A. Petri in 1962 [23] have been proposed both to increase the class of problems that can be represented (modeling power) and to the ability to represent real-system behavior (modeling convenience).

Extensions which affect only modeling convenience may be adopted without losing analytical tractability. Theoretically, such extensions may be regarded as simply a convenient shorthand. In practice, they may drastically improve the ability to apply PNs to real problems. Some of these extensions include arc multiplicity, inhibitors arcs, transition priorities and marking dependent parameters.

Extensions to the modeling power of a Petri net were obtained by associating stochastic and timing information to it in such a way as to make the PN formalism correspond to a wide range of well-known stochastic processes. Specifically, continuous-time Markov chains underlie Stochastic Petri Nets (SPN) [2], Generalized Stochastic Petri Nets (GSPN) [2] and Stochastic Reward Net (SRNs) [10], semi-Markov processes underlie a subset of Extended Stochastic Petri Nets (ESPN) [12] and Markov regenerative processes underlie Deterministic and Stochastic Petri Nets (DSPN) [8]. Recently, we introduced a new class of stochastic Petri nets, called Markov Regenerative Stochastic Petri Nets (MRSPNs) that can be analyzed by means of Markov regenerative processes and constitutes a true generalization of all the above classes [9]. The main feature of a MRSPN is the capability to model generally distributed timed events, thus allowing Petri nets to be used to model a larger range of real situations.

5 Model solution

In this section we will discuss solution methods for the generalized Markov renewal equation. We will discuss and compare both time-domain and transform methods. We will first discuss solution methods in general and then concentrate on MRGPs generated from a DSPN specification. We will concentrate on the transient analysis.

5.1 Transient Analysis

The generalized Markov renewal equation (Equation (11)) represents a system of coupled integral equations (Volterra integral equations of the second kind [13]) that are in general hard to solve in time-domain. A discretization approach would involve numerical evaluation of the integral using some approximation rule such as trapezoidal rule, Simpson's rule or other higher order methods:

$$\mathbf{V}(t_n) = \mathbf{E}(t_n) + \sum_{i=0}^{n} a_i \mathbf{K}'(t_i)\mathbf{V}(t_n - t_i) \tag{21}$$

where $\mathbf{K}'(t_i)$ denotes the derivative $\frac{d\mathbf{K}(x)}{dx}$ evaluated at point t_i [1]. The coefficients a_i depend on the integration technique used. For example, when the trapezoidal rule is used $a_0 = a_n = \frac{h}{2}$ and $a_i = h, i = 1, 2, \cdots, n-1$. h is the discretization step and it is assumed constant. Then for any time $t = t_n = nh$, a

---

[1]When the derivative of matrix $\mathbf{K}(t)$ is difficult to obtain Equation can be approximated as: $\mathbf{V}(t_n) = \mathbf{E}(t_n) + \sum_{i=0}^{n}[\mathbf{K}'(t_i) - \mathbf{K}'(t_{i-1})]\mathbf{V}(t_n - t_i)$.

137

linear system of the form:

$$[\mathbf{I} - a_0\mathbf{K}'(0)]\mathbf{V}(t_n) = \mathbf{E}(t_n) + \sum_{i=1}^{n} a_i\mathbf{K}'(t_i)\mathbf{V}(t_n - t_i)$$
(22)

needs to be solved. Note that if $a_0\mathbf{K}'(0) = 0$, then the method is explicit otherwise it is implicit.

A potential problem with this approach is the right-hand side of the above equation can be in general expensive to compute. Nevertheless, there exist cases where the generalized Markov renewal equation has a simple form and the time-domain solution can be carried out.

An alternative to the direct solution of the Markov renewal equation in time-domain is the use of transform methods. In particular, if we define $\mathbf{E}^{\sim}(s) = \int_0^\infty e^{-st}d\mathbf{E}(t)$ and $\mathbf{V}^{\sim}(s) = \int_0^\infty e^{-st}d\mathbf{V}(t)$, Equation (11) becomes [2]:

$$[\mathbf{I} - \mathbf{K}^{\sim}(s)]\mathbf{V}^{\sim}(s) = \mathbf{E}^{\sim}(s)$$
(23)

After solving the linear system for $\mathbf{V}^{\sim}(s)$, transform inversion is required. In very simple cases, a closed-form inversion might be possible but in most cases of interest, numerical inversion will be necessary.

The transform inversion however can encounter numerical difficulties especially if the time domain function has discontinuities or its derivative is not continuous [1]. Systems with deterministic parameters often give rise to such discontinuities.

Another time domain alternative is to construct a system of partial differential equations (PDEs), using the method of supplementary variables [11]. This method has been considered for steady-state analysis in [14] and subsequently extended to the transient regime in [15, 16].

The system of integral equations, can simplify considerably if systems with deterministic parameters (as opposed to general distributions) are considered.

We now turn our attention to the DSPN system description. Note that we can identify four different cases as shown in Figure 2. We will show that in the DSPN framework if there is exactly one deterministic transition enabled (not necessarily the same) that is never preempted, the time-dependent behavior of the marking process of the DSPN can be described by a series of matrix multiplications. More generally, assuming non-preemptible deterministic transitions, but allowing for at most one deterministic transition to be enabled in a marking, the time-dependent solution of the marking process of the DSPN is also carried out in a relatively simple manner. The other two cases with preemptible deterministic transitions do not simplify.

6   Examples

In this section we present DSPN examples with special structure that can be solved effectively using the

---
[2]Note that there is an alternative form of the Equation (11) with LST given by $\mathbf{V}(s) = \mathbf{E}(s) + \mathbf{V}(s)\mathbf{E}^{-1}(s)\mathbf{K}(s)\mathbf{E}(s)$. This Equation is referred to as the backward equation as opposed to Equation (11) that is referred to as the forward equation.

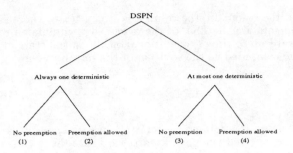

Figure 2: Various cases in Petri Nets

time domain approach. The first example requires exactly one non-preemptible deterministic transition not necessarily with the same firing time to be enabled in each marking. The second example also allows for markings where no deterministic transition is enabled.

6.1   DSPN model with exactly one deterministic transition enabled

In Figure 3 we show an example of a DSPN in each of whose marking exactly one deterministic transition is always enabled. We view the overall DSPN as partitioned into two subnets. One subnet, (D-subnet), is cyclic and consists of only deterministic transitions. Another subnet, (SRN-subnet), is arbitrary except that it contains only exponential and immediate transitions, i.e. it is a Stochastic Reward Net (SRN). Note that for each marking of the D-subnet, the evolution of the system is completely described by the SRN-subnet. Further, the SRN-subnet can change its parameters (transition rates, guards, reward rates) according to the execution state of the D-subnet, while instead the D-subnet marking cannot be affected by the SRN-subnet evolution. Additionally, each deterministic transition cannot be preempted.

There are several applications where this model can be used, e.g., as a Markovian queue with periodic arrivals [24], phased-mission systems [3] or time-limited polling systems [25]. Note that if transition t_5 and place P_5 do not exist then P_4 will give rise to an absorbing marking and the model will correspond to a phased-mission system. When transition t_5 and place P_5 do exist then the model will correspond to a periodic arrival process or a time-limited polling system.

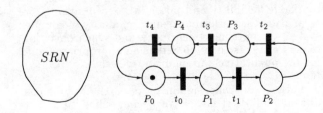

Figure 3: Petri Net model

Let Ω denote the state space of the marking process of the DSPN of Figure 3. Define also $\Omega_i, 0 \le i \le 4$ to be the set of markings in which deterministic transition t_i is enabled. Since $\forall i, j \in (0,1,2,3,4), i \neq j$ deterministic transitions t_i and t_j are not concurrently enabled and sets Ω_i and Ω_j, $i \neq j$ do not have any common elements. This will imply that matrices $\mathbf{K}(t)$ and $\mathbf{E}(t)$ can be represented by a block structure of the form:

$$\mathbf{K}_{ij}(t) = \begin{cases} \mathbf{P}_i(\tau_i)u(t-\tau_i) & \begin{array}{l}0 \leq i \leq 3 \\ j = i+1\end{array} \\ \mathbf{P}_4(\tau_4)u(t-\tau_4) & \begin{array}{l}i = 4 \\ j = 0\end{array} \\ 0 & \text{otherwise} \end{cases} \quad (24)$$

$$\mathbf{E}_{ij}(t) = \begin{cases} \mathbf{P}_i(t)f(t,\tau_i) & \begin{array}{l}0 \leq i \leq 4 \\ j = i\end{array} \\ 0 & \text{otherwise} \end{cases} \quad (25)$$

where $\mathbf{P}_i(t) = e^{\mathbf{Q}_i t}$, $\mathbf{Q}_i$ is the infinitesimal generator matrix of the corresponding Markov chain of the reduced reachability graph when transition t_i is enabled, $u(t - \tau_i)$ is the delayed unit step function and $f(t, \tau_i) = 1 - u(t - \tau_i)$ and τ_i (i=0,1,2,3,4) is the deterministic firing time of transition t_i. The size of the block matrices $\mathbf{K}_{ij}$ and $\mathbf{E}_{ij}$ is $p \times p$, where p is the cardinality of the reduced reachability set of the SRN.

Now since matrix $\mathbf{K}(t)$ depends on time only through delayed unit step functions $u(t - \tau_i)$ the generalized Markov renewal equation is simplified to:

$$\mathbf{V}(t) = \begin{cases} \left[\prod_{i=0}^4 \mathbf{P}_i(\tau_i)\right]^n \mathbf{E}_0(s) \\ \qquad nT < t < nT + \tau_0 \\ \left[\prod_{i=0}^4 \mathbf{P}_i(\tau_i)\right]^n \left[\prod_{i=0}^j \mathbf{P}_i(\tau_i)\mathbf{E}_{j+1}(s)\right] \\ \qquad nT + \tau_0 < t < nT + \sum_{l=0}^j \tau_l, 0 < j \leq 4 \end{cases} \quad (26)$$

where $n = \lfloor \frac{t}{\sum_i \tau_i} \rfloor$, $T = \sum_i \tau_i$ and $s = t - nT$. As n tends to infinity the above expression becomes periodic with period T:

$$\mathbf{V}(s) = \begin{cases} \mathbf{\Pi}\mathbf{E}_0(s) & 0 < s < \tau_0 \\ \mathbf{\Pi}\left[\sum_{i=0}^j \mathbf{P}_i(\tau_i)\mathbf{E}_{j+1}(s)\right] & \tau_0 < s < \sum_{l=0}^j \tau_l, \\ & 0 < j \leq 4 \end{cases} \quad (27)$$

where

$$\mathbf{\Pi} = \lim_{n \to \infty} \left[\prod_{i=0}^4 P_i(\tau_i)\right]^n$$

As a special case, we have equations for the D/MAP/1/L+1 queue [20].

6.2 DSPN with marking having no DET transitions enabled

Now we relax the restriction that exactly one DET transition is always enabled. Let Ω_e denote the set of markings in which no DET transition is enabled and Ω_d the set of markings in which DET transitions are enabled. Clearly, $\Omega_e \cup \Omega_d = \Omega$, the state-space of the marking process of the DSPN. To simplify our analysis we assume all deterministic transitions have the same duration and none of them are preempted. A further generalization that allows transitions with different firing times and preemption of deterministic transitions is also possible but leads to more complex equations.

Matrix $\mathbf{V}(t)$, $\mathbf{K}(t)$ and $\mathbf{E}(t)$ can be partitioned in parts, $\mathbf{V}^{(e)}(t)$, $\mathbf{K}^{(e)}(t)$ and $\mathbf{E}^{(e)}(t)$ with size $n_1 \times n$ and $\mathbf{V}^{(d)}(t)$, $\mathbf{K}^{(d)}(t)$ and $\mathbf{E}^{(d)}(t)$ with size $(n - n_1) \times n$, where n_1, n the cardinalities of Ω_e and Ω, respectively. The Markov renewal equation can be written as:

$$\mathbf{v}_i(t) = \begin{cases} e^{-\Lambda_i t} + \sum_j \int_0^t \lambda(i,j)e^{-\Lambda_i x}\mathbf{v}_j(t-x) & i \in \Omega_e \\ \mathbf{p}_i \mathbf{V}(t-\tau) & i \in \Omega_d \end{cases}$$

$$(28)$$

where $\lambda(i,j)$ is the transition rate from state i to state j of the subordinated Markov chain, $\Lambda_i = \sum_j \lambda(i,j)$ and $\mathbf{v}_i(t)$, $\mathbf{p}_i$ the ith row of matrices $\mathbf{V}(t)$ and $\mathbf{P} = \mathbf{K}(\infty)$, respectively.

The above equations denote the fact that the behavior of the system when only exponential transitions are enabled is described by a system of integral equations, while its behavior when deterministic transitions are enabled is governed by a simple difference equation. The above system of integral equations can be converted to a system of differential equations as follows:

$$\frac{d\mathbf{V}^{(e)}(t)}{dt} = \mathbf{\Lambda}^{(e)}\mathbf{V}^{(e)}(t) + \mathbf{\Lambda}^{(d)}\mathbf{V}^{(d)}(t) \quad (29)$$
$$\mathbf{V}^{(d)}(t) = \mathbf{P}^{(d)}\mathbf{V}(t-\tau) \quad (30)$$

where $\mathbf{\Lambda}^{(e)}$ is the size $n_1 \times n_1$ matrix with entries the transition rates from states of Ω_e to states in Ω_e while $\mathbf{\Lambda}^{(d)}$ is the size $n_1 \times (n - n_1)$ matrix with entries the transition rates from states Ω_e to states in Ω_d. Equation (29) represents a system of first order differential equations with a forcing term $\mathbf{\Lambda}^{(d)}\mathbf{V}^{(d)}(t)$.

As an example we consider the MMPP/D/1/L+1 queue [22]. A DSPN model for the MMPP/D/1/L+1 queue is shown in Figure 4. Place P_1 and transitions t_1 and t_2 represent the modulating process. Whenever there is a token in place P_1 the rate of transition t_{arr} is λ_2; otherwise it is λ_1. The number of tokens in place P_2 represents the total number of customers in the queueing system.

The analysis of the MMPP/D/1/L+1 queue can be seen as a matrix generalization of the analysis of M/D/1/L+1 queue. If the state representation is

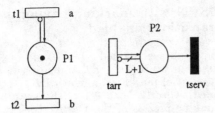

Figure 4: MRSPN for the the MMPP/G/1/L+1 queue

given by the pair (# of customers in the queue, phase of the modulating process) then we can give the following representation in terms of an MRGP.

We define matrices $\mathbf{E}(t)$ and $\mathbf{K}(t)$ as follows:

$$\mathbf{E}_{ij}(t) = \begin{cases} \mathbf{A}(0,t)u(t) & i = 0, \\ & j = 0 \\ \mathbf{A}(j-i,t)[1-u(t-\tau)] & i > 0, \\ & i \le j < L+1 \\ \breve{\mathbf{A}}(i,t)[1-u(t-\tau)] & i > 0, \\ & j = L+1 \\ 0 & \text{otherwise} \end{cases}$$
(31)

$$\mathbf{K}_{ij}(t) = \begin{cases} \left(\mathbf{I} - e^{(\mathbf{Q}-\Lambda)t}\right)(\Lambda - \mathbf{Q})^{-1}\Lambda u(t) & i = 0 \\ & j = 1 \\ \mathbf{A}(j-i+1,\tau)u(t-\tau) < i < L+1 \\ & i-1 \le j < L \\ \breve{\mathbf{A}}(i,\tau)u(t-\tau) & 0 \le i \le L+1 \\ & j = L \\ 0 & \text{otherwise} \end{cases}$$
(32)

with:

$$A_{l,m}(n,t) = P\{N(t) = n, J(t) = m | N(0) = 0, J(0) = l\},$$
(33)

where $N(t)$ denotes the number of arrivals in the interval $(0,t)$ and $J(t)$ the stochastic process that keeps track of the phase of the auxiliary process at time t,

$$\breve{\mathbf{A}}(n,t) = \sum_{l=L+1-n}^{\infty} \mathbf{A}(n,t),$$

$\mathbf{Q}$ is the infinitesimal generator matrix of the modulating process (CTMC) and Λ is the diagonal matrix with entries equal to the arrival rates at a given state of the CTMC. A time-domain algorithm for the computation of transient queue length distribution at time t is given in [21]. The algorithm is summarized as follows: For t in the interval $[0,\tau]$:

$$\mathbf{V}_{ij}(t) = \begin{cases} \mathbf{A}(j-i,t) & i \ge j \\ 0 & i < j \end{cases}$$
(34)

Let $\mathbf{P} = \mathbf{K}(\infty)$ and let $\mathbf{V}_l(t)$, $\mathbf{P}_l$, $l = 0, 1, 2, \cdots L+1$ the lth row matrix of matrices $\mathbf{V}(t)$, $\mathbf{P}$ respectively. Then, for $t > \tau$ $\mathbf{V}_l(t)$ can be computed as follows:

$$\mathbf{V}_l(t) = \begin{cases} \mathbf{P}_l\mathbf{V}(t-\tau) & 0 < l \le L+1 \\ \int_0^t e^{(\mathbf{Q}-\Lambda)x}\Lambda\mathbf{V}_1(t-x)dx + \mathbf{E}_0(t) & l = 0 \end{cases}$$
(35)

where $\mathbf{E}_0(t) = (e^{(\mathbf{Q}-\Lambda)t}, 0, \cdots, 0)$. We can show by direct substitution that the second part of the above equation represents a solution of the following differential equation:

$$\frac{d\mathbf{V}_0(t)}{dt} = (\mathbf{Q} - \Lambda)\,\mathbf{V}_0(t) + \Lambda\mathbf{V}_1(t)$$
(36)

Application of an implicit method such as backward Euler for the solution of the above differential equation requires the solution of a linear system. We will use a higher order explicit method known as the fourth order Runge-Kutta.

$$\mathbf{V}_0(\alpha+2\Delta\alpha) = \mathbf{V}_0(\alpha) + (\mathbf{F}_1+2\mathbf{F}_2+2\mathbf{F}_3+\mathbf{F}_4)\frac{2\Delta\alpha}{3}$$
(37)

with

$$\begin{aligned} \mathbf{F}_1 &= (\mathbf{Q}-\Lambda)\mathbf{V}_0(\alpha) + \Lambda\mathbf{V}_1(\alpha) \\ \mathbf{F}_2 &= \Lambda\mathbf{V}_1(\alpha+\Delta\alpha) + (\mathbf{Q}-\Lambda)(\mathbf{V}_0(\alpha)+\mathbf{F}_1\Delta\alpha) \\ \mathbf{F}_3 &= \Lambda\mathbf{V}_1(\alpha+\Delta\alpha) + (\mathbf{Q}-\Lambda)(\mathbf{V}_0(\alpha)+\mathbf{F}_2\Delta\alpha) \\ \mathbf{F}_4 &= \Lambda\mathbf{V}_1(\alpha+2\Delta\alpha) + (\mathbf{Q}-\Lambda)(\mathbf{V}_0(\alpha)+\mathbf{F}_3 2\Delta\alpha) \end{aligned}$$

In Figure 5 we plot transient loss probabilities for a

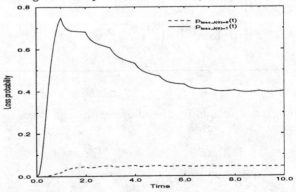

Figure 5: Transient loss probabilities for a two-state MMPP

two state MMPP and $L = 2$. The parameters chosen are: $\lambda_1 = 5$, $\lambda_2 = \frac{5}{9}$, $a = 0.9$ and $b = 0.1$. The above parameters lead to a mean arrival rate $\lambda_m = 1$. We also chose a (deterministic) service time equal to one time unit. The two curves correspond to different values of the modulating process at t equal to 0.

7 Conclusions

In computer/communication systems, the existence of deterministic and exponentially distributed parameters gives rise to stochastic models that are non-Markovian in nature. A non-Markovian model can be studied analyzing its underlying process. In many cases this process can be shown to be a Markov regenerative (MRGP) one and therefore Markov renewal theory can be applied for its long-run as well as time-dependent behavior.

In this paper we surveyed the MRGP literature and focused on the different solution techniques that can be adopted for their transient analysis. Computational methods for systems with deterministically and exponentially distributed event times were presented and some interesting applications, described by using the Petri net notation, were discussed.

References

[1] J. Abate and W. Whitt. The Fourier-Series Method for Inverting Transforms of Probability Distributions. *Queueing Systems*, Vol. 10, Nos. 1-2, 5-88, 1992.

[2] M. Ajmone Marsan, G. Conte and G. Balbo. A Class of Generalized Stochastic Petri Nets for the Performance Evaluation of Multiprocessor Systems, *ACM Trans. on Computer Systems*, Vo. 2 No. 2, 93-122, 1984.

[3] M. Alam, U. Al-Saggaf. Quantitative Reliability Evaluation of Repairable Phased-Mission Systems Using Markov Approach. *IEEE Transactions on Reliability*, Vol. 35, 498-503, 1986.

[4] A. Bobbio and M. Telek. Transient Analysis of a Preemptive Resume M/D/1/2/2 through Petri Nets. *Technical report*, Dept. of Telecommunication, Technical University of Budapest, 1994.

[5] V. Catania, A. Puliafito, M. Scarpa, L. Vita. *Concurrent Generalized Petri Nets*. In *Proc. 2nd Int. Workshop on the Numerical Solution of Markov Chains*, Raleigh, NC, 1995.

[6] G. Ciardo, R. Marie, B. Sericola and K. Trivedi. Performability Analysis Using Semi-Markov Reward Processes. *IEEE Transactions on Computers*, Vol. 39, No. 10, 1251-1264, October 1990.

[7] P. Chimento and K. Trivedi. The Completion Time of Programs on Processors Subject to Failure and Repair. *IEEE Transactions on Computers*, Vol. 42, No. 10, 1184-1194, 1993.

[8] H. Choi, V. Kulkarni, K. Trivedi. Transient Analysis of Deterministic and Stochastic Petri Nets. *Proc. of the 14th Intnl. Conference on Application and Theory of Petri Nets*, Chicago, IL, 166-185, 1993.

[9] H. Choi, V. Kulkarni, K. Trivedi. Markov Regenerative Stochastic Petri Nets, *Performance Evaluation*, Vol. 20, Nos. 1-3, 337-356, 1994.

[10] G. Ciardo, J. Muppala, and K.S. Trivedi. SPNP: Stochastic Petri net package. *Proc. Int. Conf. on Petri Nets and Performance Models*, pp. 142-150, Kyoto, Japan, Dec. 1989.

[11] D. Cox. The Analysis of Non-Markov Stochastic Processes by the Inclusion of Supplementary Variables. *Proc. Camb. Phil. Soc.*, Vol. 51, 433-441, 1955.

[12] J. Dugan, K. Trivedi, R. Geist and V. Nicola. Extended Stochastic Petri Nets: Application and Analysis, *Proc. of the PERFORMANCE '84*, Paris, France, 507-519, 1984.

[13] C. Fröberg. *Introduction to Numerical Analysis*, Second Ed., Addison-Wesley, Reading Massachusetts, 1969.

[14] R. German and C. Lindemann. Analysis of Stochastic Petri Nets by the Method of Supplementary Variables. *Performance Evaluation*, Vol. 20, Nos. 1-3, 317-335, 1994.

[15] R. German. Transient Analysis of Deterministic and Stochastic Petri Nets by the Method of Supplementary Variables. *Proc. of MASCOTS '95*, Durham, NC, 1995.

[16] R. German. New Results for the Analysis of Deterministic and Stochastic Petri Nets. *Proc. Int. Computer Performance and Dependability Symp.*, Erlangen, Germany, 1995.

[17] D. Jagerman. An Inversion Technique for the Laplace Transforms. *Bell System Technical Journal*, Vol. 6, No. 8, 1995-2002, 1982.

[18] V. Kulkarni. *Modeling and Analysis of Stochastic Systems*. Chapman-Hall, 1995.

[19] C. Lindemann. An Improved Numerical Algorithm for Calculating Steady-State Solutions of Deterministic and Stochastic Petri Net Models. *Performance Evaluation*, Vol. 18, No. 1, 79-95, 1993.

[20] D. Logothetis and K. Trivedi. Transient Analysis of the Leaky Bucket Rate Control Scheme Under Poisson and On-Off Sources. *Proc. of Infocom '94*, Toronto, CANADA, 1994.

[21] D. Logothetis and K. Trivedi. Time-Dependent Behavior of Redundant Systems with Deterministic Repair. In *Proc. 2nd Int. Workshop on the Numerical Solution of Markov Chains*, Raleigh, NC, 1995.

[22] D. Logothetis. *Transient Analysis of Communication Networks*, Ph.D. Thesis. Dept. of Electrical Engineering, Duke University, 1994.

[23] C. Petri. *Kommunikation mit Automaten*. PhD thesis, University of Bonn, Bonn, West Germany, 1962.

[24] A. Rindos, S. Woolet, I. Viniotis and K. Trivedi. Exact Methods for the Transient Analysis of Non-homogeneous Continuous-Time Markov Chains. In *Proc. 2nd Int. Workshop on the Numerical Solution of Markov Chains*. Raleigh, NC, 1995.

[25] H. Takagi. Queueing Analysis of Polling Models: An Update. *Stochastic Analysis of Computer and Communication Systems*, Elsevier Science Publishers (North-Holland), 1990.

[26] M. Telek. Some Advanced Reliability Modelling Techniques. *Ph.D Thesis*, Tech. Univ. of Budapest, 1994.

[27] K. Trivedi, A. Puliafito and D. Logothetis. From Stochastic Petri Nets to Markov Regenerative Petri Nets. *Proc. of MASCOTS '95*, Durham, NC, 1995.

[28] K. Trivedi, J. Muppala, S. Woolet and B. Haverkort. Composite Performance and Dependability Analysis. *Performance Evaluation*. Vol. 14, Nos. 3-4, 197-215, 1992.

Session 5:
Distributed Systems

Session Chair: Günter Haring

Design and Analysis of Efficient
Fault-Detecting Network Membership Protocols

Martin Leu

Universität Dortmund, Fachbereich Informatik, 44221 Dortmund, Germany
email: leu@ls4.informatik.uni-dortmund.de

Abstract

Network membership protocols determine the present nodes and links in a computer network and, therefore, contribute to making the huge amount of general distributed systems and their inherent redundancy available for fault tolerance. In this paper two different protocols, GNL and GLV, are described in detail which solve the problem for a very general set of assumptions not covered by existing solutions of related research areas like network exploration, system level diagnosis and group membership:

- *Neither the topology nor a superset of the nodes are known in advance.*

- *Nodes do not require any special initial knowledge except a unique relative signature [Leu 94a] for authentication.*

- *Faults may affect any number of nodes and can cause arbitrary behaviour except for breaking cryptographic fault detection mechanisms like digital signatures.*

The protocols are compared in terms of execution time and global communication costs based on simulation experiments on randomly generated topologies. It is shown that the GLV protocol dominates the GNL protocol clearly for nearly all practically relevant cases.
Keywords: Distributed systems, fault detection, network membership, relative signatures, simulation.

1 Introduction

Due to the lively development in the last decades from centralized to distributed systems nowadays computer networks often provide a large amount of structural redundancy which enables the implementation of various fault tolerance techniques like fault masking, backward recovery, reconfiguration, etc. and combinations thereof. We seek to exploit these hugh resources by investigating how to get fault-tolerant process systems (FTSs) started within such an environment. The following typical properties of general distributed systems makes the problem more difficult compared to dedicated systems which are traditionally employed for fault tolerance:

- General distributed systems are usually also spatially distributed and not surveyable. The operationality of nodes cannot be proven directly.

- General distributed systems are reconfigured every once in a while for a number of purposes (maintanance, adaption, inclusion of new equipment, removal of old equipment, etc.). Usually, a dependable view of the current topology or even the subset of operational components is not available.

Each FTS requires a certain amount of structural redundancy, namely the number of nodes and disjoint communication paths [Hadz 87, MePr 87] between them, to tolerate the specified number of faults during operation. Before a FTS can switch to fault-tolerant operation the operationality of the required components (primary and stand-by components if reconfiguration is employed) must be checked in order to prevent that the redudancy required for fault tolerance is consumed by non-operational components. Hence, a "green light condition" for fault tolerance operation is to be established [EcLe 94].

This can be achieved by so-called *network membership protocols* that equip its *initiator* with a dependable view of the currently present components of the underlying network as well as their topology.

A component is *present* if it is existing and operational (i. e. it has sent or transferred at least one message). Clearly, failed-silent components are tagged non-present but we do not claim that present components are generally faultless.

A view of the present components is *dependable* if an allocation for an FTS can be derived from this view in which the specified amount of components are guaranteed to stay faultless for the specified amount of time with respect to the fault assumptions of the FTS. Note, that for this purpose the view is not required to contain only proven faultless components.

Since the topology and, hence, the available redundancy is assumed to be initially unknown a fault tolerant solution to the problem is excluded. Instead, the presented protocols are fault-detecting, which is adaquate for the required "green light condition", by employing cryptographic means like digital signatures [DiHe 76].

Nevertheless, depending on the faults actually occuring during protocol execution the resulting view may deviate from reality in two ways by

- neglecting some present components or by

- reporting non-present or even non-existing components.

The first kind of deviations cannot be avoided since the network can be partitioned by faulty nodes. Furthermore, there is an obvious tradeoff between the efficiency of such a network membership protocol and its robustness against the loss of messages even if the network is not partitioned [Leu 93]. On the other hand, such deviations are not critical since they might prevent a possible allocation but never result in starting an FTS on less than the required redundant structure. The second kind of deviations may occur more rarely since it can only result from errors in the value domain [Powe 92] but is indeed critical. A statement on the number of components remaining faultless during operation cannot be given if this type of deviations is unbounded. Hence, a view of the present components is *dependable* if this kind of deviations is bounded in terms of the number of actually faulty components.

We intend to use the view resulting from a fault-detecting network membership protocol for the fault-detecting startup and initialization of a statically redundant FTS, the _configuration manager_ (CM), which continuously maintains a view of the currently present components. Dynamical changes of the topology during operation can be captured by insertion or removal protocols between the respective node and the CM. When the CM operates in a fault-tolerant way its dependable view can serve to install further FTSs.

This paper introduces two fault-detecting protocols which solve the network membership problem under a very general set of assumptions (see A1 to A9 and F1 to F3 in section 2.1). Known solutions of related research areas lack the required generality:

- _Group membership_ [Cris 88] determines the presence of nodes and/or processes in a fault-tolerant way. Transparent and fault-tolerant communication are presupposed. Known solutions [AlCi 93, Cris 91, KGRe 89] do not consider faults in the value domain.

- _System level diagnosis_ [MaMa 81, PMCh 67] is a well-established research field which addresses the problem of determining the fault state of components. Most solutions assume perfect fault coverage. Usually nodes, which have been diagnosed as faultless, are trusted, especially when disseminating the syndrome [SBBi 92, BaHa 91, BiBu 91, VaPr 91, SeDa 89, SHOS 88, MMWi 86, HKRe 84]. Some of the work exclude new fault events during protocol execution [Pelc 93, BaHa 91, SHOS 88] or presuppose a known or even fully connected topology [BuBi 93, FuRa 89, BSMa 88].

- _Network exploration_ [Chan 82, Sega 83] is neccessary whenever a network with unknown topology begins operation. Most of the solutions are optimized for efficiently detecting the structure of nodes and links, but do not provide appropriate reactions on fault occurences.

The two network membership protocols presented in this paper differ in the number of sent messages and in the way the membership information is represented which influences the length of the sent messages. In order to compare the protocols in terms of efficiency simulation experiments on randomly chosen topologies were carried out. This also clarified the behaviour of the protocols dependent on several input parameters like the number of nodes, the number of links, the fixed costs per message transfer, etc.

The remainder of this paper is organized as follows: Section 2 introduces the basic assumptions and definitions. The two network membership protocols as well as a method for obtaining dependable information about a node´s neighbourhood are described in section 3. In section 4 the simulation model is given and the results of the simulation experiments are discussed in section 5. The paper concludes with section 6.

2   System model

2.1   Assumptions

In this paper we focus on two different protocols (see section 3), GNL (growing node lists) and GLV (gathering local views), that solve the network membership problem under the following very general set of assumptions:

A1   The underlying network is a partially connected point-to-point network with bidirectional links.

A2   The topology is not known in advance.

A3   The nodes of the CM are pre-defined.

A4   Nodes are not unexpectedly switched off but follow a switch-off protocol.

A5   Authentication within the unknown network is enabled by _relative signatures_ [Leu 94a].

A6   An upper bound on message transfer times between to neighbouring nodes is known.

A7   Each node can distinguish its adjacent links and determine the message transfer times of his sent and received messages.

A8   An upper bound on the time for generating a relative signature is known.

A9   The time between the sending of a message and the reception of a corresponding acknowledge (handshake) can always be measured with the given accuracy.

We restrict ourselves to point-to-point networks (A1) since the GNL protocol is not applicable when broadcast-oriented communication structures (busses) occur. More exactly, the underlying network may contain busses, but these will not be reported by the GNL protocol. Note, that point-to-point networks are indeed practically relevant, particularly in the field of fault tolerance. However, the GLV protocol can handle both, point-to-point links and busses [Leu 94b], but a discussion of this topic is excluded because of space limitations. Assumption A4 does not really exclude the switching off of components but treats this cases as node failures. Note, that this assumption is generally unavoidable for fault tolerance. Authentication (A5) is neccessary since errors in the value domain have to be detected. Relative signatures (see section 2.2) enable authentication within unknown topologies. Assumption A6 is needed for a time-driven protocol termination detection technique (see section 3.2). Without A6, an application dependent termination detection is still possible [EcLe 94]. The assumptions A7 to A9 are basically needed for a technique to dependably determine the structure of the neighbourhood of a node (see section 3.1) and are therefore only indirectly related to the network membership protocols themselves.

As already explained, the presented protocols are fault-detecting. Since the view resulting from a network membership protocol is intended to serve the installation of further FTSs with individual reliability requirements its own fault model is very pessimistic. The fault assumptions are:

F1   The number of faulty components is not bounded.

F2   The behaviour of faulty nodes is in no way restricted except for the unforgebility of relative signatures of faultless nodes.

F3   Faulty links cannot alter the message contents without invalidating the contained relative signatures.

2.2   Definitions

Let the network be given by the pair $(\mathcal{N}, \mathcal{L})$ with
$\mathcal{N} := \{N_1, N_2, \ldots, N_n\}$ and $\mathcal{L} := \{L_1, L_2, \ldots, L_m\}$
where $\mathcal{N}$ is a set of n nodes and $\mathcal{L}$ is a set of m bidirectional point-to-point links. Each link is represented by a subset of $\mathcal{N}$ with two elements:

$\forall L \in \mathcal{L}: \; L \subseteq N \; \wedge \; |L| = 2 \,.$

The individual knowledge of a node about the structure of the network (or parts thereof) is called a *network view* and is defined in analogy. We have to distinguish the local and the global view of a node N_i which are denoted by

$$(\mathcal{N}_{loc,i}, \mathcal{L}_{loc,i}) \quad \text{and} \quad (\mathcal{N}_{glob,i}, \mathcal{L}_{glob,i}) \,,$$

respectively. The *local view* contains information about the neighbourhood of N_i and has to be maintained by N_i locally (see section 3.1) whereas the *global view* results from the execution of a network membership protocol and is, therefore, only relevant for the nodes of the CM. The sets of faultless nodes and links are denoted by

$$\mathcal{N}^c \subseteq \mathcal{N} \quad \text{and} \quad \mathcal{L}^c \subseteq \mathcal{L} \,.$$

For detection of faults in the value domain authentication is required. The so-called *relative signatures* [Leu 94a] enable authentication in unknown topologies since a reliably distributed complete list of authentication functions is not required. Instead, relative signatures can be checked by a single globally known authentication function. A relative signature σ consists of two parts: the *actual signature* σ_1, which is message dependent, and an *authenticator* σ_2, which identifies the sender of the message. Messages with the same authenticator originate from the same sender such that all subsequent messages of a sender N_x can be authenticated relative to the first one. Let

$$W_i := \{0, 1\}^i \quad \text{and} \quad W := \bigcup_{i:=1}^{\infty} W_i$$

be the set of words of length i and the set of words of arbitrary length, respectively. Relative signatures consist of a set of signature functions

$$\text{sig}_i \colon W \to W_{ls} \times W_{ls} \,, \quad i \in \{1, 2, \dots, n\} \,,$$

where it is assumed that both, the actual signature and the authenticator, have the same length ls, and a single authentication function

$$\text{auth} \colon W \times (W_{ls} \times W_{ls}) \to \{true, false\} \,.$$

The functions are chosen such that

$$\text{auth}(x, (\sigma_1, \sigma_2)) \Leftrightarrow \exists\, i \in \{1, 2, \dots, n\} \colon (\sigma_1, \sigma_2) = \text{sig}_i(x)$$

holds with very high probability. It is assumed that each node N_i possesses a single individual signature function sig_i. Like any other signature scheme this scheme relies on the fact that a faultless node will never reveal its signature function or any secret information related to it. Its properties are (with very high probability):

- A faulty node cannot forge the relative signature of any faultless node.
- A faulty node cannot generate a new valid signature function on its own.

Since authenticators are unique it is assumed in the following that the *node identifier* of a node N_i is equal to the authenticator σ_2 of its relative signature:

$$N_i := \sigma_2$$

Note, that faulty nodes in a computer network do not pose the same threat on a signature scheme as intelligent adversaries which take planned actions to break the scheme [Echt 86, Nieu 91]. This fact enables much more efficient implementations of digital signatures for fault-tolerant applications than the ones given in [RSAd 78, ElGa 85, GMRi 88]. See [Leu 94a] for details on efficient relative signatures for fault tolerance.

3 Two network membership protocols

The investigated network membership protocols, GNL and GLV, are based on the so-called *echo algorithm* [Chan 82] and are started by an initiating node, the *initiator*. It is assumed that each node N_i owns a dependable view $(\mathcal{N}_{loc,i}, \mathcal{L}_{loc,i})$ of its neighbourhood, called a *local view*. A local view contains the node identifier of the node itself, the node identifiers of its neighbours and a description of the respective links. A method of obtaining a local view automatically and a discussion of its dependability properties are given in section 3.1. Of course, an automatically generated local view can only contain components which were present since the node became operational.

In both protocols, GNL and GLV, the initiator distributes exploring messages (*explorers*) by flooding (also: diffusion [CASD 85]). Each explored node contributes *membership information* about the present components within its neighbourhood based on its local view. This information is returned to the initiator by so-called echo messages (*echoes*).

Let T_B and T_E be the points in time when the initiator starts the protocol (begin) and when the initiator detects the termination of the protocol (end), respectively. The interval $[T_B, T_E]$ is called the *protocol window*. To ensure that messages are indeed created within the protocol window the initiator distributes a random number, the so-called *protocol identifier*, within the explorers. The membership information returned to the initiator must be signed together with this protocol identifier. Since the protocol identifier cannot be foreseen and is long enough to exclude the probability of "guessing", any valid signature received in time (before T_E) is guaranteed to have been created after T_B and trivially before T_E and is therefore called a *current signature*. Clearly, different and may be overlapping instances of a network membership protocol must use different protocol identifiers. Hence, nodes participating in different protocols can distinguish them by their protocol identifier. Therefore, not only the explorers but all messages of the same protocol carry the protocol identifier.

The initiator N_i considers a node N_j to be present and, hence, a member of the network if it has received a current signature of N_j. A link $L := \{N_x, N_y\}$ is considered to be a member of the network if both adjacent nodes, N_x and N_y, witness that at least one message has been transferred on L during the protocol window by reporting this link in a currently signed message. So far the common ground between the GNL and the GLV protocol. The details and differences are given in sections 3.2 and 3.3, respectively.

3.1 Generating dependable local views

When a node N_i becomes operational it has to establish a dependable local view $(\mathcal{N}_{loc,i}, \mathcal{L}_{loc,i})$ before being able to participate in a network membership protocol. Furthermore, the neighbours have to be informed to include the new node into their own local views. Obviously, when a node N_i establishes or updats its local view each link can be considered separately.

A protocol which determines the identity of a neighbour accessible via a link L is called *identity request protocol*. In the following a fault-detecting identity request protocol is introduced and the properties of the resulting local view are stated formally.

The protocol must prevent that a faulty neighbour pretends the identity of a different faultless node. A faulty node can pretend such an identity by the following ways:

- If signatures are resisted the faulty node can just send the node identifier of a faultless node since this information is public. Hence, signatures are needed – in our solution relative signatures, of course.

- If signatures are used and a publicly known value is to be signed, signatures of this value are also publicly available. Hence, an unforseeable random value is to be signed.

- If a random value is to be signed by the neighbour then the identity request can be forwarded to a faultless node whose correct answer is in turn forwarded to N_i. Hence, a timeout mechanism for fault detection is required.

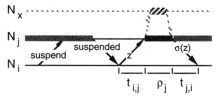

Fig. 1   A fault-detecting identity request protocol for dependably obtaining the identity of a neighbour.

These arguments lead to the solution depicted in fig. 1. The node N_i starts the identity request protocol by asking N_j to suspend its other activities (grey bars). This ensures the applicability of the timeout mechanism. It particularly prevents that N_j becomes involved in several identity request protocols at the same time. After receiving an acknowledging message from N_j the node N_i sends its random value z and starts to measure the time (assumption A9) until the reception of the signed value $\sigma(z)$. It is assumed that N_i can estimate (e. g. by knowing the message length and the transfer rate) the message transfer times $t_{i,j}$ and $t_{j,i}$ (A7) such that the time ρ_j in which N_j calculates its signature can be determined quite exactly, since the link $\{N_i, N_j\}$ does not transfer any other messages during the protocol. Let the inaccuracies due to time granularity, measuring and/or estimation be subsumed in the (very small) value δ. Let

$$\tau_{min} \text{ and } \rho_{max}$$

be the *minimum message transfer time* (for short messages) in the network and the *maximum time a node needs to calculate a relative signature* (assumption A8), respectively. Obviously, this approach requires that

$$2 \cdot \tau_{min} > \rho_{max} + \delta .$$

Informally, message transfer times must be greater than signature calculation times within the whole network. Otherwise, it would be possible for a faulty node N_j to forward the identity request to a another node N_x and to forward the answer message of N_x to N_i in time (hatched part of fig. 1). This property is called *time homogeneity*. Obviously, this requirement excludes the utilization of this approach in heterogeneous systems containing both high speed links and slow computers.

In order to get rid of the time homogeneity requirement one has to eliminate the dependence between message transfer times and signature calculation times. This can be achieved by introducing a fictitious signature calculation time

$$\rho > \rho_{max}$$

which is to be obeyed by faultless nodes as exactly as possible

– if neccessary by waiting the remaining time. Hence, a faultless node N_j will perform its calculation in ρ_j time units with

$$| \rho_j - \rho | < \delta'$$

where δ' again reflects possible (very small) inaccuracies. Now, a faulty node has exactly $\rho + \delta + \delta'$ time units to forward an identity request and get an appropriate answer. Since this time is even longer than in the former protocol this time may well be sufficient if the node to which the request is forwarded is also faulty and does not obey ρ (in principle the request can even be forwarded several times but each participating node is neccessarily faulty). Consequently, a faulty node may present a signature of a faulty node instead of its own signature but this is not detrimental since a faulty node may reveal its signature function anyway. However, the request cannot be forwarded to faultless nodes if

$$\delta + \delta' < 2 \cdot \tau_{min} .$$

Informally, nodes must be able to measure or estimate the time accurate enough such that message transfer times are not missed (assumption A9). Obviously, this requirement is principally unavoidable when employing a timeout mechanism to detect forwarded identity requests.

Let $(\mathcal{N}_{loc,i}, \mathcal{L}_{loc,i})$ be the local view of a faultless node N_i generated with the above identitiy request protocol. Then the following validity conditions hold:

- $\mathcal{N}_{loc,i} \subseteq \mathcal{N}$

- $\forall \{N_i, N_x\} \in \mathcal{L}_{loc,i}$: $N_x \in \mathcal{N}^c \Rightarrow \{N_i, N_x\} \in \mathcal{L}$

For local views of faulty nodes at least the first condition holds, since a node cannot fake identities by generating new signatures (see section 2.2). From these properties of the local views the validity conditions of the resulting global view $(\mathcal{N}_{glob,i}, \mathcal{L}_{glob,i})$ of an initiator N_i can be derived:

- $\forall N_x \in \mathcal{N}_{glob,i}$: $N_x \in \mathcal{N} \wedge N_x$ is present

- $\forall \{N_x, N_y\} \in \mathcal{L}_{glob,i}$: $N_x \in \mathcal{N}^c \wedge N_y \in \mathcal{N}^c \Rightarrow$

$$\{N_x, N_y\} \in \mathcal{L} \wedge \{N_x, N_y\} \text{ is present}$$

From the second condition follows that each faked communication path between any pair of faultless nodes neccessarily contains at least one faulty node. Hence, the number of faked disjoint communication paths between any pair of faultless nodes is bounded by the number of actually faulty nodes. Therefore, the resulting global view is dependable in the previously defined sense.

3.2   The GNL protocol

The GNL protocol (growing node lists) expresses the membership and topology information in the form of node lists where neighbouring nodes in the node list are assumed to have a direct link. The explorers flooded by the initiator N_i carry a node list initialized with the node identifier N_i. A node N_j receiving an explorer on a link L adds its own identifier N_j (and also its relative signature which is explained later in this section) and forwards the extended explorer via a different link (if existent). Furthermore, N_j creates *new explorers* initialized only with the node identifier N_j and floods them via the remaining links (if existent). Afterwards, N_j is called *explored*. Obviously, when an explorer reaches a node with degree 1, i. e. the node possesses only one link, the explorer cannot be forwarded any further. Hence, an echo has to be generated to report the collected node list to the initiator. According to the echo algorithm [Chan 82] echoes are returned on the reverse path which the first explorer travelled.

A second reason for generating an echo is when an explorer reaches an already explored node. Let N_x be the sender and N_y be an already explored receiver. Since N_x and N_y are indeed neighbours and N_y is already explored it has also sent an explorer to N_x which in turn was received after N_x was explored (otherwise it would not have sent an explorer to N_y). This is a symmetric situation since both nodes received an explorer from each other and both were explored before. The two explorers between N_x and N_y are said to *collide*. Both nodes can detect this collision and, hence, only one of the nodes, e. g. the one with the greater node identifier, has to generate an echo containing both node lists, which is a message saving optimization. This protocol originates from the one given in [EcLe 94] but is optimized in several ways. A detailed analysis of the effects of these optimizations in terms of robustness and efficiency can be found in [Buhl 94] and [Hilb 94], respectively.

The initiator N_i receives the echoes and constructs its global view ($\mathcal{N}_{glob,i}$, $\mathcal{L}_{glob,i}$). Like the echo algorithm the GNL protocol is guaranteed to terminate unless a faulty node continuously sends spontaneous echoes with the current protocol identifier (spontaneous explorers can be tolerated since faultless nodes need only accept one explorer per link).

It is a different problem how the initiator decides from its local point of view when the protocol has terminated. Besides the application dependent termination criterion which is defined on the growing global view and is discussed in detail in [EcLe 94] a time driven termination detection technique called *incremental timeout* can be employed. This approach requires an upper bound on the message transfer time to be known (assumption A6). The basic idea is to guarantee for the initiator that, at least in the faultless case, there is an upper bound on the interarrival times of echoes. For this purpose a parameter D (distance) is introduced. Each node receiving an explorer compares the distance which the explorer travelled (the length of the contained node list) with D. If equal, an echo is generated regardless of any other criteria. Consequently, the contained node list needs not to be forwarded any further such that the node will send only new explorers. If τ_{max} is the maximum message transfer time then the interarrival times of echoes are obviously bounded by $2 \cdot D \cdot \tau_{max}$. The initiator will always receive with timeout $2 \cdot D \cdot \tau_{max}$ and if the timeout expires it detects termination. Of course, the smaller D is chosen the more additional echoes have to be generated. Hence, there is a tradeoff between efficiency and termination detection latency which can be controlled by the parameter D.

In the following the GNL protocol with the incremental timeout technique is presented more detailed but still informally for the sake of simplicity. First, the steps executed by a node N_j after receiving an explorer are given:

```
1   on reception of an explorer with node list NL on link L do
2     if last entry of NL = neighbour accessible via L then
3       enter Nj into NL
4       if degree of Nj = 1 then return echo with NL
5     else
6       if already explored then
7         if Nj > last entry of NL then
8           return echo with NL and the node list of the explorer
                                    sent to the neighbour reached via L
9         else
10          if length of node list = D then
11            return echo with NL and initialize NL with Nj
12          send explorer with NL on a link other than L and
                                    initialize  NL  with  Nj
13    send explorers with NL on all remaining links
```

The process of receiving explorers can be terminated τ_{max} time units after the first explorer has been received. Furthermore, at most one explorer per link must be accepted. The process of receiving echoes must be started after the first explorer was received and can be terminated if the interarrival time of $2 \cdot D \cdot \tau_{max}$ between two echoes is exceeded. If an echo is received it is just forwarded over the link on which the first explorer was received. The steps executed by the initiator N_i are given in the following:

```
1   choose a random protocol identifier and initialize NL with Ni
2   send explorer with NL on all links
3   loop
4     receive echo containing node list NL with timeout 2·D·τmax
5     if timeout then
6       calculate global view from the set of received node lists
7       output global view and terminate
8     check validity of NL
9     include NL into the set of received node lists
```

Figure 2 shows the structures of the explorers and echoes, respectively, of the GNL protocol. The fixed message header contains the message type and the protocol identifier (prot_id). Above that, an explorer consists of a node list and an echo consists of one or two node lists depending on whether or not the echo was generated due to an explorer collision.

A node list consists of a length field # (or alternatively of a termination character) and a respective amount of entries. Each entry consists of a node identifier (node_id) and a relative signature (rel_sig). As already mentioned in section 2.2, it is assumed that nodes are identified by the authenticator of their relative signature (node_id $\hat{=} \sigma_2$). Hence, the field rel_sig only contains the actual signature σ_1. According to the specification both adjacent nodes of a present link have to witness with their signature. Consequently, a node N_y which received an explorer from N_x and forwards the explorer to node N_z generates the signature from the value prot_id$\oplus N_x \oplus N_y \oplus N_z$ where "$\oplus$" denotes the concatenation of words. Informally, N_y signs the proven present link $\{N_x, N_y\}$ and the potentially present link $\{N_y, N_z\}$. If the message is transferred successfully to N_z then the signature for $\{N_y, N_z\}$ was justified. Otherwise, the message is lost and also the unjustified signature. If an explorer is initialized by a node N_x and sent to a node N_y the node list contains just one entry where the node identifier is N_x and the signature is generated from prot_id$\oplus N_x \oplus N_y$. Analogously, when a node N_z receives an explorer from a neighbour N_y and an echo has to be generated

explorer:

header		node list					
expl	prot_id	#	node_id	rel_sig	~~	node_id	rel_sig

echo:

header		node list 1						node list 2 (optional)					
expl	prot_id	#	node_id	rel_sig	~~	node_id	rel_sig	#	node_id	rel_sig	~~	node_id	rel_sig

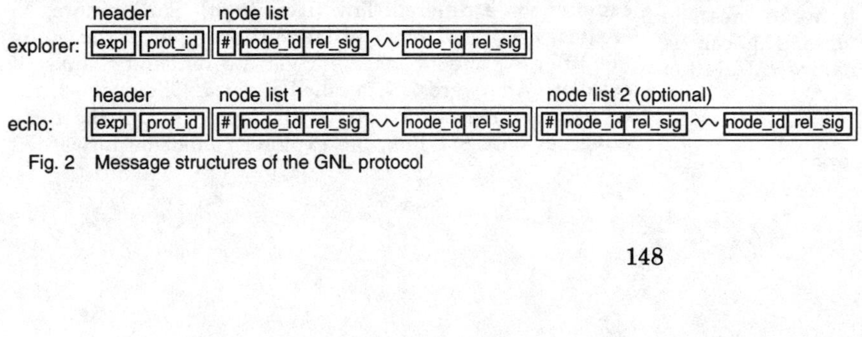

Fig. 2   Message structures of the GNL protocol

148

the last entry of the list contains N_z and a signature over $prot\_id \oplus N_y \oplus N_z$. Node lists containing such a last entry are called *complete*. The signed sequence of node identifiers is called the *scope of the signature*. Figure 3 shows an example of a complete node list with 5 elements reflecting the path N_2–N_7–N_8–N_3–N_9. Signatures are replaced by their scopes.

5	N_2	$N_2 N_7$	N_7	$N_2 N_7 N_8$	N_8	$N_7 N_8 N_3$	N_3	$N_8 N_3 N_9$	N_9	$N_3 N_9$

Fig. 3 An example of a complete node list with 5 elements. Signatures are replaced by their scopes.

The initiator only accepts node lists which obey this structure and whose signatures are valid (line 8). If valid, the node list of the above example would result in the links $\{N_2, N_7\}$, $\{N_7, N_8\}$, $\{N_8, N_3\}$, $\{N_3, N_9\}$ and the nodes N_2, N_7, N_8, N_3, N_9 to be included into the global view since from each node a current signature was received and each link was witnessed by both adjacent nodes.

3.3 The GLV protocol

In contrast to the GNL protocol the GLV protocol (gathering local views) represents the membership and topology information in the form of link lists where each link is specified by the node identifiers of the two adjacent nodes. Note, that a network view can be completely representetd by such link lists since the set of nodes is contained implicitly. The explorers flooded by the initiator N_i only have the purpose to inform the other nodes to return the present portion of their local view in the form of link lists to the initiator. Consequently, no topology information is collected during the exploration phase. Let each explorer which is the first to explore a node be called *primary explorer*. According to the flooding technique the primary explorers form a spanning tree whose root is N_i. Over each link not belonging to the spanning tree two colliding explorers are transferred. According to the echo algorithm a node will not generate an echo until it received a message on each of its links (regardless of the message type). Hence, the first nodes to generate echoes are the leaves of the spanning tree, either because they have degree 1 or due to explorer collisions. When having received a message on each link an echo containing a list of these links and, of course, a current signature is generated and returned on the link on which the primary explorer was received. Hence, echoes are only transferred on the links of the spanning tree in the reverse direction as the primary explorers. Therefore, a node N_j, which is not a leaf of the spanning tree, will receive echoes on some of its links before being able to generate its own echo. In contrast to the GNL protocol these echoes are not forwarded immediately but saved temporarily and later merged with the own echo. Hence, in the faultless case each node sends exactly one echo and consequently on each link exactly two messages are transferred, either two colliding explorers or a primary explorer and an echo. The initiator N_i detects the termination when it has received a message on each of its links.

The weak point of this pure echo protocol variant is the condition that a node must receive a message on each of its links before sending its own echo – one fail-silent component suffices to prevent the termination of the whole protocol! The appropriate countermeasure is the incremental timeout technique for termination detection (see previous section). To implement the technique we again need the

additional distance parameter D. Furthermore, an explorer must not only carry the message type and protocol identifier but also a field called "hops" which reflects the distance the explorer travelled so far (see figure 5). The value of hops of the primary explorer of a node N_j is called the *distance* of N_j. If the distance of a node N_j equals D then the node will reset the field hops to 0 before forwarding the explorer. Nodes with distance 0 will immediately acknowledge the receipt of their primary explorers by a short message with the type "ack" (see figure 5).

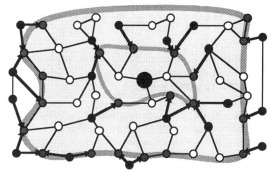

Fig. 4 Example execution of a GLV protocol with D = 2. The fat circle depicts the initiator. Nodes with distance 0, 1 or 2 are filled black, white or grey, respectively. Acknowledge messages are represented by thick arrows. The fat grey lines illuminate the "wavefronts" of generated echoes.

Figure 4 shows an example execution of a GLV protocol with $D := 2$. The initiator is depicted by the bigger circle. The shade of a node expresses its distance: black = 0, white = 1 and grey = 2. Black nodes send acknowledge messages to grey nodes which is shown by thick arrows. The grey nodes in turn generate echo messages (since they have received one message on each link). In figure 4 these nodes are connected by fat grey lines to indicate the "wavefronts" of generated echoes. Obviously, in the faultless case the echoes of the first wavefront will reach the initiator $2 \cdot [D+1] \cdot \tau_{max}$ time units after T_B (the start of the protocol) at the latest. The echoes of subsequent wavefronts are received before $4 \cdot [D+1] \cdot \tau_{max}$, $6 \cdot [D+1] \cdot \tau_{max}$, etc. The interarrival time of echoes must therefore never exceed $2 \cdot [D+1] \cdot \tau_{max}$. Hence, the initiator will always receive with timeout $2 \cdot [D+1] \cdot \tau_{max}$ and if the timeout expires termination is detected. Note, that the same criterion can be used by the other nodes as well to detect the termination of the protocol. As for the GNL protocol, we are faced with a tradeoff between additional communication and a small termination detection latency.

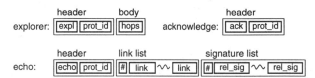

Fig. 5 Message structures of the GLV protocol.

Figure 5 shows the message structures used by the GLV protocol with incremental timeout. The echo structure consists of a link list and a signature list. Let $\{N_4, N_7\}$, $\{N_4, N_9\}$, $\{N_3, N_4\}$ be the present portion of the local view of a node N_4. Then N_4 enters these links into the link list and generates a signature from the value $prot\_id \oplus N_4 \oplus N_7 \oplus N_4 \oplus N_9 \oplus N_3 \oplus N_4$ (or an alternative value capturing the same information). Let node N_9 (a neighbour of N_4) report the links $\{N_4, N_9\}$, $\{N_2, N_9\}$. The signature has to be built from $prot\_id \oplus N_2 \oplus N_9 \oplus N_4 \oplus N_9$. If the echoes have to be merged the link lists can be unified thereby eliminating doubles like the link $\{N_4, N_9\}$. In order to check the signature of a node N_j one has to map the unified link list onto the value from which the signature was built by eliminating the links which do not contain N_j. To avoid ambiguities the node identifiers within a link as well as the links within the link list have to be sorted. This *unification technique* works as long as neighbours consistently report the link between them. Otherwise, the mapping possibly yields more links than were originally signed. In our approach such inconsistent lists are simply not unified. However, they are still transferred in the same echo requiring additional link list and signature list fields.

4 The simulation model

The major goals of the simulation experiments were to compare the two protocols in terms of communication costs and execution times as well as an analysis of the influence of the distance parameter D. On a fixed topology numerous different protocol executions yielding different communication costs and execution times are possible. Furthermore, for fixed numbers of nodes and links there is a vast amount of different topologies each yielding different communication costs and execution times in the mean. A mathematical model exactly reflecting the protocol behaviour and capturing all random influences is intractable – hence, the simulation experiments. The simulation model was supposed to concentrate on the communication expenses rather than local calculation times since the investigated protocols only require minor local calculations. The following assumptions were made in the simulation model:

- Local calculations of nodes are not considered.
- All links provide (more or less) the same message transfer rate.
- Faults are not considered.

The first two assumptions also express the independence of the experiments from a specific network. The exclusion of faults is justified since the most probable faults like processor crashes or transmission errors result in the loss of membership information but do not cause additional messages. In this sense the faultless case can be viewed as the "worse case". Furthermore, realistic probabilities for faulty nodes to produce additional messages are hard to quantify but certainly they are not likely to have a big impact on the results and a huge amount of simulation runs would have been necessary to capture this influence without gaining much information. We assume that the faultless case occurs most often by far.

The transfer time of a message is determined by the actual length of the contained data as described in the sections 3.2 and 3.3 (the so-called *variable costs*), an amount of *fixed costs* associated with the basic message transfer mechanism and a random offset to capture the inherent indeterminism of distributed systems. The exact formula for the transfer time t_{trans} of a message with length ℓ is

$$t_{trans} := \ell \cdot c_{var} + c_{fix} + exp(2 \cdot c_{var})$$

where $exp(2 \cdot c_{var})$ is an exponentially distributed random variable with mean $\mu = 2 \cdot c_{var}$. Unlike shared media point-to-point links are usually characterized by only a relatively small random variation of the message transfer time. Experience with some communication systems led to the choice of the factor 2 which on the one hand results in a relatively small variation but on the other hand proved to produce quite different protocol executions on the same topology. The fixed costs c_{fix} are an input parameter of the simulation experiments which are expressed in multiples of c_{var}, which was taken as the basic time unit and was set to 1.

The link over which a message with transfer time t_{trans} is transferred remains occupied for the duration t_{trans}. Successing messages must wait until the predecessing message transfer is completed. Waiting messages obey FIFO. The send-operator is modelled non-blocking such that a sender is not delayed by waiting messages. It is assumed that the messages are buffered and finally sent by an independent communication instance (e. g. a DMA-supported process).

The simulation outputs are the global communication costs c_{glob} and the protocol execution time t_{exec}, which equals the model time after execution of a protocol since the model time is initialized with 0. Let $m_1, m_2, \ldots, m_x$ be the messages transferred during a protocol execution and let ℓ_i be the length of message m_i. The global communication costs c_{glob} of a protocol execution is defined by the sum of the message transfer times of all transferred messages:

$$c_{glob} := \sum_{i=1}^{x} (c_{fix} + \ell_i \cdot c_{var})$$

Each simulation run is executed on a different randomly chosen topology. The input parameters of the topology generation algorithm are the number of nodes n and the number of links $m \in [n-1, \ n \cdot (n-1)/2]$ of the resulting network. A third parameter is the maximum node degree g of the resulting network, which was chosen according to n and m. For a given n and m the parameter $g(n, m)$ was determined by

$$g(n, m) := \lceil 2 \cdot m \ / \ n \rceil + 2$$

where $\lceil x \rceil$ is the smallest natural number greater or equal x. This is greater by 2 than necessary to accomodate the m links. On the one hand, this enables a quite even distribution of the links within the network. On the other hand, there is enough flexibility to guarantee a fast termination of the following random-driven topology generation algorithm:

```
1   choose randomly a pair of nodes (Nx, Ny). Add link {Nx, Ny}
2   do n-2 times
3     | choose randomly a pair of nodes (Nx, Ny) such that
      |   Nx is already connected to at least one link but does not
      |   exceed g(n, m)-1 and Ny is not connected. Add link {Nx, Ny}
4   do n-m+1 times
5     | choose randomly a pair of nodes (Nx, Ny) such that
      |   neither node exceeds g(n, m)-1. Add link {Nx, Ny}
```

The initial step in line 1 is needed for the subsequent loop (lines 2 – 3) to find a first pair of nodes. This loop provides for a spanning tree as the skeleton of the network to guarantee connectedness. The next loop (lines 4 and 5) just adds the remaining links randomly.

Table 1 summarizes the input and output parameters of the simulation model. For each set of input parameters sufficient simulation runs were executed to satisfy the specified confidence level α for the specified maximum deviation ε [LaKe 82] for both output parameters t_{exec} and c_{glob}. The values $\alpha := 0.98$ and $\varepsilon := 0.02$ have proven to be an acceptable compromise between "smooth curves" and computation costs and usually yielded from 500 to 2500 simulation runs for one set of input parameters.

description	name	value range	type
number of nodes	n	{50, 100, 150}	input
number of links	m	[n−1, n·(n−1)/2]	input
fixed costs	c_{fix}	{0, 20·c_{var}, 40·c_{var}}	input
distance	D	{1, 2, … , 10} ∪ {∞}	input
execution time	t_{exec}	–	output
global costs	c_{glob}	–	output

Tab. 1 Input and output parameters of the simulation model

5 Discussion of the results

Figure 6 and 7 show the execution times of the GNL and the GLV protocol for networks with n = 50 nodes and D = ∞ (no incremental timeout). The number of links m is varied from 50 to 1220 which nearly covers the whole possible range. The graphs show three curves each associated with different amounts of fixed costs c_{fix}. The GNL protocol is much more influenced by a growing amount of links than the GLV protocol. Both protocols generate the same amount of explorer messages, namely 2·m − n + 1 but differ in the number of echoes. In the GLV protocol each explored node generates exactly one echo.

The number of echoes transferred in the GNL protocol is mainly determined by the number of explorer collisions, which is of the order of the number of links for great numbers of links, and by the length of the return path of each echo. The increase of t_{exec} in the range from 300 to 850 links is due to "traffic jams" around the initiator. For more than 850 links t_{exec} decreases because of the shorter return paths. Due to the larger amount of echoes and the "traffic jams" of the GNL protocol it is much more sensitive to an increase of c_{fix}. Note the different scales of the ordinates.

It turns out that the GNL protocol is less efficient in practically the whole range of m if a message transfer comprises even a relatively small amount of fixed costs like $c_{fix} = 20·c_{var}$. Figure 8 magnifies the practically relevant range of m = 50, … , 320. For $c_{fix} = 0$ there is indeed a range where GNL is more efficient than GLV but exhibits a greater gradient such that there always exists a point at which GLV becomes more efficient. For $c_{fix} = 20·c_{var}$ GNL is already worse than GLV except for networks with extremely few redundant links, which are not relevant for fault tolerance.

In figure 9 the case D = 1 is shown which is the opposite extreme of D = ∞ and enables termination detection with minimal latency (see section 3). Obviously, the GLV protocol is much more affected and exhibits a similar behaviour as GNL since now the amount of echoes is also of the order of the number of links. Nevertheless, GLV remains more efficient.

When considering the global communication costs c_{glob} it is even clearer that GNL is dominated by GLV, as can be seen from figure 10. Figure 11 again magnifies the practically relevant range of m. Furthermore, GLV is shown with and without unification of link lists when merging echoes (see section 3.3). As expected, the influence of this optimization decreases as the paths of the echoes become shorter. Obviously, GNL is already worse for practically relevant cases for $c_{fix} = 0$. With increased fixed costs the difference between GNL and GLV becomes even greater.

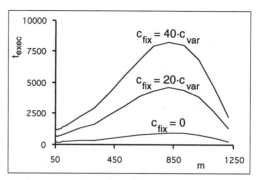

Fig. 6 Execution times of the GNL protocol for n=50, m=50…1220 and D=∞.

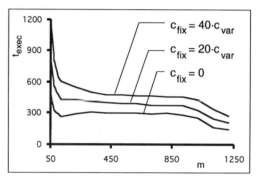

Fig. 7 Execution times of the GLV protocol for n=50, m=50…1220 and D=∞.

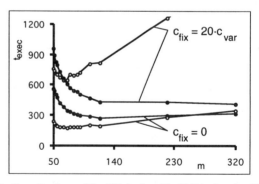

Fig. 8 Execution times of the GNL (-○-) and the GLV (-●-) protocol for n=50, m=50…320 and D=∞.

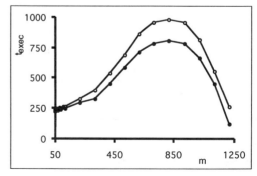

Fig. 9 Execution times of the GNL (-○-) and the GLV (-●-) protocol for n=50, m=50…1220, c_{fix} = 0 and D=1.

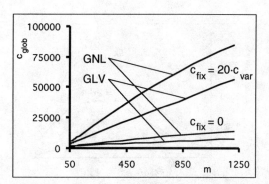

Fig. 10 Global costs of the GNL and the GLV protocol for n=50, m=50...1220 and D=∞.

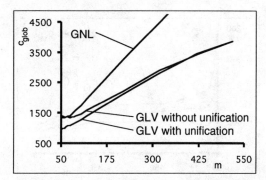

Fig. 11 Costs of the GLV protocol with and without link list unification for n=50, m=50...520, c_{fix}=0 and D=∞.

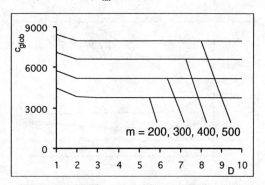

Fig. 12 Global costs of the GNL protocol for n=100, c_{fix}=0 and D=1...10.

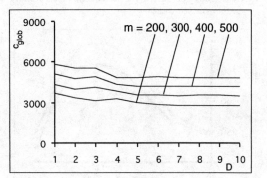

Fig. 13 Global costs of the GLV protocol for n=100, c_{fix}=0 and D=1...10.

Figure 12 and 13 show c_{glob} of GNL and GLV when varying the distance parameter D (incremental timeout technique) for a network with n = 100 nodes and c_{fix} = 0. The graphs show four curves each associated with different numbers of links in a practically relevant range. Obviously, the GNL protocol is not influenced very much. This is due to the fact that each explored node forwards the received node list at most once. For the remaining links new explorers are generated. As a result the mean explorer length is considerably low and, hence, not many additional echoes are generated due to the distance parameter, particularly when the number of links increases. Although GLV causes less costs its curves are more influenced. This becomes even more apparent when considering the execution times, as shown in figure 14. Amazingly, the execution times do not decrease monotonically.

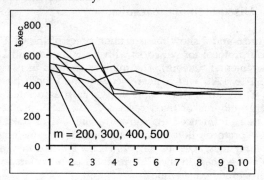

Fig. 14 Execution times of the GLV protocol for n=100, c_{fix}=0 and D=1...10.

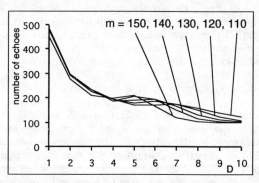

Fig. 15 Number of echoes generated by the GLV protocol for n=100 and D=1...10.

For the GLV protocol the incremental timeout technique in the mean causes equidistant wavefronts of echoes travelling towards the initiator. The observed effect is an interference of these wavefronts with the diameter of the network (which decreases with an increasing number of links m). The curves become much smoother, when considering less links, i. e. larger diameters. Figure 15 shows the number of echoes for m = 110, ... , 150. Note, that without the incremental timeout technique (D = ∞) exactly 99 echoes are generated when n = 100. A resumee is deferred to the subsequent conclusion.

6   Conclusion

In this paper two fault-detecting network membership protocols, GNL and GLV, were introduced for determining the present components of partially connected point-to-point networks. It has been motivated that such protocols are an inportant contribution to making the huge amount of non-dedicated distributed systems and their inherent structural redundancy available for fault tolerant use. Furthermore, a method has been presented to determine a dependable view of a nodes neighbourhood which is the basis for a dependable global view resulting from a network membership protocol.

It has been shown by simulation experiments that the GLV protocol is more efficient for nearly all sets of input data. Particularly in practically relevant cases where a message transfer is associated with some fixed costs the GLV protocol has clearly been shown to be the better choice. By analysis of the influence of the distance parameter D it has been shown that GLV remains more efficient even in the case when the incremental timeout technique for termination detection is applied which is important for the robustness of the GLV protocol. As the final conclusion, the GLV protocol is to be heavily recommended where applicable.

Future research will be directed to initial synchronization of the configuration manager nodes after having established a dependable global view each in order to enable the execution of Byzantine agreement protocols and, hence, fault tolerant operation. Furthermore, the indeed practically relevant broadcast-oriented communication structures (busses) are to be consistently incorporated into the model of the network.

References

AlCi 93   G. Alari, A. Ciuffoletti: Group membership in a synchronous distributed system; Fifth European workshop on dependable computing, EWDC-5, Lisboa, 1993.

BaHa 91   A. Bagchi, S. L. Hakimi: An optimal algorithm for distributed system level diagnosis; FTCS-21 digest of papers, IEEE, 1991, pp. 214 – 221.

BiBu 91   R. Bianchini, R. Buskens: An adaptive distributed system-level diagnosis algorithm and its implementation; FTCS-21 digest of papers, IEEE, 1991, pp. 222 – 229.

BSMa 88   D. M. Blough, G. F. Sullivan, G. M. Masson: Almost certain diagnosis for intermittently faulty systems; FTCS-18 digest of papers, IEEE, 1988, pp. 260 – 265.

BuBi 93   R. W. Buskens, R. P. Bianchini Jr.: Distributed on-line diagnosis in the presence of arbitrary faults; FTCS-23 digest of papers, IEEE, 1993, pp. 470 – 479.

Buhl 94   A. Buhl: Implementierung und Test von fehlererkennenden Topologieexplorationsprotokollen; diploma thesis, University of Dortmund, 1994.

CASD 85   F. Cristian, H. Aghili, R. Strong, D. Dolev: Atomic broadcast: from simple message diffusion to byzantine agreement; FTCS-15 digest of papers, IEEE, 1985, pp. 200 – 206.

Chan 82   E. J. C. Chang: Echo algorithms: depth parallel operations on general graphs; IEEE Transactions on Software Engineering, vol. SE-8, no. 4, IEEE, 1982, pp. 391 – 401.

Cris 88   F. Cristian: Agreeing who is present and who is absent in a synchronous distributed system; FTCS-18 digest of papers, IEEE, 1988, pp. 206 – 211

Cris 91   F. Cristian: Reaching agreement on processor-group membership in synchronous distributed systems; Distributed Computing, vol. 4, Springer, Heidelberg, 1991, pp. 175 – 187

DiHe 76   W. Diffie, M. E. Hellman: New directions in cryptography; Transactions on Information Theory, vol. IT-22, IEEE, 1976, pp. 644 – 654.

Echt 86   K. Echtle: Fault-masking with reduced redundant communication; FTCS-16 digest of papers, IEEE, 1986, pp. 178 – 183.

EcLe 94   K. Echtle, M. Leu: Fault-detecting network membership protocols for unknown topologies; Fourth International Working Conference on Dependable Computing for Critical Applications DCCA-4, San Diego, 1994, pp. 46 – 57.

ElGa 85   T. El-Gamal: A public key cryptosystem and a signature scheme based on discrete logarithms; Transactions on Information Theory, vol. IT-31, IEEE, 1985, pp. 469 – 472.

FuRa 89   D. Fussel, S. Rangarajan: Probabilistic diagnosis of multiprocessor systems with arbitrary connectivity; FTCS-19 digest of papers, IEEE, 1989, pp. 560 – 565.

GMRi 88   S. Goldwasser, S. Micali, R. Rivest: A digital signature scheme secure against adaptive chosen-message attacks; SIAM J. Comput., vol. 17, no. 2, 1988, pp 281 – 308.

Hadz 87   V. Hadzilacos: Connectivity requirements for Byzantine agreement under restricted types of failures; Distributed Computing, vol. 2, no. 2, Springer International, 1987, pp. 95 – 103.

Hilb 94   U. Hilbk: Leistungsbewertung von fehlererkennenden Topologieexplorationsprotokollen; diploma thesis, University of Dortmund, 1994.

HKRe 84   S. H. Hosseini, J. G. Kuhl, S. M. Reddy: A diagnosis algorithm for distributed computing systems with dynamic failure and repair; IEEE Transactions on Computers C-33, vol. 3, 1984, pp. 223 – 233.

KGRe 89   H. Kopetz, G. Grünsteidl, J. Reisinger: Fault-tolerant membership service in a synchronous distributed real-time system; Int. working conference on dependable computing for critical applications, conf. preprints, UCSB, 1989, pp. 167 – 174.

LaKe 82   A. M. Law, W. D. Kelton: Simulation Modeling and Analysis; McGraw-Hill, 1992, pp. 148.

Leu 93   M. Leu: Startup problems in fault-tolerant distributed systems; Fifth European Workshop on Dependable Computing EWDC-5, Lisboa, 1993.

Leu 94a   M. Leu: Relative signatures for fault tolerance and their implementation; First European Dependable Computer Conference EDCC-1, Berlin, Lecture Notes in Computer Science 852, Springer Verlag, 1994, pp. 563 – 580.

Leu 94b   M. Leu: Generierung verläßlicher globaler Netzsichten unter Verwendung des GLV-Netzmitgliedschaftsprotokolls; internal report, University of Dortmund, 1994.

MaMa 81   J. Maeng, M. Malek: A comparison connection assignment for diagnosis of multiprocessor systems; FTCS-11 digest of papers, IEEE, 1981, pp. 173 – 175.

MePr 87   F. J. Meyer, D. K. Pradhan: Consensus with dual failure modes; FTCS-17 digest of papers, IEEE, 1987, pp. 48 - 54.

MMWi 86   E. Maehle, K. Moritzen, K. Wirl: A graph model for diagnosis and reconfiguration and its application to a fault-tolerant multiprocessor system; FTCS-16 digest of papers, IEEE, 1986, pp. 292 – 297.

Nieu 91   L. J. M. Nieuwenhuis: Fault tolerance through program transformation; Ph. D. thesis, University of Twente, Netherlands, 1991.

Pelc 93   A. Pelc: Efficient distributed diagnosis in the presence of random faults; FTCS-23 digest of papers, IEEE, 1993, pp. 462 – 469.

PMCh 67   F. Preparata, G. Metze, R. Chien: On the connection assignment problem of diagnosable systems; IEEE Transactions on Computers, vol. 16, Dec. 1967, pp. 848 – 854.

Powe 92   D. Powell: Failure mode assumptions and assumption coverage; FTCS-22 digest of papers, IEEE, 1992, pp. 386 – 395.

RSAd 78   R. Rivest, A. Shamir, L. Adleman: A method for obtaining digital signatures and public-key cryptosystems; Communications of the acm, vol. 21, no. 2, acm, 1978, pp. 120 – 126.

SBBi 92   M. Stahl, R. Buskens, R. Bianchini Jr.: On-line diagnosis in general topology networks; IEEE Workshop on Fault-Tolerant Parallel and Distributed Systems, 1992, pp. 114 – 121.

SeDa 89   A. Sengupta, A. Dahbura: On self-diagnosable multiprocessor systems: diagnosis by the comparison approach; FTCS-19 digest of papers, IEEE, 1989, pp. 54 – 61.

Sega 83   A. Segall: Distributed network protocols; IEEE Transactions on Information Theory, vol. 29, no. 1, 1983, pp. 23 – 35.

SHOS 88   E. Schmeichel, S. L. Hakimi, M. Otsuka, G. Sullivan: On minimizing testing rounds for fault identification; FTCS-18, digest of papers, IEEE, 1988, pp. 266 – 271.

VaPr 91   N. Vaidya, D. Pradhan: System level diagnosis: combining detection and location; FTCS-21 digest of papers, IEEE, 1991, pp. 488 – 495.

On Integrating Error Detection into a
Fault Diagnosis Algorithm for Massively Parallel Computers

Jörn Altmann[‡], Tamás Bartha[†], András Pataricza[†]

[†] Department of Measurement and
Instrumentation Engineering
Technical University of Budapest
Müegyetem rkp. 9, H-1521 Budapest, Hungary
email: pataric@mmt.bme.hu

[‡] Department of Computer Science
(IMMD) III
University of Erlangen-Nürnberg
Martensstr. 3, 91058 Erlangen, Germany
email: jnaltman@informatik.uni-erlangen.de

Abstract

Scalable fault diagnosis is necessary for constructing fault tolerance mechanisms in large massively parallel multiprocessor systems. The diagnosis algorithm must operate efficiently even if the system consists of several thousand processors. In this paper we introduce an event-driven, distributed system-level diagnosis algorithm. It uses a small number of messages and is based on a general diagnosis model without the limitation of the number of simultaneously existing faults (an important requirement for massively parallel computers). The algorithm integrates both error detection techniques like <I'm alive> messages, and built in hardware mechanisms. The structure of the implemented algorithm is presented, and the essential program modules are described. The paper also discusses the use of test results generated by error detection mechanisms for fault localization. Measurement results illustrate the effect of the diagnosis algorithm, in particular the error detection mechanism by <I'm alive> messages, on the application performance.

Keywords: Error detection, distributed diagnosis, syndrome decoding, massively parallel systems

1 Introduction

The production cost of complex, highly integrated electronic components is decreasing due to the development of manufacturing technology. As a result, massively *parallel multicomputers*, capable of operating simultaneously several thousand processing elements (*PEs*), are gaining importance in computation-intensive scientific and technical applications. Beside the huge processing capacity achieved by utilizing massively parallel architectures, reliable operation over a long time period is also a crucial requirement. The large number of processors of such systems increases the probability of faults. Thus, the aim of fault tolerance is to ensure the specified operation in spite of faults by preventing detected errors from becoming failures [11].

In design and application of massively parallel computers *scalability* is a significant requirement. A multiprocessor system is called scalable, when extending it with new resources performance increases proportionally. Due to this requirement, centralized devices would limit the number of PEs. Thus, like other functions of the system, diagnosis must be *distributed* as well by using the PEs themselves for determining the system fault status: this approach is known as *distributed fault tolerance* [13][14][16]. In recent years several improvements for distributed diagnosis algorithms were published [3][7][10].

The paper presents a distributed diagnosis algorithm which integrates *error detection* mechanisms and minimizes the number of diagnostic messages. The aim of the algorithm is to generate a correct diagnostic image in every fault-free processor. If the diagnosis is correct, the fault-free processors can logically disconnect the faulty units from the system by stopping the communication with them. Employing this method, the number of tolerable faults depends only on the properties of the system interconnection topology.

The algorithm was developed for the Parsytec GCel[1]. This computer incorporates all features of a massively parallel multiprocessor, like scalability, regular distributed system structure, and a large number of PEs. Scalability is achieved by extending the hardware in units of 16 processors (called clusters) up to 16'384 processors in its full configuration [17]. The PEs (INMOS T805 transputers) are interconnected by a two-dimensional grid (see *Fig. 1*).

---

1. Supported by the EU (European Unit) as part of the Esprit Project 6731, Fault Tolerance for Massively Parallel Systems, and the Hungarian-German Joint Scientific Research Project #70 with additional support from OTKA-F007414.

154

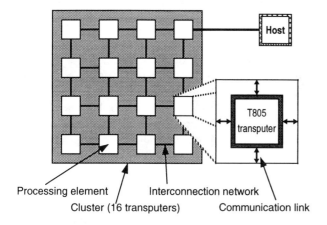

Processing element / Interconnection network
Cluster (16 transputers) / Communication link

Fig. 1. Structure of the Parsytec GCel

The following sections explain how the diagnosis algorithm fulfils the requirements from a practical view. In *Section 2*, we describe the diagnosis model of the algorithm. The structure of the diagnosis algorithm and the proof of correctness are presented in *Section 3*. The implementation aspects of the algorithm are introduced in *Section 4*, where the essential program modules are explained in detail. *Section 5.* deals with measurements results, which illustrate the impact of these fault tolerance techniques on application performance.

2 Diagnosis model

The application of the developed distributed system-level diagnosis algorithm (described in *Section 3*) requires the following conditions to be fulfilled:

- **Individual and incomplete tests**. The algorithm treats the processing elements as "intelligent units" performing tests (of less than 100% error coverage) on units directly accessible via a communication link. Since tests covering every possible errors in such complex components as the modern processors are practically impossible to implement, the proposed testing mechanism only detects:

  - cpu errors by self-test,
  - crashes of processors and links,
  - errors (e.g., data or control structure errors) on application level detected by application-dependant test.

Tests are independently performed on each processor. There is no explicit request message from a tester processor to a neighboring processor for performing a test. Results obtained by self-tests are sent by fault-free nodes within a predefined time-out limit to all neighboring processors (*<I'm alive>* messages). On receiving a message, each neighbor compares the received self-test result with the (saved or processed) local ref-

erence values. Therefore, the algorithm is prevented from a deadlock due to lost messages and test requests [8], and reduces the number of required tests [19].

Only the normal interconnection facilities may be used for testing purposes. All messages are assumed to be protected by error-correcting encodes, which serves as an additional test for both the neighboring processor and the communication link connecting the PE with its neighbor. Consequently, an error in the communication will also result in a bad test outcome, which supports the diagnosis of the interconnection network as well.

- **Symmetric test invalidation**. The algorithm uses the symmetric test invalidation model (*PMC*) introduced by Preparata et al. [18]. In this model, a fault-free tester always determines the condition of the device under test (*DUT*) correctly: the result is 0 if the test passes, 1 if the test fails. A test performed by a faulty tester may result in an arbitrary outcome. Since such test results may not correspond to the actual fault state of the DUT, they must be left out of consideration. Note, that the PMC model is the most pessimistic test invalidation model, applying the highest degree of diagnostic uncertainty in the faulty case. At the same token it is the most general one. Thus, incorporating the PMC model the algorithm is applicable in systems of other fault models as well.

- **Diagnosability**. The majority of the diagnosis algorithms introduces an upper limit on the number of simultaneously existing faults in order to simplify the handling of uncertainty originating from the pessimistic test invalidation model. The underlying assumption of this *t-limit* is that a small number of faults are more likely to occur in a properly designed multiprocessor system if the individual faults are independent, thus, uncorrelated. The t-limit is the largest number of arbitrary located faults for which a proper diagnosis is always assured (e.g., for the two-dimensional grid the t-limit is as low as 2). Note, that the t-limit is a *worst-case* diagnostic measure, in most situations it provides too pessimistic estimation [11][15]. For this reason, we introduce a model which supports the diagnosis of an arbitrary number of faulty processors.

Let us consider now the *interconnection graph* $G = (N, A)$ of the system. Its nodes $u_i \in N$ ($i = 1...n$, where n denotes the total number of processing elements in the system) correspond to the processors. A directed arc $(u_i, u_j) \in A$ exists between two nodes if direct communication is possible between the corresponding processors in the given direction. Diagnosis of the whole system is possible until G remains *strongly connected*. However, faulty PEs or links can cut the in-

155

terconnection graph into isolated subgraphs. The case of a system with three isolated connected subgraphs is presented in *Fig. 2*. If this happens, diagnosis is restricted to the group of fault-free processors located in the same connected subgraph. Since subgraphs are isolated, the host computer can access only the PEs located in the connected subgraph containing the host link (see subgraph 1 in Fig. 2).

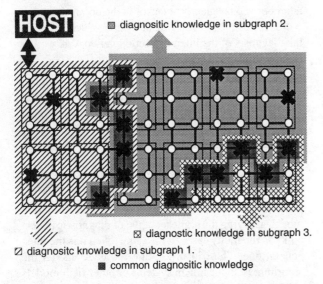

■ diagnositic knowledge in subgraph 2.

⊠ diagnostic knowledge in subgraph 3.

◪ diagnositc knowledge in subgraph 1.

■ common diagnositic knowledge

Fig. 2.   Diagnostic knowledge in different subgraphs

Messages exchanged between non-neighboring nodes are transferred via paths of processors and links. Faulty processors or communication links cannot be included in this path, because they would block the correct information flow or make it unreliable. Therefore, a set of faulty processors and links may *isolate* a group of fault-free processors. In such cases the diagnostic image of the whole system is incomplete, but a complete diagnostic image within connected subgraphs can be generated.

The algorithm does not require the limitation of the number of faults, rather it includes only the nodes in the same connected subgraph in diagnosis, classifying the state of other processors as unknown. Each fault-free PE diagnoses its own subgraph, as indicated in *Fig. 2*. Unknown processors are identified by detecting the isolating *barriers* made of faulty processors [4].

Although the host computer can access only the processors in its own subgraph, the diagnosis procedure running in other regions is also important. Due to the distributed nature of the algorithm, every processor maintains a consistent local diagnostic image. When a faulty node within a barrier is repaired or replaced, two isolated regions will be joined together. In such cases

the two different local diagnostic images can be combined in order to obtain a consistent diagnostic image of the joined subgraphs.

- **Determining the real message order**. The arrival of messages at a processor will not always correspond to the order of their creation, due to communication delays. Such a situation can occur if a PE becomes faulty during the testing process. Then, messages received in a wrong order will cause the algorithm to generate an incorrect diagnosis. To avoid this, logical time-stamps related to test execution must be attached to the diagnostic messages, and the real order of messages must be determined using a distributed event-ordering procedure [14].

3   Structure of the diagnosis algorithm

The diagnostic process described below is almost identical for the different processors (only the inhomogeneity at the grid borders has to be taken into account), so each processor can use the same diagnosis algorithm. The algorithm consists of two phases: an *initial* and a *working* phase. Two observations motivated the splitting of the algorithm:

- Current peaks during power on/off may damage the electronic components of the system. Hence, the majority of faults occurs (or already exists) in the initial phase. Moreover, typically the power-on tests serve as major means for the detection of permanent faults. The failure rate is expected to be lower during further operation.

- Processors do not have any information on the fault state of other components in the initial phase of the diagnosis algorithm (i.e., communication links and other PEs). All processors have to be tested once to generate the initial diagnosis image. Later the system fault state does not change significantly compared to the first diagnostic image due to low fault rate. For this reason, a considerable overhead in communication and administration can be saved by calculating and distributing only the *differences* between the current (diagnosed) fault state and the stored diagnostic image.

3.1   Initial phase

Inter-processor communication starts after the local diagnostic images has been generated by testing the *neighbouring* processors, and it continues until each fault-free processor has received diagnostic information from all the others in the same connected subgraph. Every PE sends the local test results to its neighbors, and further on it receives and forwards the messages sent by other units. PEs maintain a list of the processors from which they have not received a diagnostic image yet, in order to evaluate the termination criterion of communication. For this purpose they must also discover which nodes are accessible via a path of fault-free processors and links.

There are processors that meet the termination condition before others, due to the inherent inhomogeneity of the two-dimensional grid topology (i.e., processors located on grid edges do not have certain neighbors) and obstacles in communication formed by faulty components [5]. These processors must inform their neighbors before termination, otherwise the neighbors would possibly try to communicate with the already terminated processor. To avoid this *deadlock* situation, the algorithm has a *termination* period. Ready-to-terminate PEs send special messages to their neighbors during this period, so the still active nodes will not communicate with these PEs further on [4]. After the information is sent to each neighbor, processors decode the received syndromes using the algorithm described in *Section 4.4*, thus completing the initial phase.

For the transputer system, the initial phase of the diagnosis algorithm is integrated into the boot and loading process.

3.2 Working phase

The algorithm continues with the working phase after finishing the initial phase. All processors have an initial, *system-level diagnostic image* at this point. Let u_i be an arbitrary processor in the multiprocessor system which periodically tests its neighboring processors u_j, u_k, u_l, u_m. The test compares the values (results of self-test programs) received in <I'm alive> messages from the neighbors with stored or processed local reference values. Hence, an error is detected in four different ways:

- a <I'm alive> message does not arrive within the predefined time-out interval,
- a <I'm alive> message contains incorrect error correcting code,
- the value of the <I'm alive> message does not match the local reference value.

Assume, that the current result of comparison shows that u_k, u_l, u_m are fault-free and u_j is faulty. Then the local test result is $a_{i,k} = a_{i,l} = a_{i,m} = 0$, but $a_{i,j} = 1$. The processor u_i compares the obtained local test results to the stored local diagnostic image during further operation. If it finds a difference indicating a new fault occurrence, it invokes exception handling. Assume, that the local test result $a_{i,j} = 1$ indicates a new fault. In this case, processor u_i starts to broadcast messages containing the local test result $a_{i,j} = 1$. Now, two different cases can be distinguished regarding the state of the tester:

i)   processor u_i is fault-free or

ii) processor u_i is faulty.

In the first case processor u_i broadcasts a correct local test result to each neighbors indicated as fault-free in the current local diagnostic image. If there is no other new faulty processor except u_j, these processors are really fault-free. Because every fault-free processor diagnose their neighbors correctly each faulty processor can be isolated; broadcast messages are sent only between fault-free neighbors. Hence, processor u_i sends its local test results only to processors u_k, u_l, u_m. The same procedure continues until all fault-free processors within a connected subgraph receive the local test result of processor u_i.

If there are multiple new faulty processors in the system, it may happen that the local test result becomes corrupted. If this remains undetected by the coding of messages an incorrect local test result is broadcasted, falsely indicating the occurrence of a single processor fault in the system. Although some of the fault-free processors now receive an incorrect local test result, it does not result in a wrong fault localization as it will be shown in *Section 4.4*. The reason is that only changes within the system are reported by the local test results, not the fault state of a processor.

In the second case processor u_i sends either a correct or a wrong local test result to some of its neighbors. On the one hand, if the neighbor is faulty, the communication between these two faulty processors has no impact on the correctness of the diagnosis. On the other hand, if the neighbor is fault-free and the message format from processor u_i is correct, a wrong local test result will be broadcasted. The same situation as described above in the previous paragraph.

After all, every fault-free processors within a connected subgraph have received the message regarding the local test result. After receiving the first message about the local test result, the processor stops the application as soon as possible and waits for further local test results from other neighbors of the faulty processor for a fixed *time interval (time-out termination criterion)* [9]. Furthermore, all fault-free neighbors will initiate further, more exact tests on the probably faulty processor and on the processor initiating the exception handling.

All processors can determine the fault state of the whole system by processing the incoming local test results (*syndrome decoding* process), unless some faulty processors cut the system into different isolated subgraphs (*Section 4.4*).

The working phase of the diagnosis algorithm is *event-driven*, as both the local test result distribution and the syndrome decoding process are activated by the changes in the local diagnostic image [6].

4   The implemented diagnosis algorithm

The implementation details of the initial phase of the algorithm are not discussed in the paper, as the boot process (and thus the initial phase) has no impact on the application performance. During this phase no application is running, so efficiency requirements do not have high priority.

The realization of the working phase can be done in different ways, depending on the splitting of the processing power between the diagnostic process and the running application. In the following the implementation of the algorithm will be described. Alternative approaches to the testing mechanism of neighboring processors, termination rules, distribution of local test results, and processing of diagnostic information are presented to show that the algorithm can be adapted to several systems and requirements.

The main structure of the implementation for the working phase of the algorithm is shown in *Fig. 3*. If no fault event is detected, the algorithm periodically tests the neighboring processors. Testing is accomplished by assigning independent modules to each tested unit [2].

If the tests detect an error in one of the neighboring processors, exception handling is invoked by issuing an error indication from the corresponding *testing* module to the *local diagnosis* module. The local diagnosis module gives control to the *supervisor* module, which handles the exceptions caused by the detected error. The supervisor module activates the modules responsible for *terminating the current application*, for *distribution of the local test results*, and for *processing of the diagnostic information* (as described in *Section 4.4*) [1].

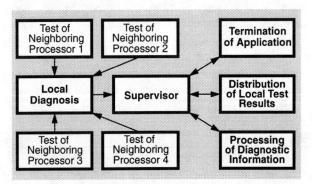

Fig. 3.   Main modules of the implemented algorithm

4.1   Test of neighboring processors

Each testing module is comprised of three threads: one for receiving local test results from the neighboring processors, one for sending such messages (<I'm alive> message), and one for evaluating the result (i.e., verifying whether the responses are delayed or incorrect), respectively. If the evaluation indicates a faulty behavior of the neighboring processor, the thread sends an error message to the local diagnosis module.

This <I'm alive> testing mechanism offers a possibility to control the testing related run-time overhead. On the one

hand very precise and thoroughgoing self-tests can be used resulting in a decreased application performance due to the more intensive diagnosis process. Such self-tests can take two forms: either realized in software or in hardware.

On the other hand, the use of <I'm alive> messages indicating the alive or dead state of a processor reduces the requirements of processing capacity to a fraction, thus yielding more computational power to the application. Although this kind of tests is easy to process, it can only detect processor and link crashs, and more post-processing is required later.

However, since the application is quickly stopped after error detection, there is a sufficient time remaining for more finely granulated tests and post-processing in a subsequent separate testing phase.

4.2   Terminating the application

The function of this module is to interrupt the execution of the application on all the PEs as soon as possible. This is necessary for the prevention of error dissemination and to decrease the fault latency in the multiprocessor. If the application is quickly suspended, the probability of error dissemination is reduced, because no further communication - with the exception of diagnostic information transfer - will take place.

For quick termination of the application, the module initiates a fast broadcast. The broadcast messages are received at every node by the local diagnosis module, which initiates immediately exception handling. No specific routing mechanism is required for the implementation of the fast broadcast, as the existing routing mechanism of the Parsytec GCel system extended with a high-level, fault-tolerant communication protocol is fully sufficient. The broadcast is based on flooding the multiprocessor with a so-called *stop message* indicating the occurrence of an error. Each processor sends this message to all of its fault-free neighbors. The neighbors forward the message to their neighbors (excluding the sender), continuing this process until the message arrives at every accessible fault-free node. The advantage of using flooding is its easy algorithm and its inherent fault-tolerant behavior; all fault-free processors within a connected subgraph are reached.

4.3   Distribution of local test results

The module for distribution of the local test results is activated after terminating the application. At first, only the neighboring processors of the faulty processor start a separate testing phase, executing fault localization tests. The assumed causes are faulty links and faulty processor components. These additional tests even assure the classification of faults as *temporary* or *permanent*. The outcome of these tests as well as the tests results obtained by the error

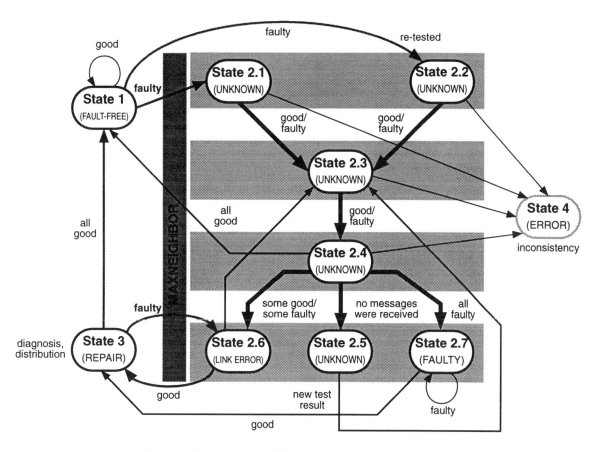

Fig. 4.   State diagram of the syndrome decoding algorithm

detection mechanism constitute the local test results.

The distribution module transfers the local test results to the supervisor module of each processor using the fault-tolerant flooding broadcast.

Different criteria can be used for terminating the distribution phase. Our first implemented criterion was to wait until all the local test results from each tester of the faulty node have been received, but we found that this method is not robust against errors during the diagnosis (e.g., lost messages due to node failure). A time-out criterion is used for elimination of this lack of robustness [8]. The distribution process waits for a certain time interval, in which all of the local test results must be received. The main advantages of this method are its safety and simplicity, but the optimal time-out limit must be estimated in the design phase.

4.4   Fault localization

It is necessary to analyze the obtained local test results in order to determine the fault state of each accessible unit of the system. This task is accomplished by a syndrome decoding algorithm (defined by the state diagram in *Fig. 4*). Syndrome decoding is invoked by the supervisor module on

receiving a new local test result. This way the local test result distribution and the fault localization modules are executed alternatively. Therefore, even if the time-out limit used in the distribution process is not optimal, the processor will not be idle.

Fig. 4 describes the different states of the classification process of a unit under diagnosis (*UUD*). Three possible fault classifications are taken into consideration: the UUD can be *faulty*, *fault-free*, or a *link fault* in the communication link between the testing processor and the UUD may occur. (Note, that actually there is a fourth classification for the inaccessible PEs: *unknown*.) In each state (represented by nodes in the graph) the actual classification is shown in parentheses. Transitions between states are indicated by directed arcs in the graph. A transition is enabled by receiving a local test result.

There are four possible starting states in the diagnosis of a UUD: State 1, State 2.5, State 2.6, and State 2.7; depending on the classification created in the initial phase of the diagnosis algorithm. If the UUD was found to be *fault-free* in the initial phase (i.e., State 1 is the starting state), this classification remains unaltered, until a message indicating a fault in the UUD has been received from one of its neighboring processors. Two different activities must be performed after receiving a fault indication, depending on the topological relationship between the diagnosing PE and the UUD:

- if the PE is one of the neighbors of the UUD (i.e., it is assigned to test it), the PE executes a new test, then it broadcasts the local test result in the system, as well as the received test result. This procedure assures that each processor will receive an up-to-date test result from all the testers of the UUD. These activities are performed in State 2.2.

- if the PE is not one of the neighbors (State 2.1), it only forwards the received local test result to its neighbors and enters the next state.

Test results from the testers of the UUD are obtained and then analyzed during the subsequent four state classes (from State 2.1 to State 2.7, marked by gray background). The number of these state classes (indicated as MAXNEIGHBOR in *Fig. 4*) equals to the number of neighboring (testing) processors. Transitions are independent of the received test results, as the purpose of these states is to obtain all information from the tester processors. A time-out mechanism is used in receiving the local test result messages. During the obtaining of local test results, the classification of the UUD is set to *unknown*. Decision is made when all local test results are received, or the time-out period used in the distribution phase expires. Local test results not received within the time-out period due to an extremely large communication delay are assumed to be missing.

Missing messages which generate diagnostic inconsistency are taken into consideration as indications of a new error occurrence during diagnosis (State 4). In this case the diagnosing processor broadcasts a fault indication in the system. All processors receiving the message will begin to test their neighbors.

If no messages are received within the time-out limit, the UUD is inaccessible, so its classification remains unknown (State 2.5). This classification is valid, till a new local test result related to the UUD is received from one of its testers later on, then the algorithm continues the diagnosis of the unit in State 2.3.

If every tester found the UUD to be faulty, then the unit itself is considered to be *faulty* (in State 2.7). A processor crash, and the simultaneous fault in all of its communication links are equivalent as they produce identical syndromes. Such syndromes are represented as processor faults.

If a tester processors produces a bad test outcome for its neighbor and vice versa, then the corresponding communication links between these testers are assumed to be faulty (classification *link fault* in State 2.6).

State 3 provides the possibility of taking on-line repairs into consideration. Here an extra diagnostic process is required to assure consistency between the diagnostic images stored in processors belonging to different connected subgraphs. If faulty links or nodes - previously isolating two or more connected subgraphs - have repaired, the subgraphs are joined, but the diagnostic knowledge (described in *Section 2*) of the processors remains potentially different. For this reason a special broadcast procedure is performed between the nodes of previously isolated subgraphs to merge the various diagnostic knowledge into one.

5. Measurements

As stated in *Section 3*, faults seldom occur during the operation of the system. In a fault-free system the event-driven diagnosis algorithm performs only error detection. Thus, the <I'm alive> testing mechanism has the largest impact on the application performance. We have examined the run-time overhead related to testing. The minimal run-time overhead can be achieved using the <I'm alive> message. Therefore, this testing mechanism was measured.

5.1 Application run-time overhead

As the application run-time overhead is an important criterion for the evaluation of a fault tolerance mechanism, we measured the application run-time overhead by running a benchmark-like practical application (*Ising*) and the diagnosis algorithm concurrently on each processor. The Ising application calculates the spin of electrons in a gas at various temperatures. In *Fig. 5* the run-time overhead is displayed as a function of the time between two consecutive <I'm alive> messages.

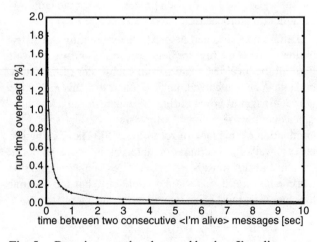

Fig. 5.   Run-time overhead caused by the <I'm alive> testing mechanism (Ising application)

The overhead is approximately inversely proportional to the time between two consecutive <I'm alive> messages.

160

The sending of <I'm alive> messages has a very little impact on the application run-time, if the interval between two messages is longer than one second. If the <I'm alive> messages are sent in every 500 milliseconds, the overhead is larger, but does not exceed 0,2 percent.

The reason for the coarse of the curve is the increasing usage of computational power for receiving, sending, and evaluating <I'm alive> messages by the <I'm alive> mechanism, if the time interval between the two consecutive <I'm alive> messages decreases.

Furthermore, performance measurements were made with various other benchmark-like applications, differing in the intensity of communication. The shape of curves describing the overhead corresponding to the different applications are similar to the curve in *Fig. 5*. The collection of these curves can be represented by the grey marked region in *Fig. 6*, bounded by two curves of the application overhead. The curve at the lower border of the marked region represents the run-time overhead of the *whetstone* benchmark program, which does not communicate. The curve at the upper border describes the run-time overhead of a dummy program which performs only communication.

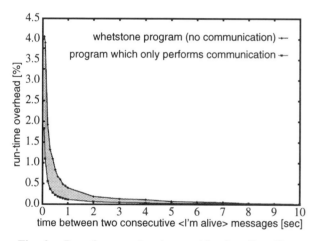

Fig. 6.   Run-time overhead caused by the <I'm alive> mechanism for various applications

The reason for the difference in the run-time overhead between the whetstone and the dummy application is the load of the communication network.

5.2   Impact of the application on the <I'm alive> message testing mechanism

Additionally to the influence of the <I'm alive> mechanism on the application performance, the inverse effect is another important criterion for the assessment of diagnosis software. Since the same communication network is used for sending the <I'm alive> messages as well as the application messages, and since both kind of messages are sent

with the same priority on the multiprocessor Parsytec GCel, the impact of the application messages on the <I'm alive> message testing mechanism has to be examined.

The time between two consecutive <I'm alive> messages has been measured. This time is composed of the *<I'm alive> time interval* and the communication time needed for sending this <I'm alive> message to the neighboring processor. The <I'm alive> time interval was chosen to be one second to have a small run-time overhead as indicated in *Fig. 6*.

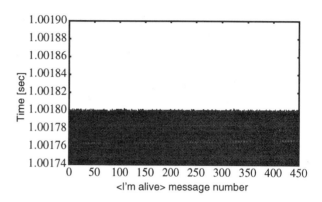

Fig. 7.   Time between two consecutive <I'm alive> messages running the whetstone application

For the whetstone application (*Fig. 7*), the time between two consecutive <I'm alive> messages is nearly constant, with a variance only in the microsecond range. The average time is 1.00180 seconds. That could be expected because the whetstone application does not communicate. Therefore, the average time will be used as the base for the comparison with the following measurements.

In a dummy application exclusively performing communication, the average time is 1.00187 seconds (*Fig. 8*). This shows that the time between two consecutive <I'm alive> messages is only a little bit larger running the dummy application than for the whetstone benchmark program.

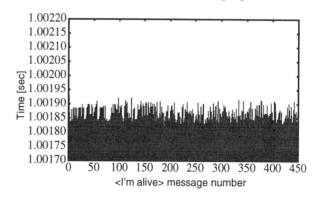

Fig. 8.   Time between two consecutive <I'm alive> messages running an application which only communicates

Furthermore, even the measured time values vary not much more than the values displayed in *Fig. 7*. They are in the range between 1.00182 and 1.00193 seconds (see *Fig. 8*). Considering these results, it can be stated that the messages sent by the applications have a moderate impact on the <I'm alive> message testing mechanism. An upper limit for the delay of the messages can easily be found. For the example given, the maximal delay is 0.00193 seconds which can be recognized in *Fig. 8*.

5.3   Fault latency

The *fault latency (T_l)* in a processor is defined as the time interval between the fault occurrence and the error detection by a neighboring processor (tester). The latency depends on the time *(T_c)* between two consecutive checks of incoming messages *(check time interval)* and the <I'm alive> time interval *(T_{ia})* where $T_{ia} < T_c$. The model of fault latency is shown in Fig. 9.

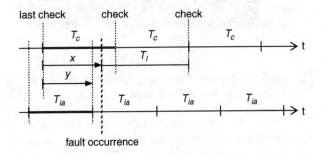

Fig. 9 Model of fault latency

As the checking process in the tester processor runs asynchronously to the <I'm alive> message generating process in the processor under test, we assume that the remaining time y from the last check to the next <I'm alive> message is an equiprobable distributed random variable.

Additionally, as faults are assumed to be uncorrelated with both the message sending and the checking process, the random variable x denoting the time between the last check and the occurrence of an error is assumed to be equal distributed, and the distributions of x and y are independent.

Then, two cases concerning the latency T_l have to be distinguished:

i)   the latency T_l is $T_l = 2T_c - x$ and $0 \le x \le T_c$ or

ii) the latency T_l is $T_l = T_c - x$ and $0 \le x \le T_{ia}$.

The density functions for the two cases are:

case i)
$$f_i(x) = \begin{cases} x > T_{ia} & f_{i1}(x) = 1 \\ x \le T_{ia} & f_{i2}(x) = \dfrac{x}{T_{ia}} \end{cases}$$

case ii)
$$f_{ii}(x) = \begin{cases} x > T_{ia} & f_{ii1}(x) = 0 \\ x \le T_{ia} & f_{ii2}(x) = 1 - \dfrac{x}{T_{ia}} \end{cases}$$

The desity functions $f_i(x)$ and $f_{ii}(x)$ show: if x is in the range $0 \le x \le T_{ia}$ than both cases of latency are possible depending on y; if x is in the range $T_{ia} \le x \le T_c$ than only case i) happens.

The *theoretical mean fault latency T_{ml}* can now be calculated by $T_{ml} = T_{ml1} + T_{ml2}$, where T_{ml1} and T_{ml2} are:

$$T_{ml1} = \frac{1}{T_c} \int_0^{T_{ia}} \left((2T_c - x)\frac{x}{T_{ia}} + (T_c - x)\left(1 - \frac{x}{T_{ia}}\right) \right) dx$$

$$T_{ml2} = \frac{1}{T_c} \int_{T_{ia}}^{T_c} (2T_c - x)\, dx$$

After completing the above integration, the following formula results for the theoretical mean latency T_{ml}:

$$T_{ml} = \frac{3}{2}T_c - \frac{1}{2}T_{ia}$$

Assume an <I'm alive> message period time of 1.0 second and a check time interval of 1.1 second. Then, a mean latency T_{ml} of 1.15 seconds would result.

The model suggests, that the mean fault latency can be reduced in two ways. Firstly, the <I'm alive> message interval T_{ia} must be closely equal to the check time interval T_c. But here, the variance caused by the communication (ΔT_{max}) must be taken into account:

$$T_c \ge T_{ia} + \Delta T_{max}$$

Secondly, the check time interval (and so the <I'm alive> message interval) can be decreased. However, reducing T_c and T_{ia} the application run-time overhead will increase. Therefore, the trade-off between the reduction of the check time interval and the application run-time overhead has to be taken into consideration determining the *optimal mean latency*.

The theoretical mean latency of the <I'm alive> message testing mechanism was computed using our model. Fault injection experiments were performed to validate the result. Permanent faults, always resulting in crash failure of a processor, were injected. The measured latency and its mean value (*computed mean latency*) for the above example are shown in *Fig. 10*.

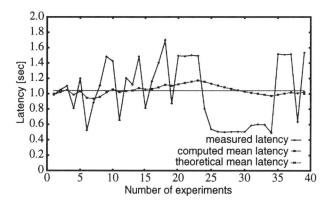

Fig. 10.   Fault latency

The measured latency varies between 0.5 and 1.7 seconds. These values are in the theoretical latency range between 0.1 and 2.2 seconds. After 39 measurements the computed mean latency is close to its theoretical value.

5.4   Run-time of the broadcast needed for stopping the application

A important aspect of the diagnosis, as already mentioned in *Section 4*, is the time needed for stopping the application after the occurrence of an error. To reduce the latency in a multiprocessor system and the probability of error propagation, the mechanism for stopping the application has to work fast. That is achieved by a fast broadcast.

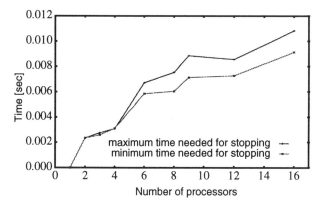

Fig. 11.   Time needed for stopping the application

In *Fig. 11* run-time measurements of this broadcast are shown. The run-time depends on the grid structure and on the location in which the broadcast is initiated after the occurrence of an error. Therefore, in *Fig. 11* two curves of the run-time are given, the upper one describing the maximum run-time, the lower one describing the minimum run-time. Considering the dependencies of the run-time, it is obvious that the curves are nonlinear; the number of hops performed by the broadcast does not increase linearly on increasing the number of processors.

6   Conclusions

In this paper we introduced a new system-level diagnosis algorithm. The algorithm is distributed, which makes it applicable in scalable systems; and event-driven, thus it processes diagnostic information fast and efficiently, requiring small amount of communication and computation. Additionally, we concentrated on the relation between the tests for error detection and the tests for error localization.

The general structure of the algorithm consisting of two separate phases has been described. A new syndrome decoding method, which produces the diagnosis gradually was given. Furthermore, we presented an extended diagnosis model, which makes possible to obtain all accessible diagnostic information without limiting the number of tolerated faults within the system.

Additionally, we presented an implementation based on the algorithm which uses different tests for error detection and localization, using a separate testing phase after quick termination of the running application. It executes the local test result distribution and the syndrome decoding procedures alternatively, thus creating diagnostic images gradually, taking every test outcome into consideration during diagnosis. The implementation was examined, highlighting the advantages and disadvantages. Furthermore, we have proven the efficiency of our algorithm by some measurement results. The measurement results show that the testing causes only a small overhead.

References

[1]   Altmann, J., "Diagnoseprotokolle in Multiprozessorsystemen," Diploma Work, University of Erlangen-Nürnberg, February 1993.

[2]   Altmann, J., F. Balbach, and A. Hein, "An Approach for Hierarchical System Level Diagnosis of Massively Parallel Computers Combined With a Simulation-Based Method for Dependability Analysis," *IEEE 1st European Dependable Computing Conference*, Berlin, October 1994.

[3]   Bagchi, A. and S. L. Hakimi, "An Optimal Algorithm for Distributed System-Level Diagnosis," *IEEE Proc. 21st Int. Symposium on Fault-Tolerant Computing*, pp. 214-221, Montreal, June 1991.

[4]   Bartha, T., "Diagnostic Algorithms of Multiprocessor Systems," Diploma Work, Tech. University of Budapest, 1993.

[5]   Behr., P. M., W. K. Giloi, and W. Schröder, "Synchronous versus Asynchronous Communication in High Performance Multicomputer Systems," *Aspects of Computation on Asynchronous Parallel Processors*, pp. 239-247, North-Holland, 1989.

[6]   Bianchini, R. and R. Buskens, "An Adaptive Distributed System-Level Diagnosis Algorithm and its Implementation," *IEEE Proc. 21th Int. Symposium on Fault-Tolerant Computing*, pp. 222-229, Montreal, June 1991.

[7]   Bianchini, R., R. Buskens, and M. Stahl, "On-Line Diagnosis in General Topology Networks," *Proc. IEEE Workshop on Fault-Tolerant Parallel and Distributed Systems,* pp. 114-121, Amherst, July 1992.

[8]   Ciompi, P., F. Grandoni, and L. Simoncini, "Distributed Diagnosis in Multiprocessor System: The MuTeam approach," *IEEE Proc. 11th Int. Symposium on Fault-Tolerant Computing,* pp. 25-29, Portland, June 1981.

[9]   Cristian, F., H. Aghili, and R. Strong, "Atomic Broadcast: From Simple Message Diffusion to Byzantine Agreement," *IEEE Proc. 15th Int. Symposium on Fault-Tolerant Computing,* pp. 200-206, Ann Harbor, June 1985.

[10]   Dal Cin, M. and F. Florian, "Analysis of a Fault-Tolerant Distributed Diagnosis Algorithm," *IEEE Proc. 15th Int. Symposium on Fault-Tolerant Computing,* pp. 159-164, Ann Harbor, June 1985.

[11]   Dal Cin, M. and A. Pataricza, "Increasing Dependability in Multiprocessors," *Proc. of the 8th Symp. on Microcomputer and Microprocessor App. µP'94,* pp. 55-64, Budapest, October 1994.

[12]   Kime, C. R., "System Diagnosis," in *Fault-Tolerant Computing: Theory and Techniques,* Prentice-Hall, New York, pp. 577-623, 1985.

[13]   Kuhl, J. G., and S. M. Reddy, "Distributed Fault-Tolerance for Large Multiprocessor Systems," *ACM-Sigarch Newletter 8,* no. 3, pp. 23-30, 1980.

[14]   Kuhl, J. G., S. M. Reddy, and S. H. Hosseini, "On Self Fault-Diagnosis of the Distributed Systems," *IEEE Proc. 15th Int. Symposium on Fault-Tolerant Computing,* pp. 30-35, Ann Harbor, June 1985.

[15]   Malek, M. and Y. Maeng, "Partitioning of Large Multicomputer Systems for Efficient Fault Diagnosis," *IEEE Proc. 12th Intl. Symposium on Fault-Tolerant Computing,* pp. 341-348, Santa Monica, June 1982.

[16]   Meyer, F.J. and G. Masson, "An Efficient Fault Diagnosis Algorithm for Symmetric Multiprocessor Architecture," *IEEE Transaction on Computer,* vol. EC-27, pp. 1059-1063, November 1978.

[17]   Parsytec Computer GmbH., "The Parsytec GCel Technical Summary," Version 1.0, Aachen, 1991.

[18]   Preparata, F., G. Metze, and R. Chien, "On the Connection Assignment Problem of Diagnosable Systems," *IEEE Transaction on Computer,* vol. EC-16, no. 6, pp. 848-854, December 1967.

[19]   Rangarajan, S. and D. Fussell, "A Probabilistic Method for Fault Diagnosis of Multiprocessor Systems," *IEEE Proc. 18th Int. Symposium on Fault-Tolerant Computing,* pp. 278-283, 1988.

Performance Evaluation of The Quorum Consensus Replication Method

Abdelsalam Helal
Computer Science & Engineering
University of Texas at Arlington
Arlington, TX 76019
helal@cse.uta.edu

Bharat Bhargava
Dept. of Computer Sciences
Purdue University
W. Lafayette, IN 47907
bb@cs.purdue.edu

Abstract

The goal of data replication in distributed database systems is to increase data availability in the presence of failures. Using the quorum consensus method, up to $\lfloor \frac{(n+1)}{2} \rfloor$ site failures can be tolerated, in an n-site system, without loss of data accessibility. Quorum consensus can however be very expensive to use, especially in large-scale systems. This is because multiple sites in the system must be accessed to perform the read or write operations.

This paper describes an actual implementation of the quorum consensus method and gives an experimental evaluation of its performance. The implementation was done in the context of the Purdue Raid, which is a LAN-based distributed database system with extensive experimentation infrastructure. We focus our description on the particularities of managing version numbers and choosing object weights and thresholds. We also present a performance evaluation study, where the message traffic overhead, throughput and response time, and availability of the quorum consensus method is studied and compared to the read-one-write-all method.

1 Introduction

The replication of data in distributed database systems is used to increase data availability in the presence of site and/or communication link failures. Replication, however, creates consistency problems among the replicas of the same data object, especially in the presence of failures. Moreover, it results in a performance penalty due to the increased time that is needed to access and update multiple remote copies, instead of single copies. To maintain mutual consistency among data replicas in the presence of failures, a replication control method is used. Many replication control methods have been proposed in the literature [4, 2, 16, 9, 1, 14, 10]. A survey of these methods can be found in [12].

Replication methods vary in the degree of availability that they provide. They also vary in their message exchange and delay overhead. Efficient methods

usually provide limited availability while ultra fault-tolerant methods are penalized with high overhead. In fact, a non-optimized implementation of a highly-available method can result in an overhead so high that it can hinder transaction processing to the extent that defeats the main purpose of replication [13].

In this paper we will focus on the availability and performance of the quorum consensus replication method [9]. Quorum consensus (QC) is a general mechanism for managing replicated data objects. It is also known as weighted voting. Under quorum consensus, each data object is assigned a read threshold and a write threshold. Also, each copy of the data object is assigned a weight and a version number. In order to read(write) a data object, a read(write) quorum must be available. Any set of available copies with total weight greater than or equal to the read(write) threshold constitutes a read(write) quorum. Weights are chosen so that any write quorum of a data object intersects any other read or write quorum of the same object. This requirement is called the quorum intersection rule. The rule guarantees that any pair of conflicting operations will have quorums that intersect and therefore will always be synchronized by the concurrency control at the sites on which the intersected copies reside. The most up-to-date copy of the read quorum is returned by the read operation. This is the copy with the highest version number. When writing the value for an object, all copies of the write quorum are assigned a same version number greater than their current maximum version number. Quorum consensus can be adapted to implement read-one-write-all (ROWA) and read-same-as-write (QC-RSW) policies, among others [6]. The QC-RSW will be explained in section 2.3. The main characteristics of the quorum consensus method are qualitatively described below:

- *Availability:* Quorum consensus can achieve higher availability than the ROWA method. This is because it is sufficient that a quorum of copies be available to perform an operation. Unlike the ROWA method, quorum consensus availability can be tuned to favor the read operation over the write operation. Furthermore, this tuning can be done on a per object basis. This allows for utilizing knowledge of transaction workload to further enhance data availability.

- *Message Traffic:* Quorum consensus requires access to multiple remote copies in order to process a read operation. Unfortunately, the quorum sizes increase linearly with the number of copies for an object. This leads to heavy message traffic that can become a bottleneck in the communication subsystem. The hierarchical quorum consensus [15] method can improve scalability by reducing the message traffic overhead. This is done by organizing the copies in a multi-level hierarchy, and requiring that a quorum for an object at a certain level in the hierarchy be assembled by gathering a vote of sub-objects at the previous level in the hierarchy.

- *Computation Cost:* The computation cost attributed to message processing is proportional to the total volume of message traffic. The technique of *deferred writes* can reduce the computation cost of processing *write* messages. To reduce the cost of the *read* operations, read requests of the same transaction can be buffered in a piggyback message in the communication subsystem. For example, consider a transaction with 5 read operations, three of which have site 4 as a member of their quorums. A single message that contains three read requests can be sent to site 4, instead of three separate messages. Unfortunately, per-site piggyback messages require a priori knowledge of the read set of transactions.

2 RAID Implementation of Quorum Consensus

The implementation of the quorum consensus method in the Raid distributed database system is presented in this section. We focus our description on the particularities of managing version numbers and choosing object weights and thresholds. We first give a brief description of the Raid system.

2.1 Raid

Raid [7, 5] is a server-based, relational, distributed database system that has been developed at Purdue University. Each database site in the Raid system consists of seven servers, each of which encapsulates a subset of the functionality of the system. The seven servers are the User Interface (UI), the Action Driver (AD), the Access Manager (AM), The Concurrency Controller (CC), the Atomicity Controller (AC), the Replication Controller (RC), and the Surveillance Controller (SC). The user interface is a front-end that allows a user to invoke SQL-type queries on a relational database. The action driver translates parsed queries into a sequence of low-level read and write actions. The access manager is responsible for the storage, indexing, and retrieval of information on a physical device. The concurrency controller checks that read and write actions of different transactions do not conflict. The atomicity controller is responsible for ensuring that transactions are committed or aborted atomically across all sites. The replication controller manages multiple copies of data objects to provide system availability and mutual consistency of replicated data. The Surveillance controller collects connectivity information about Raid sites, and advertises view changes to the replication controller. The details of Raid design and implementation can be found in [5].

2.2 Version numbers

Version numbers are implemented at the tuple-level granularity in Raid. This choice was made to accommodate re-using the replication controller for the O-Raid project that implements objects as tuples that possibly contain persistent pointers [8]. The storage location of version numbers in quorum methods is a critical problem. Our approach in Raid was to encapsulate the version numbers inside the tuples by enforcing and including a system-wide integer attribute in all users and system relations.

This approach though simple, has the restriction of requiring every write to be preceded by a read on the same object in order to determine the maximum version number needed by the write operation. Therefore, in this approach, $Read\_Set(t) \supseteq Write\_Set(t)$, for a transaction t. In this case, a transaction with a read-to-write ratio $\frac{r}{w}$, will always have this ratio adjusted to $\frac{1}{w}$. As will be shown in section 2.3, this adjustment affects our replication policies under the QC method.

We believe that other alternatives that would allow the replication controller to determine the maximum version number without any inter-server communication are not feasible to pursue in a server-based, layered implementation like Raid. For example, if the version numbers are to be stored in RC's address space, it would be necessary to duplicate concurrency control as well as atomicity control inside the replication controller in order to regulate concurrent access and atomic update of the data relations and their corresponding version numbers.

2.3 Weights and thresholds

In Raid, weights and thresholds are chosen not only to satisfy the quorum intersection rule mentioned in section 1, but also to specify and control the availability-performance compromise of the QC method. Two optimization problems are involved in this compromise. Both can be formulated as integer programming problems. Let R_T and W_T be the read and write thresholds of an object, respectively. Also, let r and w be the fraction of operations which are reads and the fraction of operations which are writes, respectively. Assuming equal weights of unity for all copies of all objects, let M be the sum of weights of any object's copies. M can then be interpreted as the degree of replication.

The first problem deals with performance and can be formulated as follows:

$$\text{Minimize} \quad rR_T + wW_T$$
$$\text{subject to:}$$
$$
\begin{aligned}
W_T &> \frac{M}{2} \\
R_T + W_T &> M \\
R_T &\leq M \\
W_T &\leq M
\end{aligned}
$$

$$R_T > 0, \quad W_T > 0, \quad \text{integers.}$$

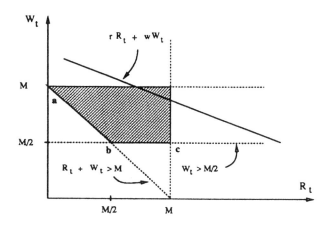

Figure 1: Performance Optimization of Quorum Consensus

The objective function represents the expected number of message exchange to perform an operation. The convex set of all feasible solutions is shown as the shaded region in Figure 1. Depending on the values of r and w, the objective function can be minimized at:

$$a = (1, M) \qquad : \quad -\infty \leq -\frac{r}{w} \leq -1$$

or,

$$b = (\lceil \frac{M+1}{2} \rceil, \lceil \frac{M+1}{2} \rceil) \quad : \quad -1 \leq -\frac{r}{w} \leq 0.$$

The second problem is to maximize the tolerance to failure. That is to maximize $M - max(R_T, W_T)$, subject to the same set of constraints. Obviously, the extreme point $b = (\lceil \frac{M+1}{2} \rceil, \lceil \frac{M+1}{2} \rceil)$ gives the maximum tolerance. Both optimal solutions suggest that under QC, performance and availability are contradictory goals for update percents less than 50%. Optimal performance is realized at $(R_T, W_T) = (1, M)$ while optimal availability is realized at $(R_T, W_T) = (\lceil \frac{M+1}{2} \rceil, \lceil \frac{M+1}{2} \rceil)$. For higher update percents, both goals merge and the optimal thresholds to use are $(R_T, W_T) = (\lceil \frac{M+1}{2} \rceil, \lceil \frac{M+1}{2} \rceil)$.

Through this examination of the QC method, we determined two polices to use in Raid regarding the quorum parameters:

- First, we decided to restrict our choices of the thresholds to one of two values. Either $(R_T, W_T) = (1, M)$, which is the quorum version of the read-one-write-all, or $(R_T, W_T) = (\lceil \frac{M+1}{2} \rceil, \lceil \frac{M+1}{2} \rceil)$, in which both reads and writes are majority. We call the first QC-ROWA, and the second QC-RSW (to be read: reads same as writes).

- Second, because the read-to-write ratio in Raid is always greater than 1.0, performance and availability cannot both be met by adjusting only the

quorum parameters. Partial replication has to be used to improve the availability of the QC-ROWA method, and to not impair the performance of the QC-RSW method. We assign thresholds on a per object basis in the following way:

- when performance is most important or when the object is read-only or unlikely to be updated, we will use QC-ROWA (or ROWA).

- when availability is most important or when the object is likely to be updated, we will use QC-RSW.

The next section presents a performance evaluation study of the Raid implementation of the quorum consensus method.

3 Performance Evaluation of Quorum Consensus

We conducted a series of experiments to measure the performance of the QC method. The experiments were executed on an instance of the Raid system that runs on five Sun 3/50s and four SPARCstation1's, all with local disks. All the machines were connected through an Ethernet segment. On some of the Sun 3/50 machines, measurements were facilitated by microsecond resolution timers that were obtained from Zytec Corporation. To conduct the experiments, we used the industry standard DebitCredit benchmark [3] and an action driver simulator. The next section briefly describes the benchmark and the driver simulator, along with the experimental procedure.

3.1 Experimental Infrastructure
The DebitCredit Benchmark: DebitCredit transactions read and write a single tuple from each of three relations: the teller relation, the branch relation, and the account relation. In addition, a tuple is appended to a special write-only sequential history file describing the transaction. In our experiments, each of these relations was a 100-tuple long. Details of the relation schemas can be found in [3]. The benchmark requires that the entire transaction be serializable and recoverable.

The Action Driver Simulator: In place of Raid action driver (AD), we used an action driver simulator to provide an easily controllable experiment. The details of the simulator can be found in [17]. The simulator runs in two modes. In the open-system mode, it simulates *Poisson* arrival of transactions. In the closed-system mode, it simulates a job queue that limits the maximum degree of concurrency. The simulator parameters and their setting are explained in Table 1. Default values are bold-faced. Unless otherwise stated, the experiments in this paper assumed the default values.

Parameters' Default Values: Pilot experiments were performed to determine the appropriate default values of the simulator parameters.

Table 1: Action Driver Simulator Parameters

Parameter	Value
simulation type	open, closed
total number of transactions	250
transaction arrival rate	[0.1 ... 2.0]
maximum degree of concurrency	3
hot spot percentage	20%
hot spot access %	80%
update percent	Read-only, 17%, 20%, 50%, Write-only
average transaction size	1 ... 6
timeout value	20 seconds
RC method	ROWA, QC
AC method	2PC, 3PC
AC logging	on, off
CC method	TS/O, 2PL, OPT
restart policy	rolling average

- One set of experiments showed that a total of 250 transactions was sufficient to produce reliable results in a reasonable amount of time. For instance, the maximum relative 90%-confidence interval of the majority of the pilot experiments did not exceed 30% in an average of six minutes. Larger number of transactions would unnecessarily slow down the experiments.

- Another experiment showed that three is the appropriate maximum degree of concurrency to use in Raid. Higher degrees of concurrency resulted in a linear increase in the number of aborts, a linear increase in response time, and a saturation in throughput. Results from this experiment are shown in Figure 2.

- Through open experiments, we observed that it was difficult to gain confidence in the results for average transaction arrival rate greater than two transaction per second.

- The hot spot size and the hot spot access percentages were chosen as 20% and 80%, respectively, as suggested in [17].

- As the number of operations per transaction is limited (by the DebitCredit benchmark), it was not possible to experiment with a wide spectrum of update percentages. For example, a four-operation transaction can have 25% or 50% update percentages, but it cannot have 10%, 20%, 30%, or 40% update percentages. For this reason, we chose read-only, 17%, 20%, 50%, and write-only update percentages.

- A 20 seconds timeout value was chosen, which was reasonably large since deadlocks are rare.

The Experimental Procedure: The experiments were run in the early morning to minimize the effects of network traffic from external sources. All of the machines were rebooted before the experiments were started to provide a consistent, uniform operating environment. After the reboot, an experiment specification file was read. Each line in that file defines a single Raid experiment, for which a new Raid instance was started. Upon completion of the provided transaction stream, each server in the instance wrote its performance statistics to a log file. A new Raid instance was used for the next experiment. Confidence interval analysis was automatically generated to test the acceptability of the averaged results. Accordingly, some experiments were repeated for improvements.

The Output Data: Each experiment involved some 250 transactions and lasted for about 6 to 12 minutes. Measurements of the experiments are therefore sample means over 250 data points. To gain more confidence in our measurements, we replicated each experiment 6 to 10 times. This shows as 6 to 10 repeated lines in the experiment specification file. The experiment output that we reported was the average over the 6

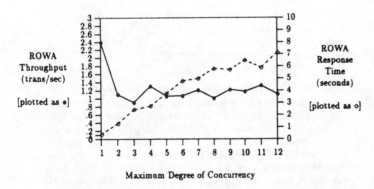

ROWA Throughput (trans/sec) [plotted as •]

ROWA Response Time (seconds) [plotted as ◦]

Maximum Degree of Concurrency

Figure 2: Determining the Maximum Degree of Concurrency

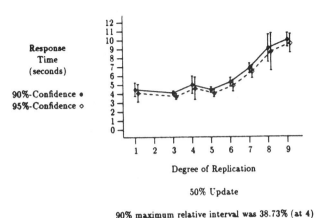

50% Update

90% maximum relative interval was 38.73% (at 4)
95% maximum relative interval was 50.43% (at 4)

Figure 3: 90% and 95% Confidence Interval of Output Data

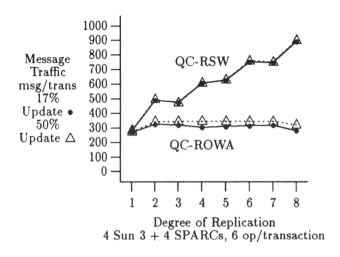

Degree of Replication
4 Sun 3 + 4 SPARCs, 6 op/transaction

Figure 4: Message Traffic of The QC-RSW

to 10 repeated measurements. The confidence of that average was checked by 90% (and some times 95%) confidence interval analysis. Figure 3 shows the kind of confidence that we obtained in our output data. The Figure shows the results of an experiment that investigates the effect of the degree of replication on the average transaction response time. The experiment consisted of 9 measurements, each repeated 6 times. The Figure shows a 90% and 95% confidence intervals of the averaged data. Even though the 90% and the 95% curves are identical, we offset the 95% curve in order to better clarify the difference between both intervals. The maximum relative intervals of both curves are also shown. In this paper, we only report the maximum 90% relative interval over all experiments, instead of depicting the confidence interval on each experiment.

3.2 Experiment I: Message Exchange Overhead

The QC-RSW method requires access to multiple remote copies to process either a read or a write operation. Unfortunately, the quorum sizes increase linearly with the number of copies. This leads to heavy message traffic that can become a bottleneck in the communication subsystem.

To measure the effect of the QC-RSW on message traffic, we performed an experiment on an 8-site Raid system. We ran 250 transactions and measured the message traffic per transaction. Each transaction consisted of six operations. Timestamp ordering and two-phase commit were used by the concurrency and the atomicity controllers, respectively. Figure 4 shows the message traffic per transaction for 17% and 50% update ratios. For both update percentages, the message traffic sstep-wise linearly increases with an increase in the degree of replication. A 140% increase in message traffic occurs when the degree of replication is

increased from 1 to 4. A 250% increase in message traffic occurs when full replication is used.

The effect of the update percent is almost negligible, owing to using the deferred writes technique. This technique ensures that, regardless of the transaction size and regardless of the update percentage, a small number of write messages will be generated at the end of the transaction. At most $3n$ write messages can be generated from any transaction in an n-site system. These messages represent the three rounds of committing a transaction using $n-1$ participant sites. To compare, notice that an $O(n^2 s)$ read messages are generated for a transaction of length s, in an n-site system. The effect of the update percent, is therefore, negligible.

A comparison of the message traffic generated by a QC-RSW and QC-ROWA is shown in Figure 4. The traffic of the QC-ROWA is almost constant since read messages are only 2 messages, and write messages (also owing to the deferred writes technique) are at most $3n$.

3.3 Experiment II: Throughput and Response Time

To see how the excess message traffic can be interpreted in terms of performance penalty, we measured the throughput and response time.

In our measurements (Figure 5), we observed that response time increases linearly with the degree of replication. Response time increases by 12% when the degree of replication is increased from one to four, and increases by 48% when the degree of replication is increased from one to eight. Even though the effect of tripling the update percentage on the message traffic was negligible, the effect on response time was such that it increased by 8%. This increase was profiled and an interesting observation was that at higher update percentages, the same small number of write messages carry larger update lists, with possibly multiple updates per site on behalf of one single transaction. The encoding and decoding conversion into and from the

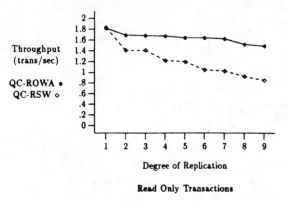

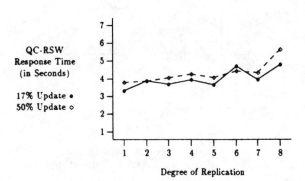

Four Sun3s + four Sparcs, 6 operations/transaction

maximum relative interval for 17 update percent was 29.75% (at 8)
maximum relative interval for 50 update percent was 16.06% (at 8)

Figure 5: Performance of The QC-RSW

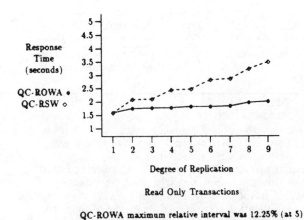

Read Only Transactions

QC-ROWA maximum relative interval was 12.25% (at 5)
QC-RSW maximum relative interval was 1.60% (at 7)

Figure 6: Response Time: QC-ROWA vs. QC-RSW

Read Only Transactions

QC-ROWA maximum relative interval was 11.60% (at 8)
QC-RSW maximum relative interval was 1.65% (at 7)

Figure 7: Throughput: QC-ROWA vs. QC-RSW

external data representation (XDR) that takes place in the communication subsystem gets affected by the length of the update lists carryed by the write messages. The XDR processing overhead is therefore what causes the update percentage to have a non-negligible effect on response time.

In another 9-site experiment, we examined the effect of the QC-RSW message traffic on performance by comparing its response time and throughput with the response time and throughput of the QC-ROWA method. In this experiment two-phase locking was used. Figures 6 and 7 compares the response time and the throughput of both methods. Under full replication, QC-RSW slows down transaction processing. It results in a 43% reduction in throughput and a 73% increase in response time with respect to the QC-ROWA method. For degree of replication five, it reduces throughput by 27% and increases response time by 36%. For degree of replication two, it reduces throughput by 16% and increases response time by 19%.

3.4 Data Availability

In general, the higher the degree of replication, the higher the availability provided by the QC-RSW method. Message traffic, however, linearly increases with increasing the degree of replication, leading to high performance penalties. Analogous to the QC-ROWA method, where partial replication was discovered to improve its availability [6], in the QC-RSW method, partial replication is used to *not* impair its performance. To determine the least partial degree of replication that provides almost the same availability that is obtained under full replication, we used an availability model that was developed by [11], and that was published in [6]. We evaluated the availability model for the QC-RSW and the QC-ROWA methods on a system which consisted of nine sites connected by a single ethernet segment with workstation

170

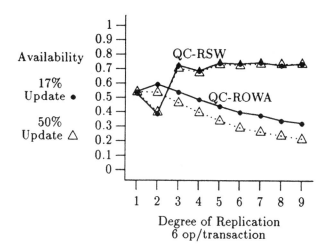

Figure 8: Availability of the QC-RSW

reliability of 0.95. Transactions of size 6 operations were considered. The model was evaluated for 17% and 50% update percents. Degree of replication was varied from one to nine copies.

Figure 8 depicts the effect of the degree of replication on QC-RSW and QC-ROWA availabilities. The comparison clearly shows the availability advantage of QC-RSW. It also shows that QC-RSW benefits from an increased replication, whereas QC-ROWA suffers from the same.

QC-RSW availability was observed to oscillate around an increasing average that almost reaches a plateau at degree of replication 5. Five, was therefore the degree of replication that we chose at the least partial degree of replication for QC-RSW. For QC-ROWA, the least partial degree of replication was only two.

The oscillatory behavior of the QC-RSW availability suggests that even degrees of replication consistently have less availability than the preceding odd ones. Therefore, tow copies are less available than one copy; three copies are more available than one and two copies; four copies are less available than three copies, and so forth. This oscillatory behavior can be explained as follows. Consider a system consisting of three sites that are completely connected. Assume that each site has a reliability factor 0.9. For a degree of replication of 1, the probability that a designated site is up is 0.9 (note that the probability that any one site is up is higher). For a degree of replication of 2 (in which QC-RSW requires both copies), the probability that 2 designated sites are up is 0.81 (less than 0.9). For a degree of replication of 3 (in which QC-RSW requires any 2 copies), the probability that any 2 sites are up is the sum of the probabilities that the configurations 011, 101, 110, and 111 occur. This amounts to $3*(0.9^2)+0.9^3$ or 0.972 (greater than 0.9 and 0.81). The computation of these probabilities directly affect the availability as measured by our model.

4   Conclusion

An actual implementation of the quorum consensus replication method has been presented. Important implementation details concerning the management of version numbers and the choices of the weights and thresholds of copies and objects have been detailed. An experimental performance evaluation study has been presented to assess the message exchange overhead, throughput and response time, and availability of the quorum consensus method. In addition, a comparison has been held between the quorum consensus and the read-one-write-all (ROWA) method. Some of the findings are listed below. Explanations of these finding can be found in sections 3.2, 3.3, and 3.4. The reader is reminded that the scope of these findings is the particular implementation on the Raid system.

- The message exchange overhead of QC is almost invariant to the transaction update percent. That is almost the same number of messages will be exchanged for update intensive or query transactions. This finding is contrary to the common belief.

- The above conclusion does not apply for response time. Response time (which is a delay overhead) is rather sensitive to the transaction update percent.

- The message exchange overhead of QC increases linearly with the number of replicas of a replicated object. The overhead of the ROWA method is almost invariant to the number of replicas. ROWA is also insensitive to the update percentage.

- The difference in response time and throughput when QC is used instead of the simple ROWA method is as expensive as 73% increase in response time, and 43% decrease in throughput!

- The availability of the QC method benefits from higher degrees of replication (actually this is known in theory), while ROWA does not. ROWA does not benefit from one copy implementation either, and *two* is a magical number if ROWA is to be used. Also, we found that the availability of the QC with equal read/write quorum sizes (QC-RSW), exhibits a zigzag effect, where even degrees of replication consistently offered lower availability than their immediate odd predecessors.

References

[1] Amr El Abbadi and S. Toueg. Availability in partitioned replicated databases. In *Proc. Fifth ACM SIGACT-SIGMOD Symp. on Principles of Database Systems*, pages 240–251, March 1986.

[2] P. Alsberg and J. Day. A principle for resilient sharing of distributed resources. *Proceedings of the 2nd Int'l Conference on Software Engineering*, pages 562–570, October 1976.

[3] Anon. A measure of transaction processing power. *Datamation*, 31(7):112–118, April 1985.

[4] P. A. Bernstein and N. Goodman. An algorithm for concurrency control and recovery in replicated distributed databases. *ACM Transactions on Database Systems*, 9(4):596–615, December 1984.

[5] Bharat Bhargava, Karl Friesen, Abdelsalam Helal, Srinivasan Jagannathan, and John Riedl. Design and implementation of the RAID V2 distributed database system. Technical Report CSD-TR-962, Purdue University, March 1990.

[6] Bharat Bhargava, Abdelsalam Helal, and Karl Friesen. Analyzing availability of replicated database systems. *International Journal of Computer Simulation*, 1(4):393–418, December 1991. A special issue on distributed file systems and database simulation.

[7] Bharat Bhargava and John Riedl. A model for adaptable systems for transaction processing. *IEEE Transactions on Knowledge and Data Engineering*, 1(4):433–449, December 1989.

[8] Prasun Dewan, Ashish Vikram, and Bharat Bhargava. Engineering the Object-Relation Model in O-Raid. In *Proceedings Of the International Conference on Foundations of Data Organization and Algorithms*, pages 389–403, June 1989.

[9] D. K. Gifford. Weighted voting for replicated data. *Proceedings of the 7th Symposium on Operating System Principles*, pages 150–162, December 1979.

[10] Abdelsalam Abdelhamid Heddaya. *Managing Event-based Replication for Abstract Data Types in Distributed Systems*. PhD thesis, Harvard University, October 1988. TR-20-88.

[11] Abdelsalam Helal. *Experimental Analysis of Replication in Distributed Systems*. PhD thesis, Purdue University, May 1991.

[12] Abdelsalam Helal and Bharat Bhargava. *Advanced Replication Techniques in Distributed Systems*. IEEE Computer Society Press, 1995.

[13] Abdelsalam Helal, Jagannathan Srinivasan, and Bharat Bhargava. SETH: A quorum-based replicated database system for experimentation with failures. *Proceedings of the 5th IEEE Int'l Conference on Data Engineering*, pages 677–684, February 1989.

[14] Maurice Herlihy. A quorum-consensus replication method for abstract data types. *ACM Transactions on Computer Systems*, 4(1):32–53, February 1986.

[15] Akhil Kumar. Hierarchical quorum consensus: A new class of algorithms for replicated data. *Proceedings of the 10th IEEE symposium on Distributed Computing Systems*, May 1990.

[16] T. Minoura and G. Wiederhold. Resilient extended true-copy token scheme for a distributed database system. *IEEE Transactions on Software Engineering*, 9(5):173–189, May 1982.

[17] John Riedl. *Adaptable Distributed Transaction Systems*. PhD thesis, Purdue University, May 1990.

Session 6:
Performability of Real-Time Systems

Session Chair: Lui Sha

Enhancing the Performance and Dependability of Real-Time Systems

D. L. Hull, W. Feng, and J. W.-S. Liu
Real-Time Systems Laboratory
Department of Computer Science
University of Illinois at Urbana-Champaign
1304 W. Springfield Ave.
Urbana, IL 61801
{*hull, feng, janeliu*}@cs.uiuc.edu

Abstract

The imprecise-computation technique was proposed as a way to handle transient overloads and enhance the dependability of real-time systems. In a system based on this technique, each time-critical task produces an approximate but usable result whenever a failure or overload prevents the system from producing a precise result. This approach makes meeting deadlines easier, increases the availability of data and services, reduces the need for error-recovery operations, and minimizes the costs in replication. In this paper, we provide an overview of ways to implement and schedule imprecise computations. We then describe the Imprecise Computation Server (ICS) and how it is used to ensure real-time performance of time-critical applications.

1 Introduction

A real-time system contains tasks which must produce logically correct results by certain timing deadlines. If a time-critical task fails to deliver its result by its deadline, a timing fault occurs. A real-time system functions properly only in the absence of timing faults. For many such systems, having an approximate but usable result on a timely basis is better than having a late and precise result. An example is the Traffic Alert and Collision Avoidance System (TCAS), which is used in commercial aircrafts to alert pilots of potential collisions. TCAS must be able to tell the pilot of a potential collision and the necessary evasive action by a certain time. A failure to do so in time is not tolerable. On the other hand, TCAS maintains an acceptable level of performance if it issues a timely warning together with an estimated location of the conflict traffic

An approximate but usable result can often be produced with much less processor time than a precise result. This observation is the basis for the imprecise-computation technique [9-11]. By trading off precision for timeliness, the imprecise-computation technique prevents missed deadlines by ensuring that an approximate result of an acceptable quality is available whenever the exact result cannot be produced in time.

The imprecise-computation technique can also enhance fault tolerance and provide graceful degradation for real-time systems. For example, in a tracking and control system, a transient fault may cause a tracking computation to terminate prematurely and produce an approximate result. The fault can be tolerated and no recovery action is needed if the result allows the system to maintain track of the targets. In embedded systems, this technique can be used with traditional checkpointing and replication techniques [9, 15]. The result is a reduction of the costs for providing fault tolerance and enhanced availability.

After describing ways to implement imprecise computations, we provide an overview on methods to schedule imprecise computations. We then present an architecture which integrates the storage and return of intermediate, *imprecise* results of computations with traditional checkpointing and replication for fault tolerance and error recovery and how such a system would be used in a real-time environment.

2 Implementation of Imprecise Computations

We call a system based on the imprecise-computation technique an *imprecise system*. A task in an imprecise system can be implemented using the milestone method, sieve method, or multiple-version method. Each method is appropriate for different types of real-time applications.

A task and its underlying computational algorithm are said to be *monotone* if the quality of the intermediate result produced by it is non-decreasing as it executes longer. A monotone task produces a precise result when the entire task completes; the error in the result, also referred to as the error of the task, is zero. An approximate result can be made available by recording the intermediate results produced by the task at appropriate instants of its execution, i.e., *milestones*. What variables to record and when to record them are specified by the programmer. In addition to the result variables, the programmer also specifies accuracy-measure variables to be recorded at the same time. The values of the accuracy measures give an estimate of the result accuracy. If the task is terminated before completion, the approximate result recorded at the latest milestone before the time of termination is the best among all the intermediate results produced during its execution. The portion of the task that must be completed in order to produce an acceptable result is mandatory. The remainder of the task is optional; this part may be left unexecuted or partially executed. This method for returning approximate results is called the *milestone method*. It is applicable whenever there are monotone (or simply incremental) algorithms, including all iterative algorithms, statistical detection and estimation, incremental voice and video transmissions [14], incremental query processing [21], and AI anytime algorithms [2]. In particular, a task based on an anytime algorithm is either entirely optional or has a mandatory portion that takes a negligible amount of time to complete compared with the rest of the task.

Not all computations are monotone, but we can still trade off result quality for processing time by making use of either sieve functions or multiple versions. A computation or set of computations whose sole purpose is to produce outputs that are at least as precise as the corresponding inputs is called a *sieve function*. If a sieve function is executed, it improves the accuracy of its inputs. If it is skipped, processing time is saved but at the expense of having less accurate values. Hence a task that carries out a sieve function is optional. The multiple-version method provides at least two versions of each task — the primary version and alternate version(s). The primary version produces a precise result but has a longer processing time while an alternate version has a shorter processing time but only produces an approximate but acceptable result. During a transient overload, when it is not feasible to complete the primary version of every task by its deadline, the system may choose to schedule an alternate version of some of the tasks.

While the sieve and multiple-version methods may be more widely applicable, they are not ideal for two reasons. First, the system must anticipate and decide ahead of time whether to schedule a sieve or primary version. This leads to a higher scheduling overhead [19]. Second, and more importantly, these methods, unlike the milestone method, cannot be easily integrated with traditional fault-tolerance methods. For these reasons, we prefer to use the milestone method whenever possible.

3 Scheduling Methods

We logically divide each task T_i into two parts: a mandatory task and an optional task, and let M_i and O_i represent these tasks, respectively. The processing times of T_i, M_i, and O_i are p_i, m_i, and o_i, respectively, where $p_i = m_i + o_i$. The traditional real-time model is a special case of the imprecise-computation model where all tasks are mandatory (i.e., $o_i = 0$ for all i). A task implementing a sieve function or an anytime computation is entirely optional (i.e., $m_i = 0$).

The quality of the result produced by a task T_i is a function of two independent parameters: the processing time of the executed portion of the task and the quality of the input of the task. Let σ_i denote the amount of processor time assigned to the optional task O_i. Most of the existing scheduling algorithms assume that the inputs to every task are precise; that is, the quality of the result produced by T_i depends solely on σ_i and how the quality of the result depends on σ_i. Oftentimes, the exact behavior of the quality as a function of σ_i is not known. In this situation, rather than trying to maximize the quality of the result produced by each task T_i, we try to minimize the fraction of discarded work $(o_i - \sigma_i)/o_i$ or the amount of discarded work $o_i - \sigma_i$. The *total amount of discarded work* of the task set $\{T_i\}$ is $\Sigma_{i=1}^{n} w_i (o_i - \sigma_i)$ where w_i denotes the weights of the tasks. These weights allow the real-time system to account for the varying degrees that the quality of the results of individual tasks impact the overall quality of the result produced by all the tasks in the system. Examples of optimal and suboptimal algorithms which minimize the total amount of discarded work can be found in [3, 18, 19].

The qualities of results produced by some tasks (e.g., those based on most iterative algorithms and statistical methods) improve faster during the early part of their execution, and the rates of improvement slow as the tasks execute. In this case, the average quality of the results produced by the tasks can be kept small by making the maximum fraction of discarded work among of all the tasks as small as possible. The *maximum fraction of discarded work* of a set of tasks $\{T_i\}$ with identical weights is $max_i\{(o_i-\sigma_i)/o_i\}$. Polynomial-time algorithms for finding optimal schedules with the smallest maximum fraction of discarded work can be found in [6, 17].

On the other hand, the result of a task may improve in quality at a faster as it executes longer. The optional part of such a task should be scheduled as much as possible or not at all. Hence, the execution of the optional task approximates that of a task with the *0/1 constraint*. A task with this constraint is to be scheduled entirely or discarded entirely. A task that implements a sieve function is a task with the 0/1 constraint. From a scheduling point of view, a task with two versions is a mandatory task followed by one with this constraint. Algorithms for scheduling tasks with the 0/1 constraint can be found in [7, 19].

All the aforementioned scheduling algorithms assume that the inputs of the tasks are precise and that the release times and deadlines of individual tasks are given. In many applications, however, these assumptions are not valid. The result produced by a task may be an input to its immediate successors. When this result is imprecise, the input to the successor tasks are imprecise. A task may need to do additional work to compensate for the imprecision in its input. Moreover, a poorer input may slow down the rate at which its result converges to the precise one. As a result, the processing times of M_i and O_i may increase as the quality of the input decreases. Once the quality of the input drops below some threshold, the processing times of the mandatory task and/or the optional task may become infinite. When the processing time of the mandatory task becomes infinite, the imprecision in the input has fatal consequences. We can prevent this occurrence by making the processing times of the predecessor tasks larger so that the quality of the input never drops below the fatal threshold. When the processing time of an optional task becomes infinite, the task can never produce a precise result no matter how long it executes.

The timing constraints which can be derived directly from high-level requirements are typically not that of individual tasks, but rather are timing constraints over sets of tasks. These timing constraints are called *end-to-end timing constraints*. As long as the last task(s) in a task set completes before its end-to-end deadline, the completion times for the individual tasks in the set are unimportant. This gives us the freedom to assign intermediate deadlines to the individual tasks. This freedom to advance and postpone the executions of individual tasks gives us an added dimension in the tradeoff between result quality and timing requirements and makes the problem of scheduling imprecise computations more difficult. Several heuristic algorithms for scheduling tasks with imprecise inputs and end-to-end timing constraints can be found in [4]. These algorithms deal with composite tasks, each of which is a chain of component tasks. The composite tasks are independent of each other. The ready time of a composite task is the ready time of its first component task, and the deadline of the composite task is the deadline of its last component task. The jth component task becomes ready when the $(j-1)$th component task completes, and its input is the output of the $(j-1)$th component task. The heuristic algorithms in [4] support a two-level scheduling strategy. At the higher level, the scheduler uses an algorithm, such as those that minimize the maximum fraction of discarded work [6, 17], to distribute the total available processor time among independent composite tasks as evenly as possible subject to their ready times and deadlines. The time allocated to each composite task is then partitioned among component tasks. After accounting for all the extended mandatory and optional processing times caused by poor input quality, the algorithms try to make the fraction of discarded work of the last component task as small as possible, and hence the quality of the output of the composite task as good as possible.

4 Integrating Imprecise Computation with Checkpointing and Replication

An imprecise task that is implemented using the milestone method must save its imprecise results at its milestones, specified by the designer, as it executes toward completion. The milestones may occur periodically or at irregularly spaced time instants. We observe that the repeated return of intermediate, imprecise results is similar to the checkpointing traditionally used to enhance the fault-tolerance of a system. We call the user-defined mechanism for the return of intermediate, imprecise results *user-directed checkpointing*, and the traditional checkpointing mechanism *system-directed checkpointing*.

In an imprecise system, user-directed checkpointing can be used together with system-directed checkpointing to reduce the overall cost of providing fault tolerance. At a system-directed checkpoint, the operating system must save the complete state of the task so that the task can be restarted later from this state. Since user-directed checkpointing is done under designer control and at a time specified by the designer, it is generally not necessary to save as much state as is required when checkpointing is done by the operating system at an arbitrary time. Consequently, the cost of a user-directed checkpoint is typically lower than for a system-directed checkpoint. Since fault recovery can make use of both user-directed and system-directed checkpoints, system-directed checkpoints need not be taken as often. Moreover, if an imprecise task fails in its optional part, it is not necessary to restart the task. Instead, the system can use the last recorded result — since the task was executing in its optional part, it must be of acceptable quality.

Imprecise computation can also be used to reduce the cost of replication in systems with multiple processors. We have a choice once one of the copies of the task has finished its mandatory part: we can terminate the other copies because a result of acceptable quality is now guaranteed, or we can allow all of the copies to continue. Another possibility is to have each of the replicated tasks run a different version of the algorithm, as is done in the multiple-version method. For example, one step in tracking is track association. It takes as inputs a set of established tracks, which indicate the past positions and velocities of the targets, together with the new radar returns, which indicate the current positions and velocities of possible targets. It produces a new, updated set of established tracks. There are many algorithms to compute the new tracks, with different processing time requirements and accuracy measures. By replicating the different versions on separate processors, we can use the best result obtained by the deadline for that step.

5 An Imprecise Computation Server

We have implemented an environment, called the Imprecise Computation Server (ICS), for the integration of user- and system-directed checkpoints. ICS requires that computations are implemented using the milestone method.

5.1 Architecture

The architecture of ICS is an extension of the client-server model, as shown in Figure 1. Each imprecise server in the system is an instance of a server type; there may be more than one server of the type. Each (imprecise) server is composed of a callee and a supervisor. A client task which makes use of the result of the server is composed of a caller and a handler. The caller and the callee are application-specific; they are provided by the programmer. The supervisor and the handler are part of the underlying system. They are produced automatically by ICS. A supervisor may be for more than one server. Similarly, a handler may take care of more than one client.

As in traditional systems, the server executes whenever it is called by the client. A client calls a server through its handler, which sends an invocation request on the client's behalf to the server's supervisor. When the supervisor grants the request, it activates the callee. If the callee has not completed when the time allocated for its execution has expired, the supervisor terminates it.

The programmer defines the variables that hold the intermediate results and a measure of their accuracy. During its execution, the callee performs user-defined checkpointing by recording the values of these variables at time instants specified by the programmer and making them accessible to the client.

If the callee terminates normally, the client has the callee's final, precise result. If the system terminates the callee before the end of its optional part, the client has the best imprecise result produced by the callee before it was terminated. Based on the last recorded value of the accuracy-measure variable, the handler can decide whether the imprecise result is acceptable and return it to the caller or whether the callee needs to be restarted.

In addition to participating in the callee's result-saving process, the supervisor also periodically performs sanity checks on the callee and checkpoints it. If a failure is detected before the mandatory portion of the callee completes, recovery is necessary. The supervisor restores the callee's state to the state saved by the last checkpoint operation and resumes its execution from that state.

5.2 Implementation

The Imprecise Computation Server (ICS) is implemented on top of the Mach operating system [1]. It makes use of IMIG, a modified version of the Mach Interface Generator (MIG) [13].

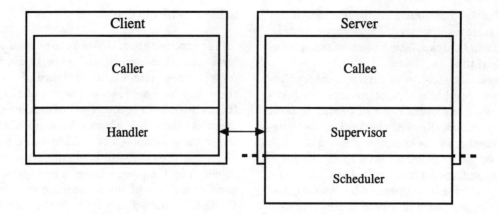

Figure 1: An imprecise computation server and its client

	Client Side	Server Side
ICS-supplied	*service_stub*	*service*_server
		*service*_save
User-supplied		*service*
		*service*_checkpoint
		*service*_restart

Table 1: ICS functions and their classifications

There is a server type for each imprecise service provided by the application system. To develop an imprecise application system in the ICS environment, the programmer writes an interface description for each server type in the system. This interface description describes the input and output arguments of all servers of the type. IMIG also inserts into the interface for each server an argument that contains ICS-specific information, such as the server's deadline and the maximum amount of error allowed in the output arguments. From this interface description, IMIG generates the server-specific handler and supervisor code for each service.

For example, Table 1 describes the interface between ICS and the application code for a service called *service*. The ICS-supplied routines are generated by IMIG; the user-supplied routines are called by the IMIG-generated code. A brief description of each of these routines follows.

The *service_stub* routine is the client's interface to the server. As such, it implements the handler for the client of the server. When called, it packages the input arguments into a message and sends the message to the appropriate supervisor. It then collects intermediate imprecise results. If the server fails in its mandatory part, it restarts the request. The *service*_server routine implements the supervisor of the servers of the type. It listens for invocation requests from clients, chooses a server, schedules the callee's execution, and performs system-directed checkpointing. During its execution, the callee calls the *service*_save routine to return results to the client. An argument to the routine indicates the imprecision in the results being returned. When the result is precise, the imprecision in the result is zero.

The routine *service* is written by the programmer. This routine performs the work done by the callee. In addition, the programmer provides the routine *service*_checkpoint, which is often substantially lighter weight than the application-independent checkpointing routines used by the operating system. The supervisor calls service_checkpoint to request that the callee perform a sanity check and then checkpoint itself. Similarly, the programmer provides the routine *service*_restart to direct the recovery of the server in a lightweight manner. The supervisor calls *service*_restart when it is necessary to restart the computation from a saved state.

We now illustrate the use of ICS with an example. This example is an imprecise service which finds the root of a function using Newton's method (e.g., the client uses this service to determine when the path of a rover whose trajectory is given by the function, will intersect the path defined by a beacon beam). The interface description for the service would include the definition shown in Figure 5.2 When IMIG is run on this interface, it generates the client routine **newton_stub** and the server routines **newton_server** and **newton_save**. The definition of the **imprecise_info_t** data type is:

```
impreciseRoutine newton (
    server : mach_port_t;            /* Port to talk to server on.  */
    icsinfo : imprecise_info_t;      /* ICS-specific information.  */
    in initPoint : double_t;         /* Initial guess for Newton's method.  */
    out rootPoint : double_t;        /* Root found by Newton's method.  */
);
```

Figure 2: `newton`'s IMIG interface definition

```
typedef struct impreciseInfo {
  long imprecision;
  time_value_t deadline;
  time_value_t mandatoryTime;
  long resources;
  long maxFaults;
} imprecise_info_t;
```

The `imprecision` parameter is a measure of the maximum imprecision allowed in the result. The server also uses this field to return the accuracy measure of its result. The `deadline` parameter is the deadline of the callee (which is an imprecise task in our previous terminology). The deadline gives either a relative deadline to the invocation time of the service or an absolute deadline. The supervisor uses this information to determine when the callee is to be terminated and a result must be returned. The value of `mandatoryTime` is an upper bound on the time required to execute the mandatory part of the callee. The supervisor and the operation system make use of this information in scheduling and controlling the execution of the task. The `resources` parameter is a bitmap that represents the resources required by the callee. It can be used to specify a count of the number of resources needed by a particular server or to force the selection of a particular server when there are multiple servers for the service. The client may specify how fault tolerant the server should be. It does so through the parameter `maxFaults`, which is the maximum number of faults the server must be able to tolerate during the execution of the mandatory part of the callee.

To implement the Newton-method service, the programmer must provide several routines. They are the following:

```
newton(
  mach_port_t server;
  imprecise_into_t *icsinfo;
  double_t initPoint;
  double_t *rootPoint;
) { ... }
```

```
newton_checkpoint() { ... }

newton_restart(
  mach_port_t server;
  imprecise_info_t *icsinfo;
  double_t initPoint;
  double_t *rootPoint;
  void *state;
) { ... }
```

The `newton` routine implements the callee. Its interface matches that given in the IMIG interface definition above. Logically, `newton_restart`'s arguments are identical to those in `newton` with the addition of the state variable, which points to the saved state from which to continue execution. The `newton` routine calls `newton_save` to return its imprecise results. The code for the body of the function `newton`, shown in Figure 3, saves the intermediate, imprecise results as it progresses towards a precise root of the function `f`.

To invoke the Newton-method service, the client sets up the `imprecise_info_t` structure and calls the `newton_stub` routine as shown in Figure 4. In operation, when the `newton_stub` routine is called, the handler uses the scheduling information passed to it to select a server to handle the request. It then sends this server's supervisor a message containing the scheduling information and the request's input arguments. The supervisor creates a new thread of control for the callee and passes the callee's processing requirements to the scheduler. During the callee's execution, it calls its result-saving routine to record a set of imprecise results at points specified in the callee's code.

To generate system-directed checkpoints, the supervisor sets a timer to expire at the time for the next system-directed checkpoint. When the timer expires, it calls the callee's checkpoint routine. If the callee calls its result-saving routine in the interim, the timer is reset, delaying the next system-directed checkpoint. If the handler finds that the server has died or missed its deadline, it can decide whether to return the last

179

```
extern double f();
double x0, x1 = initPoint, x2 = initPoint + 0.1;
double f1 = f(x1), f2 = f(x2);

do {
  x0 = x1 - f1 * (x1 - x2) / (f1 - f2);
  x2 = x1; f2 = f1; x1 = x0; f1 = f(x0);

  *rootPoint = x1;
  icsinfo->imprecision = imprecision(f1));
  if (newton_save(icsinfo, rootPoint) != MACH_MSG_SUCCESS)
    return KERN_FAILURE;
while (icsinfo->imprecision > 0);

return KERN_SUCCESS;
```

Figure 3: The implementation of newton

```
icsinfo.imprecision = 5;              /* some imprecision allowed.  */
icsinfo.deadline.seconds = 0;         /* deadline = .02 seconds.  */
icsinfo.deadline.microseconds = 20000;
icsinfo.mandatoryTime.seconds = 0;    /* mandatory time = .01 seconds.  */
icsinfo.mandatoryTime.microseconds = 10000;
icsinfo.resources = 0;                /* no resources required.  */
icsinfo.maxFaults = 1;

if ((rv = newton(server, &icsinfo, guess, &answer)) != KERN_SUCCESS)
  fprintf(stderr, "newton failed, %s\n", mach_error_string(rv));

printf("guess %f produced answer %f, imprecision %d\n",
  guess, answer, icsinfo.imprecision);
```

Figure 4: An example of calling newton

imprecise result produced by the server or to restart the request from the saved state on another server.

6 Usage and Future Work

ICS is a work in progress. We plan to experiment with several extensions; these include heuristic scheduling algorithms, algorithms for server selection in systems with multiple identical servers, and replicated execution on multiple servers. In particular, the scheduling algorithms described in [6, 17, 7, 19, 4] can be seamlessly integrated with ICS by treating the algorithms as a preprocessing step to the client's call to the service stub routine.

Many real-time applications can benefit from using ICS by taking advantage of the services that it offers. For example, in constraint-based graphics such as Rockit [8], GITS [16], and Oak [20], the constraint solver must be fast enough to produce interactive response. Specifically, it must be fast enough for constrained visual objects (e.g., two lines constrained to be perpendicular to one another) to follow the motion of the mouse cursor in real time. When constrained objects are more complex in nature, real-time response is difficult due to the extensive computations involved in satisfying complex geometric constraints. A possible solution would be to restrict the power of the constraint solver by employing propagational algorithms [5] whose implementation can be simplified with ICS.

Radar tracking is another real-time application which would benefit from ICS. In this application, the mandatory part consists of processing the returned radar signal and creating track records for detected targets by a signal processor. The optional part attempts to associate these targets with established tracks using a data processor. If the returned radar signal is noisy, then the amount of time required to process the signal remains the same (i.e., the processing time of the mandatory part stays the same). However, the track records will be noisy. There may be more false returns — records associated with non-existent targets. As a result, the data processor must spend additional processing time in associating tracks. We plan to implement the algorithms for end-to-end scheduling of dependent tasks described in [4] in ICS to make it ideally suited for these types of applications.

7 Acknowledgements

This work was partially supported by the NASA contract NAG1613, by the US Navy ONR contract N00014-92-J-1146, and by a fellowship from TRW System Development Division.

References

[1] A. Accetta, R. Baron, W. Bolosky, D. Golub, R. Rashid, A. Tevanian, and M. Young. Mach: A new kernel foundation for Unix development. In *Proceedings of the Summer USENIX Conference*, July 1986.

[2] M. Boddy and T. Dean. Decision-theoretic deliberation scheduling for problem solving in time-constrained environments. *Artificial Intelligence*, 1992.

[3] J.-Y. Chung, J. W.-S. Liu, and K.-J. Lin. Scheduling periodic jobs that allow imprecise results. *IEEE Transactions on Computers*, 19(9):1156–1173, September 1990.

[4] W. Feng and J. W.-S. Liu. Algorithms for scheduling tasks with input error and end-to-end deadlines. Technical Report UIUCDCS-R-94-1888, University of Illinois at Urbana-Champaign, September 1994.

[5] B. N. Freeman-Benson, J. Maloney, and A. Borning. An incremental constraint solver. *Communications of the ACM*, 33(1):54–63, January 1990.

[6] K. I. J. Ho, J. Y. T. Leung, and W. D. Wei. Minimizing maximum weighted error of imprecise computation tasks. Technical report, University of Nebraska, 1992.

[7] K. I. J. Ho, J. Y. T. Leung, and W. D. Wei. Scheduling imprecise computation tasks with 0/1 constraints. Technical report, University of Nebraska, 1992.

[8] S. Karsenty, J. Landay, and C. Weikart. Inferring graphical constraints with Rockit. Technical report, Digital Equipement Corporation, Paris Research Laboratory, March 1992.

[9] B. Koo and S. Toueg. Checkpointing and rollback-recovery for distributed systems. *IEEE Transactions on Software Engineering*, January 1987.

[10] K.-J. Lin, S. Natarajan, and J. W.-S. Liu. Imprecise results: Utilizing partial computation in real-time systems. In *Proceedings of 8th IEEE Real-Time Systems Symposium*, December 1987.

[11] J. W.-S. Liu, K.-J. Lin, and C. L. Liu. A position paper for the 1987 IEEE workshop on real-time operating systems. In *Proceedings of the 1987 IEEE Workshop on Real-Time Operating Systems*, May 1987.

[12] J. W.-S. Liu, K.-J. Lin, and S. Natarajan. Scheduling real-time, periodic jobs using imprecise results. In *Proceedings of 8th IEEE Real-Time Systems Symposium*, December 1987.

[13] Keith Loepere, editor. *Mach 3 Server Writer's Guide*. Open Software Foundation and Carnagie Mellon University, 1990.

[14] G. Mongatti, L. Alparone, G. Benelli, S. Baronti, F. Lotti, and A. Casini. Progressive image transmission by content driven laplacian pyramid encoding. *IEE Proceedings-I*, 139(5), October 1992.

[15] M. Obradovic and P. Berman. Voting as the optimal static pessimistic scheme for managing replicated data. In *Proceedings of 9th IEEE Symposium on Reliable Distributed Systems*, October 1990.

[16] D. R. Olsen and K. Allan. Creating interactive techniques by symbolically solving geometric constraints. In *Proceedings of ACM SIGGRAPH Symposium on User Interface Software and Technology*, 1990.

[17] W.-K. Shih and J. W.-S. Liu. Algorithms for scheduling imprecise computations with timing cons traints to minimize maximum error. *To appear in IEEE Transactions on Computers*.

[18] W.-K. Shih and J. W.-S. Liu. On-line scheduling of imprecise computations to minimize error. In *Proceedings of the 13th IEEE Real-Time Systems Symposium*, December 1992.

[19] W.-K. Shih, J. W.-S. Liu, and J.-Y. Chung. Algorithms for scheduling imprecise computations to minimize total error. *SIAM Journal on Computing*, 20(3), July 1991.

[20] T. Tonouchi, K. Nakayama, S. Matsuoka, and S. Kawai. Creating visual objects by direct manipulation. In *Proceedings of ACM SIGGRAPH Symposium on User Interface Software and Technology*, 1992.

[21] S. V. Vrbsky and J. W.-S. Liu. Approximate: A query processor that produces monotonically improving approximate answers. *IEEE Transactions on Knowledge and Data Engineering*, 5(6):1056–1068, December 1993.

Performability Analysis of Formal Graphical Specifications

K. Waedt, J. Richter, A. Graf, U. Mertens

SIEMENS KWU NL–R, Frauenauracher Str. 85, 91056 Erlangen, Germany

Abstract

The advantages of forward documentation with a toolkit for graphical block oriented specification of software and hardware for performability analysis and automation of safety critical technical processes are described in the following. Main topics are the timing analysis and pre runtime scheduling employed by the distributed, responsive TELE-PERM XS Digital Safety I&C for Nulear Power Plants.

Key words

Automatic Code Generation, Dependability, Formal Graphical Specification, Forward Documentation, Hard Real Time, Performability, Safety I&C, Timing Analysis, V&V

1. Introduction

As noted by Malek, in the past questions of fault tolerance and real time applications for digital computer systems were analyzed and as far as possible solved separately:

"The architects of space and the architects of time need to unite their efforts in development of systems, where faults and time are considered at the conceptual and specification levels. With promising theories being put into practice, ... " [32]

Systems characterized by this "marriage of real time and fault tolerance" [31] are denominated as *responsive systems*. This paper will restrict itself to performance and dependability issues for *hard* real time fault tolerant systems. As an example of such a responsive system the Digital Safety I&C [9] for the reactor protection system [20] of NPPs from the Nuclear Division of SIEMENS Power Generation Group (KWU) will be considered.

The reactor protection system ensures that a NPP operates without danger to human life, health and environment. A major task of a reactor protection system is to keep the NPP in a safe state for 30 minutes *without the necessity of intervention by human operators*, irrespective of the incident concerned [10]. The reliability of the software to be used to control these extremely safety critical technical processes must be demonstrated. This is a major goal of TELEPERM XS engineering system SPACE.

Section 2.1 touches some problems of modelling the safety critical, responsive system. Section 2.2 briefly describes the formal specification method employed by

SPACE. Section 3 handles performance and timing analysis for local scheduling plans (Section 3.1) and the global scheduling plan (Section 3.2). Section 4 covers reliability and dependability analysis based on the formal specification method described in section 2.2. Finally, Section 5 elucidates the advantages of formal specification for the V&V of the reusable code and particularly the generated code, which has to guarantee performability.

2. Performability

2.1 Modelling safety critical, responsive systems

For new systems to be developed the performability characteristics can not be measured but have to be estimated from adequate models of the target system. In some cases these models can be quite precise, as for the fail–safe duplex system [4]. In the duplex system example analytical solutions to performability questions exist [6]. However, practical safety critical applications as the Digital I&C for a NPP are much more complex and an analytical approach is rather inpracticable. For these cases there are currently already tools or toolkits available, like RISK SPECTRUM ([36], used by SIEMENS), Tomspin [30], PANDA [33] or CLAIRE [35] which to give an example, evaluate generalized stochastic petri nets (GSPNs) with up to millions of internal states.

In our opinion, modelling all the dependability and performability characteristics of a comprehensive safety critical system is an exhaustive, error–prone and expensive procedure. On the other hand a simplified, inexact model of the target application is generally not adequate to demonstrate important characteristics, like timeliness. Our approach is to start with a formal specification of a complete I&C system. This specification must accomplish the following requirements. It must

- be formal,
- serve as single source for hardware ordering,
- serve as single source for automatically generating the non reusable software,
- contain an abstraction level familiar and unequivocally understandable to those process and fluid system engineers, which formulated the system requirements,

- contain an abstraction level suited as concise (and consistent) end user documentation,
- support validation through simulation and
- support automatic performability and dependability analysis.

A general introduction to such a forward documentation technique is given in [14, 46]. Section 2.2 will restrict to the last of the above requirements, which implies an automatic derivation of the analysis model. But first let us representatively consider the modelling of LAN load.

Due to the nature of CSMA/CD protocols at high load collisions of data packets result in a decreasing of throughput, since all collided packets have to be retransmitted. As increasing load exceeds an upper limit, throughput degrades due to increasing collisions. Thus one cannot give an upper bound for packet transmission time. For modelling the CSMA/CD throughput the analytical results of [41] are used. This formula models the throughput of the standard (1–persistent unslotted) CSMA/CD protocol [21]. Unlike the original model in [43], this formula is corrected in [41, 44]. A compilation of analytical models for other CSMA/CD variants can be found in [38].

Fig. 2.1 shows the calculated throughput $S(a,G)$. Parameter a denotes the signal propagation delay of the medium normalized to the packet transmission time. The rate of generated packets per packet transmission time is given by G. As Fig. 2.1 shows, even at burst load the throughput S remains at a high level for small signal delay times. This is reasonable, as collisions are speedily detected with a small signal propagation delay. Transmission of collided packets can then be rescheduled. For a conventional coax cable signal propagation delay is about 5 µs/km.

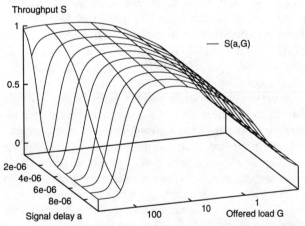

Fig. 2.1: Throughput according to analytical models [37]

In [40] measurements on a real Ethernet implementation have shown that throughput is much better in real world systems than the analytical model predicts. Due to assumptions of the analytical model measurements and model correspond mainly for small and high loads [16]. Our actual timing analysis implementation uses the analytical model only for calculating the degradation of the throughput in case of high loads. For the throughput calculation the signal propagation delay and offered load are derived out of the HW/SW–specification under analysis. The preceding discussion shows that collision detection is handled more quickly as signal propagation on the medium becomes small. Use of fibre optic and active star couplers (collision detection in the star coupler rack) provide a small signal propagation delay and quick collision handling.

Restricting the maximum load (to 20%) is a prerequisite and first step toward avoiding nondeterministic behaviour. Timing analysis assures that this maximum load is never exceeded. The local and global scheduling plans (cf. section 3) combined with clock synchronization assure the implementation of sparse time and thus collision avoidance.

2.2 Formal specification of safety critical, responsive systems

In 1988, shortly after our research and development project "Digital I&C" for SIEMENS NPPs started, one of the first questions was, whether the available digital techniques were suitable for implementation of the responsive system described in [11]. The HW of this distributed system contains hundreds of CPUs (the majority of which are communication processors) and dozens of LANs. The main SW requirements were available from SIEMENS KONVOI PWRs allowing an estimation to be made. The assignment of computers to different rooms and buildings was likewise derived from PWRs already constructed. Additionally, SW for different processing levels, such as data acquisition, preprocessing, subsystem control, deviation monitoring, voting, message distribution and data concentration was assigned to CPUs of different racks. The performance requirements were approximated manually using shell scripts and a relational database. After several weeks the performance requirements were finally estimated and revealed that several HW platforms were not suitable as a basis for the Digital I&C. The main weak points were: LAN and/or bus bandwidth, CP performance and processing performance (filtering of analog signals).

In the meantime, the engineering tools for integrated HW and SW specification have become available. The above procedure of manual estimation of performance characteristics of a large distributed, responsive system is now replaced by a comprehensive performability analysis. The formal graphical specification contains detailed and complete reliability and timing attributes of elementary components (not further decomposed in the formal specification). This allows the performability analysis to be automated. The results are precise, so that they are even used while automatically generating SW (cf. Section 3.1).

The HW is specified hierarchically. The top level diagram contains pictograms, which denominate buildings

184

relevant for the distributed responsive system. The second level contains the relevant rooms. The third level contains the HW cabinets placed in the relevant rooms. The next level contains the racks of each cabinet and finally the boards of each rack. There are further HW elements modeled, such as transceivers, power supplies, fans and submodules of boards, such as measurement modules. In addition to these diagrams, which model mainly the hierarchical HW composition, we introduced interconnection diagrams, which contain the relations between the individual HW elements.

Fig. 2.2 is an extract from a single page interconnection diagram, as diagrams are usually printed in DIN A3 format, as recommended in [45].

For each pictogram of the HW interconnection diagram there is a corresponding pictogram in the hierarchical HW specification. A hyperlink facility in the engineering tool's diagram editor supports editing this correspondence. The content of a diagram is stored not only as graphics, but also as objects with persistent attributes.

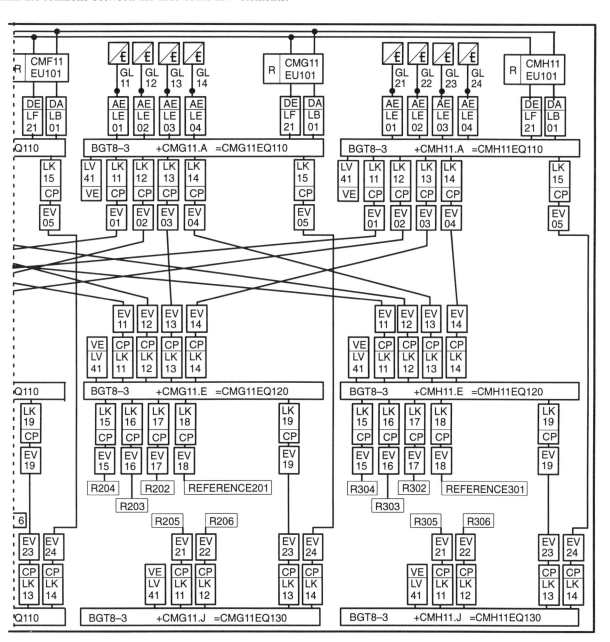

Fig. 2.2: HW interconnection diagram example (40% extract from one page)

The safety I&C SW is specified according to the technique of forward documentation. This is based on the initial researches of Welfonder [48, 49] and Herden [18] which are recognized as documentation guidelines by most large energy supply companies in the meantime [45]. With regard to the hierarchical approach of forward documentation one aim here is to obtain a homomorphous mapping between functional documentation entities and coherent fluid system engineering process segments.

SW diagrams of the documentation hierarchy's overview and area level are quite close to process and fluid system engineering (containing pictures of pumps, valves, motors, etc.). SW diagrams of the individual level are close to I&C. The I&C hierarchy is subdivided into the process, group and individual level. For most functional entities the main I&C assignments measurement, open–loop control and closed–loop control are distinguished.

Code is generated only for SW diagrams of the individual level, which are called **functional diagrams** (FDs). A FD is a documentation and at the same time specification entity, which manages a set of interconnected **function blocks** (FBs). FBs and connections are the basic elements for graphical block–oriented specification with SPACE. The FD editor contains navigation facilities and a hyperlink facility for redundant FDs. Redundant HW nodes are not restricted to processing exactly the same SW. There have to be explicitly specified FDs which are redundant to FDs processed on other CPUs. Thus sideward error recovery based on automatic code generation is feasible.

3. Timing analysis

A FB can be represented by an imperative language function with restricted syntax in terms of programming language constructs, formal parameters and variables. The source code for one FB is referred to as an **FB module**. The most important components of an FB module are shown in Fig. 3.1 which simultaneously outlines its main structure. Within an FB module the allocation of memory is prohibited. Static variables are kept in data structures outside the FB module and local variables are restricted to a predefined total size per FB module. Inside a FB module recursive functions and unbounded loops are forbidden. FB modules are not allowed to call each other.

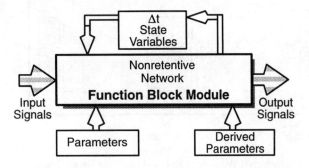

Fig. 3.1: Basic components of a function block module

3.1 Local Scheduling Plans

Hard real time systems function either event– or time–triggered [27]. Thereby, all events are or are initiated by states or changes in state of the equipment to be controlled by the responsive system. A time–triggered approach usually means that tasks are processed periodically with the smallest period in the range of milliseconds (e.g., 400 μs for the MAFT system [23] and multiples of one ms for the MARS system [25]). The commitment to the event–triggered or time–triggered approach is a basic overall design decision for responsive systems and has a major influence on further problems which have to be solved for distributed responsive systems [28].

While in event–triggered systems, as in DELTA–4 [34], conventional on–line scheduling is performed (e.g. earliest deadline first scheduling or least laxity first scheduling [22], eventually enhanced by a pre runtime schedulability test [19]) for hard real time time–triggered systems pre runtime scheduling is feasible. Thereby dependencies due to common resources may be summarized in a so called Gantt Diagram [5] as is performed in the MAFT system for groups of tasks and even for subatomic periods [24].

As in MARS and MAFT our basic approach concerning the time dimension is also time–triggered with pre runtime scheduling. But there is one essential difference that results from the way in which the end user specifies the SW that has to be executed on the real time system. While in the MARS system (as well as in the MAFT system [47]) SW is specified at the task level, we favour a formal SW *and* HW specification as described in Section 2.2. As an example in [12] a vessel control system is described, in which the tasks of the first dependency graph are responsible for filling the vessel, those of the second dependency graph are responsible for heating the vessel content according to given gradients, those of the third dependency graph for preparing and supervising the heater, etc. A MARS dependency graph considers the precedence constraints between tasks, such as the so–called stimulus–tasks, which process data from peripheral input devices, and response tasks which prepare the output data. The time delay from the stimulus task to the response task is called MART (maximal response time). Thus the dependencies between tasks which process one given real time problem are comprised in a directed acyclic, not necessarily coherent dependency graph.

Fohler [12] underlines that in the MARS system, unlike in other conventional real time systems, it is possible to define an individual dependency graph for each operating mode of a HW node. Since the transitions between operating modes are subject to application–specific restrictions (switching must not be abrupt), they are covered by additional dependency graphs (cf. Fig. 3.2).

The MARS dependency graphs are determined pre runtime. For this each task is assigned a number of time slices which is sufficient for completion in one period. At runtime the MARS scheduler checks all dependency graphs at the end of each time slice and starts the next task according to priority and dependency–constraints.

With TELEPERM XS the above vessel example would be solved on a more abstract level. Open– and closed–loop control would be specified using adequate FBs inside FDs. This formal specification inherently includes the transition between application–specific operating states. This is due to the way in which fluid and process engineers are used to solving their problems. They would use for example a PRIORITY FB to select a closed–loop control which should be active at a given time. But no programmer's view to implementation details as tasks is required. Tasks are determined automatically prior to code generation.

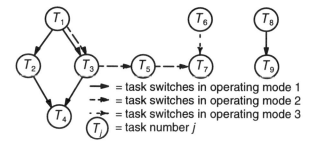

Fig. 3.2: Pre runtime scheduling in MARS [29]

Fig. 3.3 illustrates a simple example where two **functional diagram group** (FDG) modules with different periods are processed in a single task. An FDG is defined as the set of those FDs which must be processed with the same period on the same CPU. The **FDG module** is the SW which implements an FDG. Dependencies between FDs of the same FDG are determined automatically by topological sorting and sequentialization [13]. The same holds for FBs which are processed inside an FD.

Dependencies between FBs may not only imply dependencies inside of FDs but also between FDs and FDGs. These dependencies may even include multiple closed–loop directed cycles, where, however, each cycle must contain at least one so called DELAY FB. Thus analogous signal flow graphs can be simulated by discrete differential equations. Inconsistent SW specifications containing incomplete or invalid dependencies, such as cycles over FBs which contain no DELAY FB, are flagged as erroneous and rejected prior to code generation.

Instead of application–specific operation modes we distinguish various operating modes per **runtime environment** (RTE). Three of these operating modes are relevant for scheduling:

- **Initialization**. Different initializations are performed at FB module, FDG module and RTE level.
- **Parametrization**. During initialization or after a FB parameter change state variables and so called derived parameters (cf. Fig. 3.1) are computed.
- **Run**. The periodic part of FB, FD and FDG modules is executed.

State variables are used to store results of heavily–used expressions, which depend only on FB parameters. Only after an FB parameter has been modified — which can happen during runtime — the values of derived parameters are computed and checked again. Since in practice FB parameters are modified rather seldom, with a frequency of days or weeks, this is in essence a runtime optimization.

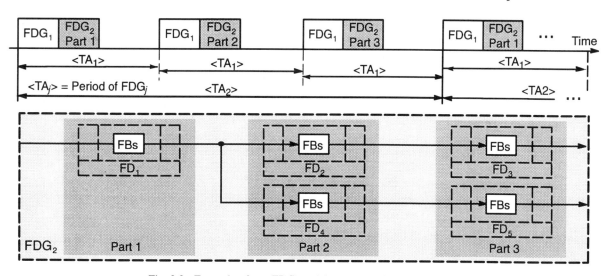

Fig. 3.3: Example of two FDG modules processed in the same task

The worst case runtimes of FB modules are determined by measurement in a suitable test environment on representative target machines. The runtimes are determined for each of the three above named RTE operation modes. The values of input signals, parameters, derived parameters and state variables which yield the worst–case runtimes for an

FB module must be evaluated individually for each FB. This means that, say the runtimes of a SORT FB with eight input signals whose FB module implements an ascending bubble sort will yield the worst case runtimes when the analog input signals are by chance descending.

The fortuitous combination of FB module inputs which will lead to the worst case runtimes is usually a bit more complicated, since each signal is enhanced by an accompanying status. Some FB modules perform so–called active status processing. Their computations depend on attributes set in the signal status. The status may contain the attributes "error" or "test". The value of a signal marked as erroneous in its status will not be considered by a FB module with active status processing.

Depending on the FB module in question, the consequence of the error attribute being set in one or more input signal's status could be computation of a substitute value, modification of the FB modules behavior (e.g. 2–of–3 logic instead of 3–of–4 logic) or simply ignoring the invalid input signal. The influence of the signal status on the control flow inside an FB module is also simple, since it must be reflected by the FB's pictogram(s). The status must be considered when determining the FB module's worst case runtimes.

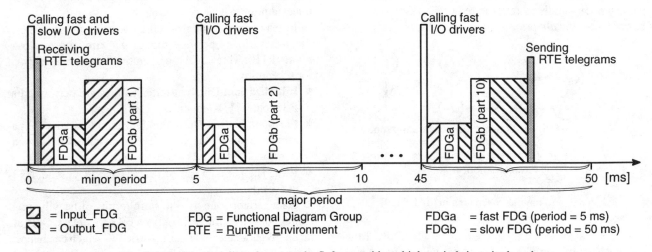

Fig. 3.4: Local scheduling plan example: Software with multiple periods in a single task

The conditions under which the final worst case run–times are determined depend not only on the target CPU but also on the target operating system. In the case of TELE-PERM XS, this is the minimal operating system MICROS, developed by SIEMENS and employed in many different automation applications. This operating system for safety critical applications manages most resources in a static way. For example the maximum number of tasks (e.g. 16) is specified prior to compiling the operating system and can not be changed during runtime. In addition, all I/O drivers processing analog, digital or binary signals are not integrated into the operating system's kernel, nor into the operating system itself. They are integrated into the target system's RTE which is also generated automatically. This means that processing of input and output drivers (cf. Fig. 3.4) is handled in the same way as calling of an FB module. In fact, I/O drivers for FDG input or output signals could also be implemented as FB modules, just as was implemented in 1991 in a first prototype of the FDG code generator.

Since all computations as well as the actual control flow are determined inside FB modules, only a few types of elementary operations need to be considered during timing analysis. These are mainly copying of data (e.g. signals between FDs of the same FDG), negation of signals, trans-forming the test attribute in a signal or FDG telegram status into an error attribute and initializing the signal values with defaults.

Since all these elementary operations are simple, their duration can be measured by performing a large number of representative runs per elementary operation. The number of occurrences of each elementary operation can be determined automatically, because the operations themselves are also generated automatically.

As illustrated in Fig. 3.4, FDG modules with different periods can be joined in a single task. Thus the requirement of [7] for a minimum number of interrupts (even of supervisor calls) can be approached quite well. Theoretically the number of FDGs per CPU is not limited. The only restriction is that each FDG's period must be an integer multiple of the fastest FDG period — not the period of the fastest FDG multiplied with a power of 2, as in the MAFT system. In practice, however, a large number of FDGs per CPU is not required, even for the Safety I&C of a NPP. But at least two different FDGs should be supported with regard to the Nyquist criteria [39]: one containing FDs for sampling analogous I/O signals (e.g., with a period of 5 ms) and one slower FDG responsible for the network traffic. Local scheduling plans are determined completely automatically.

3.2 The global scheduling plan

As *global scheduling plan* we denote the rules by which the initial starting times of tasks from different nodes of a distributed, responsive system are determined. The main restrictions are given by

- signals exchanged between FBs which are executed on different CPUs,
- sets of redundant FDs, which must be started simultaneously and
- clock synchronization.

Generally, if computation is distributed, a number of processing levels can be distinguished. With an eye to fault tolerance on each processing level, redundant FDs are processed on different CPUs and decisions based on diverse input signals (such as from neutron flux, pressure, level or frequency) are also computed on different CPUs. As a result, it is finally necessary to consider not only the execution time of one CPU's FDG modules but also the maximum response time (MART, cf. section 3.1) of the overall distributed, responsive system (cf. Fig. 3.5).

Usually the overall worst case runtimes of the FDG modules, including the runtime environment (RTE), amount to only a predefined fraction of the total available computation power (e.g. 50%). All remaining resources are used for a low priority background task which performs self–monitoring. Thus telegrams can be sent from one processing level to the next before the period has finished. This holds for each processing level. Since computation is not event–triggered, an FDG starts its computation not necessarily at the moment when all input telegrams are available, but only when its period starts — in fact one or more of the telegrams may be lost or may not be received due to the source HW node being in a repair or test state. Theoretically, complex dependencies mean that evaluation of an optimal global scheduling plan requires backtracking. By adding further restrictions, as higher priority for messages from lower to upper processing levels, the evaluation of an appropriate global scheduling plan is simplified.

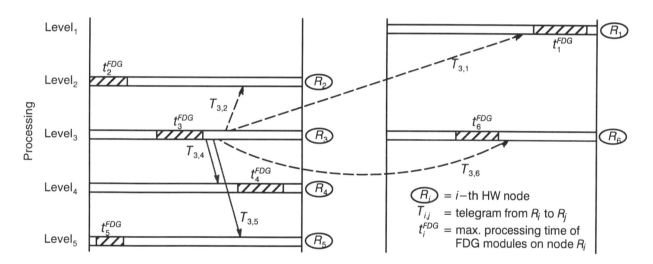

Fig. 3.5: Global scheduling plan example: Influence of sending times on throughput

As recommended by [17], we evaluate the network traffic by exact analysis of the used network protocol, in our case based on IEEE 802.3 and Futurebus. Due to performance considerations we use only a protocol stack up to ISO/OSI level 2, cf. Fig. 3.6. Further ISO/OSI levels are either empty or handled at application level. Since the data structures for all transmitted information as well as the broadcast times are determined automatically, an exact analysis of the network traffic is feasible. This is once again a consequence of the formal and integrated specification of SW and HW. Thus compared with conventional approaches for network performance analysis, no inexact assumptions about user profiles are required (e.g. the percentage of graphics and database application started over a IEEE 802.3 backbone with 50 workstations).

As described above, the network traffic analysis serves not only to identify network performance bottlenecks, which in conventional applications are diminished by adding bridges and routers [17], but also to determine optimal startup time offsets for CPUs from neighboring processing levels.

The pre runtime network performance analysis considers all details, like:

- Very short user telegrams. For example: since the minimum frame size of IEEE 802.3 packets is 64 bytes there is no difference if 1 or 43 bytes of user data are transmitted on IEEE 802.2 level.
- Long user telegrams. These are split into packets during automatic code generation of the RTE.

Clock synchronization is very important for distributed, responsive systems. This is of paramount importance, especially when collisions are to be avoided in CSMA/CD based networks. Precise clock synchronization together with an extremely high percentage of network bandwidth usage can be obtained with HW based approaches, as described in [26]. However, if off–the–shelf HW is to be used due to its good service record, continuous internal synchronization based on regulation theory is then feasible, provided that the specification is formal. The low–level, distributed SW for handling the dedicated synchronization telegrams is automatically generated as a part of the RTE. This kind of clock synchronization is fully adequate if only a predefined maximum percentage of each network's bandwidth (such as 20 to 38 % [17]) is used. This is always the case in safety critical applications.

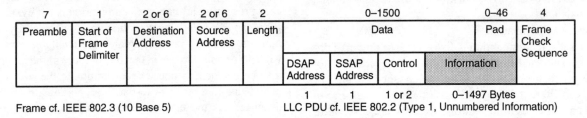

Fig. 3.6: Characteristics of a typical protocol [42]

There is no clock synchronization method which guarantees an internal clock synchronisation $\Delta_{int} = 0$ [46]. The interdependencies between clock synchronization, collisions (if possible for the given MAC layer) and network performance or timeliness are considered explicitly prior to code generation.

An exact timing analysis is performed not only for LANs, but also for backplane busses, local busses and local extension busses. After each change in either the SW or the HW specification the automatic timing analysis is restarted prior to code generation.

4. Dependability analysis

The implementation of some functional entities (cf. Section 2.2) may require a high computing power which is not available on a single CPU. Therefore multiple CPUs or host CPUs connected over local extension busses with slave CPUs may be employed (cf. Fig. 4.1). Performance is increased, but at the same time the number of HW entities in which a fault could potentially cause a functional entity failure is increased.

All HW entities which must be error free to ensure the availability of a given functional entity must be considered. The extraction of a failure model (e.g. fault tree or GSPN) can be done automatically. Thus the common problem of having discrepancies between the model and the implementation vanishes. The evaluation of the generated model can be accomplished by any commercial evaluation tool with a batch mode interface (preferably based on a relational database). To facilitate the overview of the quite detailed model, modularization could be supported in the generated failure model (such as master/checker or pair/spare).

Since the HW specification includes the modelling of buildings and rooms, the toolkit will accept questions like "What's the influence of a fire restricted to room X?".

Currently automatic dependability analysis is under development.

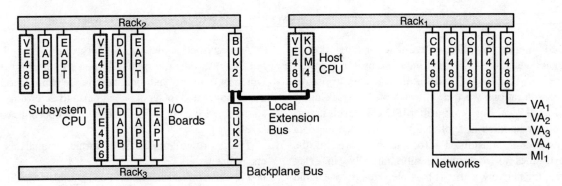

Fig. 4.1: Increasing performance through host CPUs and subsystems

5. Verification and validation

While we use redundant HW to cope with HW faults we try to obtain error free SW without the use of SW diversity. The verification is simplified due to:

- Use of a small number of simple FB modules (about 50) which allow complete coverage tests with tools such as IDAS–TESTAT [15],

- Restriction to a small number of simple programming constructs (subset of ANSI C),
- Formal, integral specification of SW and HW,
- Formal specification of the overall program structure using syntax diagrams,
- Automatic code generation of non reusable SW
- Use of inverse code generators, which take the generated code as input and reconstruct the specification. As a result, the process of code generation is verified.
- Commitment to block–oriented programming. As a result, the number of combinations of basic high level programming language elements (that is FBs) is smaller by some orders of magnitude than for conventional programming. According to Halstead's theory [8], the program volume V is directly proportional to the number of composition steps N and logarithm base 2 of the number of elementary statements (FB modules) η, $V := N \cdot \text{ld } \eta$.

Validation is based on generated testbeds. SIEMENS KWU real time simulator OPAL is used as front end. This simulator is currently in use in several NPPs. It is one of about 150 simulators worldwide, which are used for NPP personnel training [50]. Using the simulator language, transients for individual input signals are specified by different means such as data streams or trigger functions. The periodic data exchange between the simulator and the generated I&C SW to be validated is performed by a generated interface.

Validation of the timing analysis has been performed for several representative specifications. For validation of the timing analysis methodology itself, computed and measured execution times have been compared not only for our target architecture but also for the following architectures: HP 9000/715 (33, 50, 75 and 80 MHz), Intel 386SX20, Intel 486DX33 and Motorola 68020/25, 68030/50 and 68040/25.

The quite interesting results are satisfying. However a detailed discussion of the influence of cache sizes, compiler optimizations etc. goes beyond the scope of this paper. The most important result is, that the computed execution times are indeed always equal or larger than the measured execution times. For individual specifications the worst case execution times of different FB modules can not be obtained at the same time for some given FDG input signals and FB parameter combinations. An exact execution time estimation for such FD and FDG modules is complicated. It requires to persistently store the worst case context for each FB module and consider all dependencies between these contexts. Currently we do not compute this exact worst case context for FDG modules. Thus proving the correctness of such a complicated algorithm is avoided. In this sense — as the discrepancy between the estimated and measured worst case execution times may sum up to a few percents — our actual solution is suboptimal.

The complete toolkit was developed according to the OOA/OOD methodology of Coad/Yourdon [1, 2, 3] and implemented in C++.

6. Acronyms and shortcuts

CP, CPU = Communications Processor, Central Processing Unit
FDG = Functional Diagram Group
GSPN = Generalized Stochastic Petri Net
HW, SW = Hardware, Software
I&C = Instrumentation and Control
KWU = SIEMENS' Power Generation Group
LAN, LLC = Local Area Network, Logical Link Control
MAC = Medium Access Control
NPP, PWR = Nuclear Power Plant, Pressurized Water Reactor
OOA, OOD = Object Oriented Analysis, OO Design
OPAL = On–line Predictor with Active Learning Facility
PDU, RTE = Protocol Data Unit, Run–Time Environment
SPACE = Specification and Coding Environment
V&V = Verification and Validation

7. References

[1] Coad, P; Yourdon, E. *Object–oriented Analysis*, Prentice Hall, 1991

[2] Coad, P; Yourdon, E. *Object–oriented Design*, Prentice Hall, 1991

[3] Coad, P; Nicola, J. *Object–oriented Design*, Prentice Hall, 1993

[4] Dal Cin, M., *Fehlertolerante Systeme,* Teubner Verlag, '79

[5] Dal Cin, M., *Systemnahe Programmierung*, Teubner '88

[6] Dal Cin M., *Bewertung fehlertoleranter Systeme*, Univ. Erlangen–Nürnberg, IMMD III, April 1994

[7] Deutsches Institut für Normung, *DIN IEC 880, Software für Rechner im Sicherheitssystem von Kernkraftwerken,* Beuth Verlag, Berlin, August 1987

[8] Ehrenberger, W.; Saglietti, F., *Architecture and Safety Qualification of Large Software Systems*, ESREL '93, pp. 985–999, München, Mai 1993

[9] Fischer, H.D.; Graf, A.; Mertens, U., *Siemens–KWU works towards digital I&C for safety systems*, nuclear engineering internat., pp. 35–36, February 1991

[10] Fischer, H.D., *Special Features of a Computer–Based German Reactor Protection System*, Fault–Tolerant Computing Systems 5, pp. 266–287, 1991

[11] Fischer, H.D.; Hellmerichs, K.; Parry, A., *Digital instrumentation and control for future nuclear power plants within the French–German cooperation*, Int. Symp. on NPP I&C, Tokyo, pp. (1–2–1)–(1–2–15), Mai 1992

[12] Fohler, G., *Realizing Changes of Operational Modes with a Pre Run–Time Scheduled Hard Real–Time System*, Hrsg.: Kopetz, H., Proc. of the 2nd Int. Workshop on Responsive Computer Systems, pp. 287–300, Saitama, Japan, 1992

[13] Gehringer, T., *Ein Werkzeug zur funktionsgestützten Automatisierung*, VDI Berichte Nr. 937, STAK, pp. 93–101, '92

[14] Graf, A., *Software development method for safety critical applications*, Advanced Control and Instrumentation systems in Nuclear Power Plants: Design, Verification and Validation, Vol. I, Session 3/20, pp. 1–12, Helsinki, 6/94

[15] Hahn, D.; Werner, U., *IDAS–TESTAT für C, Systembeschreibung und Benutzerhandbuch Version 2.6*, IDAS GmbH, D–65549 Limburg, Holzheimer Str. 96, 1993

[16] Hammond, J.L.; O'Reilly, P.J.P., *Performance Analysis of Local Computer Networks*, Addison–Wesley, 1988

[17] Held, G., *Local Area Network Performance: Issues and answers*, Wiley, 1994

[18] Herden, W.; Welfonder, E., *Herstellerunabhängige online–Dokumentation digitaler Leittechniksysteme*, Prozeßrechensysteme '88, pp. 625–643, Springer, 1988

[19] Herrtwich, R.G., *Betriebsmittelvergabe unter Echtzeitgesichtspunkten*, Informatik–Spektrum, Band 14, Heft 3, pp. 123–136, Juni 1991

[20] Hoffmann, H.; Fischer, H.D.; Lochner, K.–H.; Mertens U., *Microprocessor–Based Information and Control System for Safety and Non–Safety Applications in Nuclear Power Plants of the Nineties*, Trans. ENS/ANS–Foratom Conf., pp.1820–2830, 1990

[21] IEEE Standard 802.2: Logical Link Control

[22] Jöhnk, M., *Echtzeit–Geist. Grundlagen der Echtzeitverarbeitung in Unix–Systemen*, iX, pp. 114–119, 12/91

[23] Kieckhafer, R.M.; Walter, C.J.; Finn, A.M.; Thambidurai P.M., *The MAFT Architecture for Distributed Fault Tolerance*, IEEE Tr. on Comp., Vol. 37, No. 4, pp. 398–405, '88

[24] Kieckhafer, R.M., *Fault–Tolerant Real–Time Task Scheduling in the MAFT Distributed System*, IEEE, 22dt Hawaii Int. Conf. on System Sciences, pp. 143–151, 1/89

[25] Kopetz, H.; Damm A.; Koza C.; Mulazzani, M.; Schwabl, W.; Senft C.; Zainlinger, R., *Distributed Fault–Tolerant Real–Time Systems: The Mars Approach*, IEEE MICRO (0272–1732/89/0200–0025501.00), pp. 25–40, 2/89

[26] Kopetz, H., *Loosely Coupled Distributed Computer System with Node Synchronization for Precision in Real Time Applications*, USA Patent No. 4 866 606, 9/89

[27] Kopetz, H., *Sparse time versus dense time in distributed real–time systems*, Proceedings of the 12th Internat. Conf. on Distributed Comp. Syst., pp. 460–467, Yokohama, 1992

[28] Kopetz, H., *Six Difficult Problems in the Design of Responsive Systems*, Proceedings of the Second Int. Workshop on Responsive Comp. Syst., pp. 3–15, Japan, 10/92

[29] Kopetz, H.; Fohler, G.; Grünsteidl, G.; Kantz, H.; Pospischil, G.; et. al., *The Programmer's View of MARS*, IEEE Real–Time Systems Symposium, pp.223–226, USA, 1992

[30] Lepold, R., *Performability Evaluation of a Fault–Tolerant Multiprocessor Architecture Using Stochastic Petri Nets*, Springer, FTCS 5, pp. 253–265, 1991

[31] Malek, M., *Responsive Systems: A Challenge for the Nineties*, Microprocessing and Microprogramming 30, North–Holland, pp. 9–16, August 1990

[32] Malek, M., *Responsive Systems: A Marriage Between Real Time and Fault Tolerance*, Springer, Fault–Tolerant Computing Systems 5, pp. 1–17, September 1991

[33] PANDA Toolkit, Univ. Erlangen–Nürnberg, IMMD III

[34] Powell, D., *Delta–4: A Generic Architecture for Dependable Distributed Computing*, Springer, 1991

[35] Raguideau, J.; Dominique Schoen, *CLAIRE, An event–driven simulation tool for testing software*, Advanced I&C systems in NPPs: Design, V&V, Vol. II, Session 4/24 pp. 1–8, Helsinki, June 1994

[36] RELCON TEKNIK AB, *RISK SPECTRUM PSA, Version 1.1*, November 1992

[37] Richter, J., *Zeit– und Betriebsmittelanalyse von formalen Leittechnikspezifikationen*, Diplomarbeit, Univ. Erlangen–Nürnberg IMMD III, 1. Februar 1995

[38] Rom, R.; Sidi, M., *Mulptiple Access Protocols – Performance and Analysis*, Springer, 1990

[39] Schüßler, H.W., *Digitale Signalverarbeitung, Band 1*, Springer, 1989

[40] Shoch, J.F.; Hupp, J.A., *Measured Performance of an Ethernet Local Network*, ACM, 23(12):711–721, 1980

[41] Sohraby, K.; Molle, M.L.; Venetsanopoulos, A.N., *Comments on "Throughput Analysis for Persistent CSMA Systems"*, IEEE COM–35(2):240–243, 1987

[42] Tanenbaum A.S., *Computer Networks*, Prentice–Hall, 1989

[43] Takagi, H.; Kleinrock, L., *Throuput Analysis for Persistent CSMA Systems*, IEEE COM–33(7):627–638, 1985

[44] Takagi, H. Kleinrock, L., *Correction to "Throughput Analysis for Persistent CSMA Systems"*, IEEE COM–35(2):240–243, 1987

[45] VGB, ETG/VDE, *Richtlinie VGB – R 170 C: Leittechnik für Kraftwerke. Funktionsbezogene Dokumentation*, 1989

[46] Waedt, K.; Stöcker, S., *SPACE, Specification and Coding Environment. A Toolkit allowing the Graphical Specification of Safety Critical Programs for Automation*, ESREL '93, pp. 825–839, München, 1993

[47] Walter, C.J., *MAFT: An Architecture for Reliable Fly–by–Wire Flight Control*, Proc. AIAA/IEEE Eighth Digital Avionics Systems Conference, pp. 415–121, Oktober 1988

[48] Welfonder, E.; Herden, W., *Leittechnik–Dokumentation aus Betreibersicht*, ETG/VGB–Fachtagung "Betriebliche Dokumentation in Kraftwerken, Einfluß der modernen Leittechnik und der Planungsmittel", Baden–Baden, '86

[49] Welfonder, E.; Herden, W.; Kocher, P.; Förster, T., *Hierarchische funktionsbezogene Leittechnik–Dokumentations– und Planungs–Methode*, Prozeßrechensysteme '88, Stuttgart, pp. 603–624, Springer Verlag, März 1988

[50] Wendl, H.; Zienert, J., *Echtzeit–Simulatoren für die Schulung von Kraftwerkspersonal*, Siemens Verlag, power journal, pp. 44–48, Dezember 1992

Session 7:
Fault Injection Environments

Session Chair: Kent Fuchs

System-Level Modeling in the ADEPT Environment of a Distributed Computer System for Real-Time Applications

Anup K. Ghosh and Barry W. Johnson

Center for Semicustom Integrated Systems
Department of Electrical Engineering
University of Virginia
Charlottesville, Virginia 22903

Joseph A. Profeta, III

Union Switch and Signal, Incorporated
A Member of the Ansaldo Group
Pittsburgh, Pennsylvania 15237

Abstract

The design of complex systems in safety-critical applications requires an integrated design and assessment environment. This paper presents the ADEPT environment for designing dependable systems from concept to implementation. An application of ADEPT to modeling a distributed computer system used in real-time embedded train control applications is described. Results from a performance analysis of the distributed computer system model are illustrated. Dependability results are also presented for a second example application.

1   Introduction

The design of complex systems in safety-critical applications requires an integrated design and assessment environment [1]. As requirements for safety and reliability become more stringent, system designs become more complex, and the ability to accurately validate a system design against requirements becomes increasingly difficult, if not impossible [2]. In many design environments, a different set of tools is used for reliability evaluation, performance evaluation, and gate-level design and simulation [3].

A number of software tools exist for evaluating dependability metrics such as reliability and availability for system architectures used in computation-critical applications. Some examples described in the literature are CARE III [4], HARP [5], SHARPE [4], FIGARO [6], UltraSAN [7], DEPEND [9], FIAT [10], and MEFISTO [11]. Similarly, many software tools exist for evaluating performance of system architectures. A few examples described in the literature are SHARPE [4], SARA [8], RESQME [12], SES/Workbench [13], and Ptolemy [14]. It is apparent that many software tools exist to evaluate either dependability or performance.

Few tools, however, exist to evaluate both dependability and performance from a single model. Two examples are SHARPE and START [15]. SHARPE utilizes combina-torial models such as fault-trees and reliability block diagrams together with Markov and semi-Markov models at different levels of abstraction to model a system. START also allows reliability and performance evaluations from a single system architecture model. Neither SHARPE nor START, however, provide a path from the system dependability/performance model to the design of systems at lower levels in the design process. As a result, the design process is fragmented between different modeling and design environments and inconsistencies between models and levels of abstraction can cause costly design errors. The software tools mentioned above lack a single design path that permits incremental refinement of the model from concept to implementation in an integrated performance/dependability evaluation environment. Also the expertise necessary to use the tools is uncommon to most system designers.

In an integrated performance/dependability evaluation design environment, changes in one model are automatically reflected in the other. Using a design environment that permits assessment of performance and dependability measures from a single behavioral model, the design engineer can study trade-off issues between performance and dependability, reliability and safety, and hardware and software designs at an early stage of design [2]. This feature should allow quick exploration of the design space for viable candidate alternatives. The ADEPT (Advanced Design Environment Prototyping Tool) environment described in the next section supports the hierarchical development of systems in an integrated performance/dependability evaluation design environment.

The hierarchical development of complex system designs permits complexity management through abstraction. System-level models constructed quickly can be used for rough performance evaluation to identify bottlenecks in system components. System-level models can also be used to evaluate the reliability of complex systems to aid in redundancy management issues, such as fault detection, isolation and reconfiguration [3]. Dependability measures of complex systems can be extracted from system-level models via simulation at early stages of the design in order to determine if dependability requirements can be satisfied.

194

Sensitivity analysis of assessment metrics against system parameters is especially useful during early stages of design in order to guide design decisions. As design decisions for system components are made, more complex models can be constructed at lower levels of the design using hardware description languages to replace the simpler models without affecting other parts of the model [2]. The step-wise refinement of the model allows incremental validation against performance, dependability, and functional requirements through simulation.

This paper presents the application of ADEPT to the design of a distributed computer system to be used in an embedded train control application. The ADEPT design environment is first presented in Section 2. Next, the distributed computer system architecture employed for the train control application is presented in Section 3. The ADEPT model of the distributed computer system is described in Section 4. A performance analysis of the ADEPT model is given in Section 5. Section 6 presents interpreted ADEPT modules used in modeling dependable systems and a dependability analysis example. Summary, conclusions, and future work are discussed in Section 7.

2 ADEPT design methodology

ADEPT is a design environment that supports hierarchical design from system level abstraction down to instruction set architecture level and gate level design. The design methodology uses the VHSIC (Very High Speed Integrated Circuit) Hardware Description Language (VHDL) IEEE Standard 1076 to model systems at the system, register transfer, logic and circuit levels [16]. ADEPT provides a single path design environment from which behavioral models of systems are used to assess performance and dependability metrics. The integrated modeling environment reduces the need for multiple translators between different modeling environments for design and performance/dependability modeling. Changes in the design are automatically reflected in the performance and dependability models. As a result, inconsistencies between models are eliminated. Additionally, performance and dependability modeling can be performed during the early stages of design. The single-path environment encourages design for dependability and step-wise concurrent validation rather than ad hoc design methodologies which often add redundancy to enhance dependability late in the design process.

The ADEPT environment facilitates mixed-mode simulation of uninterpreted (system-level) models and interpreted (functional) models by using a common hardware description language. This hybrid modeling methodology facilitates hierarchical design and incremental refinement. High-level uninterpreted models can be rapidly constructed for initial performance and dependability measures in order to quickly explore the design space and evaluate trade-offs between designs and alternative candidates. As the design is refined, interpreted models may replace uninterpreted high-level models without affecting the rest of the model to allow more precise simulation results [16].

2.1 ADEPT modules

ADEPT provides a library of building blocks called ADEPT modules. Systems can be constructed from interconnecting the ADEPT modules to model the behavior of the system. The building blocks provide the capability of modeling complex systems using data/control concepts. The ADEPT modules utilize a token-based handshaking protocol to exchange tokens between modules. Tokens are used to represent the flow of data and control information through a system. Each token has a STATUS and COLOR field. The STATUS field is used to implement the handshaking between modules. The COLOR field is used to provide additional information associated with the token.

ADEPT *Color* modules are provided that permit the manipulation of these fields. ADEPT *Control* modules are used to control the flow of tokens through the system. *Delay* modules are used to model the temporal aspects of a system such as those from hardware, software, and hardware/software interactions. Delays can be constant or data dependent. The set of *Fault* modules is used in dependability modeling. The Simple Fault module allows fault injection by selecting a failure density function reflecting the fault arrival process. The Fault Injection module is a more sophisticated version of the Simple Fault module that permits the system designer to model the probability density function of the fault process, the latency, duration, sensitivity, and fault type (transient or permanent) [3]. Error Detection and Error Correction modules are also provided to model self-checking systems [17]. The Repair module can be used to restore failed components based on the component's repair rate. Similarly, the Reconfigure module is used to reconfigure a system after a failure has occurred. This module will essentially remove a component, for example a processor, from the system by switching off its output once the fault module signals that the processor has failed.

Miscellaneous modules are provided for data collection and monitoring. The data collected by these modules can be used for post-simulation analysis. Finally, *Hybrid* modules are used to support mixed-mode simulations of uninterpreted and interpreted models.

2.2 VHDL and Petri net description

Underlying each ADEPT module is a VHDL description and a Colored Petri Net (CPN) representation. Both representations may be directly simulated to obtain performance and dependability metrics. Alternatively, the CPN model may be used to obtain analytical solutions for performance and dependability metrics. The analytical and simulation-based methods to evaluating performance and dependability from the CPN and VHDL models are shown in Figure 1. The CPN representation provides a mathematical foundation for the methodology, allowing formal analysis for performance and reliability [18]. From the CPN model, fault-tree or Markov models may be constructed from provably correct transformations in order to extract dependability metrics such as reliability and safety using classical analytical techniques or simulation [16].

Research in progress has interfaced the ADEPT environment with the Reliability Estimation System Testbed

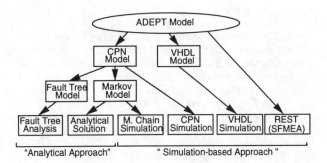

Figure 1: ADEPT Performance and Dependability Analysis Approaches from [16].

(REST) developed at NASA-Langley and the College of William and Mary [19]. The goal of this effort is to perform a Simulatable Failure Modes and Effects Analysis (SFMEA) by observing erroneous tokens that reach system outputs. The REST engine supports SFMEA and automatically generates a Markov model used for determining lower and upper bounds on system unreliability.

Alternatively, the VHDL model of the system can be simulated to obtain performance or dependability measures. The underlying representations are transparent to the user. Thus, no knowledge of Petri Nets or VHDL is required to construct and simulate the models. The ADEPT environment also allows custom VHDL models to be constructed and interconnected with the rest of the model, providing designers with additional flexibility.

The ADEPT design environment provides a graphical schematic capture interface in which system models are constructed by interconnecting ADEPT module instantiations. Currently, Mentor Graphics' Design Architect™ is used as the front-end schematic capture system [20]. Once the design is captured, VHDL code is automatically generated by invoking menu options from the interface. The

VHDL code can be simulated using an IEEE Standard 1076 VHDL simulator. Performance and reliability analysis programs are provided for post-simulation analysis of the model.

3 Distributed system for train control

The railroad industry is actively replacing electromechanical relay-driven safety interlocking systems with microprocessor-controlled interlocking systems. The ultra-safe and time-critical requirements for transit train control demand a safety-critical approach to the design of real-time distributed computer systems used in executing these control applications. Train control functions, in general, need to ensure that a train safely transports passengers and cargo to the proper destination. Train control functions exist at the wayside and on-board trains.

Figure 2 shows the wayside and carborne embedded train control environment. Zone Control Computers (ZCC) at the wayside are responsible for ensuring trains do not enter an unsafe route which may lead to train derailment or collision and catastrophic loss of life or assets. The switches controlled by the ZCCs determine which path a train will take along its destination route. The ZCCs also set signals to warn train drivers when to stop before entering a block of track. A set of Boolean equations is evaluated to control the interlocking of switches and signals so trains can proceed safely along a route.

An architecture of a distributed train control system designed to meet safety-critical and performance requirements is shown in Figure 3. The figure shows VME card cages interconnected by the FDDI high speed serial network. The card cages consist of a variable number of processors and input/output (I/O) devices. The number of processors placed in a card cage is determined by the real-time and dependability requirements of the application. In the wayside application, typically a single processor can execute all the application equations within the real-time

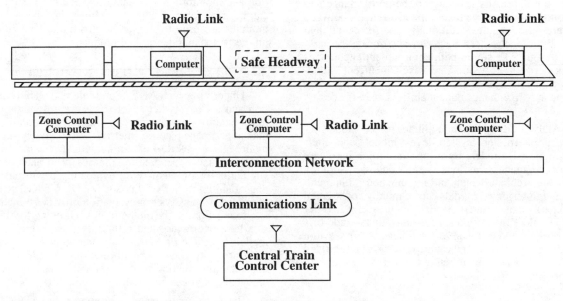

Figure 2: Wayside and Carborne Embedded Train Control Environment

requirement. In some carborne applications such as moving block reference systems, multiple processors may be required to concurrently execute application equations in order to meet the real-time requirements. Additionally, fault-tolerant operation may be necessary in carborne applications in which redundant processors may be used for majority voting of system outputs.

Input devices are sensor systems used for sensing train occupancy of a track, switch setting, track integrity, and signal aspects. Example output devices are actuator systems used to control switches, and highway grade crossing warning systems in wayside systems. In carborne applications, input devices are used to sense velocity and position, while output devices control acceleration and braking. The network interface unit (NIU) is the interface between the FDDI serial network and the VME parallel backplane. The processor, input/output devices, and communication systems are all commercial off-the-shelf (COTS) components.

The system performs its functions according to a time-triggered schedule implemented by the software executive on the processor. System events such as writing outputs, writing input polls, and control equation evaluation are activated by the system executive at fixed periodical intervals of time to facilitate deterministic system behavior.

4 ADEPT model of the system

The uninterpreted ADEPT model of the distributed computer system models the behavior of each component in Figure 3. Separate models exist for the FDDI serial network and media access control (MAC) protocol, the network interface unit (NIU), the processor, the input/output devices, and the VME bus and arbitration unit. This section

first describes the system-level ADEPT model. Next the implementation of the FDDI MAC protocol in ADEPT is described. Lastly, other resource-sharing features of the ADEPT model are briefly mentioned.

4.1 System-level ADEPT model

A top-level diagram of the distributed computer system captured in the Mentor Graphics' Design Architect^{TM} graphical front-end of the ADEPT environment is shown in Figure 4. In this model, a 4-node system is shown, where a node corresponds to a card cage. The system models a typical configuration which may be found in a small wayside application where a single processor node controls the I/O devices in its own card cage and those in remote I/O card cages. A token initialization module creates a network token at the start of simulation. Whenever the token is captured by a node on the network, the node is given access to the network media to transmit messages. A Network Delay element models the transmit delay of data due to the physical distance between nodes. The modules described are all hierarchical modules built up from ADEPT modules.

Larger configurations of distributed systems are easily created by instantiating network nodes and interconnecting them at the top level. Performance results from simulating 4, 8, 16, 32, and 64 node networks are presented in Section 5.

4.2 Modeling the FDDI MAC protocol

The FDDI ANSI X3T9.5 standard guarantees that each active node on the network gains access to the media by allocating synchronous bandwidth to each node. Synchronous bandwidth is the amount of bandwidth measured

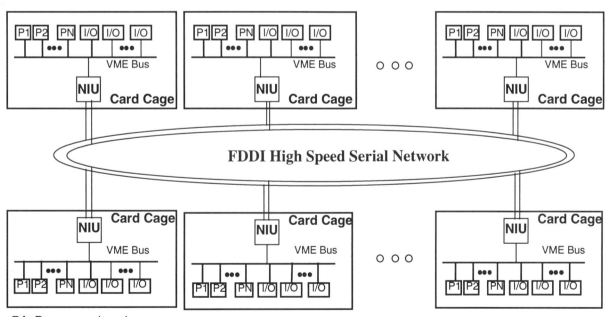

Pi : Processor i card
I/O : Input/Output Cards
NIU: Network Interface Unit

Figure 3: Architecture of a Distributed Computer System Used in Train Control Applications

in milliseconds that is guaranteed to be allocated for a node to transmit data whenever the network token arrives. When a node does not use some or all of its synchronous bandwidth, the unused bandwidth allocated for that node gets added to a pool of asynchronous bandwidth which is time divided among network nodes. The asynchronous bandwidth is determined from the target token rotation time (TTRT) and a token rotation timer (TRT).

The TTRT is a measure of how frequently a node needs to transmit on the network, typically dependent on a node's application. Each node measures the time for the token to rotate around the ring. This time is held in the TRT. As the token arrives at a node, this node subtracts the value in the TRT from the TTRT. This value is placed in the Token Holding Timer (THT). The THT is a measure of how much asynchronous bandwidth is available to a node during this token capture. Once the THT is determined, the TRT is reset and started and the node can now begin synchronous transmission of data limited by the synchronous bandwidth. Asynchronous bandwidth determined from the

THT may then be utilized by the node for remaining data transmissions. The token is then passed to the next node in the network and the process is repeated again. This dynamic allocation of bandwidth results in efficient use of bandwidth which guarantees network latency [22].

The timed token passing protocol of FDDI is modeled in ADEPT by timing network token arrivals. When the network token arrives at a node, the time at which the token arrives is noted by the FDDI Timer module shown in Figure 5. Data frames whose destination is addressed to this node are copied to the FDDI/VME interface module of this node, then passed on to the next node downstream. Data frames originating from this node are consumed or "stripped" from the network. These functions are performed by the Data_Pres2 module in Figure 5. Outgoing data from this node is also sent to the TXR via the FDDI/VME interface. The outgoing data tokens are forwarded to the next node downstream.

The TTRT and synchronous bandwidth allocation is set by the user from the top level shown in Figure 4. These

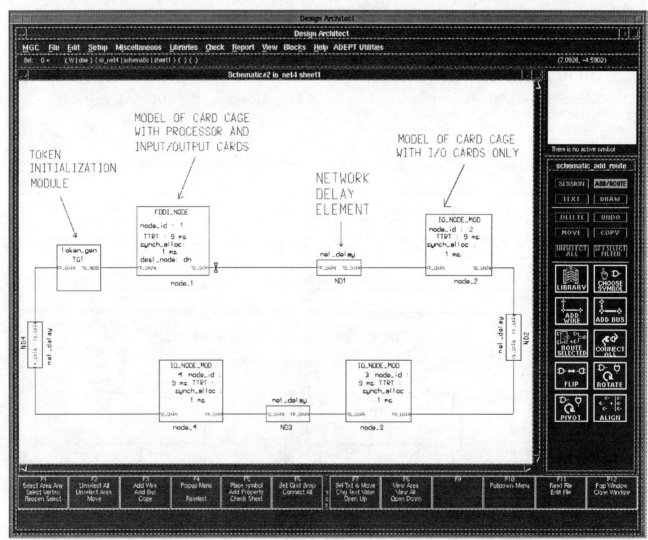

Figure 4: Design Architect Schematic Capture of 4-Node Distributed Computer System ADEPT Model

parameters are passed to the FDDI Timer in Figure 5 which dynamically calculates the token rotation time based on the previous network token arrival time. If the token rotation time is less than the TTRT for the node, then the amount of asynchronous bandwidth available is equal to the difference between these two times. The FDDI Timer performs this calculation and sends the amount of synchronous and asynchronous bandwidth available to the FDDI/VME interface module. The FDDI/VME interface module regulates outgoing data frames from the VME backplane to allow only the maximum number of bytes corresponding to the sum of the synchronous and asynchronous bandwidth to enter the FDDI network.

4.3   Other features modeled by ADEPT

Other resource sharing functions were modeled using ADEPT modules. A VME Bus Arbitration Unit is modeled to perform bus master arbitration between the FDDI/VME Interface and the two possible processor cards. This module determines which device is allowed to be bus master at a given moment in time. Furthermore, the VME master/slave cycle is implemented by this module so that a bus master maintains control of the bus until the slave responds with data to the bus master.

The cyclic polling paradigm of the time-triggered architecture was also modeled using ADEPT modules. Input polls are sent to input cards in local and remote card cages concurrently with output data at the beginning of every I/O cycle. The output data updates actuators at fixed times every cycle. Input cards respond to the polls with a fixed-length data packet to the processor which sourced the poll. Once the input data reaches the processor of origin, a processor delay equivalent to the processing time for the application is incurred. This cycle repeats itself with a fixed period.

5   Performance analysis

The performance metrics of interest in this real-time system are *latency* and *response time*. Latency is a measure of the time it takes for a network node to gain access to the network once data is queued to transmit. Response time is a measure of the time between when a network node sends a request to another node and receives the corresponding data back. The response time includes the network latency. Network throughput and utilization do not become significant performance metrics until network capacity becomes highly loaded.

The response time for receiving data back from a polled card is the sum of network latencies and transmission times for the poll and the data. This sum includes VME bus latency and transmission times and FDDI latency and token rotation times from processor to input card and back to processor. The VME bus is a non-deterministic communication bus and the average token rotation time of the FDDI can vary significantly based on the network loading. Given the complexity of a distributed system that uses different communication media and protocols, this metric is difficult to calculate analytically. Therefore, in order to achieve realistic response times, the network was modeled in the ADEPT environment and the response time for a variable number of nodes was determined through simulation.

A few different configurations of the architecture in Figure 3 were modeled and simulated. Each different model consists of a variable number of I/O nodes of which only 4 input and 4 output cards are utilized. Every configuration contains one node with a processor card and 4 input and 4 output cards. The single processor polls all input cards and writes outputs to all output cards on the network. The architecture configurations were designed to emulate a simplex processing system for a wayside train control application in which the wayside signals and switches are

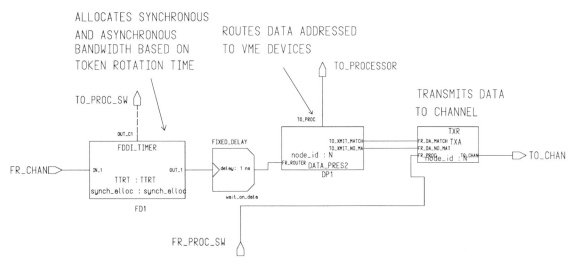

Figure 5: Network Interface Unit

distributed geographically and remotely controlled by the single processor. The models reflect applications from small to moderately large size. The distance assumed between nodes is 1 kilometer.

Figure 6 shows the FDDI *network latency* and *I/O response time* for two different VME bus throughput rates. The data shows that the maximum network latency increases nearly linearly with the number of nodes added to the network. Note that the horizontal axis is not linear. The latency trend shown in Figure 6 is a characteristic of token ring networks. As the number of active nodes on the network increases, the time to access the FDDI network also increases [23]. The second graph shows the I/O response time for two different VME throughput rates. The I/O response time is the time it takes to write all outputs, poll all input devices and receive input data back into the processor. This metric is important in determining the performance of a real-time system based on a time-triggered paradigm with a static I/O cycle. The I/O response time reveals the amount of time necessary to dedicate to I/O tasks in the static I/O cycle. The remainder of the time is spent executing application equations and performing auxiliary tasks such as diagnostics and maintenance. The trend indicated by the data shows that the I/O response time increases nearly linearly with the number of nodes attached to the network for the configuration described in this section. The I/O response times measured through simulation are essential data that the system designer needs in order to plan a conservative yet efficient I/O cycle period.

As a demonstration of a sensitivity analysis using this ADEPT model, the VME bus throughput capacity was initially specified based on a theoretical VME throughput of 50 megabytes per second (MB/s). As the design of this sys-

tem matured, the VME bus throughput capacity was measured at 3 MB/s in a lab prototype. After modifying this parameter in the VME bus model, the results in Figure 6 show that the maximum FDDI network latency for a VME throughput of 3 MB/s is reduced by an order of magnitude from the 50 MB/s VME bus, while the I/O response time for the 3 MB/s VME bus increased by a factor of three over the 50 MB/s VME bus. This phenomena is explained by considering the effect of decreasing the throughput of the VME bus on FDDI network traffic. By decreasing the VME throughput, a lower number of packets will be queued for transmission over the FDDI network at a given point in time compared to a scenario with a higher VME throughput. With less packets waiting to be transmitted, the waiting time for transmission, or network latency, will be reduced.

Conversely, by increasing the delay in transmitting data over the VME bus, all I/O transactions will be delayed because this traffic must use the VME bus. The reduced latency of the FDDI network is not enough to compensate for the increased delay of the 3 MB/s VME bus. As a result, the I/O response time is increased. This example illustrates an application of ADEPT to sensitivity analysis in which varying an input parameter of the model shows a corresponding change in a performance metric.

6   Dependability analysis example

In addition to performance analysis, ADEPT now provides a set of error modules to evaluate system dependability including Mean Time Between Failures (MTBF), Mean Time Between Hazardous Events (MTBHE), and error coverage estimation.

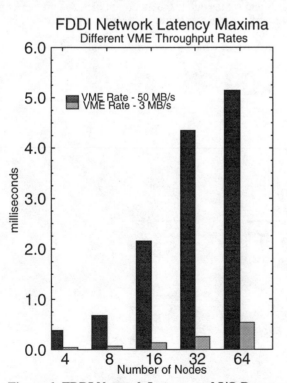
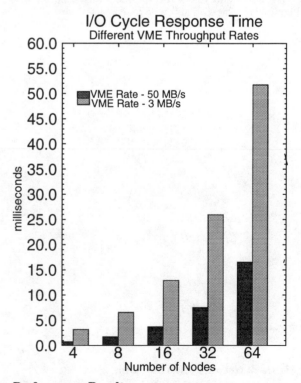

Figure 6: FDDI Network Latency and I/O Response Time Performance Results

200

At a high-level of abstraction used in uninterpreted modeling, the set of fault modules described in Section 2.1 and [17] mark data tokens as either corrupt or error-free by coloring a Boolean field of the token record. For example, the Fault Injection module determines the fault arrival time by sampling the specified failure density function randomly. Once this time in the simulation is reached, any tokens flowing through the fault injection module are marked as corrupt by coloring the Boole1 field of the token record as TRUE. The Error Detection module reads the Boole1 field of tokens and sets its error detected output control line if the token is marked as corrupted. The coverage of the Error Detection module may be entered as a parameter, so that corrupted tokens are flagged only the percentage of time specified by the coverage parameter.

This section presents results from modeling systems at the interpreted information flow level. In the interpreted level of abstraction, the actual data values of information are carried in a record field of each token to allow functional behavior of components to be modeled. For example, the Error Detection module may now be replaced with a Decoder module which performs cyclic redundancy checks on codewords stored in a data field of tokens. Modeling at the interpreted level does not change any of the functionality or behavior of the model used at the uninterpreted level.

Several modules have been written to support fault injection and detection at the interpreted level. The Error Injection module allows the user to select distributions and ranges for sampling a random value to determine the error arrival time, error latency, error duration, error type (transient or permanent), and error vector. At the time randomly generated from the error arrival distribution, an error, whose value is determined from the error vector distribution, is injected into a data field of an arriving token after the error latency time. If the error type is permanent, the

error persists for all arriving tokens, or else the error type is transient and persists for the duration determined by the duration parameter. Similar to the uninterpreted Fault Injection module, the Boole1 field of corrupted tokens is colored TRUE.

Two modules have been written to allow modeling of code-based systems. The Encoder module encodes the data field of arriving tokens in a (7,4) Hamming code. The Decoder module performs a cyclic redundancy check of arriving tokens to ensure that the data field contains a valid (7,4) Hamming code. If the data field contains an invalid codeword, a control token is placed on the control output line of the Decoder module.

Figure 7 illustrates the use of these interpreted modules in a Triple Modular Redundancy (TMR) coded voting system. Input tokens are generated by a Source module and colored with a data value randomly selected from a uniform distribution. Three copies of every input token are fanned out from the Wye module to the three distinct channels. Each channel contains an encoder, a computer, and an Error Injection module. The function of the computer is unspecified in this diagram, but each computer executes an identical algorithm on the input data tokens before producing output tokens. The Error Injection module corrupts the data field of the tokens using the specified distributions for error arrival times, latency, duration, error type, and error value.

The output from each channel is sent to a Majority Voter module. This module waits for all three input tokens to arrive, then performs a bit-wise majority vote on the data fields. Errors in a single channel are masked by the voter. The voted result is written to a single token which is placed on the output of the voter. The voter also performs a vote on the Boole1 field of each of the tokens. If at least two out

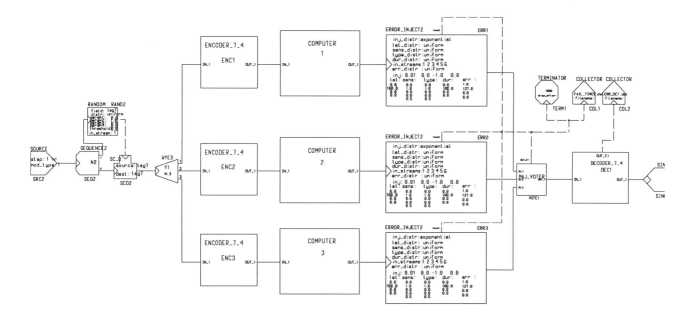

Figure 7: ADEPT Model of a Coded Triple Modular Redundant System

of three of the Boole1 fields are true, then the voter places a control token on the fail line to indicate the system has failed. The time of the failure is recorded by the Collector attached to the fail line. The Terminator module is used to terminate the simulation after the specified number of failures is reached.

The tokens output from the voter are sent to the Decoder. The Decoder checks the data field of the tokens in order to detect errors in the data field. When two out of three inputs to the voter are corrupted, the system has failed, and an incorrect codeword may result on the output. Errors detected by the Decoder are recorded by the Collector module attached to the error line of the Decoder. This configuration models a system whereby a safe shutdown would ensue by detecting codeword corruptions after the TMR system failed. An unsafe failure can occur, however, when the TMR system fails and the voter produces a valid, albeit incorrect codeword. In this case, the error is not detected by the Decoder, and an unsafe failure can result.

The TMR system shown in Figure 7 was simulated with the following parameters: exponential error arrival times with parameter $\lambda = 0.01$, uniform error vector distribution, all tokens are sensitive to the error process, zero error latency and duration, and permanent faults only. In addition, a simplex system consisting of a single channel of the TMR system was simulated for comparison. The 95 percent confidence interval based on the simulation results for the true MTTF of the TMR system is [82.42, 84.08]. The 95 percent confidence interval for the true MTTF of the simplex system is [97.95, 100.63]. The theoretical MTTF for a TMR system has been calculated to be 83.33 for exponential failure parameter $\lambda = 0.01$ [21]. Similarly, the theoretical MTTF for a simplex system with exponential failure parameter $\lambda = 0.01$ is 100.0. In this respect, the simulation results closely mirror the theoretical results.

Although the MTTF for the simplex system is greater

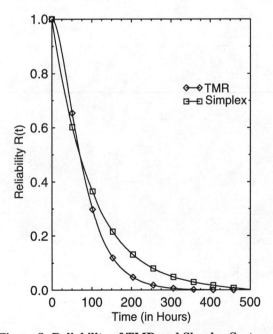

Figure 8: Reliability of TMR and Simplex Systems

than the MTTF for the TMR system, the reliability of the TMR system is greater than the reliability of the simplex systems for short mission times. The reliability of the two systems can be calculated from the simulation data based on the methodology described in [17]. Figure 8 plots the reliability of the TMR and the simplex system as a function of time. The crossover point where the reliability of the TMR system equals the reliability of the Simplex system is approximately 70 hours, as expected from analysis. For mission times less than 70 hours, this TMR system is more reliable than the simplex system.

The MTBHE is calculated from the times when the system failed and the Decoder did not detect an error. The 95 percent confidence interval for the MTBHE for the TMR system is [487.37, 520.46]. The 95 percent confidence interval for the MTBHE of the simplex system is [813.53, 880.43]. The coverage of the Decoder can also be easily quantified as the ratio of the number of errors detected to the number of failures that occurred in the system. The coverage of the Decoder in the TMR system is 0.835, while the coverage for the simplex system is 0.882. These measures are effective in determining the additional benefit of employing a simple Hamming code to increase system safety.

7   Summary and conclusions

The complexity of distributed systems mandates the need for system-level abstraction for the design and assessment of systems employed in computation-critical applications. The ADEPT design methodology described in Section 2 provides an environment for hierarchical design from system-level abstraction to implementation. The ADEPT design environment also allows integrated performance/dependability evaluation of a design model of a system so that changes in the design are automatically reflected in the performance and dependability models. As the design process for a system matures, uninterpreted submodels may be replaced by interpreted hardware description models without affecting the rest of the model. This form of mixed-mode or hybrid modeling permits incremental development of systems from high-levels of abstraction to gate-level models.

The ADEPT environment was used to model a distributed computer system for a real-time train control application. The uninterpreted model allows different configurations of the system to be easily constructed and evaluated. Performance results of interest were obtained via simulation of the model. The FDDI network latency and I/O cycle response times obtained allow the system designer to determine a static I/O cycle that will meet real-time deadlines for variable-sized applications.

Section 6 presented ADEPT modules which were used in constructing an interpreted model of a TMR system. Dependability metrics such as MTBF, MTBHE, and error coverage in addition to reliability plots were obtained from the ADEPT model.

Currently, the interpreted ADEPT error modules are being integrated with an interpreted model of the distributed train control system. The goal of this effort is to determine the safety and reliability of the distributed system through a simulation-based approach.

8   Acknowledgment

We would like to acknowledge the support of the Advanced Technology Group at Union Switch and Signal, Pittsburgh, PA without whom this research effort would not have been possible. We would also like to thank Sanjaya Kumar, of the University of Virginia, for editing and making suggestions in the development of this paper.

References

[1]   R.K. Iyer and W.H. Bryant, Co-Chairs "Computer-Aided Design of Dependable Mission Critical Systems," *Proceedings of the 19th Fault-Tolerant Computing Symposium* (FTCS-19), pp. 416.

[2]   J.B. Dugan, Panelist, "Techniques for Facilitating the Design of Fault Tolerant Systems," *Proceedings of the 19th Fault-Tolerant Computing Symposium* (FTCS-19), pp 417-418.

[3]   E.D. Cutright and B.W. Johnson, "A Simulation-Based Approach to Integrated Performance & Reliability Modeling Using VHDL," *1994 Proceedings Annual Reliability and Maintainability Symposium (RAMS)*, pp. 402- 408.

[4]   R.A. Sahner, K.S. Trivedi, "A Hierarchical, Combinatorial-Markov Method of Solving Complex Reliability Models," *Proceedings of the Fall Joint Computer Conference*, Nov. 1986, pp. 817- 825.

[5]   J.B. Dugan, R. R. Geist, K.S. Trivedi, M. Smotherman, "The Hybrid Automated Reliability Predictor," *AIAA Journal on Guidance Control and Dynamics*, 1986.

[6]   M. Bouissou, "Knowledge modelling and reliability processing: presentation of the FIGARO language and of associated tools," *SAFECOMP 91*, Trondheim, Norway, Nov. 1991.

[7]   W.H. Sanders and W.D. Obal II, "Dependability Evaluation Using UltraSAN," *Proc. of the 23rd FTCS*, 1993, pp. 674-679.

[8]   M.K. Vernon, G. Estrin, "The UCLA Graph Model of Behavior: Support for Performance-Oriented Design," *Proceedings IFIP WG10.1 Working Conference on Methodology for Computer System Design*, Lille, France, Sep. 1983, pp. 47-65.

[9]   K.K. Goswami and R.K. Iyer, "DEPEND: A Simulation-BAsed Environment for System Level Dependability Analysis," Tech Report No. CRCH-91-11, Univ. of Illinois at Urbana-Champaign, 1992.

[10]   Z. Segall, et al., "FIAT - Fault Injection Based Automated Testing Environment," *Proc. 18th Intl. Symp. Fault-Tolerant Computing*, June, 1988, pp.

[11]   E. Jenn, J. Arlat, M. Rimen, J. Ohlsson, and J. Karlsson, "Fault Injection into VHDL Models: The MEFISTO Tool", in *Proceedings of the 24th Fault-Tolerant Computing Symposium* (FTCS-24), pp. 66-75.

[12]   R.F. Fordon, A. McNair, P.D. Welch, "Examples of Using the Research Queuing Package Modeling Environment (RESQME)", *Proceedings 1986 Winter Simulation Conference*, 1986, pp. 494-503.

[13]   Scientific Engineering Software, Inc., *SES/Workbench User's Guide*, Austin, Texas, April 1989.

[14]   B.L. Evans, A. Kamas, and E.A. Lee, "Design and Simulation of Heterogeneous Systems Using Ptolemy," *Proceedings of the 1st Annual RASSP Conference*, Arlington, VA, August 15-18, 1994, pp. 97-105.

[15]   R.T. Goettge and E.W. Brehm, "START - A Tool for Performance and Reliability Evaluation of Hardware/Software Designs," *1991 Workshop on Hardware/Software CoDesign, Austin, Texas, May 1991*, pp. 1-6.

[16]   S. Kumar, R.H. Klenke, J.H. Aylor, B.W. Johnson, R.D. Williams, and R. Waxman, "ADEPT: A Unified System Level Modeling Design Environment," *Proceedings of the 1st Annual RASSP Conference*, Arlington, VA, August 15-18, 1994, pp. 114-123.

[17]   E.D. Cutright, "A Simulation-Based Approach to Integrated Performance & Reliability Modeling Using VHDL," *Ph.D. Dissertation*, University of Virginia, May 1994.

[18]   K. Jenson, "Colored Petri Nets: A High Level Language for System Design and Analysis," in K. Jensen and G. Rozenburg (Eds), *High-Level Petri Nets: Theory and Application*, Springer-Verlag, 1991, pp. 44-119.

[19]   D. Nicol, D. Palumbo, and A. Rifkin, "REST: A Parallelized System for Reliability Estimation," *Proc. of the 1993 RAMS*, Jan. 1993, pp. 436-442.

[20]   Mentor Graphics Corporation, *Design Architect Reference Manual*, Oregon, April, 1992.

[21]   B.W. Johnson, *Design and Analysis of Fault Tolerant Digital Systems*, Addison Wesley Publishing Company, Reading MA, 1989.

[22]   T. Madron, *LANs: Applications of IEEE/ANSI 802 Standards*, John Wiley & Sons, Inc., New York, N.Y., 1989.

[23]   R. Jain, "Performance Analysis of FDDI Token Ring Networks: Effect of Parameters and Guidelines for Setting TTRT," *IEEE Lightwave Telecommunications Systems*, Volume 2, Number 2, May 1991, pp 16-22.

DOCTOR: An IntegrateD SOftware Fault InjeCTiOn EnviRonment for Distributed Real-time Systems *

Seungjae Han, Kang G. Shin, and Harold A. Rosenberg
Real-Time Computing Laboratory
Department of Elec. Engr. and Computer Science
The University of Michigan
Ann Arbor, Michigan 48109–2122.
email: {sjhan, kgshin, rosen}@eecs.umich.edu

Abstract

This paper presents an integrateD sOftware fault injeCTiOn enviRonment (DOCTOR) which is capable of (1) generating synthetic workloads under which system dependability is evaluated, (2) injecting various types of faults with different options, and (3) collecting performance and dependability data. A comprehensive graphical user interface is also provided. The software-implemented fault-injection tool supports three types of faults: memory faults, CPU faults, and communication faults. Each injected fault may be permanent, transient or intermittent. A fault-injection plan can be formulated probabilistically, or based on the past event history. The modular organization of tools is particularly designed for distributed architectures. DOCTOR is implemented on a distributed real-time system called HARTS [1], and its capability has been tested through numerous experiments.

1 Introduction

In real-time systems the correctness of a computation depends not only on the logical correctness of the result but also on the time at which the result is produced [2]. There are a wide range of real-time applications, including continuous-media, transaction processing, and life- and mission-critical controls. Distributed architectures have proved to be well suited for meeting the timing and reliability requirements of these real-time applications. One of the major problems which the designers of distributed real-time systems face is the difficulty of evaluating their dependability. Numerous approaches have been proposed to evaluate system dependability, such as formal methods, analytical modeling, simulation, and experimental measurements.

Validating distributed real-time systems is a challenging task, since both performance and reliability constraints should be considered simultaneously, and their software and hardware architectures are very complex. In fact, the growing complexity of distributed real-time systems, due mainly to their inter-component communications, makes most of the existing evaluation approaches intractable except for fault injection into actual prototype systems. With a common goal to accelerate the occurrence of faults or errors in the system to be tested during operation, numerous fault-injection tools have been developed using both software and hardware techniques [3, 4, 5, 6, 7, 8, 9, 10]. Although hardware-implemented fault injectors closely mimic the real world by producing actual hardware faults, they require additional hardware which is often very expensive and inflexible. Moreover, it is difficult to use them to force a distributed system into certain states, which are essential for testing distributed protocols, because the effect of hardware fault injection is usually unpredictable and hard to reproduce. Hence, more systematic error injection at a higher-level than hardware-component level is necessary for the validation of distributed real-time systems.

Based on the above observations, we have developed a software-implemented fault injection tool which can inject communication faults as well as traditional hardware faults such as memory and CPU faults. The temporal behavior of a fault may be specified as transient, intermittent, or permanent. Beside this basic fault model, it also provides a convenient

---

*The work reported here is supported in part by the Office of Naval Research under Grants N00014-91-J-1115 and N00014-94-1-0229, the National Aeronautic and Space Administration under Grant NAG-1493, and the National Science Foundation under Grant MIP-9203895. Any opinions, findings, and conclusions or recommendations expressed in this paper are those of the authors and do not necessarily reflect the views of the funding agencies.

user interface that allows the user to specify fault-injection timing, thus enabling the user to construct more complicated fault-injection scenarios. Another point we would like to emphasize is the importance of supporting tools for an integrated experiment environment. For example, using only a few application workloads is not sufficient to assess the effects of a wide range of applications on the underlying fault-tolerance mechanisms. The dependence of experimental results on the executing workloads has to be dealt with in a systematic manner.

For ease in generating workloads of various operational characteristics under which system dependability may be evaluated, we have developed a synthetic workload generation tool [11]. Also, to facilitate the collection of both performance and reliability data, an efficient data-collection tool is developed. We have been developing an automated test case selection tool [12] for systematic fault generation on a formal basis. All these tools are controlled through a unified graphic user interface. In contrast to others [5, 6, 10], we integrate tools in a distributed environment.

In real-time systems where time is the most precious resource, fault injection and data collection must be performed with minimum overhead to the target system. Otherwise, the correctness of the validation itself becomes questionable. To minimize the performance overhead of fault injection, only essential functions are performed on the same processor under test and relatively simple fault-injection techniques are employed, which enhances the portability of tools as well. To increase the accuracy and to minimize the overhead of data collection, we have designed a dedicated hardware for data collection.

The proposed software-implemented fault-injection environment, called an integrateD sOftware fault-injeCTiОn enviRonment, or DOCTOR for short, is implemented on HARTS. In the duplicate-match fault-detection experiment, the evaluated dependability measures such as detection coverage & latency are compared with other fault-injection tools. Communication fault injection is used to evaluate a probabilistic distributed diagnosis algorithm. The results show that the algorithm performs better than its predicted worst case, but it is quite sensitive to various coverage and inter-processor test parameters.

The paper is organized as follows. Section 2 presents the motive of our approach by discussing new requirements for fault injection in distributed real-time systems. Section 3 describes the organization of DOCTOR and its components. Section 4 presents the fault model used in DOCTOR. In Section 5, we discuss the implementation issues. Section 6 presents experiments and their results to demonstrate the usefulness of DOCTOR. The paper concludes with Section 7.

2 Fault-Injection Requirements

There are four major attributes of fault injection: a set of faults F, a set of activations A which specify the workload used to exercise the system, a set of readouts R, and a set of derived measures M which correspond to dependability measures such as MTTF [5]. The $FARM$ sets for fault injection in distributed real-time systems are more complex than those for single processor systems, because the fault-tolerance mechanisms of distributed real-time systems utilize multiple processors connected by communication networks. Considerable complexities or difficulties exist in evaluating distributed diagnosis, processor group membership, replicated process group for fault masking or recovery, fault-tolerant communication, and so on. A sophisticated fault-injection scenario in both time and space dimension should be constructed to test execution paths that may occur very rarely during normal operation.

The requirements for fault injection in distributed real-time systems are enumerated below.

1. The fault model should include faults on communication links and communication adaptor circuitry as well as faults inside a processing node such as memory faults, CPU faults, or bus faults.

2. The fault injector should be able to coerce the whole target system to follow a certain intended execution path, which requires it to orchestrate all participants' behaviors. This is not achievable by randomly selecting fault type and injection timing. A systematic fault-selection aid tool and a flexible user interface are necessary for this purpose.

3. The operational characteristics of workload should be easily adjustable, especially in terms of the communication activities.

4. Fault injection or data collection must require as little modification to the target system code as possible. The performance overhead or interference by these two should also be minimized and quantifiable.

5. To obtain high-resolution timing data such as error-propagation delay or error-recovery latency, a special time-stamping technique should be employed, because clock-synchronization skews

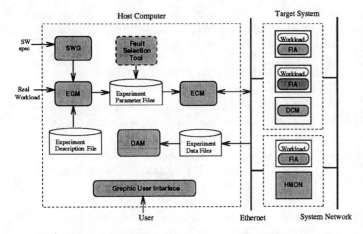

Figure 1: The organization of DOCTOR

among different processing nodes may cause unacceptably inaccurate time measurements. We solve this problem by using dedicated hardware.

3 Integrated Experiment Environment

We provide a complete set of tools for automated fault-injection experiments. As mentioned earlier, this tool set is intended for use in distributed real-time systems (whereas most of other existing tools are intended for single processor systems). Figure 1 shows the organization of DOCTOR which forms a modular software architecture. In the distributed system architecture assumed, a host computer works as a console node and several processing nodes are connected via a system communication network and linked to the host node by an Ethernet. Each node can be a bus-based multiprocessor group.

One distinct feature of this organization is the separation of components of the host computer from those of the target system. It has the advantage of reducing the run-time interference with the target system caused by fault injection, because each component runs separately and only essential components are executed on the target system. It also increases the portability of DOCTOR, since the highly system-dependent part is isolated from the rest.

The fault injector, the core part of DOCTOR, consists of three modules: Experiment Generation Module (EGM), Experiment Control Module (ECM), and Fault Injection Agent (FIA). Data Collection Module (DCM) collects experimental data during each experiment, and they are analyzed off-line after completing the experiment by Data Analysis Module (DAM). To obtain more accurate timing data with smaller performance overhead, Hardware MONitor (HMON) can be used in the place of DCM. Synthetic Workload Generator (SWG) [11] is provided to generate various artificial workloads. A tool for systematic fault selection [12] is currently under development. In addition, a comprehensive Graphic User Interface (GUI) and an automated multi-run experiment facility are provided to facilitate and automate the design and execution of fault-injection experiments. Fault-injection experiments are completely transparent to the workloads.

Each fault-injection experiment with specific workloads is called a *run*. In a fault-injection experiment, one of the factors that determine the quality of analysis results will be the number of runs. Therefore, it is very useful to automate multi-run experiments. The key problem in experiment automation is the synchronization and re-initialization of several processes involved. The level of re-initialization required depends on the status of the target system after completing each run. In some cases, it may be necessary to reset the whole system, and in some other cases, the restart of workloads may suffice. We support both levels.

3.1 EGM

The first role of EGM is to generate executable images of workloads which will be downloaded (from the host) to the target system. A workload could be run on a single processing node or be distributed among a number of nodes. The user can use real programs as workloads, or can rely on SWG for artificially-generated workloads. In either case, when the workloads are compiled, the symbol-table information is extracted to be referenced by ECM.

The second role of EGM is to parse the experiment description file supplied by the user. The experiment description file describes the experiment plan which contains the information about the fault type and injection timing. EGM generates an experiment parameter file for each node involved in the experiment. These files are used by ECM to determine when to start fault injection, which type of fault to be injected, and how many times the experiment will be run, and so on.

3.2 FIA & ECM

FIA receives commands from ECM via Ethernet and executes them by injecting faults or making workloads wait/start/stop. It also reports its activities to DCM or HMON, such as the injection time, location, type, etc. FIA is a separate process which runs on the same processor where the workload is running.

ECM functions as an external controller. It synchronizes the start/end of each run among several nodes, and sets up an experiment environment by downloading executable images of the workload, FIAs, DCMs, and even system software if needed. ECM utilizes the experiment parameter files and the information received from FIAs to create proper commands to FIAs. For example, the symbol-table information which is contained in the experiment parameter files is used to decide memory fault-injection locations. At the same time, the information about run-time stack location from FIA is used. FIA and ECM share the responsibility of past event history management, which is particularly important for communication fault injection.

3.3 SWG

To evaluate the dependability of fault-tolerance mechanisms, we must measure dependability parameters like detection coverage and latency while executing appropriate workloads. A workload produces demands for the system resources, so the structure and behavior of the workload may affect the experimental result significantly. In DOCTOR, the user can use a synthetic workload produced by SWG instead of real programs, so that experiments can be conducted under various workload conditions. Because a synthetic workload is parameterized in the high-level description format, the user can easily control the workload characteristics.

3.4 DCM & HMON

The basic function of these tools is to log the events generated by the monitored object. The FIAs and fault-tolerance mechanisms under test generate such events, and if performance is monitored together with dependability, the event triggering instructions need to be placed in the operating system kernel. These events are the categorized, time-stamped information about the activities which we want to monitor. For example, in fault-detection experiments, two types of data are needed for the post analysis. One is the history of fault-injection reports, and the other is that of error-detection reports. Generation of events is the only overhead to the monitored object. DCM/HMON runs continuously during experiments, and its function is fairly passive. [1]

If the goal of an experiment requires very high-resolution timing measurements, the time-stamp resolution supported by the underlying operating system or hardware may not be sufficient. Moreover, if the objects to be monitored are distributed among several nodes, the time-stamps of collected events are difficult to compare, because the tightness of clock syn-

---

[1] To minimize performance interference, DCM usually runs on a processor different from those on which workloads or fault-tolerance mechanisms run, but on the same backplane-bus(on the same node). The collected data are stored in files and used later for post data analysis.

Fault types		Location
Single bit	Set	Stack/Heap
Compensating	Reset	Global variables
Single byte	Toggle	User-code
Multi bytes	User defined	OS Kernel area
User defined		User defined

Table 1: Memory fault options

chronization among the nodes may not reach the desired time-stamp resolution. In order to obtain high-resolution time-stamps (e.g., 25 $n$sec), a hardware-implemented monitor (HMON) is developed. When a log request arrived through the backplane-bus, HMON generated a time-stamp and stores the time-stamped event into its local memory. It also maintains its own synchronization network so that necessary events are signaled to other HMONs. As a result, the measurement accuracy becomes independent of the system clock synchronization.

4 Fault Model

Hardware or software faults affect the various aspects of the system state or operational behavior, such as memory or register contents, program control flow, clock value, the condition of communication links, and so on. Modifying memory contents has been a basic technique used in software-implemented fault injectors. Faults are likely to (eventually) contaminate certain parts of memory, so memory faults can represent not only RAM errors but also emulate faults occurring in the other parts of the system. Though the memory fault model is quite powerful, some faults may affect system memory contents in a very subtle and nondeterministic way, and hence, it is very difficult to emulate such a faulty behavior with memory fault injection alone. A more sophisticated fault model is therefore required.

Currently, DOCTOR supports three types of faults: memory faults, CPU faults, and communication faults. The user can choose any combination of these three types to induce appropriate abnormal conditions. For each fault type, one can specify a number of options as shown in Tables 1, 2 and 3. We are also adding the capability of system-level error injection, such as making processes slow or fast, terminating or suspending processes, corrupting clock/timer services, corrupting system-call services, and so forth.

4.1 Memory Faults & CPU Faults

A memory fault can be injected as a single bit, two-bit (compensating), whole byte, or burst (of multiple bytes) error. The contents of memory at the selected

Fault types		Location
Single bit	Set	Data registers
Compensating	Reset	Address registers
Single byte	Toggle	Stack pointers
Whole word	User defined	Program counter
User defined		Status register

Table 2: CPU fault options

Fault types	Options
Lose messages	Faulty-link selection
Duplicate messages	Faulty-direction selection
Alter messages	Altered location
Delay messages	Altering operation
User defined	Delay control

Table 3: Communication fault options

address are partially or totally set, reset, or toggled. Beside the fault type, it is important to control the location of memory to be contaminated. The injection location either can be explicitly specified by the user, or can be chosen randomly from the physical memory space. It is sometimes desirable for a fault to be injected only into a memory section, such as the user program code, the user stack/heap, or the system software area.

CPU faults can occur in data registers, address registers, the data fetching unit, control registers, the op-code decoding unit, ALU, and so on. The exact effect of faults in each processor component is highly architecture-dependent. Therefore, to emulate actual faults more directly, the utilization of detailed knowledge about the specific CPU architecture is required. However, depending on the underlying hardware and system software, accessibility to hardware components varies widely. One way to overcome this limitation is to inject erroneous effects rather than faults themselves. We chose to emulate the consequences of CPU faults in the architecture-independent level. For example, the control flow may be altered by bus line errors, instruction decoding logic errors, condition code flag errors, or control register errors (e.g., program counter). Instead of dealing with each possible case, the contents of CPU registers are used as the targets of fault injection.

4.2   Communication Faults

The communication faults in DOCTOR can cause messages to be lost, altered, duplicated, or delayed. If a node has multiple incoming and outgoing links, as in point-to-point architectures, different fault types can be specified separately for each link. The user can specify whether outgoing, incoming, or all messages are lost at the faulty link. Messages can be lost intermittently, with a probability distribution specified by the user, or alternately, every message can be lost during a certain period. Messages may be altered in a similar manner as memory faults, i.e., by corrupting single bit, two-bit compensating, or burst errors. The user can specify whether the error is to be injected into the body of a message or into its header. For delayed messages, the delay time can either be deterministic or follow some probability distribution. In addition to this set of predefined communication fault types, the user can define additional communication faults. These user-defined faults may be combinations of the predefined fault types, and may be based on the contents of individual messages or on the past message history. This variety of communication failures, and the ability to combine existing fault types and define new fault types, allow for the injection of a variety of failure semantics, including Byzantine failures.

4.3   The Control of Injection Timing

One important aspect of our fault model is its fine controllability of the fault-injection timing. In fact, the capability of injecting a proper fault instance into a proper location at a proper time is essential to the fault-injection experiments. Our fault model supports three temporal types of faults: transient, intermittent, and permanent. A transient fault is injected only once, and an intermittent fault is injected repeatedly. When injecting an intermittent fault, the user can specify the probability distribution of the fault recurrence interval. Several types of distributions like uniform distribution, exponential distribution, normal distribution, Weibull distribution and binomial distribution are provided. The user can specify the necessary constants of each distribution type, and similar probability distributions are provided for fault durations. Besides its (pre-defined) probabilistic injection timing control, DOCTOR allows the user to design fault-injection scenarios with user-specified timing control in either time-based specification or history-based specification. So, the user can directly control injection timing and fault durations with absolute or relative specifications.

5   Implementation on HARTS

The first target system[2] of DOCTOR is HARTS. HARTS is comprised of multiprocessor nodes connected by a point-to-point interconnection network. Each HARTS node consists of several Application

---

[2]We are currently porting DOCTOR to a VxWorks based distributed real-time system.

Processors (APs) and a Network Processor (NP). The APs are used for executing application tasks, and the NP handles most of communication processing. In the current configuration, the nodes of HARTS are VMEbus-based Motorola 68040 systems. Each HARTS node has 1–3 AP cards, an NP card, and a communication network interface board. Each node of HARTS runs an operating system called HARTOS[3] [15]. A Sun workstation serves as a console. Applications and system software are downloaded from this workstation through a dedicated local Ethernet. In implementing the fault injector on HARTS, we use three techniques to inject faults concurrently with the execution of workloads. Simple memory overwrites are used for injecting memory faults, a special fault-injection protocol layer is used for injecting communication faults, and modification of CPU registers is used for injecting CPU faults.

For memory fault injection, when a pre-determined time is reached, ECM sends the corresponding FIA a message, which contains the address, the fault duration and the mask pattern. The content of the addressed location is masked by the specified pattern using AND (reset) operation, OR (set) operation, or XOR (toggle) operation. HARTS does not have any memory protection,[4] so FIA can easily overwrite any memory area. If the type of fault to be injected is permanent, the problem is not so easy, because the only way to facilitate true-permanent memory faults is to make use of system-provided memory protection support. Because HARTS is not equipped with memory protection support, we use pseudo-permanent memory faults. A permanent fault is emulated as an intermittent fault with a very small recurrence interval. FIA refreshes the contents of the fault location periodically. Another issue in injecting a memory fault is the problem of deciding the location of injection. Again, because HARTS does not use virtual memory, the symbol-table information can be used in an absolute address form.

A transient/intermittent type of CPU fault requires fault injection at run-time. The way we use is invoking a trap to the associated process and performing fault injection while the process is frozen, then allowing the process to continue execution again, which is similar to [7, 10]. In HARTOS, some of the CPU registers contents are saved in the task control block and others are saved in the run-time stack, when a context switch occurs. The necessary location information about the task control block and run-time stack is obtained through call-out functions provided by the operating system. Since FIA is assigned a higher scheduling priority than other processes, it can force a process to be context-switched and return the control to the trapped process after modifying the saved register values. This can be done very quickly because the context-switching in real-time systems is usually very fast. However, the efficient injection of permanent CPU faults is difficult to achieve. One possible way (that we chose) is changing program instructions at compile time. For example, modifying all of the instructions using a faulty ALU can emulate the permanent ALU fault, and overwriting a register's contents in the middle of the program execution whenever it is used can emulate the permanent register fault. By replacing or adding instructions at the assembly language level, more types of permanent CPU faults can be emulated.

Communication faults are injected by a special protocol layer, which accepts commands from FIA to determine fault instances to be injected and to build the message history structure. The fault-injection layer may be placed between any two protocol layers in the protocol stack, but is normally inserted directly below the protocol or user program to be tested. The current implementation takes advantage of the features of the x-kernel, in which our communication protocols are implemented. The fault-injection layer is transparent to other protocol layers and does not add or modify the message header or data at all. The fault-injection layer need not be modified when it is placed between different protocol layers. If more complex fault scenarios are desired, copies of the fault-injection layer may be placed in multiple places in the protocol graph. The fault-injection layer operates by intercepting the UPI [5] operations between the protocol under test and the lower layer protocols. If it detects an operation during which a fault should be injected, based on commands from the FIA, it performs the appropriate fault injection operation. All other operations are simply passed through without modification. Outgoing and incoming messages are lost by intercepting the appropriate send and receive operations, and then discarding the message. Messages are altered by intercepting the send or receive operation, and then changing the mes-

---

[3] HARTOS is primarily an extension of the functionality of pSOS^{+m} [13]. While pSOS^{+m} provides system support within a node, an extended version of the x-kernel [14] coordinates communication between nodes.

[4] Like most other real-time systems, HARTS does not employ virtual memory or memory protection to reduce the unpredictability in memory access caused by page faults.

---

[5] All protocols in the x-kernel are implemented using same interface between layers, called the Uniform Protocol Interface (UPI).

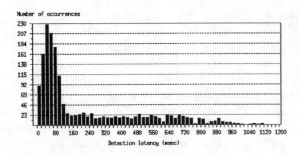

Figure 2: Error latency histogram of case 4

	case 1	case 2	case 3	case 4
matrix size	30x50x30	30x50x30	40x80x40	40x80x40
sampling freq	1/50	1/150	1/50	1/150
total runs	3000	1000	1000	3000
detection	2032	323	574	1756
error latency				
min(msec)	6	6	6	6
max(msec)	476	440	1018	1218
mean(msec)	89.10	118.49	206.76	251.57
variance	95.96^2	111.81^2	263.34^2	272.58^2

Table 4: Summary of error latency data

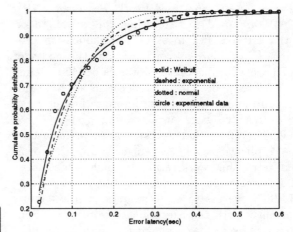

Figure 3: Fitting *cdf* of case 1

sage contents before passing it on to the next protocol layer. Messages are delayed by stopping the current message and then scheduling a future message with the same contents, using the x-kernel event library. In order to support the user-defined fault classes, we allow messages to be stored in a message history. All references to past messages in the user-defined fault description are translated into the x-kernel map library operations.

6 Experiments and Analyses
6.1 Error Latency Measurement

The goal of this experiment is to illustrate how the dependability parameters of a fault-tolerance mechanism can be measured with DOCTOR. Specifically, we measure error latency and analyze its probabilistic distribution. Error latency is the elapsed time between a fault/error injection and its detection. The

	Weibull			Exponential		Normal		
case	λ	α	error	λ	error	μ	σ	error
1	7.73	0.82	0.11	11.5	0.18	0.07	0.09	0.30
2	6.66	0.89	0.18	8.09	0.21	0.09	0.15	0.16
3	3.01	0.59	0.35	5.06	0.67	0.06	0.43	0.40
4	3.06	0.76	0.31	4.00	0.45	0.18	0.33	0.54

Table 5: Estimated distribution function parameters

experiment specification is described below. The error-detection scheme used in this experiment is the duplicate-match detection mechanism. Two identical workloads are executed simultaneously on two distinct APs of a HARTS node, and each time an element of the result matrix is generated, it is sent to the comparator program which is run on a third AP of the same HARTS node. In this experiment, a program for floating-point matrix multiplication is used as a workload. It consists of an infinite loop of the initialization step of input matrix data and the multiplication step. Since the software-implemented comparator has only limited capability of data comparison, buffers are used to store the data from workload executions and only part of the stored data are compared, so that others are discarded.

The size of matrices to be multiplied and the frequency of data sampling for comparison are the factors to be altered. Memory faults are injected into the memory section allocated for matrix data. For simplicity, we chose to inject one byte toggling transient memory faults. Because the workload keeps on re-initializing input matrix data after completing the whole multiplication, some of injected faults are overwritten in the re-initialization step. It is why the injected faults are not always detected. Four cases are tested and measured, and the results are summarized in Table 4. One observation is that the larger matrix case has a larger mean error latency, even if the same sampling frequency is used. This is because it takes longer to generate each element to be compared. Increasing the sampling frequency also shortens the mean of error latency. Figure 2 shows the histogram of error latency for case 4 (screen dump of GUI).

The latency of fault recovery is often assumed to

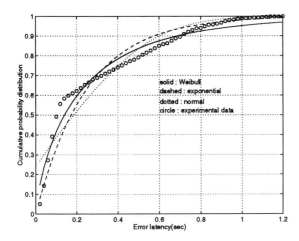

Figure 4: Fitting *cdf* of case 4

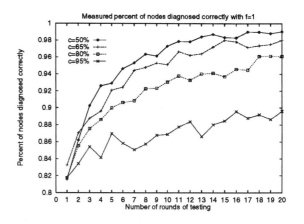

Figure 5: Percent of nodes diagnosed correctly with 1 failure mode, measured

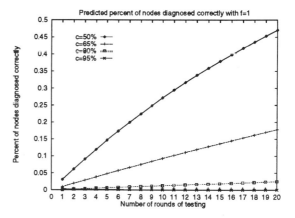

Figure 6: Percent of nodes diagnosed correctly with 1 failure mode, predicted

be distributed exponentially. However, the authors of [4, 6] observed that this was not true. In [4], Finelli showed that error latency did not fit an exponential distribution, but it rather followed the Gamma or Weibull distribution. On the other hand, in [6], Barton showed that error latency followed the normal distribution. To compare our experimental results with the others mentioned above, we performed the least-squares fit of our data to three types of distribution: normal, Weibull, and exponential distributions.

The estimated parameters of each distribution is given in Table 5 by minimizing the mean square errors. The experimental data and fitted cumulative distribution curves are plotted in Figures 3 and 4. The analysis shows that the Weibull distribution fits our data best except for case 2. Normal and exponential distributions have "inconsistent" fitting errors. Only when most errors can be detected soon after fault injection like case 1, the exponential distribution fits well, as expected. When matrix size is small but the result is compared infrequently as in case 2, or when matrix size is large but the result is compared frequently as in case 3, the normal distribution fits well, as compared to other cases. This may be because the randomness of latency increases in these cases. These results conflict Barton's result which also utilized software-implemented fault injection, but rather match Finelli's result which was obtained by hardware-implemented fault injection. This difference can be explained by the detection mechanism and experiment tools. Although the size of data set is not large enough and the workload characteristics are varied only in a limited way, the experimental results indicate that the experimental accuracy of DOCTOR is close to that of hardware-implemented fault injector.

6.2 Evaluation of a Diagnosis Algorithm

In this section, we demonstrate the usefulness of software fault injection as a tool for validating dependability models of distributed protocols. By using the communication fault injection capabilities of DOCTOR, we are able to collect data on the behavior of a distributed diagnosis algorithm under a wide range of conditions. This data can then be used both to validate the predicted performance of the algorithm, and to assist in the selection of various parameters used during the execution of the algorithm.

The algorithm we chose to test is the probabilistic distributed diagnosis algorithm given in [16]. This algorithm is intended for the diagnosis of distributed systems of arbitrary connectivity. A run of the diagnosis algorithm consists of a number of rounds of testing. For the purposes of the diagnosis algorithm, a test graph, which is a subgraph of the undirected processor connectivity graph, is selected. Each node runs an identical test task on each round, and then exchanges the results with its neighbors in the test graph. The local result is then compared with the results received, and, if the number of mismatches is greater than some threshold, the node is considered to have failed that round. This is repeated for some number of rounds. If the number of rounds in which the node failed is greater than a second threshold, then the node is considered to be faulty.

This algorithm has a number of parameters that determine the effectiveness of the algorithm. Some of these parameters are selectable by the user, while others are functions of the system environment. The parameters that we look at in this experiment are: the number of rounds of testing (r), the coverage of interprocessor tests (c), and the number of failure modes of a test (f). The coverage of a test is the probability of a faulty processor generating an incorrect result on that test. The number of failure modes of a test is the number of possible incorrect results that a faulty processor can generate for that test. Other parameters, which we will fix for these experiments, are the probability of failure of a processor (p), the interconnection topology, and the test graph.

In the experiment, the diagnosis algorithm has two parameters to be altered, the probability of failure of a processor, and the interprocessor test coverage. The fault injection scenario is described in the following. Each time a run of experiment is initialized, the fault status of each node is independently chosen, with a probability of failure, p. On a faulty node, whenever a diagnosis-message is sent out by the diagnosis algorithm, the message history is checked to determine whether any previous diagnosis-message of the same round has been sent to another node. If not, the diagnosis-message contents are altered to a randomly selected value from the range of failure modes, with a probability equal to the test coverage. If any message of the same round had already been sent out, then the message history is used to ensure that all messages from the same round are same.

In our experiments, we chose to connect the processors of HARTS in a 9-node wrapped-square mesh. We fixed the probability of node failure at 25%. Selecting such a high figure allows us to test the algorithm under worse than expected conditions. The values of the other parameters were selected to be: $c = 50\%$, 65%, 80%, and 90%; $f = 1, 10, 20$; $r = [1..20]$. We ran 500 iterations of the diagnosis algorithm with each combination of these parameters. The results of these experiments are summarized in Figures 5 through 8. There are a number of observations to be drawn from

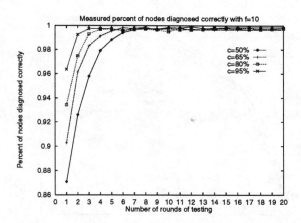

Figure 7: Percent of nodes diagnosed correctly with 10 failure modes, measured

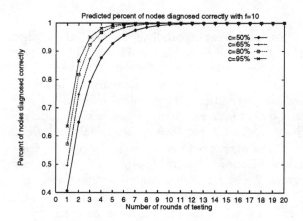

Figure 8: Percent of nodes diagnosed correctly with 10 failure modes, predicted

this data.

The first thing to notice is that in almost all cases, the measured diagnostic accuracy of the algorithm exceeded that predicted by the probabilistic model in [16], in many cases by a significant percentage. This is because the model makes a number of pessimistic assumptions, and therefore predicts only the worst-case performance of the algorithm. As a result, this distributed diagnosis algorithm may actually be appropriate for use in more systems than might be expected based only on the probabilistic model. As we see in Figure 7, using tests with 10 failure modes, even with interprocessor test coverage as low as 50%, the algorithm achieves nearly 100% correct diagnosis within 7 rounds of testing. When the test coverage is 95%, only 3 rounds are required to reach 100%. As predicted by the asymptotic analysis of the algorithm in [16], both the measured and predicted diagnostic accuracy converge to 100% as the number of tests increase, but the measured accuracy starts much higher, and converges more quickly than predicted.

One other interesting observation can be made by comparing the graphs in Figures 5 and 6 to those in Figures 7 and 8, respectively. In the cases where f, the number of failure modes, is 1, we observe that the accuracy of the diagnosis actually improves as the interprocessor test coverage decreases. This is because, when $f=1$, the faulty processors will always match when comparing their results with other faulty processors, and thus will be more likely to diagnose themselves as correct when the test coverage is high. This effect appears both in the predicted and observed behavior of the algorithm. When f is increased to 10, this effect disappears. These results indicate that tests with simple binary (e.g., good/bad) results are not a good choice when using comparison-based distributed diagnosis algorithms.

7 Conclusion

In this paper, we have presented an integrated flexible fault-injection environment called DOCTOR. It utilizes software-implemented fault injection and is intended for the validation and evaluation of distributed real-time systems. We implemented a fault injector which supports a wide range of fault type and injection options, and also developed several supporting tools such as the data-collection tool, the synthetic workload generator, and the graphic user interface. DOCTOR was implemented on a real-time distributed system, HARTS, and extensive experiments were conducted, demonstrating its power and utility. In addition, we are extending the functionality of DOCTOR in various directions. A hardware-implemented data collecting mechanism is developed, which provides high-resolution time-stamps with minimum performance overhead. We are also exploring the issues involved in formalizing both the specification of fault injection experiments, and the systematic selection of the faults to be injected. Once these extensions are completed, we will conduct more practical experiments, particularly in the area of fault-tolerant real-time communication.

References

[1] K. Shin, "HARTS: A distributed real-time architecture," *IEEE Computer*, vol. 24, no. 5, pp. 25–35, May 1991.

[2] J. Stankovic, "Misconceptions about real-time computing," *IEEE Computer*, vol. 21, no. 10, pp. 10–19, October 1988.

[3] K. Shin and Y. Lee, "Measurement and application of fault latency," *IEEE Trans. Computers*, vol. C-35, no. 4, pp. 370–375, April 1986.

[4] G. Finelli, "Characterization of fault recovery through fault injection on ftmp," *IEEE Trans. Reliability*, vol. 36, no. 2, pp. 164–170, June 1987.

[5] J. Arlat, Y. Crouzet, and J. Laprie, "Fault injection for dependability validation of fault-tolerant computing systems.," in *Proc. FTCS*, pp. 348–355, June 1989.

[6] J. Barton, E. Czeck, Z. Segall, and D. Siewiorek, "Fault injection experiments using fiat," *IEEE Trans. Computers*, vol. 39, no. 4, pp. 575–581, April 1990.

[7] G. Kanawati, N. Kanawati, and J. Abraham, "FER-RARI: A tool for the validation of system dependability properties," in *Proc. FTCS*, pp. 336–344. IEEE, 1992.

[8] K. Echtle and M. Leu, "The EFA fault injector for fault-tolerant distributed system testing," in *Workshop on Fault-Tolerant Parallel and Distributed Systems*, pp. 28–35. IEEE, 1992.

[9] H. Rosenberg and K. Shin, "Software fault injection and its application in distributed systems," in *Proc. FTCS*, pp. 208–217. IEEE, 1993.

[10] W. Kao, R. Iyer, and D. Tang, "FINE: A fault injection and monitoring environment for tracing the UNIX system behavior under faults," *IEEE Trans. Software Engineering*, vol. 19, no. 11, pp. 1105–1118, November 1993.

[11] D. Kiskis, *Generation of Synthetic Workloads for Distributed Real-Time Computing Systems*, PhD thesis, University of Michigan, August 1992.

[12] H. Rosenberg and K. Shin, "Specification and generation of fault-injection experiments," in *Proc. FTCS*. IEEE, 1995. Submitted for publication.

[13] *pSOS+/68K User's Manual*, Integrated Systems Inc., 1992.

[14] N. Hutchinson and L. Peterson, "The x-Kernel: An architecture for implementing network protocols," *IEEE Trans. Software Engineering*, vol. 17, no. 1, pp. 1–13, January 1991.

[15] K. Shin, D. Kandlur, D. Kiskis, P. Dodd, H. Rosenberg, and A. Indiresan, "A distributed real-time operating system," *IEEE Software*, pp. 58–68, September 1992.

[16] D. Fussell and S. Rangarajan, "Probabilistic diagnosis of multiprocessor systems with arbitrary connectivity," *Proc. FTCS*, pp. 560–565, 1989.

Assessing the Effects of Communication Faults on Parallel Applications[1]

João Carreira, Henrique Madeira, and João Gabriel Silva
Departamento de Engenharia Informática
Universidade de Coimbra
Vila Franca -Pinhal de Marrocos. 3000 Coimbra - Portugal
Email:{jcar, henrique, jgabriel}@mercurio.uc.pt

Abstract

This paper addresses the problem of injection of faults in the communication system of disjoint memory parallel computers and presents fault injection results showing that 5% to 30% of the faults injected in the communication subsystem of a commercial parallel computer caused undetected errors that lead the application to generate erroneous results. All these cases correspond to situations in which it would be virtually impossible to detect that the benchmark output was erroneous, as the size of the results file was plausible and no system errors had been detected. This emphasises the need for fault tolerant techniques in parallel systems in order to achieve confidence in the application results. This is especially true in massively parallel computers, as the probability of occurring faults increase with the number of processing nodes. Moreover, in disjoint memory computers, which is the most popular and scalable parallel architecture, the communication subsystem plays an important role, and is also very prone to errors. CSFI (Communication Software Fault Injector) is a versatile tool to inject communication faults in parallel computers. Faults injected with CSFI directly emulate communication faults and spurious messages generated by non fail-silent nodes by software, allowing the evaluation of the impact of faults in parallel systems, and the assessment of fault tolerant techniques. The use of CSFI is nearly transparent to the target application as it only requires minor adaptations. Deterministic faults of different nature can be injected without user intervention and fault injection results are collected automatically by CSFI.

1. Introduction

Parallel computing systems are widely used nowadays as platforms for running complex scientific programs as well as other computing-intensive applications. These systems can basically be divided in two classes: those where processors access a single shared memory, and those with physically distributed memory, interconnected by some network, where processors communicate through message passing.

Shared memory machines are limited to a small number of processors since the accesses to the centralised memory create a bottleneck in the system. As opposite, machines with distributed memory scale well to a larger number of processors as there is no centralised storage and the communications bandwidth is larger.

On both cases, the user must be aware that the likelihood of a processor failure during a long-running application increases with the number of processors, and the failure of a single processor can crash the entire system. Detecting errors and recovering from faults is thus a major concern on these systems. Furthermore, in disjoint memory parallel computers there is a new system element which is an additional source of errors regarding traditional computers: the communication system.

In fact, communication media are usually very prone to electrical interferences. Their consequence is the activation of errors in the transmitted data, which is delivered to a processing node and can cause node failures or computational errors. The effect of such errors can be as critical as errors which occur in processor circuitry.

Fault injection in the communication subsystem is a powerful approach to assess the consequences of communication faults in distributed applications and the validation of specific fault tolerant techniques as well.

This paper addresses the problem of injection of faults in the communication system of disjoint memory parallel computers and presents CSFI - Communication Software Fault Injector. The CSFI is a comprehensive set of tools which fulfils all the steps required to inject communication faults, including definition of sets of faults, automatic fault injection and collection of results. The results are saved in a file for posterior statistical analysis.

CSFI is not limited to the emulation of physical inter-

---

[1] This work has been supported by the FTMPS Esprit III project Nº 6731.

ferences. There are errors internal to the processors that result in the generation of erroneous messages; a behaviour which violates the fail-silent assumption [1]. These type of errors can also be simulated in a straight way using CSFI. In addition, it allows full controllability over the time and location of the injection, enabling the user to define deterministic fault injection experiments, i.e. which can be exactly reproduced.

The current version of CSFI has been implemented in a transputer based system running the PARIX OS. The execution of fault injection experiments on the target system is controlled from an *host* computer, presently a SUN Sparc running SunOS.

We start by discussing related research in the field of software fault injection in Section 2. The design, methodology and implementation of CSFI are discussed in Section 3. Section 4 describes several fault injection experiments performed using a mix of parallel applications, and Section 5 presents and analyse the obtained results. Finally, some concluding remarks are presented in Section 6.

2. Related Research

Experimental evaluation by fault injection has became an attractive way of validating fault tolerance mechanisms [2]. Several fault injection techniques have been proposed, which can be roughly divided in three main classes:

- Physical fault injection
- Simulation based fault injection
- Software fault injection

Physical faults can be injected in several ways: by environmental stress, interfering at the pin level, and interfering at the power supply pins.

Environmental stress, allows the injection of realistic hardware faults inside the processor circuitry. Studies were performed by exposing target chips to heavy ion radiation [3]. The main disadvantages of this technique are the lack of control over the faults and the limited observability.

Pin level fault injection [2][4] requires special hardware equipment and direct access to the target system. It consists roughly in injecting different electrical levels at selected pins (usually processor pins). This technique is very powerful and can lead to interesting results [5], but it has become increasingly more difficult to implement due to the high degree of integration and complexity in contemporary processor architectures. This trend makes pin-injection virtually impossible in many processors as more and more logic moves inside chip. Another simple method for injection of physical faults is to interfere with the power supply [6][7]. However it is quite difficult to control the extension of the errors caused inside the chip with this method.

In Simulated Fault Injection [8], faults are injected into simulation models of the system. This technique involves a huge development effort and can be very time consuming.

Finally, *Software Fault* Injection (SFI) also know as fault emulation [9][10][11][12] is being increasingly used as an alternative to the others. It consists in introducing faults or errors in the system by means of specific injection software.

Software fault injection main advantages are:

- Low complexity and development efforts.
- Low cost (no specific hardware)
- Increased portability (at least of higher-level SW modules)
- Easy expandability (for new classes of faults)
- No problems with physical interferences.
- No risk of damaging the system under test.

The main drawback of this technique is its limited ability to emulate gate-level faults. However, a recent study [13] suggest that approximately 80% of gate-level fault manifestations (errors) can be represented by software injected faults. SFI's were mainly used in the past to inject errors in the task memory image or CPU registers. Communication fault injection was also included in some studies to evaluate distributed diagnosis algorithms [14] and the fault tolerant capability of algorithms [15].

CSFI was designed to inject faults in the communication subsystems of disjoint memory multiprocessors interconnected by point-to-point packet based links. Although we have implemented CSFI for a specific transputer system, the same principles can be applied to other distributed memory system as well. Of course it's impossible to achieve a complete hardware independence and therefore full portability. Nevertheless we tried to reduce the porting effort by designing a modular structure which separates as much as possible the system dependent parts from the rest.

3. CSFI Architecture

CSFI is implemented as several modules running on the target system and in a *host* computer. Basically, modules running on the *host* are used for experiment definition, control, and result collection. CSFI modules residing on the target system are responsible for the fault injection itself and were designed to cause minimum interference on the measured applications. CSFI works roughly by inserting a piece of software on the communications layer of a processing node, which monitors the flow of packets on that node and corrupts their contents on demand. The overhead introduced by CSFI in the system is only due to this software which checks for each packet received in the target node if the fault trigger condition was reached.

The basic CSFI concept is valid for general disjoint memory parallel computers. These systems have all some common characteristics, such as information being carried between nodes in packets consisting of a payload and a control section (header). CSFI can be used in different parallel systems following this model and the task of porting the CSFI software from one specific target system to another is typically reduced to the lower level SW module.

In order to better understand the CSFI architecture, the present implementation for transputer networks will be used during the following sections as a vehicle to describe the general concepts. However, it is worth to stress that the same discussion can be applied to other disjoint memory systems as well.

3.1. The Target System

The target system of the current implementation is based on the T805 transputer [16]. It is composed of a processing unit plus four independent serial communication links and associated communication processors which can transmit data at a rate of 20 Mbits/s. A low-level communication protocol is implemented in hardware which transmits one-byte data units through the links along with acknowledge packets for transmission confirmation and flow control.

The target system uses PARIX 1.2 [17], a commercial operating system which is being increasingly used in academy and enterprises. It implements an higher level packet protocol responsible for features such as virtual channels, packet routing and delivery/acceptance of messages to/from user processes. PARIX packets consist of a 120 bytes body along with a 4 bytes header which contain the destination processor and virtual link.

At the present, PARIX does not include any error detection capability either in the communication subsystem or processing nodes. Nevertheless, several improvements are being implemented.

3.2 Fault Model

Communication faults are emulated in CSFI by a modified PARIX communication protocol layer. The alternative of emulating communication faults from inside the application, e.g. by corrupting buffer contents, was rejected due to its limited capabilities, lack of generality and application dependency. At this protocol level its possible to generate the most common faults in the communication subsystem with total application independence.

One main feature of the CSFI is that injected faults are deterministic, i.e. the user is capable of reproducing any fault injection experiment. To completely describe a fault the user should provide the following information:

- A Fault Location (processor *where* the monitorization and injection is performed).
- A Fault Trigger (*when* to inject the fault) .
- A Fault Type (*what* to corrupt and *how* to do it).
- A Fault Duration (*how long* to perform the corruption).

The different aspects of a fault and their associate parameters will be described with detail on the following paragraphs. Table 1 summarises the discussion.

Fault Location	Processor Number	
	Physical Link Number	(0..3, All)
Fault Trigger	Virtual Link Number	
	Mth Message received	
	Pth Packet of message	
Fault Type	Packet Type	(Data,Ack)
	Error Level (Payload)	Word Offset
		Number of Bits
		Method(Stuck0/1,Flip)
	Error Level (Header)	New ProcID
		New VLink
Fault Duration	Number of packets	

Table 1. CSFI fault definition parameters

3.2.1. Fault Location. CSFI provides fault injection capabilities on all point-to-point links of any node of the system. However, as having simultaneous injection on several processors at the same time would hardly be a deterministic process, we opted for limiting fault injection on one node at a time, i.e. for each experiment and application run, CSFI only monitorizes and injects faults on the links of one processor. The CSFI fault location within the system is defined by the *Processor Number* and the *Physical Link Number (0..3,All)* parameters.

The user can choose to monitorize all four physical links simultaneously or only one individually. The later case is useful to emulate for instance a link breakdown.

3.2.2. Fault Trigger. After startup, the CSFI module on the target system waits for a user specified trigger condition to occur. In classical processor fault injectors, the trigger is usually defined in spatial or temporal terms. Fault injection is triggered by the program's access to a specific address, or alternatively, simply after expiring some predefined time. In CSFI, although we intend to inject faults in a completely different context (serial packet stream instead of parallel bus data), the same basic ideas can still be used. Therefore, defining trigger conditions is done in CSFI through the following parameters: *Virtual Link Number, Mth Message received* and *Pth Packet of message.* In other words, fault injection start after the Pth data packet of the Mth message is received in the Vth Virtual Link.

We decided not to provide fault definition in temporal terms because again it wouldn't allow determinism on the injection. In fact, it's highly improbable that the same message would be flowing through the link after a fixed time since startup, for consecutive runs of the same application. This is due to the asynchronous nature of the system itself.

3.2.3. Fault Type. If the trigger condition is ever detected by CSFI in the target node, the trigger packet and optionally a specified number of subsequent packets are corrupted. The corruption can affect different types of packets and different sections within one packet. The two types of PARIX packets can alternatively be selected for injection through the parameter P*acket Type (DATA,ACK)*.

Within each packet the user can select which of the sections of the PARIX packets to corrupt using the parameter *Error Level (Payload,Header)*. For Ack packets, of course it doesn't make sense to inject Payload errors, as there is no payload at all. For data packets both levels can be selected.

CSFI provides different error types for each of the injection levels. The rational is that corrupting information on either level usually has very different consequences, and while at the Payload a simple bit-level mutation is enough, in the Header it is useful to specify faults at a somewhat higher level. Therefore the parameters given for errors at the payload level are: *Word Offset* (from payload start), *Number of Bits* (to corrupt), and *Method* used in bit corruption which can in turn be bit Stuck or flip.

Alternatively, for header level errors the user only provides the new values to replace in the headers fields: *New ProcID* and *New VLink*.

The capability of selectively modifying the packet destination, instead of just doing some blind bit-level corruption allows the user to simulate for instance erroneous situations within the nodes which lead to the transmission of messages with wrong destinations, but still valid from the protocol point of view.

3.2.3. Fault Duration. Additionally, CSFI enables the user to easily define transient or permanent faults on the links simply by specifying single/multiple packet fault durations respectively. This is accomplished through the *Duration* parameter which specifies for how many packets will the error be repeated.

3.3 CSFI Modules

The CSFI system has a modular structure and is composed by the following parts:
- Experiment Definition Module (EDM)
- Experiment Management Module (EMM)
- Injection Agent (IA)
- Altered PARIX Router

The first two modules run on the *host* computer while the latter ones run on the target system. Concerning portability, both the Experiment definition and Experiment Management modules can be almost directly used with other target systems without modifications. The Injection Agent, of course would need to be recompiled for the new target, but again with minimum source code alterations. Finally, the lower level CSFI component - the altered PARIX Router - is the only module which cannot be reused. For each different target system this module which is highly system dependent must be rewritten, though keeping the same interface with the Injection Agent.

3.3.1. Experiment Definition Module. To collect statistically meaningful results from fault injection experiments the user has to define large quantities of faults and realise extensive experiments. The CSFI Experiment Definition Module (EDM) enables the user to define either archive fault files with large amounts of fault descriptors, used in multi-run experiments, as well as single fault descriptor files for *ad hoc* experiments.

To easily define multiple fault descriptors, the user simply specifies intervals of variation for each of the above described fault parameters. EDM uses this information to create fault descriptors with parameters randomly generated within the specified intervals.

3.3.2. Injection Agent and altered Router. To use the CSFI capabilities with benchmarks running on the target system, the user must first make a minor modification in the benchmark code. In fact the CSFI programmers interface consists on only two functions, *StartCSFI(..)* and *StopCSFI()* which should be inserted in the application source code. These functions are archived in a C library to be linked with the user application.

The invocation of the *StartCSFI(..)* function activates the CSFI Injection Agent (IA) and starts the monitorization at the links. The following paragraphs give a brief description of the all process.

The IA starts by looking for a system file named *.fault* on the host file system, which contains the description of a single fault (Figure 1). This action can be performed at several nodes simultaneously, as PARIX loads an identical main program onto all processors. However, the Injection Agent will remain active only at the processor which is specified in the fault descriptor. Afterwards, the IA copies the fault parameters to a memory region known as the *parameter area* and triggers the monitorization start, which is effectively performed by the modified PARIX Router.

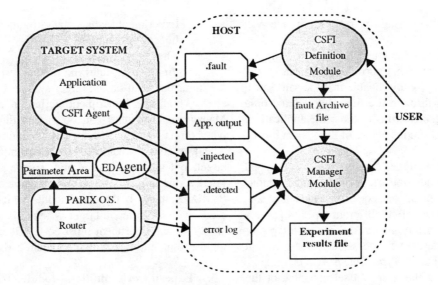

Figure 1. Interfaces of CSFI automatic fault injection.

When the trigger condition is reached, and the fault effectively injected, the Router signals the IA again by setting a flag in the *parameter area*. Finally, the IA saves the information about whether the fault was effectively injected or not (trigger condition never reached) in a system file named *.injected*. Fault injection terminates either implicitly, according to the fault definition parameters, or explicitly by invoking the *StopCSFI()* function within the application. Furthermore, this function should always be invoked before the applications termination, as it is responsible for some CSFI garbage collection. Still, a common user requirement consists in starting fault injection only after the applications/system initialisation phase or after some other specific task. This issue is handled in CSFI simply by inserting the *StartCSFI(..)* call at the appropriate location in the source code. Monitorization (and injection) will only start after this statement.

3.3.3. Experiment Manager Module.
CSFI enables the user to automate the process of fault injection and perform multi-run experiments without further operator intervention. This task is accomplished by the Experiment Manager Module (EMM). First it gets general input information about the experiment from the operator, namely: *benchmark command line, benchmark output file* and *input fault archive file*.

Thereafter, the benchmark is run once without any fault injection and some execution data is collected: *Exit code (status), execution time* and *benchmark output file*. The output file generated during this *gold* run is saved in the *.reference* system file for posterior comparison with results generated under fault injection. After this step, and based on the collected results, the user should define a timeout for application termination to cope with cases

where faults crash and hang the target system. Next, the EMM will automatically read a fault descriptor from the specified fault archive file, copy it to the *.fault* file (current fault), start the application and wait for its termination (or alternatively kill it after the specified timeout expires). This procedure is repeated for every fault described in the fault archive file (Figure 1).

For each injected fault, the EMM collects some output data which includes: *benchmark exit code (status), execution time, benchmark output file, information in .injected* file, *PARIX error log file*, and optional EDM information. This data is directly stored in a CSFI results file.

3.4 Data Collection and Analysis. The fault injection results are highly dependent on the type of experiments and the evaluated fault tolerant technique. Nevertheless there is a set of results which are common to most of the experiments. Therefore, an additional task of CSFI is to collect these results and provide means for the user to easily include more specific fault injection results. All the results are stored in a Microsof Excel formatted file, enabling the user to perform the most appropriate statistical analysis for each application.

. Each line of this file contains the fault parameters and the results collected upon the injection of the correspondent fault. In the remaining of this Section we will describe in detail the meaning of the collected information and how it is obtained by the CSFI.

The first step is to find out whether a fault has been activated or not. This information is provided whenever possible by the Injection Agent in the *.injected* file. Of course, if a fault crashes the entire system, the IA will not be able to provide this information and the EMM will report *NO INFO* for that run. Nevertheless, there is no ambiguity as these cases correspond to application termination by timeout, which is also provided as a result, and clarifies the user about the fault effectiveness. This information is stored in the results file in the *Injection Status* field. Lines corresponding to faults that had not been injected due to trigger conditions which never occurred can be removed from the results file.

For each run, the EMM also measures the application *Execution Time*. This parameter is useful to verify whether the fault delayed, crashed or hanged (terminated by timeout) the system, but has to be used carefully because it is measured in the *host* and is thus subject to interferences external to the target.

Another result always collected by the EMM is the application's *Exit Code*. This is can be very useful to the user, because it is normally through the exit code that programs, function libraries or the operating system signal to the outside any erroneous event that lead to application termination. Therefore, it can be effectively used to identify the source of several system crashes.

PARIX can detect some erroneous situations in the system. On such events and whenever possible, it sends messages to *stderr* to alert the user. CSFI redirects this messages to a file which is scanned after each run by the EMM. The *PARIX Error* parameter identify cases where the OS detected errors and gave feedback to the operator.

The impact of the faults on the application results is a major concern. Therefore, the EMM also collects the output file generated by applications (if any) and performs a built-in comparison procedure against the *.reference* file in order to produce five different results (Table 2). The comparison can be performed automatically by an EMM built-in procedure or alternatively by a user-provided specific comparison program, which can be designed to handle any particular situation. In our experiments, the most relevant is the *DIFFERENT* result which represents a fault that caused the generation of incorrect results.

This field in conjunction with *Exit Code, Parix Error,* and *Execution Time* is used to identify the most dangerous cases: faults that lead to incorrect results whilst everything apparently terminated correctly.

After the injection of each fault, the EMM also checks the *.detected* system file for an error detection code. Although in the experiments described in the next section no error detection mechanisms (EDM) has been used, we have decided to provide specific fields in the results file for storing error detection information for future use. Similarly, an additional field for more specific results has also been considered (see Table 2).

4. Study of the impact of communication faults on parallel applications

Massively parallel computers (MPC) are a promising approach to achieve very high computational performances. However, the probability of occurring faults increase with the number of processing nodes, which makes error detection and recovery a prominent issue in parallel systems. The evaluation of the impact of communication faults on parallel applications is of utmost importance, as most of the existing parallel systems do not have fault tolerant techniques.

The goal of the presented experiments is to assess the percentage of faults that cause the parallel application to produce wrong results in a typical commercial parallel system without fault tolerant techniques. To determine the amount of faults which lead to incorrect results generation and mislead the operator making him think that they are correct, we have to eliminate those cases where the erroneous system behaviour can be perceived by the operator. In our case study, these include abnormal Exit Codes, OS error messages during execution, system hang-up, and absence/incorrect size of application results.

4.1. Fault Parameters

Several fault types affecting both the payload and the header of transmitted packets were repeatedly injected into

Injection Status (YES,NO,NO INFO)	Injection effectiveness. Provided (when possible) in the *.injected* system file by the Injection Agent.
Execution Time (X sec, TIMEOUT)	Execution time of the application measured from the host.
Exit Code (N)	Application's Exit Code returned by the exit() call in the C Language .
PARIX Error (YES, NO)	Error detected and reported by Parix.
Output Correctness	Result of byte-to-byte comparison with the *.reference* file. BIGGER: Bigger size SMALLER: Smaller size DIFFERENT: Same size but different contents EQUAL: Same size and contents NONE: No output file found EMPTY: Empty output file
Error Detection Status (EDM code)	Error detected by an Error Detection Mechanism.
Other Type of Results	Fields available for storing more specific fault injection results, depending on the experiment.

Table 2. Application run symptoms collected by the CSFI.

a mix of applications representative of real distributed programs.

We concentrated mainly on faults affecting the packet payload which represents 96,8% of the complete Parix packet contents (120 bytes payload plus 4 header). This choice was also driven by the earlier observation that errors in the header always lead to incorrect application termination, as Parix does not provide any mechanism for timeout or repetition of lost packets. Finally, we defined payload oriented faults in order to affect the all range of payload bytes either with single bit or burst errors, comprising bit stuck-to-0/1 and bit-flip mutations. The study was restricted to transient faults, i.e. faults with one-packet duration, as transient faults are much more frequent than permanent ones. A typical fault injection experiment starts with the injection of faults covering a wide range of fault locations/triggers and evolves by shortening the interval of fault parameters to a level where the majority of defined faults are activated. For instance, the user can find from these preliminar experiments that the application only uses virtual links numbers up to 20, and therefore restrict the Vlink parameter given during fault definition to this set.

The experiments were performed in a Pasytec X'Plorer with a grid of 4x2 T805 transputers and 4 Mb RAM per node. The presented results have been obtained with the injection of 3000 faults per benchmark.

4.2. Test Applications

The benchmarks used in the experiments were selected in order to comprise both fine and coarse granularities. Additionally, the applications are required to have the following characteristics:
- Produce results capable of being stored in a file
- Be deterministic, i.e. produce the same results for consecutive runs with the same input parameters.
- Generate relatively small results in order to accelerate the comparison process and the overall injection experiment.

We chose to develop some of the benchmarks using a parallel programming library build on top of PARIX, called ParLin [18], which follows the Linda paradigm. Linda is widely used in the parallel programming world because it provides practical means for process creation, synchronisation and data sharing at a high level of programming abstraction. We also developed other benchmark in C directly using PARIX message passing primitives.

1. Nqueens (Linda)
Counts the number of solutions to the N-Queens problem, i.e. the number of possible placements of N Queens in a chess board in such a way that they cannot affect each other. This is a typical master-worker program in which the problem to solve is distributed by several independent jobs. Each job is assigned a possible placement of the first two queens. The application has the advantage of being simply tuned to be either a coarse grained problem (few big jobs) or a fine grained one (many small jobs).

2. π Calculation (Linda)
Computes an approximate value of π by numerically calculating the area under the curve $4/(1+X^2)$. The area is partitioned in N strips by a Master program and each job is assigned a subset of the total strips. This jobs will be carried out by Workers that return to the Master their part of the total sum. The final calculated value for π is stored in a file by the master.

3. Matrix Multiplication (Linda)
This is a master-worker application. Multiplicates two matrixes by assigning to each worker a sub-part of the result matrix. The generated result (matrix) is much bigger than the other benchmark results (about 57 Kbytes), and implies a slightly longer comparison.

4. Bizance (Message Passing)
Agreement problem with three processes. Each process generates a random number (opinion), and send it to the other participating processes. Upon receipt of both opinions, each process generates a conclusion by ORing both received opinions and their own which is saved in a file. All processors should reach the same conclusion and thus the file should contain three similar values when the program terminates. In this problem, instead of comparing the results of a run under fault injection with the faultless case, we check if the three values stored in the output file are equal. Therefore an alternate user-defined comparison program was used instead of the built-in EMM procedure.

5. Experimental Results

Although the used target system does not have any specific error detection/correction mechanism, some critical erroneous situations can be detected at the OS level, programming library level, and by the EMM through a timeout mechanism. Upon detection of any error through this simple mechanisms, the application is immediately aborted and consequently the final application result is not generated to file (NONE cases). In the discussion that follows we will distinguish among the different erroneous terminations for the cases in which no output result is generated by the application (NONE cases).

Figure 3 shows the impact of payload level faults on the output results produced by the Nqueens and π Calculation applications.

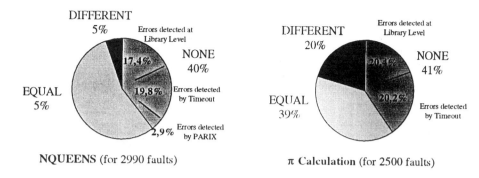

NQUEENS (for 2990 faults)   **π Calculation** (for 2500 faults)

Figure 3. Output results for Nqueens and π Calculation

As can be noticed, 20% of the faults injected in the π calculation caused erroneous results (DIFFERENT). This figure is quite important as it represents the most critical situation in which wrong application results have been produced and no errors have been detected by the system. This means that in actual circumstances these erroneous results would be assumed as being correct. In the case of the Nqueens application only 5% of the injected faults caused wrong application results. Again, no error have been detected for all these faults. On the other hand, 20% of the faults injected in the π application corrupted the results. One possible reason why the results of the π Calculation are more affected by faults than the Nqueens is related with the higher accuracy of the value calculated. Any small corruption on an intermediate calculation will be always reflected on the final result.

Another interesting fact is that a significant number (55% for Nqueens and 39% for Pi Calculation) of faults do not affect the application results. It should be noted that all these faults have corrupted packets in the payload. Most of these faults correspond to cases where the inherent redundancy of the system masked the faults. For instance, Linda applications use a small set of high level primitives to coordinate parallelism, but in a Linda implementation for a disjoint memory system theses primitives are converted in patterns of message passing. This is much like high level language constructs which are converted to assembly instructions by compilers. Messages generated by the Linda runtime system are general templates which accommodate dissimilar information, and therefore much faults affect unused fields without any consequences for the computed result. We call these faults *"null"* and should not be confused with *"latent"* or *"dormant"* faults which are usually used in processor/memory fault terminology. The *null* faults, effectively disappear from the system due to the transient nature of messages, as opposite to *latent* ones.

One interesting point is to analyse in more detail what happens in the cases where the target have not outputted any results (NONE). In Nqueens, only 2,9% of the errors

were detected by the Parix Operating System. These errors correspond to Critical/Fatal errors which are reported by Parix on stderr and lead to program abortion. As shown in Figure 3, the Linda library error detection mechanisms, mainly consistency checks on received messages and error checks on system calls, were able to detect 17,4% of the errors. We can identify this particular termination type because the library aborts the program with a specific exit code upon detecting an error. The remaining faults - 19,7% - caused the program to hang-up and were detected by the timeout mechanism.

For the π Calculation benchmark, the analysis of the faults in which the system did not produce any output lead to similar results than Nqueens. However in this case Parix did not detect any errors.

The impact of faults injected at the payload level in the MATMULT and BIZANCE benchmarks results are shown in Figure 4. For MATMULT, in which large quantities of data is moved around the processing nodes, the percentage of faults in which the application terminates normally (without any error being detected) but the produced results were erroneous (DIFFERENT) raised up to 30%. This figure is even larger than the ones obtained for the Nqueens and π calculation benchmarks. About 35% of the faults did not affect the results and for 35,8% of the faults the target system had not output any results (NONE).

Among these faults 21% have been detected by error checks at the library level, 1,5% have been detected by Parix error codes, and 13,3% caused the system to crash and were detected by timeout.

In the case of faults injected in the Bizance benchmark, only 5% of the faults caused the application to generate erroneous results (DIFFERENT) without any error being detected (everything seemed to be normal). The percentage of faults that lead to erroneous results (SMALLER) but were detected by the system was 78,6%. Among these faults, 38,6% were detected by Parix, and 40,0% by application level checks.

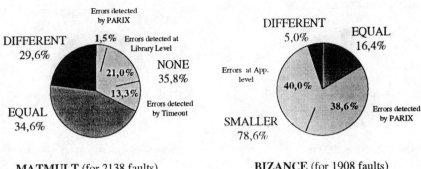

MATMULT (for 2138 faults)   **BIZANCE** (for 1908 faults)

Figure 5. Output results for MATMULT and BIZANCE.

This last case corresponds only to simple application checks made on system primitives return values as this application directly uses the Parix OS services This suggests that even fairly simple error detection checks can greatly reduce the percentage of faults that cause wrong results without being detected. In fact, we tested the same benchmark without those checks and obtained 45% of cases in which the output results were erroneous as opposite to the 5% obtained in the present case.

Faults injected in the packet header have a dramatic impact on the application. In fact, most of these faults caused the system to crash without producing any results. .

For instance, in the nqueens application, the percentage of faults which lead to application crash was 74,7%, and for the remaining 25,3% of the faults the results have not been affected (EQUAL). Similar results were obtained for the other benchmarks. It should be noticed that this faults were defined in order to corrupt the packet header fields - Destination Processor and Virtual Link - , what caused packets to be routed to wrong destinations and explains the high percentage of system crashes. The error distribution obtained with the Linda benchmarks show that programming libraries simple built-in error detection mechanisms can play an important role on overall error detection. Moreover these mechanisms are easily included since they are basically consistency checks on Linda-built messages and OS primitives error checking.

The last one, checking of OS primitives return values should be always done for the sake of programs robustness, but it is usually neglected by the programmer. By encapsulating these error checking in the library we are freeing the programmer from these concerns and potentially increasing error detection capabilities.

Figure 7 summarises the percentage values for errors which caused wrong result generation without being detected obtained on each of the four benchmarks used in the experiments. The results are highly application dependent, as was already emphasised on previous researches of dif-

ferent natures [3][13][19]. Moreover, the results show quite clearly that in a typical commercial system without any particular fault tolerant mechanisms there is a real danger of producing wrong results.

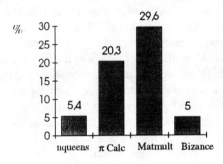

Figure 7. Undetected Errors summary for the set of benchmarks.

6. Conclusions

This paper presents CSFI (Communication Software Fault Injector), a software implemented communication fault injection tool. Faults injected with CSFI directly emulate by software communication faults and expurious messages generated by non fail-silent nodes, allowing the evaluation of the impact of faults in parallel systems, and the assessment of fault tolerant techniques. The use of CSFI is nearly transparent to the target application as only requires minor adaptations. Deterministic faults of different nature can be injected without user intervention, and CSFI collects fault injection results automatically. The current CSFI version was implemented on a T805 transputer system. However, as the fault injector has a modular structure, it can be adapted to other systems with a small effort.

The paper also presents fault injection experiments assessing the effects of communication faults on parallel applications. It was shown that 5% to 30% of the faults injected at the packet payload level in the communication subsystem of a commercial parallel computer caused undetected errors that lead the application to generate erroneous results. All these cases correspond to situations in which it would be virtually impossible to detect that the benchmark output was erroneous, as the size of the results file was plausible and no system errors had been detected. This emphasises the need for fault tolerant techniques in parallel systems in order to achieve confidence in the application results.

Faults injected at the header level had a strong impact on the target system causing the system to crash in most of the cases. However, no application wrong results were ever observed for this class of faults.

References

[1] D. Powel et al, "The Delta-4 Approach to dependability in open distributed computing systems", Intern. Symp. on Fault-Tolerant Computing Systems, FTCS-18, Tokyo-Japan, June 1988.

[2] J.Arlat et al., "Fault injection for dependability validation: a methodology and some applications", IEEE Trans. on Software Eng., Vol 16, No 2, Feb. 1990, pp. 166-182.

[3] U.Gunneflo, J.Karlsson and J.Torin. "Evaluation of error detection schemes using fault injection by heavy-ion radiation", Proc. Fault Tolerant Computing Symp., FTCS-19, pp 340-347, Chicago, June 1989.

[4] H.Madeira, M.Rela, F.Moreira, J.Silva. "RIFLE: A General Purpose Pin-Level Fault Injector", Proc. First European Dependable Computing Conference, pp 199-216, Berlin, Germany, October 1994.

[5] H.Madeira and J.G.Silva, "Experimental Evaluation of the Fail-silent behaviour in Computers without Error Masking", Proceedings of the 24th International Symposium on Fault-Tolerant Computing Systems (FTCS-24), Austin, Texas, USA, 15-17 June 1994, pp 350-359, IEEE Computer Society Press, ISBN 0-8186-5520-8.

[6] M.Cortes and McCluskey, "Properties of transient errors due to power supply disturbances", Proc. Int. Symp. on Circuits and Systems, IEEE, pp 1064-1049, May 1986.

[7] A.Damm, "Experimental Evaluation of error-detection and self-checking coverage of components of a distributed real-time system", Phd thesis, Univ. of Vienne, Oct 1988.

[8] E.Czeck, D.Siewiorek, "Effects of Transient Gate-Level Faults on Program Behaviour", Intern. Symp. on Fault-Tolerant Computing Systems, FTCS-20, pp 236-243, 1990.

[9] T.Lovric, K.Echtle, "ProFI: Processor Fault Injection for Dependability Validation", Presented at IEEE International Workshop on Fault and Error Injection for Dependability Validation of Computer Systems, Gothenburg, Sweden, June 1993.

[10] G.Kanawati., "FERRARI: A Tool for the Validation of System Dependability Properties", FTCS-22, Digest of papers, IEEE 1992, pp. 336-344.

[11] S.Han, H.Rosenberg, K.Shin, "DOCTOR: an Integrated Software Fault Injection Environment", Technical Report-University of Michigan, 1993.

[12] Z.Segall, T.Lin, "FIAT: Fault Injection Based Automated Testing Environment". In Proc.. 18th Int. Symp. Fault - Tolerant Computing., June 1988, pp 102-107.

[13] E.Czeck, "Estimates of the Abilities of Software-Implemented Fault Injection to Represent Gate-Level Faults", Presented at IEEE International Workshop on Fault and Error Injection for Dependability Validation of Computer Systems, Gothemburg, Sweden, June 1993.

[14] H.Rosenberg, K.Shin,"Software Fault Injection and its Application in Distributed Systems", in Proc. Int. Symp. on Fault-Tolerant Computing, pp 208-217, 1993.

[15] K.Echtle, Martin Leu. "The EFA Fault Injector for Fault-Tolerant Distributed System Testing", in Workshop on Fault-Tolerant Parallel and Dist. Systems, pp 28-35, IEEE 1992.

[16] "Transputer Technical Notes", Prentice Hall International, ISBN 0-13-929126, 1989 INMOS Limited .

[17] "PARIX 1.2 Reference Manual and User Manual", Parsytec GmbH, 1993.

[18] João Gabriel Silva, João Carreira, Francisco Moreira,"ParLin: From a Centralized Tuple Space to Adaptive Hashing".Transputer Applications and Systems'94, pp 91-104, IOS Press, 1994.

[19] R.Iyer and D.Rosseti, "A measurement-based model for workload dependence of CPU errors", IEEE Transactions on computers, vol C-35, pp. 511-519, June 1986

[20] "Networks, Routers and Transputers", IOS Press 1993, ISSN: 0925-4986.

[21] J.Lala, "Fault detection isolation and reconfiguration in FTMP: Methods and experimental results", 5thAIAA/IEEE Digital Avionics System Conf., pp 21.3.1-21.3., 1983.

[22] J.Barton, E.Czeck, Z.Segall, D.Siewiorek,"Fault Injection Experiments using FIAT", IEEE Transactions on Computers, Vol. 39, No.4, April 1990, pp 575-582.

[23] H.Madeira,"Behaviour based error detection", Phd Thesis, University of Coimbra, 1993.

[24] A.Steininger, "Evaluation of Error Detection Mechanisms by Fault Injection: Literature Survey and definition of an Experiment", Internal Report 93/05 Dept. for Measurement Technology, Vienna University of Technology, Austria 1993.

[25] H.Madeira, F.Moreira, P.Furtado, M.Rela, e J.G.Silva. "Pin-level Fault injection: Some Research Results at the University of Coimbra", IEEE International Workshop Fault and Error Injection for Dependability Validation, Gothenburg, June 1993.

Dependability Evaluation using Hybrid Fault/Error Injection*

Nasser A. Kanawati

Computer Advanced Technology
GENIX
Dearborn, MI 48034

Ghani A. Kanawati, Jacob A. Abraham

Computer Engineering Research Center
The University of Texas at Austin
Austin, TX 78712

Abstract

This paper presents a new hybrid fault/error injection technique which overcomes the limitations of both software-based and hardware-based approaches. The logic for the hardware fault injection circuitry is implemented using Field Programmable Gate Arrays, and the software is an extension of FERRARI, the software-based fault injection system. The combination of these techniques allows the incorporation of new capabilities by the use of mechanisms to trigger and synchronize the injection of a fault or error with events in the system. Results of physical fault/error injection experiments on a SPARC1 system are presented. The injection was synchronized to the executing modes and load conditions of the system. These results show that the system behavior is very sensitive to the internal state and load. Therefore, in order to validate the dependability properties of a system, it is imperative to inject faults/errors while the system is in critical conditions and different execution modes.

Keywords: fault/error injection, software-based, hardware-based, hybrid, FPGAs, performance, critical conditions

1 Introduction

Validation of the dependability properties of fault-tolerant computer systems during the development of these systems has become a requirement. The validation process provides: 1) a measure of the ability of a system to detect, locate and recover from errors, 2) confidence in a system before it is deployed, 3) a measure of the effectiveness of embedded fault tolerance mechanisms, and 4) feedback during the development stage for improving the design and implementation of a system.

Several techniques have been adopted to evaluate the dependability properties of a system [1] - [17]. Fault/error injection has been recognized as the best approach to evaluate the behavior and performance of complex systems under faults and to obtain statistics on parameters such as coverage and latencies. There are several advantages in adopting the fault/error injection approach for evaluating these systems. These advantages include: 1) the effects and latencies of errors can be determined when executing realistic programs, 2) the overhead of recovery algorithms under permanent faults as well as transient errors and system performance can be evaluated, 3) the effects of errors occurring during the recovery process can be studied, and 4) analytical models can be refined by utilizing data such as fault coverage and recovery coverage.

The objective of fault/error injection is to mimic the effects of faults originating inside a processor chip as well as those faults affecting the external buses of the processor circuitry. It was found in [19] that a significant percentage of the injected faults inside a sample processor are manifested as "address and data line errors". Fault/error injection then emulates these errors using two approaches, hardware-based and software-based. The hardware-based fault/error injection approach emulates these errors by forcing logic values on external buses[1] [3], [5], [6] or at pins of chips on a board. The software-based fault/error injection approach, on the other hand, either corrupts the program image in memory, or mutates the instruction stream in real-time in order to emulate the behavior of the errors [8]-[13], [16], [17]. One of the main drawbacks of these hardware implemented techniques is that they do not monitor the software activity of the system and, as a result, are not able to inject faults for the critical conditions and states of the system. Examples of these critical conditions are high CPU utilization, pending I/O requests, pending acknowledged interrupts, high page swapping rates, execution of recovery routines, etc. It is imperative to inject faults into these systems not only during normal conditions, but also while they are running under these critical conditions. Other disadvantages of existing hardware fault injection techniques are: 1) they are unable to inject faults inside processors[2], 2) they require special hardware, 3) they require access to the hardware of the target system, which may be difficult or extremely expensive and/or time-consuming to accomplish, 4) they

---

*This research was supported in part by the U.S. Air Force Space and Missile Center, through contract No. PPDC57246UT with the Computer Sciences Corporation and in part by the Naval Air Warfare Center Under contract bN62269-93-C-0531.

[1] Other researchers injected faults/errors inside the chip using heavy-ion radiation [4].

[2] Heavy-ion radiation is an exception where faults are injected inside a processor; however, the location of the fault inside the processor is not controllable

increase the possibility of damaging the system under study, and 5) it is difficult to automate the fault/error injection process.

Software based fault/error injection techniques ([8] - [13], [17]), on the other hand, have shown the viability of software techniques for the validation of coverage and latency. Since hardware functionality is largely visible through software, faults at various levels of the system can be emulated. Hence, this method of fault injection is less expensive in terms of time and effort than hardware implemented fault injection techniques. A software-based technique is designed to inject error patterns into executing software. These error patterns are representative of errors that are likely to be generated by software and hardware. This technique emulates the process of injecting errors in the external circuitry of the processor by mutating the instruction stream of the application while it is running.

There are limitations, however, to the software-based fault/error injection approaches. These are: 1) they fail to inject faults in peripheral devices, supporting logic circuitry (circuitry that controls memory cycles, especially address logic), selection circuitry and clock circuitry, 2) they do not emulate faults while external events are taking place, (e.g., during hardware interrupts, and 3) they cannot be used to validate highly redundant fault-tolerant systems, (e.g., a processor assembly in a "dual configuration," an N modular redundant system, parity check circuitry, or error detection and correction circuitry).

This paper presents a fault/error injection technique that has been developed to address the drawbacks of hardware-based and the limitations of software-based fault/error injectors for the validation of the dependability properties of complex systems. Our objective is to highlight the advantages of the new technique rather than to compare the hardware-based and software-based approaches. The new technique is a hybrid approach which combines software-based and hardware fault/error injection techniques in order to induce fault/error conditions on external buses and signals that cannot be injected through software techniques. These external buses include local processor buses and control lines for supporting logic circuitry. In addition, the new approach provides a mechanism to synchronize the injection of a fault/error with the execution modes (defined later) of a system.

In this study Logic Cell Arrays (LCAs), also known as Programmable Gate Arrays (FPGAs), were utilized in order to inject faults into a SUN SPARC1 system. Fault injection circuitry was implemented using an LCA. The advantages of implementing the circuitry using an LCA include: 1) any change to the circuit can be immediately checked[3] in the target system, 2) there is no lengthy wait for a custom device to be manufactured, 3) there is no waste of components as with one-time-programmable solutions, and 4) there is no need for a long erase time using ultraviolet light as with EPROM-based logic. The configured hardware was constantly modified to induce a fault/error in the

targeted system and to study the effects of several parameters such as fault duration and fault type stuck-at on the output.

Section 2 presents the hybrid fault/error injection tool developed in this work. In Section 3, an illustration of the mechanism to inject faults/errors into the SPARC1 system is presented. Physical fault/error injection experiments are presented in Section 4. We present our conclusions in Section 5.

2 Hybrid Fault/Error Injection Tool

In Figure 1, the hybrid fault/error injection tool used in this work is presented. A *controller* coordinates the activities and flow of information across four modules. These modules are: 1) Software-based fault/error injector, 2) Software monitor, 3) Hardware monitor, and 4) Hardware-based fault/error injector,

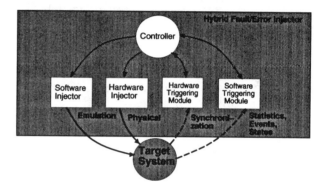

Figure 1: A hybrid fault/error injection scheme

Software-based fault/error injection module: This module emulates hardware faults and errors through software, by executing sequences of instructions to emulate the hardware fault so that when the new modified code is executed, the behavior of the system would be the same as if the internal fault had been present [17].

Software monitor: This module measures activities of the target system such as the number of processes, network traffic, context switching frequency, and I/O utilization percentage. In addition, this module has several control programs that will drive the system to critical conditions by increasing the activity of the system to a selected level. Once the system reaches that level[4], the *controller* activates the hardware-based fault/error injection module to start injecting faults/errors into the system.

Hardware monitor: In addition to fault/error injection of a system under certain critical conditions, the hybrid tool is able to synchronize the fault/error injection process to certain bus activities on the target system. An example of

---

225

these activities is a rising/falling edge of a control signal[5]. This module is implemented on the same LCA used to implement the hardware-based fault/error injection module.

Hardware-based fault/error injection module: This module applies logic signals at selected lines and buses in the target system. The logic circuitry of this module, as mentioned earlier, was implemented on an LCA. A detailed description of the procedure followed to implement this module is further discussed in [21].

3 Description of Test Environment

Experiments to evaluate the capability of the hybrid fault/error injection technique were conducted on a SUN4 SPARC1 (Risc Architecture) running SUNOS 4.1.3 (Solaris 1.1). Selection of the SPARC1 system was due to several reasons. These include: 1) the software-based fault/error injector and the software monitor were previously implemented on the SUN4 SPARC1 machine. 2) the SUN4 SPARC1 system has extension connectors to its internal SBUS bus, which allows direct access to some of the SPARC1 control signals and address and data system buses. Note that although the SBUS does not exist in other systems, the knowledge and the experience gained in these experiments can be extended to other hardware implementations.

Our objective in these experiments was not to validate the dependability properties of the SPARC1 system (although the SPARC1 system traps many irregular conditions, it is not designed to be fault tolerant), but to investigate the plausibility of the developed hybrid fault/error injection technique for other more complex systems designed to be fault tolerant.

The experimental setup used to inject faults/errors in the SPARC1 is shown in Figure 2. The user selects either the software-based or the hardware-based fault/error injection technique. The procedure and results of the software-based technique were presented in [17]. In the hardware-based technique, the user can select a condition or a state of the hardware and/or software before fault/error injection proceeds.

When a triggering event occurs, the *controller* of the hybrid tool initiates fault/error injection by sending a message to the fault/error injection circuitry via a serial port connector[5] as shown in Figure 2. For every run of the selected application, the fault/error injection circuitry injects one fault/error (logic-0/logic-1) into the SBUS bus line(s).

The mechanism to inject faults/errors in the system is shown in Figure 3. In this figure, the user application executes a system call to access the fault/error injection device driver[6]. This step forces the application to execute a trap instruction which will switch the processor to start executing in the kernel mode[7]. Later, the device driver (executing in the kernel mode)

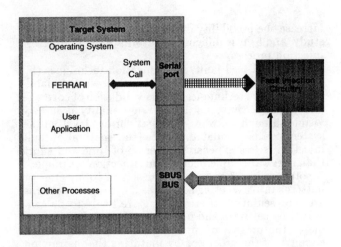

Figure 2: A mechanism to inject faults/errors in the SUN4 SPARC 1 system

tests the state of the serial port and sends a signal to the serial port once the port becomes ready. The timing diagram in Figure 3(A) illustrates the case when the fault/error injection circuitry is ready to force logic values on its output ports before the kernel returns to the selected application, whereas in Figure 3(B), the fault/error injection circuitry is delayed and becomes ready to force logic values on its output ports only after the system returns to the user application.

In order to control the instant at which a fault/error is injected, hence generate repeatable experimental results, the period between the application making a system call (Figure 3) and the fault/error injection circuitry becoming ready to inject a fault/error should be kept constant. This can be achieved if the application makes a non-blocking system call (do not block on write), where the serial port is always ready (not waiting) to send a signal to the fault/error injection circuitry[8].

4 Fault/Error Injection Experiments

The experiments and results presented in this work are intended primarily as a vehicle for testing the capability of the hybrid technique to validate fault tolerant systems. Hardware faults were injected into the SUN SPARC1 SBUS bus while the system was running different applications. In these experiments, the effect of the injected fault/error and the error detection coverage was observed against several parameters. These parameters are enumerated in the next subsection.

4.1 Experiment Parameters

1. Fault/error duration: the behavior of the system was studied for several fault duration periods that ranged from 21 nsec to 67 msec. Small duration

---

[5] The serial port on the SUN4 SPARC1 was selected because it is a popular interface to several systems.

[6] serial port

[7] Note that this process does require context switching the

application. The processor is simply switched to the kernel mode in order to execute on behalf of the application to trigger the fault/error injection circuitry.

[8] The duration between two successive system calls to inject faults/errors was always larger than the serial port baud rate.

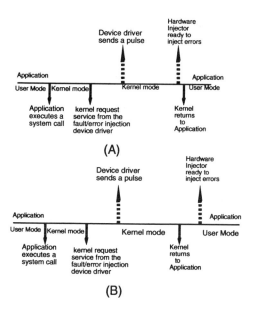

Figure 3: A mechanism to inject faults/errors in the SUN4 SPARC 1 system. [In (A) the hardware injector is ready to inject faults/errors before the kernel switches to the user application while in (B) the hardware injector is ready to inject faults/errors while the user application is executing.]

faults (21 nsec to several SBUS clock cycles [9]) induce transient errors, whereas those lasting 67 msec look like permanent stuck-at faults as they span close to a million instruction cycles.

2. Fault/error type: the system behavior exhibited different responses when injected with either logic-1 or logic-0 transient errors, as will be shown later.

3. Fault/error model: data, address, and control lines were injected.

4. Processor mode: the system was injected during two modes. These modes are determined by signals generated by the processor whenever an address is asserted on the address bus. These signals identify to the memory management unit and other devices the address space that the processor is accessing during every cycle [20] and whether or not privileged instructions[10] may be used. The selected modes are *user instruction, supervisor instruction* [20].

5. System utilization resources statistics: these include load average (the number of jobs in the run queue averaged over a period of time), frequency

of page swapping, CPU context switching, disk I/O operations, and network traffic[11].

4.2 The Response of the SPARC1 Under Fault/Error Injection

In this subsection we present the response of the system to fault/error injection. The system was running several applications when it was injected with faults and transient errors. These applications include a *quicksort* algorithm for sorting integer numbers, and *system calls* that access *kernel* tables. These tables hold information about the activities in the system. The *quicksort* application was embedded with several executable assertions. Executable assertions have proved to be an effective system level concurrent error detection technique against intermittent hardware faults [18]. These assertions are typically derived from the program design and are introduced into the program to monitor the correct operation of the system. The *system calls* were selected to search into the system and report statistics about processes, virtual memory, traps, and CPU activity.

Most of the injected faults/errors produced *traps* (error conditions and exceptions) and were detected by the built-in error detection capabilities of the SPARC processor and its memory management unit and the resident operating system. These errors caused the processor to: 1) halt execution of all processes, 2) jump to the trap handler of the detected error, and discontinue acknowledging other interrupts, 3) indicate the nature of the trap, 4) dump all memory pages to the swap area[12], and 5) reboot the machine. In a few cases, upon detecting an error, the processor sent a message to the console indicating the nature of the error (such as "Parity Error was detected"), and later resumed execution of the suspended processes without rebooting the machine. The following is a brief description of some of the system responses observed during fault/error injection experiments and referred to later in this paper as "observed errors".

- "Watchdog Reset"[WReset]: is the case when the processor encounters a trap while traps are disabled [20], it enters into an ERROR state and then halts (stops executions of all processes). The processor then, asserts a *reset* signal and enters into the monitor mode (diagnostic mode). Once in this mode, the user has to boot the machine manually.

- "Instruction Access Exception"[Inst Access Excpt]: this trap occurs when the memory system is unable to supply a valid instruction during an instruction fetch cycle.

- "Data Access Exception"[Data Access Excpt]: this trap occurs when the memory system is unable to supply valid data during a data fetch cycle.

---

[9]The SBUS clock cycle was 76 nsec.

[10]Privileged instructions restrict access to control registers to supervisor software, thus, preventing user programs from accidentally modifying the state of the machine [20].

[11]Normally measured by the number of buffers allocated for received and transmitted messages.

[12]An example of a swap area is a file (located on a special disk partition) on which paging and swapping are to take place.

- "Text Error"[Text Error]: this trap occur 1) when the UNIMP (unimplemented) instruction is encountered, 2) when an unimplemented instruction which is not an FPop or CPop is encountered, and 3) when an instruction is fetched which, if executed, would result in an illegal processor state (e.g. writing a wrong control word to the processor status register).

- "Asynchronous Memory Error"[Asyn Mem Error]: this is caused by a delayed memory access initiated by the cache controller. The error is caused by a delayed write to main memory initiated by the write buffer.

- " Memory Address Alignment"[Mem Addss Align]: this trap occurs when a load or store instruction generates a memory address that is not properly aligned for the data type (single or double integer).

- "System Hangs"[HANGS]: this situation occurs when the processor halts execution of all processes and does not accept any command from the keyboard. The processor seems to enter into an endless wait state. Once in this situation, the system was manually reset by turning power off.

- "Window Underflow"[Win Undf]: this trap occurs when the continued execution of a RESTORE instruction causes the current window pointer [13] to point to a window marked invalid [20].

- "Window Overflow"[Win Overf]: this trap occurs when the continued execution of a SAVE instruction would cause the current window pointer to point to a window marked invalid [20].

- "User Detection"[User Detect]: this is the case when an error detection mechanism in the user application code detects an error and sends a message to the console. Examples of these mechanisms are: checking the monotonic order of the quicksort application results, checking file descriptors of opened, read, written, and closed files, executable assertions, etc.

  "Undetected Error": this is the case when faults/errors were injected into the system while it was running a quicksort application (integer numbers) and the output generated by this run was different than a reference output.

In many cases, while the processor is servicing one of the above traps [14] another trap with a higher priority occurs (due to another error or to a latent error). In these cases the processor traps to the Watchdog Reset trap.

---

[13] the SPARC implements a register file stack as a circular stack composed of several windows. The current window pointer points to the active window. To prevent overwriting the oldest window as the stack wraps around, a bit is set in a special register to mark windows that will trigger underflow or overflow traps.

[14] excluding the Watchdog Reset trap

4.3 Experimental Results

Results for over 10,000 runs[15] are summarized in this subsection. The SBUS bus was injected with faults/errors at several instances while the processor was either in the user mode (running user application) or in the kernel mode. In addition, the duration of the fault/error was constantly modified for some of the experiments. In the following figures and tables, selected SBUS lines are presented; other SBUS signals have exhibited similar responses.

For the majority of the experiments conducted, faults/errors were injected in the user application Figure 3(B). We were inclined to adhere to this preference in order to avoid crashing the system frequently. In addition, these injected faults/errors will have no effect on subsequent runs since the user application will be loaded into memory for every run. Injecting these faults/errors when the processor was executing in the kernel mode, on the other hand, precipitated frequent system crashes, as will be presented later. In addition, in order to account for latent errors that may affect the system in subsequent runs, the state of the machine (memory, internal registered) has to be saved and later compared for every run[16].

4.3.1 Permanent faults

Table 1 lists the effect of permanent faults injected on several signals of the SUN SPARC1 SBUS bus[17]. The duration of the fault was set to 67 msec. As shown in this table, most of the injected faults generated a "Watchdog Reset" trap.

Table 1: Effects of stuck-at faults of a 67 millisecond cycle injected on SBUS bus signals while the system is running different applications.

Name of signal	Effect of fault stuck-at-1	Effect of fault stuck-at-0
intReq[7:1]	Disrupts the screen	no effect
Bus Request	System hangs	System hangs
Read	Watchdog Reset	System hangs
Transfer Ack	Watchdog Reset	System hangs
LateErr	No effect	Watchdog reset
PA[27:0]	Watchdog Reset	Watchdog reset
Data[31:0]	Watchdog Reset	Watchdog reset

---

[15] each experiment consisted of a number of runs that ranged between 50 and several hundreds.

[16] For those experiment that inject faults/errors while the processor is in the kernel mode, we choose to boot the system after every run in order to nullify the effect of generated latent errors, if any.

[17] In Table 1, "intReq" (interrupt Request), "Bus Request," "Read," "Transfer Ack," "LateErr," and "DataPar" are control signals of the SBUS bus, "PA" is the physical address bus, and "Data" is the data bus of the SBUS bus. A description of the function of each signal is detailed in [21].

4.3.2 Effect of error duration

Figure 4 shows the response of the system when transient errors of various duration were injected into the system. In this figure and for the remaining figures presented in this paper, the y-axis denotes the percentage of injected errors that were either: 1) detected by a particular error detection mechanism, 2) produced wrong output, 3) resulted in the system hanging (explained earlier), or 4) crashed the system (observed by complete disruption of the console). The response of the system was studied for two execution modes of the processor. These are: 1) *supervisor instruction*, i.e. the processor is executing an instruction while it is in the supervisor mode, 2) *user instruction*.

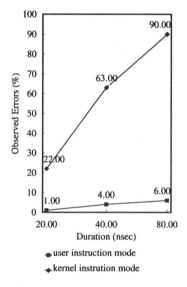

Figure 4: SPARC1 behavior when transient errors of varying duration were injected into the system.

As shown in Figure 4, the response of the system varies considerably when the duration of the transient error is prolonged. More obvious in this figure is the different behavior the system has exhibited when it was in the *supervisor instruction* mode than when it was in the *user instruction* mode. The system was far more sensitive to injected errors when it was in the supervisor mode than when it was in the user mode. Thus, in order to validate the dependability properties of a system while it is running in a critical state or mode, it is imperative to inject faults/errors into the system when it is executing in the *supervisor* mode.

4.3.3 Effect of error type

Figure 5 shows the response of the system when logic-0 and logic-1 transient errors were injected. The duration of the error for this experiment and for later experiments was set to one instruction cycle. Error injection in this experiment and in later experiments was not synchronized to a particular processor mode.

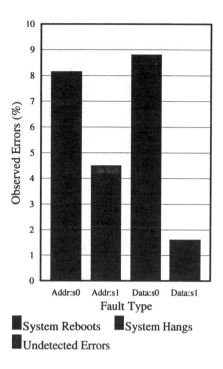

Figure 5: The SPARC1 behavior under logic-1 transient and logic-0 transient errors.

Addr:s0 is the average response for several address line error models when logic-0 errors were injected and Data:s1 is the average response for several data line error models when logic-1 errors were injected. A similar definition holds for the other two bars in the figure. In this experiment, logic-0 errors caused the system to reboot and hang more often than logic-1 errors for both injected address and data lines and buses.

There are two reasons for the different behavior obtained when injecting the system with logic-1 and logic-0 errors. The first is related to charging and discharging a logic node. In Figure 6 we show a simplified implementation of a "bus" node under fault/error injection. Figure 6(a) depicts the case when there is a logic-1 established on the targeted node and the fault/error injection buffer is driving that node to logic-0. In this case, the buffer simply provides a path to ground on that node, thus sinking the charge on the targeted node. In Figure 6(b), on the other hand, the current supplied by the buffer in order to drive the node to a logic-1 level, has to exceed the current discharging capability of the output transistor of the targeted node. Note that this behavior holds only when the output transistor of a logic node is implementing a bus node; it is anticipated that for other types of transistors (for example a p-MOS transistor), the effects of logic-0 and logic-1 are symmetrical. The other reason is related to the address space allocated for running processes. Most systems consume lower memory pages before allocating higher memory pages for new processes. Consequently, inject-

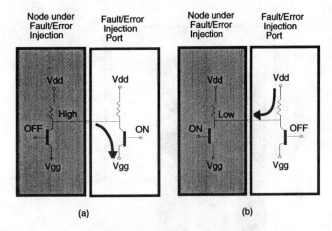

Figure 6: A simplified view of a logic node under fault/error injection

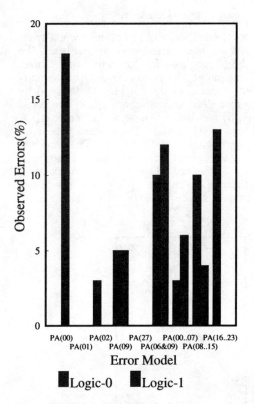

Figure 7: The SPARC1 behavior against several address error models. In this figure, PA(00..07) indicates that address lines PA(00) through PA(07) are injected simultaneously.

ing logic-0 errors corrupts these frequently addressed pages more often. Although this result is obvious when fault/error injecting address lines, it is more subtle when injecting data lines. In addition to modifying data variables, instructions, etc., injecting data lines with faults/errors mutates pointer variables that are used to access operands as well as the destination addresses for jump instructions.

Another finding, not shown in Figure 5, was that a very small number of injected errors (0.1%) were detected by the user application detection mechanism when logic-0 type errors were injected into the address lines (results of the quicksort application were not monotonically increasing). Undetected errors (results were different from a reference output), on the other hand, were more than 0.3% when logic-1 transient errors were injected into the address lines.

4.3.4 Effect of error model

In addition to the error type (logic-0/logic-1), the system response was also dependent on the the error model (single bit, two bits, multiple bits) as well as the SBUS line selected for fault/error injection. Figures 7 and 8 show the response of the system when transient errors were injected into selected SBUS address and data lines. These lines were selected to show the different responses observed when these lines were injected with transient errors.

In Figure 7, a logic-1 transient error on address line PA(00)[18] produced 18% observed errors, and no effect when logic-0 errors were injected [19]. On the other hand, PA(09) produced 6% observed errors for both logic-0 and logic-1 errors. Another example is the result obtained when D(24..31) were injected with transient errors. In this case, logic-0 errors produced 18%

observed effect while logic-1 errors produced no effects. Note that D(00..07) indicates that data lines 0 through 7 were injected simultaneously, whereas D(00/..15) indicates that data lines 0 through 15 were injected one at a time. Also note that PA(06&09) indicates that address lines (06) and (09) were injected simultaneously. Note that injected logic-0 and logic-1 errors on PA(01) and PA(27) produced no effects.

4.4 Synchronization of Fault Injection with Internal/External Events

It was argued in Section 1 that in order to validate the dependability properties of a system, it is imperative to inject faults/errors into the system when it is in critical conditions. As was shown earlier in Figure 4, the system becomes more sensitive to injected errors when it is in the *supervisor mode* than when it is in the *user mode*. In the following we identify certain critical conditions or events that were found to affect the system behavior under error injection. The selected events depend on utilization percentages of the resources of the system. The following is a list of some of the conditions that were used to trigger the fault/error injection process:

- Heavy load determined by a large number of 1) jobs in the run queue, 2) processes and pages

---

[18]We are using the same notation used by SUN for the SBUS lines and signals. In this notation, PA(00) is the SBUS bus address line 0.

[19]Note that the SPARC system fetches words from memory at two bytes boundaries.

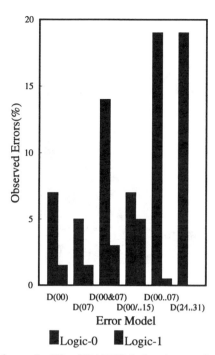

Figure 8: The SPARC1 behavior against several data error models. In this figure, D(00..07) indicates that data lines D(00) through D(07) are injected simultaneously, whereas D(00/..15) indicates that data lines D(00) through D(15) were injected one at a time.

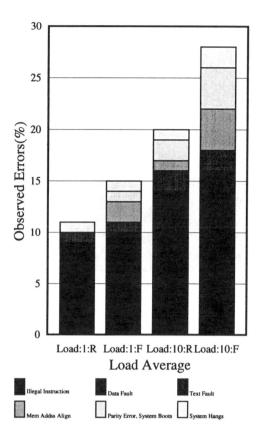

Figure 9: The behavior of the SPARC1 when its load average was varied while injecting transient errors into address lines (16) through (23).

swapped in and out of main memory, 3) CPU context switching, 4) device interrupts, 5) traps, and system calls.

- Packet traffic on configured network interfaces measured by the number of buffers allocated for receiving and sending messages across the network.

- A large number of I/O system calls which can be measured by the percentage of time the system has spent running I/O operations requested by the user application.

In order to determine the effect of the system load on the response of the system during faults/errors injection, transient errors were injected into the SBUS bus while running additional processes[20]. In Figure 9, the response of the system for several load averages is shown when PA(16) through PA(23) were injected with transient errors. Another variable considered in this experiment is the transition (rising and falling edge) of the SBUS bus clock. In Figure 9, Load:1:R is the case when the load of the system was measured to be 1 and the error was injected at the rising edge of the SBUS bus cycle, whereas Load:10:F is the case when the load of the system was measured to be "10"

and the error was injected at the falling edge of the SBUS bus cycle. As shown in Figure 9, the number of observed errors was doubled when the load average increased ten fold. The behavior of the system did not, however, change considerably when the load average was increased five times[21]. Note that in this figure the response of the system was different when the error was injected at the rising/falling edges of the SBUS clock signal. The system was more sensitive to injected errors at the falling edge of the clock (almost 1.5 times) which suggests that address lines are asserted at the falling edge of the SBUS bus cycle[22].

Similar experiments were conducted to measure the effect of disk and network traffic utilization when the system was fault/error injected. In Figure 10, Mbuf:125 denotes the case when the system was utilizing 125 network private buffers when the system was injected with a logic-0 transient error at the rising edge of the SBUS cycle. Similarly, in Figure 11, U10% is

---

[20]Normally these additional processes are run in the background.

[21]Apparently the first five processes were loaded entirely into memory, hence, swapping rate did not increase. As a result, the SBUS activity did not increase either.

[22]to the knowledge of the authors, this information is proprietary for SUN.

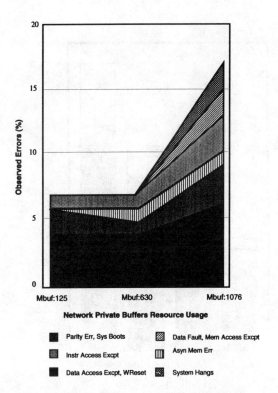

Figure 10: The behavior of the SPARC1 when the network buffer usage was varied while injecting transient errors into data line (07).

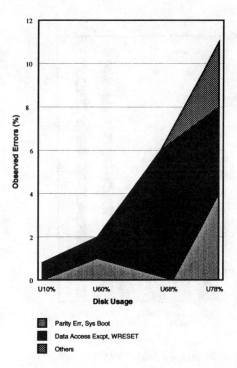

Figure 11: The behavior of the SPARC1 when the disk utilization was varied while injecting logic-1 transient errors at the rising edge of the SBUS cycle into data line (00).

the case when the disk I/0 utilization was measured at 10%. As shown in these figures, the system exhibited a similar response to the load average experiment shown in Figure 9. In all three experiments, the system is prone to crash due to injected errors when it utilizes more of its memory and resources. Note that in Figures 9, 10, and 11 we decided not to increase the load average, disk and network utilization beyond the values indicated as this was degrading the performance of the system tremendously.

The response of the system under fault/error injection during critical conditions can be explained by understanding the SUN implementation of the SPARC1 system. This implementation, shown in Figure 12, is quoted from the SPARC manual [20]. Consider a system running a small application or a small number of processes to be operating under a normal condition. In this condition, the system is utilizing a small part of the memory address space, network buffers, disk I/O buffers, and temporary files. As a result, the text and data for the application may all reside in the cache and the system does not need to access its main memory while executing the application, Figure 12. Injecting errors in the external buses (between main memory and the memory management unit) in this case, does not alter the the execution of the application. Furthermore, since the fault/error injection circuitry was inducing errors randomly on the SBUS lines, many of these errors were mutating locations

outside the address space allocated for that application. When the system is in a heavy load condition, however, the processor is accessing its address and data buses constantly while swapping pages in and out of main memory. Hence, injecting faults/errors on external buses when their activities have increased will alter the execution of other running applications and will ultimately force the system to crash more often.

5 Conclusion

In this paper we have presented the methodology, design and implementation of a hybrid fault/error injection technique. This technique was able to inject, in

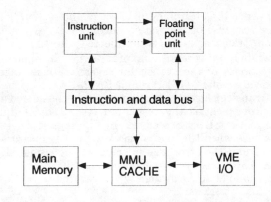

Figure 12: Implementation of the SPARC1 system.

real time, a wide range of transient errors and permanent faults at selected pins of the targeted system. A variety of experiments which illustrate the capability of the physical fault/error injection of the new hybrid technique was also presented. Results have shown that the system behavior was different when logic-0 transient errors and logic-1 transient errors were injected on the SBUS bus of the SPARC1 system. These results have also revealed that the system behavior was different when injected with faults/errors when it was running in critical conditions defined as high load, disk and network resources usage. These experiments have shown that as the system utilizes more of its memory and resources, it becomes more vulnerable to crash due to injected errors. The results of these experiments have also shown that the system behavior was far more sensitive to injected errors when it was in the *supervisor* mode than when it was in the *user* mode. Hence, when constructing fault/error injection experiments to validate the dependability properties of a system, it is imperative to inject faults/errors into these systems not only while they are running during normal conditions, but also while they are running under critical conditions and execution modes. Finally, although the SBUS bus targeted for fault/error injection does not exist in other systems, it is anticipated that these systems have similar buses, for example memory buses, that can be utilized to induce physical faults/errors into these systems.

References

[1] X. Castillo and D. Siewiorek, "Workload Performance, and Reliability of Digital Computer Systems," *Proc. 11th Int'l Symp. on Fault Tolerant Computing,* June 1981, pp. 84-89.

[2] D. Heimann and K. Trivedi, "Availability and Reliability Modeling for Computer Systems," *Advances in Computers,* VOL. 31, 1990, pp. 175-233.

[3] M. Schuette, J. Shen, D. Siewiorek, and Y. Zhu, "Experimental evaluation of two concurrent error detection schemes," in *Proc. 16th Int. Symp. Fault Tolerant Computing.,* Vienna, Austria, July 1986, pp. 138-143.

[4] U. Gunneflo, J. Karlson, and J. Torin, "Evaluation of Error Detection Schemes Using Fault Injection by Heavy-ion Radiation," in *Proc. 19th Int. Symp. Fault Tolerant Comput.,* Chicago, IL, June 1989, pp. 340-346.

[5] J. Arlat, Y. Crouzet, and J. Laprie, "Fault Injection For Dependability Validation of Fault - Tolerant Computing Systems," in *Proc. 19th Int. Symp. Fault Tolerant Comput.,* Chicago, IL, June 1989, pp. 348-355.

[6] J. Arlat *et al.,* "Fault Injection for Dependability Validation: A Methodology and Some Applications," *IEEE Trans. on Soft. Eng.,* VOL. 16, NO. 2, February 1990.

[7] K. Shin, and Y. Lee, "Measurement and Application of Fault Latency," *IEEE Trans. on Compt.,* VOL. C-35, NO. 4, April 1986.

[8] Z. Segall *et al,* "FIAT - Fault Injection Based Automated Testing Environment," in *Proc. 18th Int. Symp. Fault Tolerant Computing,* June 1988, pp. 102-107.

[9] J. Barton, E. Czeck, Z. Segall, and D. Siewiorek, "Fault Injection Experiments Using FIAT," *IEEE Trans. on Compt.,* VOL. 39, NO. 4, April 1990.

[10] R. Chillarege and N. Bowen, "Understanding Large Systems Failures - A Fault Injection Experiment," in *Proc. 19th Int. Symp. Fault Tolerant Computing,* Chicago, IL, June 1989, pp. 356-363.

[11] , J. Geradin, "The DEF Injector Test Instrument, Assistance in the Design of Reliable and Safe Systems," *Computers in Industry,* North Holland 1989, pp. 311-319.

[12] H. Rosenberg K. Shin, "Software Fault Injection and its Application in Distributed Systems," *Proc. 23nd Int'l Symp. on Fault Tolerant Computing,* Toulouse, June 1993, pp. 208-217.

[13] L. Young, and R. Iyer, "A Hybrid Monitor Assisted Fault Injection Environment," *3rd IFIP Working Conference on Dependable Computing for Critical Applications,* Sicily, Italy, September 1992.

[14] W. Kao, and R. Iyer, "DEFINE: A Distributed Fault Injection and Monitoring Environment," *IEEE Workshop on Fault-tolerant Parallel and Distributed System,* June 1994.

[15] R. Iyer and D. Tang, "Experimental Analysis in Computer System Dependability," *Fault-Tolerant Computing,* second Edition, D.K. Pradhan, Ed., Prentice Hall, 1994.

[16] J. Marshall, "The Fault Tolerance Validation for an Autonomous On board Spaceborn Computer," *AIAA Computing in Aerospace 9 Conference,* San Diego, CA, October 1993, pp. 1307-1317.

[17] G. Kanawati, N. Kanawati, and J. Abraham, "FERRARI-A Fault and ERRor Automatic Real-time Injector," in *in Proc. 22nd Int. Symp. Fault Tolerant Computing,* Boston, 1992, pp. 336-344.

[18] A. Mahmood, E. McCluskey and D. Lu., "Concurrent Fault Detection Using A Watchdog Processor and Assertions," *Proc. Int'l Test Conf.,* 1983, pp. 622-628.

[19] G. Kanawati, N. Kanawati, and J. Abraham, "EMAX: An Automatic Extractor of High-Level Error Models," *AIAA Computing in Aerospace 9 Conference,* San Diego, CA, October 1993, pp. 1297-1306.

[20] SUN, "SPARC architecture manual," ver 7. part no. 800-13900-08 revision Oct , 1987.

[21] N. Kanawati, G. Kanawati, and J. Abraham, "Hybrid Fault Injection Techniques," Technical Report UT-CERC, September 1993.

Session 8:

Performance and Reliability Analysis

Session Chair: Edgar Nett

PERFORMANCE ANALYSIS OF THE RAID 5 DISK ARRAY

Anand Kuratti and William H. Sanders
Center for Reliable and High-Performance Computing
Coordinated Science Laboratory
University of Illinois at Urbana-Champaign
1308 W. Main St., Urbana, IL 61801
(kuratti,whs)@crhc.uiuc.edu

Abstract

While the processor and memory performance of computers continues to improve, I/O performance has remained relatively constant. Strategies to achieve better I/O performance than current disk systems have been investigated to address the growing I/O bottleneck. One effort is the RAID (Redundant Arrays of Inexpensive Disks) Level 5 disk array. RAID 5 offers increased parallelism of I/O requests through the disk array architecture and fault tolerance through rotated parity. Although RAID 5 offers the promise of improved I/O performance, such gains must be quantified. Accurate analytical modeling can be used to quantify and predict the I/O request response time for different workloads. While previous analytical models to calculate the I/O request response time have been constructed, they often rely upon simplifying assumptions or computational bounds, which are accurate for certain values of the possible workload parameters. This paper presents an analytical performance model to compute the mean steady state response time of a RAID 5 I/O request under a transaction-processing workload. By carefully considering individual disk accesses, the arrival process of disk requests, and correlation between disk requests, an accurate model for a wide range of the workload parameters is developed.

1 Introduction

Over the past decade, it has been recognized that as CPU and memory performance of computers continue to dramatically increase, I/O performance has improved at a much slower pace. To address the growing gap between processor/memory and I/O performance, new strategies for mass data storage have begun to be developed. One way to increase I/O performance is to use an array of disks. By interleaving data across many disks, both throughput (megabytes per second) and the I/O rate (requests per second) are improved. However with more disks, the reliability and availability of disk arrays is lower than for single disks. Because disk arrays hold the promise of improved performance, different ways to design and organize disk array architectures have been investi-

gated. One effort is Redundant Arrays of Inexpensive Disks (RAID).

Introduced in [1, 2], Patterson, Gibson, and Katz present five ways to introduce redundancy into an array of disks: RAID Level 1 to RAID Level 5. For each level, data is interleaved across multiple disks, but the incorporated redundancy ranges from traditional mirroring to rotated parity. Using a simple model of maximum throughput, the authors suggest that RAID 5 with rotated parity offers the best performance potential of the organizations considered.

Although it appears that RAID 5 can achieve lower I/O request response times than single disks, tools for modeling and analyzing response time under different operating conditions are important to be able to compare RAID 5 and current disk systems. In particular, analytical models combined with a realistic assessment of workload would allow a system architect to accurately design and predict the performance of a RAID 5 disk array. But like many parallel systems, disk arrays are difficult to model because of the effect of *queuing and fork-join synchronization*. Since data is placed on multiple disks, each I/O request requires several disk requests. Each disk request waits to access a disk then waits for the other disk requests to complete before the I/O request can complete. Under general conditions, exact analysis of the effect of these non-independent delays on the I/O request response time is not possible. However, approximate analysis such as computation of upper and lower bounds of the mean I/O request response time is possible by careful consideration of the characteristics of the system.

This paper presents an analytical model to calculate the mean steady state response time for a RAID 5 I/O request under a transaction-processing workload. By systematically deriving the distribution of time for a disk to service a request, the arrival process of requests to individual disks in the array, and the time for all disk requests in an I/O request to complete, a model which considers both queuing and fork-join synchronization is developed. Based on this model, analytical values for the mean overall, mean read, and

236

mean write response times for I/O requests are computed over a wide range of the workload parameters and compared to results obtained from a detailed simulation model.

Previous analytical models of I/O request response time include [3, 4, 5, 6]. In particular, Lee and Katz [3] constructed a closed queuing model and compared several disk utilization approximations to results from a detailed simulation model. Although a formula for response time based on disk utilization is derived, it is based on the mean service time for a disk request which is not determined. Chen and Towsley [4, 5] modeled RAID 5 performance using queuing analysis and determined the mean overall, mean read and mean write I/O request response times. They considered write synchronization, the effect of different request size distributions, and disk access skewing. Thomasian and Menon [6] developed a model for I/O request response time under normal, degraded, and rebuild modes based on an $M/G/1$ queue with server vacations.

In [4, 5, 6], the authors assume that arrivals to each disk in the array can be approximated as independent Poisson processes with a uniform rate. Although both report accurate results for the mean I/O request response time based on the workloads considered, we show how such assumptions can lead to inaccurate results when a larger range of the workload is considered. In our model, we illustrate how the workload influences the arrival and service of disk requests. As a result, we can analytically determine the regions of the workload where such assumptions are appropriate and verify these conclusions by detailed simulation.

The organization of this paper is as follows: section 2 briefly describes the RAID 5 architecture, including data and parity assignment and I/O methods. Using this description, the workload and assumptions used in developing the analytical models are presented in sections 3 and 4. Section 5 develops a model for individual disk accesses, including derivation and approximation of the time to service a disk request. In section 6, we show how disk requests are distributed to individual disks given Poisson arrivals of I/O requests and a transaction processing workload. Based on the arrival process and disk service time for disk requests, section 7 demonstrates that response time for an I/O request is the maximum of the completion times of the resulting disk requests. Using the completion time for an I/O request, formulas for the mean overall, mean read, and mean write response times are derived. Section 8 presents graphs of the analytical and simulated mean I/O request response times. Finally, section 9 gives conclusions and directions for future research.

2 RAID 5 Architectecture
2.1 Data and Parity Placement

A RAID 5 disk array consists of N identical disks on which data is interleaved. The unit of data interleaving, or amount of data that is placed on one disk before data is placed on the next disk, is a *stripe unit*. Since disks are organized into rows and columns, the set of stripe units with the same physical location on each disk in a row is a *stripe*. Each stripe contains data stripe units and a *parity stripe unit*. A parity stripe unit is the *exclusive-or* (XOR) of all the data stripe units in the stripe. The presence of a parity stripe unit in each stripe allows a RAID 5 disk array to tolerate single disk failures in each row of disks. When a single disk in a row fails, a data stripe unit can be reconstructed by reading the corresponding data and parity stripe units from the other disks in the stripe. The number of stripe units in a stripe is defined as the *stripe width* (W_s), where the number of data stripe units in each stripe is $W_s - 1$.

Parity stripe units in a RAID 5 disk array are rotated, i.e. distributed uniformly across all disks in a RAID 5 disk array. This helps to balance the increased load at each disk caused by requests that update parity. Another advantage of rotated parity is that data is also distributed more evenly. A more uniform distribution of data increases the probability that a disk will participate in an I/O operation, which increases the throughput and I/O rate of the array.

2.2 I/O Methods

Given a description of how data and parity are placed on a RAID 5 disk array, operations to read data from and write to the array can be defined. A read request for data results in read requests for data stripe units at individual disks. When all stripe units have been accessed, the I/O request is complete. For a write request, data stripe units must not only be written, but the corresponding parity stripe units must be updated. Depending on how much of a stripe is written and how many stripes are accessed, three different cases can occur.

1. If the request starts at the first data disk in a stripe and the request size is $W_s - 1$ data stripe units, all data stripe units in the stripe are written. This is called a *full stripe write*. Since the parity stripe unit is the exclusive-or of all data stripe units in the stripe and all data stripe units are written, the new parity stripe unit is generated entirely from new data. The request completes when all data and parity stripe units are written.

2. If the request consists of less than $W_s - 1$ data stripe units and all stripe units belong to the same stripe, the stripe is partially modified. Since the new parity stripe unit is a combination of the new and old data stripe units, the new parity is computed by reading the old data and parity stripe units, then XORing the old and new data. The

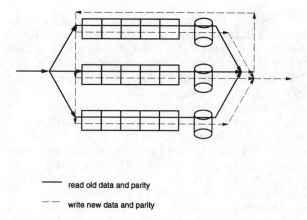

——— read old data and parity

- - - write new data and parity

Figure 1: Write Synchronization

request completes after the new data and parity stripe units have been written.

3. If the request accesses two or more stripes, i.e. data stripe units requested are allocated across stripe boundaries, two or more partial and/or full stripes must be updated. Because an operation on one stripe does not effect the data and parity stripe units in another stripe, a write I/O request that accesses multiple stripes is divided into several partial and/or full stripe writes. The I/O request is complete when all operations finish.

A potential problem that arises during a partial stripe write is how the parity stripe unit is updated. If the old data stripe units are overwritten by new data before the new parity stripe unit is calculated, the parity stripe unit will be incorrect. To ensure that old data and parity stripe units are read before new data is written, the write request must be *synchronized* between read and write phases. Several methods have been proposed to ensure synchronization [7]. For example, Chen and Towsley [4] model the disk-first with priority scheme, in which parity requests are issued when the data accesses reach the head of the disk queues, but the parity access is given higher priority than non-parity accesses at the same disk. In our model shown in Figure 1, synchronization is ensured by waiting for all reads for old data and parity, then issuing the write requests for the new data and parity. As opposed to [4], this method incurs higher response time for the parity update requests by not using priority, but reduces the response times for other requests at the same disk.

3 System Workload

The workload we consider is determined by the size and arrival pattern of I/O requests. Since the arrivals of I/O requests to the disk array depend on the characteristics of the application(s) which read from and write data to the array, it is impossible to give a general model for the arrival of I/O requests. However,

for many applications, the stream of I/O requests can be approximated by a Poisson process. In [4, 5, 6], they also assume that the arrival of I/O requests is Poisson but further assume that arrivals to each disk are also Poisson and independent with a uniform rate. In this paper, we assume that the arrival of I/O requests is Poisson but compute the arrival process of requests to individual disks in section 6.

The second component of the system workload is the size of an I/O request. For many applications, request sizes can be classified as either *supercomputer-based*, where requests are large and infrequent, or *transaction-based*, where small amounts of data are frequently accessed. For this work, it is assumed that requests are transaction-based, where the number of data stripe units requested is less than or equal to the number of data stripe units in a stripe, $W_s - 1$. A distribution which reflects this type of workload is a quasi-geometric distribution [4, 5]:

$$P\{N = n\} = \begin{cases} \sigma & n = 1, \\ (1 - \sigma)\frac{\rho(1-\rho)^{n-1}}{(1-\rho)-(1-\rho)^{W_s-1}} & n = 2, \ldots, W_s - 1, \end{cases}$$

where N is a random variable representing the request size ($1 \leq n \leq W_s - 1$), σ is the probability that one data stripe unit is requested ($0 \leq \sigma \leq 1$), and ρ is the parameter of the geometric distribution ($0 \leq \rho < 1$). Since we assume that the maximum number of data stripe units in an I/O request is $W_s - 1$ and a request for data can overlap stripe boundaries, at *most* two stripes can be accessed during any I/O request.

4 Model Overview

Using a description of a RAID 5 disk array, including data and parity mapping, I/O methods and system workload, we can develop a model to compute the mean response time of a RAID 5 I/O request. In doing so, the following assumptions are made:

1. Although our approach works with any RAID 5 configuration, we assume that the array contains 20 disks with a stripe width of 5 disks and a stripe unit size of 4 KB to obtain numerical results.

2. For many transaction-processing workloads, such as scientific databases, a majority of requests are queries to read data. The ratio of reads to writes for such systems is typically 2 or 3 to 1. In this paper, the probabilities for read and write requests are assumed to be 0.7 and 0.3.

3. Each disk can service only one request at a time. Other requests wait and are serviced in first come-first served (FCFS) order.

4. The arrival of I/O requests to the system is Poisson with rate λ.

5. I/O requests access data throughout the disk array in a uniform pattern. Since an I/O request

requires multiple stripe units, this means that the starting stripe unit is assumed to be random and that each disk in the array is equally likely to contain the starting stripe unit in a request.

6. Since the focus of this paper is the performance of the array, we assume that the response time for I/O requests is only affected by the disk subsystem, i.e. memory and data paths are fast enough to have little impact on the response time of a request.

Based on a description of the data and parity placement, I/O methods, workload, and model assumptions, we can construct a model to calculate the response time for a RAID 5 I/O request. Recall that an I/O request generates several disk requests. Each request may wait for several disk requests to complete before service for that request begins. Once the data for a request has been located and transfered to memory, it must wait for the remaining disk requests in the I/O request to complete before the I/O request can complete. In the following sections, we will analyze each of the non-independent delays that contribute to the response time of an I/O request.

To do this, we first develop a model of the time for a disk to service a disk request. Second, based on the Poisson arrival of I/O requests, we derive the arrival process of requests to individual disks and the probability that a disk is accessed by an I/O request, subject to the request size distribution. Third, using the arrival process and service time for a disk, the completion time for a disk request is viewed as the virtual waiting time of a queue with the same arrival and service time distribution. Finally, we compute the response time for an I/O request as the maximum of the dependent completion times of the accessed disks.

5 Disk Model

Since an I/O request is composed of multiple disk requests, a model of the I/O request response time must consider the time for individual disk accesses. Although a disk access involves many complex electrical and mechanical interactions, the seek time, rotational latency, and transfer time dominate the time to service a disk request. At a high level, the time for a disk to service a request can be viewed as the time to locate the correct track and sector where the data is located and the time to transfer the data to memory. To precisely define the time needed for disk service, let S, R, T, and Y be a set of random variables representing seek time, rotational latency, transfer time and disk service time. As stated above, a disk request involves locating the correct track and sector, then transferring the data to memory, or $Y = S + R + T$. Because the track location is independent of sector placement, density of Y, $f_Y(y)$, can be written as a convolution $f_S(s) * f_R(r) * f_T(t)$. Using previous results for the probability densities (pdf) for seek time,

maximum disk rotation time (R_{max})	16.7 ms
number of disk cylinders (C)	1200
total disk storage	500 MB
single cylinder seek time (a, S_{min})	3 ms
average seek time ($\bar{S}$)	11 ms
maximum stroke time (S_{max})	18 ms
sustained transfer rate (T_r)	3 MB/s

Table 1: Assumed Disk Parameters

rotational latency, and transfer time, we can evaluate the convolution to determine the pdf of the disk service time.

5.1 Seek Time

In considering a model for seek time, there exists a possibility that the disk arm does not move during a disk access. This is called the *sequential access probability* p_s [4, 5]. This probability changes according to the data access pattern for disk requests and the disk scheduling policy. When requests access data in uniformly and the disk scheduling is first-come, first-served, the disk arm tends to move to any other cylinder with equal probability during a request. Given these assumptions, the pdf of seek distance can be expressed as [4, 5]

$$P\{D = i\} = \begin{cases} p_s & i = 0 \\ (1 - p_s)\left\{\frac{2(C-i)}{C(C-1)}\right\} & i = 1, 2, \ldots, C-1, \end{cases}$$

where C is the total number of disk cylinders.

To determine a relationship of seek time to seek distance, Chen and Katz [8] empirically derive a formula for the disk profile, $s \approx a + b\sqrt{i}$, $i > 0$, where s is the seek time, i is the seek distance in cylinders, a is the arm acceleration time, and b is the seek factor of the disk. In terms of the parameters listed in table 1, a is equivalent to the single cylinder seek time. The seek factor b can be expressed as $-10a + 15\bar{S} - 5S_{max}$ where a is the single cylinder seek time, $\bar{S}$ is the average seek time, and S_{max} is the maximum seek time [8]. Because seek time is a function of seek distance, the seek time pdf can be written as a transformation of the seek distance pdf

$$f_S(s) = \begin{cases} 0 & s = 0 \\ \frac{(1-p_s)2[C-((s-a)/b)^2]}{C(C-1)} & 0 < s \le S_{max}. \end{cases}$$

5.2 Rotational Latency

Under a variety of workloads and disk scheduling policies, rotational latency is commonly assumed to be uniformly distributed in $[0, R_{max}]$, where R_{max} is the time for a full disk rotation. However, in [9], the authors note that the uniform distribution is an accurate approximation for rotational latency when requests at a disk are independent. Since we assume that the starting data stripe unit of each I/O request is random, the locations of data for successive requests at a disk will tend be scattered across the disk. Thus, we use the uniform distribution to model the rotational latency of a disk.

5.3 Transfer Time

Once the location for the data has been determined, the data is transferred to memory. Because each disk request involves a request for a stripe unit of fixed size, the transfer time is constant. The transfer time is $T = bT_r$, where b is the stripe unit size in bytes and T_r is the sustained transfer rate. Using the parameters in table 1, the transfer time for a 4 KB stripe unit is approximately 1.3 ms.

To determine the probability density for the disk service time, we convolve the each of the densities. Because the transfer time is constant, the disk service density depends on the convolution of the seek time and rotational latency. The transfer time will shift the disk service time, but will not change the shape of the probability density. Since seek time is based on the number of cylinders that the disk arm moves, S is not a continuous random variable. Due to the discrete nature of seek time, the regions of integration for $f_Y(Y)$ depend on a, S_{max}, and R_{max}. For the case where $R_{max} \leq b\sqrt{C-1}$, which corresponds to the parameters in table 1, the density of Y can be written as a set of polynomial equations. This set of equations is similar to those derived in [4], but different behavior is observed at the boundaries of integration as p_s increases.

Figure 2 shows a graph of $f_Y(Y)$ using the parameters listed in table 1. To interpret this graph, we consider how seek time, rotational latency, and transfer time affect the disk service time. Note that seek time and rotational latency are both larger than the transfer time of a disk request. As p_s increases, the seek time becomes smaller and rotational latency dominates the disk service time of the request. If the disk arm does not move, rotational latency is effectively the only component of time for a disk request, and the density of disk service time equals the uniform density of the rotational latency. When $p_s=1/C$, where C is the number of disk cylinders, the probability that the disk arm does not move equals the probability of moving to any other cylinder, making the function continuous. To determine which of the curves in Figure 2 reflects the service time of a disk in our RAID 5 disk array model, we consider the locations of data accessed by successive requests. Since we assume that the starting stripe unit of an I/O request is random and requests for a disk are serviced in first come, first served order, the data locations accessed between successive requests will tend to be scattered across the disk. Therefore, during a request, the disk arm will tend to move to any other cylinder (including not move) with equal probability. This is equivalent to

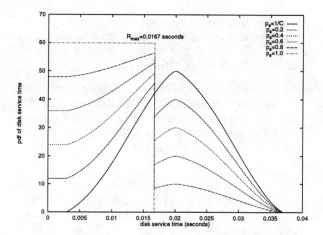

Figure 2: Disk Service Time for Different Values of p_s

the case where $p_s = 1/C$. When the sequential access probability p_s is $1/C$, the pdf of disk service time can be approximated by an Erlang density of order k and mean μ. Figure 3 shows an optimized fit of the Erlang pdf to the actual pdf using the least squares curve fitting method. By shifting the mean slightly, the peak

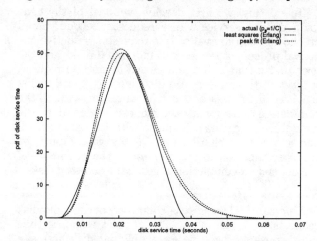

Figure 3: Erlang Approximation for Disk Service Time Density

can be more closely matched (peak fit), while sacrificing the error on the right side of the curve. The peak fit parameters of the Erlang density are order (k) 8 and mean (μ) 42. We will use the peak fit parameters for the Erlang density as an approximation to the disk service time pdf. Using this approximation, we will derive analytical expressions for the mean steady state I/O request response time in section 7.

6 Disk Arrival Process

Since the response time for an I/O request depends on completion times for disk requests, it is important to characterize the arrival process of disk requests. In this section, we will show how requests arrive at individual disks given a Poisson stream of I/O requests in a RAID 5 disk array.

Let $\{N(t)|t \geq 0\}$ be the Poisson stream of I/O requests. Let $\{N_k(t)|t \geq 0\}, 1 \leq k \leq n$, be n output processes, where each output process is a group of k of disks accessed by an I/O request. p_k is the probability that a group of k disks is accessed by an I/O request. Since only one out of a possible n groups of disks may be accessed by each I/O request, selections of groups of disks during successive I/O requests form a sequence of generalized Bernoulli trials.

Multiplying by the probability that there are m requests in $(0, t]$, the probability mass function that m_1 requests access group 1, m_2 requests access group 2,... m_n requests access group n in $(0, t]$ is a multinomial partitioning of I/O requests that results in mutually independent Poisson arrivals at groups of disks. Thus, the rate of arrivals for group 1, group 2,... group n are $p_1\lambda, p_2\lambda, \ldots p_n\lambda$. Because an individual disk is part of different groups of disks that can be accessed during a request, the superposition of these Poisson group requests results in Poisson arrivals at an individual disk. The arrival rate of requests at a disk is $p_j\lambda$, where p_j is the probability that disk j, $1 \leq j \leq N$, is accessed during an I/O request and N is the number of disks in the array. Although the arrival process to each disk is Poisson, it is important to note that these processes are not independent, since the probability that an individual disk is accessed depends upon the group of disks that is accessed. The effect of the dependence between arrivals to individual disks on the I/O request response time will be addressed in section 7.

The probability p_j that disk j is accessed depends on the number of data stripe units requested and whether the request is a read or write. p_j is expressed as

$$p_j = \sum_{n=1}^{W_s-1} P\{N = n\}p_r q_{r_n,j} + \sum_{n=1}^{W_s-1} P\{N = n\}p_w q_{w_n,j}$$

where $P\{N = n\}$ is the probability that an I/O request accesses n data stripe units, p_r and p_w are the probabilities that an I/O request is a read or write, and $q_{r_n,j}$ and $q_{w_n,j}$ are the probabilities that disk j is accessed during a read/write request for n data stripe units. Both $q_{r_n,j}$ and $q_{w_n,j}$ depend on how a disk is accessed during an I/O request. A simple approach to compute p_j would be to enumerate all possible I/O requests that access disk j, then divide by the total number of I/O requests. However, for even small arrays, the number of possible I/O requests becomes large and calculations become complicated. A better approach is to look at how I/O requests access stripes of data.

Because disks are organized into rows and columns, any disk can be referenced by the row r and the disk k within that row. Recall that at most two stripes can be accessed by an I/O request. We can separate

the probability that disk j is accessed during an I/O request into the probabilities that row r is accessed, q_r, the probability that n data stripe units are requested, $P\{N = n\}$, and the probability that disk k of row r is accessed during a request for n data stripe units, q_{k_n},

$$p_{k,r} = q_r \left\{ \sum_{i=1}^{W_s-1} P\{N = n\}q_{k_n} \right\}.$$

To evaluate q_{k_n}, recall that an I/O request can access one or two stripes. By enumerating all possible read and write requests that directly access a stripe and those that overlap from the adjacent stripe, we can determine the requests that access a specific disk of a row. Multiplying by the probability that a specific row is accessed gives the probability that disk j is accessed, p_j,

$$p_j = q_r P\{N = n\} \sum_{n=1}^{W_s-1} \{p_r q_{r_n,k} + p_w q_{w_n,k}\}$$

where $q_{r_n,k}$ is the probability that disk k of row r is accessed during a read I/O request for n data stripe units and $q_{w_n,k}$ is the probability that disk k of row r is accessed during a write I/O request for n data stripe units. Since the probability that a specific row is accessed by an I/O request is assumed to be uniform, the set of q_r probabilities are equal and the access probability of a disk k in a row is equal to the probability for disk k of any row. By considering how I/O requests access stripes of data, we are able to compute disk access probabilities based on a row of disks rather than all disks in the array.

A graph of the disk access probabilities, for a representative row of disks, is shown in Figure 4. The parameters of the request size distribution, σ and ρ of the quasi-geometric distribution in Chapter 2, are placed on the x-axis. For each σ from 0.1 to 0.9 in increments of 0.1, ρ varies from 0.1 to 0.9 in increments of 0.1. To verify the accuracy of the analytical computations, disk access probabilities for all disks in the array are also obtained from a detailed simulation model of I/O requests (Figure 5) with a confidence level of 99% and relative confidence interval width of $\pm 1\%$. As σ and ρ are varied, the graph separates into nine regions where σ is fixed and ρ varies within each region. As σ increases, the probability that one data stripe unit is accessed by an I/O request increases. Since a disk is less likely to be accessed during smaller sized requests, the disk access probabilities for each region are higher when σ is lower. Within a region for a given σ, as the parameter of the geometric distribution ρ increases, the probability that one data stripe unit is requested increases and the disk access probabilities decrease. Therefore, as reflected in the graphs, disk access probabilities are highest when $< \sigma, \rho >$ is

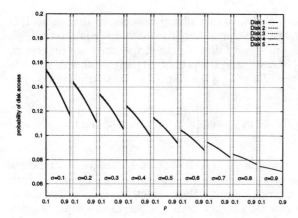

Figure 4: Analytical Disk Access Probabilities

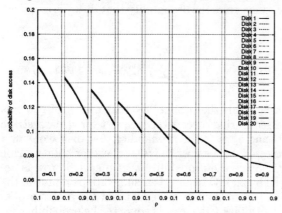

Figure 5: Simulated Disk Access Probabilities

lowest. An important point is that only at the smallest request sizes are the disk access probabilities close to a uniform value. Disk access probabilities are more than three times larger than a uniform value when the request sizes are largest.

Comparing analytical and simulation results, probabilities computed analytically are extremely close to the the simulated probabilities for all disks. It is clear that since the probability that a particular row is accessed is uniform, access probabilities for the ith $(1 \leq i \leq W_s)$ disk in each row are equal and the access probabilities for each disk in the array are approximately equal. However, as shown in the graph and calculated in [10], there are slight differences in the disk access probabilities for disks of the same row since all combinations of n data stripe units are not possible in an I/O request for n data stripe units.

7 Response Time
7.1 Analytic Computation

Given how requests arrive and are serviced by a disk, we can calculate the response time for an I/O request. Based on the number of disks accessed, the type of I/O request, and completion time for a disk

request, we will determine expressions for the mean overall, mean read, and mean write response times of an I/O request.

Depending on the number of data stripe units accessed and whether a request is a read or write, a request for n data stripe units results in l disk requests, where $l \geq n$. For a read request, a request for n data stripe units results in n disk requests. The request completes when all n disk requests are complete. A write of n data stripe units may be a partial stripe write, a full stripe write, or a partial write of two stripes. A partial write of a single stripe requires $n+1$ data and parity stripe units to be read and written in two separate operations. A full stripe write requires W_s requests to write data and parity since the new parity is completely determined from new data. When two stripes are accessed, the operation can be separated into two independent partial stripe operations because stripe units in one stripe do not depend on those in another stripe.

If we represent a disk as a queue, the completion time for a disk request is equivalent to the *virtual waiting time* of a queue. The virtual waiting time is defined as the time for both the requests ahead of and a request itself to be serviced [11]. Since the disk service time can be approximated by an Erlang distribution and arrivals to each disk are Poisson, the steady state distribution of the completion time for a disk request can be viewed as the virtual waiting time distribution of an $M/E_k/1$ queue in steady state ($V_{M/E_k/1}$). Furthermore, since the arrival rates of requests and disk service time for each disk are approximately equal, the virtual waiting times of each disk are also approximately equal. Based on the fact that the virtual waiting times of each disk are approximately equal, the response time for both read and full stripe write requests can be formulated as the maximum of l identical virtual waiting times.

Although the calculation is similar for a partial write of a single stripe, the request requires data and parity to be read then written in two separate operations. Thus, the response for the I/O request is the maximum of the virtual waiting times for the disk requests to read old data and parity and the maximum of the virtual waiting times for disk requests to write the new data and parity. An important consideration is the distribution of virtual waiting times for requests to read old data and parity and the distribution to write new data and parity.

Because requests for a partial stripe write are fed back to write new data and parity, the combined arrival process of I/O requests to the array of new and feedback arrivals is not Poisson. However, we conjecture that since the percentage of partial write requests is small compared to read and full stripe write requests and that disk requests are fed back once after synchronization, the overall arrival process will remain approximately Poisson. This differs from analyses of single server queues in which jobs are fed back with a fixed probability. When jobs are fed back multiple times for the same arriving task, the percentage of customers that are fed back over steady state is large enough to destroy the Poisson process. However, for RAID 5 partial write, disk requests are fed back once after synchronization. Furthermore, this synchronization step tends to smooth out the feedback arrival process and preserve the overall Poisson arrival process of requests to groups and individual disks in the array.

Assuming that the arrival process remains Poisson, the mean time to write the new data and parity will be the same as to read the old data and parity because of the *PASTA (Poisson Arrivals See Time Averages)* property of Poisson arrivals. Therefore, the mean response time for a partial stripe write request is $2\times$(maximum l $V_{M/E_k/1}$). By comparing analytical and simulated response times for write I/O requests in section 8, we will investigate the assumption that the feedback of requests caused by a partial write I/O request does not markedly change the overall Poisson arrival process to disks in the array.

To determine the distribution of the virtual waiting time for the steady state $M/E_k/1$ queue, we refer to [11]. If W is a random variable denoting the virtual waiting time of the $M/E_k/1$ queue in steady state, where k is the order and μ is the mean of the Erlang distribution and λ is the disk request rate, distribution of W is written as a series expansion

$$F_W(t) = 1 - e^{-k\mu t} \sum_{i=0}^{\nu} \frac{\beta_i [k\mu t]^i}{i!}$$

where the coefficients β_i have the form

$$\beta_i = \begin{cases} 1 & \text{if } i = 0, 1, \ldots k-1 \\ \frac{\lambda}{k\mu} \sum_{j=1}^{r} \beta_{i-j} & \text{if } i = r, r+1, \ldots \end{cases}$$

and ν is chosen to be large relative to k. Since $k = 8$ as described in the Erlang approximation in section 2, ν was chosen as 60, sufficiently accurate for all numerical calculations [11].

As stated above, calculation of the response time of an I/O request is based on the maximum of the virtual waiting times of the l disks accessed during a request for n data stripe units. However, for the general case, computation of the maximum of l non-independent random variables becomes difficult if the distribution is complicated or l is large. As an approximation, we use the method in [12] to compute an upper bound for the expected value of the maximum of l identical random variables. Using the expression for the virtual waiting time for the steady state $M/E_k/1$ queue, the expected maximum of l $M/E_k/1$ virtual waiting times is

$$M_l = \frac{\nu+1}{k\mu} \left\{ 1 + \frac{[\nu+1]k\mu m_l \beta_{\nu+1}/(\nu+1)!}{\sum_{i=o}^{\nu}(k\mu m_l)^i \beta_i/(i)!} \right\}$$

where m_l is such that

$$l e^{-k\mu m_l} \sum_{i=0}^{\nu} \frac{\beta_i [k\mu m_l]^i}{i!} = 1$$

Based on the upper bound for the mean time for l disk requests to complete, the mean overall, mean read, and mean write response times for an I/O request can be written as

$$\begin{aligned} \overline{t_r} &= \sum_{l=1}^{W_s-1} P_r\{A=l\} M_l \\ \overline{t_w} &= \sum_{l=2}^{W_s+1} P_w\{A=l\} 2 \times M_l \\ \overline{t} &= p_r \overline{t_r} + p_w \overline{t_w} \end{aligned}$$

where $P_r\{A=l\}$ and $P_w\{A=l\}$ are the probabilities that l stripe units are accessed during a read request and write request, and M_l is an upper bound for the expected maximum of the virtual waiting times for l disk requests.

Note, that since parity must be updated during a write request, the minimum number of stripe units that can be accessed is a data stripe unit and the corresponding parity stripe unit, or two stripe units. Since $W_s - 1$ is the maximum number of data stripe units in a request and at most two stripes can be accessed given the transaction-processing workload based on the quasi-geometric distribution, two parity stripe units must also be updated in addition to the W_s data stripe units, making the maximum number of stripe units accessed in a write request, $W_s + 1$.

7.2 Model Validation

In order to compare and validate analytical results, a detailed event-driven simulator was constructed. The simulator is designed to mean the average steady state throughput and response time of a RAID 5 I/O request. We will describe how the simulator models I/O requests and point out key differences from the analytical model.

Although an I/O request is generated according to the same workload as in the analytical model, the simulator and analytical model differ in how requests are assigned to a disk and how disks service a request. Once the number of data stripe units in the request has been determined from the quasi-geometric distribution, the starting data stripe unit for the request is randomly chosen from all possible data stripe units. For the number of data stripe units in the request, requests are assigned to successive disks. If the request is a read, disks where a parity stripe unit is located are skipped; requests to read the old parity are assigned if the request is a write. This differs from the probabilistic assignment of requests used in the analytical model.

Each disk services requests in first-come, first-served order and maintains the current disk position (track, sector). When a new request is received, the new sector and track are computed and the seek time and rotational latency to position the read/write head at this new position is calculated. Then the time to transfer the stripe unit to memory is added to the completion time. When the disk request completion time becomes the minimum next event time, the request is removed from the disk queue and the next disk request is serviced; otherwise the disk remains idle. By explicitly maintaining disk position, we check the Erlang disk service time approximation used in the analytical model.

In the same manner, each disk request of an I/O request is serviced. Once all requests have completed, the time at which the last disk request finished is recorded. The time from when the I/O request was generated to this time is recorded. If the request is a read, this is the response time of the I/O request. If the request is a write, the disk requests are reassigned to the same disks and the time until all disk requests complete again is the response time for a write I/O request. When a sufficient number of I/O requests have been generated, the mean overall I/O request response time is calculated by summing the completion times of all the I/O requests and dividing by the total number of I/O requests. In a similar manner, the mean read and write response times are the sum of the completion times of the read and write requests divided by the number of read and write requests.

The *batch means* method [13] was used to statistically determine whether a sufficient number of I/O requests had completed for the steady state response time to lie within a specified confidence interval and relative confidence interval width. Using an initial batch of 1000 I/O requests to complete the transient period and a batch size of 1000, the simulation was sequentially lengthened by increasing the number of batches until a confidence level of 99% and relative confidence interval width of 1% was reached. Since we are careful to achieve a high degree of accuracy with the simulator, differences between the analytical results and simulation results are due to the probabilistic assumptions of the analytical model rather than statistical inaccuracies in the simulation.

8 Results

Graphs of the analytical and simulated values of the steady state mean overall I/O request response time are shown in Figures 6 and 7; graphs for the steady state mean read and write I/O request response times are given in the appendix. In addition, graphs of the percent difference are shown for each set of graphs of the mean overall, mean read, and mean write I/O request response times. For each graph, the x-axis represents the parameters of the request size distribution, σ and ρ. For each σ from 0.1 to 0.9, ρ varies from 0.1 to 0.9. The y-axis represents the mean steady state response time for an I/O request. The separate curves on each graph represent the I/O request rate, λ, ranging from 20 requests/second to 180 requests/second.

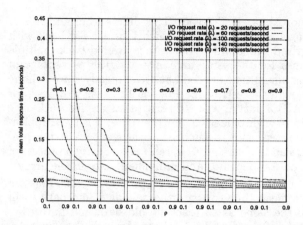

Figure 6: Mean Overall Response Time - Analytical

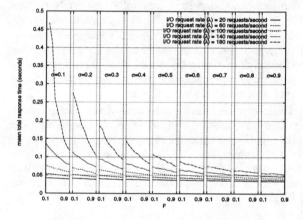

Figure 7: Mean Overall Response Time - Simulation

It can be seen that as the rate of I/O requests increases, response time increases and jumps caused by the disk access probabilities illustrated in Figures 4-5 become more pronounced. As σ and ρ increase, the number of stripe units for an I/O request decreases, causing the mean response time of the I/O request to decrease. For the range of I/O request rates and sizes, the percent difference between the analytical and simulation response times is less than 10%, where the percent difference is highest when the request rate is highest and request size is largest. In addition, we point out that the analytical values are slightly larger than the simulation results, since their computation is based on an upper bound for the expected maximum.

An important point is the relationship between the read and write I/O request times. Since a write request requires two phases to read then write data and parity, we would expect that the write response time would be approximately two times greater than the read response time for an I/O request of n data stripe units. Although this is true at low I/O request rates, the write response time is approximately three times greater at the highest request rates and sizes [10]. Due to additional queuing at a disk at higher request rates,

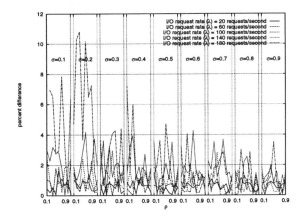

Figure 8: Mean Overall Response Time - Percent Difference

additional disk accesses for parity update(s) cause the response time for an I/O request to increase dramatically. This illustrates why it is important to consider the actual I/O request rate and disk access probabilities for read and write requests rather than assuming a uniform distribution of arrivals, as was done in previous studies [4, 5, 6].

9 Conclusions

This paper has presented an accurate analytical model to compute the mean response time of an I/O request during steady state. By analyzing and deriving the components needed for an I/O request to access data, a higher degree of accuracy when compared to measurement and detailed simulation than previous studies was obtained.

First, given previous work for different components of a disk access, the probability density of the time to locate and transfer data during a disk request was derived. Second, given that I/O requests are Poisson, it was determined that requests to groups and individual disks were also Poisson with a rate equal to the probability that the group or disk is accessed during a request times the I/O request rate, where disk access probabilities were calculated from the behavior of a representative row of disks. Third, since an I/O request resulted in multiple disk requests, it was observed that response time for l disk requests can be expressed as the maximum of l virtual waiting times of a queue. Since requests were shown to be Poisson and disk service time distribution was approximated by an Erlang density, an upper bound for the expected maximum of l virtual waiting times of the steady state $M/E_k/1$ queue was determined and used to calculate the completion time of l dependent disk requests.

Based on this approach, we can analyze other aspects of RAID 5 performance. Although we do not discuss degraded and rebuild modes in this paper, RAID 5 can tolerate single disk failures in each row. An important consideration of RAID 5 design is how the response time for an I/O request is affected when one or more disks have failed and are undergoing reconstruction. We are currently extending this work to investigate different ways to balance response time and total reconstruction time for the RAID 5 disk array.

References

[1] D. Patterson, G. Gibson, and R. Katz, "A Case for Redundant Arrays of Inexpensive Disks (RAID)," in *Proceedings of the 1988 ACM SIGMOD Conference on Management of Data*, (Chicago, IL), pp. 109–116, June 1988.

[2] D. Patterson, G. G. P. Chen, and R. Katz, "Introduction to Redundant Arrays of Inexpensive Disks (RAID)," in *Proceedings of the Spring 1989 COMPCON*, (San Francisco, CA), pp. 112–117, April 1989.

[3] E. Lee and R. Katz, "An Analytic Performance Model of Disk Arrays," in *Proceedings of the 1993 ACM SIGMETRICS Conference on Measurement and Modeling of Computer Systems*, (Santa Clara, CA), pp. 98–109, May 1993.

[4] S. Chen and D. Towsley, "The Design and Evaluation of RAID 5 and Parity Striping Disk Array Architectures," *Journal of Parallel and Distributed Computing*, vol. 17, January 1993.

[5] S. Chen and D. Towsley, "A Performance Evaluation of RAID Architectures," UM-CS-1992 067, University of Massachusetts, Amherst, MA, September 1992.

[6] A. Thomasian and J. Menon, "Performance analysis of RAID 5 disk arrays with a vacationing server model for rebuild mode operation," in *Proceedings of the IEEE International Conference on Data Engineering*, (Houston), pp. 111–119, February 1994.

[7] A. Mourad, W. Fuchs, and D. Saab, "Performance of Redundant Disk Array Organizations in Transaction Processing Environments," in *Proceedings of the 1993 International Conference on Parallel Processing*, (Boca Raton, FL), August 1993.

[8] P. Chen, E. Lee, G. Gibson, R. Katz, and D. Patterson, "RAID: High-Performance, Reliable Secondary Storage," *ACM Computing Surveys*, vol. 26, June 1994.

[9] C. Ruemmler and J. Wilkes, "An Introduction to Disk Drive Modeling," *IEEE Computer*, vol. 27, March 1985.

[10] A. Kuratti, "Analytical Evaluation of the RAID 5 Disk Array," Master's thesis, University of Arizona, Tucson, AZ, August 1994.

[11] C. Kim and A. Agrawala, "Virtual Waiting Time of an Erlangian Single Server Queuing System," UMIACS-TR-1986 6, University of Maryland, College Park, MA, December 1985.

[12] A. Gravey, "A Simple Construction of an Upper Bound for the Mean of the Maximum of N Identically Distributed Random variables," *Journal of Applied Probability*, December 1985.

[13] A. Law and W. Kelton, *Simulation Modeling and Analysis*. New York: McGraw Hill, second ed., 1991.

Routing Among Different Nodes Where Servers Break Down Without Losing Jobs

Nigel Thomas   Isi Mitrani

Computing Science Dept, University of Newcastle, Newcastle upon Tyne NE1 7RU
Email: n.a.thomas@newcastle.ac.uk , isi.mitrani@newcastle.ac.uk

Abstract

Jobs generated by a single Poisson source can be routed through N alternative gateways, modelled as parallel $M/M/1$ queues. The servers are subject to random breakdowns which leave their corresponding queues intact, but may affect the routing of jobs during the subsequent repair periods.

The marginal equilibrium queue size distributions are determined by spectral expansion. This can be done, at least in principle, for any number of queues. Several routing strategies are evaluated and compared empirically. Numerical results, including optimal routing, are presented and possible generalizations are considered.

1 Introduction

The modelling literature contains many studies dealing with the performance and availability of systems subject to breakdowns and repairs. Problems of this type arise in areas as diverse as computing, communications, manufacturing and transport. However, most of the work has concentrated on models involving a single job queue served by one or more processors (e.g., see [1, 8, 13, 14]). Very few results are available for systems with more than one queue. An approximate solution for a general Jackson network of unreliable nodes was suggested in [7]. Mikou [5] analysed a tightly coupled two-node network with simultaneous breakdowns and repairs, by a far from trivial reduction to a boundary value problem. More recently, Mitrani and Wright [11] examined a system with N parallel queues where the consequences of a breakdown are (a) the loss of all jobs in the corresponding queue and (b) the re-direction or loss of all arrivals to that queue during the subsequent repair period. Those assumptions imply that the queue of a broken server is necessarily empty. Idrissi-Kacemi et al. [6] have studied the case of two queues, only one of which is subject to breakdowns; all jobs present are transfered, and new jobs are redirected, to the other queue after a breakdown.

Of the above citations, only [11] obtains exact performance measures for a model with more than two queues.

Here we consider a system where jobs from a common incoming stream may be directed to one of N alternative nodes, each of which consists of a single server and an unbounded queue. The service, breakdown and repair processes at the different nodes are independent of each other and have different parameters, in general. The consequences of a breakdown at a server are not too catastrophic: service stops and the existing jobs remain in place; new arrivals during the subsequent repair period may or may not be re-directed to other nodes, depending on the routing policy. There are no job losses.

The routing policies that are examined are *almost static*. That is, the choice of where to send an incoming job is Bernoulli, independent of past history and of the current queue sizes. However, the probability of selecting a given node may depend on the current server configuration, i.e. on which servers are operative and which are not.

Our motivation for studying this system comes from the field of networking: the jobs are messages generated by some source, and the servers are alternative gateways through which those messages may be routed. Gateways are subject to failures that interrupt service for random periods of time. The source finds out about such failures and may redirect traffic. This naturally raises the question of how to set the routing probabilities. The main purpose of the analysis, therefore, is to determine performance measures so that different routing policies can be evaluated and compared.

The model and its parameters are specified in section 2. Ideally, one would like to find the joint stationary distribution of the set of operative servers and the numbers of jobs in the corresponding queues. To determine that distribution, it is necessary to solve a non-separable multidimensional Markov process, which is an intractable problem in the general case. The only case for which the joint distribution may be attainable is $N = 2$.

On the other hand, the performance measures of practical interest are mainly concerned with local or global averages, e.g. the average number of jobs present at a given node or the overall average response time. To calculate such performance measures, it is enough to determine the marginal queue size distributions. This last problem can be solved, at least in principle, for arbitrary N (section 3). Problems of comparison and optimization of routing policies can thus be tackled numerically. Several such numerical evaluations are reported in section 4. Various generalisations of the model, where the same solution methodology applies, are mentioned in section 5.

2 The model

Jobs arrive into the system in a Poisson stream with rate λ. There are N servers, each with an associated unbounded queue, to which incoming jobs may be directed. Server k goes through alternating independent operative and inoperative periods, distributed exponentially with means $1/\xi_k$ and $1/\eta_k$, respectively. While it is operative, the jobs in its queue receive exponentially distributed services with mean $1/\mu_k$, and depart upon completion. When a server becomes inoperative (breaks down), the corresponding queue, including the job in service (if any), remains in place. Services that are interrupted in this way are eventually resumed from the point of interruption. The system model is illustrated in figure 1.

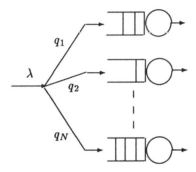

Figure 1: A single source split among N unreiable nodes

The *system configuration* at any moment is specified by the subset, σ, of servers that are currently operative (that subset may be empty, or it may be the set of all servers): $\sigma \subset \Omega_N$, where $\Omega_N = \{1, 2, \ldots, N\}$. There are of course 2^N possible system configurations. The steady-state marginal probability, p_σ, of configuration σ is given by

$$p_\sigma = \prod_{k \in \sigma} \frac{\eta_k}{\xi_k + \eta_k} \prod_{k \in \overline{\sigma}} \frac{\xi_k}{\xi_k + \eta_k} \ , \quad \sigma \subset \Omega_N \ , \quad (1)$$

where $\overline{\sigma}$ is the complement of σ with respect to Ω_N and an empty product is by definition equal to 1. These expressions follow from the fact that servers break down and are repaired independently of each other.

If, at the time of arrival, a new job finds the system in configuration σ, then it is directed to node k with probability $q_k(\sigma)$. These decisions are independent of each other, of past history and of the sizes of the various queues. Thus, a routing policy is defined by specifying 2^N vectors,

$$\mathbf{q}(\sigma) = [q_1(\sigma), q_2(\sigma), \ldots, q_N(\sigma)] \ , \quad \sigma \subset \Omega_N \ , \quad (2)$$

such that for every σ,

$$\sum_{k=1}^{N} q_k(\sigma) = 1 \ .$$

The system state at time t is specified by the pair $[I(t), \mathbf{J}(t)]$, where $I(t)$ indicates the current configuration (the configurations can be numbered, so that $I(t)$ is an integer in the range $0, 1, \ldots, 2^N - 1$), and $\mathbf{J}(t)$ is an integer vector whose k'th element, $J_k(t)$, is the number of jobs in queue k ($k = 1, 2, \ldots, N$). Under the assumptions that have been made, $X = \{[I(t), \mathbf{J}(t)] \ , \ t \geq 0\}$ is an irreducible Markov process. The condition for ergodicity of X is that, for every queue, the overall arrival rate is lower than the overall service capacity:

$$\lambda \sum_{\sigma \subset \Omega_N} p_\sigma q_k(\sigma) < \mu_k \frac{\eta_k}{\xi_k + \eta_k} \ , \ k = 1, 2, \ldots, N \ . \ (3)$$

When the routing probabilities depend on the system configuration, the process X is not separable (i.e., it does not have a product-form solution). Consequently, the problem of determining its equilibrium distribution is intractable for $N > 2$. In the case $N = 2$, a solution may be possible, but both the mathematical analysis and the implementation would be difficult. On the other hand, the quantities of principal interest are expressed in terms of averages only; they are the steady-state mean queue sizes, L_k, and the the overall average response time, W, given by

$$W = \frac{1}{\lambda} \sum_{k=1}^{N} L_k \ . \quad (4)$$

To determine those performance measures, it is not necessary to know the joint distribution of all queue sizes; the marginal distributions of the N queues in isolation are sufficient. Unfortunately, the isolated queue processes, $\{J_k(t) \ , \ t \geq 0\}$ ($k = 1, 2, \ldots, N$), are not Markov. However, the performance measures can be determined by studying the stochastic processes $Y_k = \{[I(t), J_k(t)] \ , \ t \geq 0\}$ ($k = 1, 2, \ldots, N$), which model the joint behaviour of the system configuration and the size of an individual queue. The state space of Y_k is infinite in one dimension only, which simplifies the solution considerably and makes it tractable for reasonably large values of N. The important observation here is that Y_k is an irreducible Markov process, for every k. This is because the arrivals into, and departures from queue k during a small interval $(t, t + \Delta t)$ depend only on the system configuration and the size of queue k at time t, and not on the sizes of the other queues.

The next task, therefore, is to find the equilibrium distribution of Y_k:

$$p_k(i, j) = \lim_{t \to \infty} P[I(t) = i \, , \, J_k(t) = j] \ ,$$

$$i = 0, 1, \ldots, 2^N - 1 \ , \quad j = 0, 1, \ldots \ . \quad (5)$$

Given the probabilities $p_k(i,j)$, the average size of queue k is obtained from

$$L_k = \sum_{j=1}^{\infty} j \sum_{i=0}^{2^N-1} p_k(i,j) . \quad (6)$$

3 Queue size distributions

The process Y_k is of the *block tri-diagonal*, or *Quasi-Birth-and-Death* type. Its possible transitions are:

(a) from state (i,j) to state (i',j), where i' is a configuration with either one more, or one fewer operative server;

(b) from state (i,j) to state $(i,j+1)$, if the routing probability to queue k in configuration i, $q_k(i)$, is non-zero;

(c) from state (i,j) to state $(i,j-1)$, if $j > 0$ and server k is operative in configuration i.

The balance equations for Y_k are best written in vector and matrix form. Define the (row) vector of equilibrium probabilities of all states with j jobs in queue k :

$$\mathbf{v}_k(j) = [p_k(0,j), p_k(1,j), \ldots, p_k(2^N-1,j)] ,$$

$$j = 0, 1, \ldots . \quad (7)$$

Let $A = (a_{i,i'})$ $(i, i' = 0, 1, \ldots, 2^N - 1)$ be the matrix of instantaneous transition rates corresponding to transitions (a). If in configuration i the subset of operative servers is σ, and in i' it is $\sigma + \{\ell\}$, for some server ℓ, then $a_{i,i'} = \eta_\ell$; similarly, if in i' the configuration is $\sigma - \{\ell\}$, for some server ℓ, then $a_{i,i'} = \xi_\ell$. It is also useful to introduce the diagonal matrix, D_A, whose i'th diagonal element is the i'th row sum of A $(i = 0, 1, \ldots, 2^N - 1)$.

Let B_k be the diagonal matrix whose i'th diagonal element is equal to $\lambda q_k(i)$; these elements are the instantaneous transition rates corresponding to transitions (b). Also, let C_k be the diagonal matrix whose i'th diagonal element is equal to μ_k if server k is operative in configuration i, and 0 otherwise; these are the instantaneous transition rates corresponding to transitions (c).

When $j > 0$, the vectors (7) satisfy the balance equations

$$\mathbf{v}_k(j)(D_A + B_k + C_k) = \mathbf{v}_k(j)A + \mathbf{v}_k(j-1)B_k$$

$$+ \mathbf{v}_k(j+1)C_k , \quad j = 1, 2, \ldots . \quad (8)$$

For $j = 0$, the equation is slightly different:

$$\mathbf{v}_k(0)(D_A + B_k) = \mathbf{v}_k(0)A + \mathbf{v}_k(1)C_k . \quad (9)$$

In addition, all probabilities must sum up to 1:

$$\sum_{j=0}^{\infty} \mathbf{v}_k(j)\mathbf{e} = 1 , \quad (10)$$

where e is a column vector with 2^N elements, all of which are equal to 1.

The above equations can be solved by several methods. Perhaps the best approach is to use *spectral expansion* (see [9, 10]). Rewrite (8) in the form

$$\mathbf{v}_k(j)Q_{k,0} + \mathbf{v}_k(j+1)Q_{k,1} + \mathbf{v}_k(j+2)Q_{k,2} = \mathbf{0} ,$$

$$j = 0, 1, \ldots , \quad (11)$$

where $Q_{k,0} = B_k$, $Q_{k,1} = A - D_A - B_k - C_k$ and $Q_{k,2} = C_k$. This is a homogeneous vector difference equation of order 2, with constant coefficients. Associated with it is the characteristic matrix polynomial, $Q_k(z)$, defined as

$$Q_k(z) = Q_{k,0} + Q_{k,1}z + Q_{k,2}z^2 . \quad (12)$$

Denote by $z_{k,\ell}$ and $\psi_{k,\ell}$ the *generalized eigenvalues and left eigenvectors* of $Q_k(z)$. These quantities satisfy

$$\psi_{k,\ell}Q_k(z_{k,\ell}) = 0 , \quad \ell = 1, 2, \ldots, d , \quad (13)$$

where $d = degree\{det[Q_k(z)]\}$.

The eigenvalues do not have to be simple, but it is assumed that if $z_{k,\ell}$ has multiplicity r, then it has r linearly independent left eigenvectors. This is invariably observed to be the case in practice. Under that assumption, any solution of (11) is of the form

$$\mathbf{v}_k(j) = \sum_{\ell=1}^{d} x_{k,\ell}\psi_{k,\ell}z_{k,\ell}^{j} , \quad j = 0, 1, \ldots , \quad (14)$$

where $x_{k,\ell}$ $(\ell = 1, 2, \ldots, d)$, are arbitrary (complex) constants.

Moreover, since only normalizeable solutions are acceptable, if $|z_{k,\ell}| \geq 1$ for some ℓ, then the corresponding coefficient $x_{k,\ell}$ must be set to 0. Numbering the eigenvalues of $Q_k(z)$ in increasing order of modulus, the spectral expansion solution of equation (11) can be written as

$$\mathbf{v}_k(j) = \sum_{\ell=1}^{c} x_{k,\ell}\psi_{k,\ell}z_{k,\ell}^{j} , \quad j = 0, 1, \ldots , \quad (15)$$

where c is the number of eigenvalues strictly inside the unit disk (each counted according to its multiplicity).

In the numerical experiments carried out with this model, the eigenvalues and eigenvectors of $Q_k(z)$ have always been observed to be simple, real and positive.

Substituting (15), for $j = 0$ and $j = 1$, into (9), yields a set of homogeneous linear equations for the unknown coefficients $x_{k,\ell}$. There are $2^N - 1$ independent equations in this set (rather than 2^N) because the generator matrix of the Markov process is singular. A further, non-homogeneous equation is provided by (10), which now becomes

$$\sum_{\ell=1}^{2^N} \frac{x_{k,\ell}\psi_{k,\ell}\mathbf{e}}{1 - z_{k,\ell}} = 1 .$$

These equations can be solved uniquely for the coefficients $x_{k,\ell}$, if $c = 2^N$. This turns out to be the case when (3) is satisfied. Indeed, the ergodicity condition is equivalent to the requirement that $Q_k(z)$ has exactly 2^N eigenvalues strictly inside the unit disk.

Having determined the coefficients $x_{k,\ell}$, the average number of jobs in queue k is obtained by substituting (15) into (6):

$$L_k = \sum_{\ell=1}^{2^N} \frac{x_{k,\ell} z_{k,\ell} \psi_{k,\ell} \mathbf{e}}{(1 - z_{k,\ell})^2} \quad . \tag{16}$$

4 Evaluation of scheduling strategies

In order to reduce the number of parameters that have to be given values when defining the routing strategy, we shall evaluate and compare several strategies based on a single routing vector, $\mathbf{q} = (q_1, q_2, \ldots, q_N)$. In each case, the optimization problem is to chose the elements of that vector so as to minimize the average response time, given by (4).

1. *The fixed strategy*

The most straightforward way of splitting the incoming stream is to send each job to node k with probability q_k, regardless of the system configuration. Then the N nodes are independent of each other; node k can be considered in complete isolation, as an M/M/1 queue with breakdowns and repairs. In this simple case, there is a well known explicit formula for the average queue size (see [1, 8, 14]):

$$L_k = \frac{\lambda q_k[(\xi_k + \eta_k)^2 + \xi_k \mu_k]}{(\xi_k + \eta_k)[\eta_k \mu_k - \lambda q_k(\xi_k + \eta_k)]} \quad . \tag{17}$$

2. *The selective strategy.*

Intuitively, it seems better not to send jobs to nodes where the server is inoperative, unless that is unavoidable. This suggests the following strategy: If the subset of operative servers in the current system configuration is σ, and that subset is non-empty, send jobs to node k only if $k \in \sigma$, with probability proportional to q_k:

$$q_k(\sigma) = \frac{q_k}{\sum_{\ell \in \sigma} q_\ell} \quad , \quad k \in \sigma \quad .$$

If σ is empty (i.e. all servers are broken), send jobs to node k with probability q_k ($k = 1, 2, \ldots, N$).

3. *The fixed(m) strategy.*

It is possible that some nodes are unable, under any circumstances, to receive jobs when broken. Suppose that the last $N - m$ nodes are of this type ($m > 0$), and jobs are sent to the first m nodes regardless of their state. Thus, when the system configuration is σ, an incoming job can be directed to any node k for which $k \le m$ or $k \in \sigma$, or both, with probability

$$q_k(\sigma) = \frac{q_k}{\sum_{\ell \in \{1,2,\ldots,m\} \cup \sigma} q_\ell} \quad , \quad (k \le m) \lor (k \in \sigma) \quad .$$

4. *The selective(m) strategy.*

This strategy, like the selective one, does not send jobs to broken nodes unless that is unavoidable. In addition, the last $N - m$ nodes are completely unable to receive jobs when broken ($m > 0$). In other words, if the system configuration is σ, and $\sigma \ne \emptyset$, an incoming job is directed to node k, only if $k \in \sigma$, with probability proportional to q_k:

$$q_k(\sigma) = \frac{q_k}{\sum_{\ell \in \sigma} q_\ell} \quad , \quad k \in \sigma \quad .$$

If σ is empty, the job is sent to one of the first m nodes, with probability

$$q_k(\sigma) = \frac{q_k}{\sum_{\ell=1}^{m} q_\ell} \quad , \quad k = 1, 2, \ldots, m \quad .$$

Clearly, the fixed strategy is a special case of the fixed(m) one, when $m = N$. Similarly, the selective strategy is a special case of the selective(m) one, when $m = N$. All strategies except the fixed are evaluated by the spectral expansion method.

Intuitively it would seem that, for a given routing vector, the selective strategy should perform better than the others, since it appears to make the best use of all servers. The fixed strategies may be expected to perform poorly, since they largely or completely disregard the current availability of servers. When the majority of the servers are quite reliable, the performance of a selective(m) strategy should not depend much on m and should resemble that of the selective strategy (since the only differences arise when all servers are broken).

This intuition is confirmed by the results in figure 2, where a 3-node model is solved under the three fixed and three selective scheduling strategies. In all cases, the overall average response time, W, is plotted against the job arrival rate. The nodes have different characteristics (see caption), but no advantage is taken of those differences. The routing vector is $(\frac{1}{3}, \frac{1}{3}, \frac{1}{3})$, i.e. the *a-priori* splitting of the input stream is into three equal sub-streams.

There is a clear separation between the two groups of curves; every selective strategy out-performs every fixed one. The selective strategies are quite close, although the servers are not very reliable. Within the fixed strategies, it is worth noting that fixed(1) and fixed(2) start off better than fixed, but become worse when the load increases. This is because the prohibition on sending jobs to some servers when they are broken helps to balance the load at low arrival rates, but saturates the other servers when the load is high. If, instead of keeping the routing vector constant, it is optimized for each value of λ, then the corresponding plots do not cross: fixed(1) becomes uniformly better than fixed(2), which in turn becomes better than fixed.

Despite their plausibility, the above remarks are not universally valid. In particular, it is possible to construct examples where the fixed strategy performs better than the selective (e.g. $N = 2$, $\lambda = 10$, $\mu_1 = 30$, $\mu_2 = 10$, $\xi_1 = 100$, $\xi_2 = 1$, $\eta_1 = 100$, $\eta_2 = 100000$; admittedly, that example is rather contrived, with one fast and fairly unreliable server, while the other is slower and extremely reliable).

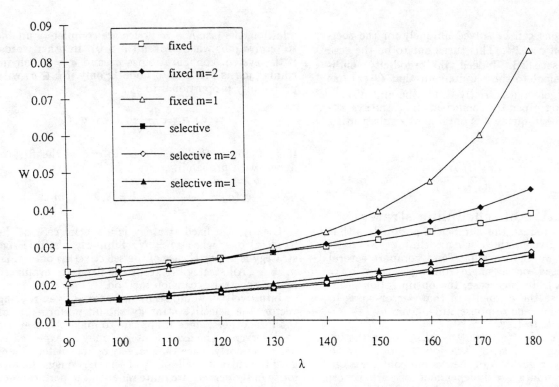

Figure 2: Average response time as a function of the job arrival rate.
$\mu_1 = 150, \mu_2 = 170, \mu_3 = 190, \xi_1 = 20, \xi_2 = 30, \xi_3 = 40, \eta_1 = \eta_2 = \eta_3 = 50$

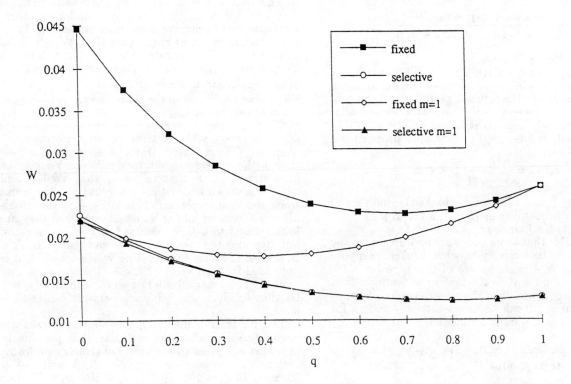

Figure 3: Average response time in a 2-node system, as a function of the routing vector $(q, 1 - q)$.
$\lambda = 50, \mu_1 = 150, \mu_2 = 100, \xi_1 = \xi_2 = 1, \eta_1 = \eta_2 = 10$

The rest of the experiments illustrate various aspects of optimal routing.

Figure 3 concerns a 2-node system where the routing vector, $(q, 1-q)$, is varied on the range $0 \le q \le 1$ (remember that that vector is used in making routing decisions only when both servers are operative or, in the case of the selective strategy, when both are broken). The average response time is plotted against q. The system parameters (see caption) are such that each server is operatove approximately 90% of the time, while server 1 is 50% faster than server 2. The figure suggests the following observations, of which the first is obvious (from the definitions of the strategies), the next two are quite intuitive, and the last is somewhat counter-intuitive:

(a) When $q = 1$, the fixed and fixed(1) strategies are identical, as are the selective and selective(1) ones; when $q = 0$, the fixed(1) and selective(1) strategies are identical.

(b) The curves corresponding to the selective strategies are not only lower, but also *flatter* than those of the fixed ones; in other words, the selective strategies are less sensitive to changes in the routing vector.

(c) For the fixed and two selective strategies, the best routing vector sends the majority of the jobs (70% - 80%) to the faster server.

(d) For the fixed(1) strategy, it is best to send fewer jobs (40%) to the faster server than to the slower one.

To explanain (d), note that under the fixed(1) strategy, node 1 is obliged to receive all jobs whenever server 2 is broken, regardless of its own state. This load should be compensated by sending it fewer jobs when there is a choice, i.e. when both servers are operative.

Figure 4 shows the performance of a 5-node system as a function of the job arrival rate, under an approximately optimal routing vector. For each value of λ, a gradient search method was used to get close to the optimal vector, and the corresponding value of the average response time was plotted. The parameters are chosen so that the faster servers are also more reliable. As in figure 2, there is almost no difference between the selective strategies. However, the fixed strategy curves no longer cross each other. The general conclusion concerning those strategies seems to be that the more one avoids sending jobs to broken servers, the better the performance that can be achieved, provided that an appropriate routing vector is employed.

A numerical search for the optimal routing vector is expensive, and rapidly becomes more so when the number of nodes increases. It is desirable, therefore, to find a good heuristic that avoids the search and yet produces a nearly optimal performance. One candidate for such a heuristic is the following: Assign to node i a weight, w_i, given by

$$w_i = \frac{\mu_i \eta_i}{\xi_i + \eta_i} \ , \quad i = 1, 2, \ldots, N \ .$$

This is the available service capacity of server i (the average amount of service it can provide per unit time). Let the ith element of the routing vector be

$$q_i = \frac{w_i}{\sum_{j=1}^{N} w_j} \ , \quad i = 1, 2, \ldots, N \ .$$

Thus the suggestion is to ignore the job arrival rate and simply split the input stream in proportion to the available service capacities.

In figure 5, the performance of the above heuristic is compared to that of the optimal routing vector (which does depend on λ), and also to the 'dumb' splitting based on the vector $(\frac{1}{N}, \frac{1}{N}, \ldots, \frac{1}{N})$. The experiment is carried out on a 5-node system under the selective routing strategy. The servers have the same breakdown and repair characteristics (about 90% operative), but different speeds. The average response time is plotted against λ.

It can be seen that, while the heuristic is very close to the optimal performance throughout the range of arrival rates, the equal splitting clearly fails to balance the loads at the different servers. The penalty of not using a good routing vector can be very large.

Unfortunately, the fine performance of the heuristic under the selective routing strategy is not replicated under the fixed ones. In particular, it performs very poorly with the fixed(m) strategy for small values of m. Another heuristic, better able to handle those strategies, is needed.

We combine the attempt to improve the heuristic with that of finding an approximate, but much faster solution of the model. The idea is to treat node i as an isolated single server queue modulated by a two-state Markov process. During operative periods, distributed exponentially with mean $1/\xi_i$, jobs arrive in a Poisson stream at rate λ_{i1}, and are served at rate μ_i. During inoperative periods, distributed exponentially with mean $1/\eta_i$, jobs arrive in a Poisson stream at rate λ_{i0}, and the service rate is 0. For a given strategy and routing vector, the two arrival rates are easily determined. Let $\Omega(i)$ be the set of all server configurations in which server i is operative, and $\overline{\Omega(i)}$ be the set of all configurations in which it is inoperative. Then

$$\lambda_{i1} = \frac{\xi_i + \eta_i}{\eta_i} \lambda \sum_{\sigma \subset \Omega(i)} p_\sigma q_i(\sigma) \ ,$$

$$\lambda_{i0} = \frac{\xi_i + \eta_i}{\xi_i} \lambda \sum_{\sigma \subset \overline{\Omega(i)}} p_\sigma q_i(\sigma) \ ,$$

where the probabilities p_σ are given by (1).

Thus the approximation consists of replacing a modulating process with 2^N states (all possible server configurations), by one with just 2 states. It should be pointed out that this approximation affects only the arrival process, not the services. Moreover, in the case of the fixed routing strategy, the approximation coincides with the exact solution. The two arrival rates are then equal: $\lambda_{i1} = \lambda_{i0} = \lambda q_i$.

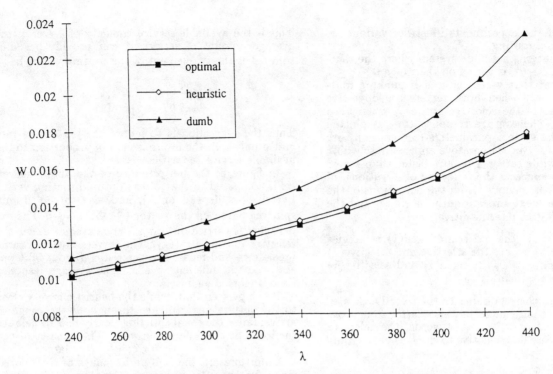

Figure 4: Optimised average response time as a function of the job arrival rate.
$N = 5$, $\mu_1 = 150$, $\mu_2 = 160$, $\mu_3 = 170$, $\mu_4 = 180$, $\mu_5 = 190$, $\xi_1 = \xi_2 = \xi_3 = \xi_4 = \xi_5 = 50$,
$\eta_1 = 50$, $\eta_2 = 60$, $\eta_3 = 70$, $\eta_4 = 80$, $\eta_5 = 100$

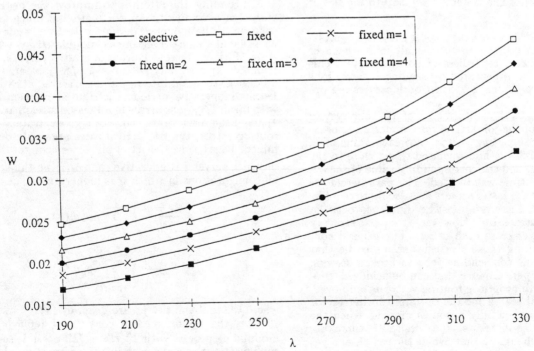

Figure 5: Comparisom between the heuristic, optimal and equal (dumb) routing, for different
arrival rates.
$N = 5$, $\mu_1 = 120$, $\mu_2 = 140$, $\mu_3 = 160$, $\mu_4 = 180$, $\xi_1 = \xi_2 = \xi_3 = \xi_4 = 10$,
$\eta_1 = \eta_2 = \eta_3 = \eta_4 = 100$

Under the simplifying assumption, it is not difficult to derive a closed-form solution for the isolated node i. The average number of jobs in it is given by

$$L_i = \frac{\eta_i \lambda_{i1} + \xi_i \lambda_{i0} + \frac{\xi_i}{\xi_i + \eta_i} \lambda_{i0}(\mu_i + \lambda_{i0} - \lambda_{i1})}{\eta_i \mu_i - \eta_i \lambda_{i1} - \xi_i \lambda_{i0}} \ . \quad (18)$$

Note that if $\lambda_{i0} = 0$, i.e. if node i does not accept jobs while broken, then (18) reduces to the standard result for the average queue size in an M/M/1 queue with parameters (λ_{i1}, μ_i).

The following optimization procedure is now suggested: for a given strategy, find the routing vector which minimizes the *approximate* average response time, W_{approx}. The search for that vector is considerably facilitated by the ease of computing W_{approx}.

This procedure performs extremely well, not only for the selective strategy (where the crude heuristic is already quite good), but also for the various fixed(m) and selective(m) strategies. The exact value of W computed after the approximate optimization is practically indistinguishable from that obtained by optimizing exactly. The relative error is much less than 1%, and would not show up on a figure.

Another question of interest concerns the accuracy of the approximation itself, as opposed to that of its optimal routing vector. A comparison between the exact and approximate values of W, in the context of a 5-node system under several routing strategies, is illustrated in Figures 6 and 7. In figure 6, the fixed(2), fixed(4) and selective strategies are evaluated for different arrival rates, λ, and the corresponding optimal routing vector. In all cases, the approximation underestimates the exact response time. The relative error is greater for the selective strategy than for the fixed ones. These observations are not surprising, since the approximation reduces the variability of the arrival stream, and that reduction is greater for the selective strategy. Even the larger error does nor exceed 10%.

Figure 7 shows the effect of changing m in the fixed(m) and selective(m) strategies. In the former, the variability of the arrival stream increases when m decreases, and so the accuracy of the approximation decreases. The influence of m on the selective strategies is negligible because in this system the probability that all servers are broken is very small. Again, the error is on the order of 10% or less.

Before we leave this section, some remarks on the complexity of the exact numerical solution are in order. To compute the distribution and/or the mean of one queue in an N-node system requires the determination of 2^N eigenvalues and eigenvectors, and the solution of a set of 2^N simultaneous linear equations. The complexity of that task is on the order of 2^{3N}. Since there are N queues, the total complexity of the full solution, for one set of parameters, is $O(N2^{3N})$. This is a large computational effort even for systems of moderate size. In addition, when the number of eigenvalues is very large, one begins to encounter numerical problems associated with ill-conditioned matrices.

The largest system we have been able to tackle had 8 nodes (256 server configurations); then the solution for a single queue took an hour.

The approximate solution is of course applicable for much larger values of N.

5   Generalizations

The solution methodology described in section 3 can be applied to more general models involving routing and breakdowns. For example, a breakdown may be accompanied by the loss of the job in service (if any), with a given probability. The only effect of that assumption is to complicate slightly the *Death* transitions of the process Y_k: these can now be from state (i, j) to state $(i', j - 1)$ ($i' = i$ if the departure is due to a service completion and $i' \neq i$ if to a breakdown). The matrix C_k is no longer diagonal but the solution procedure remains unchanged.

Similarly, a breakdown may be *caused*, with a certain probability, by the arrival of a job into a node. That complicates the *Birth* transitions of Y_k, making them from state (i, j) to state $(i', j + 1)$. The matrix B_k is then no longer diagonal. Both the above effects may be present in the same model.

It would be easy to modify the selective and selective-m strategies by making them lose incoming jobs when all servers are broken. In all these models where losses are possible, the average number of jobs lost per unit time is an important performance measure. That quantity is obtained directly from the probabilities (1) and from the distributions of the processes Y_k.

Another possible generalization concerns the introduction of more operative states. For instance, instead of being just operative or broken, a server may be *fully operative*, *partially operative* and *broken*. Perhaps when fully operative the server can both accept and serve jobs, when partially operative it can accept but not serve, and when broken it can neither accept nor serve. In general, a server could be in one of n possible opperative states, with different arrival and service characteristics in different states, and with transitions between states governed by an arbitrary Markov chain. Provided that those transitions, and the routing decisions, do not depend on how many jobs are present at other queues, the analysis would proceed as in section 3.

Of course, the price paid for such an increase in generality is a corresponding increase in complexity. Changing the composition of the matrices A_k, B_k and C_k does not alter significantly the computational complexity of the solution, but changing their size does. That size is determined by the number of system configurations. If, instead of the 2 possible operative states for each server there are n states, the total number of system configurations grows from 2^N to n^N. This imposes obvious limitations on the size of problems that can be solved numerically.

6   Conclusions

The system considered here has a property which may loosely be described as *quasi-separability*. An individual node can be analysed in isolation of the others, provided that the full server configuration is included as a state variable. Because of that property,

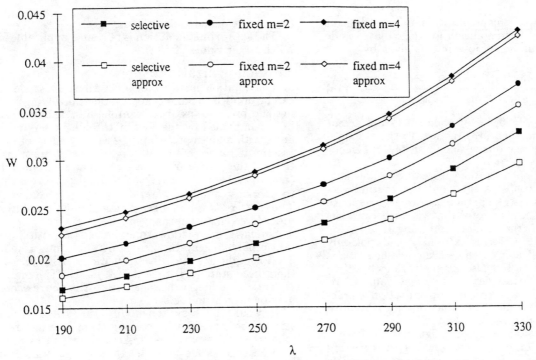

Figure 6: Exact and approximate solutions of average response timewith optimal routing vector
for different strategies.
$N = 5$, $\mu_1 = 150$, $\mu_2 = 160$, $\mu_3 = 170$, $\mu_4 = 180$, $\mu_5 = 190$,
$\xi_1 = \xi_2 = \xi_3 = \xi_4 = \xi_5 = 50$, $\eta_1 = 50$, $\eta_2 = 60$, $\eta_3 = 70$, $\eta_4 = 80$, $\eta_5 = 100$

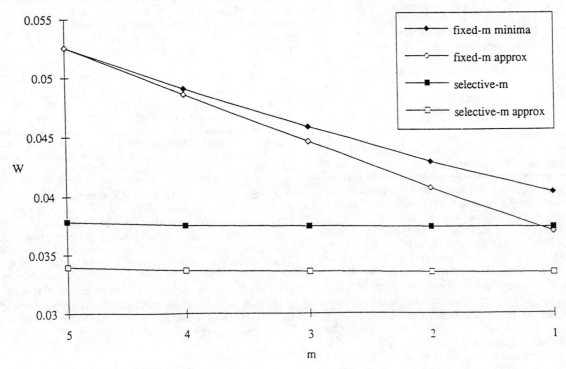

Figure 7: Exact and approximate solutions of average response time, with optimised routing
vector, as a function of job arrival rate.
$N = 5$, $\lambda = 350$, $\mu_1 = 150$, $\mu_2 = 160$, $\mu_3 = 170$, $\mu_4 = 180$, $\mu_5 = 190$,
$\xi_1 = \xi_2 = \xi_3 = \xi_4 = \xi_5 = 50$, $\eta_1 = 50$, $\eta_2 = 60$, $\eta_3 = 70$, $\eta_4 = 80$, $\eta_5 = 100$

one can determine exactly the performance measures in models with more than two nodes. It is also possible to optimize the splitting of the input stream among the nodes, under different routing policies. However, such an optimizations involves a search in a multidimensional space, together with the solution of many instances of the model. Computationally, this can be very expensive. A simple heuristic has been proposed, that appears to work well for selective routing policies, but not for fixed ones. Further progress can be made either by discovering more generally applicable heuristics, or by developing fast approximate solutions whose complexity does not grow exponentially with N. Both these avenues of further research are worth pursuing.

Acknowledgement

This work was carried out in connection with the Basic Research projects QMIPS (Quantitative Methods In Parallel Systems), and PDCS 2 (Predictably Dependable Computer Systems), funded by the European Union. The first author is supported by a CASE scholarship and is sponsored by British Telecom.

References

[1] B. Avi-Itzhak and P. Naor, "Some Queueing Problems with the Service Station Subject to Breakdowns", *Operations Research*, 11, pp. 303-320, 1963.

[2] J.W.Cohen and O.J. Boxma, *Boundary Value Problems in Queueing System Analysis*, North-Holland (Elsevier), 1983.

[3] G. Fayolle and R. Iasnogorodski, "Two Coupled Processors: The reduction to a Riemann-Hilbert Problem", *Z. Wahrsheinlichkeitstheorie*, 47, pp. 325-351, 1979.

[4] F.D. Gakhov *Boundary Value Problems*, Addison Wesley, 1966.

[5] N. Mikou, "A Two-Node Jackson Network Subject to Breakdowns", *Stochastic Models*, 4, pp. 523-552, 1988.

[6] O. Idrissi-Kacemi, N. Mikou and S. Saadi, "Two Processors Only Interacting During Breakdown: The Case Where the Load is Not Lost", submitted for publication.

[7] I. Mitrani, "Networks of Unreliable Computers", in *Computer Architectures and Networks* (eds. E. Gelenbe and R. Mahl), North-Holland, 1974.

[8] I. Mitrani and B. Avi-Itzhak, "A Many-Server Queue with Service Interruptions", *Operations Research*, 16, 3, pp. 628-638, 1968.

[9] I. Mitrani and R. Chakka, "Spectral Expansion Solution for a Class of Markov Models: Application and Comparison with the Matrix-Geometric Method", to appear in *Performance Evaluation*.

[10] I. Mitrani and D. Mitra, "A Spectral Expansion Method for Random Walks on Semi-Infinite Strips", in *Iterative Methods in Linear Algebra* (Eds R. Beauwens and P. de Groen), North-Holland, 1992.

[11] I. Mitrani and P.E. Wright "Routing in the Presence of Breakdowns", *Performance Evaluation*, 20, pp. 151-164, 1994.

[12] N.I. Muskhelishvili *Singular Integral Equations*, P. Noordhoff, 1953.

[13] B. Sengupta, "A Queue with Service Interruptions in an Alternating Markovian Environment", *Operations Research*, 38, pp. 308-318, 1990.

[14] H.C. White and L.S. Christie, "Queueing with Preemptive Priorities or with Breakdown", *Operations Research*, 6, pp. 79-95, 1958.

An Analysis of Impact of Workload Fluctuations on Performance of Computer Systems

Guang-Liang Li *

Institute of Computing Technology

Academia Sinica, P. O. Box 2704–1, Beijing 100080

P. R. China

gli@mimi.cnc.ac.cn

Abstract

This paper presents an analysis of system performance degradation induced by workload fluctuations. The basic idea of the analysis is based on catastrophe theory. Conventional performance models typically express workload only by using its average properties. However, we may not be able to predict system performance simply by using average workload properties, since computer systems are nonlinear systems and workload of computer systems usually fluctuates. The interaction between workload fluctuations and the nonlinearity may greatly affect system behavior. Our analysis shows that fluctuations in workload may change the dynamic structure of the system state space and cause the system performance to vary drastically.

1 Introduction

Performance degradation is a phenomenon that has been observed in many practical computer systems for a long time [3,17,2,16]. When performance degradation occurs, the system moves abruptly from a stable state with an optimal performance to another stable state but with a worse performance. This phenomenon is especially typical in some distributed systems such as compter networks [16]. Although in some systems the cause of such multistability may be deterministic [5], there exist systems for which deterministic factors may not be appropriate explanations. Systems modeled by queueing models [20] typically fall into this categrory; the existence condition of queueing model solution excludes the deterministic causes of such multistability. If this existence condition holds for a system, then the system should settle down in a unique stable state corresponding to an optimal performance; otherwise, the system would crash. The existence condition of queueing model soluion usually corresponds to average workload properties of systems. Even in a system designed according to average workload properties to have a unique optimal performance, we may still observe performance degradation. Since deterministic factors may not be the cause of multistability in these systems, fluctuations in workload may be responsible for such behavior. Conventional perfor-

mance models typically express workload by using its average workload properties. This treatment of workload is based on an assumption that we might be able to average out the effect of fluctuations in workload and the system would adjust its behavior to its average workload properties. However, computer systems are nonlinear systems where system performance does not vary linearly with system load and workload of computer systems usually fluctuates. We may not be able to predict system performance simply by using average workload properties, since the interaction between workload fluctuations and the nonlinearity may greatly affect system behavior.

We present an analysis of system performance degradation induced by workload fluctuations. The basic idea of the analysis belongs to catastrophe theory [29]. The analysis shows that there exists a certain relation between fluctuations in workload and system performance degradation, which has not been addressed in the literature.

Some authors have already used catastrophe-theoretic ideas to analyze performance of computer systems [24,25,19]. Other authors have analyzed the impact of the fluctuations in the arrival process to a queueing system on the stability of the system [27]. There are also a number of approaches that can be used to capture workload fluctuations, such as the Markov modulated Poisson process used in [9,26], Markov fluids developed in [1,22], and the work by Hsueh et al. [11]. Our work differs from theirs in that we model the interaction between the nonlinearity of system behavior and fluctuations in system workload and analyze the impact of such interaction on sytem performance.

In Section 2, we introduce an analytical model and outline the assumptions. Based on the model, we analyze the impact of workload fluctuations on system performance in Section 3. In Section 4, we summarize the results and briefly discuss the further research.

2 Modelling Nonlinearity and Workload Fluctuations

We model the system with a one-dimensional diffusion process. For distributed systems, this model cannot capture the interaction among the subsystems;

---

*This work was supported by Academia Sinica.

256

however, we conjecture that the interaction may not be able to exclude performance degradation induced by workload fluctuations and intuitively, it would aggravate the phenomenon. Therefore, for the purpose of this study, the one-dimensional diffusion model is sufficient.

Let $x(t)$ be the number of jobs to be finished in the system at time t. We are interested in systems with moderate or heavy load. Similar to the diffusion approximation to queueing models under the heavy traffic assumption [18], we may consider x as a continuous variable. For a real-world system, there exists a maximum number of jobs that the system can carry. For simplicity and without loss of generality, let this maximum number of jobs equal one. So x is in the closed interval $[0, 1]$. We may interpret x as the number of jobs in the system scaled by the maximum number of jobs that the system can carry. Let $x_1(t)$ be the number of jobs accepted by the system and $x_2(t)$ be the number of jobs finished by the system in time interval $(0, t)$. We have

$$\frac{dx(t)}{dt} = \frac{dx_1(t)}{dt} - \frac{dx_2(t)}{dt}, \quad (1)$$

where

$$\frac{dx_m(t)}{dt} = g_m(x)\lambda_m(t), \ m = 1, 2. \quad (2)$$

The function $g_1(x)$ denotes the ratio of the number of jobs accepted by the system to the number of jobs arrived, the stochastic process $\lambda_1(t)$ is the job arrival rate at time t (jobs / time unit), the function $g_2(x)$ is the effective processing capacity of the system (basic operations / time unit), and the stochastic process $\lambda_2^{-1}(t)$ is the processing demand of the job (basic operations / job) being processed by the system at time t. The stochastic processes $\lambda_m(t), m = 1, 2$ describe the impact of fluctuations in workload of the system.

The assumptions for the analysis are as follows:

1. The stochastic processes are stationary with means $\overline{\lambda}_m$ and variances $\sigma_m^2, m = 1, 2$, because user environments do not evolve systematically in general, at least over the time span concerned by performance analysts. So

$$\lambda_m(t) = \overline{\lambda}_m + \xi_m(t), \quad (3)$$

where $\xi_m(t), m = 1, 2$ represent fluctuations in workload.

2. Fluctuations in workload are the cumulative effect of numerous different factors and vary on a much faster time scale than systems, so we could model them as Gaussian white noises with

$$E[\xi_m(t)] = 0, \ m = 1, 2, \quad (4)$$

$$E[\xi_m(t)\xi_n(\tau)] = \delta_{mn}\delta(t - \tau)\sigma_m^2, \ m, n = 1, 2, \quad (5)$$

where

$$\delta_{mn} = \begin{cases} 1, & m = n \\ 0, & \text{otherwise,} \end{cases}$$

$$\delta(t - \tau) = \begin{cases} \infty, & t = \tau \\ 0, & \text{otherwise.} \end{cases}$$

For the purpose of this study, we assume that fluctuations in the workload are not too large. This is because arbitrarily large fluctuations may cause the stochastic processes $\lambda_m(t), m = 1, 2$ that characterize the job arrival and the processing demand to take negative values, which is meaningless. In addition, if the fluctuations are too large, one may not be able to define stable states of the system properly. Therefore, we focus on a situation in which although workload fluctuates, the fluctuations are reasonably small. So the stochastic processes can remain nonnegative and stable states of the system can be well-defined.

3. The functions $g_m(x), m = 1, 2$ have the following qualitative properties:

   (a) According to the definition,

   $$0 < g_1(x) < 1, \ 0 \le x < 1. \quad (6)$$

   (b) It is necessary to control the input of the system, that is, the number of jobs accepted by the system, in order to achieve an optimal performance [16]. Therefore, the number of jobs allowed to be accepted by the system decreases as the number of jobs already in the system increases, and the system would not accept any job when the total number of jobs in the system reaches the maximum number of jobs that the system can carry. So

   $$\frac{dg_1(x)}{dx} < 0, \ 0 \le x \le 1; \ g_1(1) = 0. \quad (7)$$

   (c) According to the definition,

   $$g_2(x) > 0, \ 0 < x < 1. \quad (8)$$

   (d) If there is no jobs in the system, then the effective processing capacity of the system is zero. If the number of jobs in the system reaches the maximum number of jobs that the system can support, then the system would collapse due to deadlock so caused [16]. Therefore, $x = 1$ represents the worst case of performance degradation in which the effective processing capacity of the system drops to zero. So

   $$g_2(0) = g_2(1) = 0. \quad (9)$$

(e) The effective processing capacity of the system increases as the system state variable x grows below a critical value x_0. However, with the constraint of resource limitation, the effective processing capacity of the system would decrease after the state variable exceeds the critical value. That is,

$$\frac{dg_2(x)}{dx} \begin{cases} > 0, & 0 \le x < x_0 \\ = 0, & x = x_0 \\ < 0, & x_0 < x \le 1. \end{cases} \quad (10)$$

The above properties of the function $g_m(x), m = 1, 2$, are typical for many computer systems. Previous studies have substantiated these properties [2,3,6,14,15,16,8,12]. Properties (d) and (e) are the qualitative description of the observation of these systems. Specifically, property (e) describes the intrinsic nonlinearity of the system behavior caused by resource limitation. Although one may keep the system state from exceeding the critical value, we may not be able to exclude this property from a real-world system.

Thus, the following stochastic differential equation holds:

$$\frac{dx(t)}{dt} = f(x) + g_1(x)\xi_1(t) - g_2(x)\xi_2(t), \quad (11)$$

where

$$f(x) = g_1(x)\overline{\lambda}_1 - g_2(x)\overline{\lambda}_2. \quad (12)$$

If on the interval $[0, 1]$ the functions $g_m(x), m = 1, 2$, are twice continuous and differentiable, then with the Ito interpretation [10,23], we may switch equation (11) to the forward Kolmogorov equation governing the temporal evolution of the probability density $P(x, t)$ of the stochastic process $x(t)$:

$$\frac{\partial P(x,t)}{\partial t} = -\frac{\partial[f(x)P(x,t)]}{\partial x}$$
$$+ \frac{1}{2}\frac{\partial^2}{\partial x^2}\sum_{m=1}^{2}\sigma_m^2[g_m^2(x)P(x,t)]. \quad (13)$$

We only consider the steady-state behavior of the system. The stationary solution of equation (13) is

$$P_s(x) = \frac{N}{G(x)}\exp\left[2\int^x \frac{f(u)du}{G(u)}\right], \quad (14)$$

where

$$G(x) = \sum_{m=1}^{2}\sigma_m^2 g_m^2(x), \quad (15)$$

and N is the normalization constant. The existence of the stationary solution will ensure that the state variable is well-defined.

The basic idea of the model developed here belongs to catastrophe theory [29]. In fact, the probability density $P_s(x)$ has the properties of potential functions in the sense of Thom. This stochastic potential function depends on not only the parameters describing the deterministic factors influencing the system but also the parameters characterizing the stochastic fluctuations in workload of the system. Therefore, based on this model, we can analyze the impact of workload fluctuations on system performance.

Let C denote the space from which all these parameters take their values. Corresponding to an open set C_s in C, the behavior of the system is *structurally stable* [7,4]. This means especially that the number and type of the extrema of $P_s(x)$ do not change if the parameters vary in C_s. On the other hand, the system behavior is structurally unstable if the parameters belong to the complement $C_u = C - C_s$. The dimensionality of C_u is typically one less than that of C_s. When the parameters cross C_u and re-enter C_s, the shape of $P_s(x)$ changes in quality and the behavior and the performance of the system change drastically. This phenomenon is called *bifurcation*. The set C_u is called *catastrophe set* or *bifurcation set* and defined for some x as

$$C_u = \left\{ u \in C : \frac{dP_s(x)}{dx} = \frac{d^2P_s(x)}{dx^2} = 0 \right\}. \quad (16)$$

The change of the dynamic structure of the system state space may affect not only the behavior and the performance of the system but also the results obtained from models that do not consider workload fluctuations. In such models, the performance metric is usually the function of the mean value of the system state variable corresponding to the average workload properties. If the probability distribution of the state variable is unimodal, then these models are valid and the mean state and the average performance are useful approximations to the most probable state and the most probable performance, respectively. Otherwise, the mean state may only be a compromise state of several most probable states. The probability of such a state may be rather small, and the average performance may not be likely to appear. Therefore, in this case, the average performance analysis and the optimization as well as control based on such analysis may have little use in practice. The analysis presented in the next section will show that fluctuations in workload can indeed destroy the unimodal shape of the probability distribution of the system state variable.

3 Bifurcation Caused by Workload Fluctuations

To obtain more general conclusions, we analyze the model under only a few qualitative assumptions made in Section 2. We may interpret $P_s(x)$, the stationary solution of equation (13), as a measure of the fraction of time an arbitrary realization of $x(t)$ spends in an infinitesimal vicinity of x [10]. So we may identify the extrema of $P_s(x)$ with the steady state of the system. The maxima, in whose neighborhood the system tends to reside, are the *stable* steady states and preferentially observable. These states are also called *most probable states.* On the other hand, the minima, which the system leaves rather quickly, are unstable steady states. We may describe the stable behavior and performance of the system by the maxima of $P_s(x)$.

We determine the extrema of $P_s(x)$ according to $dP_s(x)/dx = 0$, that is

$$f(x) - \sum_{m=1}^{2} \left[\sigma_m^2 g_m(x) \frac{dg_m(x)}{dx} \right] = 0. \quad (17)$$

The most probable states have to fulfill the further condition $d^2 P_s(x)/dx^2 < 0$, that is

$$\frac{df(x)}{dx} < \sum_{m=1}^{2} \sigma_m^2 \left[\left(\frac{dg_m(x)}{dx} \right)^2 + g_m(x) \frac{d^2 g_m(x)}{dx^2} \right]. \quad (18)$$

According to the qualitative properties of the functions $g_m(x), m = 1, 2$, we may re-write the extrema condition equation (17) as follows

$$G_1(x)\psi_1(x) = G_2(x)\psi_2(x), \quad (19)$$

where

$$G_m(x) = \overline{\lambda}_m g_m(x), \ m = 1, 2 \quad (20)$$

represent the input and output flows of the system, respectively, corresponding to the average workload properties. The following equations

$$\psi_1(x) = 1 + \theta_1 \left| \frac{dg_1(x)}{dx} \right|, \ 0 \le x \le 1, \quad (21)$$

$$\psi_2(x) = \begin{cases} 1 + \theta_2 \left| \frac{dg_2(x)}{dx} \right|, & x \le x_0 \\ 1 - \theta_2 \left| \frac{dg_2(x)}{dx} \right|, & \text{otherwise}, \end{cases} \quad (22)$$

$$\theta_m = \sigma_m^2 / \overline{\lambda}_m, \ m = 1, 2, \quad (23)$$

reflect the impact of the workload fluctuations. Since $G_2(x)\psi_2(x)$ represents the output flow affected by the workload fluctuation, its value should not be negative. This requires $\psi_2(x) \ge 0$. Therefore, for $x > x_0$, if $\psi_2(x) < 0$, then we set $\psi_2(x) = 0$.

If we do not consider the workload fluctuations, then the steady states of the system are determined by the common points of the curves G_1 and G_2. For practical systems, we may not be able to exclude the steady state $x = 1$, which represents the crashing state. The best we may expect is to keep the crashing state unstable. Based on the average workload properties, if we require

$$\max G_1(x) < \max G_2(x), \ 0 \le x \le 1; \quad (24)$$

$$G_1(x) < G_2(x), \ x_0 \le x < 1, \quad (25)$$

and

$$\frac{dG_1(1)}{dx} > \frac{dG_2(1)}{dx}, \quad (26)$$

then the system will have only one stable steady state $x = x_s$, representing the stable (and perhaps optimal) operation point of the system; the crashing state $x = 1$ is an unstable steady state, as shown in Fig. 1. For the purpose of this study, in the following analysis, we assume that inequalities (24), (25) and (26) hold, so in the absence of fluctuations, the system has only one stable state with an optimal performance and the crashing state is unstable. This assumption represents a desirable property in the system optimal design and excludes the deterministic causes of multistability.

If we take the workload fluctuations into account, then the steady states of the system are determined by the common points of the curves

$$\Psi_m(x) = G_m(x)\psi_m(x), \ m = 1, 2. \quad (27)$$

They are the curves G_m deformed by the workload fluctuations. The stability condition [inequality (18)] now becomes

$$\frac{d\Psi_1(x)}{dx} < \frac{d\Psi_2(x)}{dx}. \quad (28)$$

Fig. 2 shows the deformation of the curve G_1. Since for $0 \le x \le 1$ inequality $\psi_1(x) > 1$ holds, we have $G_1(x) \le \Psi_1(x)$.

Fig. 3 shows the deformation of the curve G_2. If $0 \le x \le x_0$, then $\psi_2(x) \ge 1$, and $\psi_2(x) = 1$ when $x = x_0$. Therefore, $G_2(x) \le \Psi_2(x)$ for $0 \le x \le x_0$. If $x_0 < x < 1$, then $\psi_2(x) < 1$, so $G_2(x) > \Psi_2(x)$. If $\psi_2(x) > 0$ for $x_0 < x < 1$, we see that $G_2(x) > \Psi_2(x) > 0$. However, if σ_2^2, the fluctuation in the processing demand, is large enough such that $\psi_2(x) = 0$, then the fluctuation will force $\Psi_2(x)$ to remain zero on a subinterval of $(x_0, 1]$. In the following, we analyze the impact of the workload fluctuations on the performance of the system. Specifically, we show that although according to average workload properties the system might settle down in a unique stable state with an optimal performance, multistability may still appear to cause performance degradation if the workload fluctuations are sufficiently large.

Without loss of generality, we consider the throughput as the performance metric of the system defined as a non-negative function of the system state variable. According to the nonlinear behavior of the system, the performance metric is zero when $x = 0$, and will approach 0 as x approaches 1. Otherwise, the performance metric remains positive. We define the *steady-state performance* as the performance calculated at the extrema of $P_s(x)$. The performance calculated at the maximum is stable, preferentially observable, and called the *most probable performance*. Whereas the performance corresponding to the minimum is unstable.

If the fluctuations are small, then the curves $G_m, m = 1, 2$ change only slightly as shown in Fig. 4. From a comparison of Fig. 1 and Fig. 4, we see that $P_s(x)$ has a maximum at $x = x_{m1}$ and a minimum at $x = 1$. Due to the fluctuations, $x_{m1} = x_s$ need not hold. Yet, the system still has a unique stable steady state, and accordingly, the behavior and the performance of the system only change slightly. The system

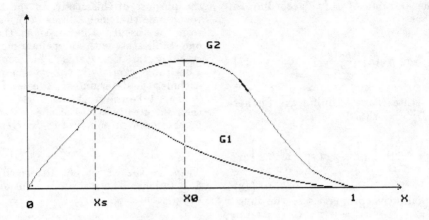

Figure 1: The steady states of the system in the absence of workload fluctuations.

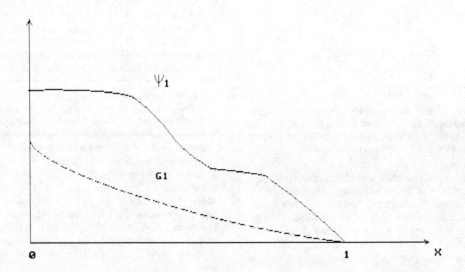

Figure 2: The deformation of the curve G_1.

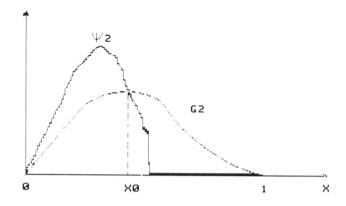

Figure 3: The deformation of the curve G_2.

can operate stably in a neighborhood of that state and has a unique most probable positive performance. The crashing state $x - 1$ is unstable. This is the behavior typically predicted by queueing models. In addition, if the fluctuations are sufficiently small, we have in fact $P_s(1) = 0$. Although all points in the system state space are *recurrent*, that is, as $t \to \infty$, the system will approach any $x \in [0, 1]$ with probability 1, arbitrarily closely, infinitely often, the system will spend most of its time near the unique stable state.

If the fluctuations are large enough, then they may significantly deform the curves $G_m, m = 1, 2$, and some interesting phenomena may appear. Accordingly, the behavior and the performance of the system may change drastically. On the one hand, for a fixed value of σ_1^2, if σ_2^2 increases to a value large enough such that the curves $\Psi_m, m = 1, 2$, have at least two points of intersection for $0 < x < 1$ besides the trivial common point $x = 1$, and if

$$\left| \frac{dg_2(1)}{dx} \right| \left[\overline{\lambda}_2 - \sigma_2^2 \left| \frac{dg_2(1)}{dx} \right| \right] < \left| \frac{dg_1(1)}{dx} \right| \left[\overline{\lambda}_1 + \sigma_1^2 \left| \frac{dg_1(1)}{dx} \right| \right], \quad (29)$$

then $d^2 P_s(1)/dx^2 < 0$ holds. The above conditions imply that the system parameters have crossed the bifurcation set. Now $x = 1$ becomes a maximum of $P_s(x)$ and $P_s(x)$ has more than two maxima, so multistability appears. The system has at least two stable steady states, including the crashing state. There may exist several different performances for identical average workload properties. The system may move abruptly from one most probable state to another, causing the performance to degrade and even causing the system to crash. Fig. 5 shows a simple example. In contrast to the situation described in Fig. 4, we see that in Fig. 5, the system behavior has changed drastically. In this example, $P_s(x)$ has two maxima: $x = x_{m1}$ and $x = 1$, with a minimum at $x = x_{m2}$. Bistability appears in the system. Yet, all points in $[0, 1]$ are still

recurrent; however, since the crashing state has become stable, the system may also spend much time near the crashing state. In practice, such a large excursion arbitrarily near $x = 1$ may in fact lead to a system crash. The system performance deteriorates.

On the other hand, if we fix σ_2^2 and let σ_1^2 increase, then all other extrema except the maximum $x = 1$ of $P_s(x)$ will gradually disappear as shown in Fig. 6. The system will lose all the steady states with positive performance metrics. The only most probable state left is the crashing state. This phenomenon occurs if

$$\Psi_1(x) > \Psi_2(x), \ 0 \le x < 1. \quad (30)$$

When (30) holds, if we have

$$\int_0^1 G^{-1}(x) \exp \left[2 \int^x \frac{f(u)du}{G(u)} \right] dx < \infty, \quad (31)$$

then although the system will spend most of its time near the crashing state $x = 1$, all points $x \in [0, 1]$ are still recurrent. The system may still work, but with a much worse performance. However, if (31) does not hold, then the total stationary probability mass will be entirely concentrated on $x = 1$:

$$P_s(x) = \delta(1 - x). \quad (32)$$

In this case, only the crashing state will remain recurrent, all other points $0 \le x < 1$ in the system state space will cease to be recurrent and become *transient*; the system will visit these states only a finite number of times. The system will collapse, that is, as $t \to \infty$, the system state x converges to the crashing state $x = 1$ with probability 1.

In summary, the variance of the intensity of the workload fluctuations may create, destroy, and change the type of the extrema of $P_s(x)$ and change the property of points in the system state space. This may cause the system behavior to change drastically and greatly affect the system performance. The above analysis also shows that in order for a system with

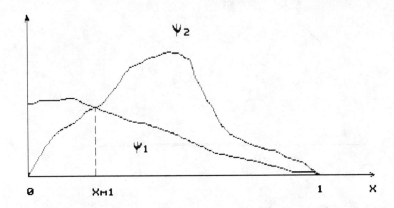

Figure 4: Small fluctuations deform the curve $G_m, m = 1, 2$, only slightly.

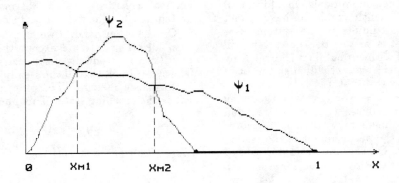

Figure 5: An example of bistability induced by workload fluctuations.

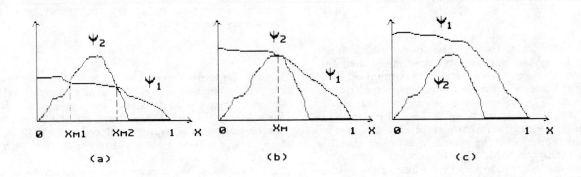

Figure 6: The disappearance of steady states. (a) Bistability. (b) x_{m1} and x_{m2} coincided and became x_m. (c) x_m disappeared.

262

fluctuating workload to have a unique stable operation point, the average workload properties may not be sufficient, since the stability condition [inequality (18)] includes the parameters characterizing the workload fluctuations. We may have to adjust control parameters to adapt to the impact of workload fluctuations.

4 Conclusion

According to the theory of complex systems, it is the rule rather than the exception that the behavior of any complex system is nonlinear. This is also true for computer systems. The causes of the nonlinear behavior of systems may include the resource limitation, the control mechanism that controls the competition for the limited resources by different users, workload fluctuations, as well as the interaction between the control mechanism and workload fluctuations. Understanding the nonlinear behavior of the system is important to the system design and analysis. Multistability and bifurcation are typical nonlinear behaviors, which may lead to performance degradation. Our analysis shows that multistability and bifurcation induced by workload fluctuations may be the cause of performance degradation observed in systems designed based on average workload properties to have a unique stable operation point. According to our analysis, the system may gradually lose all its steady states with positive performance metrics if the fluctuation in the job arrival increases; whereas if the fluctuation in the processing demand grows, multistability may appear in the system behavior. Performance models based on average workload properties may not be able to capture the impact of workload fluctuations. Although there are some methods that can be used to capture workload fluctuations, the impact of the interaction between workload fluctuations and the nonlinearity of systems on system performance have not been addressed in the literature. Our work supplements the conventional analysis and theoretically explains the system behavior under the influence of workload fluctuations. Yet, as the first step toward the exploration of the performance impact of workload fluctuations, this work is still in its early stages. In the following, we discuss briefly a number of interesting open problems that need further research.

1. Perhaps the most important problem is to construct more detailed models to analyze and design appropriate control mechanisms, so we may be able to adapt to the performance impact of workload fluctuations in practice.

2. In our analysis, we model the workload fluctuations as white noises based on the assumption that fluctuations in workload vary on a much faster time scale than systems. This may not be suitable for some systems for which modeling workload fluctuations as colored noises may be more appropriate. Recent measurements indicate that there may exist correlation in workload for some systems [21]. Yet, we conjecture that the correlation in workload may not be able to exclude multistability induced by workload fluctuations. However, the performance impact of workload fluctuations modeled as colored noises is subject to further research.

3. Our exploration of the performance impact of workload fluctuations is based on an analytical approach. Although we have gained some insights from the analysis, some analytical assumptions may appear stringent. For some systems a simulation approach may be more suitable. However, conventional techniques may not be very useful for modeling catastrophe or bifurcation phenomena, because conventional simulation models are subject to the continuity test or sensitive analysis, which requires the output of a simulation model not to change drastically if the parameters of the model are changed only slightly [13] . Therefore, the conventional techniques may only be able to model the system behavior corresponding to the situation in which all the system parameters take their values only within a connected subset of the parameter space C_s not separated by the bifurcation set C_u. So these models may exclude the catastrophe or bifurcation phenomena subject to study. The method developed by Takens [28] may be useful for this purpose. Takens proved that for an n-dimensional system, if there are sufficient observation data of one of the state variables $x(t)$, then we may construct an m-dimensional system, $m \leq n$, with state variables $x(t), x(t+T), ..., x[t+(m-1)T]$ for almost every time lag T, which has the same dynamical properties as the original n-dimensional system. With a simulation model based on this technique, we may be able to reconstruct the bifurcation or catastrophe properties from simulation data and detect such phenomena in an experimental setting.

References

[1] D. Anick, D. Mitra, and M. M. Sondhi, "Stochastic theory of a data-handling system with multiple sources", *Bell Syst. Tech. J.*, vol. 61, pp. 1871–1894, 1982.

[2] P.-J. Courtois, "On time and space decomposition of complex structures". *Commun. ACM*, vol. 28, no. 6, pp. 590–603, June 1985.

[3] P. J. Denning, "Thrashing: its causes and prevention", in *Proc. AFIPS Fall Joint Compt. Conf.* San Francisco, Cali. Dec. 9–11, AFIPS Press, Arlington, Va., 1968, pp. 915–922.

[4] W. Ebeling, "Structural stability of stochastic systems" in *Chaos and Order in Nature*, Springer-Verlag, 1981.

[5] M. Garzia and C. Lockhart, "Nonhierachical communication networks: an application of compartmental modeling", *IEEE Trans. Commun.*, vol 37, no. 6, pp. 555–564, June 1989.

[6] M. Gerla and L. Kleinrock, "Flow control: a comparative survey", *IEEE Trans. Commun.*, vol. com-28, no. 4, pp. 553–574, Apr. 1980.

[7] J. Guckenheimer and P. Holmes, *Nonlinear Oscillations, Dynamical Systems, and Bifurcations of Vector Fields*, Springer-Verlag, 1983.

[8] A. Giessler et al., "Free buffer allocation — an investigation by simulation", *Comput. Netw.*, vol. 2, pp. 191 – 208, 1978.

[9] H. Heffes and D. Lucantoni, "A Morkov modulated characterization of voice and data traffic and related statistical multiplexer performance", *IEEE J. Select. Areas Commun.*, vol. SAC-4, pp. 856–867, Sept. 1986.

[10] W. Horsthemke, *Noise-Induced Transitions*, Springer-Verlag, 1984.

[11] Hsueh et al., "Performability modeling based on real data" *IEEE TC*, April 1988.

[12] R. Jain, "Congestion control in computer networks: issues and trends", *IEEE Network*, vol. 4, no. 4, pp. 24–30, May 1990.

[13] R. Jain, *The art of Computer System Performance Analysis*, John Wiley & Sons, 1991.

[14] L. Kleinrock, "On flow control in computer networks", in *Conference Record of the International Conference on Communication*, vol. 2, June 1978, New York, pp. 27.2.1–27.2.5.

[15] L. Kleinrock, "Power and deterministic rules of thumb for probabilistic problems in computer communications", in *Conference Record of the international Conference on Communications*, IEEE, New York, June 1979, pp. 43.1.1–43.1.10.

[16] L. Kleinrock, "Distributed systems", *Commun. ACM*, vol. 28, no. 11, pp. 1200–1213, Nov. 1985.

[17] L. Kleinrock and S. Lam, "Packet switching in a multiaccess broadcast channel performance evaluation", *IEEE Trans. Commun.*, vol. 23 no. 3, pp. 410–423, Apr. 1975.

[18] H. Kobayashi, "Application of the diffusion approximations to queueing networks I: Equilibrium distributions", *J. ACM*, vol. 21, no. 2, pp. 316–328, Apr. 1974.

[19] J. Kaniyil, Y. Onozato and S. Noguchi, "Input buffer limiting: behavior analysis of a node throughout the range of blocking probabilities", *IEEE Trans. on Commun.*, vol. 39, no. 12, pp. 1813–1822, Dec. 1991.

[20] S. S. Lavenberg, "A perspective on queueing models of computer performance", *Performance Evaluation*, vol. 10, pp. 53–76, 1989.

[21] W. Leland et al., "On the self-similar nature of Ethernet traffic", *Proc. ACM/SIGCOMM'93*, San Francisco, 1993.

[22] D. Mitra, "Stochastic theory of a fluid model of producers and consumers coupled by a buffer", *Adv. Appl. Prob.*, vol. 20, pp. 646–676, 1988.

[23] F. Moss and P. V. E. McClintock, eds. *Noise in Nonlinear Dynamical Systems*, three volumes, Cambridge University Press, 1989.

[24] R. Nelson, "Stochastic catastrophe theory in computer performance modeling", *J. ACM*, vol. 34, no. 3, pp. 661–685, July 1987.

[25] Y. Onozato and Noguchi, "On the thrashing cusp in slotted ALOHA system", *IEEE Trans. Commun.*, vol. com-33. no. 11, pp. 1171–1182, Nov. 1985.

[26] R. Nagarajan, J. F. Kurose, and D. Towsley, "Approximation technique for computing packet loss in finite-buffered voice multiplexers", *IEEE J. Select. Areas Commun.*, vol. 9, no. 3, pp. 368–377, April 1991.

[27] C. Rosenberg, R. Mazumdar, and L. Kleinrock, "On the analysis of exponential queueing system with randomly changing arrival rates: stability conditions and finite buffer scheme with a resume level", *Performance Evaluation*, vol. 11, pp. 283–292, 1990.

[28] F. Takens, "Detecting strange attractors in turbulence", in *Lecture Notes in Mathematics*, eds D. A. Rand and L-S Young, Springer-Verlag, New York, 1981.

[29] R. Thom, *Structural Stability and Morphogenesis*, W. A. Benjamin, Reading, Mass., 1975.

Evaluation of Performability Measures for Replicated Banyan Networks *

Amiya Bhattacharya
CSE Department

Ramesh R. Rao
ECE Department

Ting-Ting Y. Lin
ECE Department

University of California, San Diego
La Jolla, CA 92093

Abstract

Performability, a composite measure that evolved from the synergy between performance and reliability, can capture the cumulative performance of a degradable multistage interconnection network over its operational life. In this paper, we present a technique for conservative analysis of performability measures for the replicated banyan network. Assuming uniformly distributed message generation at unblocked sources, we make a reward assignment for synchronous circuit-switched operation that translates the cumulative performance to total number of messages routed. The analytical results and simulated values for the average level of the cumulative performance of a replicated banyan are compared. The analysis technique is capable of handling non-Markovian model of component failure. The effect of perturbation from the Markovian model on the cumulative performance has been studied.

1 Introduction

Multistage interconnection networks (MIN), a low-cost alternative to full crossbar, have been used to set up connections between two groups of modules in a wide range of computer and communication systems. The shared memory multiprocessor system is the most common example, where every memory access for a processor takes place through a MIN placed between the processors and memory modules. Banyan networks [13] (also referred to as delta networks by some authors [3]), a class of blocking MINs with unique path property, have received the widest publicity for their self-routing capability. A simple multipath banyan can be constructed by replicating the single-path pro-

totype and coupling them at the input and output. Each layer of a *replicated* banyan inherits the self-routing and blocking properties, and together they achieve higher permutation capability and fault tolerance. The fault-free MINs offer better performance and reliability, but the performance-reliability trade-off plays an important role when the system operates in a degraded mode as a consequence of component failure.

The traditional performance analysis of fault-free multipath banyans [5, 9] left out reliability issues. On the other hand, the degraded modes of operation were ignored by structural reliability analysis techniques [11]. The gap was bridged by the introduction of a composite measure called performability [1] and its wide acceptance [18]. This measure is essentially the probability that the system reaches an accomplishment level over a mission time. Under this framework, the system configuration under successive faults is characterized by a stochastic process. Even if the system is potentially repairable, the designer is concerned with the transient behavior of the system over the mission. So the quantification reduces to the evaluation of the distribution or moments of some accumulated performance metric (reward) defined on this stochastic process.

The closed form solution to performability can be obtained by conditioning on the state trajectories (sample paths) [4, 6]. This involves a number of integral evaluations that grows linearly with the number of trajectories. An exponential growth of trajectories is quite common. The tradition is to do performability analysis under a Markov reward model [4, 8, 10, 14, 16], where the problem reduces to the transient analysis of the underlying Markov chain. However, due to the memoryless property of Markov process, it implies an exponential distribution of sojourn time, and a constant hazard rate. The valid-

*Supported by ONR under grant N0001491-J1017 and NSF under grant NCR-8904029

ity of this assumption is oftentimes questionable. In practice, system components have been better characterized by varying hazard rate over the lifetime, often modelled by Weibull distribution [12, 19]. The use of exponential approximation to non-exponential distribution is known to be a cause of considerable error in transient analysis [15].

The method outlined in this paper is a very reasonable trade-off in this regard. In [21], we developed a technique based on order statistics for exact analysis of performability measures for an unstructured multicomponent system. It imposes no assumption on the component life other than mutual independence, and we deduced the distributions of the sojourn times from the distributions of individual component lifetimes. Here we present a technique that creates a conservative bound for performability of replicated banyans based on a reduced state-space, and evaluates it under a similar analytical framework. For completeness, the order statistics formulation has been partially reproduced.

For illustration, we consider the synchronous circuit switched operation of a non-repairable replicated MIN in all analyses and simulations throughout this paper. However, there is absolutely no loss of generality, because factors such as switching, timing, protocol and source behavior that affect the performance, only change the reward rates. We formulate the performance models of replicated banyans for all configurations using a reduced state-space. Subsequently, a meaningful delay oriented reward rate assignment is chosen that conforms to the bounding argument used in state-space reduction. Unlike some previous works which drop requests at the point of conflict [3], we analyse blocking and its effect on delay under resubmission as in [20]. This leads to a bound on mean delay at each degraded state under consideration, that is conservative in estimating the accumulated reward over successive levels of degradation.

2 Performability and Related Measures

Let $\{X_t\}_{t\geq 0}$ be a continuous-time discrete-space stochastic process representing the state of the degrading system. The state-space Q is finite for any practical system, however large it may be. Each state $q \in Q$ represents a possible configuration of the system with some components failed, and has an associated *reward rate* $\rho_q = \rho(q)$, a non-negative real number reflecting the level of performance per unit time, when the system is in state q. Performability of the system over

a *mission time* t is defined as the *probability density function (pdf)* of the accumulated reward (cumulative performance)

$$Y_t = \int_0^t \rho(X_t)\, dt. \qquad (1)$$

The *cumulative distribution function (cdf)* of Y_t is called the *performability distribution function*. The mean value of Y_t, which we would call *mean reward in mission* (MRIM), is a useful characterization. In this paper we focus our attention on the accumulated reward until the complete system failure, and consider the value of Y_t as t approaches infinity. We use the abbreviation *mean reward until failure* (MRUF) for $E[Y_\infty]$.

For a nonrepairable system reentry to a state is not feasible. The *sojourn time* or the *residence time* τ_q, which is the total time spent by the system in configuration q over the mission time $t = \sum_{q \in Q} \tau_q$, is therefore contiguous. As $t \to \infty$, equation (1) reduces to

$$Y_\infty = \sum_{q \in Q} \rho_q \tau_q, \qquad (2)$$

which also provides a simple expression for MRUF

$$E[Y_\infty] = \sum_{q \in Q} \rho_q E[\tau_q]. \qquad (3)$$

One implicit assumption in formulating the composite performance-reliability measure as above is that the performance and failure rates are functions of only the system state. This means that increasing load or stress during the degradation due to component failure would not affect the lifetime distribution of the surviving components. This is not only a feature which makes the analysis tractable, but also a desired characteristic in many implementations.

3 Multipath Banyan Networks

A $N \times N$ (where $N = m^K$) symmetric MIN is constructed by arranging $m \times m$ crossbar switches in K stages, with N/m switches in each stage. We adhere to $m = 2$ henceforth, as 2×2 switches are most common. Switches of adjacent stages are connected by an interconnection pattern, so that a path can be established between any pair of input and output [3, 13]. MINs with unique paths between any input-output pair form the class of *banyan* or *delta* networks, that includes well-known topologies such as *flip*, *omega* and *baseline* networks. The unique path gives rise to their self-routing capability — switches at successive stages can complete routing over the network by locally checking the successive bits of the destination addresses. However, paths between disjoint input-output pairs share links, and two propagating message headers may conflict. The situation is usually resolved by blocking one of the messages randomly. As a result, these networks are called *blocking networks*.

An *r-replicated* banyan (also known as layered banyan) consists of r identical distinct copies of the single-path prototype [5, 9]. Figure 1 illustrates the construction of a 8×8 multistage shuffle-exchange (or omega) network, each of the layers shown as rectangles in (b) is individually a single-path omega as shown in (a), coupled at the inputs and outputs by the distributors and collectors. The MIN is considered corrupted if there exists a single fault in every one of the layers, because at this point complete biconnectivity cannot be guaranteed.

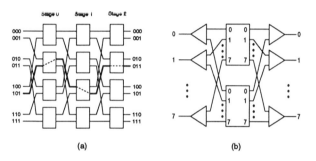

Figure 1: Replicated omega network

In this paper we consider the *synchronous circuit switched* operation of the MINs [3]. The source modules can submit requests for setting up circuits only at periodically occurring instants. This period is the *network cycle* or *sweep* time t_c [20]. Starting from the beginning of a sweep, the tips of partially set up circuits propagate together, at steps of switch delay t_d, through successive stages creating a wavefront. After they pass through K stages, circuits get set up and are subsequently released together after a hold time t_h. The network cycle or sweep length is given by $t_c = Kt_d + t_h$. Sources whose requests are blocked, become aware of their failed attempts, when an indicator signal back-propagates through the partially set-up circuit to reach them within the same sweep, and they are ready to resubmit the blocked requests at the beginning of the next sweep. We assume that the distributors make copies of the request and load onto all layers (multiple loading), as opposed to randomly choosing a layer to submit (random loading). A success results if at least one copy reaches the destination [7].

4 Reward Model

Let us recall that the reward rate reflects the steady level of performance per unit time, while the MIN is under some specified configuration. The assumption that the configuration does not change before this steady state is reached is critical in decomposing the performability problem into subproblems of performance evaluation. However, the solvability and complexity of these subproblems dictate the reward assignment so that the performability measure is both meaningful and tractable.

4.1 Choice of reward

In a shared-memory multiprocessor environment, the initial distribution of traffic is governed by the memory reference pattern imposed by the running processes. We assume a uniform distribution that has become a standard in the literature [3, 5]. Moreover, we adhere to strict *data-dependency* in memory reference within a processor. This ensures that blocked requests are not dropped and the net effect of their resubmission is taken into account. We proposed a resubmission protocol earlier [20] that extends the analysis of probability of success [3, 5] to an upper bound analysis for delay, provided it is assumed that the destinations are also re-randomized during resubmission. We have observed that the average delay in any active configuration settles down to a value very close to this analytical bound.

The key assumption that the reward rate must be a function of only the system state means that the performance metric to be used as reward should attain a steady state value between state changes. Since the network cycle time is extremely small as compared to component lifetime, resubmissions when ignored at the end of the sojourn time has no effect on the mean delay. All requests generated can thus be considered successful over the long run, and the network becomes lossless. Under this condition, the choice of $Y_t = \sum_q (N\tau_q)/(\delta_q t_c)$ represents the total number of requests routed during the mission time, where N is the number of sources, δ_q is the delay (in network cycles) and t_c is the network cycle time. This leads to an obvious choice of reward rate [22]

$$\rho_q = \frac{N}{\delta_q t_c}. \qquad (4)$$

4.2 Delay analysis

A resubmission protocol proposed in [20] has been used to derive an upper bound on the mean delay.

To enforce the uniform traffic distribution in successive network cycles, this protocol dictates the following modification in source behavior. Blocked sources, not being allowed to generate a new request in the next sweep, resubmit the unserviced request with some probability q. However, they are assumed to re-randomize the choice of destination. Unblocked sources have a probability p for generating new request ($p \leq q$). For the analysis, however, they are also assumed to submit a new request independently with probability q, effectively loading the network with spurious requests. This leads to an overestimation of the mean delay, and the upper bound has been found to be

$$\hat{\delta} = 1 + \frac{1}{qp_s} - \frac{1}{q}, \qquad (5)$$

where p_s is the probability of success, defined as the probability that a request survives at the output of the MIN, given it is submitted at the input.

Computation of p_s for replicated banyan can be simplified if we make the independence approximation as in [5]. For a single layer, define $\{q_i, 0 \leq i < K\}$ to be the probability that an input port of an ith stage switch in that layer carries a request, while q_K is the probability that a request appears at any of the output ports of the kth stage (i.e. the output of that layer). Initialize $q_0 = q$ when requests are multiply loaded. Success through any of the layers results in a success, and as a result p_s is given by

$$p_s \;=\; 1 - (1 - \frac{q_K}{q})^r,$$

where

$$q_{i+1} \;=\; 1 - (1 - \frac{q_i}{2})^2, \;\; 0 \leq i \leq K - 1. \qquad (6)$$

Clearly, $\hat{\delta}$ in equation (5) is a function of q, a design parameter to be chosen within the range $[p, 1]$.

4.3 Reduction of state-space

Substituting the value of p_s in the equation (5) we have $\hat{\delta}$ as an upper bound for the average delay of the MIN. Since the result has been derived based on a uniform request distribution over uniformly replicated banyan [20], p_s needs to be recomputed for all levels of replication or dilation, and we have the reward assignment for certain configurations only. However, we can argue that the reward rates for any configurations in between can be conservatively estimated by the reward rates of one of those known configurations. As a result, we consider only those configurations for which an exact value of the assigned reward is known, and

all other configurations can be identified to be in between two of those. This leads to the development of the order statistics formulation, described next.

5 Order Statistics Formulation of Performability

Our goal is to have a modelling scheme that can potentially handle more general distribution of component lifetime than the traditional Markov reward model. The Markovian transient analysis essentially involves formulation of a system of differential difference equations from the directed acyclic graph representing the degradation. The system of equations are usually solved in a transformed domain. However, if the degradation graph is a chain, it is easy to represent the order statistics of lifetimes in time domain and relate them to the sojourn times. Closed form expressions for the marginal and joint distributions of the order statistics are known in terms of the distribution of component lifetimes with any arbitrary distribution. We exploit this generality and attempt to embed by conditioning a number of such degradation chains into the reduced degradation graph of the replicated MIN.

5.1 State-space

A r-replicated banyan network has r unique-path banyan layers. Each layer has $S = (N \log_2 N)/2$ switches and $L = N(\log_2 N + 1)$ links. The degradation of the MIN can be conservatively decomposed as follows. A layer gets corrupted by a single failure of any of its switches or links, in the sense that at least one pair of source and destination cannot be connected through that layer. For a conservative bound on performability, we ignore the contribution of such a defective layer, and assume that the network has as many layers as the perfect ones. Thus the MIN reduces to an r-component system, where each layer can be considered as a component. In what follows, we show how the analysis technique for multicomponent systems as developed in [21], can directly be applied to derive a closed form integral expression for the bound.

$F(t)$, the cdf of lifetime of the layer, can be obtained using the argument that it would require all S switches and L links to be fault-free at time t so that the layer does not fail until time t. i.e.

$$F(t) \;=\; 1 - \{1 - F_s(t)\}^S \{1 - F_l(t)\}^L \qquad (7)$$
$$f(t) \;=\; \{1 - F_s(t)\}^S L \{1 - F_l(t)\}^{L-1} f_l(t)$$
$$\quad + S\{1 - F_s(t)\}^{S-1} \{1 - F_l(t)\}^L f_s(t) \qquad (8)$$

where $F_s(t)$ and $F_l(t)$ are the cdf's of the lifetime of the individual switches and links; $f_s(t)$ and $f_l(t)$ are the corresponding pdf's.

Let q_k denote the configuration of k faulty and $(r-k)$ perfect layers. The state space consists of $\{q_k, k = 0, 1, \ldots, r\}$. For reward assignment, we can choose

$$\rho_k = \frac{N}{\hat{\delta}_{r-k} t_c} \qquad (9)$$

where $\hat{\delta}_{r-k}$ is the upper bound on mean delay for a $(r-k)$-replicated banyan. It should be noted that $\rho_r = 0$ in a conservative way.

The boundaries of the sojourn times can be identified with the time of successive failure of the layers. These are precisely the order statistics of the random variables representing lifetime of the layers. In what follows, we first introduce the order statistics, and show how their distributions relate to the distributions of the component lifetimes. Subsequently the closed form expressions for the performability distribution and MRUF are derived in terms of the distributions of the order statistics of component lifetimes.

5.2 Distribution of order statistics

If a family of random variables $T_1, T_2, \ldots, T_r$ are arranged in ascending order of magnitude and renamed as $T_{1:r} \leq T_{2:r} \leq \cdots \leq T_{r:r}$, the new random variable $T_{k:r}$ is called the *kth order statistic* for $k = 1, 2, \ldots, r$. Suppose $T_i, i = 1, 2, \ldots, r$ represents the lifetime of the i-th layer. They are independent and identically distributed (iid) if we make the assumption of independent failure. Let $F(t) = Pr[T_i \leq t]$ be the common cdf of component lifetime, and $f(t)$ be the corresponding pdf.

An extensive treatment of the distributions and moments of order statistics can be found in [2] and [17]. The cdf of the kth order statistic $T_{k:r}$ is given by

$$F_{k:r}(t) = \sum_{i=k}^{r} \binom{r}{i} \{F(t)\}^i \{1 - F(t)\}^{r-i}, \qquad (10)$$

The corresponding pdf (marginal) is given by

$$f_{k:r}(t) = \frac{r!}{(k-1)!(r-k)!} \{F(t)\}^{k-1} \{1 - F(t)\}^{r-k} f(t). \qquad (11)$$

The marginal pdf is a special case of the general expression for the joint pdf of any k order statistics out of the r. For $1 \leq r_1 < r_2 < \cdots < r_k \leq r$ and

$t_1 \leq t_2 \leq \cdots \leq t_k,$

$$f_{r_1, \ldots, r_k}(t_1, \ldots, t_k)$$
$$= \frac{r!}{(r_1 - 1)!(r_2 - r_1 - 1)! \cdots (r - r_k)!}$$
$$\{F(t_1)\}^{r_1 - 1} f(t_1) \{F(t_2) - F(t_1)\}^{r_2 - r_1 - 1} f(t_2) \cdots$$
$$\cdots \{1 - F(t_k)\}^{r - r_k} \qquad (12)$$

5.3 Conservative analysis

We are now ready to evaluate the performability measures of the r-layer banyan. For simplicity, let us first start with the assumption that the distributors and collectors holding the r layers never fail. The system degrades strictly through the state sequence $q_k, k = 0, \ldots, r$. Clearly $T_{k:r}, k = 1, \ldots, r$ are the sojourn time boundaries. Defining $T_{0:r} = 0$, the sojourn time τ_k at state q_k is

$$\tau_k = T_{k+1:r} - T_{k:r}, \qquad k = 0, \ldots, r-1 \qquad (13)$$

A lower bound $\hat{Y}_\infty$ on the accumulated reward is given by

$$
\begin{aligned}
\hat{Y}_\infty &= \sum_{k=0}^{r-1} \rho_k \tau_k \\
&= \sum_{k=0}^{r-1} \rho_k (T_{k+1:r} - T_{k:r}), \quad T_{0:r} \triangleq 0 \\
&= \sum_{k=1}^{r} (\rho_{k-1} - \rho_k) T_{k:r}, \quad \rho_r \triangleq 0 \qquad (14)
\end{aligned}
$$

so that

$$
\begin{aligned}
\Pr[\hat{Y}_\infty \leq y] &= \Pr\left[\sum_{k=1}^{r} (\rho_{k-1} - \rho_k) T_{k:r} \leq y\right] \\
&= \int \cdots \int_{\sum_{k=1}^{r}(\rho_{k-1}-\rho_k) t_k \leq y} f_{1,\ldots r:r}(t_1, \ldots, t_r) \, dt_1 \cdots dt_r \qquad (15)
\end{aligned}
$$

Similarly, a lower bound on MRUF is found to be

$$
\begin{aligned}
E[\hat{Y}_\infty] &= E\left[\sum_{k=1}^{r} (\rho_{k-1} - \rho_k) T_{k:r}\right] \\
&= \sum_{k=1}^{r} (\rho_{k-1} - \rho_k) E[T_{k:r}] \\
&= \sum_{k=1}^{r} (\rho_{k-1} - \rho_k) \int_0^\infty t f_{k:r}(t) \, dt \qquad (16)
\end{aligned}
$$

5.4 Critical fault

Until now we have not considered system failure caused by faulty distributors or collectors, which act as the critical components. The effect of such a component fault is an abrupt system failure — the graceful degradation gets truncated at that point. To incorporate the effect of critical components, we have to change the expression for the sojourn time by

$$
\begin{aligned}
\tau_k &= 0, & T_c \leq T_{k:n} \\
&= T_c - T_{k:n} & T_{k:n} \leq T_c \leq T_{k+1:n} \qquad (17) \\
&= T_{k+1:n} - T_{k:n} & T_{k+1:n} \leq T_c
\end{aligned}
$$

where T_c denotes the lifetime of the critical component, distributed with cdf $F_c(t)$ and pdf $f_c(t)$.

It is quite straightforward to handle multiple critical components. One can lump the effect onto a single critical component of effective lifetime T_c with cdf $F_c(t)$, by considering the hypothetical critical component to be active until the first real critical component failure. As there are $2N$ distributor/collectors with individual cdf $F_d(t)$, the effective distribution of critical component is given by

$$F_c(t) = 1 - \{1 - F_d(t)\}^{2N} \tag{18}$$
$$f_c(t) = 2N\{1 - F_d(t)\}^{2N-1} f_{\text{mux}}(t) \tag{19}$$

Given that $T_{m:r} < T_c \le T_{m+1:r}$, $\hat{Y}_\infty$ reduces to

$$
\begin{aligned}
\hat{Y}_\infty &= \sum_{k=0}^{m} \rho_k \tau_k \\
&= \sum_{k=0}^{m-1} \rho_k (T_{k+1:r} - T_{k:r}) + \rho_m (T_c - T_{m:r}) \\
&= \sum_{k=1}^{m} (\rho_{k-1} - \rho_k) T_{k:r} + \rho_m T_c. \tag{20}
\end{aligned}
$$

As $T_{m:r} < T_c \le T_{m+1:r}$ are disjoint, by the axiom of probability

$$
\begin{aligned}
&\Pr[\hat{Y}_\infty \le y] \\
&= \Pr[\{\hat{Y}_\infty \le y\} \cap \{T_c \le T_{1:r}\}] \\
&\quad + \sum_{m=1}^{r-1} \Pr[\{\hat{Y}_\infty \le y\} \cap \{T_{m:r} < T_c \le T_{m+1:r}\}] \\
&\quad + \Pr[\{\hat{Y}_\infty \le y\} \cap \{T_r < T_c\}] \\
&= \Pr[\{\rho_0 T_c \le y\} \cap \{T_c \le T_{1:r}\}] \\
&\quad + \sum_{m=1}^{r-1} \Pr[\sum_{k=1}^{m}\{(\rho_{k-1} - \rho_k)T_{k:r} + \rho_m T_c \le y\} \\
&\qquad\qquad\qquad \cap \{T_{m:r} < T_c \le T_{m+1:r}\}] \\
&\quad + \Pr[\sum_{k=1}^{r}\{(\rho_{k-1} - \rho_k)T_{k:r} \le y\} \cap \{T_{r:r} < T_c\}] \\
&= \iint_{\substack{\rho_0 t_c \le y,\ t_c \le t_1}} f_{1:r}(t_1) f_c(t_c)\, dt_1\, dt_c + \sum_{m=1}^{r-1}
\end{aligned}
$$

$$
\begin{aligned}
&\left\{ \int \cdots \int_{\substack{\sum_{k=1}^{m}(\rho_{k-1}-\rho_k)t_k + \rho_m t_c \le y,\ t_m < t_c \le t_{m+1}}} f_{1,\dots,m+1:r}(t_1,\dots,t_{m+1}) f_c(t_c)\, dt_1 \cdots dt_{m+1}\, dt_c \right\} \\
&\quad + \int \cdots \int_{\substack{\sum_{k=1}^{r}(\rho_{k-1}-\rho_k)t_k \le y,\ t_r < t_c}} f_{1,\dots,r:r}(t_1,\dots,t_r) f_c(t_c)\, dt_1 \cdots dt_r\, dt_c \tag{21}
\end{aligned}
$$

An expression for MRUF can be obtained by conditioning on the same set of disjoint events as

$$
\begin{aligned}
&E[\hat{Y}_\infty] \\
&= E[\hat{Y}_\infty \mid T_c \le T_{1:r}] \cdot \Pr[T_c \le T_{1:r}] \\
&\quad + \sum_{m=1}^{r-1} E[\hat{Y}_\infty \mid T_{m:r} < T_c \le T_{m+1:r}] \\
&\qquad\qquad\qquad \cdot \Pr[T_{m:r} < T_c \le T_{m+1:r}] \\
&\quad + E[\hat{Y}_\infty \mid T_{r:r} < T_c] \cdot \Pr[T_{r:r} < T_c] \\
&= E[\rho_0 T_c \mid T_c \le T_{1:r}] \cdot \Pr[T_c \le T_{1:r}] \\
&\quad + \sum_{m=1}^{r-1} E[\sum_{k=1}^{m}(\rho_{k-1} - \rho_k)T_{k:r} + \rho_m T_c \\
&\qquad \mid T_{m:r} < T_c \le T_{m+1:r}] \cdot \Pr[T_{m:r} < T_c \le T_{m+1:r}] \\
&\quad + E[\sum_{k=1}^{r}(\rho_{k-1} - \rho_k)T_{k:r} \mid T_{r:r} < T_c] \cdot \Pr[T_{r:r} < T_c]
\end{aligned}
$$

$$
\begin{aligned}
&= \rho_0 \iint_{\substack{t_c \le t_1}} t_c f_{1:r}(t_1) f_c(t_c)\, dt_1\, dt_c \\
&\quad + \sum_{m=1}^{r-1} \Big\{ \sum_{k=1}^{m-1}(\rho_{k-1} - \rho_k) \cdot \\
&\qquad \iiiint_{\substack{t_k \le t_m < t_c \le t_{m+1}}} t_k f_{k,m,m+1:r}(t_k, t_m, t_{m+1}) f_c(t_c)\, dt_k\, dt_m\, dt_{m+1}\, dt_c \\
&\qquad + (\rho_{m-1} - \rho_m) \cdot \\
&\qquad \iiint_{\substack{t_m < t_c \le t_{m+1}}} t_m f_{m,m+1:r}(t_m, t_{m+1}) f_c(t_c)\, dt_m\, dt_{m+1}\, dt_c \\
&\qquad + \rho_m \iiint_{\substack{t_m < t_c \le t_{m+1}}} t_c f_{m,m+1:r}(t_m, t_{m+1}) f_c(t_c)\, dt_m\, dt_{m+1}\, dt_c \Big\} \\
&\quad + \sum_{k=1}^{r-1}(\rho_{k-1} - \rho_k) \iiint_{\substack{t_k \le t_n < t_c}} t_k f_{k,r:r}(t_k, t_r) f_c(t_c)\, dt_k\, dt_r\, dt_c \\
&\quad + (\rho_{r-1} - \rho_r) \iint_{\substack{t_r < t_c}} t_r f_{r:r}(t_r) f_c(t_c)\, dt_r\, dt_c. \tag{22}
\end{aligned}
$$

5.5 Over-approximation: Critical failure

Let us recall that we ignored the contribution of a corrupted layer in the lower bound analysis. Oftentimes the cause of this layer corruption is only one or two switch or link faults. The resulting performance deterioration is imperceptible, and one can over-approximate all ρ_k other than ρ_r by ρ_0. This in turn results in the following over-approximation for MRUF

$$
\begin{aligned}
E[Y_\infty] \simeq \rho_0 \Bigg\{ &\iint_{\substack{t_c \le t_1}} t_c f_{1:r}(t_1) f_c(t_c)\, dt_1\, dt_c \\
&+ \sum_{m=1}^{r-1} \iiint_{\substack{t_m < t_c \le t_{m+1}}} t_c f_{m,m+1:r}(t_m, t_{m+1}) f_c(t_c)\, dt_m\, dt_{m+1}\, dt_c \\
&+ \iint_{\substack{t_r < t_c}} t_r f_{r:r}(t_r) f_c(t_c)\, dt_r\, dt_c \Bigg\}. \tag{23}
\end{aligned}
$$

Evaluation of the approximate expression is computationally less complex as it has $O(r)$ dominating terms involving triple integrals, whereas the lower bound has $O(r^2)$ dominating terms with quadruple integrals. Moreover, the reward value and the integral factor in the approximation characterize the performance and the reliability components respectively.

6 Results

It remains now to observe how well the methodology developed here can model the operation of a replicated MIN under arbitrary distribution of component lifetime. Particularly, it is necessary to pay close attention to components with increasing and decreasing hazard rates and their impact on the system performability. For illustration, we assume Weibull distributed lifetimes for all components,

$$\Pr\left[T \le t\right] = 1 - e^{-(\lambda t)^{\alpha}}, \mathrm{MTTF} = E\left[T\right] = \frac{\Gamma(1 + \frac{1}{\alpha})}{\lambda}.$$

With $\alpha = 1.0$, Weibull reduces to the exponential distribution that corresponds to the Markovian model. In contrast, we study the effect of the increasing and decreasing hazard rates by using two other values of α, viz. 0.8 and 1.2 respectively. However, instead of using the same λ values in those three cases, we use the same values for the component MTTFs. The reason for this choice is that component MTTFs are more direct results of reliability measurement. While MTTFs of components remain unchanged, $\alpha > 1$ depicts an increasing hazard rate that causes more faults to occur later as compared to the constant hazard rate ($\alpha = 1$). $\alpha < 1$ stands for a decreasing hazard rate that has the opposite effect, i.e. the failures happen earlier. Of course, we assign different MTTFs for different components — 300 days for the links and 1000 days for both the switches and the distributors/collectors. We study a 4-replicated banyan of size 64×64 implemented with 2×2 switches, operating at 100 million network cycles per second. In practice, this can reflect a 64 processor 64 module shared memory multiprocessor environment (one of a moderate size), with exactly four distinct paths between any PE-MM pair.

An event-driven simulator has been developed to study the MRUF as the replicated banyan degrades under component failure. A pattern generator creates a fault pattern by randomly choosing the life of the components so that they follow any given distribution. A fault-injector creates the state-trajectory of network degradation under such a specific pattern. The state-space is not the reduced state-space used for analysis, i.e. all possible degraded configurations of the MIN can be in the trajectory. The fault that causes the MIN to break down is always the last fault in the pattern. Each state corresponds to a reward assigned in equation (4). The transition into a new state is an event. At the core, there is a network cycle emulator which is called upon any such event. The emulator runs until the average delay settles to a steady value, and then uses that value to compute the reward rate for that state until the next event. The accumulated reward for each fault pattern is computed, which contributes to the MRUF as a large number of patterns are generated and observed. The number of network cycles simulated on each fault, and the number of random fault patterns can be controlled for the simulation runs. The effect of these two simulation pa-

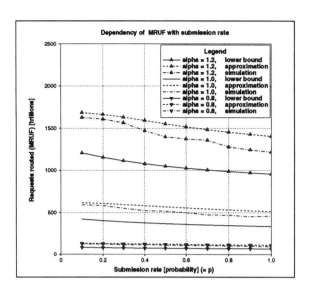

Figure 2: Effect of submission rate

rameters on the convergence of MRUF has been studied in [22]. The simulation results in this paper have been obtained by averaging over 1000 fault patterns, and 1000 network cycles emulated on each fault. The event-driven design is a necessity, as there is a huge order of magnitude difference between the network cycle time and the time between faults (a few nanoseconds vs. a few days).

We have studied the effect of variation in the rate of new request generation on MRUF. The value of resubmission rate q has been chosen to be unity, i.e. unsuccessful requests are resubmitted in the following network cycle. The value of $E[Y_{\infty}]$ shows the maximum message transfer capability of the MIN. Along with this we plotted the lower bound $E[\hat{Y}_{\infty}]$ from equation (22) and the over-approximation from equation (23). This is shown in figure 2. Table 1 shows the percentage difference of the lower bound and the over-approximation with respect to the simulation results.

The most important observation of all is the high sensitivity of MRUF towards the shape parameter α. An increase of only 0.2 in α from unity almost triples MRUF, whereas an equal amount of decrease reduces it to less than one-fourth. Markovian approximation can thus be too costly in terms of error margin. The flatness of the curves is a consequence of blocked user model. Variation of resubmission rate also has little effect, so that the analytical upper bound in [20] is a good estimate for mean delay.

p	α					
	0.8		1.0		1.2	
	l.b.	app.	l.b.	app.	l.b.	app.
0.1	-32.3	5.4	-28.7	4.2	-25.7	3.6
0.2	-34.6	5.2	-31.0	4.2	-28.0	3.5
0.3	-32.7	10.0	-29.5	8.1	-28.8	4.1
0.4	-34.8	7.3	-28.0	11.3	-26.7	8.0
0.5	-33.4	9.8	-29.0	10.0	-24.9	11.0
0.6	-31.9	12.2	-28.3	11.1	-25.3	10.4
0.7	-32.9	10.2	-25.7	15.0	-26.0	9.2
0.8	-31.3	12.6	-26.6	13.2	-22.8	13.7
0.9	-30.3	13.9	-24.9	15.6	-21.9	14.8
1.0	-27.1	18.7	-27.1	12.0	-21.4	15.3

Table 1: Percentage difference in MRUF

7 Conclusions

In this paper, we have proposed a reward structure which shows that the total number of messages routed over a MIN under fault can serve as a performability measure. We have also developed a methodology based on order statistics to analytically evaluate the mean reward for a replicated banyan network. We question the traditional Markovian model of component failure that assumes memorylessness. Our approach does not call for making assumptions about the sojourn time distributions, whether memoryless or otherwise. The key assumption is that of the independence of component lifetime, which is more tangible to a system designer. Lifetime of a component can have any general (known) distribution, possibly to be supplied by the manufacturer. Simulation results obtained using the proposed reward rate justifies our concern showing that perturbation from Markovian lifetime has pronounced effect on the cumulative measure that cannot be ignored.

Performability analysis is complex even for the Markovian model because of an exploding state-space — and it becomes harder when we relax the assumption. The order statistics approach makes use of state-space reduction and stochastic ordering to analyze a conservative bound, that has been compared against the simulation results. Detail knowledge of network operation helps in designing an over-approximation that is computationally much less expensive. Specifically for the replicated MIN, the approximate value decomposes into two distinct performance and reliability factors. However, this behavior cannot be expected of every system in general.

References

[1] J.F.Meyer, "On evaluating the performability of degradable computing systems." *IEEE Transactions on Computers*, vol. 29, pp. 720-731, August 1980.

[2] H.A.David, *Order statistics*, 2nd ed., John Wiley & Sons, 1981.

[3] J.H.Patel, "Performance of processor-memory interconnections for multiprocessors," *IEEE Transactions on Computers*, vol. 30, pp. 771-780, October 1981.

[4] J.F.Meyer, "Closed-form solution of performability." *IEEE Transactions on Computers*, vol. 31, pp. 648-657, July 1982.

[5] C.P.Kruskal and M.Snir, "The performance of multistage interconnection networks for multiprocessors," *IEEE Transactions on Computers*, vol. 32, pp. 1091-1098, December 1983.

[6] D.G.Furchtgott and J.F.Meyer, "A performability solution method for degradable nonrepairable systems." *IEEE Transactions on Computers*, vol. 33, pp. 550-554, June 1984.

[7] M.Kumar and J.R.Jump. "Performance of Unbuffered Shuffle-Exchange Networks." *IEEE Transactions on Computers*, June 1986, pp. 573-578.

[8] L.Donatiello and B.R.Iyer, "Analysis of a composite performance reliability measure for fault-tolerant systems." *Journal of the ACM*, vol. 34, pp. 179-189, January 1987.

[9] T.H.Szymanski and V.C.Hamacher, "On the permutation capability of multistage interconnection networks," *IEEE Transactions on Computers*, vol. 36 pp. 810-822, July 1987.

[10] R.M.Smith, K.S.Trivedi and A.V.Ramesh, "Performability analysis: measures, an algorithm and a case study." *IEEE Transactions on Computers*, vol. 37, pp. 406-417, April 1988.

[11] J.T.Blake and K.S.Trivedi, "Reliability analysis of interconnection network using hierarchical decomposition," *IEEE Transactions on Reliability*, vol. 38, pp. 111-120, April 1989.

[12] I.B.Gertsbakh, *Statistical Reliability Theory*, Mercel Dekker Inc., 1989.

[13] J.Y.Hui, *Switching and Traffic Theory for Integrated Broadband Networks,* Kluwer Academic Publishers, 1990.

[14] K.R.Pattipati and S.S.Shah, "On the computational aspects of performability models of fault-tolerant computer systems," *IEEE Transactions on Computers,*vol. 39, pp. 832-836, June 1990.

[15] G.Ciardo, R.Marie, B.Sericola and K.S.Trivedi, "Performability analysis using semi-Markov reward processes." *IEEE Transactions on Computers,*vol. 39, pp. 1251-1264, October 1990.

[16] L.Donatiello and V.Grassi, "On evaluating the cumulative performance distribution of fault-tolerant computer systems," *IEEE Transaction on Computers*, vol. 40, pp. 1301-1307, November 1991.

[17] B.C.Arnold, N.Balakrishnan and H.N.Nagaraja, *A First Course in Order Statistics*, John Wiley & Sons, 1992.

[18] J.F.Meyer, "Performability: a retrospective and some pointers to the future," *Performance Evaluation*, vol. 14, pp. 139-156, February 1992.

[19] D.P.Siewiorek and R.S.Swarz, *Reliable Computer Systems: Design and Evaluation*, 2nd ed., Digital Press, 1992.

[20] A.Bhattacharya, R.R.Rao and T.-T.Y.Lin. "Delay analysis in synchronous circuit-switched delta networks," *Proc. 7th International Parallel Processing Symposium*, pp. 666-670, April 1993.

[21] A.Bhattacharya, R.R.Rao and T.-T.Y.Lin. "Performability analysis of non-repairable multicomponent systems using order statistics," *Proc. 6th IEEE Symposium on Parallel and Distributed Processing*, pp. 646-653, October 1994.

[22] A.Bhattacharya, R.R.Rao and T.-T.Y.Lin. "Cumulative performance measure for gracefully degradable multistage interconnection networks," *Proc. 1st International Workshop on Parallel Processing*, pp. 234-239, December 1994.

Panel 2:

Responsiveness in Automotive and Communication Systems

Moderator: Paul J. Kühn, TU Stuttgart

Session 9:
Practical Issues

Session Chair: Kumar Goswami

Large Complex System Test

Mei-Chen Hsueh

Digital Equipment Corporation

—Abstract—

Because the complexity of today's systems is so high, the changes in technology so fast, and the use of technology so broad, systems are no longer defined and bounded by their physical form, nor by their components. Instead, systems are defined by the characteristics of their use. Depending on the requirements, the quality of a system may vary from one configuration to another and from one usage to another. System testing, therefore, must be designed to include differences within and between application domains, and the testing process must be designed to evolve with changes in technology and requirements. This paper presents an approach to testing and evaluating large, complex systems and demonstrates it by using two real cases. The approach is based on usage models derived from the customer's perspective. In contrast to traditional black-box and random testing, structure testing and controlled experiments are used to explore the non-functional aspects of systems.

1 Introduction

Building a system is an exercise in problem solving and testing is a technique commonly used to determine if the solution solves the problem. System testing focused, in the past, on the functionality and performance of a single-box system, and it was sufficient during the mainframe and minicomputer era because of the relatively simple services provided by today's standards.

Today, systems are complex because of both the large number of components and the rich set of services [1,2]. It is not uncommon for a system to consist of distributed, heterogeneous, and autonomous hardware and software systems. These systems reflect the distributed nature of modern business and the heterogeneity and autonomy of its computational and information processing needs. For example, a computerized news management system enables reporters to submit news or stories from remote locations electronically and chief editors to access information across continents while editing and publishing news locally [3]. In this environment, new issues involving verifying, validating, and testing large, highly complex systems are rapidly emerging [1,4].

1.1 Problems

The difficulty stems from the fact that:

1. Today's systems contain not only boxes of hardware, system software (for example, operating systems and system utilities), and user applications, but many layers of software products. Each of these software products exists in the system as one or many interrelated processes. These software products—often initially developed independently to solve narrower problems—are put together to provide a basic set of services for today's open, distributed, client-server computing.

2. The use of computing technology is changing. Computer-based systems are no longer the privilege of a few communities, such as scientific, engineering, and financial; other professionals, such as animation creators, use computers to increase their productivity and creativity as well. Furthermore, the same system can support different application environments; conversely, the same application can run on different system structures.

The challenge is to ensure that all components are working together harmoniously and predictably in production environments—environments that may differ, depending on the usage of the systems, even though the systems have exactly the same configuration.

1.2 Approach

This paper presents a domain-driven, usage-model approach to test and evaluate today's complex systems. The usage models define possible application system environments, sequences of user operations, and computing services needed. The adoption of the usage-model approach is due to the fact that the confidence level in system quality is restricted to the degree to which the test system resembles the actual environments of the production systems. The key concept is that systems must be accountable and dependable for customers' businesses. A good understanding of various applications, their system environments, and specific uses and requirements is essential.

The contributions of this paper are summarized as follows:

- Introduce usage-model, scenario-driven testing methodology for today's system testing.

- Define four test objectives other than functionality for today's complex systems; interoperability, integrity, availability, and performance.

- Introduce a combination of the structure testing and functional testing technique at the system level and tightly controlled experiments to effectively explore the system's dependability.

The layout of the rest of this paper is as follows. In Section 2, goals for system testing and four nonfunctional test objectives are defined, followed by two case studies in Section 3 and Section 4. The case study in Section 3 demonstrates the system test from the vendor perspective. Usage-model selection, test design technique, and focuses are also discussed in this section. A system test for a specific customer focusing on the performance aspects of the system is demonstrated in Section 4. Finally, a conclusion is provided in Section 5.

2 Goals and Objectives

The primary goal of the system test is to evaluate the capability and dependability of a system by a bounded effort at a given point in time. Thus, the confidence level in system quality is restricted to the degree to which the test system resembles the actual environment of the production systems. In summary, the goals of system testing are to:

1. Determine the validity of the final system with respect to user needs and requirements,

2. Examine and evaluate the system behavior by executing a set of selected data.

3. Reduce the risk of unexpected outcomes.

It is not unusual to see a long list of requirements from a customer stipulating specific services, response time, throughput, down time, security, particular platforms and networks, and so on. These requirements portray the customer's expectations for dependability in the context of the intended use of the system. Thus, in addition to system functions, four other system attributes are identified to be the core test objectives for

testing today's large, complex systems. Briefly, they are:

- Interoperability — the extent to which the components interoperate and communicate with each other through an agreed-upon mechanism and protocol.

- Integrity —the extent to which the system, as well as data, is in a consistent state at any given point in time.

- Availability —the extent to which the system is available to provide services.

- Performance—the extent to which the system responds to requests and delivers acceptable services.

In the next two sections, this approach is demonstrated through two real cases—one from the vendor perspective and the other from the customer perspective.

3 Case 1—the vendor perspective

The system under test (SUT) was a system which contained more than twenty layered products (called middleware), providing the following services:

1. Database management services, e.g., Rdb.

2. Application control and management services, e.g., ACMS.

3. Network and communication services, e.g., PATHWORKS and MailWorks.

4. Presentation services, e.g., DECforms, SQL Services, and DECwindow/Motif.

5. Other services, e.g., DECtrace and VMS Volume Shadowing.

3.1 SUT — Configuration & Environment

The first challenge was to construct a SUT which included the user environment (i.e., applications) and the physical configuration. Because the use of technology is so broad, a system is no longer defined and bounded by its physical form, nor by its components. Instead, it is defined by the characteristics of its usage. Therefore, system testing, must be designed to include differences within and between application domains, and the testing process must be designed to evolve with changes in technology. With this in mind, the strategy was to create a SUT which would represent a majority of the real use.

A survey was conducted to gather information from customers, account managers, and field engineers to determine a viable SUT. The information gathered included application type, computing style (current and near future), configuration, platforms, workload, and system characteristics essential to customers.

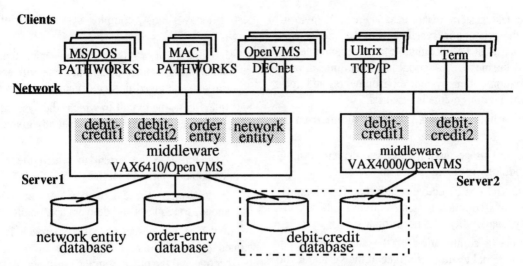

Figure 1   SUT configuration & environment

Three applications—order-entry, debit-credit, and network management—were selected to create the user environment. The key to this selection was the broadness and representativeness. For example, order-entry was an application widely seen in most businesses. Similarly, debit-credit type of practice was not limited to the banking industry. In fact, even today, these two applications are functions performed daily by most businesses. The third application, network management, was chosen to add background activities and workload to the system.

Figure 1 shows the SUT. It should be noted that the determination of this configuration was constrained by (1) the availability of equipment, (2) the cost of allocating them and (3) the following criteria:

- The SUT must support the client-server environment.

- Client devices must include MS/DOS PCs, Macintosh computers, and UNIX-based workstations to support an open environment.

- The SUT must contain at least two server machines to support a geographically separated database.

- One of the servers must have sufficient capacity to run all selected applications simultaneously.

In this configuration, the two server machines were VMS-based while the client machines consisted of various desk-top computers and terminals. Two banking application environments, shown as debit-credit1 and debit-credit2 in Figure 1, were duplicated in both

Table 1   Application characteristics

Application	debit-credit1 (banking)	debit-credit2 (banking)	order-entry (car-rental)	network entity management
Type	TP/DB	DB	TP/DB	DB
Database	distributed & shared	distributed & shared	centralized	centralized
Database Operation	update & query	query	update & query	update & query
Computing Style	interactive & batch	interactive	interactive & batch	interactive
Concurrent User	yes	yes	yes	yes
Desktop Device	terminal	MS/DOS, Mac Ultrix, OpenVMS	MS/DOS, Mac Ultrix, OpenVMS	OpenVMS
User Interface	Form	Interactive SQL	Form	DECwindow/Motif
Server Software Required	ACMS, Rdb, DECforms, DECdtm, DECnet	Rdb, SQL-Services, PATHWORKS, UCX, DECnet	ACMS, Rdb, DECforms, PATHWORKS, UCX, DECnet	Rdb, DECnet

servers to support a distributed database, but the data access must pass through Server1. Both implementations shared one database—a single logical entity, physically partitioned into two parts to attach to different servers. The other two applications were running only on Server1. Detailed characteristics of each of the applications are shown in Table 1.

It should be noted that all of the application software was home-grown, which meant the effort could concentrate on designing test cases rather than developing the software

3.2 Test Cases & Design

Test cases were aimed at exploring the non-functional aspects of the system, because each of the services, often with its underlying dependency, had been individually tested, and exercising the applications would also explore the functional aspects of the system.

The following requirements were provided:

1. Interface coverage
   a. user—form, window, and structural query language (SQL).
   b. communication —TCP/IP, DECnet, and PATHWORKS.

2. System components coverage
   a. hardware—all clients and servers
   b. software—all TP/DB sensitive software
   c. database—all three databases

3. Failures—server, network, process, and power

4. Dependency coverage

These requirements ensured that the tests would sufficiently cover those key components or characteristics that were of interest. In order to obtain the most value with given resources and time, it was further required that:

- Design should concentrate on those circumstances in which the complexity, the uncertainty, or the vulnerability could be high.

- Each of the test cases could be used for more than one purpose. For example, test cases for interoperability testing could be used for performance testing. Similarly, test cases for availability testing could also be used for integrity testing.

In the next two subsections, two examples of the case design are explored while providing a general guideline.

3.2.1 Example 1

To conduct the case design, the structure of the middleware was unveiled, shown in Figure 2, based on the product dependency. It should be noted that excluded from this graph are those components which are either standalone (i.e., required only operating system, such as VMS Volume Shadowing) or TP/DB insensitive. This diagram provides an insight into the relationship of the components and thus helped in understanding the system's complexity. For example, how many different ways will a component invoke

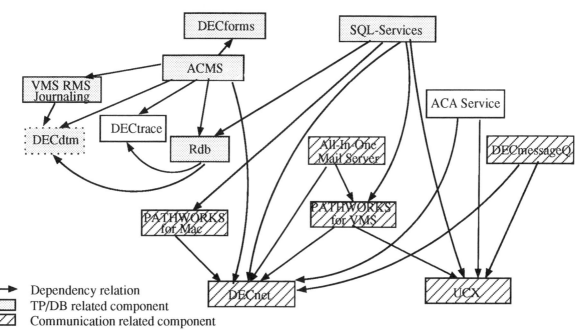

Figure 2 Dependency graph of the middleware

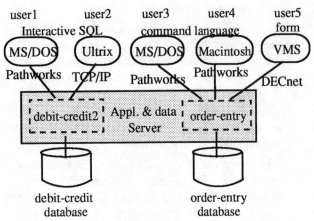

Figure 3   Example 1

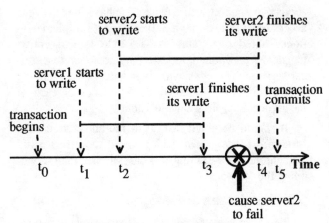

Figure 4   Example 2

other components? Where is the concurrency coming from? What are the most complicated scenarios?

Figure 3 illustrates a test case for interoperability. The significance of this test is not only in the platform coverage, but also in the software components involved. For example, TCP/IP, DECnet, and PATH-WORKS are used to provide communication interfaces and DECforms, SQL, and command line language are used for the user interface. In the server, the TP monitor, ACMS, provides control and management services to the order-entry users while Rdb provides database management services for both types of users. It should also be noted that test generators were used from each of the desk-tops to generate test inputs simultaneously for 30 minutes to create a sufficient workload, as well as to create concurrent events.

3.2.2 Example 2

To design test cases for integrity testing, those components—for example, DECdtm—needed to be studied in order to understand how the integrity was kept during the normal operation and with the presence of failures as well. Furthermore, under what circumstances would the integrity be imperiled and what would the system do if an inconsistency occurred? This was also necessary because we wanted to focus on high vulnerability cases. Figure 4 illustrates a test case with a high vulnerability.

This case simulates a remote server failure while the server is performing a remote update to the database as a part of a distributed transaction. One of the very crucial elements of this test is the timing of the failure. For example, it is expected that the database is in an inconsistent state after server2 fails. It is also expected that the database recovery takes place after the server machine comes back up. The only time window in which the database is vulnerable is between t_3

and t_5. In other words, if the failure falls outside the $[t_3, t_5]$ window, no harm will be done because either no updates have been done or the transaction has already been committed.

Although a randomly induced failure may result in the same effect, the probability is very low because of the short transaction nature of these types of applications; about one second each. To guarantee the desired effect, the approach was to extend a particular transaction's execution time long enough to allow a carefully calculated system call executed automatically to crash the server at the right time. In addition to the vulnerability, the uncertainty in this case was also high because of a newly developed product, DECdtm, and the support to other products shown in Figure 2.

3.3 Summary

The structure testing technique, other than the traditional black-box functional testing technique, makes possible the design of a set of test cases with an ultimate value based on a set of pre-defined criteria. The significance of this technique includes the following:

1. An effective mechanism to help gain insight into the system complexity based on the component's structure.

2. A powerful mechanism to conduct cause-effect analysis and event exploration through the component's dependency.

3. A viable method to identify system states in which events can be seeded accurately to ensure the occurrence of the events.

4. A way to quickly identify the true causes of the problems when tests fail, particularly, for non-functional tests, such as integrity and availability.

As a result, nineteen tests were developed for interoperability testing; nineteen for integrity testing;

and fifteen for availability testing. All non-destructive cases were used to conduct performance tests as well. It should be noted that these tests have by no means been completed; nor are they enough. These tests, however, do represent events which are likely to happen in real environments.

Four tests failed: one produced a harmless message during the SQL compilation phase, one resulted in a database inconsistency, and the other two resulted in an availability problem due to an improper recovery. Most of the problems required fixes before the product could be released. For example, one of the unsuccessful tests was due to the inconsistency between two servers after recovery from a remote server failure. In this particular case, a process of the local server still assumed its link to its counterpart in the remote server, while the counterpart tried to re-establish a new link with it. This is an integrity problem and an availability problem as well.

Even though the usage models were carefully chosen, the real environments can be very different because of the actual implementation in the application software and the usage. This difference greatly affects performance. In the next section, a system test focusing on system performance is presented using a real customer's environment.

4 Case 2—the customer perspective

The application system under study provides information services that support the business functions of companies in the telecommunication industry. The business functions include marketing, sales, finance, engineering, installation, billing, and customer services. Some use batch processes (for example, billing) and some are interactive (for example, customer services). Here is demonstrated only the interactive part of the application. Details of this case study can be found in [5] and [6].

4.1 SUT—Configuration and Environment

The test system environment was created by copying the complete set of system images, databases, applications, and user accounts from a selected production system. Figure 5 shows the SUT configuration and environment.

Two VAX computers formed a client-server computing environment. The client, shown as the application requestor in Figure 5, received user requests through two form managers, processed them, and then forwarded the requests to the server for data services. The services provided to this particular application included database management, application control and

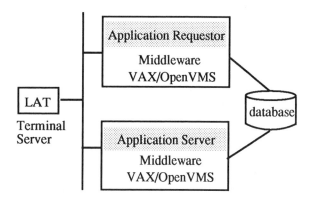

Figure 5 SUT configuration & environment

management, presentation services, and network and communication services.

4.2 Workload and Experiments

Four experiments, shown in Table 2, were designed to evaluate:

1. Impact due to the size of the database. For example, what would the response time be if the size of the database doubled?

2. Impact due to the workload. For example, could the system handle more users?

3. Acceptable maximum throughput. For example, the maximum number of transactions in a unit of time in which at least 95% of transactions are completed within one second.

Table 2 Characteristics of the experiments

(a) Experiments

Experiment	Users	DB size	Workload
Exp 1	143	5 GB	WL1
Exp 2	143	9 GB	WL1
Exp 3	286	9 GB	WL2
Exp 4	286	9 GB	WL3

(b) Workloads

User's Job Function	% of Users	Arrival Rate (users/min)		
		WL1	WL2	WL3
Order-entry	18.2	0.99	2.00	3.53
Payments	12.6	1.94	1.40	2.61
Customer Inquiry	30.1	3.53	4.00	6.67
Finance	35.7	0.69	7.54	10.00
Others	3.4	0.31	0.63	1.20
Total	100.0	7.46	15.53	24.01

Each of the job functions shown in Table 2(b) contained more than one task and each task filled more than one form. For example, the order-entry job functions included adding a new account, deleting a customer, and changing a customer's information. Adding a new account alone required 16 return key strokes. The workload, including the user job functions, the specific tasks of each of the job functions, and the job functions mix, was defined and given by the customer based on years of experience.

Six metrics were defined to evaluate the system from the end user, system, and resources standpoints.

- Response time — the time the system takes to respond to a user request.
- Throughput — the total number of transactions completed in a given period.
- Qualified throughput — the percentage of the throughput, representing those transactions in the total throughput which satisfy a pre-determined criterion.
- CPU time — the amount of time the CPU is allocated for a service.
- Direct I/O — the number of disk I/O's made for a service.
- Service time — the wall time used for a service, including delay.

4.3 Results

Table 3 shows that when the database size increased to 9 gigabytes (Exp 2) from 5 gigabytes (Exp 1), the CPU time for all the functions increased. In addition, the service times for most job types increased as well, except for Customer Inquiry. The slight improvement in the Customer Inquiry's service time

Table 3 Resource Utilization

Job Functions	Service Time		CPU Time		Direct I/O	
	Exp 1	Exp 2	Exp 1	Exp 2	Exp 1	Exp 2
Order-entry	12.13	13.61	2.10	2.38	757	770
Payments	8.93	21.73	1.53	3.76	490	2176
Customer Inquiry	3.23	3.10	0.87	1.07	202	130
Finance	7.21	10.96	0.96	1.63	357	418
Others	0.83	0.94	0.19	0.21	38	37

seemed to come from a 30% improvement in its I/O, after the database was re-organized. Exp 2's performance was still reasonably good compared to Exp 1. This can be seen in Figure 6.

Figure 6 shows the system performance of the four experiments. In these figures, the left Y-axis represents the number of transactions completed in each 60-second interval. The right Y-axis represents qualified throughput. A vertical reference line for the right Y-axis marks the 95th percentile level in the total scale of the qualified throughput. In addition to the total throughput, throughput by job function was also plotted.

The throughputs of Exp 1 and Exp 2 were about the same and the qualified throughputs were **above** 95% most of the time. When the workload increased, as in Exp 3, a slight degradation in the qualified throughput was observed; **above, but very close to,** 95% most of the time. The system, however, saturated when Exp 4 was conducted.

Figure 6 also indicates that Payments may be the job function most sensitive to the changes. For exam-

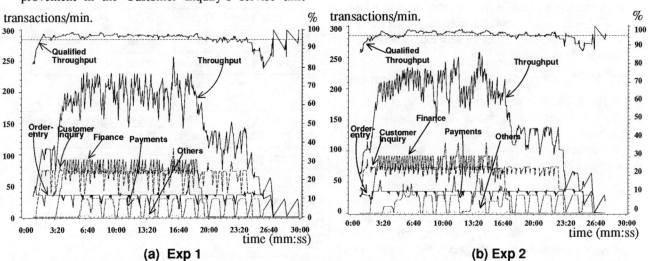

(a) Exp 1   (b) Exp 2

Figure 6 System throughput & qualified throughput

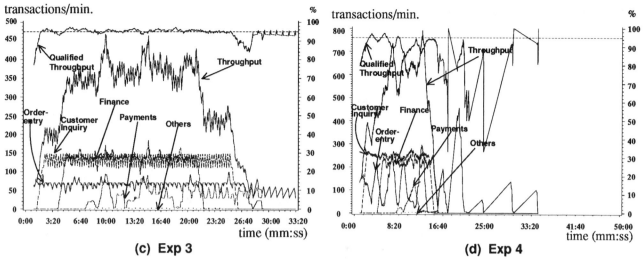

transactions/min.

(c) Exp 3

transactions/min.

(d) Exp 4

Figure 6 System throughput & qualified throughput (cont.)

ple, the Payment throughput pattern seen in Figure 6(a) was slightly disrupted in Figure 6(b) when the size of the database increased, and no pattern was found in Figure 6(c) when the workload doubled. In addition to Payments, a significant change in the Order-entry's throughput pattern was also observed; from a uniform distribution with a small variation in Figure 6(c) to a big high-low swing in Figure 6(d).

Intuitively, it is suspected that both Payments and Order-entry might compete with each other through interlocking. To verify it, two additional experiments were conducted; one without Payments and the other with Payments alone. Results are shown in Figure 7.

Figure 7 shows user activity time plots. In this figure, the X-axis represents individual users while the Y-axis represents time. For example, the first 52 users in Figure 7(a)

are order-entry operators, the next 102 users are customer representatives, who handle customer's inquiries, and so on. Each of the sticks in the figure represents the elapsed time of a user job and it also marks the begin and end times of the job activity.

Figure 7(a) shows that users of both job types, Order-entry and Payments, suffered minutes long elapsed times. Further, the step-wise pattern clearly indicates that there might be conflict between these two job types. When the Payments jobs were completely removed, shown in Figure 7(b), the Order-entry's job elapsed time decreased dramatically to a normal range. Surprisingly, no significant changes to the other job types, such as Customer Inquiry, were observed. However, in Figure 7(c), long elapsed times for most of the Payments jobs continued to occur even though there were less than 3 jobs per minute running in the system.

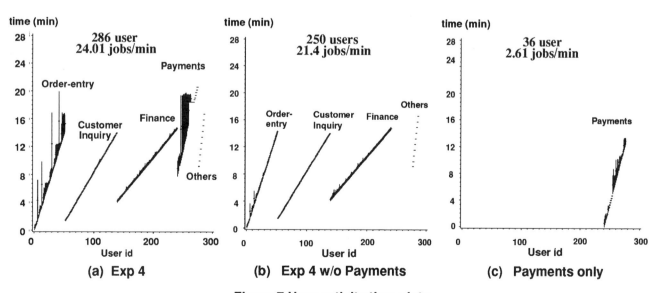

(a) Exp 4

(b) Exp 4 w/o Payments

(c) Payments only

Figure 7 User activity time plots

283

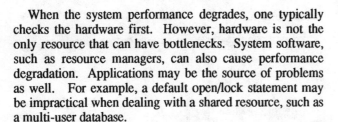

When the system performance degrades, one typically checks the hardware first. However, hardware is not the only resource that can have bottlenecks. System software, such as resource managers, can also cause performance degradation. Applications may be the source of problems as well. For example, a default open/lock statement may be impractical when dealing with a shared resource, such as a multi-user database.

5 Concluding Remarks

The confidence level of the system's capability and dependability in real use is mostly restricted to those circumstances which resemble the system environment being tested. Although each of the components was individually tested, the environment was often too simple to represent most real production environments. Moreover, the test was conducted often from the designer standpoint rather than the end-user standpoint; that is, focusing on the design functions rather than the user functions.

The domain-driven, usage-model approach presented here forces one to determine SUT and to design tests properly from the production perspective in order to gain greater confidence in the system's capability. A similar approach was also reported in [7] by Musa.

Rather than the traditional black-box testing, the structure testing technique was adopted at the system level. This technique enables one to invest the effort intelligently by providing a traceable reasoning for each of the tests; that is, the value and necessity of each of the tests must be identified first. Furthermore, the controlled experiment allows one not only to test but also to observe system behavior accordingly.

It should be noted that during the course of this work, many circumstantial justifications were made. Some were concerns regarding quality; some were issues involving cost; and some were scheduling constraint. For example, the integrity test mentioned earlier was a justification made because of the quality.

In summary, this paper presents:

1. The usage-model, scenarios-driven approach for today's complex systems testing. This approach requires designers and test engineers to look at and examine systems from the customer's perspective.

2. Four non-functional testing objectives: interoperability, integrity, availability, and performance. These reflect the modern nature of today's technology and systems sought by customers.

3. A combination of functional and structure testing technique to explore the complexity of a system through the inter-relationship of the system components.

4. Controlled experiments to examine and observe the system behavior.

System testing for today's large, complex systems can be very costly due to the infinite nature of the problem. However, this should not stop one from performing system testing. In fact, the testing process must be designed to evolve with the changes in as well as the use of technology.

References

1. IEEE Computer Society Task Force on ECBS, "Systems Engineering of Computer-Based Systems," IEEE Computer, November, 1993, pp. 54-65.

2. L. Laverdure, P. Srite, and J. Colonna-Romano, *NAS Architecture Reference Manual*, Digital Press, Digital Equipment Corporation, 1993.

3. Dow Jones Business Publications, *Global News Management System Specifications*, V 2.0, Dow Jones & Company, May, 1991.

4. B. Thome, Task Force on Engineering of Computer-Based Systems Newsletter, Vol. 1, No. 2, Winter, 1993, IEEE Computer Society.

5. K. Alden, "CMIS Application System Testing and Verification," Digital Technical Report, DEC-TR 881, Digital Equipment Corporation, March, 1993.

6. M.C. Hsueh, "Online Workload, Performance and Scalability of a Database Production System: a Case Study," IEEE Proceedings of the 17th Annual International Computer Software & Applications Conference, November, 1993, pp.306-312.

7. J.D. Musa, "Operational Profiles in Software Reliability Engineering," IEEE Software, Vol. 10, No. 2, March, 1993, pp. 14-32.

MODELING RECYCLE: A CASE STUDY IN THE INDUSTRIAL USE OF MEASUREMENT AND MODELING

Luai M. Malhis[†‡], Stephen C. West[†], Latha A. Kant[‡], and William H. Sanders[*]

[†]IBM Corporation
Storage Systems Division
Tucson, AZ 85744

[‡] Dept. of Electrical and Computer Engineering
University of Arizona
Tucson, AZ 85721

[*] Center for Reliable and High-Performance Computing
Coordinated Science Laboratory
University of Illinois
Urbana, IL 61801

Abstract

Large-scale data storage systems rely on magnetic tape cartridges to store millions of data objects. As these tapes age, the resident data objects become invalid; consequently, less and less of the tape potential capacity is effectively utilized. To address this problem, data storage systems have a facility, called "recycle" in this paper, that transfers valid data objects from sparsely populated tapes onto new tapes, thus creating empty tapes for reuse. A high performance recycle process is needed to keep the number of tape cartridges to a minimum, and to maintain a continuous supply of empty tapes for storing newly created data objects. The performance of such processes is not easy to determine, and depends strongly on the data stored on the tapes, the speed and characteristics of the computer on which recycle is executed, and the nature of the algorithms themselves. This paper documents an extensive effort to evaluate a proposed recycle algorithm, using field workload data, laboratory measurements, and modeling. The results of the study were used to improve the recycle process, and were later verified through field trials. In addition yielding the results themselves, the effort illustrated that modeling and measurement, in an industrial setting, can indeed be used successfully in the design process.

1 Introduction

While system-level model-based performance evaluation is an active research area at many universities, its use in industry is not as widespread. In many cases, large-scale systems are designed in an *ad-hoc* manner, with validation (or disappointment regarding) system performance coming only after an implementation is made. This is particularly true in the area of software development, where algorithms are often devised and implemented without a clear understanding of how they will impact the performance of the system in which they are embedded. Extensive measurement and testing is often done after an implementation is complete, but is then too late to avoid design mistakes that lead to poor performance. This does not need to be the case. Modern modeling tools and techniques, coupled with measurements done on similar software, can yield accurate performance predictions that can be used in the design process.

We illustrate the effective industrial use of modeling, coupled with measurement, by reporting on the study of an algorithm to manage a large tape archive. The system (both hardware and software) considered was responsible for the "recycle" operation in the IBM's Data Facility Storage Management Subsystem Hierarchical Storage Manager (hereinafter called HSM). Recycle is the process of moving valid data objects from partially-filled tapes (called volumes) in a data archive to output volumes and releasing the previously partially filled volumes, now empty volumes, to a pool of scratch volumes for subsequent reuse. The recycle process prevents the unbounded growth in the number of volumes in the archive, many of which may be nearly empty, and contributes to the efficient utilization of the potential archive capacity.

The activity reported herein was completed over a six-month period at IBM and at the University of Arizona. During this time, a "project team" at IBM, whose task was to revise the algorithms used in the recycle operation, interacted with a "modeling and measurement team," composed of IBM employees and University of Arizona researchers. The task of the modeling and measurement team was to build accurate models of both existing and proposed recycle algorithms, and to aid in the development of more efficient recycle algorithms. The modeling team built two models: one of the existing recycle algorithm, and one that contained many proposed changes. We obtained parameter values for these models from actual trace data collected in the laboratory, and from existing recycle customer sites while executing the existing recycle algorithm, and also from a careful study of several real-life workloads (tape archives) from customer sites.

Comparing the results of both models under the same workloads gave the project team a quantitative measure of changes of performance obtained by redesigning the system. Such measures could only come from modeling, because the proposed modifications had not yet been implemented. These results helped to guide the development effort of the project team by focusing its attention on items that would have the largest gain in performance. Furthermore, we validated the results of the model by field measurements on the revised recycle software.

We expressed the existing and proposed recycle algorithms as composed stochastic activity networks (SANs) [1], and solved using the terminating simulator in the *UltraSAN* [2] modeling environment. For more detailed discussion of SANs and *UltraSAN* see [1, 2, 3]. The results are significant because they show that modeling, coupled with measurement, can be effectively used in the industrial software design process to predict the performance of alternative algorithms and software implementations. Furthermore, they show that SANs are indeed a reasonable method to express specific software algorithms, and *UltraSAN* can be used to efficiently solve large, industrial, models.

The remainder of the paper is organized as follows: Section 2 provides an overview of the existing system and the proposed modifications, Section 3 discusses the measurement activity that provided guidance to build the models, Section 4 discusses the models, to help the reader understand how complex software can be represented as SANs, Section 5 discusses the results obtained from the models, and concluding remarks are presented in Section 6.

2 Background and Problem Definition

HSM provides facilities for managing data sets (files) on storage devices. HSM also migrates primary data between storage devices (off-loads of infrequently accessed data sets to slower media) and creates backup copies of unmigrated primary data (creates redundant copies of data sets without moving the primary data sets). The HSM storage administrator controls the migrate and the backup processes to achieve the migrate and backup rates required by the user's installation (customer site).

Over time, these backup and migrate actions result in storing large amounts of data on magnetic tape cartridges (called volumes). As volumes age, the resident data sets (also called "objects") slowly become invalid for the following reasons: 1) when data sets change frequently, they cause multiple versions of the same data set to be backed up. When the number of copies (versions) exceed some defined limit, the oldest copy becomes invalid, 2) when the primary data set no longer exists, the backup versions become invalid, 3) when a migrated data set is recalled to primary storage from a tape volume, the data set on the volume becomes invalid, and 4) when the age of a data set exceeds some predefined value, the data set becomes invalid.

Because of these invalidations, tape volumes (which may each contain tens to thousands of data sets) contain increasingly large amounts of invalid data. Consequently, the potential capacity of tape volumes in an archive is less utilized. To address this inefficiency, HSM has an operation called "recycle." The recycle operation selects valid data sets on sparsely populated volumes to be transferred onto another volume, thus aggregating valid data sets from many volumes onto a single volume. Recycle then frees the newly emptied volumes for reuse. For example, if 100 volumes with an average of 10% valid data are recycled, the process recovers these 100 volumes at the expense of 10 new full volumes, or a net tape gain of 90 volumes.

The original implementation of recycle has been distributed widely with thousands of customer installations. Recently, it became more common and necessary for customers to run their operations around the clock, leaving little idle capacity for needed, but time-consuming, operations such as recycle. To make this possible, the recycle project team within IBM was asked to propose modifications to the recycle algorithm to increase its efficiency (increasing the rate of tape gain during the execution of recycle) and, in turn, to reduce the number of tapes necessary to store a given amount of valid data.

In particular, the following changes were proposed to the existing Recycle algorithm:

Multi-tasking The original recycle implementation uses a single task to transfer valid data sets from a single input volume to a single output volume. The project team proposed that multiple, but independent, input-output pairs be supported. The intent was to obtain an increase by a factor equal to the increased number of input-output pairs.

List Building and Sorting The original recycle implementation processes the meta-data catalog in a specific collating order. Each new invocation of recycle starts the new recycle search at the beginning of this collating order. In particular, volumes are selected by searching the catalog, looking for volumes that meet the recycle criteria (the fraction of valid data on the volume is less than some value). When a volume that meets the recycle criteria is encountered, the search operation is suspended and the volume is immediately recycled. After the volume is processed, the search is resumed. Often, customers terminate the recycle process before all the volumes that meet the recycle criteria are processed, for example, when a given number of empty tapes are produced. This selection and processing algorithm causes the following: 1) many empty or nearly empty volumes not to be reclaimed (because of early termination) and, 2) volumes with a higher percent valid to be processed before volumes with a lower percent valid.

Such behavior does not provide the greatest rate of tape gain over a fixed execution period. The project team thus proposed that the catalog records be searched at the beginning of the recycle operation, and volumes that meet the recycle criteria be processed in increasing order of percent valid data. Such an implementation should produce the maximum tape gain rate over any period of execution of the recycle process, if the overhead incurred in processing the list were small relative to the time to recycle volumes.

Immediate Queue If the overhead in building the sorted list is not small, processing of volumes can be delayed significantly, which can cause a customer to perceive an inefficiency in the recycle operation. Because the overhead was unknown (prior to the modeling project), the project team proposed maintaining a second queue, which was not sorted in increasing percent valid order, but met the recycle criteria. The project team proposed an algorithm that can place certain volumes on the second queue depending on their percent valid and the current length of queue. The volumes on the second queue can then be recycled while the list is being built and sorted, avoiding the delay in the start of processing.

Input Drive Allocation The project team also recommended changing the way input drives were allocated in recycle. In particular, the original implementation requested a tape drive allocation for each input volume processed, and released the allocation following the recycle of the volume. The repeated allocations were made to allow competition for the tape drive resources and to avoid blocking other activities while the operator retrieved the next volume. With the advent of automatic tape libraries (hence reducing the time necessary to change tapes), it was deemed appropriate to consider retaining the input drive allocation over multiple input tapes.

Multiple Read/Write Buffers The original implementation uses a single fixed size memory block to buffer data from the input tape to the output tape.

This implementation required that tape reads and writes be done in a sequential fashion, with a write to the buffer beginning only after the previous read completed. It was hypothesized that this serialization contributed significantly to the inefficiency of the original implementation. Consequently, the project team proposed that multiple read/write buffers be used, in a manner that allowed parallel reads and writes to occur.

Connected Set Processing Finally, the project team recommended changing the way volumes were selected for processing, considering the basic unit of selection as a "connected set," rather than an individual volume. Connected sets are formed when a single data set spans more than one volume. To achieve maximum fullness on each migrate or backup volume, a new data set is started on a volume if the expected remaining capacity of the volume is more than some value. If the started data set is not completely written when a maximum allowed capacity is reached, the output volume is demounted and a new empty volume is mounted in the target drive. The suspended data set is continued on the new volume, which causes a single data set to span two volumes (or more, for very large data sets).

The data set that exists on more than a single volume is called a *spanned data set*. The volume set (of size one or more) with no spanned first (valid) data set, no spanned last (valid) data set, and with zero or more (valid) spanned data sets form a single *connected set*. Note that a connected set can be of size one. The original implementation based recycle selection upon an individual volume's percent valid calculation. When a selected recycle volume had one or more spanned data sets, the volumes that contained part of the spanned data sets were mounted and the partial data set was recovered. The other data sets on these incidentally selected volumes were not recycled unless the volume was selected upon its own merits later in the recycle sequence. The new method proposed was to consider each connected set as a single unit for recycle and the total connected percent valid value to be the criterion for selection.

It was thought that these changes to Recycle would increase its performance, but it was not clear the extent to which the performance would improve, or which of the proposed design changes would have the most significant impact. To investigate these options, we built a detailed model of the recycle operation, using real customer workload data (measured in the field), and software execution time measurements, collected in the laboratory and at real customer sites. We describe these workload and software measurements in the next section.

3 Source of Data and Workload

When evaluating real systems, either existing or to be implemented, determination of reasonable values for model parameters is generally the most difficult and time-consuming activity in the modeling process. Whereas a model of an academic nature may allow simplifying assumptions and a restricted focus, real systems tend to have less than ideal implementations and to require models that can address a broad spectrum of questions. It is thus important to ensure that these real-life imperfections, perturbations, and broad scopes are addressed in their models.

With an accurate understanding of the system to be modeled, it is reasonably straightforward to construct models that represent all of the necessary system steps in the proper sequence, and to make all of the correct choices for the algorithms being modeled. To also provide accurate and meaningful results, the model must be as follows: 1) constructed with the correct activity times (service, delay, wait, and so on) for all of the resources implemented in the model, and 2) exercised with a meaningful workload.

The modeling and measurement team developed a basic understanding of the existing system and the intended enhancements through extensive discussions with the project team. Though these discussions were informative and important, much more detailed and more precise timing information than was known by the developers was required to build accurate models. This detailed information was obtained from three primary sources: 1) trace data from existing user installations, 2) trace data from special test cases run in IBM's performance measurement laboratory, and 3) Control Data Set (CDS) information from four existing customer installations (a customer's CDS information specifies, precisely, the type of information stored on his tape archive).

The data that was collected was extensive, and space does not permit a detailed accounting of all measurements and analyses in this paper. Instead, we will try to highlight the types of information that went into the developed model to give the reader an indication of type, and level of detail, of information that was included.

The actual sequence of software events encountered during the execution of the recycle algorithm was determined by analyzing trace data from an existing user installation. This analysis produced both an understanding as to which steps in the sequence were significant and, in many cases, the actual timing information that was used in the model. The key sequence and timing information included: 1) volume selection sequence and times, 2) valid data set search, selection, and processing sequence and times, and 3) tape activity (waits, mounts, demounts) times.

One important issue that we needed to address was the timing associated with the physical movement of tape within a volume. Though the user installation

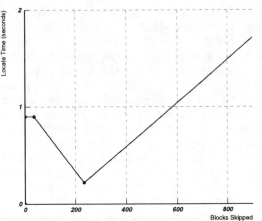

Figure 1: Tape locate time as a function of invalid blocks skipped

trace data allowed us to determine tape motion delays encountered while moving over invalid data sets, we had no way of determining how much media (that is, data blocks) was skipped. To determine these skip times to locate to the next valid data set, we conducted laboratory measurements, using the original recycle implementation, that allowed us to measure the locate time as a function of the number of invalid blocks skipped. The derived relationship, shown in Figure 1, has three distinct regions of operation: 1) The initial region, which is dominated by the tape repositioning time, has little to do with the number of blocks being skipped; 2) The middle region, where the locate time actually decreases for a period of time as a result of reduced tape repositioning; 3) The final region, which has a linearly increasing time to locate to the next valid data set.

The tests of recycle conducted in the laboratory also helped to refine some of the numbers that we had previously obtained from the user installation trace data, for example, the precise read/write buffer timings and a more precise split of what was CPU utilization time and IO or disk access time, for many of the CDS access steps.

To assure the validity and acceptance of the model results, we developed a realistic workload for the models from the user installations archive meta-data records. These records were in the CDSs. We had access to these single point-in-time CDSs from four user installations. The CDSs contain a complete set of records relating to the state of all currently valid tape data sets. These records contain data set names, dates, sizes, location, and so on. The CDS information was received in its raw, unprocessed form and custom data reduction programs were written to extract the information deemed to be interesting. We were able to determine a number of important distributions for both migrate and backup type data sets. In particular, we derived the following: 1) fraction of

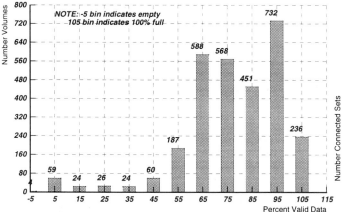

Figure 2: Percent valid distribution for volumes

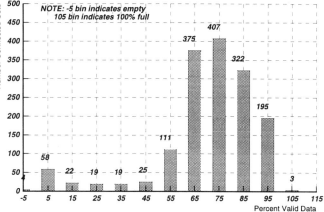

Figure 3: Percent valid distribution for connected sets

volumes containing particular amounts of valid data (10 percent resolution), 2) distribution of number of connected sets by percent valid bin, 3) distribution of number of volumes per connected set by percent valid bin, 4) probability of 0, 1, and 2 spanned data sets (per volume) by percent valid bin, 5) distribution of non-spanned data set size by percent valid bin, 6) distribution of spanned data set size by percent valid bin. All conditional distributions (conditioned upon the percent valid values) were determined for each 10 percent bin of the percent valid distributions. In addition to the distributions above, we determined the fraction of volumes that are empty among all volumes in the record.

Figures 2, 3 and 4, are examples of the type of information that we extracted from the customer installation CDSs (these are from an installation that we chose to use as a workload). Figure 2 shows the distribution of migrate volumes by percent valid bins.

Figure 3 shows the distribution of migrate connected sets by percent valid bins. As was typical in all of the installations, the ratio of volumes to connected sets was closest to 1 at low percent valid and grew progressively larger as percent valid became larger. The conditional connected set size distributions were determined, by percent valid bin, and utilized in the model. For all volumes and connected sets, the ratio was 2959/1566 or 1.9 for this installation.

Figure 4 shows the size (number of volumes per connected set) distribution for the connected sets. Most connected sets are small in size, 1 or 2 volumes, but there are some of size 10, 15, and 20 volumes. These larger connected sets are always the newest connected sets where the data sets have not started to become invalid, very close to 100% valid.

The data capture phase consumed from 40% to 50% of the total work of the modeling and measurement team. In retrospect, the substantial time spent on measurement and data analysis paid off, because it made the construction of models much easier. This

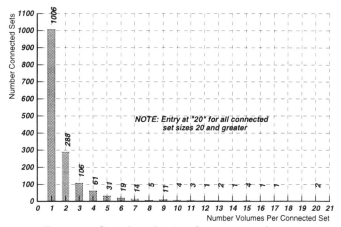

Figure 4: Size distribution for connected sets

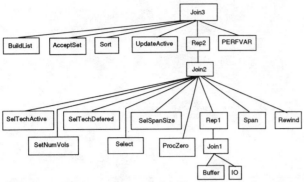

Figure 5: Composed model for Stage 1 recycle operation

activity extracted data from a number of different sources, with customer installation supplied data and local laboratory measurement data being the most significant source of data. In the next section, we discuss the models, and how they use the data discussed we presented.

4 SAN Models for Existing and Proposed Recycle Algorithms

We built two SAN models, one for the original algorithm and one for the proposed modification. We maintained as much commonality between the two models as possible, introducing differences only as necessary to implement the proposed changes in the algorithms. Because of space limitations, we are unable to discuss in detail both of the models. Instead, we describe the structure of the SAN model of the proposed algorithm, and, in some detail, a small part of the model of the proposed algorithm that implements the list building operation. In this way, we hope you will gain an appreciation of the complexity of the models, and how we integrated the algorithms and measured workload data into the SAN models. For a more detailed description of both SAN models, see [4].

Figure 5 shows the "composed model" for the proposed recycle algorithm. A composed model [5] is built from several SAN submodels using "replicate" and "join" operations. These operations permit the construction of hierarchical (or composed) models from existing SAN models. The *replicate* operation replicates a subnet a certain number of times. The replicate operation thus allows the construction of composed models that consist of several identical component subnets. The combination of several different subnets is accomplished using the *join* operation. The join operation produces a composed model that is a combination of the individual subnets.

Each subnet in the composed model in Figure 5 represents some of the processing steps in the proposed recycle algorithm. For example, the subnet labeled **buildList** represents the process of searching through the meta-data records and determining which connected sets meet the recycle criterion. The subnet labeled **acceptSet** determines whether the selected connected set for recycle should be inserted into the immediate queue, to be recycled immediately, or inserted into the defered queue, to be recycled after the completion of the list building and sorting process. Sorting the list is represented by the subnet **Sort**.

The subnets representing a single task are joined together using node **Join2**. These joined subnets are then replicated a number of times (equal the number of tasks in the system), using node **Rep2**, to represent the multi-tasking scenario. The multiple read/write buffers for each task are represented by the two subnets **buffer** and **io**, and the two nodes **Join1** and **Rep1**. The number of times **Rep1** is replicated reflects the number of read/write buffers available to each task to transfer the data blocks. Finally, the node **Join3** joins all the subnets needed to build the recycle model for the proposed algorithm.

Each leaf in the composed model is a *stochastic activity network* (SAN) [1]. Figure 6 shows an example SAN from the composed model shown in Figure 5. Stochastic activity networks are a stochastic extension to Petri nets. Structurally, they consist of *activities, places, input gates,* and *output gates*. Activities (*start-Sel* and *contBuild* in Figure 6) represent activities of the modeled system whose durations impact the ability of the system to perform. *Places (selNext* and *exit1* in Figure 6) are used to represent the "state" of a system and may contain *tokens*. *Cases* associated with activities (represented as small circles on one side of an activity, *repeat* in Figure 6) permit the realization of uncertainty with probabilistic choices concerning what happens when an activity completes. *Input gates* and *output gates* permit flexibility in defining enabling and completion rules. In this model, we use places, along with input and output gates, to control the processing flow of the recycle operation. We use activities without cases to represent the various timings in the recycle process and we use activities with cases to represent the various distributions (described in the previous section) that define the model workload.

To illustrate the use of SANs to build the recycle model, we describe in some detail the structure and the function of the subnet labeled **buildList** shown in Figure 6. Specifically, for each connected set, we must probabilistically determine a percent valid value from the density function shown in Figure 3. This determination can be accomplished by using a single *activity* with a number of cases equal to the number of possible percent valid values a connected set can have. If the percent valid values must be specified to within one percent resolution, an *activity* with 100 cases is needed. On the other hand, if the percent valid resolution is required to within 0.1 percent then an *activity* with 1000 cases (or some combination of several *activities* each with many cases) is required. This approach is impractical, especially if some flexibility is needed

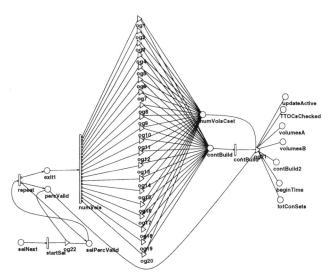

Figure 6: SAN Model: *buildList*

to decide at what resolution of the percent valid values to run the model. A more practical approach is to use conditional distribution for each percent valid value. We use the conditional distribution to compute the probability that a connected set have a percent valid value equals x, assuming that the percent valid value for that connected set is greater than or equal to x.

We modeled the percent valid value selection process using a single activity with two cases (activity *repeat* in Figure 6). Each time this activity is enabled, we compute the probability distribution function of the density function shown in Figure 3. Then two probabilities for the two cases associated with this activity. Let the variable called **accept_prob** be the probability value associated with case 1, and the variable called **reject_prob** be the probability value associated with case 2. If the model is to run with percent valid resolution equals 0.1 percent, there are 1001 different percent valid values (ranges from 0.0 percent to 100.0 percent) that a connected set can have. The place *percValid* contains a number of tokens that represents one of the 1001 possible values. For example, if the number of tokens equals 125, the percent valid value represented is 12.5 percent. The number of tokens in this place are set to zero before a percent valid value is selected for a connected set using output gate *og22* in Figure 6.

The computed PDF, conditioned on the number of tokens in place *percValid*, uses the following procedure to compute **accept_prob** and **reject_prob** values. The variable **num_tokens** represents the number of tokens in place *percValid*. If **num_tokens** equals zero, then **accept_prob** is set to the value of the PDF at zero, and the **reject_prob** is set to 1.0 - **accept_prob**. If **num_tokens** is not zero but less than 1000, the two variables **upper** and **lower** are assigned

the values **num_tokens** + 0.5, and **num_tokens** - 0.5, respectively. Also, the value of the PDF at the point **lower** is **PDF_lower** and the value of the PDF at point **upper** is **PDF_upper**, and variable **total_prob** is 1.0 - **PDF_lower**. Then, **accept_prob** is set to (**PDF_upper** - **PDF_lower**)/**total_prob**, and the **reject_prob** is set to 1.0 - **accept_prob**. Finally, if number of tokens in place *percValid* equals 1000, then **accept_prob** is set 1.0 and **reject_prob** is set to 0.0. Thus, conditioned on the number of tokens in place *percValid*, the PDF is used to determine the probability of accepting or rejecting that percent valid value for the connected set.

When activity *repeat* completes, either case 1 or case 2 is chosen. If case 1 is chosen, a token is added to place *exit1*. In this case, the connected set is assigned the percent valid value represented by the number of tokens in place *percValid*. If case 2 is chosen, then that percent valid value is rejected. In this case a token is added to place *percValid* and place *selPercValid*. Hence, the process of accepting or rejecting the next possible percent valid value is repeated. This approach gives greater flexibility in running the model at any specified resolution for percent valid.

Moreover, we use the activity *numVols*, and the cases associated with this activity to represent the conditional distributions (conditional upon the percent valid values) of the number of volumes in a connected set. The unconditional distribution of the number of volumes in a connected set by percent valid bins is shown in Figure 4. From this distribution, the possible number of volumes in a connected set can vary from one to twenty. Hence, an activity with 20 cases can be used to model 20 different possibilities.

In some activities, the time to do an operation is not a single value but rather a function of some value. For example, the time required to locate the next valid data set to be transferred from the input tape is a function of the number of invalid blocks that must be skipped to move to the next valid data set. This locate function is shown in Figure 1. In this case, the activity completion time in the SAN model must be representative of such functions. The function specifying the activity completion time of the locate operation is shown, in Table 1, example of the possible complexity of such functions.

When completed, the model of the proposed recycle algorithm consisted of 16 subnets, 162 input and output gates, 177 places and 77 activities. The timing information and the workload were then inserted into the models, and the models were simulated using the terminating simulator in *UltraSAN*. Confidence intervals are generated by the simulator, and replications are done until a desired level of confidence is reached.

5   Results

We present results here for a single workload for a single, sample migrate account, although many work-

Table 1: Activity time distributions for SAN *select*

Act.	Dist.	Parameter values
skip	det.	

	value	/* *skip time is based on number of blocks* */
		if (blkstoskip == 0)
		    return(0.0);
		if (blkstoskip < 37)
		    return(0.9007615);
		if (blkstoskip < 236)
		    return(1.029212 − 0.003453
		    ∗ blkstoskip);
		else
		    return(−0.239565 + 0.001940
		    ∗ blkstoskip);

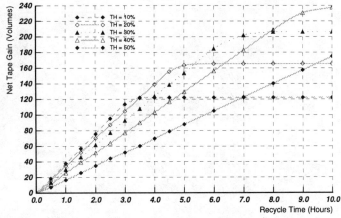

Figure 7: Net Tape Gain (Stage 0)

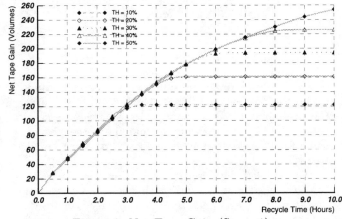

Figure 8: Net Tape Gain (Stage 1)

loads were studied in the course of our work. The number of migrate volumes managed was 6000. To illustrate the type of output available, we examine two parameters of interest in this section. Subsection A, titled **Net Tape Gain**, contains results on the rate at which tape volumes are recovered. Subsection B, titled **Multiple Buffers**, discusses the effect of multiple buffers on the Net Tape Gain.

5.1 Net Tape Gain

The measure of most interest to the development team and the user community is at what rate are tapes released for reuse, or in other terms, the number of tapes freed for new use in some period of time.

The performance variable net tape gain (NTG), is the number of tapes released during the recycle process. If we let `empties` represent the empty candidate volumes, `freed` the number of non-empty candidate volumes and `filled` the number of output tapes used to hold all of the valid data in the non-empty candidate volumes, then NTG = `freed` + `empties` - `filled`.

Net Tape Gain: Stage 0 Figure 7 gives the cumulative NTG (in volumes) as a function of recycle time (in hours) for five different preset threshold values for Stage 0.

The curves in Figure 7 illustrate the following: First, the net tape gain for a given threshold value increases linearly with recycle time until all the 6000 input tapes have been processed, after which it flattens out because there are no additional tapes to recycle. For example, the curve for 30 percent threshold rises linearly for apprximately seven hours, which represents the time to scan the 6000 input volumes and to recycle those cartridges with less than or equal to 30 percent valid data. Each plateau implies that the 6000

volumes were scanned and there are no more tapes to be reclaimed. Second, the number of tapes reclaimed per hour is inversely proportional to the threshold value because larger threshold values have a greater amount of valid data to be transferred. This implies that a greater amount of time needs to be spent in the data transfer phase, which reflects in a smaller number of tapes released per hour. Third, the recycle time increases with the threshold value, with this time varying from three and a half hours to nine hours for threshold values of 10 percent through 40 percent. Because the viewing window was restricted to 10 hours, we can not determine the completion time for the 50 percent curve.

Net Tape Gain: Stage 1 The set of curves in Figure 8 give NTG as a function of time for Stage 1. Again, the time to recycle the 6000 volumes increases as the percentage of threshold value increases, and the plateauing of the NTGs occur upon completion of the recycle process.

An important difference between Stages 0 and 1

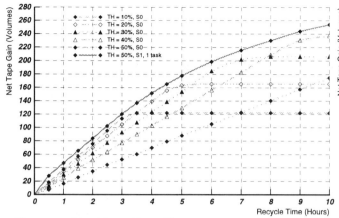

Figure 9: Net Tape Gain (Stages 0 and 1 with single task)

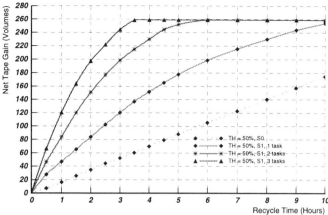

Figure 10: Net Tape Gain (Stages 0 and 1, 50% threshold, with multiple tasks)

is in the rate of NTG for different threshold values. While the rate of NTG differed between the various threshold values in Stage 0, Stage 1 exhibits little difference as the threshold value changes. This is due to the sorting process used in Stage 1, which always places the same volumes in the same order regardless of the threshold. The only effect the larger threshold values have is that they allow the recycle process to process further into the sorted list.

Thus, these curves are approximately the same and are within their simulation confidence intervals except for their completion points. For example, after the first 3 hours of recycle for the migrate account studied, the NTG in Figure 8 begins to flatten out for the 10 percent threshold value (indicating its completion). The curves for higher threshold values remain clustered until the curve for 20 percent threshold breaks away around the four and a half hour time period (marking its completion). This process continues until the maximum threshold is reached.

Comparisons between Stages 0 and 1 Figures 9 and 10 illustrate how the two recycle approaches compare. Because Stage 1 allows for the presence of multiple tasks and Stage 0 does not, Figure 9 compares both stages with 1 task, while Figure 10 compares Stage 0 with 1 task and Stage 1 with multiple tasks for a fixed threshold. We chose a threshold value of 50 percent for Stage 1 because it was consistent with the largest Stage 0 threshold and would provide the best comparison over the total threshold range.

Comparing the curves in Figure 9, we see that Stage 1 outperforms Stage 0, with the NTG of the former being higher than that of the latter for the same migrate account studied. The performance difference tends to become enhanced with increasing threshold values.

Figure 10 compares the NTG for Stages 0 and 1, with Stage 1 having multiple tasks. This figure shows

the very significant gain obtained by increasing the number of tasks. Also note that the time to obtain a given level of NTG varies linearly across the number of tasks. For example, the time taken to recover 200 net tapes in Stage 1 is approximately six, three and two hours with one, two, and three tasks, respectively.

5.2 Multiple Buffers

We show the net tape gain as a function of the number of buffers allocated to a single task in Figure 11. In this study, the recycle threshold is set to 50 percent. the number of volumes is set to 6000, and a single task processes tapes. During the first few hours (≤ four hours), the processed connected sets have a very low percentage of valid blocks. If a connected set has a very small percentage of valid blocks, the amount of time spent in moving valid data from the source volume to the target volume is very small compared to total processing time for that connected set. Most of the total processing time is spent verifying whether a data set is valid or not, mounting new volumes into the input drive, locating to the next valid data set, and rewinding volumes. Therefore, changing the number of buffers from 1 to 2 to 4 has a very small impact on the net tape gain.

However, if the connected sets have a large percentage of valid blocks, the number of buffers used has some effect on net tape gain. The reading and writing of buffers are independent operations because they operate on independent drives. Therefore, increasing number of the buffers from 1 to 2 increases the net tape gain slightly because while one buffer is being read from the input drive, another buffer can be written to the output drive.

But, the increase in net tape gain is small because, regardless of what percentage of valid blocks a connected set has, the data movement time is still small compared to other processing times per input volume. Furthermore, the change in net tape gain when the

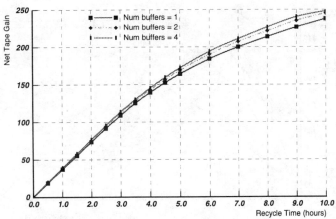

Figure 11: Changing number of buffers

number of buffers is increased from 2 to 4 is much smaller than in the case when the number of buffers is changed from 1 to 2. This minimal improvement is due to very little use of any serial resource.

To summarize, the multiple buffer concept has a small and variable impact on the recycle process. The greater the amount of valid data on the volume, the greater the enhancement. As the tape technology density increases, the usefulness of multiple buffers should increase.

The retention of the input drive allocation did not prove to be a significant enhancement in these models because we did not model contention for the drives from other applications. In a real environment with moderate to heavy drive utilizations, this approach may have noticeable performance gains for the recycle process.

Observations of system resources, such as CPUs and ATL Picker, utilization showed that there are periods during the recycle process when the host CPU, the serial IO, and the ATL picker utilizations peak to appreciable levels. These system resources may not be available at such levels and the recycle process may be adversely affected. The use of these resources has a linear increase as a function of the number of tasks in the system. The peak CPU utilization, serial I/O utilization, and picker utilization per input task are 2.7 percent, 3.1 percent, and 9 percent, respectively.

6 Conclusion

The results presented here served two purposes. First, they provided useful (and sometimes surprising) information to the project team. This information was used, wherever possible, in the current new release of recycle, and will be used in future releases. Second, the results illustrated that modeling and measurement can be used, very successfully, in an industrial setting. This realization is important, since modeling had not been used extensively in the past, due to uncertainty of its benefits for such software systems. Stochastic activity networks were shown to be an appropriate representation for the types of systems we are interested in, and made it easy to integrate measurement information collected in the field and laboratory. In addition, the work provided the necessary evidence of the utility of our approach, and resulted in the initiation of several new modeling projects, using stochastic activity networks and *UltraSAN*.

Acknowledgment The modeling team thanks Cindy Gallo, Jerry Pence, Tony Pearson, Lyn Ashton, and Don Lawver, from the IBM Storage Systems Division in Tucson, Arizona, and Bhavan Shah, originally a member of the university modeling team, now an employee of Intel in Portland, Oregon, for their support and contributions throughout the recycle modeling effort.

References

[1] Meyer, J. F., A. Movaghar, and W. H. Sanders, "Stochastic activity networks: Structure, behavior, and application", in *Proc. International Workshop on Timed Petri Nets*, pp. 106–115, Torino, Italy, July 1985.

[2] Couvillion, J., R. Freire, R. Johnson, W. D. Obal II, M. A. Qureshi, M. Rai, W. H. Sanders, and J. E. Tvedt, "Performability modeling with *UltraSAN*," *IEEE Software*, vol. 8, no. 5, pp. 69-80, September 1991.

[3] Sanders, W. H. and R. S. Freire, "Efficient Simulation of Hierarchical Stochastic Activity Network Models," in *Discrete Event Dynamic Systems: Theory and Applications*, vol. 3, no. 2/3, pp. 271–300, July 1993.

[4] Kant, L., L. M. Malhis, W. H. Sanders, B. P. Shah, and S. C. West, Reference Manual: *UltraSAN* models for recycle modeling project, PMRL Technical Report 93-18, Department of Electrical and Computer Engineering, University of Arizona, December 1993.

[5] Sanders, W. H. and J. F. Meyer, "Reduced base model construction methods for stochastic activity networks," in *IEEE Journal on Selected Areas in Communications*, special issue on *Computer-Aided Modeling, Analysis, and Design of Communication Networks*, vol. 9, no. 1, pp. 25-36, January 1991.

[6] Sanders, W. H., *Construction and solution of performability models based on stochastic activity networks*, Ph.D. thesis, University of Michigan, Michigan, 1988.

[7] Performability Modeling Research Laboratory, *UltraSAN User's Manual*, Department of Electrical and Computer Engineering, University of Arizona, August 9, 1993.

An Analysis of Client/Server Outage Data

Alan P. Wood, Tandem Computers, Inc., Cupertino, CA 95014

Abstract

This paper examines client/server outage data and presents a list of outage causes extracted from the data. The outage causes include hardware, software, operations, and environmental failures, as well as outages due to planned reconfigurations. The study spans all client, server, and network devices in a typical client/server environment. The outage data is used to predict availability in a typical client/server environment and evaluate various fault-tolerant architectures. The results are stated in terms of user outage minutes and have been validated by comparison with other outage surveys and data in the literature. The major results from the outage data study are:

- Each client in a client/server environment experiences an average of 12,000 minutes (200 hours) annual downtime.
- Server outages, especially server software failures, are the dominant cause of client/server unavailability.
- Fault-tolerance in a client/server environment can reduce user outage minutes by nearly an order of magnitude.

1.0 Introduction

Ten years ago, computer systems were relatively simple. The usual user configuration was a dumb terminal connected via an async line to a host mainframe. The world has changed. Today's typical user configuration is an intelligent workstation connected through several network devices such as bridges and routers to multiple servers and possibly a mainframe. Today's servers, and even some clients, have more processing power than the host mainframes of ten years ago. Applications are spread among the clients and servers instead of all residing on the host. A single data base query often requires five or more different pieces of equipment and the associated software to all be operating properly. Instead of being a uniform, single vendor environment, the typical client/server environment contains equipment and software from many different vendors.

With all this complexity, it would seem that system availability in a client/server environment would be very poor. It is true that a complex client/server environment built from the hardware of ten years ago would be down as often as it was up, but hardware reliability has improved

dramatically in the last ten years. Hardware MTBFs have increased one to two orders of magnitude. The classical availability models that considered only hardware are no longer relevant. Software, operations, and environmental failures are all at least as important as hardware failures. Scheduled maintenance periods are being eliminated as customers demand availability 24 hours a day, 365 days a year. Availability models are complex because they must account for the myriad of ways that client/server environments can be configured and the many failure modes of client, server, and network devices. Such complexity makes it difficult to properly account for availability in client/server architecture design.

This paper presents an evaluation of client/server outage data. The data includes physical, design, operations, and environmental failures, as well as outages due to planned reconfigurations. It includes outages due to client, server, and network devices in a typical client/server environment. Based on client/server outage data, the paper indicates the most important outage causes in a client/server environment and evaluates methods for improving client/server availability. The paper also addresses basic issues, such as the definition of system failure and the appropriate measure of availability, that need to be reconsidered in this new computing paradigm.

To our knowledge, there have been no previous comprehensive analyses of outage data for a client/server environment. Previous outage data studies such as [1], [11], and [12] have focused on a host mainframe environment. This outage data will help design engineers analyze client/server availability. It also provides clues for the most effective client/server architectural improvements.

2.0 Measuring Client/Server Availability

Availability, defined as uptime/(uptime + downtime), is a standard system performance measure. Availability is usually expressed as a probability or percentage, e.g., 99.9% availability. Unavailability is defined as 1 - availability, e.g., 99.9% availability is equivalent to 0.1% unavailability. It is often more useful to use unavailability than availability to describe the effects of design or operations changes, especially if unavailability is expressed as amount of downtime per year,. For example, a design change that increases availability from 99.9% to 99.99% does not sound too exciting. However, if we describe the design change's impact as a decrease in

295

Availability	90%	99%	99.9%	99.99%	99.999%
Approximate Annual Outage Minutes	50,000	5,000	500	50	5

Table 2-1. Availability Measured in Annual Outage Minutes

downtime from 500 minutes per year to 50 minutes per year, we do a better job of conveying the true impact of the change on business productivity. Table 2-1 shows the relationship between percentages and annual outage minutes assuming continuous operation.

In a distributed client/server environment, it is difficult to measure uptime and downtime because it is hard to define a system failure. If a single PC fails, the user of the PC cannot access the application, but all other users can continue operating without any loss of performance (unless the PC has failed in a mode that causes an outage for other users.) If 1 out of a 1000 users cannot access the system, is the system down? If not, what about 10 out of a 1000 or 100 out of 1000? All outages are not equally painful from a business perspective, even if they are of equal duration. A PC failure that causes a single user outage is not as painful as a server failure that causes a 50 user outage, which is not as painful as a distributed data base failure that causes a 1000 user outage.

An appropriate measurement of client/server availability needs to include both the duration of an outage and the number of users affected. We propose that user availability, rather than system availability, is the appropriate measure. *User availability* is defined as *user uptime/(user uptime + user downtime)*, averaged across all users. If an average of 1 user out of a 1000 is down, that equates to 99.9% user availability, which is equivalent to 0.1% user unavailability or about 500 annual user outage minutes per user. Using annual user outage minutes to measure client/server availability helps us avoid having to artificially decide how many down users equates to a system outage.

3.0 Client/Server Outage Data

Surprisingly, we were able to find very few companies that kept good client/server outage data. Most companies that we approached did not keep outage data of any type. A few companies had data on the network only, a few had some data on the servers, and no one kept data on single client outages. Our best source of data was one of our large customers that has a large networking application with about 15,000 users. They keep detailed records on all outages that affected 4 or more users and provided us with their entire set of outages for 1992 and 1993. In researching our internal outage data, we found that our MIS group that supports the campus LAN kept good data on the campus LAN, but had no data on clients or servers. We found another MIS group that had good data on the servers because they were responsible for

supporting the servers. This may be typical of other companies and may explain why it is difficult to get outage data for a complete client/server environment. Some examples of the outage data we collected are contained in Section 3.1.

In a distributed computing environment, it is difficult to precisely determine whether a user is up or down. Performance that is good enough for one user may not be good enough for another user, and even if it was, the performance dynamically varies throughout the network. Rather than trying to absolutely quantify the definition of failure, we took a very simple approach for gathering data. If a user said their application was down (which means that their client, server, or path through the network was not working to their satisfaction), then we counted that user as down. This ensures that we measure client/server availability as perceived by the users. It has the drawback that two users might report the same situation differently. In practice, this was hardly ever a problem - all users felt the network was down, or all users felt the network was up.

To make sure that we properly accounted for the impact of an outage on the users, we measured user downtime rather than equipment downtime. For example, if the clients have to reboot their workstation and restart their application to recover from a server outage, that recovery time is included as part of the outage.

Since we could not find an abundance of client/server outage data, we augmented the data we had with literature surveys (e.g., [2]-[8]), articles quoting downtime figures (e.g., [9]), university studies (e.g., [10]-[12]), MTBF quotes from vendors, and our internal outage data. In Section 3.2, we describe how the data was synthesized to provide a list of outage causes.

3.1 Example Outage Data

Table 3-1 provides some examples of the raw outage data collected. Notice the wide variety of outages and the potentially disastrous effect some of these outages could have on a business, e.g., the building transformer that caused 1027 users to be down for 575 minutes = 590,525 user outage minutes! Another interesting point is that in many cases the real cause of the outage was never diagnosed - the operators just figured out how to get the users back on line.

One of the most interesting things about the data we collected was the difference between actual client/server failure causes and the user's perception of those causes. People tend to think of hardware when they think of failures, but hardware reliability has increased remarkably in the last decade. Our data showed that hardware failures

Outage Minutes	Cause/Maintenance Action	Number of Users Down
420	Construction group accidentally set off Halon system in computer room.	25
360	After power restored, Ethernet card (to File Server) did not properly restore because it had been incorrectly configured.	25
150	Circuit breaker tripped by the simultaneous use of multiple tape drives - wiring problem.	25
13	15 workstations unable to access the application. The trouble was isolated to hung file server. Operations performed a stop and start of the file server process to restore service to the client.	15
9	Clients lost access to the application due to broadcast storm on the LAN caused by a bad supervisor card in the hub. The card was replaced to restore service.	287
486	Clients lost access to the application due to a failed remote router link. Failure isolated to a cross connect problem in the link caused by a power failure. The router was reset and service restored.	40
143	60 workstations did not have access to the application due to a router problem. Operations isolated the trouble to a loose cable on the download server. This cable was tightened, routers reloaded and the clients rebooted their workstations.	60
5	Clients could not access the application. Operations bounced the name server process to allow access.	9
575	Client could not access the application due to a bad fuse in the building transformer. Due to the location of the transformer, it took several hours to replace the fuse and restore power.	1027
90	Clients could not access application due to a hub problem. Operations reset the supervisory card on the 8th floor and the Ethernet cards on the 3rd and 4th floors.	58
24	Clients lost access to the application. Operations isolated the trouble to an out of synch condition between file server and line handler processes, which occurred following a failure of the host application. Both processes were bounced to restore.	30
31	Clients experienced degraded service following an application maintenance release. The release was backed out to restore service.	205
46	Clients lost access to the application due to a broadcast storm on the internet LAN. Operations determined the cause to be a packet which caused the LAN bridges to loop. They disabled and enabled the bridges to isolate the packet and restore service.	75

Table 3-1. Example Client/Server Outage Data

caused only 10%-20% of the unplanned outages. Software, operations, and environment failures were as common or more common than hardware failures. Reconfiguration (planned) outages were also more common than hardware failures. Detailed results are contained in Section 4.

3.2 Client/Server Outage Causes

Using the data described in Section 3.2, we developed a list of outage causes for a client/server environment. These outage causes, grouped into categories, are shown in Table 3-2. Except where noted, the outage causes apply generically to clients, the network, or servers. Some of the outage cause terminology may be unfamiliar and is defined at the bottom of the table.

Most of these outage causes apply to any type of computing environment, but some are propagating type outages peculiar to the client/server computing environment. A propagating (also called multiple node) outage means that a specific item of equipment fails in a

mode that causes an outage for other equipment that should be unaffected by the failure. For example, a router failure should cause downtime for at most the users in that router zone, e.g., a maximum of 200. However, the router can fail in a mode (e.g., broadcast storm or algorithm conflict) that causes very heavy traffic on the LAN, which makes response time very poor and causes all users to think the LAN is down. These types of outages can result in very large amounts of user outage minutes because so many users are down.

Some typical propagating type outage causes are:
- Distributed data base corrupted or frozen
- Broadcast storm
- Babbling node
- Router algorithm conflict
- Duplicate network addresses (e.g., duplicate IP addresses)
- Virus
- Name/security server hung or data base incorrect
- Operations bounced the application
- Campus wide router reset.

297

	Physical	Design	Operator	Environment	Reconfig- uration
HW	• CPU, LAN card, disk, etc. fail • Babbling node	• PC with lock on DB fails • Firmware error • Self-test failure	• Cable bumped • Wrong cable pulled	• Commercial power • HVAC • Disasters • Circuit breaker trip	• Upgrade system • Add disk • Move
System SW		• OS crash • Broadcast storm • Server hung • DB corruption • Disk access error • LAN protocol error • Access denied • Router algorithm conflict • Packet errors (runts,jabbers) • Timeouts	• Duplicate or incorrect address • Data not backed up • Stopped wrong process • Table or log deleted	• Power fail recovery error • Virus	• New release • Bug fix • Workload balancing
Applica- tion SW		• Application freeze • Network paging	• Bounced application	• Power fail recovery error	• New release • Bug fix

Broadcast Storm - a broadcast is a special message or packet that all network hosts must receive and process. A broadcast storm is a condition in which broadcasts are being overused, potentially completely disabling the network. Broadcast storms usually occur because of software errors.

Babbling Node - the transmission of random, meaningless packets onto the network; often caused by a failed LAN card.

Runts - packets that are smaller than the minimum length allowed by the network protocol (e.g., 60 bytes for Ethernet).

Jabbers - packets that are larger than the maximum length allowed by the network protocol (e.g., 1518 bytes for Ethernet).

Router Algorithm Conflict - Routers use some variant of a shortest path algorithm. If (e.g.) router A thinks that the shortest path to router C is through router B and router B thinks that the shortest path to router C is through router A, packets for router C will be sent back and forth between routers A and B. This usually occurs because of some breakdown in the router shortest path updating strategy.

Network Paging - a (diskless) workstation runs a job too large for its memory and has to page over the network causing very heavy network traffic.

Table 3-2. Client/Server Outage causes

3.3 A "Typical" Client/Server Environment

Client/server environments are very diverse. They range from a small departmental LAN with a single server to E-mail networks connecting tens of thousands of users to hundreds of servers. There are, however, the following typical characteristics of a client/server environment:

• Users primarily use local servers connected via a LAN. The economics of the client/server environment generally permit the clients to be in close proximity to their primary servers. Therefore, our "typical" client/server environment is a LAN with a communications server for WAN access. Also, the clients are located near their primary server (logically if not physically).

• There are no standard client/server configurations, but there are standard client/server components. Servers are generally powerful workstations performing a specific type of service, e.g., file servers, data base servers, and print servers. Clients are generally PC-class computers.

Typical LAN components include transceivers, bridges, routers, hubs, and gateways.

• Ten to 50 clients per (data base) server is typical. We chose 25 as a reasonable average number based on the client/server environments we studied and opinions from experienced client/server operations managers.

• Equipment layering is typical, meaning that subnets are joined to form networks, which are joined to form larger networks.

It is more likely that availability would influence client/server architecture in a mission-critical environment than in a typical campus LAN environment. Therefore, we defined a representative data base server architecture as opposed to considering file servers, print servers, or other less critical servers. However, most of the conclusions also apply to other architectures and server types.

Using the typical client/server environment characteristics and our desire to examine a data base server architecture, we defined the "typical" client/server architecture shown in Figure 3-1. In Figure 3-1, the users

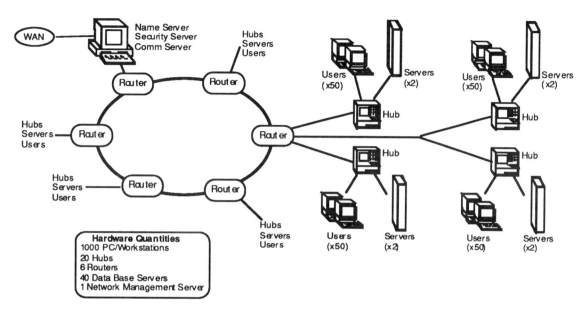

Figure 3-1. "Typical" Client/Server Architecture

and their primary servers are connected to a hub (also called a concentrator) with 50 users and 2 servers per hub. Four hubs are attached to a router for a total of 200 users per router. There are 6 routers in a ring (e.g., a FDDI ring), 5 of which connect 200 users each for a total of 1000 users. The sixth router provides a gateway for communications (comm server) outside the LAN via a WAN and also provides a server that performs network management. Although network management activities such as name services and security services are often spread throughout the network, we chose to include a single name/security/comm server for simplicity. This equipment in this architecture is more uniformly distributed than expected for a client/server environment, but it provides a reasonable basis for calculating client/server downtime and comparing architecture alternatives. The clients are considered to be PCs or workstation class machines. It is certainly possible to consider other client types such as ATM machines or hand-held devices or smart phones, but the majority of current clients are PCs or similar machines.

3.4 User Outage Minutes

For each outage cause identified in Section 3.2, the client/server outage data was used to determine the number of outage minutes that should be ascribed to that outage cause. The typical client/server environment defined in the previous section was used to determine the number of users affected by an outage. The outage minutes were then multiplied by the number of users affected, resulting in user outage minutes. These calculations were performed in a spreadsheet with each row corresponding to an outage cause. An excerpt from the spreadsheet is shown in Table 3-3, and the complete spreadsheet is contained in the [13]. The spreadsheet contains hardware, software, operations, environment, and reconfiguration (planned) outages for each type of client/server device shown in Figure 3-1 - PC/workstations, (data base) servers, name/security/comm server, hubs, and routers.

Table 3-3 shows part of the spreadsheet. For each outage cause, we used the outage data to determine the number of outage minutes that should be ascribed to that outage cause (column 2 of Table 3-3). For example, for a LAN card/connection hardware outage, vendor MTBF

Outage cause	Annual Outage Minutes	Total Number of Items for 1000 Users	Total Annual Outage Minutes	Number of Users Affected	Annual User Outage Minutes
Hub client LAN Card Failure	4	100	400	10	4,000
Hub server LAN Card Failure	4	40	160	50	8,000
Hub LAN Card Failure- Babbling node	1	140	140	200	28,000
Server Application SW Failure	280	40	11,200	50	560,000

Table 3-3. User Outage Minutes Calculation

quotes provide a 300,000 hour MTBF (customer outage data provides a similar MTBF). Customer data provides a 3 hour repair time. Annual outage minutes are (3 hours) x (60 min/hr) x (8760 hrs/yr)/(300,000 hrs) = 5 min/yr. Customer data shows 14%-50% propagating failures; 20% assumed. Therefore, the annual outage minutes for LAN card failures is 4 minutes for non-propagating failures and 1 minute for propagating failures. These outage minutes are shown in the second column of Table 3-3. Non-propagating client LAN card failures are separated from server LAN card failures because they affect a different number of users; propagating failures (babbling node) are not separated because they affect the same number of users. The complete derivation of annual outage minutes for each outage cause is contained in [13].

The client/server architecture shown in Figure 3-1 is used to determine the total number of devices to which each outage cause applies (column 3 of Table 3-3). For example, there are 10 users per client LAN card, so there are 100 client LAN cards for 1000 users. Multiplying columns 2 and 3 yields column 4, "Total Annual Outage Minutes". The number of users affected (column 5 of Table 3-3) is determined from the typical client/server architecture. For example, a hub client LAN card failure affects the 10 users attached to it, a hub server LAN card failure affects the 25 users attached to the server and an estimated additional 25 users that need remote access, and a propagating (babbling node) failure affects the entire 200

user subnet. Finally, user outage minutes are calculated by multiplying columns 4 and 5, yielding column 6.

4.0 Results

From the spreadsheet in [13], the total annual user outages minutes for 1000 users is 12,031,800 user outage minutes or about 12,000 user outage minutes per user. With 525,600 minutes per year, this is 97.7% user availability. Unplanned user outage minutes are 8,185,800 or 68% of the total. Reconfiguration (planned outages) accounts for 32% of the total.

Figure 4-1 depicts annual user outage minutes by equipment type. The operations and environment failures that are not specific to an equipment type are shown separately. Figure 4-1 shows that server outages dominate client/server availability, accounting for nearly 2/3 of user outage minutes. A surprising result is that the network only accounts for only 10% of the user outage minutes, despite the user perception that the LAN is always to blame for outages.

Figure 4-2 shows user outage minutes by outage cause category. Hardware, software, and operations outages were further categorized as client, network, and server outages. Note that software failures account for 39% of the user outage minutes, reconfiguration accounts for 32%, and hardware failures account for only 11%.

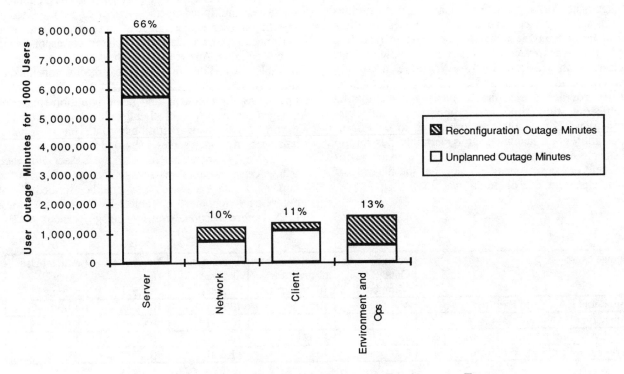

Figure 4-1. User Outage Minutes by Equipment Type

300

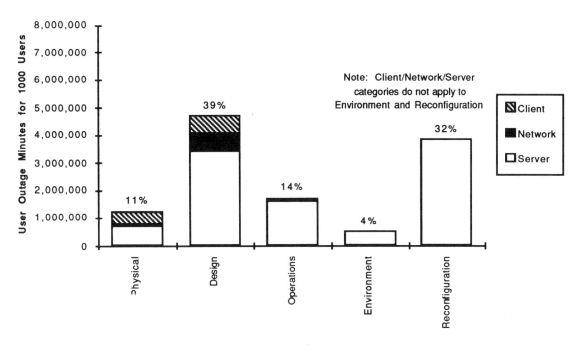

Figure 4-2. User Outage Minutes by Outage Category

4.1 Results Validation

Client/server user outage minutes were derived "bottoms-up", i.e., by defining a set of outage causes and the appropriate outage minutes based on aggregated outage data. Having done so, we need to verify that the results are reasonable by comparing them to other reported results. After all, 12,000 outage minutes (200 hours) a year for each user is a significant amount of downtime. There have been several surveys of LAN downtime (e.g., [2]-[8]) that can be used for comparison. Table 4-1 contains a detailed comparison between the results from this paper and seven surveys. User outage minutes ranges are provided in Table 4-1 when the length of a typical work week is unknown. The correlation is surprisingly good, indicating that the results are reasonable.

5.0 Improving Client/Server Availability

As shown in Section 4, servers are the dominant cause of client/server unavailability. The server outage data used in Section 4 is from commodity servers, so the obvious first step in improving client/server availability is to use fault-tolerant servers. Since server software (application and OS) failures are the dominant server outage causes, software fault-tolerance is important in reducing outage minutes. Software fault-tolerant servers can reduce server outage minutes by an order of magnitude (see the discussion of software fault-tolerant servers in [11]-[12]). Reducing user outage minutes due to servers by an order of magnitude reduces total user outage minutes by more than a factor of 2 as shown in Figure 5-1. In the Software Fault-Tolerant Server stacked column in Figure 5-1, the

Reference	Outages Included	User Outage Minutes	Equivalent User Outage Minutes from this Paper
[2]	Unplanned, no client outages, unknown work week	3,000	1,800-3,600
[3],[4]	Unplanned, "typical" work week	2,400-4,800	1,800-3,600
[5]	Unplanned, no client outages, unknown work week	3,150-6,300	1,800-3,600
[6]	Unplanned, 60-80 hour work week	2,600-5,200	2,900-3,900
[7]	Unplanned, server only	"10s of hours a year"	1,400 (=24 hours)
[8]	Standard work week	1,440-2,880	3,000

Table 4-1. Results Comparison with Outage Surveys

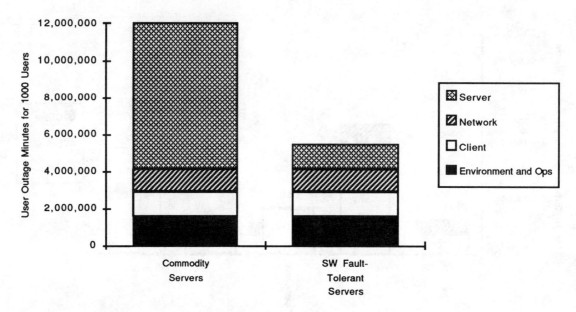

Figure 5-1. Effect of Software Fault-Tolerant Servers on Client/Server Availability

four categories (server, network, client, and environment and operations) account for relatively equal proportions of user outage minutes. Therefore, additional methods to decrease user outage minutes in all four categories need to be investigated.

There are many possible client/server architectures. In the following discussion, we consider 7 modifications to the architecture presented in Section 4. Figure 5-2 depicts some of those alternatives. Each alternative's impact on user outage minutes is estimated for each outage cause in the spreadsheet. The results are shown in Table 5-1, and the remainder of this section is devoted to describing each alternative. The spreadsheet in [13] can be used to evaluate other alternatives by estimating their impact on the user outage minutes associated with each outage cause.

Add fault-tolerant server LAN connection

An extension of server fault-tolerance is to make the server connection to the network fault-tolerant. This eliminates outage minutes due to LAN card failures in the server and the server-to-network connection (e.g., in the hub). This approach requires server software that automatically detects the loss of a server-to-network connection and switches to the alternative path without user intervention.

Add fault-tolerant client LAN connection

Fault-tolerant PCs, while available, are very expensive. A more reasonable approach is to have dual-ported or redundant LAN cards in each PC that can take advantage of redundant paths through the network. This eliminates outage minutes due to LAN card failures in the

client and the server-to-client connection (e.g., in the hub). This approach is most useful with software that automatically detects the loss of a server-to-client connection and switches to an alternative path without user intervention.

Add fault-tolerant LAN

The obvious way to reduce network outages is to make the LAN fault-tolerant. This implies multiple, independent paths among all clients and servers. It reduces user outage minutes due to network failures and reconfigurations, and also reduces user outage minutes due to propagating client and server failures such as a broadcast storms. This approach requires software that automatically detects the loss of a server-to-client connection and switches to an alternative path without user intervention.

Add client session keep-alive

The most common PC outage cause is a software failure causing a reboot or application restart. This generally takes at most a few minutes, but the user then has to reestablish the session and restart any transactions that were in process when the PC failed. Reestablishing a session may take a long time if the PC lacks suitable transaction information. If the server and client could save the necessary client information and reestablish the session for the client, client downtime would be significantly reduced. For example, if a transaction ID was kept by both client and server on disk, the client could check for unfinished transactions when rebooting. The server could reestablish the session when the PC rebooted and continue processing the transaction.

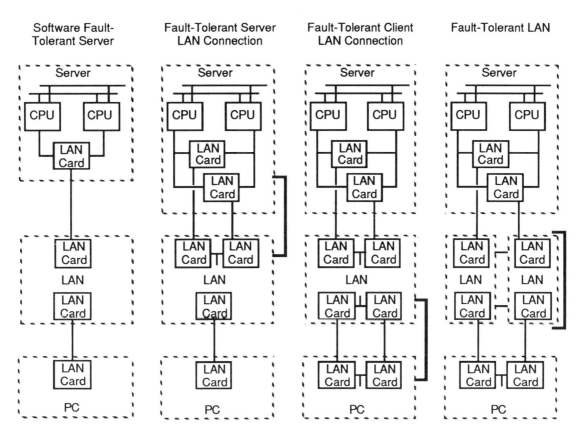

Figure 5-2. Alternative Client/Server Architectures

Architecture Alternative	User Outage Minutes Per User					Comments on Outage Minute Reductions
	Total	Server	Network	Client	Env & Ops	
Commodity Servers	12,032	7,892	1,196	1,342	1,602	From the spreadsheet in [13]
Software FT Servers	5,489	1,349	1,196	1,342	1,602	Reduce server outages by 90% based [11]-[12]
Add FT server LAN connection	5,339	1,336	1,119	1,342	1,602	Reduce server LAN card by 90% & babbling node by 50%;reduce hub & router card by 15%
Add FT client LAN connection	5,127	1,336	876	1,313	1,602	Reduce client & network LAN cards & babbling node by 50%
Add FT LAN	3,930	1,331	84	1,066	1,449	Reduce most network modes by 90-99%, router algorithm by 75%, OS broadcast storm & addressing by 50%, ops cable by 90% & ops test by 50%
Add client session keep-alive	3,638	1,331	84	774	1,449	Reduce client OS & application by 75% because recovery is much quicker
Add FT PC	3,250	1,331	84	386	1,449	Reduce PC HW by 95%
Add UPS	2,861	1,331	84	386	1,060	Reduce power outages by 90%
Add reconfiguration capability	2,084	1,331	84	386	283	Reduce system move outages by 90%

FT = Fault-tolerant; UPS = Uninterruptable power supply

Table 5-1. User Outage Minutes for Architecture Alternatives

Add fault-tolerant clients

Fault-tolerant PCs protect against most PC hardware failures including disk and power failures. However, they do not currently protect against software failures or allow on-line reconfiguration. Since fault-tolerant PCs are expensive, a more reasonable option might be to have extra PCs in a hot standby mode.

Add uninterruptable power supplies (UPSs)

Environmental outages are dominated by commercial power failures. The obvious ways to protect against these outages is to provide uninterruptable power supplies (UPSs) and to possibly improve site power filtering and conditioning. An interesting problem is that site consolidation makes it easier to protect against power outages, but the nature of client/server environments tends toward site expansion.

Add reconfiguration capability

About half of the user outage minutes in the environment and operations outage category are due to massive system reconfigurations such as building moves. A fault-tolerant server, network, and client architecture can help reduce this downtime if it can be configured as two independent client/server systems. Conceptually, half the hardware can be moved while the other half continues to run the application (possibly with degraded performance). The hardware that was moved is then configured and runs the application(s) while the other half of the equipment is being moved.

6.0 Summary

This paper contains an analysis of client/server outage data and a set of outage causes extracted from the data. By using the outage data to predict the expected annual downtime associated with each outage cause, the total user outage minutes for a typical client/server environment was estimated. The results most useful to design engineers are:

- From an equipment perspective, server outages are the most significant cause of client/server unavailability - 66% of client/server user outage minutes are caused by server outages.
- From an outage category perspective, software causes the most user outage minutes (39%), but all outage categories are important. Hardware (11%), operations (14%), environment (4%), and reconfiguration (32%) all contribute significantly to client/server unavailability.
- Fault localization is very important. Over a third of the user outage minutes are caused by propagating failures, i.e., failure such as broadcast storms that cause outages

for client/server components that should be unaffected by the failure. If the impact of an equipment failure on other equipment can be minimized, user outage minutes can be significantly reduced.
- Fault-tolerance, applied throughout the client/server architecture, can reduce annual user outage minutes by nearly an order of magnitude.

References

[1] Gray, Jim, "A Census of Tandem System Availability Between 1985 and 1990", IEEE Transactions on Reliability, Vol. 39, No. 4, Oct., 1990.

[2] Saal, Harry, "LAN Downtime: Clear and Present Danger", Data Communications, March 21, 1990

[3] Caginalp, Elizabeth G., "Downtime Problems Grow with Networks", CRN Extra, October 15, 1991.

[4] Caginalp, Elizabeth G., "The Lowdown on Downtime", CRN Extra, February, 1992.

[5] Fogel, Avi, and Michael Rothenberg, "LAN wiring hubs can be critical points of failure; but physical layer downtime can be prevented", LAN Times, January 7, 1991.

[6] Caldwell, Bruce, "Program Lifts Grounded Users", Information Week, June 22,1992.

[7] Louzon, Michelle, "How tolerant can you be?", Computerworld, May 4, 1992.

[8] META Group, Workgroup Computing Strategies, "LAN Downtime", November 26, 1993, File #340.

[9] Bowen, Charles, "Study by 3M Focuses on PC Data Loss", Online Today, October 20, 1992.

[10] Feather, Frank, "Fault Detection in an Ethernet Network via Anomaly Detectors", Doctoral Thesis, Carnegie Mellon University, 1992.

[11] Lee, Inhwan, Don Tang, Ravishankar K. Iyer, and Mei-Chen Hsueh, "Measurement-Based Evaluation of Operating System Fault Tolerance", IEEE Transactions on Reliability, Vol. 42, No. 2, June, 1993.

[12] Lee, Inhwan and Ravishankar K. Iyer, "Faults, Symptoms, and Software Fault Tolerance in the Tandem GUARDIAN90 Operating System", Proceedings of the 23rd International Symposium on Fault-Tolerant Computing (FTCS-23), Toulouse, France, June 22-24, 1993.

[13] Wood, Alan, "Client/Server Availability Study", Tandem Technical Report 94-1, 1994. Tandem Computers, Inc., Part no. 106404. This report is available from Tandem Computers, Inc., Corporate Information Center, 10400 North Tantau Ave., MS248-07, Cupertino, CA 95014-2599.

Session 10:
Low-Level Hardware Aspects

Session Chair: Mukesh Singhal

Dependability Analysis in HW-SW Codesign[1]

Gy. Csertán   A. Pataricza   E. Selényi

Dept. of Measurement and Instrument Eng.
Technical University of Budapest
H-1521 Budapest, Műegyetem rkp. 9, Hungary
e-mail: csertan, pataric, selenyi@mmt.bme.hu

Abstract

The increasing complexity of todays computing systems necessitates new design methodologies. One of the most promising methods is hardware-software codesign, that supports unified hardware-software modeling at different levels of abstraction, and hardware-software synthesis. As applications include even critical applications, dependability becomes to an important design issue.

A novel approach for the underlying modeling in hardware-software codesign is presented in this paper. The basic idea of this new method is the extension of the descriptions of the functional elements with the models of fault effects and error propagation at each level of the hardware-software codesign hierarchy.

From the extended system model various dependability measures can be extracted. This paper concerns test generation, solved by a generalized form of the well-known logic gate level test generation algorithms and extraction of the input model of integrated diagnostics, allowing testability and diagnosability analysis of the system.

Keywords: diagnostic design, integrated diagnostics, testability, test generation, dataflow, HW-SW codesign

1 Introduction

The advent of low-cost implementation technologies of application specific circuits opens new horizons for custom-tailored solutions. The availability of low-cost, but highly complex off-the-shell programmable components (PLDs) and ASIC technologies allows for the use of such a background even for small enterprises, and not only for the market leaders. Unfortunately the complexity offered by this technologies can not be dominated by traditional design methods any more. Recent efforts aim at solving this problem and reducing the cost and time of the design task by providing new design methodologies and developing integrated environments for system engineering. These offer various tools for the computer architects

and circuit designers based on a homogeneous toolbox and common engineering database for the whole design process. An important characteristic of such tools is that activities performed earlier only after the final engineering design are pushed forward into an early design phase, thus allowing a radical shortening of the design-feedback loop. Practical experiences show a 1:20 reduction in design time, while the resulting hardware overhead due to the automated design is as low as 40%. Moreover the use of automated design technologies radically improves the product's design quality. One such new design approach is hardware-software codesign (Figure 1), that denotes "the joint specification, design, and synthesis of mixed HW-SW systems" [4].

A main insufficiency of this tools (like Ptolemy [8], COSMOS, SpecSyn) originates in the lack of an integrated support of dependability analysis. This becomes crucial in safety related applications, like process control and automation. The avoidance of costly re-design cycles needs the pushing of diagnostic design (test generation, testability analysis), into early phases of system design as well. In [11] a method is presented for testability analysis as part of integrated diagnostics in early design phases, but the problem of generating the input model of this method and designing of the test set remain still unsolved.

The aim of our work is the development of a toolbox for model-based diagnostics and dependability evaluation in the form of an extension of the existing functional design tools. The basic models and technologies developed are fully coherent with those used in the original tools in order to keep the integrity of the design environment and avoiding unnecessary model transformations.

In this paper a novel approach is presented, that uses the dataflow notation as the modeling methodology of HW-SW codesign. Using this approach the behavior of the functional units of digital computing systems can be hierarchically described and aspects of faults, their effects, and error propagation can be handled during the design process. As it is shown in [6] and in this work, the following major problems can be solved concurrently with system design:

- fault simulation
- test generation, including generation of fail-safe

[1] This research is part of the EC Research Project #CP93:9624 FUTEG (FUnctional TEst Generation and diagnostics) with additional support from: Hungarian-German Joint Scientific Research Project #70 and OTKA T-3394 (Hungarian NSF)

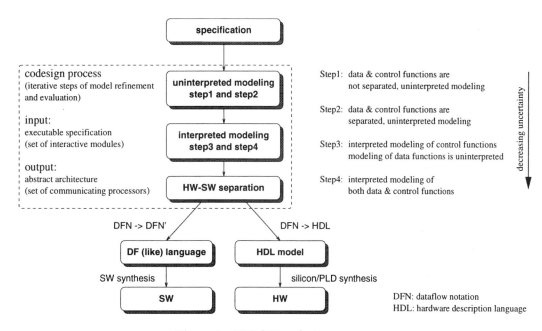

Figure 1: HW-SW codesign process

tests

- estimation of optimal diagnostic strategies
- testability analysis for both built-in and maintenance tests
- failure modes and effects analysis (FMEA), risk analysis

The paper is organized as follows: Section 2 introduces the modeling approach, and presents a simple system and its model as example. In Section 3 a representative of the family of test pattern generation algorithms is presented, and a test is generated for the example. Section 4 deals with the extraction of the integrated diagnostics model illustrated by some results of the analysis of the example. Finally Section 5 contains concluding remarks and a short overview of the future work.

2 The Modeling Approach

Since the application area of HW-SW codesign is very broad, no general solution can be found for all problems. Usually a vertical slice is taken handling a partial problem in depth and solution is given for that particular aspect. We focus our main attention on the design of digital computing and control systems, where dependability is of primary concern. In this case the system is modeled at the highest level of abstraction of the functional design process usually by dataflow models [10, 3]. Only the flow of data and the processing-related delay times are modeled in the form of token flows without any description of the individual data transformation in the components (Step 1 and Step 2 *uninterpreted modeling* in Figure 1). This phase aims primarily at performance analysis and optimization usually supported by formal analysis methods, like analysis after an automatic translation into timed Petri nets.

More and more structural and functional details are incorporated through stepwise refinement into this initial model thus defining increasingly exactly the system's structure and the data processing functions of its components. (Step 2 *mixed uninterpreted-interpreted modeling* in Figure 1). After the refinement uncertainty within the model decreases and analysis results become more exact.

Finally, when all component functions become fully specified (Step 4 *interpreted modeling* in Figure 1), separate automatic or interactive hardware and software synthesis processes can be started in parallel.

Our approach is based on the idea of modeling the fault effects and their propagation similarly to the flow of data in the functional model. In uninterpreted modeling the tokens representing the data can be marked either as correct or as faulty. A set of error propagation paths can be estimated by tracing their flow from the fault site in the network. As uninterpreted modeling does not handle data dependencies, at the highest level of abstraction diagnostic uncertainty has to be introduced in order to express conditional error propagation. This way the simulation and test generation algorithm delivers a superset of propagated fault effects in the system. In the model all potential consequences of a fault are incorporated. In the subsequent steps of model refinement this global overview of the system effectively supports test generation procedures by radically restricting the search space to the solutions of those from the coarse model.

Using a multi-valued logic a more detailed fault model and a more precise description of the reactions of functional units to erroneous input values can be defined. Therefore a global overview of the system testability and diagnostics can be estimated. As example, the tokens and component fault states can be qualitatively grouped (colored) according to the severity of the fault effects into categories like:

- catastrophic (causes a damage in a component)
- fatal (blocking the further operation, e.g. an undetected wrong opcode input of a CPU-like element)
- incorrect (may invoke only error propagation, like wrong input data to be processed by the CPU)

In such a way not only invalidation relations and potential test paths can be estimated, but a fail-safe test process can be designed as well by incorporating the inhibition of the propagation of catastrophic errors into the goals of the test generation algorithm.

It should be pointed out, that the use of other guiding attributes in this user-defined colorings of the tokens and propagation rules offers full freedom for the analysis of different user requirements.

By adding fault occurrence, fault latency and detection probabilities the model can serve as a starting for a more detailed dependability analysis.

Moreover a more detailed description allows to handle uncertainty: at a higher level the unknown behavior of a component is identified by only one color. Later this color can be split into many shades, representing the behavior of the component in more details, without modifying the structure of the component.

Later, when introducing data dependencies at the mixed and interpreted models costly heuristic or structural test generation algorithms must be invoked for the final decision. However the high-level dependability analysis provides not only an inexpensive way for comparative analysis of alternative constructs, but serves as a tool for test strategy design and can control the used heuristics. Remember, that the reduction of uncertainty during successive model refinement monotonically restricts the solution space.

2.1 The Dataflow Notation

The dataflow notation is well-suitable for conceptual modeling of computing systems in the early design phases [3], for early validation of computing systems [2], for performance evaluation, if extended with the notion of time [5], and for being the modeling base of HW-SW codesign [4]. In this work the asynchronous dataflow notation, introduced in [7], is used.

The proposed notation meets the requirements for the specification language in HW-SW codesign:

- Since dataflow can express both large grain and fine grain parallelism, homogeneous modeling in all phases of the design process is possible.
- Concurrency can be easily expressed in terms of dataflow.
- Hierarchical modeling is supported.
- Communication within dataflow networks is straightforward.
- Synchronization of communicating units is done by waiting for data from another unit.
- Performance evaluation of dataflow models is solved, the theoretical background is Petri nets.
- Scalability of the dataflow notation allows the simple description of massively parallel computing.

A *dataflow network* N is a set of nodes P_N, which execute concurrently and exchange data over point-to-point communication channels C_N. The *dataflow node* represents the functional elements of the system and describes their signal propagation behavior by a simple relation between input and output, eventually depending on the previous state of the node. The use of relations instead of input-output functions allows the modeling of non-deterministic behavior. For instance in case of diagnostics this provides a proper mean to express diagnostic uncertainty. The *channels* of the dataflow network symbolize the interaction between the functional elements of the system. Internal channels link two nodes. Input (output) channels connect a single node to the outside world representing the primary inputs (outputs) of the system. *Communication events* occur when data items (subsequently called tokens) are inserted into an input channel (input event describing the arrival of some data to the primary inputs) or data items are removed from an output channel (output event denoting the appearance of results on a primary output of the system).

The functional behavior of a node p is defined by the set of firing rules R_p over the input domain and over S_p, the set of possible states of the node. A node is ready to execute as soon as the data required by one of its firing rules are available and the node is in a proper state. The meaning of firing rule $f \in R_p$, denoted by $f = (s, X_{in}, s', X_{out})$ is that if the node p is in state $s \in S$, each of the input channels $i \in I_p$ holds at least $X_{in}(i)$ data items, then firing rule f is potentially selected for execution. The execution of firing rule f removes $X_{in}(i)$ data items from each input channel $i \in I_p$ and outputs $X_{out}(j)$ data items on each output channel $j \in O_p$, while the node changes its state from s to s'.

2.2 An example

Due to space limitation the selected example is kept very simple and can not even introduce the full modeling power of the presented approach. The system is an automaton that delivers different candies.

According to the proposed approach, the modeling is uninterpreted and for more accurate description of the complex functional units a multi-valued fault model is used. This fault model has to express uncertainties originating in the neglected data dependencies. According to the black-box modeling approach component faults are identified by the rough, and for the sake of the compactness of the example, simplified classification of the results they deliver:

- ok colored token denotes that the component delivered correct computational result.
- inc token denotes that the component delivered incorrect result.
- dead token is sent, if the component, due to a fatal fault, does not deliver results at all.
- x message is used to express uncertainty. x is sent if the result, depending on the input and on the implementation of the component, can be either correct or incorrect.

An adder component, that receives fault free inputs is considered to enlighten the meaning of the different

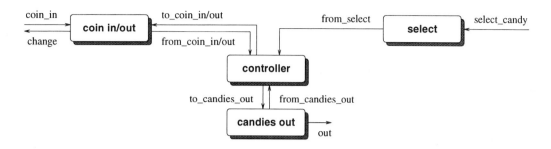

CANDY AUTOMATON:

P_N ={coin_in/out, select, controller, candies_out}
C_N ={coin_in, change, to_coin_in/out,
    from_coin_in/out, from_select
    select_candy, to_candies_out,
    from_candies_out, out}

CANDIES OUT:

I={to_candies_out}
O={from_candies_out, out}
S={ok_0, inc, dead}
R={f1 ... f12}

f1=(ok_0; to_candies_out=ok; ok_0; ok->from_candies_out, ok->out)
f2=(ok_0; to_candies_out=inc; ok_0; ok->from_candies_out, inc->out)
f3=(ok_0; to_candies_out=dead; ok_0; ok->from_candies_out, dead->out)
f4=(ok_0; to_candies_out=x; ok_0; ok->from_candies_out, x->out)
f5=(inc; to_candies_out=ok; inc; ok->from_candies_out, inc->out)
f6=(inc; to_candies_out=inc; inc; ok->from_candies_out, x->out)
f7=(inc; to_candies_out=dead; inc; dead->from_candies_out, dead->out)
f8=(inc; to_candies_out=x; inc; ok->from_candies_out, x->out)
f9=(dead; to_candies_out=ok; dead; dead->from_candies_out, dead->out)
f10=(dead; to_candies_out=inc; dead; dead->from_candies_out, dead->out)
f11=(dead; to_candies_out=dead; dead; dead->from_candies_out, dead->out)
f12=(dead; to_candies_out=x; dead; dead->from_candies_out, dead->out)

Figure 2: Data flow model of the candy automata

tokens. If the adder is fault free, an **ok** token is sent. If a faulty adder adds every time 2 to the result of the addition, an **inc** token is sent. If the 0 bit of the adder is stuck-at-0 an **x** token is sent, since depending on the values of the input the result can be either correct (8+2 is 10 in both the fault free and in the faulty case) or incorrect (8+1 is 9 in fault free and 8 in the faulty case). If the adder is implemented by an independent hardware component and the power of the component is broken a **dead** token will be sent. What can be expressed by the use of **dead** tokens? The answer gives an example for token grouping according to severity: in a responsive real-time application it is very important to have results within a defined time limit. If a component does not deliver any result, it can be considered as a severe fault, while delivering incorrect result is less severe. On the other hand, in a safety critical application such a component can be detected by a watchdog, but an incorrect result can lead to system crash.

The dataflow graph of the system and the formal definition of one of its components are shown in Figure 2. The components are assumed not having built-in fault detection capabilities, and the evaluation of the model is restricted to the case of single internal faults. The system consists of four parts:

coin_in/out sends as first step of its operation the calculated sum of coins inserted by the user to the controller. The change determined by the controller is returned to the user in the second step. Malfunctions of the component are **inc** (wrong recognition of the value of a coin) and **dead** (a coin is stuck).

select sends the identifier of the candy selected by the client to the controller. We assume, that this component can not be **dead**, but it may deliver incorrect results (keyboard fault).

controller issues an order to the candies_out component to deliver a candy according to the client's selection and the sum of coins. After delivering the candy it calculates the change. The controller delivers either correct or incorrect results (fault in the numerical computation).

candies_out delivers the candies according to the command from the controller. The end of the process is reported back to the controller. Errors of the component are **inc** (wrong type of candy is delivered) or **dead** (candy is out of stock).

Inputs of the system are: **coin_in**, **select_candy**, while **change** and **out** are its outputs. The initial state of fault-free components is ok_0. A verbal interpretation of some firing rules of the candies_out node (Figure 2) is:

f1- In a fault-free system this rule describes the candies_out node. As only error free messages are received on its input (**to_candies_out=ok**) it always remains in its error free state ok_0 and sends error free messages to its outputs (**ok-> from_candies_out** and **ok->out**)

f2- Describes the error propagation of the fault-free component in the state ok_0. An erroneous input (**to_candies_out=inc**) will result in faulty delivering of candies (**out->inc**) while the other output is assumed to remain unaffected by the error (**from_candies_out->ok**). As an external fault does not have a permanent effect on **candies_out**, it remains in its error free state ok_0.

f5- Due to an assumed internal fault, the component is permanently in the erroneous state **inc**.

309

Correct input messages (`to_candies_out=ok`) will be resulting in incorrect output `out->inc` value (wrong type of candy is delivered), but a correct signal will be sent to the controller `from_candies_out->ok` (candy is delivered successfully).

3   Test Strategy Design

The basis of effective fault detection and diagnostics is a well planned test strategy. This test strategy describes the execution order of the tests of a given subset of the system's test set. Selection of the subset is done according to some criteria, like test time minimization, maximum fault coverage, safe testing, etc. The test set of the system usually is created automatically from the system description and fault model. It contains the test vectors describing the inputs of the system being necessary to detect component faults at the outputs of the system. Inputs of the system can be either the primary inputs (PI), or special, test inputs (TI). Outputs once again are either primary outputs (PO), or test outputs (TO). Earlier test pattern generation was executed at the logic-gate level. Since in case of complex systems the very large number of logic gates prohibits the use of traditional test generation method, new approaches are necessary. In this section it will be shown that test strategy design can be done concurrently with system design even at a higher level of abstraction by using a dataflow model based automatic test pattern generation (ATPG). ATPG at the logic-gate level is a very well elaborated field of the computer science offering well-proven solutions for practical problems. As our approach uses a generalized form of gate-level ATPG, at first a comparison between logic-gate level description and the proposed dataflow description is given:

- In the gate and module-level stuck-at fault model, faults are modeled at the output of logic gates. Faults of a functional dataflow node are manifested similarly at the outputs in the form of faulty messages.
- The behavior of a dataflow functional element is described by a transfer relation, similarly to the truth or state transition tables of logic gates and modules.
- The model may contain loops that, just like in case of sequential logic have to be cut and an iterative array model can be constructed in both cases [1].
- Since dataflow components can have internal states as well, the testing of a system requires a predefined initial system state. (In practical dataflow models examined till yet there was no need for the search of a self-initialization sequence.)

Due to this correspondence, methods and solutions of logic-gate level test pattern generation can be generalized for the dataflow model and high-level ATPG algorithms can be generated. As a representative example the D-algorithm [1, 9] is selected, that is well known and widely used for test generation for stuck-at faults in logic circuits.

3.1   The high-level D-algorithm

In order to generate a test for a given fault the problem of test generation is recursively divided into the subproblems of:

- error propagation
- line justification
- implication and checking

Error propagation tries to propagate the error of a line to the POs, line justification is responsible for setting the PIs according to the fault of a given node, and implication and checking aims at the reduction of the problem space. The D-algorithm performs implication and checking after each line justification and error propagation step. Error propagation has priority over line justification. To keep track the still open problems two sets are maintained during the algorithm: the *J-frontier* containing the gates of which inputs have to be justified and the *D-frontier* containing the gates from the inputs of which the error has to be propagated towards the POs.

Due to modification during adaptation, our solution of the subproblems is slightly different from the original one:

- Due to the multi-valued fault model not only 0 and 1 values are used. (E.g. in the candy automaton example `ok`, `inc`, `dead`, `x` values are used.) In correspondence with it instead of value pairs D (1 in the good, 0 in the faulty circuit) and $\overline{D}$ (0/1), various value pairs are propagated. (In the example `ok/inc`, `ok/dead`, `ok/x`, `inc/ok`, `inc/dead`, `inc/x`, `dead/ok`, `dead/inc`, `dead/x` are propagated.)
- Instead of the truth table firing rules are used. Possible actions depend on the state of the component. States of the component have to be consistent in subsequent blocks of the iterative array model (predecessor and successor states). For this reason nodes and channels are instantiated, i.e. objects with the same instance number belong to the same block.
- Since components may have multiple outputs the J- and D-frontiers contain channels instead of gates.
- Checking has to ensure that the additional constraints imposed by the global testing requirements are fulfilled. E.g. in safe testing the propagation of a `dead` token is prohibited.
- A frame program of the high-level D-algorithm (Figure 3) is necessary because components may have multiple outputs, thus error propagation can be started in more than on direction. The set input mappings (IM), created in Step 4, contains all those input mappings for which a fault pair is activated on one or more of outputs of the component. Test generation is successful if at least for one input mapping the D-algorithm executes successfully, Step 5–8.

The high-level D-algorithm (Figure 4) recursively calls itself and at each call performs the possible implications, checks the decisions made by the previous

```
1:  test generation algorithm(N, err)
2:  begin
3:    set node N  state to err
4:    create the set of input mappings IM
5:    repeat
6:      select the next element of IM
7:      D-alg()
8:    until SUCCESS or IM is empty
9:  end
```

Figure 3: The test generation algorithm

```
1:  D_alg()
2:  begin
3:    if (imply&check()=FAILURE) then return FAILURE
4:    if (error not at PO) then
5:      if (D-frontier empty) then return FAILURE
6:      repeat
7:        select C from D-frontier
8:        if (Propagate(C)=SUCCESS) then return SUCCESS
9:      until all elements of D-frontier have been tried
10:     return FAILURE
11:   if (J-frontier empty) then return SUCCESS
12:   select C from J-frontier
13:   if (Justify(C)=SUCCESS) then return SUCCESS
14:   return FAILURE
15: end
```

Figure 4: Procedure D-alg()

```
1:  Imply&check()
2:  begin
3:    create the set N
4:    repeat
5:      select the next element of N
6:      set inputs, outputs and state of the node
         if it can be done uniquely
7:      if (input-output, state or criteria inconsistency exists)
         then return FAILURE
8:    until all elements of N have been processed
9:    return SUCCESS
10: end
```

```
1:  Justify(C)
2:  begin
3:    create the set F
4:    repeat
5:      select the next element cf F and
         set inputs, outputs and component state
6:      if (D-alg()=SUCCESS) then return SUCCESS
7:    until all elements of FP have been tried
8:    return FAILURE
9:  end
```

```
1:  Propagate(C)
2:  begin
3:    create the set FP
4:    repeat
5:      select the next element of FP and
         set inputs, outputs and component state
6:      if (D-alg()=SUCCESS) then return SUCCESS
7:    until all elements of FP have been tried
8:    return FAILURE
9:  end
```

Figure 5: Procedures for solving subproblems

call and solves an error propagation or a line justification subproblem (Figure 5).

The Imply&check() procedure selects all the components of which inputs or outputs have been changed since the last call (Step 3). Then it tries to make implications and consistency check for the selected components. If check fails for any of this components no test can be generated. When encountering such a situation this solution will be immediately rejected as if it was a contradiction and backtracking is invoked.

Suppose that channel C is an output channel of component N. The procedure Justify(C) creates the subset of firing rules of N, such that firing rules belonging to F produces the required output on C. Then D-alg() is called to continue test generation. If this fails for all elements of F, channel C can not be justified.

The function of Propagate(C) is similar to that of Justify. In this case C is an input channel of the node, and firing rule pairs from FP have to propagate the fault pair present on C to one or more outputs. If the continued test generation fails for all of the selected firing rule pairs, the fault on C can not be propagated.

3.2 Complexity issues

The algorithms, especially the error propagation, line justification, and implication procedures, are slightly more complex then the original one due to the higher complexity of functional dataflow elements. Moreover due to the multi-valued fault model the decision tree of such an ATPG algorithm is larger, e.g. for a given decision the number of alternatives is higher. This can lead to an increased number of backtracking.

Since the dataflow semantics used for the modeling maintains the compositionality property [7] these complexity issues can be managed by hierarchical test generation. Suppose that the test results of a subnetwork for a given test vector are known (a partial test

has been generated). If this is placed into a larger dataflow network, test generation can be started with error propagation from the output of the subnet to the POs and line justification can be started from the inputs of the subnet towards the PIs of the system without going inside of the subnet.

3.3 Test generation for the example

To enlighten the previously presented algorithm, test generation is presented in details (Figure 6) for the inc fault of the controller component in the simple example. The test generation procedure is shown in Figure 6 step-by-step.

Vertical partitioning of Figure 6 denotes the different steps of test generation. In horizontal partitioning the leftmost part contains the identifier of the steps. In the middle the unfolded dataflow model of the system is shown (only channel and nodes with defined state are shown) and in the rightmost column states of the nodes and the channels, the J- and the D-frontiers are enlisted. The different steps in the process are:

Step 1: State of the controller is ok_0/inc. The input mapping ($from\_coin\_in/out_0 = ok$, $from\_select_0 = ok$) is selected and outputs are set according to it: a value pair appears on the output channel of the controller ($ok/inc- > to\_candies\_out_0$). The D-algorithm can be started.

Step 2: Error propagation step: the value pair from $to\_candies\_out_0$ is propagated through the component candies_out. A value pair appears on the PO out_0, but propagation can not be stopped, there is still data on channel $from\_candies\_out_0$.

311

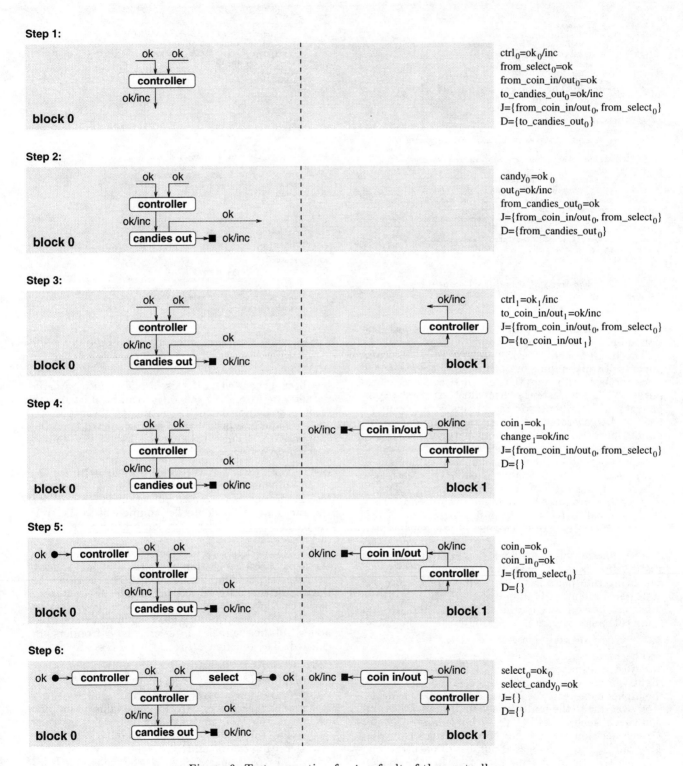

Figure 6: Test generation for inc fault of the controller

input		system state				output	
coin_in	select_candy	coin_in/out	select	controller	candies_out	out	change
ok	ok	ok	ok	ok	ok	ok	ok
ok	ok	inc	ok	ok	ok	inc	x
ok	ok	ok	inc	ok	ok	inc	ok
ok	ok	ok	ok	inc	ok	inc	inc
ok	ok	ok	ok	ok	inc	inc	ok
inc	ok	ok	ok	ok	ok	inc	ok
inc	ok	inc	ok	ok	ok	inc	x
inc	ok	ok	inc	ok	ok	inc	ok
inc	ok	ok	ok	inc	ok	x	inc
inc	ok	ok	ok	ok	inc	x	ok
ok	inc	ok	ok	ok	ok	inc	ok
ok	inc	inc	ok	ok	ok	inc	x
ok	inc	ok	inc	ok	ok	inc	ok
ok	inc	ok	ok	inc	ok	x	inc
ok	inc	ok	ok	ok	inc	x	ok

Table 1: Results of fault simulation

Step 3: Error propagation from $from\_candies\_out_0$ through the controller. This will be the second instance of the controller in the test. A value pair is propagated to $from\_coin\_in/out_1$. ($from\_coin\_in/out_1$ denotes that the channel is in the second block of the iterative array model.)

Step 4: Error propagation from $from\_coin\_in/out_1$ trough component coin_in/out. The value pair ok/inc reaches the PO $change_1$ and the D-frontier is empty. Error propagation is finished, line justification can be started.

Step 5: Line $from\_coin\_in/out_0$ is justified by setting PI $coin\_in_0$ to ok.

Step 6: Justification of $from\_select_0$ by setting PI $select\_candy_0$ to ok. The J-Frontier is empty, the system is in consistent state (components in the first block are in their ok_0 state), test generation is finished successfully.

The generated test vector maps ok on both coin_in and select_candy. As a result in the fault free system ok appears on both outputs of the system: out and change. If the components coin, candy, and select are fault free and the controller has the fault inc, after applying the test vector inc appears on both outputs of the system.

4 Testability Analysis

For testability analysis the integrated diagnostics approach of Sheppard et. al. [11] is used. This approach is based on the conclusion-test and test-test dependency relations. Conclusion is the isolation of a fault, in our case fault of a component. Test is any information source relevant to the diagnostic problem. Dependency relationships among tests and conclusions are described in form of a directed dependency graph. In the dependency graph tests and conclusions are represented by nodes (tests are denoted graphically by circles, conclusions by boxes) and dependencies are directed edges. If a test T_2 depends on T_1 (if T_1 fails T_2 will also fail), then a path exists from T_1 to T_2. Similarly if a test T_3 depends on the conclusion C_1 (if C_1 fails T_3 will also fail), then a path exists from C_1 to T_3. (A test fails, if it does not deliver the intended result). The adjacency matrix of the dependency graph, the so-called dependency matrix, has two parts, one describing test-test dependencies (upper part) and a second one describing conclusion-test dependencies (lower part). If conclusion C_3 depends on test T_1 then the [3,1] element of the lower part is set. Based on the dependency matrix different testability measures can be computed [11]:

- isolation level (ratio of diagnosable faults)
- nondetection (fault coverage)
- test leverage (robustness of the test set)
- overtesting (ratio of uniquely diagnosable faults to number of tests is relatively high)
- undertesting (ratio of uniquely diagnosable faults to number of tests is relatively low)
- test uniqueness (a test can detect/diagnose only one fault)
- test redundancy (multiple tests can detect and/or diagnose the same fault)
- false alarms (the cumulative effects of multiple faults produces an identical syndrome as a different fault)

This method of testability analysis is used in our modeling approach since all dependency relationships can be extracted from the dataflow model by means of fault simulation. For this purpose in [6] a parallel fault simulation is proposed. In the previously presented example 5 possible conclusions can be considered: C_1 is coin_in/out=inc, C_2 is select=inc, C_3 is controller=inc, C_4 is candies_out=inc, and finally the

	T$_{1a}$	T$_{1b}$	T$_{2a}$	T$_{2b}$	T$_{3a}$	T$_{3b}$
T$_{1a}$	F		F		F	
T$_{1b}$	F	F	f	f	f	f
T$_{2a}$			F		f	
T$_{2b}$	F	f	f	F	f	f
T$_{3a}$			f		F	
T$_{3b}$	F	f	F	f	F	F
C$_1$	F	f	F	f	F	f
C$_2$	F		F		F	
C$_3$	F	F	f	F	f	F
C$_4$	F		f		f	
C$_0$			F		F	

Table 2: Dependency matrix for the example

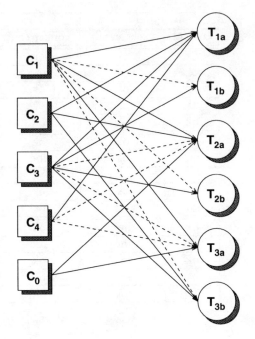

Figure 7: Dependency graph for the example

conclusion no fault is denoted by C_0. (For simplicity **dead** faults are omitted.) In the analysis of the example 3 tests are considered: T_1 (the one generated in the previous section, a test for controller=**inc**), T_2 (for the fault controller=**inc**), and T_3 (for candies_out=**inc**). They map the inputs **coin_in** to **ok, inc, ok** and **select_candy** to **ok, ok, inc**. The outputs **out** and **change** are referred to T_{1a}, T_{2a}, T_{3a} and as T_{1b}, T_{2b}, T_{3b}.

Simulation results are shown in Table 1. The corresponding dependency graph is in Figure 7 and the dependency matrix is in Table 2 respectively. In the dependency matrix F denotes "strong" dependency, i.e. when a conclusion fails the test will also fail, while f denotes "weak" dependency, i.e. when a conclusion fails failure of the test will depend on the actual value in the test vector, corresponds to an **x** output value. In the graph solid lines present "strong" dependency, and dashed lines present "weak" dependency.

How is the dependency graph extracted from the simulation results? For example, each time the inputs are **ok, ok** and coin_in/out fails, T_{1a} will also fail as denoted by the **inc** result on **out**. In the dependency graph it is represented by the solid line from C_1 to T_{1a}, while in the dependency matrix by the element [7,1]=F. In the same case test result T_{1b} is data dependent (output **change** is **x**), thus the dependency is represented by the dashed line from C_1 to T_{1b} and by the element [7,2]=f.

In the analysis the term *pessimistic* case is used, when only "strong" dependencies are considered. The term *optimistic* is used when also "weak" dependencies are taken into account. The pessimistic case is the worst case of analysis from the point of view of dependability measures. On the other hand in optimistic case the upper bound of dependability measures can be estimated.

Since the example is simple not all of the previously mentioned testability measures are really meaningful. The most important results of the analysis are:

- It can be seen from the dependency matrix, that none of the faults produce an identical syndrome as the fault-free case. Thus fault coverage is 100%, all faults can be detected in both the pessimistic and in the optimistic case. (Syndrome is the result of tests when the given fault occurs.)
- Isolation level equals the ratio of uniquely isolatable groups to all fault conclusion and denotes the ratio of diagnosable faults. In the pessimistic case failure signatures can be divided into three groups (group1: C_1, C_3; group2: C_2; group3: C_4) according to the observable fault effects enlisted in the dependency matrix. Thus the value of isolation level is $3/4 = 0.75$. In the optimistic case the number of groups is 4, thus isolation level is 1.0 indicating, that all of the faults can be diagnosed although tests have been generated only for the controller and for candies_out.
- T_1 and T_2 are redundant, since in all cases they result in identical syndrome. Thus one of them can be left out during the system test.

5 Conclusion and Future Work

In this work we presented a modeling approach which can be used in the early phases of HW-SW codesign. It supports testability and dependability analysis as an integral part of the design process, since in the proposed dataflow model both the functional and error propagation/fault effects information are incorporated. By means of a simple example we have shown that even in this phase of the design test strategy design and testability analysis can be done concurrently with the system design.

Future work incorporates the implementation of an environment in which dependable hardware-software codesign can be done. For this reason the Ptolemy [8] design environment, developed at the University of California at Berkeley, was used. As part of the future work we want to identify and examine the constraints imposed by the various testing criteria on HW-SW separation.

Acknowledgments

The authors want to express their gratitude to Prof. M. Dal Cin and Prof. L. Simoncini, whom hosted them for a period at the University of Erlangen, Germany, and at the University of Pisa, Italy respectively, where this work was started. Also their useful comments to this work are gratefully acknowledged.

References

[1] M. Abramovici, M. A. Breuer, and A. D. Friedman. *Digital Systems Testing and Testable Design*. Computer Science Press, New York, 1990.

[2] C. Bernardeschi, A. Bodavalli, and L. Simoncini. Dataflow Control Systems: An Example of Safety Validation. In *Proceedings of SAFECOMP'93*, pages 9–20, Poznan, Poland, 1993.

[3] A. Bondavalli and L. Simoncini. Functional Paradigm for Designing Dependable Large-Scale Parallel Computing Systems. In *Proceedings of the International Symposium on Autonomous Decentralized Systems, ISADS '93*, pages 108–114, Kawasaki, Japan, 1993.

[4] G. Boriello, K. Buchenrieder, R. Camposano, E. Lee, R. Waxman, and W. Wolf. Hardware/Software Codesign. *IEEE Design and Test of Computers*, pages 83–91, March 1993.

[5] Gy. Csertán, C. Bernardeschi, A. Bondavalli, and L. Simoncini. Timing Analysis of Dataflow Networks. In *Proceedings of the 12th IFAC Workshop on Distributed Computer Control Systems, DCCS'94*, pages 153–158, September Toledo, Spain, 1994.

[6] Gy. Csertán, J. Güthoff, A. Pataricza, and R. Thebis. Modeling of Fault-Tolerant Computing Systems. In *Proceedings of the 8th Symposium on Microcomputers and Applications, uP'94*, pages 95–108, October Budapest, Hungary, 1994.

[7] B. Jonsson. A Fully Abstract Trace Model for Dataflow Networks. In *Proceedings of the 16th ACM symposium on POPL*, pages 155–165, Austin, Texas, 1989.

[8] A. Kalavade and E. A. Lee. A Hardware-Software Codesign Methodology ofr DSP Applications. *IEEE Design & Test*, pages 16–28, September 1993.

[9] J. P. Roth, W. G. Bouricius, and P. R. Schneider. Programmed Algorithms to Compute Test to Detect and Distinguish Between Failures in Logic Circuits. *IEEE Transactions on Electronic Computers*, EC-16(10):567–579, October 1967.

[10] J. M. Schoen, editor. *Performance and Fault Modeling with VHDL*. Prentice Hall, Englewood Cliffs, New Jersey, 1992.

[11] W. R. Simpson and J. W. Sheppard. *System Test and Diagnosis*. Kluwer Academic Publishers, 1994.

Use of Preferred Preemption Points in Cache-Based Real-Time Systems

Jonathan Simonson and Janak H. Patel

Center for Reliable and High-Performance Computing
University of Illinois at Urbana-Champaign
Urbana, Illinois 61801-2307
USA

Abstract

Time-critical applications require known worst-case execution times to ensure that system timing constraints are met. Traditional cache memory arrangements, however, significantly impede the determination of tight upper bounds on these worst-case execution times (WCET). The difficulty comes in adequately predicting the cache miss ratio for a task in a preemptable multi-tasking environment. Caches thus increase the complexity of calculating WCET. To resolve this, caches have simply been excluded from WCET calculations. Each task must then be provided greater time in which to execute leading to lower throughput and performance. In this paper we present a cache management scheme that allows WCET calculations to more easily reflect the timing effects of caching. This is done through the appropriate selection of preemption points within a task's execution. The scheme focuses on the WCET component that is due to preemption overhead. An added benefit is a reduction in execution time of up to 10% for some tasks over traditional cache management.

1: Introduction

Cache memory is essential to real-time systems in providing the high throughput and performance needed by time-critical applications. The critical nature of the applications, however, demands worst-case execution times (WCET) to ensure that all timing requirements are met. It is therefore important that such systems be able to use cache memory while having calculable WCETs that account for the caching effects.

WCETs are essential for determining the schedulability of a task set. Therefore, they must be guaranteed to ensure system reliability. These guarantees are frequently made by allocating much more time than ever actually used. This results in lower system utilization due to idle

processor cycles. Some systems use these cycles for non-critical tasks. Alternatively greater attention can be given to the analysis of the system and the task set to obtain tighter bounds on the WCETs. Imprecise task results may be permissible when even shorter execution times are needed [1]. To obtain tighter execution bounds, however, a task must be examined to determine its longest path of execution. Also under examination must be the system resources required by the task and the time consumed by them. Here we look at the effects of the cache memory on these calculations and how the calculations can be made more tractable through the scheme that we present.

The difficulty that caches add to the calculation of WCET comes in determining the portion of memory references that are cache hits. The absolute upper bound on execution time when considering the cache is obtained using a hit ratio of zero, but this essentially negates the use of the cache. To get closer to the lowest upper bound, the system and the task set must be analyzed. One of the factors that contributes to the difficulty of this analysis is the variations in program flow within each task. Each execution path may have a very distinct memory access behavior resulting in very different cache hit rates. Preemptable multi-tasking environments also can add greatly to the variability in cache hit rates and thus to the variability of program execution times. Such environments result in significant reductions in tasks' cached state by the time the tasks resume execution. This is a consequence of task-state replacement by intervening processes. The degree of task-state reduction may be very difficult to determine due to variations in task execution and sequencing. All this can make the problem of determining cache hit rates intractable.

One of the first solutions that arose to resolve this problem was to simply exclude the cache from the timing calculations or even the actual system. As mentioned previously, this degrades performance with regard to throughput but does provide for more tractable timing calculations and thus better guarantees on WCETs. Kirk and Strosnider [2, 3, 4] approached the problem by partitioning the cache into segments that are then allocated to a set of tasks to

This research was supported in part by a grant from the National Aeronautics and Space Administration under contract NASA NAG-1-613.

meet the system requirements. Hardware modifications to the cache design are necessary in their technique to maintain the ownership and activity of these segments. A drawback of their technique is that each task is limited in the amount of cache space it can use. This is mostly compensated for by their segment allocation scheme. A more software-oriented approach was taken by Niehaus, Nahum, and Stankovic [5]. Their work focuses on calculating WCETs, taking into account the effects of instruction caching. The tasks are divided up at large subtask boundaries to provide scheduling points at which task switching can take place. A similar approach was taken by Arnold *et al.* [6]. Here again large subtask are examined by careful program flow analysis. A method referred to as static cache simulation is used to determine when a particular assembly instruction is going to be hit or miss. Of the six applications that they ran using their method, none underestimated the WCET. For five of the applications, the estimated WCETs were within 12% of the actual. The sixth application was overestimated by 99%. Liu and Lee [7] also address WCET for uninterrupted cached programs. Instruction caching is accounted for at a basic block granularity. Their work focuses more on the complexity of determining the worst-case control flow path. To reduce the complexity cost they present various approaches that stop short of exact analysis. An exact analysis is also provided. They were able to estimate the WCET for a binary search programto within 10% of the actual. Basumalick and Nilsen [8] have provided a short overview of additional techniques to predicting cache hit rates in real-time systems.

This paper focuses on the component of WCET calculations due to task switching. Preemptions often result in cache state changes between periods of program execution. This makes it difficult to determine the degree to which the cache reload overhead affects execution time. We propose a scheme that both reduces the observed cache reload overhead and permits determination of the execution time cost of preemptions. This allows one to more accurately calculate WCET in a preemptable environment. This scheme is also known to reduce task execution time by up to 10% through selection of preemption points that result in low cache reload times.

In the remainder of the paper we present our cache management scheme. Its aim is to provide for more predictable WCETs and reduce task execution time in a preemptable multi-tasking environment. We begin by presenting our scheme and its proposed implementation in Section 2. Section 3 provides an explanation of how the scheme was evaluated. The results and their interpretation follow in Section 4. In Section 5 we conclude the paper with an overview and future directions of this work.

2: Guided preemption via cached state

In an environment where tasks vie for processor cycles and preempt one another in obtaining those cycles, a task's cached working-set can be significantly reduced by the time the task regains control of the processor. This results in a cache-reload overhead when the task resumes. The extent of the cache state reduction and what state is lost can be difficult to determine. This is affected by factors such as point of preemption occurrence, preemption frequency, and task sequencing. These factors are often loosely defined and vary from one execution of a task to the next. The state loss that occurs is actually a replacement of the preempted task's cached working-set by intervening tasks. The traditional cache is one that is a shared resource and one in which the currently executing task has free range over the use of the cache lines. The following scheme was devised with the above ideas in mind.

The technique that is proposed limits preemptions to prespecified points within a task's execution. Firstly, this allows for more accurate worst-case calculations of the cost of preemptions since the possible points of preemptions are well defined. Secondly it allows for the reduction of preemption costs through appropriate preemption point selections. The second point clearly benefits any system not just one requiring guarantees on WCETs.

2.1: Technique basis

The basis of our technique lies in calculating the cost of a preemption. When a task is preempted there is the cost of context switching as well as the additional cost of restoring to the cache any active task state that has been lost when the task resumes. It is this additional cost that is the focus of our scheme. The context switching time is often a direct function of the degree of processor state that is saved and restored.

At the time a task is preempted, there exists some portion of the task's cached state that would have been accessed in the future prior to replacement by a cache miss. The cache lines that fit this description will be referred to as *live* or *active* cache lines and those that don't as *dead* or *non-active* cache lines. The definitions for these terms are as follows:

Definition 1: A *Live or Active Cache Line* refers to one that contains a block of data that will be referenced in the future prior to its replacement. In other words, it is a cache line in which the next reference is a hit had the task been allowed to run to completion.

Definition 2: A *Dead or Non-Active Cache Line* refers to one that contains a block of data that will be replaced prior to any future reference or that will not be referenced during the remainder of a task's execution. In other words, it is a cache line in which the next reference is a miss or for which there are no future references had the task been permitted to run to completion.

If the active cache lines are replaced due to the execution of other tasks, the data they contain must be fetched from main memory when referenced by the resuming task. This adds to the execution time of the task over what would have been necessary had the task not been preempted. This added execution time is equal to the actual number of active cache lines replaced times the cache miss penalty (ie. the additional time necessary to fetch the data from main memory). Since the determination of the number of active cache lines is a much more tractable problem than the determination of the number of active cache lines replaced, the remainder of this paper will use an upper bound on the cache reload overhead equal to the number of active cache lines times the cache miss penalty. How the number of active cache lines might be calculated or estimated is described in Section 2.2.

Once the number of active cache lines are determined at each instant within a task's execution, the points of preemption can be chosen to decrease preemption costs. These points will be referred to as *preferred preemption points* and are defined as follows and illustrated in Figure 1.

Definition 3: A *Preferred Preemption Point* for a given interval of task execution t_i to t_j is the instant within that interval having the minimum number of live cache lines for the interval.

Only one preemption point is needed per task switching if it is known when in each task's execution a higher priority task will be ready to run. On the other hand, preemption points are necessary at frequent intervals and possibly

throughout a task's execution in systems that exhibit a high degree of variability and where higher priority tasks may need to gain control of the processor quickly. In either case, by knowing the maximum number of preemptions for each individual task and the maximum cost of those preemptions, a upper bound on the added time due to the effects of preemptions on caching can be determined. This can be expressed as given below for the highly variable case. The equation does not account for other system effects of preemptions, such as a possible increase in paging and possible contention for system resources (eg. secondary storage devices). The overhead due to preferred preemptions above that without preemptions is then

$$E_P = (max(p_{l0}, \cdots, p_{ln-1})\, t_m + t_c)\, P \qquad (1)$$

where

E_P = *Time due to preferred preemption points above that necessary without preemptions*

p_{li} = *Number of live lines at preferred preemption point i*

n = *Number of prespecified preferred preemption points*

t_m = *Cache miss penalty*

t_c = *Context switch time*

P = *Maximum number of preemptions*

If the number of live lines per preemption point is known and the exact points of preemptions are known, E_p becomes

$$E_P = Pt_c + t_m \sum_R p_{li} \qquad (2)$$

where

R = *Actual points at which preemptions occur*

2.2: Determining number of active cache lines

In the previous section it was shown that the knowledge of the number of active cache lines during a task's execution permits better worst-case execution calculations. To make use of this, however, there must be some method of determining or predicting the number of active cache lines. This section presents a possible method of addressing this issue. The method assumes a data cache but can be similarly performed for a instruction cache.

Since the active cache line behavior is linked to the activity of program variables, it is natural to look here for a solution. As a starting point it will be assumed that the

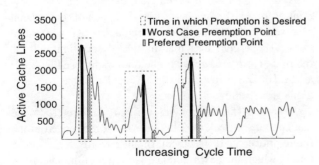

Figure 1: Preferred preemption points

task control flow paths are available in order of decreasing execution time for a non-preempting system with cache memory. From here the activity of the program variables are determined and correlated or translated to active cache lines. To determine this activity, the life times of the program variables need to be ascertained. This is similar to performing live variable analysis for register allocation but here cache lines are the resource allocated. Dynamically addressed variables may require profiling or programmer assistance to determine their life times. The life times of a variable are the times for which the variable is resident and active within the cache. For non-fully associative caches the secondary effects of mapping conflicts may need to be considered but some preliminary simulation results show that this effect should be small. The analysis of variable activity and their mapping to cache lines is performed on a per control path basis. The end result is the cache line activity along each path.

The above analysis is first applied to the worst-case execution path and the preferred preemption points are determined along this path based on cache line activity. The WCET with preferred preemption points is then calculated. The next worst-case execution path is then examined. At this point to reduce calculation costs, the cost due to all preemptions along this new path is first calculated using a cache line activity equal to the number of cache lines. If the execution time with this upper bound on preemption costs does not exceed the first worst-case execution path with preferred preemption points, further analysis of this path and others are unnecessary. If it does, then the same analysis is necessary on this path as on the worst-case execution path. If this path then exceeds the worst-case execution path, it becomes the case of comparison for the remaining paths. The analysis then proceeds to the next worst-case execution path and the above steps are repeated comparing this path to the worst-case execution path of comparison. It is likely that since execution paths share segments of code, portions of the analysis done for one path can be shared with that of other paths having overlapping segments. This leads to further reduction in calculation costs. To reduce the memory cost necessary for such compilations, it may be possible to use a smaller cache for the actual calculations and scale the results.

The steps necessary in determining the WCETs so that they account for the effects of caching are best incorporated into the compiler. This enables them to be transparent to the user. Further work is in progress in this area with respect to detail and implementation, but it is felt that a reasonable approach to the problem has been found.

2.3: Preferred preemption point selection

For best results preferred preemption points should be determined as indicated in the previous section. More relaxed techniques can be used to determine the selection of preferred preemption points for tasks where lower guarantees on deadlines are allowed or where tighter upper bounds on WCETs are unnecessary. This also applies to task that can afford to have longer execution times.

Perhaps one of the easiest techniques of selecting preemption points under these conditions is by the insertion of traps within the source code by the programer to check for ready to run tasks of higher priority. Since the programer will often have at least an intuitive feeling as to where in the code there are likely to be significant changes in the working set and consequently reductions in number of live caches lines, performance improvements will result. A slightly more complicated technique, along similar lines, is to select subroutine boundaries as the preemption points. Often at such boundaries the working-set is noted to go through significant changes. With either method if tighter bounds on WCETs are desired, further analysis would be necessary to determine the cost of the preemption points chosen. The frequency of these points would also need to be checked to determine if they met the needs of the system.

One technique, that provides perhaps the greatest performance improvements but which is probably the most computationally intensive, is to determine preferred preemption points for each control path through a task. This would be done almost identically to how preemption points were selected in the previous section, with the exception that no comparison of execution times would be necessary between paths unless tighter WCETs were desired.

The technique chosen depends on the system requirements. Take for instance a task which must use imprecise results because it can not meet its deadline but whose results are crucial to the system. Such a task would require a thorough analysis to find preferred preemption points along all program control flow paths. Systems are likely to use multiple techniques to obtain the greatest benefits.

2.4: Scheduling with preemption points

Once the preemption points are chosen the scheduling algorithm of choice must be adjusted to incorporate them. Task sets previously unschedulable may now through their reduced execution time meet the timing requirements. What follows is a modification to the rate monotone scheduling algorithm [9] that accounts for predetermined preemptions points.

The rate monotone scheduling algorithm has been modified to first allow tasks to preempt each other only at prespecified preemption points and secondly to provide the maximum time distance between preemptions such that all tasks will still meet their deadlines. The steps to the algorithm are as follows:

Step 1: Ensure the schedulability of tasks under the unmodified rate monotone scheduling algorithm without accounting for the cost of preemptions.

Step 2: Determine the maximum allowable preemption spacing for each task:

    a: Form groups of tasks consisting of each task and the tasks of higher priority.

    b: Beginning with the smallest group perform the following for each group. Apply the rate monotone schedule to the task group, but allow the lowest priority task to begin first at the critical instant (ie. a point when all tasks are ready to run). Determine the maximum time this task may execute such that all higher priority tasks in the group meet their deadlines. Already determine maximum preemption intervals should be used to define the preemption points of the higher priority tasks. Preemptions are allowed only at these points for this step of the proceedure.

Step 3: Find preferred preemption points for each task such that their maximum allowable preemption interval is not exceeded.

Step 4: Schedule tasks using the rate monotone scheduling algorithm but allow preemptions only at prespecified preemption points with the time cost for such points accounted for.

Step 1 can be determined using the work of Lehoczky, Sha, and Ding [10] for task set schedulability under the rate monotonic scheduling algorithm. The justification for Step 2 is as follows. It is possible for a lower priority task to begin execution one time unit before its higher priority tasks become ready to run. The higher priority tasks would then need to wait until this lower priority task reached a preemption point before they could begin execution. This preemption point must come in a sufficient amount of time such that all the higher priority tasks meet their deadlines. By allowing the lowest priority task to begin execution first when all higher priority tasks are ready to run, this situation is reproduced and the maximum time of execution without preemption can be determined. Step 2 was found to be very similar to work done in [11] for the schedulability of a task set using the rate-monotonic algorithm under the priority ceiling protocol. The blocking that occurs with preferred preemption points has a scheduling effect similar to the blocking that occurs with priority inheritance or semaphores. A theorem is provided in [11] for determining task schedulability under blocking.

An illustrative example of the modified rate monotone algorithm given here is depicted in Figures 2 through 5. In Figure 2, it is seen that all tasks within the task set meet their deadlines under the unmodified rate monotone scheduling algorithm. The execution times given are

Ti = Task Period
Ci = Execution Time
Di = Task Deadline = Ti

T1 = 8, C1 = 2   *T1>T2>T3>T4 (Priority Ordering)*
T2 = 20, C2 = 9
T3 = 60, C3 = 12
T4 = 120, C4 = 9

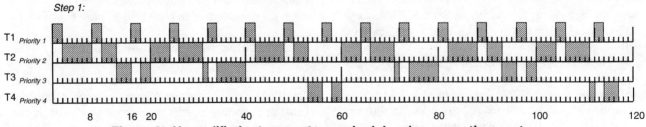

Figure 2: Unmodified rate monotone schedule w/o preemption costs

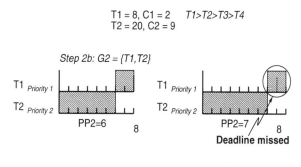

T1 = 8, C1 = 2   T1>T2>T3>T4
T2 = 20, C2 = 9

Step 2b: G2 = {T1,T2}

PP2 = Maximum Preemption Interval for Task T2 = 6

Figure 3: Step 2 of modified rate monotone scheduling algorithm for task T2

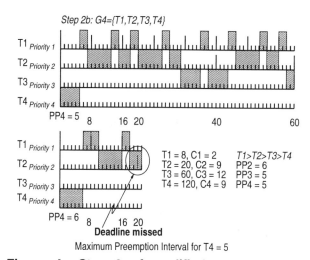

Step 2b: G4={T1,T2,T3,T4}

T1 = 8, C1 = 2   T1>T2>T3>T4
T2 = 20, C2 = 9   PP2 = 6
T3 = 60, C3 = 12   PP3 = 5
T4 = 120, C4 = 9   PP4 = 5

Maximum Preemption Interval for T4 = 5

Figure 4: Step 2 of modified rate monotone scheduling algorithm for task T4

WCETs that account for caching but not for preemptions. This figure corresponds to Step 1. It can be seen that there are 15 preemptions and three remaining time units. The total cost of preemptions can not exceed three time units if the tasks are to meet their deadlines. By using preferred preemption points the chances of meeting the deadlines are increased.

Step 2 results in the following groups G1={T1}, G2={T1,T2}, G3={T1,T2,T3}, G4={T1,T2,T3,T4}. The maximum preemption interval for task T1 is always equal to its execution time. Figures 3 and 4 show the determination of the maximum preemption intervals for task T2 and T4 respectively. The maximum preemption interval for T3 can be done similarly. For task T2, it is seen from Figure 3 that if the preemption interval exceeds 6 time units, T1 misses its deadline. Therefore the maximum preemption interval for task T2 is 6. For task T4 in Figure 4, a preemption interval exceeding 5 time units causes T2 to miss its deadline. It should be noted that when T4 reaches one of its preemption points the ready to run task of highest priority above T4 replaces T4 as the executing process. This coincides with the unmodified rate monotone scheduling algorithm with the exception that tasks now preempt only at preemption points. In determining the maximum preemption intervals for lower priority tasks, the preemption points for higher priority tasks are set at a spacing equal to their respective maximum preemption intervals.

At this point the maximum preemption intervals have been determined for all four tasks and the preferred preemption points can be selected. For this illustration, the preferred preemption points will be set to the maximum preemption intervals. Task T1 is always non-preemptable. Task T2 has a preemption point at 6 time units into its execution. Task T3 has preemption points at 5 and 10 time

units into its execution. Task T4 has a preemption point at 5 units into its execution. Figure 5 shows the tasks as they would be scheduled under Step 4 with the exception that preemption overhead is not taken into consideration in this figure. It should be noted that in this case the number of preemptions has been reduced to 11. In addition, the preemption cost will be less than the original schedule under the unmodified algorithm due to the appropriate selection of preemption points that reduce preemption costs.

Further work is in progress to refine this modification to the rate monotone scheduling algorithm. Other scheduling algorithms are also under examination to determine the modifications necessary for them.

3: Experimental evaluation

In order to verify that preferred preemption points exist and to confirm the effects that these preferred preemption points have on program execution and cache miss rate, a cache simulation was run with five programs from the PERFECT Benchmark Suite [12]. Program analysis as discussed in Sections 2.2 and 2.3 could have been used instead had it been in place at that time. The trace driven cache simulation is also intended to provide a point of comparison for the results of program analysis in future work. The simulation model was written in C++. The processor was modeled to stall on cache misses. Each miss resulted in a 10-cycle latency for accessing data from main memory. Cache hits had a 1-cycle cache access latency. A cache write-allocate scheme was used for accesses. The cache write-back scheme was setup such

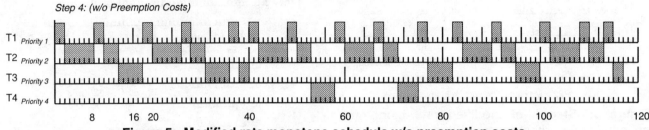

Figure 5: Modified rate monotone schedule w/o preemption costs

that it did not affect the execution time. The traces used in the simulation contained data references only and thus the simulation was restricted to that of a data cache. The cache size was set to 128K Bytes with 32-byte cache lines and direct mapping.

First simulations were done without preemptions to view the live cache line behavior of the task. Whether a cache line was active or not at any particular instant in time was not known until its replacement. For each cache line, a record was maintained of the time of the last load to the line and the last access. At the time of a cache line replacement, a period of activity for the cache line was recorded. The line was considered non-active or dead from the point of last access up until the point at which a new block was loaded. Therefore, in order to know the live line count during each cycle of execution, it was necessary to run the simulation through to completion. It was found, however, that a individual period of cache line activity was almost if not always determined within 200,000 cycles or less. This provided the plots of live cache lines versus cycles given in the next section.

Separate simulations were used to set the actual preemption points and observe the performance improvements. These simulations were run to determine the effects of preempting at preferred preemption points versus immediate and worst-case preemption points. The cache was purged at each preemption point chosen during the simulation. For a large task set, this is a reasonable approach since most of the cache lines have been replaced by intervening tasks. For each simulation run, a set interval was chosen to preempt the task. The other simulation variable was the amount of time allowed before the running task must relinquish the processor at the end of its interval of execution. It is during this time after the end of the interval that the preferred and worst-case preemption

points are sought. Live cache lines are calculated for this period requiring the simulation to run until the end of the next interval where the cache is purged. At this point the active times of all cache lines within the search period can be determined. Purging the cache at the end of the next interval is reasonable because it is to be purged soon after that interval completes anyway. At this point the simulation is returned to the state at the end of the last interval, and simulation resumes, preempting the running task at the determined point. For each task preemption interval and search length, preferred preemption points were chosen and worst-case preemption points were chosen. In addition for each preemption interval, preemptions were made immediately at interval boundaries. This method of determining preferred preemption points was used purely as a way of determining the performance improvements that could be seen with our technique. Additionally, the execution paths taken were not necessarily worst-case but it is believed that this is unnecessary for seeing the performance gains achievable.

The PERFECT Benchmarks used were ADM, BDNA, TRACK, ARC2D, and DYFESM. These memory traces were obtained using an Alliant simulator on a Alliant FX/80 [13]. The traces from ADM, BDNA and TRACK were approximately 110 million continuous data references. ARC2D and DYFESM traces were composed of 40 sample traces each. These samples comprised a total of approximately 9 million data references for each application. In the cache simulations with ARC2D and DYFESM, the cache was flushed before the start of each sample. The Alliant simulator was set to emulate execution on an Alliant FX/8 single processor. TRACK is probably most representative as an application of a real-time process. TRACK contains 33770 lines of signal processing code that is used for tracking objects. ADM is an application for air pollution analysis and contains 6142 lines of code. BDNA is a nucleic acid simulation with 3962 lines of code. ARC2D is computational fluid dynamics with 3605 lines of code and DYFESM is structural dynamics with 7599 lines of code.

4: Results

The simulation runs of ADM, BDNA, and TRACK without preemptions are shown in Figures 4, 5, and 6. The horizontal axis is the time line in millions of processor cycles. As can be seen from these plots, TRACK exhibits less frequent live cache line variance than does ADM or BDNA. This suggests that the effects of preferred preemption points will have less of a impact on the performance of TRACK than ADM and BDNA. This is supported by the results of simulations with preemptions to be shown below.

ADM, BDNA, and TRACK were run with preemption frequencies of 1/2500, 1/5000, and 1/10000 (in 1/processor-cycles). It was with this frequency that the actual preemption points where sought. Each search extended for a period of program execution equal to 10%, 50%, and 90% of the preemption interval. The preferred and worst-case preemption points were chosen from this search period. A worst-case preemption point exhibits the largest number of live cache lines within the search period. Simulations were also run with preemptions occurring immediately at the start of the search period. These preemptions are referred to as immediate preemptions. Table 1 shows percent decrease in execution time over worst case and

Table 1: Percent reduction in execution time via preferred preemption points relative to immediate (Ime) & worst-Case (Max) execution

Preemption Freq.†		1/2500			1/5000			1/10000		
Search Length ††		10%	50%	90%	10%	50%	90%	10%	50%	90%
ADM	Ime	1.8%	5.5%	8.2%	1.0%	4.6%	8.4%	0.7%	2.5%	6.2%
	Max	3.6%	9.8%	12.8%	1.8%	7.1%	11.0%	1.4%	4.1%	7.8%
BDNA	Ime	0.8%	4.6%	8.4%	0.6%	2.7%	6.9%	0.4%	1.9%	4.8%
	Max	1.6%	6.4%	10.4%	1.0%	3.9%	8.3%	0.7%	2.8%	5.8%
TRACK	Ime	0.5%	1.7%	2.6%	0.4%	1.1%	1.9%	0.3%	1.0%	1.7%
	Max	0.9%	2.7%	3.8%	0.7%	2.0%	2.9%	0.5%	1.6%	2.5%

† Preemption Frequency in 1/Processor-Cycles
†† Search Length as Percentage of Preemption Period

ime - preempt immediately upon request
max - assuming worst-case preemption point

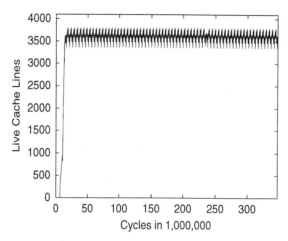

Figure 4: Simulation of ADM w/o preemptions

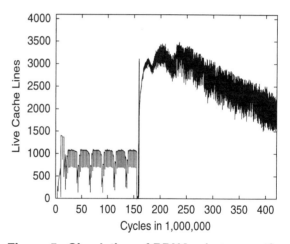

Figure 5: Simulation of BDNA w/o preemptions

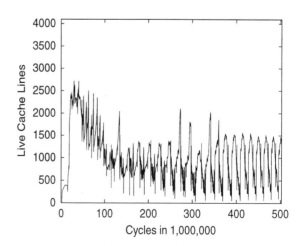

Figure 6: Simulation of TRACK w/o preemptions

immediate preemption achieved via preferred preemption points. The miss ratio for worst-case preemption points, immediate preemption, and preferred preemption points are given in Table 2. Figure 7 presents the percent reduction in execution time for preferred preemption points relative to using worst-case preemptions points when a search length of 50% of the preemption interval is used. It also gives performance numbers for ARC2D and DYFESM not shown in Table 1.

These results show greater performance gains with preferred preemption points at higher preemption frequencies. This is expected due to the larger accumulated cost of poor preemption point selection that occurs at higher preemption frequencies. This, however, does not always hold true. For tasks that have a greater stability in their live cache line activity with occasional fluctuations, the performance improvement will be seen to be greater at the frequency of these fluctuations. It should also be noted that systems with greater cache miss penalties will enjoy even greater performance benefits from preferred preemption point usage. No matter what the performance improvement, however, predetermined preferred preemptions points provide a means of calculating tighter bounds on WCETs thus allowing for greater system throughput. It should also be noted here that even without predetermined preemption points, having the cost of the worst-case preemption point for the entire program execution permits tighter execution time bounds when there exists a bound on the number of preemptions.

Table 2: Miss ratio

Preemption Freq. †		1/2500			1/5000			1/10000		
Search Length ††		10%	50%	90%	10%	50%	90%	10%	50%	90%
ADM	Max	.25	.27	.27	.19	.20	.20	.13	.13	.13
	Ime		.24			.18			.12	
	PPP	.23	.21	.20	.18	.16	.14	.12	.11	.10
BDNA	Max	.32	.32	.33	.23	.23	.24	.17	.17	.17
	Ime		.31			.23			.17	
	PPP	.30	.28	.25	.22	.21	.18	.17	.16	.14
TRACK	Max	.11	.12	.12	.09	.09	.10	.07	.08	.08
	Ime		.11			.09			.07	
	PPP	.11	.10	.10	.09	.08	.08	.07	.07	.06

† Preemption Frequency in 1/Processor-Cycles
†† Search Length as Percentage of Preemption Period
PPP - Preferred Preemption Point

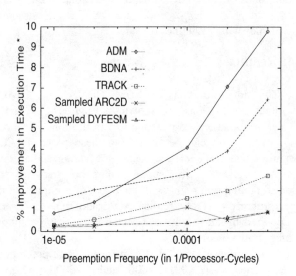

* % Improvement in Execution Time with Preferred Preemption Points over Worst-Case Preemption Points

Figure 7: Comparison at search length of 50% preemption period

5: Conclusion and future work

Caches are instrumental in providing high system performance. At the same time they add greatly to the difficulty of obtaining tight bounds on worst-case execution times. WCETs are essential in real-time systems in order to guarantee that system timing constraints are met. Past real-time systems designs have not included the effects of caching in their timing calculations. This circumvents the added difficulty of calculating WCETs due to caching but unfortunately leads to under utilization of processor power and memory hierarchy. Since real-time systems are often designed for time critical applications requiring quick response times, it is important that caches be considered in WCETs so that these times can be reduced.

The unpredictable nature of cache memory accesses lies in the variability of the cache state in a multi-tasking preemptable environment. Whether a cache access is a hit or a miss at a particular point of program execution can change as a result of task sequencing, preemption frequency, and point of preemption occurrence. A task's working set can be partially or even completely replaced when preempted by the time it resumes execution, thus requiring it to restore part or all of the working set from main memory. It is this cache-reload time that is difficult to determine. The significance of the changes in cache state due to preemptions can be minimized through the use preferred preemption points which we have outlined in this paper. Preferred preemption points are those points within a task's execution that exhibit large variances in the working set. Since the working set is in the process of changing at such times, the cached working set need not be restored in its entirety when the task resumes. By determining an upper bound on the number of active cache lines at these chosen preemption points, we can predict the time cost of these preemptions.

The use of preferred preemption points, in comparison to worst-case preemptions points, resulted in improvements in execution time as high as 12%. It was also found, however, that with preemption frequencies lower than 1/100,000 processor-cycles, the percent improvement with preferred preemption points over worst-case preemption points is minimal. Even so, WCETs with preemptions can still be predicted taking into account the cache memory, thus reducing the WCET used for a task.

Currently the direction of this work focuses on developing methods of selecting preferred preemptions points both dynamically and statically, as well as looking at adjusting various scheduling algorithms to account for this technique. There are also plans to examine this technique more closely with regards to instruction caching. As the work proceeds other approaches to this problem will be sought. These approaches may make use of multi-level caches, code reorganization, and other preexisting architecture performance improvement techniques. The objective is to make a more predictable system while maintaining the same performance level or even achieving greater performance.

References

[1] Wei-Kuan Shih, Jane W. S. Liu, and Jen-Yao Chung, "Algorithms for Scheduling Imprecise Computations with Timing Constraints," *SIAM J. Computing*, vol. 20, no. 3, pp. 537-552, June 1991.

[2] David B. Kirk, "SMART (Strategic Memory Allocation for Real-Time) Cache Design," *Proceedings of the Real-Time Systems Symposium*, pp. 229-237, IEEE, December 1989.

[3] David B. Kirk and Jay K. Strosnider, "SMART (Strategic Memory Allocation for Real-Time) Cache Design Using the MIPS R3000," *Proceedings of the Real-Time Systems Symposium*, pp. 322-330, IEEE, December 1990.

[4] David B. Kirk, Jay K. Strosnider, and John E. Sasinowski, "Allocating SMART Cache Segments for Schedulability," *Proceedings of the Euromicro'91 Workshop on Real-Time Systems*, pp. 41-50, IEEE, June 1991.

[5] D. Niehaus, E. Nahum, and J.A. Stankovic, "Predictable Real-Time Caching in the Spring System," *Proceedings of the IFAC Workshop on Real Time Programming*, pp. 79-83, May 1991.

[6] Robert Arnold, Frank Mueller, David Whally, and Marion Harmon, "Bounding Worst-Case Instruction Cache Performance," *Proceedings of the Real-Time Systems Symposium*, pp. 172-181, IEEE, December 1994.

[7] Jyh-Charn Liu and Hung-Ju Lee, "Deterministic Upperbounds of the Worst-Case Execution Times of Cached Programs," *Proceedings of the Real-Time Systems Symposium*, pp. 182-191, IEEE, December 1994.

[8] Swagato Basumalick and Kelvin Nilsen, "Incorporating Caches in Real-Time Systems," *Proceedings of the Workshop on Architectures for Real-Time Applications.*, IEEE, April 1994.

[9] C.L. Liu and J.W. Layland,, "Scheduling Algorithms for Multiprogramming in a Hard-Real-Time Environment," *Journal of the Association of Computing Machinery*, vol. 20, no. 1, pp. 46-61, January 1973.

[10] John Lehoczky, Lui Sha, and Ye DIng, "The Rate Monotonic Scheduling Algorithm: Exact Characterization and Average Case Behavior," *Proceedings of the Real-Time Systems Symposium*, pp. 166-171, IEEE, December 1989.

[11] Lui Sha, Ragunathan Rajkumar, and John Lehoczky, "Priority Inheritance Protocols: An Approach to Real-Time Synchronization," *IEEE Transactions on Computer*, vol. 39, no. 9, pp. 1175-1185, IEEE, September 1990.

[12] M. Berry *et al.*, "The Perfect Club Benchmarks: Effective Performance Evaluation of Supercomputers," *The International Journal of Supercomputer Applications*, vol. 3, no. 3, pp. 5-40, MIT Press, 1989.

[13] John W. C. Fu and Janak H. Patel, "Trace Driven Simulation Using Sampled Traces," *Proceedings of the 27th Hawaii International Conference on System Sciences*, pp. 211-220, 1994.

Performance Recovery in Direct - Mapped Faulty Caches
via the Use of a Very Small Fully Associative Spare Cache

H. T. Vergos & D. Nikolos

Computer Technology Institute, Kolokotroni 3 , Patras, Greece
&
Computer Engineering and Informatics Department,
University of Patras, 26500 Rio, Patras, Greece.

Abstract

Single chip VLSI processors use on-chip cache memories to satisfy the memory bandwidth demands of CPU. By tolerating cache defects without a noticeable performance degradation, the yield of VLSI processors can be enhanced considerably.

In this paper we investigate how much of the lost hit ratio due to faulty block disabling in direct-mapped caches can be recovered by the incorporation of a very small fully associative spare cache. The recovery percentage that can be achieved as a function of the primary cache's parameters (cache size, block size), the number of faulty blocks and the size of the spare cache is derived by trace driven simulation. The results show that when the number of the faulty blocks is small the use of a spare cache with only one block offers a hit ratio recovery of more than 70%, which increases further with cache size. A spare cache with two blocks is justified only in the case of a large number of faulty blocks.

1. Introduction

Single-chip VLSI processors use on-chip cache memory to provide adequate memory bandwidth and reduced memory latency for the CPU [4 - 10]. The area devoted to some on-chip caches is already a large fraction of the chip area and is expected to be larger in the near future. For example, in the MIPS-X processor [6] more than half of the chip area is devoted to an on-chip instruction cache.

Since in the near future a large fraction of the chip area will be devoted to on-chip caches, we expect that in a large fraction of VLSI processor chips the manufacturing defects will be present in the cache memory portion of the chip. Application of yield improvement models [11] suggests that, by tolerating cache defects without a substantial performance degradation the yield of VLSI processors can be enhanced considerably.

A technique for tolerating defects is the use of redundancy [25]. The use of redundancy to tolerate defects in cache memories was discussed in [1, 2]. Redundancy can have the form of spare cache blocks where if a block is defective it can, after the production testing, be switched out and substituted by a spare block using electrical or laser fuses. Instead of sparc cache blocks, spare word lines and/or bit lines may exist that are selected instead of faulty ones. The overhead of these techniques includes the chip area for the spare blocks or word lines/bit lines and logic needed to implement the reconfiguration. Another form of redundancy is the use of extra bits per word to store an error correcting code [26]. Sohi [1] investigated the application of a Single Error Correcting and Double Error Detecting (SEC-DED) Hamming code in an on-chip cache memory and found out that it degrades the overall memory access time significantly. Therefore the classical application of a SEC-DED code in the on-chip cache for yield enhancement does not seem to be an attractive option for high-performance VLSI processors. In [27] it was shown that the defects in the tag store of a cache memory may cause significantly more serious consequences on the integrity and performance of the system than similar defects in the data store of the cache. To this reason a new way of the SEC-DED code exploitation well suited to cache tag memories was proposed. During fault free operation this technique does not add any delay on the critical path of the cache, while in the case of a single error the delay is so small that the cache access time is increased by at most one CPU cycle. Unfortunately, this technique is effective only in the case that the defects cause single errors per word as for example in the case of a bit line defect.

Another technique to tolerate defects in cache memories is the disabling of the faulty cache blocks that was investigated in [1, 2]. It has been shown in [1, 2] that the mean relative miss ratio increase due to disabling a few defective blocks decreases with increasing cache size and is negligible unless a set is completely disabled. Therefore, the effectiveness of the method of disabling the faulty blocks depends on the number of faulty blocks and whether a set is completely disabled. Unfortunately, as we will show in the following, a large number of faulty blocks may exist. In the case of random spot defects [20] we have to consider a very small number of defects because chips with a large number of defects will usually suffer defects in other critical resources. However, we can easily see that even a very small number of defects in the tag store of a cache memory can affect a large number of tags, leading to disabling of a large number of cache blocks. Also, taking into account the fact that the area devoted to the cache may be a large portion of the chip (50% or more) and the clustering of manufacturing defects [20 - 24] we conclude that it is possible in VLSI processor chips a large number of defects to appear in the caches while all the critical resources of the chips are defect-free. Besides the above, in direct-mapped caches, a set contains just one block, thus disabling a faulty block means the disabling of a set. Direct-mapped caches offer smaller average access time than set-associative ones for sufficiently large sizes [3]. Thus as the size of the on-chip caches increases, the use of direct-mapped caches is favored [12].

Block disabling does not increase the cache access time and permits all non-faulty blocks to be used. However it increases both the mean and the variability of cache's miss ratio [2]. The main performance metric of a memory hierarchy is the average memory access time, T_{av}. For a non-faulty cache with a miss ratio m,

$$T_{av} = T_{cache} + m \, T_{memory},$$

where T_{cache} is the access time of the cache and T_{memory} the average access time of the subsequent memory hierarchy levels. In a faulty cache where faulty block disabling has occurred, the average memory access time will be :

$$T'_{av} = T_{cache} + m' \, T_{memory},$$

where m′ is the resulting cache miss ratio after faulty block disabling. That is,

$$m' = m + \delta,$$

where δ is the increment of miss ratio due to the disabled blocks. Combining the above relations we get :

$$T'_{av} - T_{av} = \delta \, T_{memory}.$$

Since T_{memory} is large the above relation implies that faulty block disabling increases the average memory access time significantly, even when δ is very small. The value of δ depends heavily on the cache associativity, block size and the number of faulty blocks [1, 2]. For direct-mapped caches even a very small number of disabled blocks can result in a substantial value of δ.

Jouppi [12] has proposed the use of a small fully associative (called victim) cache for enhancing the hit ratio of non-faulty direct-mapped caches. The function of the victim cache is to buffer the blocks that leave the main cache due to replacement. The reason of incorporating the victim cache in [12] is for direct-mapped cache performance enhancement and not for performance recovery, since faulty conditions are not considered.

In this work we investigate the subject of recovering the performance of a direct-mapped cache lost due to some disabled faulty blocks by incorporating a very small fully associative spare cache -hereafter called spare cache- *that only serves as spare for the disabled faulty blocks*. More specifically the following problems are examined :

1. How does the performance recovered relate to the primary cache's size, block size and the percentage of faulty blocks ?
2. What is the size of the spare cache required and how does it relate to the above mentioned factors ?

The use of the spare cache described later in Section 2 does not add any delay to the operation of the cache. The size of the spare cache will be measured by the number of blocks that it contains.

The results presented and analyzed in this paper are based on extensive trace driven simulation that is regarded the best way to determine a cache hit ratio [13]. Results for the ATUM traces [14], indicate that hit ratio recovery of more than 70% is feasible by a spare cache with only one block when the number of faulty blocks is small and increases with the size of the cache. The results of trace driven simulation also indicate that the incorporation of a spare cache with two blocks is justifiable only for large number of faulty blocks.

The paper is organized as follows. Section 2 presents the function of the spare cache. Section 3 discusses the simulation methodology, the traces used and presents the simulation results along with an investigation of them. Section 4 concludes our discussion.

2. The suggested cache operation

In this section we will describe the use of the spare cache along with the primary on-chip cache for hit ratio recovery.

Figure 1 presents the block diagram of the primary on-chip cache along with the spare cache. As it is obvious from this figure, the only changes to the original configuration reside in the cache control logic. Suppose that the primary on-chip cache has suffered a number of defects and that during production testing the faults caused by those defects have been discovered. One approach to implement the disabling of cache blocks is to use a second valid (availability) bit [15]. The blocks that contain one or more faults will be disabled by resetting their availability bit. All the non-faulty blocks will have the corresponding bit set and can be used during cache operation.

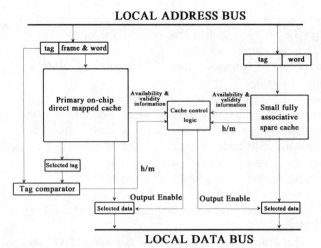

LOCAL ADDRESS BUS

Figure 1. Block diagram of the primary and the spare on-chip caches.

All accesses (either reading or writing) are in parallel propagated to both the primary and the spare caches. Any access that does not refer to a faulty block (the cache controller logic can discover if that is the case by examining the availability bit) is serviced by the primary cache as in the case that no spare existed. This modification does not increase the cache's access time.

Suppose now that an access to a faulty block happens. The cache controller logic will take notice of it due to the status of the availability bit. Off-chip memory access would be required in this case when only block disabling was performed. Such an access may not have to take place even when using a very small spare cache. The controller logic in this case takes account of the hit or miss signal generated by the spare cache along with the validity and availability information. In a hit case the control logic only needs to activate the tristate output data buffer of the spare cache and long off-chip memory access is avoided. LRU updating for the spare cache can be done in parallel with sending the required data to the microprocessor. The spare cache is a very small fully associative cache consisting from (as will be shown in the next section) only one or two blocks thus the hit/miss signal (h/m signal in figure 1) of it will be asserted much faster than the hit/miss signal of the primary on-chip cache [16].

When a disabled primary cache faulty block is referenced and the access of the spare cache results in a miss, the control logic has all the time required to discover the LRU block, update the LRU contents and replace the LRU block data with those from the slower off-chip memory hierarchy when they become available on the local data bus. No overhead delay is imposed to the non-faulty cache's miss penalty.

We must notice that the description given above can equally well be applied to both real and virtual addressed

caches. Since the primary cache's organization remains undisturbed the above description is also free from any specific implementation details.

3. Simulation and results

The best way of determining the miss ratio of a certain cache configuration is through trace driven simulation [13]. In our simulations we used the ATUM traces because they include both operating system references and multiprogramming effects. Moreover, the way that those traces were gathered introduces fewer distortions of the address trace [14]. Table II in [2] lists the features of each individual trace used. We present results only for the combined trace, denoted by *all* in [2] due to the large number of traces. For this specific trace we combined the individual ATUM traces by concatenating them and inserting cache flushes before a new trace was appended. The combined trace is about 8 million references long. Since the individual traces are up to 400000 references we simulate cache sizes up to 32 Kbytes. Larger cache simulation would be impossible without inserting much error [2, 17].

Trace driven simulation is known to be a time-consuming process [13] and several techniques have in the past been proposed to shorten the required simulation time (see for example [2, 17, 18]). These techniques though can not be applied in our case. For caches with large numbers of blocks and/or enough large number of faulty blocks, all the possible faulty blocks combinations can not be taken into account in the simulation because then the required time is prohibitively large. In such cases simulation for a subset of all the possible faulty blocks combinations should be performed.

Therefore, we have to determine how many faulty blocks combinations should be examined so that the miss ratio measurement to be close enough to the values measured by simulating all possible faulty blocks combinations (exhaustive simulation). To this end, for several cache sizes, we examined 10, 100 and 1000 faulty blocks combinations and compared both the accuracy of the results and the required simulation time against the results and the required time of the exhaustive simulation. We found the one hundred limit to be a very good compromise in producing the average miss ratios but improper for the minimum and maximum values. The extra simulation time required by the one thousand limit was not justified, since the average miss ratios were extremely close to that of the one hundred and both minimum and maximum values of miss ratio although closer, still far enough from those of the exhaustive simulation. The one hundred limit was therefore chosen. Exhaustive simulation was used when affordable.

Figure 2 shows the percentage of the lost hit ratio due to block disabling, recovered by using a spare cache with only one block, for block sizes 8, 16 and 32 bytes. Specifically the

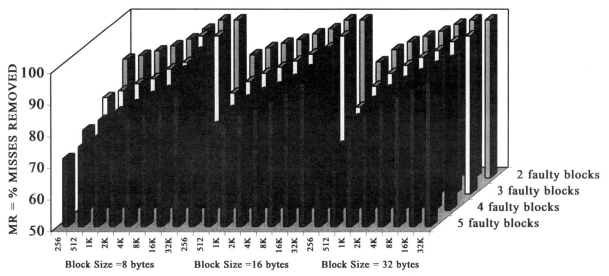

Figure 2. Percentage of the lost hit ratio due to block disabling, recovered by one spare block for 2 to 5 faulty blocks, for caches with block sizes 8, 16 and 32 bytes.

percentage of the Misses Removed (MR) is equal to :

$$MR = (m_1 - m_2) / m_1 * 100$$

for $m_1 = m' - m$,

where   m are the average misses of the non-faulty primary cache.

m′ are the average misses of the primary cache with the faulty blocks disabled.

and $m_2 = m'' - m$,

where   m″ are the average misses of the faulty primary cache supported by a spare cache.

The number of faulty blocks is varied from two to five (results for one faulty block have no meaning since recovery of 100% would be the outcome in any case).

In all cases the recovery percentage exceeds 64 %. When the primary cache size is greater than 1 Kbytes the recovery percentage is well over 75 %. (This is the most common case in today's commercial microprocessor chips). Three more observations must be made from this figure :

a.   The percentage of the misses removed (MR) increases as the number of faulty blocks decreases for the same primary cache and block sizes. This is because less faulty blocks means less possible candidates for the single spare block and hence less conflict misses.

b.   MR for the same number of faulty blocks and block size increases as the cache size increases. This is due to the fact that a larger primary cache has a bigger number of addressable blocks than any smaller with the same block size, and so references to specific blocks are more rare. For example, when the block size is 32 bytes, a 256 bytes cache, only has 8 distinct blocks that may be referenced, while a 4 Kbytes cache with the same block size has 128 distinct blocks. If we assume that two faulty blocks exist in any of these caches, the probability of interchanging

references to the faulty blocks (that cause conflict misses in the only spare block available) in the first cache is a multiple of the corresponding probability of the second cache.

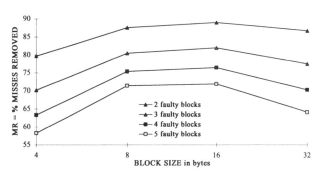

Figure 3. Percentage of the lost hit ratio due to block disabling, recovered by one spare block for 2 to 5 faulty blocks. Cache size = 256 Bytes.

c.   The relation of MR to the cache's block size though is more complicated. According to (b) above one would expect that MR will drop when moving to larger block sizes, because then we have a smaller number of blocks and thus increased conflict misses. But it has also been shown in [2], that, for a specific number of faulty blocks, the hit ratio loss is greater for caches with larger block sizes and thus the spare cache will offer a greater recovery percentage. Figures 3, 4 and 5, present MR versus block size, for cache sizes of 256 bytes, 1 and 8 Kbytes respectively and for two to five faulty blocks. We can see that for small block sizes the second of the above mentioned factors dominates and MR is increased when moving from 4 to 8 or 16 bytes block. On the other hand for large block sizes the first factor is the dominant and

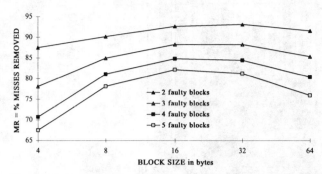

Figure 4. Percentage of the lost hit ratio due to block disabling, recovered by one spare block for 2 to 5 faulty blocks. Cache size = 1K Bytes.

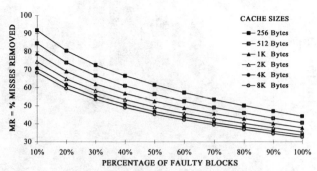

Figure 6. MR vs. the percentage of faulty blocks in caches up to 8K, with block size of 16 bytes.

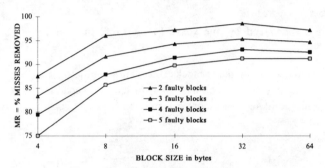

Figure 5. Percentage of the lost hit ratio due to block disabling, recovered by one spare block for 2 to 5 faulty blocks. Cache size = 8K Bytes.

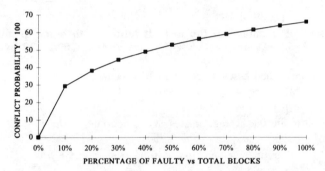

Figure 7. Conflict probability for one spare block vs. the percentage of faulty blocks. Cache size = 4 Kbytes, Block size = 16 bytes.

MR drops when moving from 32 to 64 bytes block. Depending on the cache size, a block size of either 16 or 32 bytes can maximize MR, for constant number of faulty blocks.

We will hereafter discuss how effective is the usage of the spare cache to chips with a large number of cache faulty blocks.

Figure 6 plots the recovery percentage of a single block spare cache for cache sizes up to 8 Kbytes versus the percentage of faulty blocks. For the same percentage of faulty blocks caches with larger size have a greater number of faulty blocks, thus the percentage of misses removed is smaller. Even when 20% of the total blocks are faulty, 60% of the lost hit ratio can be recovered. (A fraction of 20% of the total blocks, in a 8 Kbytes cache, means that more than 102 blocks are unavailable).

The form of the curves presented in figure 6 should have been expected, because any new faulty block that is added to the faulty blocks list will cause many more conflict misses at the spare cache. Suppose for example that two blocks A, B of the primary cache are marked as faulty. Then conflicts at the spare cache occur only by references of the form *A*B* or *B*A*, where * denotes references to any other except the

faulty blocks. If another primary cache block, suppose C, is also faulty, then any combination of the form *A*B*, *B*A*, *A*C*, *C*A*, *B*C*, *C*B*, would cause conflict misses at the spare cache.

In figure 7 the conflict probability in the competition for the single spare block is plotted against the fraction of the total blocks that are faulty in a 4 Kbytes cache. This curve was formed by counting the references and the conflict misses at the spare cache. We can observe that when the fraction of faulty blocks is less than 10% there is a great probability (> 0.7) that the spare block caches the required data. When 50% or more of the primary blocks are faulty the spare cache access will probably result in a conflict miss.

Incorporation of a second spare block is examined hereafter. Figure 8 plots the average miss ratio of a 4 Kbytes cache for three cases, namely when only block disabling is performed and when the primary cache is backed up by either one or two fully associative spare blocks, versus the number of faulty blocks. We can see that for less than 16 faulty blocks the miss ratio of the faulty cache with a spare cache of one or two blocks is almost equal to that of the non-faulty cache. The second spare block becomes attractive only when a large number of blocks is faulty. The percentage of misses

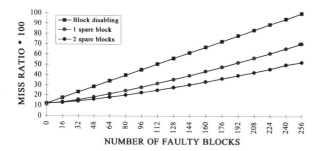

Figure 8. Miss ratio of block disabling and the use of a spare cache of 1 or 2 blocks vs. the number of faulty blocks. Cache size = 4 Kbytes, Block size = 16 bytes.

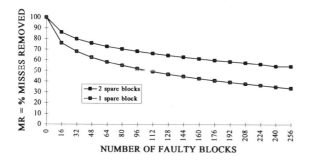

Figure 9. Percentage of lost hit ratio due to block disabling, recovered by a spare cache of 1 or 2 blocks vs. the number of faulty blocks. Cache size = 4 Kbytes, Block size = 16 bytes.

removed is plotted in Figure 9. The returns of the second spare are much smaller than those achieved by the first one and only justified for either :

a. When a great portion of the total blocks are faulty, or

b. When hit ratio sustainment is too important. Multiprocessor caches usually service misses via a multistage interconnect or a bus. When a multistage interconnect is used the miss latency can be large due to contention existence. Bus miss times with low utilization can be small, but delays due to contention among processors can become large and are sensitive to cache miss ratio [19].

Using the average memory access time, T_{av}, as a metric of performance we will now compare block disabling, and the use of spare cache. In the introduction we have shown that block disabling increases T_{av} by :

$$\delta\, T_{memory}.$$

If we denote with r the misses removed due to spare cache incorporation, using the same procedure we can get that T_{av} in this case is increased only by :

$$(1-r)\, \delta\, T_{memory}.$$

As an example suppose that T_{memory} = 6 cycles (a second level cache is supposed), T_{cache} = 1 cycle. From our simulations, for a 4 Kbytes cache with 16 bytes block and 16 faulty blocks :

$$\delta = 0.0551,$$
$$r = 76.4\%,$$
$$h = 0.8784 \text{ (non-faulty cache's hit ratio)}.$$

The overhead imposed on T_{av} in this case by block disabling is approximately 19.11%, whereas in the case of a spare cache with only one block, T_{av} increases by only 4.51%. Using a spare cache with two blocks we have an increase in T_{av} of only 2.68%. In the above example, we assumed that a second level board cache exists. In low cost systems with no board cache, the difference between the increase on T_{av} when only faulty block disabling is used and in the case of a spare cache is increased further.

4. Conclusions

To achieve high performance in single chip VLSI processors, on-chip cache memories are used. As the chip area devoted to on-chip caches increases, we expect that in a large fraction of VLSI processor chips the manufacturing defects will be present in the cache memory portion of the chip. Disabling the cache defective blocks was shown to be an attractive technique for yield enhancement of single chip VLSI processors with on-chip cache. It has been shown in [1, 2] that the mean relative miss ratio increase due to disabling a few defective blocks decreases with increasing cache size and is negligible unless a set is completely disabled. Unfortunately, the number of faulty blocks may be large and in direct-mapped caches, disabling a block means the disabling of a set. Direct-mapped caches offer the fastest access time and for sufficiently large sizes smaller average access time than the set-associative ones [3]. Thus as the size of the on-chip caches increases, the use of direct-mapped caches is favored.

In this paper we have investigated, by extensive trace driven simulation, how much of the lost hit ratio due to faulty block disabling in direct-mapped caches can be recovered by the incorporation of a very small fully associative spare cache. Four conclusions can be drawn from the work presented in this paper :

1. A spare cache with just one block is sufficient for a small number of faulty blocks.

2. A spare cache with two blocks is justified only in the case of a large number of faulty blocks.

3. For constant block size and number of faulty blocks the percentage of the removed misses increases as the cache size increases.

4. For constant number of faulty blocks a block size of either 16 or 32 bytes, depending on the cache size can maximize the misses removed.

The use of a small (with size two or four blocks) fully associative cache which will operate as a victim cache for the non-faulty blocks and as a spare cache for the faulty blocks of the primary cache is under investigation.

ACKNOWLEDGMENT

The authors would like to thank the anonymous referees for their valuable comments.

References

[1] Sohi G., "Cache Memory Organization to Enhance the Yield of High-Performance VLSI Processors," *IEEE Transactions on Computers*, Vol. 38, no. 4, pp. 484-492, April 1989.

[2] Pour F. and Hill M. D., "Performance Implications of Tolerating Cache Faults," *IEEE Transactions on Computers*, Vol. 42, no. 4, pp. 257-267, March 1993.

[3] Hill M. D., "A Case for Direct-Mapped Caches," *IEEE Micro*, pp. 25-40, December 1988.

[4] Phillips D., "The Z80000 Microprocessor," *IEEE Micro*, pp. 23-26, December 1985.

[5] Berenbaum A. D., et al., "CRISP : A Pipelined 32-bit Microprocessor with 13-Kbit of Cache Memory," *IEEE Journal of Solid-State Circuits*, Vol. SC-22, no. 5, pp. 776-782, October 1987.

[6] Horowitz M., et al., "MIPS-X : A 20-MIPS Peak, 32-bit Microprocessor with On-Chip Cache," *IEEE Journal of Solid-State Circuits*, Vol. SC-22, no. 5, pp. 790-799, October 1987.

[7] Kadota H., et al., "A 32-bit CMOS Microprocessor with On-Chip Cache and TLB," *IEEE Journal of Solid-State Circuits*, Vol. SC-22, no. 5, pp. 800-807, October 1987.

[8] Shoemaker K., "The i486 Microprocessor Integrated Cache and Bus Interface," *In Proc. of the COMPCON '90 IEEE International Conference*, pp. 248-253.

[9] Dopperpubl D. W., et al., "A 200-MHz 64-bit Dual-issue CMOS Microprocessor," *Digital Technical Journal*, Vol. 4, no. 4, pp. 35-50, Special Issue 1992.

[10] Intel, *i860 XP Microprocessor, Multimedia and Supercomputing Microprocessors Data Book*, Intel 1992.

[11] Koren I. and Pradhan D. K., "Modeling the Effect of Redundancy on Yield and Performance of VLSI Systems," *IEEE Transactions on Computers*, Vol. C-36, no. 3, pp. 344-355, March 1987.

[12] Jouppi N. P., "Improving Direct-Mapped Cache Performance by the Addition of a Small Fully-Associative Cache and Prefetch Buffers," *ACM Computer Architecture News*, Vol. 18, no. 2, pp. 364-373, June 1990.

[13] Smith A. J., "Cache Memories," *ACM Computing Surveys*, Vol. 14, no. 3, pp. 473-530, September 1982.

[14] Agarwal A., et al., "ATUM : A New Technique for Capturing Address Traces Using Microcode," *In Proc. of the 13th Annual Symposium on Computer Architecture*, pp. 119-127, June 1986.

[15] Patterson D. A., et al., "Architecture for a VLSI Instruction Cache for a RISC," *In Proc. of the 10th Annual Symposium on Computer Architecture*, pp. 108-116, June 1983.

[16] Wilton S. J. E. and Jouppi N. P., "An Enhanced Access and Cycle Time Model for On-Chip Caches," *Technical Report 93/5*, DEC Western Research Laboratory.

[17] Stone H. S., *High-Performance Computer Architecture*, Addison-Wesley, October 1987.

[18] Mattson R. L., et al., "Evaluation Techniques for Storage Hierarchies," *IBM Systems Journal*, 9, 2, pp. 78-117, 1970.

[19] Goodman J. R., "Using Cache Memory to Reduce Processor-Memory Traffic," *In Proc. of the 10th Annual Symposium on Computer Architecture*, pp. 124-131, June 1983.

[20] Stapper C. H., Armstrong F. M., Saji K., "Integrated Circuit Yield Statistics," *Proceedings of the IEEE*, Vol. 71, no. 4, pp. 453-470, April 1983.

[21] Stapper C. H., "Large-Area Fault Clusters and Fault Tolerance in VLSI Circuits : A Review," *IBM Journal of Research and Development*, Vol. 33, no. 2, pp. 162-173, March 1989.

[22] Stapper C. H., "Simulation of Spatial Fault Distributions for Integrated Circuit Yield Estimations," *IEEE Transactions on CAD*, Vol. 8, no. 12, pp. 1314-1318, December 1989.

[23] Stapper C. H., "Statistics Associated with Spatial Fault Simulation Used for Evaluating Integrated Circuit Yield Enhancement," *IEEE Transactions on CAD*, Vol. 10, no. 3, pp. 399-406, March 1991.

[24] Blough D. M., "On the Reconfiguration of Memory Arrays Containing Clustered Faults," *In Proc. of the 21st International Symposium on Fault-Tolerant Computing*, pp. 444-451, June 1991.

[25] Moore W. R., "A Review of Fault-Tolerant Techniques for the Enhancement of Integrated Circuit Yield," *Proceedings of the IEEE*, Vol. 74, no. 4, pp. 684-698, May 1986.

[26] Pradhan D. K., *Fault Tolerant Computing : Theory and Techniques*, Englewood Cliffs, NJ : Prentice-Hall, 1986.

[27] Vergos H. T. and Nikolos D., "Efficient Fault Tolerant CPU Cache Memory Design," *to appear in Microprocessing and Microprogramming - The Euromicro Journal*.

Addendum

Performability Evaluation:
Where It Is and What Lies Ahead

J. F. Meyer
EECS Department
The University of Michigan
Ann Arbor, MI 48109

Abstract

The concept of performability emerged from a need to assess a system's ability to perform when performance degrades as a consequence of faults. After almost 20 years of effort concerning its theory, techniques, and applications, performability evaluation is currently well understood by the many people responsible for its development. On the other hand, the utility of combined performance-dependability measures has yet to be appreciably recognized by the designers of contemporary computer systems. Following a review of what performability means, we discuss its present state with respect to both scientific and engineering contributions. In view of current practice and the potential design applicability of performability evaluation, we then point to some advances that are called for if this potential is indeed to be realized.

1 Introduction

In the context of computer system evaluation, the need to deal simultaneously with aspects of both performance and dependability was initially recognized in the mid-1970s. More specifically, it surfaced as the consequence of then-experimental architectures such as PRIME (developed at the University of California, Berkeley [1, 2]) which exhibited "degradable" performance in the presence of operational faults. Before describing this motivation in greater detail, a quick review of some terminology should help to clarify the distinctions we're making.

Performance, according to typical use of this term (both then and now) in computer science and engineering, generally refers to how effectively (e.g., throughput, delay) or efficiently (e.g., resource utilization) a system delivers a specified service, presuming it is delivered correctly. On the other hand, dependability (or what was then referred to broadly as "reliability") is the "trustworthiness of a (computer) system" [3] with respect to delivery of a specified service. With this view, a system "failure" occurs if the delivered service becomes "incorrect", i.e., it no longer complies with its specification. Moreover, since faults (via the errors they cause) are the source of failures, their existence and their effects become principal concerns.

Historically, this distinction between performance and dependability has been very useful in the development of evaluation techniques suited to each purpose. Moreover, as applied to computer systems, each has become an established technical discipline. However, if separate evaluations of performance and dependability are to suffice in determining the overall quality of a delivered service, one must place certain constraints on how properties affecting performance interact with those affecting dependability.

For example, let us suppose that a system's capacity to serve is binary (either "up" or "down") and specified service coincides with that delivered when the system is up. In this case, the quality of the delivered service, when up, is a performance concern, while the system's ability to remain up (failure-free) is a dependability issue. Further, under the above assumptions, we see that faults do not affect service quality (in the up state). Reciprocally, such performance does not affect loss of correct service (failure) and, hence, does not affect dependability. Accordingly, each can be evaluated separately, with their combination providing a relatively complete assessment of overall service quality.

Generally, however, individual evaluations of system performance and dependability are not so easily combined, particularly if performance in the presence of faults is *degradable*, i.e., consequences of faults can reduce the quality of a delivered service even though that service, according to its specification, remains satisfactory. Such degradation may result directly from fault-caused errors, may be due to additional computational demands associated with error processing, or may be the consequence of subsequent fault-related actions such as reconfiguration and repair.

As noted at the outset, the need to accommodate degradable performance was first recognized over 20 years ago. More precisely, and in contrast with the example given above, if a system has this property (in which case the system itself is often referred to as being "degradable" or "gracefully degrading"), a binary (up-down) classification of operational integrity is too coarse. Instead, a degradable system's integrity should be formally viewed as a multivalued variable representing the extent to which the system is faulty, e.g., which resources are faulty and, among them, which which are in the process of fault recovery, which are no longer being used (due to passivation), etc. With such variations, the usual concept of computer performance is too restrictive and, although dependability measures are compatible with this view, they account for service quality degradation only at the boundary of service loss (failure).

This recognition, together with encouragement provided by some earlier work concerning "computation-based" [4, 5] and "performance-related" [6, 7] reliability, led to the concept of *performability* and a proposed framework for its model-based evaluation [8, 9]. As initially employed, this term referred to a class of (probability) measures that quantify a systems's "ability to perform" in the presence of faults. As an adjective, it also qualified the type of stochastic models that could support its evaluation. Since then, there's been a natural expansion of its adjectival use, referring more generally to theory and techniques suited to this purpose.

After a summary of what performability evaluation entails (Section 2), we describe the present state of its theory and practice (Section 3). In the latter regard, our emphasis is on issues of performability model specification; this is followed a survey of recent work on model construction/solution techniques along with a variety of applications. Finally, in view of performability's potential for even more widespread development and application, we conclude with a discussion of what lies ahead.

2 Performability Evaluation

Generally, an evaluation of performability (relative to a designated performability measure) can be either model-based or conducted experimentally via measurements of an actual system. The review that follows presumes the former, permitting us to be more precise in the statements of key concepts. By a "model", here, we mean a representation (either analytic or via simulation) of a *total system*, composed of

i) an *object system*, i.e., the system that's the object of the evaluation study, and

ii) an *environment*, i.e., other systems (physical or human) which interact with the object system during its use.

Given an interacting set of physical and human resources, the distinction between i) and ii) depends on which subset of resources is being investigated as to its ability to perform. These comprise the object system which, in this context, is often referred to simply as the "system." The environment is then comprised of those remaining resources, lying outside the object system "boundary", whose interaction with the object system may appreciably affect its performability.

To describe the types of models and measures considered (except for small changes in some of the notation and terminology, this summarizes the original framework [8, 9]), let S denote the total system in question. Then, per the above distinctions, S consists of an object system C (the computer system being evaluated) and its environment E (workload, external faults, etc.). At the lowest level, the dynamics of total-system structure and behavior are represented by a

stochastic process X, referred to as the *base model* of S. More precisely, X is a time-indexed set of random variables

$$X = \{X_t \mid t \in I\}$$

with state space Q, where the *time base* (index set) I may be either discrete or continuous. Except in the case of a null environment, the state space Q can be viewed as the product space $Q_C \times Q_E$, where Q_C and Q_E are the state spaces of the object system and environment, respectively.

The restriction of X to Q_C is the (base) *object system model*, denoted X_C. Depending on the nature of the measures in question, a state $q \in Q_C$ may be further elaborated as pair of states $q = (q_s, q_i)$, where q_s is a *structure* state of C and q_i is some *internal* state of the structural configuration represented by q_s. In turn, each of these may be further coordinatized to permit even more refined distinctions. For example, q_s might describe which of the object system's resources are faulty and, among these, which have been passivated.

Similarly, the restriction of X to Q_E is referred to as the (base) *environment model*, denoted X_E, and represents the dynamics of workload, external faults, etc. that derive from sources lying outside of the object system boundary. Generally, the models X_C and X_E are highly dependent (as stochastic processes), particularly due to the influence that an environment typically has on object system behavior.

Conceptually, the base model $X = (X_C, X_E)$ should be regarded as a probabilistic description of the (total) system that's sufficiently detailed to support a particular type of evaluation. Note, however, that, up to this point, we have not presumed anything about the kind of measures involved; indeed, specializations of such models can also serve as the underlying representations for much of what is done in performance and dependability modeling. In general, the evaluation measures of interest can be defined in terms of one or more random variables Y that "sit on top" of the process X in the sense that knowledge of the probabilistic nature of X suffices to determine that of Y. In the context of performance and performability evaluation, Y is typically referred to as a *performance variable* (or a *performability variable*), where specification of a particular Y includes

a) a *utilization period* T, where T is an interval of the time base (or, in the degenerate case, an instant of time) over which object system performance is being observed, and

b) an *accomplishment set* A in which Y takes its values.

Relative to a specified Y, the *performability* of S is the probability measure *Perf* (denoted p_S in [8, 9]) induced by Y where, for any (measurable) set B of accomplishment levels ($B \subseteq A$),

$$
\begin{aligned}
\cdot Perf(B) &= P[Y \in B] \\
&= \text{the probability that } S \\
&\quad \text{performs at a level in } B
\end{aligned}
$$

Accordingly, this is the meaning of performability (in the narrow sense), where specific interpretations of a) and b) above express the intended meaning of Y. The extent to which *Perf* is actually determined depends on what's called for by the accompanying evaluation study. This can range from a complete determination of *Perf*, as supplied by the probability distribution function (PDF) of Y, to single-valued measures such as moments of Y or, for a specified set of accomplishment levels B, a single performability value $Perf(B)$.

With the rapid growth of computers and computer-based systems in the 1980s, recognition of the need for combined performance-dependability evaluation likewise grew, precipitating a broad spectrum of activities ranging from basic research through tool development and applications. Moreover, as these investigations progressed, the term "performability" (in addition to the type of adjectival use noted at the end of Section 1) acquired a somewhat broader meaning that encompassed measures other than the the ones cited above. These included, for example, important classes of measures such as "job completion time" (introduced in [10] and examined further by a number of authors) and "performability-to-go" ([11], wherein the initial instant for an interval-of-time variable is current time).

Three surveys concerning much of this work (through 1990) were presented at *First International Workshop on Performability Modelling of Computer and Communication Systems* (University of Twente, Enschede, The Netherlands; February, 1991) and subsequently published in *Performance Evaluation* (vol. 14, nos. 3-4, February, 1992). These included a 15-year retrospective of performability research and development ([12]; 105 references), a survey of performability analysis techniques ([13]; 97 references), and a somewhat more specialized review of Markov reward model construction and solution methods ([14]; 59 references).

In light of this relatively extensive coverage of earlier work, and with the exception of a few historical pointers here and there, the survey that follows is limited to progress over the past several years (1991-95). This should serve to update the previous reviews and, in doing so, provide a fairly complete picture of the current state of performability theory and practice.

3 Where It Is

Since 1991, activity concerning performability evaluation has continued to grow in both scope and intensity, ranging from basic theoretical work to interesting new applications. A key consideration, with regard to its more extensive application in a design context, is to make model-based performability evaluation less of an art and more of a science. Accordingly, increased attention is being devoted to questions of performability model specification, where one seeks techniques that are generally applicable to a variety of specific system domains. Moreover, the specification constructs employed should be both understandable to human users and, at the same time, precise enough to be unambiguously interpreted by an evaluation tool that

receives the specified information. With miminal intervention on the part of a tool user, subsequent steps of model construction (including simplification) and solution can then be carried out automatically.

3.1 Model Specification

Although the term "model specification" typically refers only to the (total) system model, per se, we take a somewhat broader view that also includes the measures in question and their relationship to the system model. Following the development in [15], an overall specification can thus be regarded as having three principal ingredients.

S1) Specification of what is to be learned about the object system from its (model-based) evaluation, i.e., the performability measures of interest.

S2) Specification of a stochastic process on which the evaluation is to be based (the base model X).

S3) Specification of how S2) relates to S1) in a manner that permits the base model (after construction) to indeed support solution of the specified measures.

Regarding S1), if measure specification is to have general applicability, it must be done in a manner compatible with a general means of relating, via S3), the base model specification to the measure specification. To achieve this, it is advantageous to view the accomplishment sets A of all performance variables Y as expressing value with respect to a common, uninterpreted unit of measure. In a stochastic process setting, a unit of this sort is typically referred to as a unit of "reward" (see [16], for example). Given that elements of A express reward then, quite naturally, Y can be referred to alternatively as a *reward variable* (see [17], for example). With this unified view of accomplishment, most any aspect Y of object system performance (quality) can then be represented by giving reward a more specific interpretation. Moreover, by our earlier remarks concerning Y specification (see items a) and b) of Section 2), it remains only to formally specify the time instant at which or the time interval over which reward is being quantified by Y. Here, in concert with how time is represented in the base model, time instants and durations associated with Y can either be elements of I (in the case of an interval $(t_1, t_2] \subseteq I$, it is assumed that $t_2 - t_1 \in I$) or, given that Y has a limiting distribution, the limit as a time instant or interval duration approaches infinity.

Specifically (again see [17], but without presuming an already-specified reward structure), three categories of reward variables can be usefully distinguished according to the nature of this time specification. A reward variable in the first category, called an *instant-of-time variable*, represents the reward experienced at a designated time during the object system's use. A second type of variable, referred to as an *interval-of-time* variable, represents the total amount of reward accumulated over a specified interval of time. The third category, called *time-averaged interval-of-time* variables, are similar to the second except that accumulated reward is now averaged over the duration of the specified interval.

Concerning S2), if the total system is even moderately complex, direct specification of a base model (e.g., its generator matrix in the case of a time-homogeneous, continuous-time Markov process) is typically impractical. Hence, most performability evaluation tools permit the base model to be specified at a higher level of abstraction, the most popular construct being some type of stochastic Petri net (SPN). These include stochastic activity networks (SANs, used by METASAN [18] and UltraSAN [19]); generalized Stochastic Petri nets (GSPNs, as employed, for example, in SPNP [20]), and combined deterministic/stochastic Petri nets (DSPNs, the specifications for DSPNexpress [21]). Combinations of queueing networks and SPNs have also been used for this purpose, e.g., the specification method used in DyQNtool [22] and the approaches described in [23] and [24]. Even higher level constructs, such as the production rules of METFAC [25], provide an alternative means of base-model specification that can likewise support performability evaluation.

Note that, once constructed, the base model X may be characterized in a form that is not literally a stochastic process, e.g., in the case of simulation, it's a computer program that simulates X. For specification purposes, however, this more general view of what's being specified is advantageous since, among other things, it allows the same specification to be used for both analytic and simulation model construction. For example, SAN specifications are employed in this manner (in both METASAN [18] and UltraSAN [19]); modular SPNs of the type considered in [26] also play this dual role.

As noted in [15], S3) is perhaps the most difficult aspect of performability model specification, particularly if the techniques employed are to apply to differing types of evaluation (including strict performance and dependability as well as performability) and, accordingly, a wide variety of specific base models and measures. Its purpose is to specify how state trajectories (sample functions) of X map to values of Y, thus permitting solutions at the base model level (e.g., state occupancy probabilities) to determine the desired value(s) of a given measure. Conceptually, this mapping is referred to in [8, 9] as a *capability function*. Although describing it as such is feasible in the case of discrete variables with relatively small accomplishment sets, its complexity typically precludes any form of direct specification.

A viable alternative, which is now the most popular way of accomplishing S3), is the use of a *reward structure*. If the base model is specified directly then such structures can have the form originally described in [16], with reward rates assigned to states and reward impulses to state transitions. Generally, however, S3) should rely only on knowledge that is explicit in S1) and S2). For example, if S2) is some type of SPN then S3) should not require details that are known only after construction of the base model is completed. Although the latter would be possible (by deferring S3)

until after base-model construction), such practice is discouraged for at least two reasons. First, there is no guarantee that the resulting base model can support evaluation of the performability measure(s) in question. Secondly, even if support is possible, when fully constructed, X may be too complicated (e.g., have too many states) to deal with effectively in this regard.

This recognition led to techniques of the type incorporated in DyQNtool [22], where reward rates are specified by "dynamic queueing models" and then determined later as part of the model solution procedure. Alternatively, if S2) is an SPN-type specification, it is possible to assign rate and impulse rewards at the SPN level. Examples of the latter are the methods used in UltraSAN [15, 19, 27] and the use of "stochastic reward nets" [28, 29].

3.2 Model Construction/Solution

Once a performability model is specified, the important steps of model construction and model solution still remain. Over the past several years, work on construction techniques has been closely associated with the development of associated performability evaluation tools (see the references cited above; also see [30] for a recent overview that covers tools for reliability as well as performability). Included here are concerns with crucial questions of model simplification, e.g., state space reduction in the case of analytic base models and the support of accurate, yet time-efficient solutions in the case of simulation.

In the recent past, however, even greater effort has been devoted to development of improved solution methods, particularly for reward models of the type discussed in the previous subsection. On the analytic side, contributions here include techniques for both GSPN-based reward models [31] and SAN-based reward models [32], where reviews of these and other reward model solution techniques may be found in [33, 34, 35]. Progress has also been made on more fundamental topics concerning numerical and closed-form solutions of performability [36, 37, 38, 39, 40, 41], solutions of completion time [42, 43], queues with breakdowns [44], sensitivity analysis [45], improved uniformization methods [46, 47, 48, 49], and state-space truncation [50].

Along with this progress on analytic and numerical methods, simulation techniques for performability solutions are now beginning to receive the attention they deserve. Examples in this regard include investigations of time warp simulation [51], simulation with active objects [52], the simulation of composed SAN-based reward models [53], and importance sampling of the type employed in UltraSAN [54].

3.3 Applications

Relative to the the entire domain of performability-related work, the most extensive activity (in terms of published contributions over the past four years) has been applications of performability evaluation to various types of computer components, computers, and computer-based systems. On the hardware side, where the concern is mainly operational faults, these include degradable microcomputers [55, 56, 57, 58], random-access memories [59], disk arrays [60], fault-tolerant multiprocessor systems (including hypercube architectures) [61, 62, 63, 64, 65, 66, 67, 68, 69], and fault-tolerant, real-time systems [70, 71, 72, 73]. Many of these studies, in addition to providing evaluation data concerning the object system in question, develop special concepts and methods that are suited to the type of application considered. There have also been some recent, more generic application-oriented studies which examine performability implications of a particular design approach. Examples in this regard include techniques such as "guarded repair" [74], a "performability manager" [75, 76], and "performability-driven" adaptive fault tolerance [77].

Until the early 1990s, relatively little attention had been paid to the effects of design faults on software performability. More recently, however, interest in this topic has started to develop, including work that has addressed structured software fault tolerance [78], release policies [79], and various schemes for enhancing the performability of fault-tolerant software [80, 81, 82, 83]. Again, as with the hardware studies, much of this material concerns methods and insights of scientific benefit as well as specific evaluation data that is useful from an engineering (design) standpoint.

Among applications to computer-based systems, another area of growing evaluation interest is manufacturing, where the object system considered is typically some form of automated manufacturing system (AMS). Examples of such studies include general treatments of AMS performability evaluation [84, 85], AMSs with multiple part types [86], SPN-specified AMS models [87], and a sensitivity analysis of failure-prone AMSs [88]. Other related applications include subsystems that support manufacturing such as motion systems [89] and local area networks [90, 91].

Finally, although we have chosen to limit this survey to computer-related applications (in keeping with the title of the symposium), it should be noted that performability evaluation is likewise of interest to other domains. These include established fields, such as telecommunications, as well as emerging disciplines such as intelligent transportation systems.

4   What Lies Ahead

In view of the above, we see that performability, both in the narrower sense (as a class of measures) and in the broader sense of unified performance-dependability, remains a viable area of research and development. It is important to note, however, that much of what's been accomplished to date is the consequence of work done at university and industrial laboratories. If interests in and applications of performability are to move outside of these confines and find their way into actual design/evaluation environments, additional progress must be made on several fronts.

Among these, and perhaps the most critical, is the development of even more efficient performability solution algorithms. Of particular concern here are analytic solutions of measures that quantify ability to perform over a bounded period of utilization. Experience has shown that these are particularly difficult to solve and, in spite of several innovative approaches taken during the past decade (and improved on over the past several years), truly practicable algorithms for this purpose have yet to evolve. Requirements for such practicality include spatial considerations, e.g., accommodation of total system (object system plus environment) models with large state spaces, as well as efficiency with respect to solution times.

Other developments which lie ahead, and would likewise help to promote more widespread use, reside in the areas of model specification and model construction. In general, just what distinguishes these two activities is somewhat arbitrary; indeed, the term "construction" is often used in a sense that implicitly encompasses the specification aspects S1)-S3) discussed in Section 3.1. However, maintaining the distinction that's implicit in our earlier remarks, model specification is "provision of input", namely the input required to construct (and subsequently solve) a model of the total system in question. Moreover, we assume that such provision is an essentially human activity, where the specifier should be sufficiently familiar with A) the total system being evaluated and B) the capabilities of the tools (and perhaps other people) responsible for the construction and solution phases.

However, adequate knowledge of both A) and B) on the part of a single specifier (or even a team of specifiers) is an assumption that seldom holds in practice. The difficulty encountered here is due, at least in part, to the fact that designers are more familiar with A) and evaluators are more familiar with B). Moreover, the types of system representations that are useful to designers typically differ from those suited to model-based evaluation.

As noted in [92], such differences did not evolve accidentally, nor were they purposely promoted as the consequence of antagonism between designers and evaluators. Instead, they are due to differing objectives. Designers describe systems in ways that facilitate their work and, in particular, what needs to be done in the next step of a design procedure. Evaluators, on the other hand, must look back to what is required of a system, identify measures that reflect these requirements, and then represent the system in a manner that yields the desired evaluation results. Other basic problems are caused by differences in the types of restrictions that favor design vs. evaluation. For example, high observability of internal behavior is good for evaluation, but this is not something that would naturally emerge as a design constraint.

Given that such differences will continue to persist, what's needed is something called for in an earlier survey [12], namely, innovative algorithmic means of translating design-oriented (D-O) models to evaluation-oriented (E-O) models (via specifications of the latter). Moreover, these will likely have to be applied at several levels of abstraction, the final step being a translation that results in the lowest level E-O model specification (e.g., an SPN that specifies the base model). Again as noted in [12], progress in this regard requires appropriate advances and integration of knowledge concerning design-evaluation interfaces, environment modeling, D-O to E-O model translation, and E-O model hierarchies.

If these can be achieved then applications of performability evaluation will certainly become more widespread. Further, given efficient and effective means of model specification, construction, and solution, there is less of a need for "general purpose" performability models. The advantage of the latter is that, by supporting a host of different measures, they reduce the amount of model building that's required. On the other hand, as the complexity of a total system increases, general-purpose models quickly become infeasible (e.g., state spaces required to support all the measures become excessively large). Instead, with evaluation tools capable of rapid model construction/solution, one can afford to "tailor" a model to a particular measure, permitting several feasible models to support an otherwise impractical study.

Acknowledgement

My sincere appreciation to a number of colleagues who unselfishly provided me with information concerning their recent work (Section 3). The extent to which this coverage is complete is thanks to them; any omissions, which are sure to exist, are the sole responsibility of the author.

References

[1] H. B. Baskin, B. R. Borgerson, and R. Roberts, "Prime - A modular architecture for terminal-oriented systems," in *1972 Spring Joint Computer Conference, AFIPS Conf. Proceedings*, volume 40, pp. 431–437, Washington, DC, August 1972, Spartan.

[2] B. R. Borgerson and R. F. Freitas, "A reliability model for gracefully degrading and standby-sparing systems," *IEEE Trans. Computers*, vol. C-24, no. 5, pp. 517–525, May 1975.

[3] J.-C. Laprie, editor, *Dependability: Basic Concepts and Terminology*, volume 5 of *Dependable Computing and Fault-Tolerant Systems*, Springer-Verlag, 1992.

[4] J. F. Meyer, "Computation-based reliability analysis," in *Proc. 5th Int'l Symp. on Fault-Tolerant Computing*, p. 123, Paris, France, June 1975.

[5] J. F. Meyer, "Computation-based reliability analysis," *IEEE Trans. Computers*, vol. C-25, no. 6, pp. 578–584, June 1976.

[6] M. D. Beaudry, "Performance-related reliability measures for computing systems," in *Proc. 7th Int'l Symp. on Fault-Tolerant Computing*, pp. 16–21, Los Angeles, CA, June 1977.

[7] M. D. Beaudry, "Performance-related reliability measures for computing systems," *IEEE Trans. Computers*, vol. C-27, no. 6, pp. 540–547, June 1978.

[8] J. F. Meyer, "On evaluating the performability of degradable computing systems," in *Proc. 8th Int'l Symp. on Fault-Tolerant Computing*, pp. 44–49, Toulouse, France, June 1978.

[9] J. F. Meyer, "On evaluating the performability of degradable computing systems," *IEEE Trans. Computers*, vol. C-29, no. 8, pp. 720–731, August 1980.

[10] V. G. Kulkarni, V. F. Nicloa, R. M. Smith, and K. S. Trivedi, "Numerical evaluation of performability and job completion time in repairable fault-tolerant systems," in *Proc. 16th Int'l Symp. on Fault-Tolerant Computing*, pp. 252–257, Vienna, Austria, July 1986.

[11] K. R. Pattipati, Y. Li, and H. A. P. Blom, "A unified framework for the performability evaluation of fault-tolerant computer systems," *IEEE Trans. Computers*, vol. 42, no. 3, pp. 312–326, March 1993.

[12] J. F. Meyer, "Performability: A retrospective and some pointers to the future," *Performance Evaluation*, vol. 14, no. 3-4, pp. 139–156, February 1992.

[13] E. de Souza e Silva and H. R. Gail, "Performability analysis of computer systems: From model specification to solution," *Performance Evaluation*, vol. 14, no. 3-4, pp. 157–196, February 1992.

[14] K. S. Trevidi et al., "Composite performance and dependability analysis," *Performance Evaluation*, vol. 14, no. 3-4, pp. 197–215, February 1992.

[15] J. F. Meyer and W. H. Sanders, "Specification and construction of performability models," in *Proc. 2nd Int'l Workshop on Performability Modelling of Computer and Communication Systems*, Le Mont Saint-Michel, France, June 1993.

[16] R. A. Howard, *Dynamic Probabilistic Systems, Vol. II: Semi-Markov and Decision Processes*, Wiley, 1971.

[17] W. H. Sanders and J. F. Meyer, "A unified approach for specifying measures of performance, dependability, and performability," in *Dependable Computing for Critical Applications*, A. Avižienis and J.-C. Laprie, editors, pp. 215–237, Springer-Verlag, 1990.

[18] W. H. Sanders and J. F. Meyer, "METASAN: A performability evaluation tool based on stochastic activity networks," in *ACM-IEEE Fall Joint Computer Conference*, pp. 807–816, Dallas, TX, November 1986, IEEE Computer Society Press.

[19] J. A. Couvillon et al., "Performability modeling with UltraSAN," *IEEE Software*, vol. 8, no. 5, pp. 69–80, September 1991.

[20] G. Ciardo, J. Muppala, and K. S. Trivedi, "SPNP: A graphical tool for performance analysis," in *Proc. 3rd Int'l Workshop on Petri Nets and Performance Models*, pp. 142–151, Kyoto, Japan, December 1989, IEEE Computer Society Press.

[21] C. Lindemann, "DSPNexpress: A software package for the efficient solution of deterministic and stochastic Petri nets," in *Proc. 6th Int'l Conf. on Modelling Techniques and Tools for Computer Performance Evaluation*, pp. 15–29, Edinburgh, Great Britain, 1992.

[22] B. R. Haverkort, I. G. Niemegeers, and P. Veldhuyzen van Zanten, "DyQNtool: A performability tool based on the dynamic queueing network concept," in *Modelling Techniques and Tools for Computer Performance Evaluation*, G. Balbo, editor, North-Holland, 1991.

[23] C. Lindemann and G. Hommel, "Combining deterministic and stochastic Petri net and product-form queueing network models for evaluating gracefully degradable systems," in *Proc. 5th European Computer Conference on Advanced Computer Technology, Reliable Systems and Applications*, pp. 880–884, Bologna, Italy, 1991.

[24] H. Szczerbicka, "A combined queueing network and stochastic Petri-net approach for evaluating the performability of fault-tolerant computer systems," *Performance Evaluation*, vol. 14, no. 3-4, pp. 217–226, February 1992.

[25] J. A. Carrasco and J. Figueras, "METFAC: Design and implementation of a software tool for modeling and evaluation of complex fault-tolerant computing systems," in *Proc. 16th Int'l Symp. on Fault-Tolerant Computing*, pp. 424–429, Vienna, Austria, July 1986.

[26] V. Catania, A. Puliafito, and L. Vita, "Modeling framework to evaluate performability parameters in gracefully degrading systems," *IEEE Trans. Industrial Electronics*, vol. 40, no. 5, pp. 461–472, October 1993.

[27] W. H. Sanders and J. F. Meyer, "Reduced base model construction methods for stochastic activity networks," *IEEE Journal on Selected Areas in Communications*, vol. 9, no. 1, pp. 25–36, January 1991.

[28] J. K. Muppala and K. S. Trivedi, "Composite performance and availability analysis using a hierarchy of stochastic reward nets," in *Computer Performance Evaluation, Modelling Techniques and Tools*, G. Balbo and G. Serazzi, editors, pp. 335–349, Elsevier Science Publishers B.V. (North-Holland), Amsterdam, The Netherlands, 1992.

[29] G. Ciardo, A. Blakemore, P. F. Chimento, J. K. Muppala, and K. S. Trivedi, "Automated generation and analysis of Markov reward models using Stochastic Reward Nets," in *Linear Algebra, Markov Chains, and Queueing Models, IMA Volumes in Mathematics and its Applications*, C. Meyer and R. J. Plemmons, editors, volume 48, pp. 145–191, Springer-Verlag, Heidelberg, Germany, 1993.

[30] K. S. Trivedi, B. R. Haverkort, A. Rindos, and V. Mainkar, "Tools for reliability and performability: Problems and perspectives," in *Proc. 7th Int'l Conf. on Techniques and Tools for Computer Performance Evaluation, Lecture Notes in Computer Science 794*, G. Haring and G. Kotsis, editors, pp. 1–24, Springer-Verlag, 1994.

[31] G. Ciardo, J. Muppala, and K. S. Trivedi, "On the solution of GSPN reward models," *Performance Evaluation*, vol. 12, no. 4, pp. 237–253, 1991.

[32] M. A. Qureshi and W. H. Sanders, "Reward model solution methods with impulse and rate rewards: An algorithm and numerical results," *Performance Evaluation*, vol. 20, no. 4, pp. 413–436, July 1994.

[33] K. S. Trivedi, G. Ciardo, M. Malhotra, and R. Sahner, "Dependability and performability analysis," in *Performance Evaluation of Computer and Communications Systems, Lecture Notes in Computer Science 729*, L. Donatiello and R. Nelson, editors, pp. 587–612, Springer-Verlag, 1993.

[34] K. S. Trivedi, G. Ciardo, M. Malhotra, and S. Garg, "Dependability and performability modeling using stochastic Petri nets," in *Proc. 11th Int'l Conf. on Analysis and Optimization of Systems – Discrete Event Systems*, pp. 144–157, Sophia-Antipolis, France, June 1994.

[35] K. S. Trivedi, M. Malhotra, and R. M. Fricks, "Markov reward approach to performability and reliability analysis," in *Proc. 2nd Int'l Workshop on Modeling, Analysis, and Simulation of Computer and Telecommunication Systems*, pp. 7–11, Durham, NC, 1994.

[36] Y. Masuda and U. Sumita, "Numerical analysis of gracefully degrading fault-tolerant computing systems: Semi-Markov and Laguerre transform approach," *Comput. Oper. Res.*, vol. 18, no. 8, pp. 695–707, 1991.

[37] L. Donatiello and V. Grassi, "On evaluating the cumulative performance distribution of fault tolerant systems," *IEEE Trans. Computers*, vol. 40, no. 11, pp. 1301–1307, November 1991.

[38] L. Donatiello and V. Grassi, "Some remarks on closed-form solutions of performability," in *Proc. 2nd Int'l Workshop on Performability Modelling of Computer and Communication Systems*, Le Mont Saint-Michel, France, June 1993.

[39] K. R. Pattipati, R. Mallubhatla, V. Gopalakrishna, and N. Viswanadham, "Markov-reward models and hyperbolic systems," in *Proc. 2nd Int'l Workshop on Performability Modelling of Computer and Communication Systems*, Le Mont Saint-Michel, France, June 1993.

[40] R. Mallubhatla and K. R. Pattipati, "Discrete-time Markov-reward models: Random rewards," in *Proc. Rensselaer's 4th Int'l Conf. on Computer Integrated Manufacturing and Automated Technology*, 1994.

[41] R. Mallubhatla, K. R. Pattipati, and N. Viswanadham, "Moment recursions of the cumulative performance of production systems using discrete-time Markov reward models," in *Proc. 1994 IEEE Int'l Conf. on Robotics and Automation*, San Diego, CA, 1994.

[42] A. Bobbio and L. Roberti, "Distribution of the minimal completion time of parallel tasks in multi-reward semi-Markov models," *Performance Evaluation*, vol. 14, no. 2-3, pp. 239–256, 1992.

[43] P. F. Chimento and K. S. Trivedi, "The completion time of programs on processors subject to failure and repair," *IEEE Trans. Computers*, vol. 42, no. 10, pp. 1184–1194, October 1993.

[44] I. Mitrani, "Queues with breakdowns," in *Proc. 2nd Int'l Workshop on Performability Modelling of Computer and Communication Systems*, Le Mont Saint-Michel, France, June 1993.

[45] V. Grassi and L. Donatiello, "Sensitivity analysis of performability," *Performance Evaluation*, vol. 14, no. 2-3, pp. 227–237, 1992.

[46] N. M. van Dijk, "Approximate uniformization for continuous-time Markov chains with an application to performability analysis," *Stochastic Processes and their Applications*, vol. 40, no. 2, pp. 339–357, 1992.

[47] E. de Souza e Silva and H. R. Gail, "The uniformization method in performability analysis," in *Proc. 2nd Int'l Workshop on Performability Modelling of Computer and Communication Systems*, Le Mont Saint-Michel, France, June 1993.

[48] A. P. A. van Moorsel and W. H. Sanders, "Adaptive uniformization," *Commuications in Statistics: Stochastic Models*, vol. 10, no. 3, pp. 619–648, August 1994.

[49] J. D. Diener and W. H. Sanders, "Empirical comparison of uniformization methods for continuous-time Markov chains," in *Computations with Markov Chains*, W. J. Stewart, editor, pp. 547–570, Kluwer Academic Publishers, 1995.

[50] B. R. Haverkort, "Approximate performability and dependability analysis using generalized stochastic Petri nets," *Performance Evaluation*, vol. 18, no. 1, pp. 61–78, July 1993.

[51] H. H. Ammar and S. Deng, "Time warp simulation using time scale decomposition," *ACM Trans. on Modeling and Computer Simulation*, vol. 2, no. 2, pp. 158–177, April 1992.

[52] H. Szczerbicka and P. Zeigler, "Simulation with active objects: An approach to combined modeling," *Simulation Practice and Theory*, vol. 1, no. 6, pp. 267–281, July 1994.

[53] W. H. Sanders and R. S. Friere, "Efficient simulation of hierarchical stochastic activity networks," *Discrete Event Dynamic Systems: Theory and Applications*, vol. 3, no. 2-3, pp. 271–300, July 1993.

[54] W. D. Obal II and W. H. Sanders, "Importance sampling simulation in UltraSAN," *Simulation*, vol. 62, no. 2, pp. 98–111, February 1994.

[55] C. Constantinescu and C. Sandovici, "Dependability prediction of a fault-tolerant microcomputer for advanced control," in *Proc. 5th European Computer Conference on Advanced Computer Technology, Reliable Systems and Applications*, pp. 442–446, Bologna, Italy, 1991.

[56] C. Constantinescu, "Analyzing the effect of permanent, intermittent, and transient faults on a gracefully degrading microcomputer," *Microelectronics and Reliability*, vol. 32, no. 6, pp. 861–866, June 1992.

[57] C. Constantinescu, "Predicting performability of a fault-tolerant microcomputer for process control," *IEEE Trans. Reliability*, vol. 41, no. 4, pp. 558–564, December 1992.

[58] C. Constantinescu and C. Sandovici, "Performability evaluation of a gracefully degrading microcomputer," *Computers in Industry*, vol. 22, no. 2, pp. 181–186, August 1993.

[59] B. Ciciani, "Fault-tolerance considerations for redundant binary-tree dynamic random-access-memory (ram) chips," *IEEE Trans. Reliability*, vol. 41, no. 1, pp. 139–148, March 1992.

[60] S. M. R. Islam, "Performability analysis of disk arrays," in *Proc. 36th Midwest Symposium on Circuits and Systems*, pp. 158–160, Detroit, MI, 1993.

[61] B. E. Aupperle and J. F. Meyer, "State space generation for degradable multiprocessor systems," in *Proc. 21st Int'l Symp. on Fault-Tolerant Computing*, pp. 308–315, Montréal, Que., Canada, June 1991.

[62] V. Grassi, "Cost effectiveness analyis of different fault tolerance strategies for hypercube systems," in *Proc. 21st Int'l Symp. on Fault-Tolerant Computing*, pp. 196–203, Montréal, Que., Canada, June 1991.

[63] J. Kim, K. G. Shin, and C. Das, "Performability evaluation of gracefully degradable hypercube multicomputers," in *Proc. 1992 IEEE Workshop on Fault-Tolerant Parallel and Distributed Systems*, pp. 140–149, Amherst, MA, July 1992.

[64] S. M. Koriem and L. M. Patnaik, "Performability studies of hypercube architectures," in *Proc. 6th Int'l Parallel Processing Symp.*, pp. 488–493, Beverly Hills, CA, 1992.

[65] N. Lopez-Benitez and K. S. Trivedi, "Multiprocessor performability analysis," *IEEE Trans. Reliability*, vol. 42, no. 4, pp. 579–587, December 1993.

[66] C. Chen et al., "Comparison of hybrid modular redundant multiprocessor systems with respect to performabilities," in *Proc. 23rd Int'l Symp. on Fault-Tolerant Computing*, pp. 66–75, Toulouse, France, June 1993.

[67] S. M. Koriem and L. M. Patnaik, "Fault-tolerance analysis of hypercube systems using Petri net theory," *Journal of Systems and Software*, vol. 21, no. 1, pp. 71–88, April 1993.

[68] I. Mitrani and A. Puhalskii, "Limiting results for multiprocessor systems with breakdowns and repairs," *Queueing Systems*, pp. 293–311, 1993.

[69] R. Chakka and I. Mitrani, "Heterogeneous multiprocessor systems with breakdowns: Performance and optimal repair strategies," *Theoretical Computer Science*, vol. 125, no. 1, pp. 91–109, 1995.

[70] S. M. R. Islam and H. H. Ammar, "Performability analyis of distributed real-time systems," *IEEE Trans. Computers*, vol. 40, no. 11, pp. 1239–1251, November 1991.

[71] S. M. R. Islam and H. H. Ammar, "Performability analysis of distributed real-time systems with repetitive task information," in *Proc. 21st Int'l Symp. on Fault-Tolerant Computing*, pp. 352–359, Montréal, Que., Canada, June 1991.

[72] S. M. R. Islam and H. H. Ammar, "Performability of integrated software-hardware components of real-time parallel and distributed systems," *IEEE Trans. Reliability*, vol. 41, no. 3, pp. 352–362, September 1992.

[73] K. M. Kavi et al., "Performability model for soft real-time systems," in *Proc. 27th Hawaii Int'l Conf. on System Sciences*, pp. 571–579, Wailea, HI, January 1994.

[74] H. de Meer, K. S. Trivedi, and M. Dal Cin, "Guarded repair of dependable systems," *Theoretical Computer Science*, vol. 18, no. 1-2, pp. 179–210, June 1994.

[75] L. J. N. Franken and B. R. Haverkort, "Dynamically reconfiguring distributed systems with the Performability Manager," *IEEE Network*, vol. 8, no. 1, pp. 24–32, Jan-Feb 1994.

[76] L. J. N. Franken, B. R. Haverkort, and R. Pijpers, "Modelling aspects of model-based dynamic quality of service management by the Performability Manager," in *Proc. 7th Int'l Conf. on Techniques*

and Tools for Computer Performance Evaluation, Lecture Notes in Computer Science 794, G. Haring and G. Kotsis, editors, pp. 89–110, Springer-Verlag, 1994.

[77] A. T. Tai, "Performability-driven adaptive fault tolerance," in *Proc. 24th Int'l Symp. on Fault-Tolerant Computing*, pp. 176–185, Austin, TX, June 1994.

[78] A. Bondavalli and L. Simoncini, "Structured software fault-tolerance with BSM," in *Proc. 3rd Workshop on Future Trends of Distributed Computing Systems*, pp. 278–286, Taipei, Taiwan, 1992.

[79] P. K. Kapur, R. B. Garg, and V. K. Bhalla, "Release policies and random software life cycle and penalty cost," *Microelectronics and Reliability*, vol. 33, no. 1, pp. 7–12, January 1993.

[80] A. T. Tai, A. Avižienis, and J. F. Meyer, "Evaluation of fault-tolerant software: A performability modeling approach," in *Dependable Computing for Critical Applications*, L. Simoncini, C. E. Landwehr, and B. Randell, editors, volume 6 of *Dependable Computing and Fault-Tolerant Systems*, pp. 113–135, Springer-Verlag, Wien, Austria, 1993.

[81] A. T. Tai, J. F. Meyer, and A. Avižienis, "Performability enhancement of fault-tolerant software," *IEEE Trans. Reliability*, vol. 42, no. 2, pp. 227–237, June 1993.

[82] S. Chiaradonna, A. Bondavalli, and L. Strigini, "On performability modeling and evaluation of software fault tolerance structures," in *Proc. 1st European Dependable Computing Conference*, pp. 97–114, Berlin, Germany, October 1994.

[83] A. T. Tai, A. Avižienis, and J. F. Meyer, *Software Performability: A Model-Based Approach*, Kluwer Academic Publishers, Boston, MA, 1995.

[84] N. Viswanadham, Y. Narahari, and R. Ram, "Performability of automated manufacturing systems," *Control and Dynamic Systems*, vol. 47, pp. 77–120, 1991.

[85] N. Viswanadham and R. Ram, "Composite performance-dependability analysis of cellular manufacturing systems," *IEEE Trans. Robotics and Automation*, vol. 10, no. 2, pp. 245–258, April 1994.

[86] N. Viswanadham, K. R. Pattipati, and V. Gopalakrishna, "Performability studies of automated manufacturing systems with multiple part types," in *Proc. 1993 IEEE Int'l Conf. on Robotics and Automation*, pp. 89–94, Atlanta, GA, May 1993.

[87] C. Lindemann et al., "Performability modeling of an automated manufacturing system with deterministic and stochastic Petri nets," in *Proc. 1993*

IEEE Int'l Conf. on Robotics and Automation, pp. 576–581, Atlanta, GA, May 1993.

[88] V. Gopalakrishna, N. Viswanadham and K. R. Pattipati, "Sensitivity analysis of failure-prone flexible manufacturing systems," in *Proc. 1994 IEEE Int'l Conf. on Robotics and Automation,* pp. 181–186, San Diego, CA, 1994.

[89] Y. Sugasawa, M. Katsumata, and N. Takeshita, "Behavior analysis and performability of a co-operative motion system modeled by Petri net," *Computers and Industrial Engineering,* vol. 24, no. 4, pp. 523–529, October 1993.

[90] K. H. Prodromides and W. H. Sanders, "Performability evaluation of CSMA/CD and CSMA/DR protocols under transient fault conditions," in *Proc. 10th Symp. on Reliable Distributed Systems,* pp. 166–176, Pisa, Italy, 1991.

[91] K. H. Prodromides and W. H. Sanders, "Performability evaluation of CSMA/CD and CSMA/DR protocols under transient fault conditions," *IEEE Trans. Reliability,* vol. 42, no. 1, pp. 116–127, March 1993.

[92] J. F. Meyer, "The role of modeling and evaluation in the design process," in *Information Processing 92: Proc. 12th IFIP World Computer Congress,* volume I, pp. 636–644, 1992.

Author Index

Notes

Notes

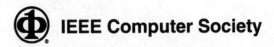